Handbook
of
Educational Administration

A Guide for the Practitioner

Emery Stoops

Max Rafferty

Russell E. Johnson

Allyn and Bacon, Inc.   Boston · London · Sydney

371.2
S 882h

Library of Congress Cataloging in Publication Data

Stoops, Emery.
    Handbook of educational administration.

    Includes bibliographies and index.
    1. School management and organization—United
States.   I. Rafferty, Max Lewis, joint
author.   II. Johnson, Russell E., joint author.
III. Title.
LB2805.S759   371.2   74-23250

ISBN 0-205-04469-7

Second Printing . . . June, 1977

Contents

Preface

American schools need qualified leadership. School systems seldom rise above the vision and competency of the superintendent, and individual schools seldom rise above the leadership qualities of the building principal.

Careful study of this book is recommended for practicing administrators, students of American school administration, and concerned and scholarly laymen. The emphasis is upon school district operations, rendering the book indispensable reading for superintendents, assistant superintendents, principals, assistant principals, supervisors, board members, and all who would understand or succeed to administrative responsibilities in America's schools.

The book is designed to prepare today's administrator for informed and competent leadership. It uses the past and deals with the present. However, it is unique in that it explores more than one hundred trends that promise to be areas in which the administrator will become involved in the upcoming decades.

Throughout the book, the authors have sought to maintain a balance between theory and practice. Elements of theory that can be tested in administrative practice have been extensively covered. Research is included to suggest innovative possibilities and to validate existing procedures. Numerous forms, figures, and illustrations for adaptation by administrators are provided in this volume, making it a handy reference for the administrator's desk.

Thirty chapters cover educational responsibilities and relationships at the federal, state, intermediate-unit, and district levels. Education, both public and private, is considered a federal concern, a state responsibility, an intermediate-unit service, and a district operation. Each of these levels and its specialized role in achieving better instruction, adequate financing, effective personnel management, and reciprocal community relations are described in detail.

The importance of placing administrative procedures on a policy basis is stressed throughout the book. The cooperative formulation of policies that give direction to administration is possible only when the superintendent exerts creative team leadership. The book's emphasis upon leadership, policies, and teamwork is a contribution intended for both practicing administrators and for graduate students.

The authors appreciate the help and encouragement of such educators as John Dunworth, C. C. Trillingham, Maynard Bemis, Calvin Grieder, Harlan L. Hagman, Steven Knezevich, John Stallings, and James R. Marks. Appreciation is also extended to Joyce King-Stoops for her technical assistance in the preparation of the manuscript and to M. L. Cushman, Dean Emeritus and Professor of Education at the University of North Dakota who reviewed the manuscript.

The authors join in wishing success and satisfaction to all administrators, administrators-to-be, and laymen who read this book.

Emery Stoops
Max Rafferty
Russell E. Johnson

PART ONE

Introduction

1

An Introduction to
School Administration

Education is a local operation, an intermediate-unit service, a state responsibility, and a national concern. The education of children is primarily accomplished at the local level; other levels are supportive. Each level — local, county, state, and federal— must be effectively administered. The school administrative structure and process have been evolving since early colonial times.

This chapter includes a discussion of the following topics:

Constitutional Origins of School Control
Court Decisions and the School Administrator
What Is School Administration?
Why Administer Schools?
Who Administers Schools?
Evaluating Administration
Organization of the Handbook
Trends

Constitutional Origins of School Control

The people, through their legislators, have enacted constitutional provisions and statutes for the establishment and control of public and private education. Either by default or design, education became chiefly the responsibility of state government.

The Tenth Amendment to the United States Constitution passed in

1791 clearly states, "The powers not delegated to the United States by the Constitution, nor prohibited by it to the states, are reserved to the states respectively, or to the people." The amendment implies that where the United States Constitution is silent, such powers are automatically the responsibility of state government. Although responsibility for education is left to the states, the courts have consistently ruled that under the "general welfare" clause of the Constitution, Congress may enact laws to express its concern for public education. This concern generally is translated into the form of financial subsidy.

A long list of court decisions provides that state legislatures, elected by the people, have plenary control over the establishment and maintenance of schools within the state. To establish and maintain effective educational programs within the state, legislatures have found it necessary to provide a central educational agency, the state department of education. To express its concern for education, the Congress has established the United States Office of Education within the Department of Health, Education, and Welfare. This office performs various functions, the chief of which is the distribution of funds to state and local educational agencies.

The people's legislators in each state, charged with the responsibility for education, have provided for intermediate units and local school districts. The intermediate unit is essentially a service arm of the state department of education. The local district has been delegated the function of operating schools through a board of education and a staff of administrators and teachers. Technically, each board of education and its administrators have only those powers that have been delineated by the state legislature. In this sense, the people, through their legislators, own and control the schools.

Although legislators have responsibility for schools, their power is not absolute; they must design legislation in harmony with state and federal constitutions. Enacted legislation is not the final word for local school administrators; before it has finality, it must be tested in the courts. The United States Supreme Court renders the final decision with respect to policies or procedures at the local, intermediate, state, or federal levels.

Court Decisions and the School Administrator

The modern school administrator—whether at the federal, state, intermediate, or local level—must function with the *Education Code* in one hand

and a battery of court decisions in the other. Since our system of checks and balances gives the courts power to review legislative enactments, administrators must function in harmony with decisions handed down by the United States Supreme Court.

The support of public and nonpublic (private or parochial) schools has always been an issue in American education. Historically, and until fairly recently, all public funds have been withheld from nonpublic schools and from children who attended nonpublic schools. In 1930, the United States Supreme Court held that children attending nonpublic schools may receive free textbooks, thus establishing, in effect, a new doctrine that has since been termed the "child benefit theory." This decision, resulting from the Cochran case,[1] opened up many possibilities for taxpayer support to nonpublic schools. Seventeen years after the Cochran case, the legislature of New Jersey provided that both public and private school pupils were entitled to free transportation. This legislation eventually was tested in the United States Supreme Court, and by a vote of 5 to 4 the theory of child benefit was upheld.[2] Many Supreme Court decisions have sustained the child benefit theory as established in the Cochran case and expanded by the Everson case, but have limited the extent to which nonpublic schools can secure free textbooks, transportation, and other aids under the child benefit theory. Recent years have witnessed continuing demands for the use of public funds in nonpublic schools.

The right to attend public schools has been tested in two landmark decisions. The right of pupils to attend public schools regardless of race was tested in the United States Supreme Court in the Plessy v. Ferguson case in 1896. Out of this decision came the "separate but equal" doctrine. In 1954, the Brown case[3] upset the "separate but equal" doctrine and declared that all pupils of whatever race, religion, or nationality are entitled to attend public schools. In the period between the Plessy and Brown cases, other decisions had direct bearing on the "separate but equal" doctrine: *Sweatt* v. *Painter, Sipuel* v. *Oklahoma Board of Regents, Alston* v. *School Board of the City of Norfolk,* and *Missouri ex rel. Gaines* v. *Canada.* Following the historic Brown case, various decisions have not only demanded equal rights of attendance for all races and for pupils of whatever backgrounds, but have gone one step further and insisted that

---

[1] *Cochran et al.* v. *Louisiana State Board of Education et al.,* 281 U.S. 370 (1930).

[2] *Everson* v. *Board of Education of Ewing Township et al.,* 330 U.S. 1 (1947).

[3] *Brown* v. *Board of Education of Topeka,* 347 U.S. 483, 74 Sup. Ct. 686.

schools not only avoid segregation but take positive means to integrate pupils on the basis of race. The courts demanded integration on the basis both of *de jure,* or legal, separation and of *de facto,* or circumstantial, segregation. This has led to the issue of "busing" to achieve racial balance.

Out of this discussion, it would seem reasonable to conclude that although legislators have plenary power to control education, legislative enactment does not constitute final authority until tested in the courts. The United States Supreme Court is the final authority in all school matters at all school levels.

What Is School Administration?

Halpin characterized school administration as a social process involving both problem solving and decision making.[4] Others have described administration as management, leadership, organization, manipulation, and control. None of these terms, however, are comprehensive or restrictive enough to properly define the role of the school administrator in his various capacities. A definition of administration at the local, county, state, and federal levels would differ somewhat depending upon the legal and functional roles of the several levels. For purposes of a working definition, the authors have chosen to focus on educational administration in the operation of schools.

Stoops and Rafferty define public school administration as *"The organization and leadership of all community personnel concerned with public education in such a manner as will effectively make for sound education within the framework of policy set up by the board of education."*[5] The authors believe that this definition, widely used since its formulation, is basically sound. It is restricted, however, to *public* education. The authors would like to refine and shorten the definition to read:

> *Administration at the local level mobilizes personnel and resources to provide maximum learning opportunities in harmony with legal stipulations.*

This definition stresses the mobilization of personnel and resources. It implies that teachers, classified workers, community supporters, and all

---

[4] Andrew W. Halpin (ed.), *Administrative Theory in Education.*

[5] Emery Stoops and M. L. Rafferty, Jr., *Practices and Trends in School Administration,* p. 5.

others join in the improvement and maximizing of learning opportunities. Resources refer to finance, transportation, facilities, equipment, and supplies. Learning opportunities are not limited to children, but should be made available to adults as well. All learners should be given greater opportunity regardless of interest, ability, race, age, nationality, or other defining condition. In essence, it means that learning opportunities should be provided to all. The administration of learning opportunities provided for all must be handled in harmony with legislative enactment and court decisions. The board of education, the superintendent, principals, teachers, and classified workers must function in ways made possible, or not prohibited by, tested statutes. The details of such an administrative operation will be delineated in later chapters of this book.

Why Administer Schools?

This may seem like a rhetorical question, but it is not. Recently, militant teachers have made frontal attacks on the size and function of local administration. Concerned taxpayers have also questioned the worth of the administrative function. School administrators must pause to assess the need for their positions.

To justify administration, there must be a consideration of the goals and objectives of the program to be administered. This is a question which many school people, private and public, have been woefully evasive in answering. It is not uncommon to ask a teacher or administrator to name the philosophy, goals, or objectives of the school and receive a blank stare. On the contrary, educators should have a clear idea of where they are going and their means of getting there.

In California, the governor's office attempted to set up goals and objectives for public education for kindergarten through the twelfth grade. During the course of the study, the California legislature defined "philosophy," "goal," and "objective" (in Assembly Bill No. 2430, April 3, 1970, Sections 7561–7563), as an addition to the *Education Code*. A portion of the assembly bill reads:

> 'Philosophy' means a composite statement of the relationship between the individual and society based upon beliefs, concepts, and attitudes from which the goals and objectives of the [school] district are derived.
>
> 'Goal' means a statement of broad direction or intent which is general and timeless and is not concerned with a particular achievement within a specified time period.

'Objective' means a devised accomplishment that can be verified within a given time and under specifiable conditions which, if attained, advances the [school] system toward a corresponding goal.

These definitions were considered by the Governor's Task Force to be appropriate and helpful in setting up further goals and objectives. Members of the task force labored through many sessions to find, expectably, their goals and objectives similar to past goals echoed throughout history. The task force reported to the governor that although goals can never be completely inclusive or mutually exclusive, the following goals were recommended for public education in California:

Communication (symbol) skills
Information
Personal values
Social values
Decision making

They were described in the task force report as *student-centered* goals; some may argue that not all are statements of a broad direction. These goals were followed by broad objectives designed to implement the intent of the goals within a specified time.

It is only through the acceptance of a philosophy, goals, and objectives that a program can be held *accountable* for any desired degree of achievement. Administration must have clear-cut goals if it is to achieve accountability. The philosophy, goals, and objectives defined and established in California might well be used in other states and school districts.

At a time when schools are underfinanced, voters are turning down bond issues, increasing numbers of teachers are critical of administration, and the public is bewildered, administrators must give more attention to accountability. When goals and objectives are established for the educational program, and when operational goals and objectives are established for the most effective conduct of the school system, then it is possible to evaluate the administration and the administrators themselves. They must be evaluated with respect to the extent to which they have achieved their goals and objectives.

In a well-operated public or private school, no employee should ever be in doubt concerning the philosophical point of view, the general goals, or the specific objectives of the program. When the purposes are clearly understood, it is more likely that they can and will be accomplished.   Then we can answer the question, "Why administer schools?"

Who Administers the Schools?

Large schools are administered by numerous administrative specialists in line with statutes and policies.   Small schools have fewer administrators who perform a multiplicity of functions.   As the size of the school system grows, specialization replaces generalization.   If one considers a reasonably large school, one begins with the board of education.   Since the board members are laymen and have other full-time jobs, they set policies and delegate the implementation of the policies to a superintendent.   The superintendent is generally faced with four or five discernible areas of responsibility.   First, according to the *Education Code* and usual board policy, he should provide a good instructional program.   Second, provision of a good instructional program requires competent certificated and classified personnel.   Third, when personnel are employed, salaries and other phases of finance are involved.   Fourth, when finances are involved, the schools have a public relations problem.   So the superintendent must appoint assistant superintendents in charge of instruction, personnel, and finance.   Ordinarily, the superintendent handles the overall public relations tasks, although public relations is everyone's job.   As school systems grow larger, they often appoint an assistant superintendent in charge of the remaining miscellaneous functions, grouped together as special services; his title is sometimes "administrative assistant."   In larger school systems, an assistant superintendent for pupil personnel services is often appointed to handle the testing program, the multitude of special classes, the health services, counseling and guidance programs, and educational research.   Other members of the administrative complex are staff supervisors, coordinators, and technicians with special skills in such areas as instructional technology, instruction of the handicapped, data processing, schoolhouse planning, art, and science.

At the school building level, there are principals, vice-principals, registrars, and coordinators.   The administrative complex and the teaching faculty are supported by a classified staff of secretaries, custodians, cafeteria workers, and bus drivers.

Administrative personnel increases not only with the size of school enrollment, but as a means of keeping up with new and expanded administrative duties. Every time a state legislature meets, it enacts statutes that require more administrative study and time. Extensive federal programs that require proposals and complex administrative techniques create heavy workloads for the administration.

Evaluating Administration

The administration of every school system is continuously evaluated. Evaluation may be formal and planned, or it may be informal, spasmodic, and uncontrolled. The formal evaluation is characterized by objectivity and approved techniques, with assessment at regular intervals and for specified purposes. The evaluation of the administration, and of administrators, should be constructive and pointed toward a level of management that will maximize learning opportunities.

As suggested earlier, the administration mobilizes personnel and resources to enhance achievement in classrooms. This is done by clarifying philosophy and setting long-term goals supported by obtainable objectives. For the achievement of these, the administration should be held accountable. The administration should be considered successful to the extent that goals and objectives are attained.

When an unbiased and constructive evaluation of the administration is completed, teachers, classified personnel, and community patrons will have greater confidence in the effectiveness of the management of the school system.. One of the greatest values of well-planned evaluation is that it helps administrators to strengthen needed and important elements of the program and to eliminate those that have become archaic. Such an evaluation is also an excellent means of inservice improvement for the administrators themselves. Pupils, custodians, and teachers feel more comfortable when they know that administrators are evaluated in the same manner that they are.

The Appendix illustrates a principal rating checklist designed to help a principal in cooperation with the superintendent and his staff to look at himself in action. It can be adapted for any administrative position.

Organization of the Handbook

Part Two deals with the broad problems of control and organization. Of first importance in school administration is the placing of the local system in proper perspective, relative to national and statewide education. Chapters in this part consider federal concern for education, the state's relation to education, the intermediate unit (county school administration), the school district's role in education, administering school district organization, and the administration of urban schools.

Part Three is concerned with school finance and business administration, traditional administrative areas of competence. Chapters deal with financial support for schools, school district budgeting, accounting procedures, supply administration, school district insurance, and technology in school practice.

Part Four discusses the kinds of knowledge and skills needed in the areas of school plant administration. The amount of tax money allotted to school buildings and sites makes this an important administrative responsibility. Chapters explain the planning, constructing, and financing of school buildings, and their maintenance and operation.

Part Five deals with the administration of special services and programs. This field has grown so much in recent years that it requires specialized knowledge and skills on the part of the administrator. Chapters discuss school district transportation, school health and nutrition, administering co-curricular programs, special education classes, and pupil personnel, and preschool educational programs.

Part Six considers personnel administration as one of the basic tasks of the school executive. The ability to solve problems involving school personnel is perhaps the most difficult competence for the average administrator to acquire. Chapters describe preservice and inservice teacher education, the administration of certificated and classified personnel, employee organizations, and negotiations.

Part Seven examines the areas of instruction, the public, and the future of American education. Chapters describe the administrator's role in the instructional program, school public relations, educational reform and innovations, and the cutting edge of educational administration.

This book will emphasize practices in the administrative field currently under discussion. An attempt is made to show a consensus of modern authorities and research regarding the best practice. Topics regarding controversies and militancy that may cause problems for the administrator are examined as objectively as possible. A summary of apparent trends is made at the end of each chapter. No apology is made for attempting to foresee the future, and no claim is made for the infallibility of such predictions. The trends listed in the volume are justified insofar as possible by the opinions of authorities, the professional experiences of the authors, and the available data and statistics. It is hoped that the presentation and discussion of such trends within the profession will at least serve the purpose of alerting administrative practitioners to their existence; and so help those persons interested in the important and complex career of school administration to approach more nearly their goal of guiding and overseeing the nation's schools.

Following the summary and trends, several "in-basket" administrative problems are presented.

Trends

School administration is growing up. For the past fifty years there has been evidence of, and increasing development in, the formulation and use of better administrative policies and procedures. This development has more recently been characterized by emphasis upon definition of purpose, evaluation, and accountability.

TOWARD BETTER COORDINATION BETWEEN LOCAL, INTERMEDIATE, STATE, AND FEDERAL LEVELS. In the past, there have been uncertainty and confusion concerning the jurisdiction of the several administrative levels. Much of the uncertainty has existed over which responsibilities fall under the domain of the state or federal agency, and over which responsibilities are those of the state or intermediate unit. At present, a greater clarity of responsibilities and jurisdictions is developing among all levels to replace the uncertainties that have existed.

TOWARD GREATER FOCUS ON ADMINISTRATIVE ACTIVITIES THAT IMPROVE LEARNING OPPORTUNITIES. The definition of educational administration as set forth in this chapter directs the energies of personnel and the potential of resources toward the maximization of learning opportunities. More and more, all levels of administration are pointed toward the improvement of classroom activities. Other functions, such as financial affairs, personnel management, and public relations, must be supportive, not an end in themselves. They have value only as they contribute to the one overriding goal of providing better learning situations. This trend has developed significantly and will develop further.

TOWARD A GREATER DEGREE OF LEGAL COMPLEXITY. Every time the state legislature or the Congress meets, additional statutes are enacted which augment the complexity of school administration. Increasing amounts of administrative time must be expended to understand new legislation and to adapt the provisions of new laws to existing programs. As a result, the state *Education Code* grows both in volume and in complexity. All indicators point to further development in this trend.

TOWARD MORE OBJECTIVE POLICIES AND PROCEDURES WITH STATED GOALS AND PROVISION FOR EVALUATION. School administration can no longer be a subjective operation. It is becoming a more scientific, objective process of establishing workable policies and procedures which follow written and board-approved goals. School administration must be accountable and responsible to teaching faculties, to school patrons, and to state authorities. To test this accountability, evaluation procedures are being developed and will be developed further in the future. The school administrator must demonstrate objectively *how* good his management is. This trend of adopting a philosophy, setting up goals and objectives, and evaluating administrative procedures will continue.

TOWARD MORE PUBLIC SUPPORT FOR NONPUBLIC SCHOOLS. The constitutional debate over federal support for public and nonpublic schools continues to be defined by the courts. This breakdown of the separation between public and nonpublic education has come about largely through the greater participation of the federal government in support programs. It is highly likely that the federal government and some state governments will grant direct subsidies to nonpublic preschools, K–12, vocational schools, colleges, and universities.

TOWARD MORE RELEVANCE TO CHANGING CONDITIONS. It is not enough for administration to be concerned only with its professional functions of handling finances, organizing educational programs, employing personnel, and keeping informed of the latest theories of learning, counseling techniques, and teaching methods. Administration must feel the pulse of the community and become conversant with its social, cultural, economic, and political aspects. The pressures and counter-pressures of various community groups must be understood as they pertain to the school district and its educational program. Administration must be more aware of all the forces and changing conditions that become evident in the fabric of community and national life. When administration becomes aware of community forces and the power structure of various groups, it can help avoid the problems of managing crises.

Change, *per se,* is not necessarily good, and there is no assurance that the new will be better than the old. However, awareness of change is necessary; but it must be evaluated in terms of its effect on improving the education of students. If there is no commitment to change and innovation, nothing remains but the continuation of the status quo and the abandonment of progress.

TOWARD INFINITELY MORE COMPLEX ADMINISTRATION. Tomorrow's schools will be administered by professionals trained to deal with community power structures, faculty militancy, student involvement, and revolutionary new aids to learning. Computerized administration and programmed learning are only two of the many facets of increased complexity in what was once a relatively unspecialized profession. Administrative complexity will stress in-depth understanding and utilization of the widest variety of resources.

TOWARD DECENTRALIZATION OF BOTH SCHOOLS AND ADMINISTRATION. The old idea of the school as a self-contained instructional unit is on the way out, and with it the concept of the superintendent sitting in the center of a line-and-staff power web. Education tomorrow will have many bases in the community, not all of them schools in any conventional sense. To serve such a diverse structure, administration will become much more mobile and task force oriented.

Administrative Problems   In Basket

At the end of each chapter, the reader will find "In-Basket (simulated) Administrative Problems." They are typical of the situations and problems that administrators may encounter in their schools or school district. Seminar leaders can assign the problems to individuals or committees for solution. The facts stated in the problem should not be changed, but any data may be assumed if no contrary information is provided. Solutions should answer the question, "What will you do when given the facts listed in the problem?" It is possible that there might be several solutions to a problem.

The problems encountered in this book may encourage seminar members to draw upon their personal experience to develop their own "in-basket administrative problems." The leader can help the group determine the facts and present possible solutions for discussion.

Problem 1

McKinley School District has an enrollment of 10,000 and consists of ten elementary schools, one junior high school, and one senior high school. The district administrative staff consists of a superintendent, a business manager, an assistant superintendent for educational services, a curriculum coordinator, a director of pupil personnel, a supervisor for music education, and a director of certificated personnel. The teacher's association believes that the central office is overloaded with high-salaried administrators and that this situation prevents them from receiving the salary increase that they are demanding. They have asked the Board of Education to eliminate some of these positions. On the other hand, the administrators believe that they are overworked and have asked for more administrative help such as a psychometrist, a reading consultant, a psychologist, a research assistant, a federal project coordinator, and a director for classified personnel.

As superintendent, how would you proceed to handle this problem?
What would you tell the Board of Education?

Problem 2

You are the new superintendent of a school district in a rural area. There are four elementary principals, a junior-senior high school principal and assistant principal. All live in the area and are well-known and respected. As the year progresses, you find that one elementary principal and the secondary assistant principal are not performing up to your expectations. You decide to develop an administrative evaluation program since there is no evidence that administrators have been evaluated previously.

How would you proceed in the development of an administrative evaluation
*   program?*
Whom would you involve?
How would you handle the ineffective administrators?

Selected References

BENNIS, WARREN, et al. *The Planning of Change.* New York: Holt, Rinehart, and Winston, 1969.

CAMPBELL, ROALD F.; CUNNINGHAM, LUVERN L.; and MCPHEE, RODERICK F. *The Organization and Control of American Schools.* Columbus, Ohio: Charles E. Merrill Publishing Co., 1965.

DRURY, ROBERT L., and RAY, KENNETH C. *Principles of School Law, with Cases.* New York: Appleton-Century-Crofts, 1965.

FREY, SHERMAN H., and GETSCHMAN, KEITH R. *School Administration: Selected Readings.* New York: Thomas Y. Crowell Co., 1968.

HALPIN, ANDREW W. (ed.). *Administrative Theory in Education.* Chicago: Midwest Administration Center, University of Chicago, 1958.

MARKS, JAMES R.; STOOPS, EMERY; and KING-STOOPS, JOYCE. *Handbook of Educational Supervision: A Guide for the Practitioner.* Boston: Allyn and Bacon, 1971.

JOHNS, ROE L., director. *National Educational Finance Project.* Vols. 1–5. Gainesville, Florida, 1971.

MCGARTH, J. H. *Planning Systems for School Executives: The Unity of Theory and Practice.* Scranton, Penn.: Intext Educational Publishers, 1972.

STALLINGS, JOHN W. "The School with Accountability." Los Angeles County Schools *Bulletin* 30 (December 1971).

STOOPS, EMERY, and RAFFERTY, M. L., Jr. *Practices and Trends in School Administration.* Boston: Ginn and Company, 1961.

————, and JOHNSON, RUSSELL E. *Elementary School Administration.* New York: McGraw-Hill Book Co., 1967.

PART TWO

Control and Organization

2

The Federal Government
and Public Education

Although American schools belong to the people, the federal government
has a national concern for public education. The many public education
laws and the grants of federal money to state and local districts attest to an
increasing interest. This has created problems, both real and imaginary.
Many educators express a concern about how much control the federal
government will exert at the local level. There is a need for better
coordination between the federal government, state government, and local
school districts in relation to educational issues, finances, and laws.

This chapter includes a discussion of the following topics:

American Schools Belong to the People
American Education Is Big Business
Federal Interest in Education
Direct Federal Involvement in Education
Types of Federal Grants to Public Schools
Public Laws and Acts
The Issue of Federal Participation
Federal Interest in Integration
The United States Office of Education
The Need for a Secretary of Education
Summary
Trends

American Schools Belong to the People

The underlying principle of the American system of public education is its lack of a system.   It is at once the despair of the logical French, the scientific Germans, and the traditional English.   In other nations, the schools belong to the government and are administered by government bureaus and appointees.   They are financed through national taxes and directed by a secretary of education.   This enables the school systems in these countries to operate independently of local whims and upheavals and simultaneously ensures a maximum of uniformity in school procedures. Indeed, some ministers of education boast that at any moment of the school day they can state with confidence the subject, unit, and text chapter being studied in every classroom of the nation.   Such uniformity of necessity involves the granting of huge powers to the national government in the field of education, and a corresponding loss of local control.

Americans have developed attitudes that stress local, rather than national, control of schools.   Where other nations have set up monolithic educational structures, the United States has a separate school system for each state and territory, each of which is more or less independent and the master of its own fate, except as affected by court decisions.   In finance, organization, and control, a national school system does not exist in this country.

American Education Is Big Business

More and more people go to school each year.   From a meager colonial beginning of Dame Schools and Bible study for a negligible percentage of the population, school enrollments rose above the 42 million mark in 1957–58 and were nearly 59 million in 1973 (*see* Table 2–1).   More than 88 percent of school-age children and youth from 5 to 17 years of age were enrolled in public schools in 1972–73.   The greatest expansion in school enrollments in the last half century has occurred in secondary, higher, and adult education.

The total cost of private and public education provides an index to the size of the operation.   Expenditures at the elementary and secondary levels, both public and nonpublic, exceeded 61 billion dollars in 1973–74. This amount is considered less than adequate by serious-minded people

TABLE 2–1. *Estimated Enrollment in Educational Institutions in the United States for the Fall of 1973*[a]

SCHOOL	PUBLIC	NONPUBLIC	TOTAL
Elementary schools (K–8)	31,470,000	3,630,000	35,100,000
Secondary schools	14,170,000	1,340,000	15,510,000
Higher education (degree-credit enrollment in universities, colleges, professional schools, teachers colleges, and junior colleges)	6,260,000	2,110,000	8,370,000
Grand Total	51,900,000	7,080,000	58,980,000

[a] W. Vance Grant and C. George Lind, *Digest of Educational Statistics, 1973 Edition,* U.S. Department of Health, Education, and Welfare, Office of Education (Washington, D.C.: U.S. Government Printing Office, 1974), p. 6.

when compared to military budgets and public expenditures for amusements; it therefore does not serve as a good index of the size and importance of the national educational effort.

It is difficult to determine exact amounts that are spent on education because of the different fiscal and tax characteristics of the various states. For example, some states do not permit the budgeting of expenditures that are based on revenues that have not been received; others do permit this. Most of the figures that are used for national comparisons are based on "best estimates."

One of the most difficult figures to arrive at is the federal expenditure for education. (*See* Table 2–2.) In 1965, for example, the federal

TABLE 2–2. *Estimated National Expenditure on Education, 1973–74, in Billions*[a]

SCHOOL	EXPENDITURES, INCLUDING INTEREST		CAPITAL OUTLAY		TOTAL EXPENDITURES	
	Public	*Nonpublic*	*Public*	*Nonpublic*	*Public*	*Nonpublic*
Elementary and Secondary	50.6	5.1	5.4	.5	56.0	5.6
Higher education	19.2	10.3	3.8	1.4	23.0	11.7
Total for the U.S.	69.8	15.4	9.2	1.9	79.0	17.3

[a] Grant and Lind, *Digest of Educational Statistics, 1973 Edition,* p. 22.

government was reported as having spent $4.9 billion[1] or $6.3 billion[2] for education and in fiscal 1966, $8.7 billion[3] or $9.1 billion.[4]   One can only say with certainty that the federal government is spending billions on education.

The figures on school enrollment and educational expenditures show the magnitude of education in America.   However, there is an inequality of educational opportunity among the states.   For example, in 1970–71, eleven states were spending $950 per pupil, while five other states were spending only $600 per pupil.[5]   Advocates of federal support for education believe that since approximately 75 percent of the tax dollar goes to the federal government, it would be appropriate that a share of the total national wealth be spent to equalize educational opportunity at the state and local level.

SIMILARITIES AMONG AMERICAN SCHOOLS.   Though differing in many details, state school systems are strikingly similar in their fundamental characteristics.   Most children study similar subjects, and most American schools are governed by locally selected boards of trustees.   Most rely on some variation of the real property tax for local financial support.   More important, a common goal has been set before the varying districts by the people.   This goal is the free and compulsory education of every individual through the secondary level.   With this ideal in view, American public schools have tended to become increasingly similar.

Communities have had a tendency to watch what other communities were doing in the area of education, and to adopt policies that have proved successful.   Experimentation has thus tended to produce constructive imitation; the result has been the essential standardization of the American system of education along certain broad, accepted lines.   This is in no sense a "national" system as it is understood in foreign countries.

UNIQUE FEATURES OF AMERICAN EDUCATION.   There are some features that are unique to American education: The control of education is rela-

---

[1] William G. Land, "Can Federal Programs Be Coordinated?" *Phi Delta Kappan,* p. 348.

[2] Francis Keppel, *What We Don't Know Can Hurt Us* (Washington, D.C.: U.S. Office of Education, Government Printing Office, 1965), p. 3.

[3] Keppel, *What We Don't Know,* p. 3.

[4] U.S. Department of Health, Education, and Welfare, Office of Education, *Federal Funds for Education and Related Activities* (Washington, D.C.: Government Printing Office, 1966).

[5] American Association of School Administrators, *The School Administrator* (April 1971), p. 3.

tively decentralized. The people at the local level, rather than educators or government officials, are ultimately responsible for all of the basic policies relating to education, as well as the educational program of the local schools. Although the primary emphasis is placed on public schools, provision is also made for the existence of private schools. As far as possible, the public schools are safeguarded from partisan political control or influence. Education in the public schools is nonsectarian. Education at public expense is made available for all students at least through the secondary grades.

THE CONSTITUTION DID NOT PROVIDE FOR "NATIONAL" EDUCATION. The framers of the Constitution pointedly did not make any mention of education. State and local control of education and federal involvement are by implication. The basis for federal involvement in education is implied in Section 8 of Article I of the Constitution which provides that Congress shall have the power to provide, among other things, for the general welfare. From the power implied there, Congress has derived the authority to tax and spend for public education.

The Tenth Amendment reserves to the states or to the people all the powers not delegated to the United States by the Constitution. The power of each state to provide and maintain public schools is thus inherent in this amendment.

There are several reasons for silence on educational provisions in the Constitution. Schooling in the 18th century was not considered a government function in any sense of the word; it was conducted under the aegis of church and home. Thus, almost by default, public education in America fell into a state and local framework, where it has remained ever since. To change the situation at this date would probably require a constitutional amendment.

Federal Interest in Education

Despite the silence of the Constitution, the federal government has always shown considerable interest in education. President John Adams was most forceful in his espousal of the cause of public education.

> The whole people must take upon themselves the education of the whole people and must be willing to bear the expense of it. There should not be a district of one mile square without a school in it at the expense of the people themselves.

Washington and Jefferson made similar statements, and the government traditionally has proved willing to give certain types of aid to the public schools.[6]

LAND GRANTS FOR PUBLIC SCHOOLS.   The colonies had definite policies involving the grant of public lands for local schools.   Under the Articles of Confederation of 1781, one lot out of every township was reserved for the maintenance of public schools.   Beginning with the admission of Ohio into the Union in 1802, the granting of school sections was part and parcel of the system of admission under which the new states entered the Union. These land grants reached the considerable total of 121,130 square miles, and, including the land set aside in Alaska for education, have achieved a value that is estimated to be worth more than a billion dollars.

MORRILL ACT.   In 1862 Congress provided for the erection of land grant colleges by awarding 30,000 acres of government land for each member of Congress to which a state was entitled.   The law provided that the states, in order to qualify for the free land, must provide buildings and equipment with their own funds.   There are now sixty-nine land grant institutions; one out of every five college students in America attends a land grant institution.

SECOND MORRILL ACT.   The amount of aid given such colleges has been increased greatly from time to time.   In 1890, the second Morrill Act gave a flat continual grant of $25,000 to each state and territory; in 1907 and 1935 supplementary grants were made.   They now total over five million dollars a year.

SMITH–HUGHES ACT.   The federal government in 1917 took a big step toward extending national influence in education with the Smith–Hughes Act.   This act, together with supplementary statutes in 1929 and 1934, supported the teaching of agriculture and home economics, and the mechanical arts and trades at the high school level.

GEORGE–DEEN AND GEORGE–BARDEN ACTS.   Annual appropriations exceeding 75 million dollars were provided through the George–Deen and George–Barden Acts (1937 and 1946, respectively).   The first act helped

---

[6] "Expressions on Education by American Statesmen and Publicists," *U.S. Bureau of Education Bulletin,* no. 28 (1913).

to subsidize education for distributive (buying and selling) occupations; the second greatly increased the sums previously allotted for agriculture, home economics, and trade and industrial education.

Direct Federal Involvement in Education

While the government aids education only through categorical financial means, as in the examples cited above, there are certain areas in which it works directly in conjunction with local districts, and, occasionally, educates directly.

PUBLIC LAWS 874 AND 815. Following the Second World War, school districts in which federal defense projects or installations attracted multitudes of families were unable to solve financial problems arising from such a population impact without some sort of aid. In 1950 Public Law 874 reimbursed schools for the education of children who, without the presence of certain types of federal enterprises, could not have been accommodated in the local schools. Public Law 815 was intended to accomplish a similar function in the area of school building and capital outlay. Thus, the United States government found itself in the position of supplying the financial needs of a number of local school districts by paying out a definite sum each year for the instruction and educational housing of federally connected pupils.

INDIAN EDUCATION. The federal government supports the education of more than 77,000 Indian children. Almost half of this number are enrolled in the 300 Indian schools operated by the government. The remainder attend public schools, with tuition paid by the government. Federal funds spent annually for Indian education total over $10,000,000.

TERRITORIES AND POSSESSIONS. In Puerto Rico, the Virgin Islands, Samoa, Guam, and the Canal Zone, education is supported in part or largely by federal grants and appropriations.

ARMED FORCES SCHOOLS. The United States operates various armed forces schools: West Point Military Academy, Annapolis Naval Academy, Air Force Academy, Army Medical School, Army War College, National War College, and the Air University. The government also establishes schools at posts, foreign garrisons, or camps for the benefit of the armed services personnel or for their dependents.

EMERGENCY FEDERAL EDUCATIONAL PROJECTS. During the depression and World War II, certain short-lived educational projects were undertaken by the national government and subsequently terminated when the original need for them ceased to exist. Among these were the Civilian Conservation Corps, the National Youth Administration, the Public Works Administration, the Works Progress Administration, the Servicemen's Readjustment Act.

Types of Federal Grants to Public Schools

There are two basic types of federal grants-in-aid for public schools. The categorical grant is awarded for specific purposes. It has been criticized because it is divisive and fragments the overall educational program; proliferates programs that are difficult to change; reduces the choice of alternatives at the local level; requires an inordinate amount of time to prepare proposals and evaluate programs that are requested by those outside the system; oversimplifies programs and services in the "national interest"; and requires external controls, contrary to the American educational system.[7] Some of the categorical grants are considered to be of a temporary nature, such as Title II (library resources) and Title III (supplementary centers) of the Elementary and Secondary Education Act (ESEA), and Title V (counseling and testing) of the National Defense Education Act. Others which the federal government believes contribute to important national goals are of a continuing nature.

The second type is the general purpose grant, intended to strengthen the total educational program by compensating for deficiencies in the public school tax base while continuing local control. The funds are provided with no strings attached and with minimum limitations on their use so that the local school districts can use them as they see fit. The Elementary and Secondary Education Act of 1965 is considered to be a historic breakthrough in federal funding since it comes close to being a general grant. Although there are some restrictions, school districts have the flexibility to use certain portions of the funds for salaries, construction, textbooks, and curriculum aids according to their needs.

---

[7] William P. McLure, "Financing Education at the Federal Level," *The School Administrator,* p. 46.

Since 1968, Congress has been considering "block grants" as a type of general aid. In that year, it approved a block-grant approach to vocational education. Under a block grant, money would be distributed to the states for education with the federal government either prorating the funds between the blocks or leaving this decision to the state legislatures.

Present categorical and other federal grants-in-aid would be consolidated into four major blocks: (1) general elementary and secondary education, (2) higher education, (3) vocational education, and (4) education for the handicapped and disabled. Some propose that all federal assistance be divided into the first two blocks.

Block grants, it is argued, would provide general federal fiscal assistance without control. Channeled through the states and through local districts, they would permit flexibility in their use and help release creative potential to improve education in each school district. They would eliminate some of the time-consuming paperwork, the period of waiting to see what happens to applications, and late funding, all of which have been prevalent with categorical assistance programs.

Public Laws and Acts

In 1969, federal money for education was authorized for 118 programs that were administered by the U.S. Office of Education. There were 10 programs for school construction; 62 programs for programs, instruction, and administration; 31 programs for teacher and other professional training and student assistance; and 15 programs for research. Several of these programs might be authorized by one public law. It would be impractical to list or explain all of these programs in this book. Those who want additional, up-to-date information concerning federal appropriations for education should write to the Budget and Manpower Division, Office of Administration, U.S. Office of Education. However, a few of the more important public laws are described here.

PUBLIC LAW 346. Commonly called the G.I. Bill, it provides liberal educational opportunities for veterans.

PUBLIC LAW 507. In 1950, it established the National Science Foundation that provides loans, grants, fellowships, and institutes to strengthen research in mathematics, science, and engineering for the purpose of securing the national defense.

PUBLIC LAW 83–531.   This law established the Cooperative Research Program and provides financial contracts with universities, colleges, and state educational agencies for conducting research, surveys, and demonstrations in the field of education.

PUBLIC LAW 85–864.   The National Defense Education Act of 1958 (NDEA) authorizes a little more than one billion dollars in federal aid to schools.   Its avowed intention is to find and encourage talent at all levels of education.   The act was originally composed of ten titles, but was raised to eleven when it was amended in 1964.

PUBLIC LAW 88–204.   The Higher Education Facilities Act of 1963 authorizes funds for public and private nonprofit institutions, cooperative centers, and boards of higher education.

PUBLIC LAW 88–452.   The Economic Opportunity Act of 1964, also called the Anti-Poverty Bill, authorizes funds for programs from preschool to adult education.   Its purpose is to eliminate deprivation and poverty and to give everyone an opportunity to work and to live in decency and dignity.

PUBLIC LAW 88–352.   The Civil Rights Act of 1964 provides funds to aid school boards in hiring advisers and training employees for problems incident to school desegregation.

PUBLIC LAW 88–210A.   The Vocational Education Act of 1963 provides funds to maintain, extend, and improve vocational education programs and to develop new programs.   This act was amended in 1968 as Public Law 90–576.

PUBLIC LAW 89–10.   The Elementary and Secondary Education Act of 1965 (ESEA) has been considered one of the most significant educational achievements in the history of the nation.   For the first time, federal law recognized the national responsibility for educating all of America's children.   Under this law, federal control is prohibited.

PUBLIC LAW 90–538.   The Handicapped Children's Act of 1958 authorizes grants to public and private nonprofit agencies for the development and implementation of experimental programs.   It provides for the establishment of from 75 to 100 model programs designed to develop successful approaches to assist preschool handicapped children.

PUBLIC LAW 90–35.   The Education Professions Development Act of 1967 (EPDA) provides funds to attract teachers, train and retrain teachers, and to strengthen school administration and curriculum development.   It established 11 major priority areas for fiscal 1970.

There are so many federal laws and acts that one can become confused.   Many school districts are not aware of the federal funds that are available or the procedure for attaining them.   A national survey made in 1969 regarding the use of federal funds found:

1.   Only 40 percent of the administrators questioned were aware of the funds available.
2.   Twenty percent of the school districts surveyed received more than the average of federal aid per student, and 50 percent of the metropolitan school systems received less than the national average.
3.   The amount of federal aid received by the school districts surveyed ranged from $1,800 to $25,000,000.
4.   The amount received per student ranged from $1 to $228.
5.   Districts that employed a full-time federal aid specialist received 32 percent more federal funds than school districts without such specialists.[8]

Because of the problems in handling federal assistance, some districts have found it practical to employ an administrator for the sole purpose of handling federal funds.   His duties are to determine what funds are available; how to get them; to write the necessary projects to become eligible; to apply for the funds; to handle the extra paperwork; and to administer the funds at the local level.

The Issue of Federal Participation

A controversy that seems destined to agitate the country for many years centers around the degree to which federal participation in education shall be permitted.   It should be noted that the argument focuses on the *degree* of participation, not the actual fact of participation.   No one seriously

---

[8] "Many School Districts Shorted on Federal Aid," *Los Angeles Times* (Oct. 20, 1969), p. 15.

proposes that our government withdraw from its myriad educational interests as they now exist.   No longer can one overlook the role of the federal
government in its influence on education.   However, the role of federal,
state, and local governments in education needs to be redefined.   The
question might be asked, "How far and to what extent should the federal
government help the state and local school districts solve their own
problems?"   Or, "Are their problems the concern of the federal government?"

In answer to the question of whether the federal government should
play a role in education, Campbell states that "education is too closely
linked to the national well-being, particularly in terms of trained manpower
and economic growth, for any answer other than federal participation."[9]
Such legislative enactments as Public Law 874, the Smith–Hughes Act,
and the various statutes designed to support vocational and distributive
education have become part of America's educational pattern and receive
the general support of most people.   The purpose of the newer federal
programs is to change educational institutions and to develop skills that are
applicable to the new technology.   This trend differs from the traditional
mode of solely stabilizing and strengthening existing educational programs.
National participation in education is, through the increasing speed and
magnitude of federal grants-in-aid, approaching national federalism of
education.   The present volume of educational legislation indicates that
a national educational policy may not be far off.

Education in the United States has traditionally been handled by local
communities and generally controlled by the states.   Nevertheless, the
widely divergent standards of educational competence in different sections
of the country, coupled with the equally contrasting abilities to finance
adequate educational programs, have given rise to proposals for greater
federal financial aid to general education.   A so-called "federal equalization" program, designed to assist states and local districts to establish
certain minimum standards for salaries, school plants, curriculum improvement, and equipment, is seriously proposed by many educators.   Legislation to this effect has been introduced and hotly contested in Congress.

Of the several objections that have been raised to large-scale federal
aid to education, the most potent is that which invokes the specter of
federal control.   The argument assumes that the gift of national funds to
the states for educational use will inevitably result in the abdication of

---

[9] Roald F. Campbell, "Federal–State Educational Relations," *Phi Delta Kappan,*
p. 17.

local and state control of the people's schools, and the immersion of public education in an unwieldy and insensitive federal bureaucracy. Protagonists of this theory also warn against the imminent danger of political propaganda emerging within the framework of federal control of the schools.

Menacker has pointed out some of the complexities of congressional behavior as they affect educational legislation. He states that "a review of federal activity reveals a piecemeal approach in which support is forthcoming only when improving education seems a necessary response to a real or imaginary national emergency. Corollary to this is the fact that federal aid is not primarily intended for the improvement of education *per se,* but rather for the achievement of certain specific objectives for which the educational structure provides the most suitable vehicle."[10] The use of the word "defense" in the National Defense Education Act of 1958 is an example. The war on poverty and civil rights have been other considerations. Race relations, the public–private school controversy, and the issue of federal control are the chief political issues relating to federal aid to education, according to Menacker.[11]

School districts have problems in predicting what federal assistance they will receive. Congress changes and cuts appropriations, making it difficult for a school district to plan ahead. Many children are deprived because the costs of education go up, but federal assistance either remains static or is cut. Many projects have been dropped when federal funds were decreased or withdrawn. Plans should be made for worthwhile programs to be continued. Perhaps the particular federal agency should require the local school district to commit itself to maintaining its new programs before the original funds are granted. Otherwise, state and local governments must take on the added burden of supplying funds to establish new programs. The federal share of education reached an all-time high of 8 percent of the school dollar in 1967–68; it dropped to 7.4 percent in 1968–69, to 7.2 percent in 1969–70, and was estimated to be only 6.9 percent in 1970–71.[12] School districts cannot operate efficiently under this arrangement. There are those who believe that the federal government should raise the support of public education to a minimum of one-third of the total cost of education.

---

[10] Julius Menacker, "The Organizational Behavior of Congress in the Formulation of Educational Support Policy," *Phi Delta Kappan,* p. 78.

[11] Menacker, "The Organizational Behavior," p. 80.

[12] National Education Association, Research Division, *Estimates of School Statistics, 1970–71,* Research Report 1970–R15 (Washington, D.C., 1970).

Proponents of federal aid hasten to disassociate themselves from what they call the "straw man" of federal control. They point out that virtually no one advocates any form of federal control over education, and that the coupling of federal aid with federal control is a prime example of *non sequitur* reasoning. It is difficult to demonstrate that the granting of national monies to land grant colleges, or to vocational and distributive education, or directly to the schools through subsidies for federally connected pupils, has resulted in the supplanting of local by federal control to any perceptible degree. The friends of federal aid point to the low standards of schooling in certain states, analyze the correspondingly high tax rates and lowly assessed valuations in the same areas, and challenge the opposition to demonstrate any conceivable way to solve the problem on a purely local level.

Dr. James E. Allen, Jr., Assistant Secretary for Education and U.S. Commissioner of Education, made this statement in 1970:

> The unique feature and obligation of Federal participation in education is that of perspective—perspective which allows for identification of those problems and needs that transcend State borders and thus require a broader approach; perspective which permits the overall appraisal of the needs and progress of education that can serve as a basis for the continuing improvement and renewal of the educational enterprise, and the marshaling of the resources to facilitate it.[13]

He also stated that federal responsibility falls into two major areas of action:

1. Research and development, planning, demonstration, and dissemination . . . in order to provide practical answers and technical assistance for use of the State and local levels.
2. Finance that is more equitable, efficient, and adequate.[14]

Federal Interest in Integration

For many years the national government has been moving slowly toward the abolition of racial segregation in all of its many agencies and projects. In pursuing this policy, it is encountering apparently immovable opposition in certain states. At almost the same time the movement for

---

[13] James E. Allen, Jr., "It Must Be a Three-way Partnership," *CTA Journal,* pp. 18–19.

[14] Allen, "It Must Be a Three-way Partnership," p. 18.

integration began, it received a massive boost from recent Supreme Court decisions that outlawed all forms of segregation.

The resulting conflict has posed the most serious threat to federal authority since the Civil War.   At the present time, all government-operated schools are being integrated, with every indication that further federal extension into various areas of public education will carry with it unalterable opposition to the principle of racial segregation.   In the area of state-supported education, complete integration may be a generation off.

The United States Office of Education

Established in 1867, the "Office of Education" (existing under various names) has now been established for over a century.   During that time, its three chief functions have been research, publication, and the furnishing of educational leadership.

1867–1906.   The first period of the Office of Education's development saw the production of a large amount of biographical and historical research conducted and published under its auspices.   The Indians of Alaska came under the jurisdiction of the Office at this time, providing for the education of their children.   The administration of $5,000,000 annually in the form of federal subventions, to the land grant colleges also was a responsibility of the Office.

1906–33.   A considerable enlargement of the activities and personnel of the Office of Education took place during this period.   The services of its experts for the purpose of surveying school districts were first made available in 1911, and the importance of that activity was underlined by numerous requests for similar surveys in succeeding years.   New divisions were constantly being added to the Office, notably in the fields of rural education, higher education, and education for blacks.   A monthly publication, *School Life,* was issued, and the Biennial Survey of Education was first issued in 1918.   Concomitantly, a marked rise in the Office's annual appropriations occurred, from $300,000 to $1,600,000.

SINCE 1933.   The administration of vocational education under the Smith–Hughes Act was added to the responsibilities of the Office of Education in 1933.   The Great Depression and the war that followed brought many new duties and obligations to the Office, including a burgeoning of requests for technical assistance on many fronts. The modern period of the Office's history has seen three supplementary functions added to its traditional interests: the establishment and administration of experimental centers; cooperation with state and local school systems in the areas of vocational education and land grant colleges; and the handling of emergency education programs.

Since 1953 the Office of Education has been part of the Department of Health, Education, and Welfare. In 1972, Congress established the Education Division within HEW. The division consists of the Office of Education and a new agency, the National Institute of Education, devoted to the promotion of educational research.

Over the years, the responsibilities of the Office of Education have increased greatly with the enactment of federal laws authorizing it to make grants and loans and to administer programs designed to improve the quality of education at every level throughout the country. Today, the Office provides support to elementary and secondary education in broad areas of strong national interest, such as compensatory education for the disadvantaged, education of the handicapped, vocational education, and assistance in federally affected areas. It makes grants to school districts to help them meet the special needs incident to the elimination or prevention of minority-group student segregation; bestows grants to developing institutions of higher education; and administers several programs of financial assistance to college students.

In the field of services, however, the Office probably will play its most important role. A city or district superintendent of schools today owes much of his success as an educational planner and tactician to the research findings released at periodic intervals by the United States Office of Education. Statistics on almost every conceivable subject, however remotely related to education, are painstakingly collected, correlated, and charted by the Office personnel, and made available without cost to educators in the field. Such services remove much of the guesswork from school administration and make possible scientific planning by administrators.

The Need for a Secretary of Education

For the past ten or more years, various educational associations have been discussing the need for a Secretary of Education to head up a cabinet-level

Department of Education. The movement gained strength in 1971 when the "Big Six," composed of the American Association of School Administrators, the Council of Chief State School Officers, the National Association of State Boards of Education, the National Congress of Parents and Teachers, the National Education Association, and the National School Boards Association, unanimously endorsed the establishment of a cabinet-level Department of Education.

There are 42 federal agencies involved in some type of educational activity. A cabinet department would provide a means for coordinating the various activities, improving the administration of federal programs, eliminating duplication of effort, and raising the status of education in America. The "Big Six" recommended the establishment of a national advisory commission on education, appointed by the President to encourage lay participation in education on the national level. It also proposed a legislative program that included the following items:

1. The amending of all applicable federal legislation to provide for a minimum of a three-year authorization with funds to be appropriated one year in advance, on a level at least equal to the appropriation of the previous year.
2. Full funding of all federal education programs.
3. Increase of federal funding of education programs to at least one-third of total education expenditures within the next five years.
4. Support of comprehensive manpower-training legislation.
5. Increased federal funding to public schools for the encouragement of early childhood development programs.
6. Full funding of the federal share in the amended National School Lunch Program.
7. Recognition of the continuing need for federal financial aid in lieu of taxes impacted by federal activities and low-rent housing.
8. Support of the revision and extension of higher education legislation.[15]

Summary

American education, although increasingly a big business, has always been decentralized and essentially local in nature. Despite this fact, the com-

---

[15] American Association of School Administrators, *Hot Line*.

mon goals of citizenship, literacy, and productivity have led to a surprising similarity in educational structure, curriculum, and output.

One reason for this is the involvement of and the interest taken in education by the national government, dating back before the adoption of the Constitution in 1789. Though education is not mentioned in that document, the "general welfare" clause has prompted Congress to exert leadership over the years in such areas as land grants to schools, vocational education, and more recently in the broader sectors of curriculum, library science, and racial integration.

A great national debate is presently occurring over the degree of federal participation in education, especially concerning the need to equalize educational opportunities in different parts of the country. The question is an old one: How much federal control would and should accompany this kind of participation?

Any controls would doubtless be administered by the U.S. Office of Education, which, since its inception more than a century ago, has shown a steady growth, especially in the post-Sputnik period when federal concern over the quality of American schools was spurred by the Cold War. Such growth has led in recent years to an increasing demand for a Secretary of Education who would enjoy cabinet status.

Trends

Clearly defined trends in the relation of the federal government to public education are discernible.

TOWARD AN INCREASE IN FEDERAL SUPPORT OF EDUCATION. Everything points to eventual adoption of the principle that the birthright of every American is a decent education. There are strong indications that the vast majority of Americans have already adopted this as a part of the American ideal, although Congress may be the last to recognize it. With the increasing acceptance of this doctrine, federal aid to needy states and school districts on some sort of equalization basis will be natural and inevitable. In the century and a half since the first steps were taken that involved the United States government in education, the trend has been clear. Federal interest and financial contributions have intensified and multiplied in areas undreamed of by the founders of our form of government. It remains now only to implement the principle logically and efficiently.

Local school districts can no longer support education with funds derived from a local tax base. To aid the local district sufficiently, federal assistance will need to reach 25 or 30 percent of the cost of education at the local level. The alternative (an unlikely one) would be to have the federal government return to the states some of the tax sources that it has been preempting for the past forty years.

TOWARD LITTLE, IF ANY, EXTENSION OF FEDERAL CONTROL. In the American democracy, it is extremely difficult, if not impossible, to put something into effect that most of the people dislike and mistrust. Therefore, a way must be found to pour the nation's wealth into local schools without sacrificing the sturdy independence of the individual districts and their governing boards.

Federal control of public education is universally abhorred; and practically speaking, it would be extraordinarily difficult to implement and to operate. Controls that are found necessary probably will prove to be extensions of the existing, very tenuous authority exercised in the administration of present federal aid to education. Such items as minimum credentialing of teachers and minimum standards of curriculum and instruction may be affected favorably by increasing federal participation in education, but the overall influence should be barely perceptible. America's schools will continue to be the responsibility of the local communities.

However, in conjunction with large foundations and private industry, there may be a move toward the development of curricula at the national level. Because local control is basic to our educational system, educators at the local and state level must be involved if national curricula are developed.

TOWARD FURTHER EXPANSION OF THE OFFICE OF EDUCATION. Since its inception in 1867, the role of the United States Office of Education has been a steadily expanding one. This trend should continue as long as the economy and population of the nation continue to grow. Its past and present work in the field of surveys and research should go on without interruption; succeeding generations should see more actual authority placed in its hands. It may actually succeed in becoming at once the guide and the conscience of American education.

It appears that the Office will place more emphasis on research and development. In cooperation with private industry, decentralized research and development centers could be established in several regional places in the country. Data from these centers could be fed into the Office's computer system and provide information for the Congress as it discusses educational appropriations. School districts could also benefit from such a central data system.

TOWARD INCREASED FEDERAL INTERVENTION IN SPECIAL FIELDS OF EDUCATION. The lessons learned as the result of successful adventures in educational and quasi-educational projects in time of war and depression will be applied in the future to problems of the atomic age. As new and presently unheard-of problems arise in our relations with our fellowmen or with the physical universe, the federal government will undoubtedly mobilize and finance the educational manpower and facilities necessary for solving new problems.

TOWARD MORE COORDINATION BETWEEN GOVERNMENT AGENCIES AND LOCAL SCHOOL DISTRICTS. The relationships between federal and state governments and local school districts will be delimited, clarified, and streamlined more carefully to ensure minimum confusion and maximum effectiveness.

TOWARD MORE GENERAL AID. Federal assistance will move more toward general support than toward categorical aid which often has been given for political purposes (whatever the public reason). General support will have the purposes of equalizing educational opportunities among the states as well as within states; it will also help support the basic programs of public schools at the local level.

Administrative Problem   In Basket

Problem

Mr. Jones is superintendent of a school district in a disadvantaged area. There are many bilingual and learning problems. The superintendent and his staff want to apply for federal funds under Title I of the Elementary and Secondary Education Act to provide a better educational program. However, the Board of Education has always been violently opposed to all federal aid and has indicated that it will not approve such a request.

What can Mr. Jones do to convince the Board of Education of the need for federal assistance?

If the Board rejects the application for federal funds, what should the superintendent attempt to do to gain support for the needed program?

Selected References

ALLEN, JAMES E., JR. "It Must Be a Three-way Partnership." *CTA Journal* 66 (January 1970).

AMERICAN ASSOCIATION OF SCHOOL ADMINISTRATORS. *Hot Line 4* (February 1971).

Brown, Rex v. *Research and the Credibility of Estimates.* Homewood, Ill.: Richard D. Irwin, 1971.

CAMPBELL, ROALD F. "Federal–State Educational Relations." *Phi Delta Kappan* 49 (September 1967).

Federal Funds for Education and Related Activities. Washington, D.C.: U.S. Office of Education, 1966.

HUTCHINS, CLAYTON D., and BARR, RICHARD H. *Statistics of State School Systems, 1965–66.* Washington, D.C.: U.S. Department of Health, Education, and Welfare, 1968.

KIMBROUGH, RALPH B. *Political Power and Educational Decision-making.* Chicago: Rand McNally and Co., 1961.

LAND, WILLIAM G. "Can Federal Programs Be Coordinated?" *Phi Delta Kappan* 46 (March 1965).

MCCLURE, WILLIAM P. "Financing Education at the Federal Level." *The School Administrator* 24 (February 1967).

MENACKER, JULIUS. "The Organizational Behavior of Congress in the Formulation of Educational Support Policy." *Phi Delta Kappan* 48 (October 1966).

MORPHET, EDGAR L. *Relationship of Education to Government.* Forty-Fourth Yearbook of the National Society for the Study of Education, Part II. Chicago: University of Chicago Press, 1945.

NATIONAL SCHOOL PUBLIC RELATIONS ASSOCIATION. *Federal Aid: New Directions for Education in 1969–70.* Washington, D.C.: The Association, 1969.

QUATTLEBAUM, CHARLES A. *Federal Education Policies, Programs, and Proposals.* Washington, D.C.: U.S. Government Printing Office, 1960.

STOOPS, EMERY, and RAFFERTY, M. L., JR. *Practices and Trends in School Administration.* Boston: Ginn and Co., 1961.

3

The State's Relation to Education

Each state has a responsibility for its educational program which it operates according to specific laws. All states have a definite organizational structure, consisting of an education department, a chief school officer, and numerous divisions headed by administrators. There is debate regarding the amount of control that the state should exert on local school districts. However, all districts look to the state for leadership and service.

This chapter includes a discussion of the following topics:

Similarity of State Organization
The Chief State School Officer
The State Department of Education
State Controls over Private Education
Historical Function of the State in Education
Public Education and State Laws
Degree of State Control of Education
The State's Role in Educational Services
Summary
Trends

Similarity of State Organization

The first state to establish a means for the supervision and control of education was New York, in 1784. Although called the University of the State of New York, it actually functioned as a state board of education and has continued to operate as such. Since that time, every state in the Union has set up an educational department with at least one board having responsibility for the supervision of schools. In 1964, all states except Illinois and Wisconsin had a state board of education.

Sections concerning education appear in all state constitutions. The legislature establishes the enabling acts for a state's system of public education, specifies laws for local boards of education, appropriates the money for financing education, and passes laws. Although it delegates power to local boards of education, it retains absolute authority over public schools. The amount of delegated power varies from state to state.[1]

QUALIFICATION FOR STATE BOARD MEMBERSHIP. Several states have set up qualifications for membership on state boards of education. Some require all congressional districts to have equal representation; some require a certain percentage of members to be professional educators; and some prohibit membership of professional educators. No state requires any educational qualifications, but the vast majority of state board members throughout the country have attended college. It is the general consensus that board members be persons interested in public education, of high character, and without political axes to grind. Americans favor lay state boards of education, composed of laymen selected from various walks of life. The National Council of Chief State School Officers states that, "In each state there should be a non-partisan, lay state board of education composed of seven to twelve able citizens, broadly representative of the general public and unselfishly interested in public education, elected by the people in a manner prescribed by law."[2]

SIZE OF STATE BOARDS OF EDUCATION. The number of members of state boards of education ranges from 3 in Mississippi to 27 in Indiana. Thirty states range from 6 to 10 members, with 9 being about the average.[3] An uneven number is desirable so that voting stalemates do not occur.

METHOD OF SELECTING STATE BOARD MEMBERS. The method of selecting state board members varies from state to state. They may be appointed by the governor with or without legislative approval; elected by

---

[1] Robert E. Wilson, *Educational Administration,* p. 198.

[2] National Council of Chief State School Officers, *Our System of Education* (Washington, D.C.: The Council, 1950), p. 20.

[3] Clayton D. Hutchins and Richard H. Barr, *Statistics of State School Systems,* OE–20020–66, U.S. Department of Health, Education, and Welfare (Washington, D.C.: U.S. Government Printing Office, 1968), p. 20.

popular vote; selected by conventions of local school board members; appointed by the state superintendent (Wyoming); or selected by the legislature. Although consensus favors the elective method of selecting state board members, in 1968 the governors of 31 states appointed all or most of the members. In four of the eleven states that elect state board members (Colorado, Louisiana, New Mexico, and Texas), they are elected on a party ballot or are affiliated with a political party,[4] despite the fact that the position should be nonpolitical. Educators favor the election of state board members over the appointive method. Whatever the method used, it is difficult to recruit competent people to serve.

TERMS OF OFFICE FOR STATE BOARD MEMBERS. The terms of office for state board members vary considerably, ranging from 2 to 14 years, with 4 to 6 years the most common.[5] If a member is to serve effectively, 4 years should be the minimum. In states where members are appointed by the governor, their tenure should.be the same as that of the governor. Terms of office should overlap in order to assure continuous operation.

FUNCTIONS OF STATE BOARDS OF EDUCATION. State boards of education are not analogous to local school boards in terms of function. They have certain legislative and policymaking powers, but most of their activities fall into three classifications: (1) the direction of the state department of education; (2) the furnishing of expert advice to the state legislature; and (3) the constant study of state educational problems. Common policy-making responsibilities include direction of state-operated schools, adoption of textbooks and courses of study, and the execution of the provisions of legislative statutes. The distinction between separate duties is not always clear. In some states, the boards also have executive duties. It is recommended that boards do not take on administrative functions because these should be the responsibility of the chief state school officer.

It is difficult in many states to determine which duties are delegated to the state board of education, the chief school officer, or the state department of education. The state legislature in California, for example, may move into educational matters by passing laws that affect education with or without consulting the state board or the state department of education, further complicating the functions of the state board. Laws of various

---

[4] Sherman H. Frey and Keith R. Getschman, *School Administration: Selected Readings,* p. 94.
[5] Wilson, *Educational Administration,* p. 199.

states are concerned with compulsory education; extension of education for all children and youth; establishment of school districts; reorganizing and enlarging school districts; and fixing minimum standards. Each state has laws that constitute a framework within which to regulate local districts.

In some states, the state board of education appoints several executive officers to carry on particular duties; they may or may not be under the direct supervision of the state school officer. Often this leads to confusion and the state board has to coordinate their administrative activities. In Hawaii, the state board of education not only is in charge of the state's educational system but also is responsible for the operation of all school districts.

The Chief State School Officer

New York pioneered the office of state superintendent of schools, appointing the first such officer in 1812. His duties were largely financial, concerned with the management of funds used to furnish grants to local districts. Maryland provided for a similar officer in 1826. Although neither of these offices proved continuous (both were abolished and then reestablished some years later), they mark the first attempt to provide a director for the ramifying operations of public education within individual states.[6]

All states today have some sort of officer whose special responsibility is to direct public education on a state level. Although the title of this officer is usually Superintendent of Public Instruction, there are local variations such as Commissioner of Education and Director of Education.

SELECTION AND TERM OF OFFICE. The chief state school officer is selected in three ways. In 21 states, he is elected by popular vote; the state board of education appoints him in 24 states; and in 5 states, he is appointed by the governor.[7] Although each method may have its advantages, the National Council of Chief State School Officers recommends that the chief state school officer be selected by the state board of education on a nonpartisan basis.[8]

When the chief state school officer has to run for office, politics are

---

[6] H. R. Douglass and Calvin Grieder, *American Public Education* (New York: Ronald Press Co., 1948), pp. 148–49.

[7] Wilson, *Educational Administration*, p. 200.

[8] National Council of Chief State School Officers, *Our System,* p. 20.

usually involved—even when the position is considered to be nonpartisan. Competent people may not run because of the necessity of campaigning and the time and money it involves.

There are advantages in having the state board select the chief state school officer: (1) The board is aware of what requirements are needed to fill the office and therefore can select the most competent person. (2) It can appoint a person who will cooperate with the state board, whereas a popular election might elect someone who would oppose the board. (3) Selection by the state board is more in accord with this country's generally accepted principles of organization and administration.[9]

Regardless of how they are selected, it is often difficult to get qualified, professional educators to accept the position because of the low salaries. District superintendents, especially in large city districts, receive much higher salaries than many state superintendents.

The term of office for chief state school officials is prescribed by law in only 31 states, ranging from 1 year in Delaware to 6 years in Minnesota. The most common term is 4 years, particularly when the official's position is an elective one.[10] Some states prescribe an indefinite tenure, especially when the state board of education makes the selection.

All chief state school officers should have legally prescribed terms of office of not less than 4 years. This is necessary in order to exercise powers and carry out duties in an effective manner. Removal from office should only be for cause according to legally established policies, and not for political reasons or at the whim of the state board. The assurance of security in office and the payment of adequate salaries should attract competent people to administer a state's educational programs.

DUTIES AND RESPONSIBILITIES OF THE CHIEF STATE SCHOOL OFFICER. The powers and duties of state school heads are not uniform, ranging from advisory (in Maryland, New Hampshire, and New York) to overall (in Massachusetts, Michigan, and Colorado). Generally speaking, the office labors under statutory and constitutional handicaps that are anachronistic today. Since almost two-thirds of the states provide for the office of state superintendent of schools in their constitutions, the functions of the office are similarly embedded in those same constitutions, whose provisions

---

9 Edgar L. Morphet, Roe L. Johns, and Theodore L. Reller, *Educational Administration: Concepts, Practices, and Issues* © 1959. By permission of Prentice-Hall Inc., Englewood Cliffs, N.J., p. 209.

10 Frey and Getschman, *School Administration*, p. 105.

remain unchanged and unmodified. Some of the features most frequently set forth by law are: title of the office, manner of selecting the incumbent, eligibility requirements, term of office, salary, and many of the powers and duties of the office.[11]

In general, the powers and duties of a chief state school officer may be described as follows:

1. Serves as executive officer of the state board of education and as administrative head of the state department of education.
2. Recommends policies and regulations for the educational programs of the state.
3. Cooperates with the state legislature and recommends educational legislation.
4. Interprets educational laws and regulations.
5. Acts as an arbitrator in disputes over educational matters.
6. Submits periodic reports and data regarding the educational system to the governor, the legislature, and other agencies.[12]
7. Serves in a leadership capacity in working with other state agencies.
8. Conducts research and collects and tabulates statistical information in the educational realm.
9. Keeps the public informed regarding educational programs of the state, the needs and accomplishments of the schools, and financial matters.
10. Advises the legislature about the financial needs of the state's school systems.
11. Distributes federal and state funds to local school districts.
12. Approves or accredits public schools and sometimes private schools.

The State Department of Education

The state department of education should consist of a state board of education, a chief state school officer, and the necessary staff to carry out its functions. It should be the legislative body of the state's educational system. Because education is a nonpolitical function, the state department should not be involved in politics.

---

11 By permission of Macmillan Publishing Co., Inc. from *The Fundamentals of Public School Administration,* 4th ed. by Ward G. Reeder. Copyright © 1958 by Macmillan Publishing Co., Inc., p. 56.

12 Morphet, Johns, and Reller, *Educational Administration,* p. 199. © 1959. By permission of Prentice-Hall, Inc., Englewood Cliffs, N.J.

It is difficult to compare programs of state departments of education because the duties of state school officers are not the same, resources vary, and programs delegated by state legislatures are different. The larger the state, the more complex the organization of the state education department becomes. Usually, several main divisions are established with their own directors or assistant superintendents, as illustrated in Figure 3–1. Some large states, like New York, may employ as many as 680 persons on the professional staff of the state department, whereas smaller ones, such as Alaska, may employ as few as 15. In addition to the professional staff, there are secretarial and clerical assistants, regional and district supervisory staffs, administrative staffs for the chief state school officer, and operation and maintenance people.[13] Generally speaking, the stronger and more universal the public school program of a given state, the more complex and well-manned is its state department.

FUNCTIONS OF THE STATE DEPARTMENT OF EDUCATION. State departments of education have four major functions: (1) leadership responsibilities; (2) regulatory responsibilities; (3) operational responsibilities;[14] and (4) service responsibilities.

Leadership responsibilities are the most important functions of the state department and lead to the improvement of education at both the state and local level. They are concerned with planning, research, advising, coordinating, and providing information. If leadership is strong, local school districts will be encouraged to do something.[15]

Regulation involves protecting children and youth, assuring efficiency in management, providing a framework for instructional programs, and assuring the growth of an educated citizenry.[16] It is concerned with minimum programs, personnel, school plants, child accounting, and finance.

Operational responsibilities refer to the operation of various programs such as vocational rehabilitation, library services, adult education, and teacher-placement and retirement services. There is disagreement as to how much the state should be involved in operational functions. Fewer problems will arise, however, if there is effective state leadership.

---

[13] Hutchins and Barr, *Statistics of State School Systems,* p. 20.
[14] Fred F. Beach, *The Functions of State Departments of Education,* p. 3.
[15] Beach, *The Functions,* p. 10.
[16] Beach, *The Functions,* p. 10.

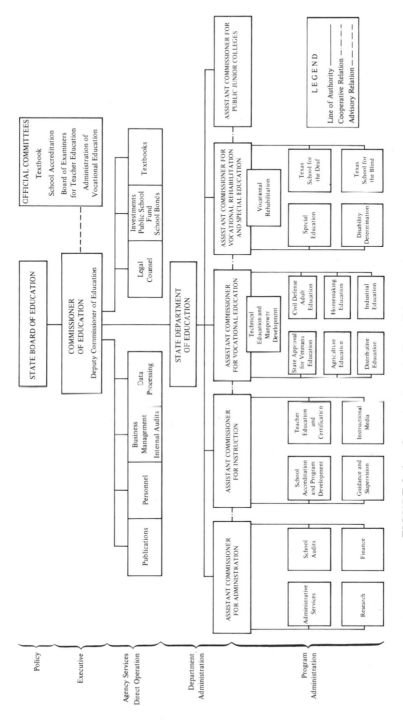

FIGURE 3–1. *Organization of a State Education Department.*

Policy

Executive

Agency Services
Direct Operation

Department
Administration

Program
Administration

STATE BOARD OF EDUCATION

OFFICIAL COMMITTEES
Textbook
School Accreditation
Board of Examiners
for Teacher Education
Administration of
Vocational Education

COMMISSIONER
OF EDUCATION
Deputy Commissioner of Education

Publications

Personnel

Business
Management
Internal Audits

Data
Processing

Legal
Counsel

Investments
Public School
Fund
School Bonds

Textbooks

STATE DEPARTMENT
OF EDUCATION

ASSISTANT COMMISSIONER
FOR ADMINISTRATION

Administrative
Services

School
Audits

Research

Finance

ASSISTANT COMMISSIONER
FOR INSTRUCTION

School
Accreditation
and Program
Development

Teacher
Education
and
Certification

Guidance and
Supervision

Instructional
Media

ASSISTANT COMMISSIONER
FOR VOCATIONAL EDUCATION

Technical
Education and
Manpower
Development

State Approval
for Veterans
Education

Civil Defense
Adult
Education

Agriculture
Education

Homemaking
Education

Distributive
Education

Industrial
Education

ASSISTANT COMMISSIONER FOR
VOCATIONAL REHABILITATION
AND SPECIAL EDUCATION

Vocational
Rehabilitation

Special
Education

Texas
School for
the Deaf

Disability
Determination

Texas
School for
the Blind

ASSISTANT COMMISSIONER FOR
PUBLIC JUNIOR COLLEGES

LEGEND
Line of Authority ————
Cooperative Relation — — —
Advisory Relation — — — —

47

Service functions may be performed for the state as a whole or for local school districts; this varies from state to state. Lane explains that:

> In some states, service to the state as a whole is rendered by the State Department of Education, acting as an educational information center for interpreting education in the state to the chief executive of the state, the state legislature, and the people through comparative studies, statistical information, advice, clarification of laws, statutes and regulations. In other states, the state department may be responsible for operating special schools (for the blind, deaf, and so on), archives, libraries, teacher-placement agencies, teacher-retirement funds, controlling interscholastic athletics, programs of rehabilitation for the handicapped, and many other activities.[17]

State departments of education are often divided into divisions, each headed by a director, to carry out their functions. Typical divisions are:

Vocational education
Vocational rehabilitation
Instruction
Administration
Secondary education
Elementary education
Special education
Certification
Finance
Teacher education
Transportation
Health and physical education
Libraries
School plant
Research
Federal programs [18]

Each division may have two or more branches. "For example, an administrative division may have branches concerned with law, school district organization, statistical studies, or business management."[19]

---

[17] Willard R. Lane, Ronald G. Corwin, and William G. Monahan, *Foundations of Educational Administration: A Behavioral Analysis,* p. 163.

[18] Roald F. Campbell, John E. Corbally, Jr., and John A. Ramseyer, *Introduction to Educational Administration,* 3rd ed. (Boston: Allyn and Bacon, 1966), p. 414.

[19] Campbell, Corbally, Ramseyer, *Introduction to Educational Administration,* 3rd ed. (Boston: Allyn and Bacon, 1966), p. 414.

The state has the responsibility of organizing the state educationally into districts or subdivisions of some sort; of determining the degree of authority to be exercised by these subdivisions; of supplying certain financial support to educational activities; of certifying teachers; and of determining the basic educational program for all schools. To perform these duties, the state needs to organize education in general conformity with the following goals:

1. A well-planned program of general education for all children and youth, and also suitable preparation for particular vocations in accordance with the needs of children and youth.
2. Instruction by carefully selected teachers who are competent and well prepared, and who are interested in the development of community life.
3. Safe and sanitary school buildings adapted to a modern program of instruction and related services.
4. Suitable school equipment and instructional materials, including books and other reading materials adequate for the needs of the children.
5. Student aid when necessary to permit able young people to remain in school at least up to age eighteen.
6. Suitable opportunities for part-time and adult education.[20]

The state department should have the ability to deal flexibly with the broad and rapidly changing array of opportunities and problems in education and administration. There must be collaboration and communication across all levels of educational administration.

PROBLEMS VEXING STATE DEPARTMENTS OF EDUCATION. Although it is agreed that state departments of education should be in strong positions of educational leadership, this is not often the case. Organizational and financial inadequacies, over which the departments themselves exercise little control, operate to circumscribe their effectiveness. Laws made by state legislatures, sometimes without consulting the state department of education, become policy. Coordination and cooperation between the legislature and the state education department need to be promoted. Among the problems vexing state departments of education are the following:

---

[20] Advisory Committee on Education, *Report of the Committee* (Washington, D.C.: U.S. Government Printing Office, 1938), pp. 17–18.

Political implications when the chief state school officer must run for
    election.
Inadequate number of qualified personnel.
Salaries too low to attract and hold outstanding educators, causing unnec-
    essary turnover.
Lack of coordination between the various departments within the state
    department of education.
Divided responsibilities and duplication of effort between state agencies.
Powers and responsibilities not clearly defined.
Departmental organization cumbersome and archaic.
Conflicts with the state legislature caused by legislative mandates and fiscal
    controls which affect long-range planning.
Inadequate budget.

DEPENDENCY ON OTHER AGENCIES.   Some states provide other agencies
or boards to carry on educational functions such as higher education,
vocational education, school plant construction, and health services.   Examples of such governmental agencies are the state Department of Justice,
Attorney General's Office, State Fire Marshal's Office, and Department of
Public Safety.   A Retirement Board may regulate teacher retirement and
pension funds.   This dispersion of functions sometimes causes problems of
red tape and lack of coordination between the various agencies.   It is
recommended that the state department of education provide all the necessary educational services.   Other agencies may provide related noneducational services, but the responsibility for coordination should rest with the
state department of education.

State Controls over Private Education

All early American schools were private.   For many decades during the
Colonial period, private school enrollment was greater than public school
enrollment.   In recent decades, and especially since universal compulsory
education laws were enacted, the percentage of the school-age population
in attendance at private schools has been decreasing.   Today, about 15
percent of the population in the elementary schools and approximately 11
percent on the secondary level attend private schools.   People have the
right to send their children to either public or nonpublic schools, and the
courts have upheld this right.

Two reasons are commonly given by parents for sending their children to private schools (where they must pay tuition simultaneously with support of the public school system with their tax dollars). One reason is the belief that the private school has higher standards and more efficient instructional methods, particularly in the academic and classical curriculum areas. A second motive is the desire to give religious instruction to one's children, in addition to the citizenship training that makes up an important part of public school training. The greatest proportion of children who are enrolled in the nation's private educational institutions attend Roman Catholic parochial schools.

All schools are subject to state control, whether public or nonpublic. Laws establishing standards for private schools, and providing for state inspection of their facilities and educational offerings have long been common in some states; in others, private schools are subject to little regulation. Private school standards vary greatly throughout the country today. Some states require the same minimum standards that exist for public schools, while others do little except check pupil attendance in the private schools.

Competition between public and nonpublic schools is unavoidable. Lack of financial assistance handicaps many private schools; they often cannot provide the books, equipment, or supplies that public schools have. Teachers may be less qualified in nonpublic schools because they do not have to be licensed by the state. Most nonpublic schools do not pay salaries high enough to attract the best qualified teachers. On the other hand, some private schools require their teachers to meet the standards for public schools. Parochial schools are often thought to be traditional and conservative, but this is not always the case. Some of the newest and most innovative educational programs exist in nonpublic schools. Public schools tend to offer a more impartial educational program. Nonpublic schools approach education from their particular bias.

The issue of how much financial support the state is obligated to provide to nonpublic schools has not been resolved. Parents who send their children to nonpublic schools complain that they are doubly taxed. Some believe that since the state does not pay for the education of their children in public schools, it would be equitable to give the private school that money (other nations do this). Others claim that because of the constitutional separation of state and church in America, this would constitute a gift of public funds to a sectarian enterprise. Because parents made the choice, it is argued, they should have no recourse. It should be noted, however, that some states provide financial assistance for textbooks and transportation. The National Defense Education Act also has some sections that apply to private schools.

COOPERATION BETWEEN PUBLIC AND NONPUBLIC SCHOOLS. Many public schools cooperate with nonpublic schools by lending materials, allowing nonpublic schools to use their facilities, enrolling nonpublic school students in some classes, and sending educational specialists to nonpublic schools. In 1966, 49 percent of the school systems with enrollments of 12,000 or more did not cooperate with nonpublic schools in any way. Of those that did cooperate, the most common practice was the lending or giving of materials. When public schools offer classes to nonpublic school students, enrollments are primarily in the following subject areas: driver training, industrial arts, home economics, vocational education, foreign languages, chemistry, physics, physical education, biology, and instrumental music. The largest enrollments are in vocational, technical, and scientific areas.[21]

Historical Function of the State in Education

As early as 1642, the colonies passed laws concerning education. It was apparently taken for granted, even in that early period, that state legislatures had the necessary power to enforce such regulations. In 1647, Massachusetts enacted a law compelling communities with a certain population to set up and maintain grammar schools, thus setting a precedent for state involvement in education.

Many settlements established local schools as the nation spread westward, but as soon as territorial or state governments became established, the larger unit assumed responsibility for the educational program. Many early schools were neither compulsory nor free. Massachusetts again led the nation in these progressive measures, establishing compulsory public education by law in 1852. Every present state constitution has a section clarifying the place of the state in education, and stressing the importance of schooling. By omission in the federal Constitution, the provision for public education is regarded as a matter for the state governments. Since 1876 Congress has required all states admitted to the Union to provide a system of public schools.

---

21 National Education Association, Research Division, "Sharing of Resources by Public Schools with Nonpublic Schools," NEA *Research Bulletin* 45 (October 1967), pp. 90–92.

Although local school control is the result of a delegation of power from the state government and operates under authority granted to it by the laws of the state, in practice such local control has been jealously guarded from state interference. However, local operation is legally, if not in actual practice, the creature of the state, and may be modified or revoked at the pleasure of the state. State preeminence in the field of education has evolved because of the ever-growing conviction of the people that education is the most important single function of the state, and cannot be carried out solely on the basis of local peculiarities. Figure 3–2 graphically depicts educational administration as a state function.

Public Education and State Laws

Legislation governing education is divided into two kinds: *mandatory* laws, which require the schools to conform to the exact specifications of the statutes; and *permissive* laws, which grant to the school district certain privileges under specified conditions. Examples of mandatory laws are those governing teacher certification, budgeting and finance procedures, the teaching of certain required subjects, and compulsory school attendance. Permissive laws enable districts to provide additions to the curriculum or basic program, such as health services, guidance programs, and adult education. Early state laws regarding education were permissive. Later, they became mandatory because local communities did not do enough. Modern thought generally holds that permissive legislation best expresses the principle of local freedom under state suzerainty. However, a dilemma is created for local school districts as they seek more state funds, while simultaneously desiring freedom of action. Certain controls inevitably accompany financial support.

Degree of State Control of Education

The amount of state control of education varies from state to state. Some have almost no controls or requirements, while others have a great deal. Every state, however, has established control over bond issues. Sometimes the state establishes requirements, but provides no financial support to implement them.

Some persons feel that the state already exercises too much control

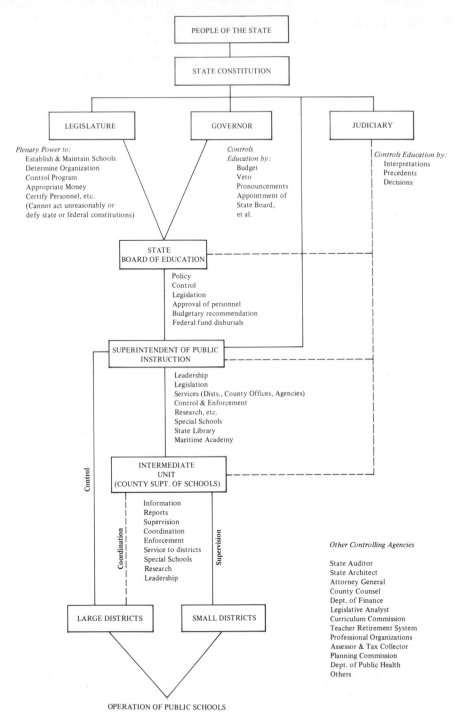

PEOPLE OF THE STATE

STATE CONSTITUTION

LEGISLATURE

Plenary Power to:
Establish & Maintain Schools
Determine Organization
Control Program
Appropriate Money
Certify Personnel, etc.
(Cannot act unreasonably or
defy state or federal constitutions)

GOVERNOR

Controls
Education by:
Budget
Veto
Pronouncements
Appointment of
State Board,
et al.

JUDICIARY

Controls Education by:
Interpretations
Precedents
Decisions

STATE
BOARD OF EDUCATION

Policy
Control
Legislation
Approval of personnel
Budgetary recommendation
Federal fund disbursals

SUPERINTENDENT OF PUBLIC
INSTRUCTION

Leadership
Legislation
Services (Dists., County Offices, Agencies)
Control & Enforcement
Research, etc.
Special Schools
State Library
Maritime Academy

INTERMEDIATE
UNIT
(COUNTY SUPT. OF SCHOOLS)

Information
Reports
Supervision
Coordination
Enforcement
Service to districts
Special Schools
Research
Leadership

Control

Coordination

Supervision

Other Controlling Agencies

State Auditor
State Architect
Attorney General
County Counsel
Dept. of Finance
Legislative Analyst
Curriculum Commission
Teacher Retirement System
Professional Organizations
Assessor & Tax Collector
Planning Commission
Dept. of Public Health
Others

LARGE DISTRICTS

SMALL DISTRICTS

OPERATION OF PUBLIC SCHOOLS

FIGURE 3–2.   Educational Administration as a State Function.

over education. State officials, they claim, cannot possibly be cognizant of the needs of local communities; and state control may lead to indoctrination of citizens with a single point of view. These arguments are similar to those advanced in opposition to federal control of education.

> The most objectionable controls are those that prevent or interfere with the development of desirable local responsibilities, that substitute state judgment for local judgment in areas where local judgment would be desirable, that tend to make all the school systems more dependent on the state for decisions, instead of strengthening the local school systems and helping them to become more able to solve their own problems.[22]

Others believe that state control should be strengthened and made more inclusive. They point out that a community's neglect of its children's education is an actual offense against the state. They feel that such a situation can be avoided only by more stringent enactments by state legislatures in the field of educational standards and procedures.

It would seem that the most practical and desirable compromise that can be reached between these two conflicting philosophies would be a situation in which a maximum amount of financial aid would be given by the state, but very little control exercised on the operational level. A set of standards defining minimum educational offerings and facilities should be set up and enforced by the state and applied to all local districts, but individual communities should be permitted to exercise initiative in exceeding those minimums. Minimum standards give the assurance that all children have an equal opportunity to be educated.

The state department should emphasize leadership, which is sorely needed in the improvement of instruction, rather than enforcement of regulations.

> What the state department of education can accomplish through state-wide planning and coordination, and through advice, assistance, and encouragement to local districts far outweighs the results obtained from mere enforcement of regulations.[23]

The major effect of all state legislation in the field of school control should be to ensure that no pupil be denied the right to a free public education because of race, creed, or economic condition. For this goal to be realized fully will require considerably more state control than is found in virtually

---

[22] Morphet, Johns, and Reller, *Educational Administration*, p. 518. © 1959. By permission of Prentice-Hall, Inc., Englewood Cliffs, N.J.

[23] Campbell, Corbally, and Ramseyer, *Introduction to Educational Administration,* 3rd ed. (Boston: Allyn and Bacon, 1966), p. 38.

any state today. In fact, states have done so little that federal legislation has been enacted to force achievement of this goal.

The State's Role in Educational Services

Resembling the federal function in education generally, but to a more localized and specific degree, the state's role in education will be increasingly that of service rather than domination. It should focus attention on functions that support constructive change. Today, the local school authorities in many parts of the nation are able to successfully call upon their state departments of education for expert aid in one or more of the following specialized areas:

1. Schoolhouse planning and site purchasing.
2. Financial accounting and bookkeeping.
3. Budgeting.
4. Providing for the needs of physically and mentally handicapped pupils.
5. Curriculum planning and development.
6. Adult education.
7. Guidance and counseling.
8. Community–school recreation.
9. Vocational education.
10. Agricultural education.
11. Business education.
12. Home economics.
13. School district reorganization.
14. School lunch programs.
15. Textbook and library services.
16. Special education program development.
17. Inservice education for teachers.
18. Technical advice in many areas.
19. Research data.
20. Teacher and administrator certification.
21. Interpretation of laws affecting education at the local level.

State consultants can help local school districts by working through the local authorities. It is increasingly important that the state decentralize its services and go out into the field, rather than remain in the state office building. In the future, local school administrators will be able to secure other and even more technical assistance from the state, especially in the fields of psychological and psychometric services, audio-visual techniques and materials, and scientific techniques and methods.

Summary

Education in the United States is a function of the state, which retains absolute authority over the public schools, although it may delegate its power to local boards of education.

Qualifications and terms of state boards of education and state school superintendents differ from state to state. In the main, however, state boards do not run local schools; rather, they concern themselves with directing their departments of education in research. State superintendents and commissioners usually act as administrators and executive officers of the state boards.

The state department of education is the legislative body of the state's educational system. It functions in leadership, regulatory, operational, and service capacities. It is typically organized into divisions, each dealing with a specialized sector of public education. Its problems center around inadequate financing and political involvement.

Private schools are also subject to state control, although to a much lesser degree than public schools. Health and safety regulations must be adhered to, for example, and many states require regular inspection of their facilities and curricula. Some states, however, do little except check pupil attendance in the private schools.

While there is considerable disagreement over the amount of state control that should be exercised over local schools, the ideal situation would be that in which a maximum amount of financial aid would be given by the state with very little control exerted, at least on the operational level.

It seems fairly certain that the state's role in education will be increasingly in the field of service, furnishing expertise in specialized areas of education upon the request of local school districts.

Trends

Most of the trends in state education are clear-cut. For the past fifty years, the tendency has been in the direction of increased state-level interest in and financial support for education.

Toward Increased State Educational Activity. As education becomes increasingly more complex, the state is being forced to provide more and more guidance and educational leadership for the local districts. Only the state can rise above the vexing and often hamstringing effects of local politics and vested interests which so often stand in the way of educational progress. Only the state can take the long-range view necessary to plan for the future. Instead of reflecting the intransigent philosophy of conservative local boards of education, the state is increasingly adopting progressive policies and gently insisting that the local districts comply. The center of leadership is slowly but surely passing from the community to the state.

Toward District Consolidation. The state system of public education will become more closely knit in future. Part of this tendency is due to the gradual disappearance of the small, poor district, and its replacement by the large, consolidated district, possessing larger administrative and support areas. The future may see each state divided into relatively few, but comprehensive, school districts. Considerable administrative and supervisory leadership will emanate from the state department of education or from the county office.

Toward School Code Revision. More states will undertake to sweepingly revise their entire program of public instruction. At present, school code commissions are working in several states to modernize the statutory and constitutional bases of public education. Various archaic provisions and relics of frontier legislation are slated to be replaced.

Toward Increased State Financial Support. The trend in most states toward shifting financial support of the public schools from the local taxpayer to the state treasury is marked and will continue. The real property tax, the traditional backbone of school support, no longer represents an adequate foundation for educational revenue. The California Supreme Court decision in *Serrano* v. *Priest* held that public schools should be financed from the wealth of the state as a whole, not from the wealth of the school district where a child lives. Other state courts have ruled that property tax financing of public education violates the equal protection clause of the Fourteenth Amendment because of the disparity of wealth between school districts. However, in 1973 the U.S. Supreme Court held in *San Antonio Independent School District et al.* v. *Rodriquez et al.* that property tax financing was constitutional and did not violate the equal protection of the law. In order to provide equal educational opportunities, states will have to supplement increasingly inadequate property tax funds with monies derived from more broadly based taxes. Related to this, the sales tax will increase in importance and administrative standards for handling the tax will be improved. The demand for equal educational opportunity on a minimum standard basis for all children inevitably leads to the provision of state funds to maintain such a program.

TOWARD AN INCREASE IN THE POWER OF THE STATE BOARD OF EDUCATION. The state board of education will slowly increase in power and in number of functions. A mere shadow organization fifty years ago, it now has general supervision over elementary and secondary education in the state. In another fifty years, greater administrative powers will be added to its present supervisory functions.

TOWARD A DECREASE OF EX-OFFICIO BOARDS. The decrease since 1900 of ex-officio boards of education, or state boards composed of persons holding other state offices, seems bound to continue. The eventual disappearance of ex-officio board members is strongly indicated.

TOWARD A UNIT TYPE OF STATE CONTROL. The supplanting of a dual type of state control by the unit type will become more marked in the future. The dual system, in which the state board of education is responsible to an authority different from the chief state school official, has produced considerable friction. The trend seems to be in the direction of a unit type of control, in which the state board appoints the state superintendent of schools.

TOWARD CHANGES IN THE STRUCTURE OF THE STATE BOARD OF EDUCATION. State boards of education in the future seem certain to be composed of either seven or nine members. The tendency in best practice today is toward this number. Board members will be elected or selected in some manner other than appointment by the governor; the length of their term will increase to 7 or 9 years on an overlapping basis; and they will serve without pay. The powers, duties, and important features of the office will be prescribed increasingly by statute, instead of by constitutional provision.

TOWARD A LEGISLATIVE STATE BOARD OF EDUCATION AND AN EXECUTIVE CHIEF STATE SCHOOL OFFICER. There will be a more distinct separation of legislative and administrative functions. This trend replaces patterns followed by some states which combine administrative and executive functions under the aegis of the state board or states where the legislature delegates both functions to either the state board or the chief state school officer.

TOWARD IMPROVEMENT OF STATUS OF STATE SUPERINTENDENT. A general upgrading of the status of the chief state school administrator is beginning, and seems likely to continue in the future. Requirements for the position may eventually include the doctor of philosophy or doctor of education degree, with several years of public school experience as a teacher and administrator. Salaries for this position will undoubtedly increase notably within a few years, on the theory that the leading school administrator of a state should be paid the highest stipend of any educator therein. The chief school officer will tend to be relieved of the necessity of running for office every few years, as his position will more and more be an appointive one. Because it appears that selection by a state board of education for an indefinite, rather than a fixed, term increases the likelihood of securing a person of high professional qualification and talent, the present trend in this direction may be expected to continue.

TOWARD STRENGTHENING THE STATE DEPARTMENT OF EDUCATION. In the interests of economy and efficiency, the future state department of education will be a single agency discharging the state's educational functions. In accordance with the trends already examined, which indicate a general increase in powers and responsibilities of all state educational offices, the state department may expect better staffing and more adequate financing in the future.

TOWARD FLEXIBILITY OF STATE CONSTITUTIONAL PROVISIONS. Gradual amending of state constitutions for the purpose of removing outdated provisions, such as those involving salaries, titles, and eligibility requirements for certain state educational offices, may be confidently expected. Few eastern states have such provisions in their constitutions; it is no coincidence that most of the more modern and efficient state departments of education are found in these states.

TOWARD MORE STATE FINANCIAL ASSISTANCE TO NONPUBLIC SCHOOLS. This trend will depend upon the attitudes in each individual state. Some now provide for textbooks and transportation. To qualify for state aid, a nonpublic school should meet the stipulation that a particular creed or dogma cannot be espoused. Nonpublic curricula must be broadened if this is to happen. Goals must be met and all teachers must be as qualified as they are in public schools.

TOWARD STRONGER EDUCATIONAL LEADERSHIP ON THE STATE LEVEL. As state department salaries gradually improve, better administrators will be attracted to such positions. Historically, state leadership in American education has not been strong. There are significant indications that this state of affairs is about to change.

Administrative Problems

Problem 1

Mayfield School District consists of two elementary schools. It must send its secondary students to the adjoining North Forks Unified School District which has 12 elementary schools, 2 junior high schools, and a senior high school. Many of the parents in Mayfield want to join North Fork in the belief that their children will have a better educational program that is coordinated through all the grades. Their school board is not interested because it would like to keep its identity as a historic small district. The North Forks Board of Education and administrators are in favor of the reorganization that would bring Mayfield's two elementary schools into its own district.

What should the North Forks Unified School District do to help bring about this reorganization?
What can the Mayfield parents do?
What role should the State Department of Education play in working with the two school districts?

Problem 2

A number of minority organizations in your state have been complaining that the tests used as a basis for assigning children to special education classes discriminate against minority children. They believe that many of their children are unfairly assigned to classes for the mentally retarded because the tests do not evaluate their real intelligence.

The state administrators' association has invited you, as the State Director of Special Education, to speak at their annual state conference regarding this growing problem.

What research would you do to prepare your speech?
Whom would you consult?
What would you propose as an answer to the test criticisms?
What would you say your office plans to do to alleviate the problem?

Selected References

BEACH, FRED F. *The Functions of State Departments of Education.* U.S. Office of Education, Miscellaneous No. 12. Washington, D.C.: U.S. Government Printing Office, 1950.

CAMPBELL, ROALD F.; CORBALLY, JOHN E., JR.; and RAMSEYER, JOHN S. *Introduction to Educational Administration.* Boston: Allyn and Bacon, 1966.

CICOUREL, AARON V. *Educational Decision-Makers.* Indianapolis: Bobbs-Merrill and Co., 1963.

EDITORIAL STAFF, U.S. SUPREME COURT REPORTS. *Decisions of the U.S. Supreme Court.* Rochester, N.Y.: Lawyers Cooperative Publishing Staff, 1973.

FREY, SHERMAN H., and GETSCHMAN, KEITH R. *School Administration: Selected Readings.* New York: Thomas Y. Crowell Co., 1968.

GRIEDER, CALVIN. *Public School Administration.* New York: The Ronald Press Co., 1961.

KIMBROUGH, RALPH B. *Political Power and Educational Decision-Making.* Chicago: Rand McNally and Co., 1964.

LANE, WILLARD R.; CORWIN, RONALD G.; and MONAHAN, WILLIAM G. *Foundations of Educational Administration: A Behavioral Analysis.* New York: The Macmillan Co., 1967.

MORPHET, EDGAR L.; JOHNS, ROE L.; and RELLER, THEODORE L. *Educational Administration: Concepts, Practices, and Issues.* Englewood Cliffs, N.J.: Prentice-Hall, 1959.

REEDER, WARD G. *The Fundamentals of Public School Administration.* 4th ed. New York: The Macmillan Co., 1958.

REUTTER, E. EDMUND, JR., and HAMILTON, ROBERT R. *The Law and Public Education.* Mineola, N.Y.: Foundation Press, 1970.

WILSON, ROBERT E. *Educational Administration.* Columbus, Ohio: Charles E. Merrill Publishing Co., 1966.

4

The Intermediate Unit:
County School Administration

The intermediate, or county, unit stands between the state and the local school district. It can provide services for those districts that lack the organization, personnel, and facilities to produce quality education. Each intermediate unit has an organizational structure comprised of a governing board, chief administrative officer, and various departments headed by administrators. Because of its position—straddling the state and local levels—it has problems and is being subjected to reorganizational considerations.

This chapter includes a discussion of the following topics:

Historical Role of the Intermediate Unit
Importance of County School Administration
Variations in Intermediate School Organization
Basic Principles of School Organization
The Intermediate Unit Characterized by Its Personnel and Functions
Problems Impeding Intermediate-Unit Functions
Personnel and Functions of the Intermediate Unit
Summary
Trends

Historical Role of the Intermediate Unit

Colonial settlers in the New World brought with them jurisdictional concepts of towns, districts, parishes, counties, and states. The town (or township) expression of a geographical unit was prevalent in New England; the parish, in French-dominated Louisiana; and the county, subdivided into townships, in the Midwest and Southwest. Public schools in the towns of Massachusetts received supervisory and inspectional service, provided by the state and, later, by subdivisions of the state. The earliest school inspectors were not educational officials, but existing governmental officials, such as the county clerk, the justice of the peace, a county judge, a land commissioner, or the chairman of the county board of school visitors.

This miscellaneous hodgepodge of county, district, or parish officials proved to be unsatisfactory as school visitors and supervisors. In 1829, legislation was enacted in Delaware providing for an official whose sole duties would be school supervision and visitation; it marked the beginning of the first intermediate unit, or county superintendency. Other states (New York in 1843) quickly followed Delaware's lead in setting up county or area superintendents.

As early as 1879, thirty-four of the existing thirty-eight states had established the office of county superintendent. Several states abandoned the office but after a short lapse re-established it. The states that allowed the office of the county superintendent of schools to lapse were Mississippi, California, Texas, Idaho, and Arizona. All of these states have since re-established some form of intermediate school administrative unit. Even states that now have a somewhat different system from the county administrative unit—Maine, New Hampshire, New York, and Vermont—at one time had the office of county superintendent. Connecticut, Massachusetts, Hawaii, and Rhode Island are the only states that have never had a county superintendent of schools and have retained the organization of the local district or group of districts, plus the state department of public instruction.

The county school administrative unit was especially well adapted to the new lands beyond the Mississippi. Many of the new states to the west had some type of county school supervisory service, even while they were still territories. The county superintendent was often an elected official and was as much an accepted part of each county's government as the county treasurer and the county clerk. The functions and personnel of the county office have changed considerably in recent years and should change even more.

Importance of County School Administration

It can be said that the United States does not have an educational system, but has fifty educational systems. The concept of education as a state function is universally accepted. However, the state department of education, from territorial and early statehood days, has proved to be geographically and psychologically too far removed from the local districts. The intermediate unit has evolved out of a need for closer supervisory help and coordination at the local level.

Early in its history the county office was called upon to keep official records, to select, to certify, and to place teachers, and to arbitrate district boundary problems. It has often been called the administrative right arm of the state department of education because it has performed the task of enforcing laws and upholding minimum standards. Such standards have applied to school finance, physical facilities, teacher preparation, pupil attendance, and the instructional program. Not only has the county office served in this capacity, but it has also functioned as a service and reporting agency to the state department. Some outstanding county superintendents with close experience at the local level have helped state departments of education to develop effective policies and procedures. The county superintendent has played an important role by maintaining two way communication between local districts and the state office.

Although the county superintendency has been limited in function and largely understaffed, the office has been of vital importance in the improvement of local district education. It is more crucial to rural and isolated schools than to urban areas, where strong school districts with well-trained personnel predominate. In rural counties, particularly, the county superintendent is considered the educational leader of the area. He is called upon to coordinate various cultural and educational activities. His advice is sought with respect to juvenile courts, county health and welfare programs, the Scouts, "Y" programs, community music, Future Farmers of America, athletics, federal support (such as the Elementary and Secondary Education Act), the National School Lunch Program, Arbor Day, the Heart Fund and the Cancer Society drives, exhibits for the county fair, and the local branch of the library. The county superintendent's office is a strategic clearinghouse for many worthwhile and constructive programs of the community, and requires considerable insight and training upon the part of the county superintendent.

The typical county superintendent's office in early times was staffed by a clerk and the county superintendent, who was expected to serve as the agent of the state department of education. Out of this semi-policing of local school districts (often dealing particularly with governing boards of one-room schools), the office has evolved into a service center for both small and large districts.

Teachers need to be trained in service. Educational supplies need to be selected and wisely used. Courses of study have to be written and interpreted. Teacher vacancies in rural areas have to be filled. Traveling libraries must be established. Audio-visual aids have to be procured, distributed, and interpreted. Pupils have to be transferred or adjusted, and district boundaries have to be adjudicated. Federal projects have to be written. Data processing equipment must be appraised, purchased, and used effectively. These educational needs have caused in recent years the county superintendent's office to emerge more as a service and leadership organization than as a primary law enforcement arm of the state.

Variations in Intermediate Unit Organization

The organization of the intermediate unit occurs in three main types of categories: (1) a supervisory union, (2) a county superintendency, or (3) a combination of county–local district units. The supervisory union is most prevalent in New England, where two or more towns have been joined together to form a supervisory or intermediate district, with a superintendent. The supervisory unions often cover rural areas, while a large city may function as an independent unit and deal directly with the state department of education. States with a supervisory union type of organization are Connecticut, Maine, Massachusetts, New Hampshire, New York, Rhode Island, and Vermont. New York has 175 supervisory unions, whereas Rhode Island has only two.

The islands of Hawaii are controlled by the State Department of Public Instruction in Honolulu, but suboffices in centers like Hilo serve functions similar to those of mainland county offices.

States that operate with the county system are largely in the Midwest, West, and Southwest, where the county was early established as a governmental unit. These states are Arizona, Arkansas, California, Colorado, Idaho, Missouri, Montana, Nebraska, North Dakota, Ohio, Texas, Washington, Wisconsin, and Wyoming. About 2,000 county superintendents serve the school administrative subdivisions of these states. It is estimated that about an equal number of other professional and highly trained personnel assist the county superintendent in these areas. California has by far the largest number of professional helpers, with a ratio of more than ten professional helpers for each county superintendent.

In some of these states an entire county has been organized as a school district, but the county–district unit is the exception rather than the rule. In the county–district unit type of organization, there is no intermediate or county office, because the county or parish jurisdictions are identical to the school district.

There are variations of the county–district organization, generally created to accommodate population concentrations. In Florida and West Virginia, for example, all school districts have been combined into districts that follow county or city boundaries. Louisiana has 3 city school parishes and Utah has 5 city school districts in addition to the larger units administered by a county–district superintendent. In Maryland all units follow county boundaries and are administered by a county superintendent, with the exception of the city of Baltimore. Virginia entitles its organizational units "divisions" that are administered similarly to the county units in other states. Ten of these divisions, however, include 2 counties each, and one contains 3 counties. Others contain city and county combined, and 22 are city school districts. Utah has a peculiar combination of county districts, city districts, and combined counties as single county unit districts. States that have the county unit system in various forms of organization are Alabama, Florida, Georgia, Kentucky, Louisiana, Maryland, Nevada, New Mexico, North Carolina, Tennessee, Utah, Virginia, and West Virginia.

The organization of the intermediate unit has developed chiefly along county lines, but with so many exceptions and variations that no single definition can include all types. The variety of organization does, however, represent a singleness of purpose—namely, the enforcement of state regulations, as adopted by the people through their legislators, and the furnishing of services, leadership, and research that the local districts cannot provide adequately for themselves. The organization of the intermediate unit has developed, not as a political expediency nor as a vestige of previous institutions, but has expanded to meet vital school needs where control is close to the people. If the intermediate unit did not exist, some stodgy professor would dream up the idea and write a book.

Basic Principles of School Organization

As a means of identifying the place and function of the intermediate unit in the American pattern, it is well to consider some basic principles that affect organization at the several levels. These principles deal chiefly with concern, responsibility, and operation. A discussion of them follows.

EDUCATION AS A NATIONAL CONCERN. A high level of education for all citizens has become a concern of the federal government and of all who exert nationwide influence. It is increasingly recognized to be essential for efficient production, wise consumption, good public health, free institutions, and national strength. In fact, without a high level of education, the survival of a people and their institutions of liberty and freedom are in jeopardy. Education must be a national concern with adequate financial support if it is to be a means of sustaining national survival and well-being.

EDUCATION AS A FUNCTION OF THE STATE. The several state constitutions, legislatures, and courts, as well as the Supreme Court of the United States, have repeatedly held that education is a function and a responsibility of the people in each state. The state has delegated that responsibility, in part, to the intermediate unit. In this sense, the intermediate unit is a partner of the state department of education, following the statutes and constitutional provisions as does any other subdivision of government. Because the intermediate unit is in fact a subdivision of state government, carrying out a state function, it should be financed by the people of the entire state, rather than by local political subdivisions. This is particularly important as counties merge into larger regions.

CHARACTERISTICS OF THE LOCAL, INTERMEDIATE, AND STATE LEVELS. The local school district is primarily operational; the intermediate unit is primarily for coordination and service; and the state department is primarily concerned with leadership, research, and enforcement.

The operation of schools should be kept close to the people, with a minimum of supervision from higher levels. Every function involved in the education of children should be performed at the lowest possible level. The intermediate unit should perform only those functions which, because of limited facilities or untrained personnel, the district level cannot carry out. Likewise, the state department should perform only those functions for which the intermediate unit lacks resources. It follows, then, that as districts grow or become consolidated or unified, they should assume more of the functions of operation. One of the chief purposes of the intermediate unit is *to help the district to help itself*. Furthermore, the state department should not bypass the intermediate unit and give direct district services, but should work through the intermediate unit.

COOPERATIVE POLICIES AND PROCEDURES. Although the state department bestows leadership and operates as a policymaking and enforcing unit, it should not formulate policies from a purely theoretical viewpoint, nor impose hampering rules and regulations. Policies should evolve out of operational practice at the lower level. Educational policies must be expressions of all the people. In this sense the people, through their legislators, determine school policies as they are observed through the experience of local school districts. It is then the function of the state department of education to define and enforce the policies that have been initiated at the local level and modified through cooperative participation in their development. All who are affected by the policies and procedures should have a voice in their formulation. The intermediate unit plays a dual role in gathering and interpreting information from the operational level, and in the legal analysis and interpretation of state legislation. In all cases, the growth and development of children should be the guide to policy formulation.

SERVICE ORIENTATION OF THE INTERMEDIATE UNIT. The best way for the intermediate unit to strengthen operation in the local district is to furnish needed services, rather than to exert punitive force. Local districts need help in the interpretation of school law, review of local budgets, certification of attendance, inservice training for teachers and classified personnel, coordination with other schools and with government and business agencies. They need assistance with federal projects, help in selecting and using instructional materials, in recruiting and selecting teachers, and in consulting service for local governing boards. The service concept in the role of the intermediate unit is growing and should grow more as local districts expand their operations. Coordination rather than domination is the best service.

Personnel and Functions of the Intermediate Unit

PERSONNEL IN THE INTERMEDIATE UNIT. The superintendent, his professional assistants, and clerical helpers constitute the personnel in the intermediate units, whether organized as supervisory unions, county superintendent's offices, county–district units, or regional areas. For the most part, the county superintendency began as a political unit and still often possesses a partisan character. Salaries for county superintendents have lagged behind those for similar positions in large city school systems. Adequate professional qualification requirements have lagged behind the needs of the expanding office, although in recent years there has been a trend toward higher professional status for the county superintendent, resulting in higher salaries. Regionalism is enhancing this trend.

Of 47 states that employ some type of intermediate-unit organization, 25 now appoint their superintendent and 22 elect him. In the early days of the office, election was the predominant way of procuring the intermediate-unit superintendent. Considerable progress has been made, and there are authoritative recommendations to point the way toward the increased practice of appointment on a professional basis.

The requirements or qualifications for the office of intermediate-unit superintendent vary considerably among 47 states. Three have no specified requirements, and others range all the way from requiring one year of college training to a requirement of six years of college training, with at least seven years of public school experience and possession of an administration certificate. The median requirement among the states is now four years of college, with experience in teaching or administration.

In too many counties, the intermediate unit is still headed by a superintendent and a clerk or a few clerical workers. There is a trend, however, for the superintendent to secure more budgetary help and to establish positions classified as assistant superintendent, director, supervisor, consultant, and coordinator. This practice strengthens the office of the county or intermediate-unit superintendent, and provides better and more specialized service to school districts. It is no longer possible for one person to be proficient in all areas. Local districts need expert consultant services in finance, legal interpretation, guidance, curriculum development, audio-visual aids, child welfare, health programs, and vocational education.

The up-to-date county superintendent of schools will secure assistance in these specialized areas. In the area of curriculum development alone, there is a place for specialists in art, music, science, remedial reading, and education of the handicapped and gifted. Judged by these needs, the personnel of many intermediate units throughout the country is woefully inadequate. This inadequacy is due chiefly to lack of finance, but also somewhat due to the lack of sufficient numbers of properly trained specialists. The level of services possible from the intermediate unit depends primarily upon the competency of its personnel. Better-trained specialists working out of the intermediate unit can do much to coordinate and improve the instructional operation of local school districts.

STATUS OF THE COUNTY SUPERINTENDENT. With respect to the relationship of the salaries of county superintendents to other aspects of status, the *Yearbook* of the Department of Rural Education of the NEA gives some striking facts. Comparisons were made between the 12 states reporting the highest salaries for county superintendents and the 12 states reporting the lowest, with the following results:

1. Every state in the highest salary group has a set minimum requirement of four or more years of college education; among the twelve in the median salary group, only three stipulate four years of college as a required minimum.
2. Ten of the states with high median salaries select the county superintendent by appointment rather than by election. All twelve states with the lowest salary medians choose the superintendent by popular vote.
3. In nine states of the highest median salary group, superintendents are chosen for four-year terms or for indefinite periods of tenure. Among the states in the lowest median salary group, seven elect their superintendents for two-year terms.
4. Of the twelve states with the highest salary medians, five have the county–unit system and three have the supervisory district or union system. All of the twelve states in the lowest median salary group have the county organization.[1]

California's large corps of professional workers at the intermediate-unit level is made possible by adequate state financing. Each county superintendent in California receives his budget from two sources: the county general fund and the school service fund provided by state formula. Authorities who witness the struggle that California superintendents go through in securing an adequate budget from local county sources, along with the struggle that county superintendents in other states are compelled to go through, are beginning to recommend that *all funds* to provide necessary services for the intermediate unit be provided by state formula.

---

[1] National Education Association, "The County Superintendent of Schools in the United States," *NEA 1950 Yearbook* (Washington, D.C.: NEA Department of Rural Education), p. 49.

FUNCTIONS OF THE INTERMEDIATE UNIT. The county superintendent of schools initially was responsible for keeping a few records and inspecting the school area. These functions were routine and "housekeeping" in nature. From this small beginning, the county superintendent's functions have multiplied, but still consist of two general types: (1) records and reports and (2) professional services.

The required records and reports are necessary in the review of budgets, auditing of accounts, control of expenditures, verification of average daily attendance, determination of district boundaries, maintenance of certificate requirements, and enforcement of school code provisions. Other recording and housekeeping functions include accounting for retirement and Social Security approval of payrolls and warrants, calling and conducting school elections, enforcing compulsory education laws and issuing work permits, assisting with quantity purchasing, transportation and housing, dissemination of information concerning county counsel or attorney general opinions and court cases, and help with data processing. These activities are largely perfunctory and mechanical, but they are necessary for the legal operation of school districts. With the meeting of each legislature the list becomes larger and more complicated. Many of the functions can be handled by classified workers without teaching or administrative certificates. In addition to these routine functions, many of the county superintendents with vision and professional point of view have established helpful services for school districts.

These services are designed primarily to improve instruction for children and youth, but are varied and complex in nature. The application of the services tends to strengthen the operational level by reinforcing teachers, counselors, and administrators with needed instructional plans, materials, techniques, and consultant help.

Some of the services that the intermediate unit can offer to the local districts are:

1. Direct supervision of classroom teachers. (This diminishes as school districts grow larger.)
2. Coordination of area programs among districts.
3. Inservice education of certificated and classified personnel.
4. Preparation of communication and publication aids.
5. Adoption or preparation of courses of study.
6. Provision of audio-visual, library, educational TV, and other materials or programs.

7. Consultant help with pupil personnel services.
8. Operation of federal programs, such as Title III (ESEA), and assistance to districts that apply for federal programs under the several titles of ESEA.
9. Cooperation with business and industry to improve vocational education.
10. Scoring, interpreting, and summarizing standardized testing.
11. Furnishing leadership toward innovations such as flexible scheduling, programmed instruction, team teaching, Head Start and preschool education, collective bargaining or professional negotiation, continuing education in business and industry, citizenship, and skills in human relations.
12. Coordination and cooperation with problem departments, law enforcement agencies, legislative committees, character-building organizations, and community support groups.

The authors made a survey of intermediate-unit function in the California counties of Los Angeles, Riverside, and San Diego, along with certain leading counties in four midwestern and two eastern states. It was found that direct supervisory help for pupils and teachers upon an individual basis is being minimized or eliminated, and that a coordinating service for district supervisors and administrators is being expanded. When the consultant from the county office works with ten supervisors who serve 300 teachers, he greatly expands his effectiveness over the former practice of going into individual classrooms to help pupils and teachers.

This shift from a lower level to a higher echelon service has come about with the strengthening and growth of local school districts, and greatly multiplies the efficiency of the intermediate unit. The effect will be to reduce the number of county consultants, but upgrade their caliber and status. Consultants who go out to work with superintendents, principals, and supervisors must have comprehensive and extended training, a variety of teaching and administrative experiences, and strong professional leadership qualifications. This shift in the level of service is commendable, because it strengthens local administrators and greatly multiplies the effectiveness of county service.

Trillingham, in reporting before the California Assembly Interim Committee, explained the two types of services by saying, "We try to lean over backwards to work under the philosophy that the center of gravity of education is within the local district. It is not the county office. We do not try to run the districts—we try to serve the districts . . . . The housekeeping division . . . handles certifications, budgets, school elections, annual reports, teacher retirement, verification of warrants, accounts and the like. . . ."[2]

HISTORICAL DEVELOPMENT OF THE COUNTY SUPERINTENDENCY IN CALIFORNIA.   Magee has traced the growth and development of the office of the County Superintendent of Schools for Los Angeles County.   The development in this case study, although it only applies to California, somewhat parallels the evolution of other county offices in the United States and brings into focus the increasing emphasis upon the county superintendent as an instructional leader.   The following is a chronology of the Los Angeles County superintendency.

1. The Office of the County Superintendent of Schools was created by the legislature in 1852; each county assessor acted in the capacity of county superintendent.
2. County superintendents were elected by the people in 1855 and are still elected in most counties.
3. Prior to 1870, the superintendent's primary duties were certifying teacher credentials and visiting schools.
4. The first Los Angeles County teachers' institute was held in 1870.
5. The County adopted all textbooks used in the schools up to 1885.
6. The Legislature increased the powers of the County Superintendent and in 1895 put the county high schools under the jurisdiction of his office.
7. In 1911, the County Superintendent was permitted to pay expenses for trustees' institutes, and county boards could pay for the transportation of students to county high schools.
8. In 1915, the County Superintendent was empowered to employ a county supervisor of attendance if a majority of districts so petitioned.
9. Supervision from the County Schools Office was authorized by the Legislature in 1921.
10. Los Angeles County was one of the first in the state to operate a county schools office.
11. The office of the County Superintendent of Schools serves as an intermediate unit between the state and local school districts.   One of its primary functions is the receiving and disbursing of school money.

---

2 C. C. Trillingham, "The County Superintendent and the County School Service Fund," Second Report of the Assembly Interim Committee on Public Education (Sacramento, 1949), p. 113.

12. The Office of the Los Angeles County Superintendent of Schools was the first to inaugurate the following educational services:

   a. Secondary curriculum coordination.
   b. Screening devices for local district boards in their selection of chief administrators.
   c. Custodial training for maintenance and operation employees.
   d. Institute programs for noncertificated employees.
   e. Appraisal of school districts, through the Regional Planning Commission, of proposed construction in the area.
   f. Preschool orientation programs for new teachers.
   g. Summer workshops for elementary school administrators.
   h. Child study workshops.
   i. Classes for mentally retarded children in small districts.
   j. Consultant services to districts for bookkeeping and accounting problems.[3]

This historical study shows that the office of the Los Angeles County Superintendent of Schools is now acting as a service organization and has pioneered many educational services. It has thereby fulfilled its instructional leadership role by stimulating better educational programs in local districts.

Problems Impeding Intermediate-Unit Functions

As with all organizational structures, everything does not always run smoothly. There are problems that must be considered and solutions sought in order to improve services. The intermediate unit has grown in service and changed its type of service, but still has various problems to meet before it can perform its functions most effectively. Some of these problems are discussed in the following paragraphs.

BETTER FINANCING. One of the chief problems besetting the intermediate unit at present is the method and amount of financing. Most intermediate units lack sufficient state support. Local boards of county supervisors, or others who provide financing from county funds, have little idea of the essential services rendered by the county superintendent of schools. These local politicians are under pressure from taxpayer groups; they tend to

---

[3] Lawrence Thomas Magee, "Historical Developments Affecting the Administration of the Office of the Los Angeles County Superintendent of Schools" (Unpublished doctoral dissertation, University of Southern California, 1955), pp. 205–208.

squeeze needed services out of the county superintendent's budget. State financing is inadequate in almost all states. Where a dual budget system exists, the state portion pays chiefly for the professional type of service, but does not pay for the so-called housekeeping functions. This puts the superintendent and his staff in the position of serving two masters, who are often in conflict with each other. It is easy for the county officials to deny the county superintendent's office its needed funds by claiming that those services should be paid for by the state, or vice versa. The county superintendent thus becomes a pawn between two political agencies. Under developing regionalism, the costs of the intermediate unit must be increasingly assumed by the state.

The financial situation is even worse in states where all revenues for the intermediate unit have to come from local sources. This puts the county superintendent of schools in competition with the sheriff, welfare agencies, the coroner, the clerk, the assessor, and the county attorney for the limited funds available. County supervisors and councilmen often see concrete results in the form of parks, hospitals, agricultural projects, law enforcement squads, and the county treasurer's office, but find it difficult to appreciate the intangible effects of improved education.

Better financing is urgently needed to provide better physical facilities, higher salaries for qualified personnel, addition of new personnel, and the financing of added professional services to local school districts. This financing should come entirely from state sources because (1) the intermediate unit is in fact a subagency of the state, and (2) one of the most effective ways for the state to fulfill its function of educating its citizens is to strengthen the intermediate unit.

IMPROVING ORGANIZATION. The organization of the intermediate unit varies over a wide spectrum of supervisory units, county offices, county–district units (large, small, urban, rural, remote), and spotty regionalism. For example, one county studied by the authors has 87 pupils, 3 teachers, and a county superintendent–teacher. In contrast, the most populated county in the same state has more than 3 million enrolled in schools. The pupil population in this one county represents a greater number than the total population in 9 of the least populated states. Between these two extremes there are many variations. Some counties are very small, representing only a few square miles, and are composed of one or two school districts. San Bernardino County, California, on the other hand, comprises 20,131 square miles and is twice as large as Vermont. The county superintendent has to travel 200 miles from one side of his county to the other. No one has determined the exact size, population, financing, and the like of the adequate or ideal intermediate unit. Hassinger, however, has set helpful limits with respect to geographical features, sociological composition, financing, instructional capabilities, population, size, and flexible area.[4]

The intermediate unit needs reorganization as much as or more than do the local districts. More progress has been made in district consolidation and reorganization than has occurred in counties, unions, or parishes.

When the county superintendent's office was created, it was thrust into an already existing set of geographical, financial, sociological, and philosophical boundaries that did not necessarily correspond to the realm of its endeavors. Tradition is hard to break; once the intermediate unit of education was confined in a county, reorganization of its physical boundaries became highly difficult.

A recent study shows considerable intermediate-unit reorganization taking place in such states as Colorado, Iowa, Michigan, New Jersey, New York, Nebraska, Ohio, Oregon, Pennsylvania, Texas, Washington, and Wisconsin. The study indicates that changes have been toward a larger geographic and population base.[5]

The regional concept of the intermediate unit has been given much consideration, and will be more prevalent in future planning. This regional concept is not a static one. The boundaries of an intermediate unit that would be realistic for the air age may be radically altered in the Space Age. The ideal intermediate unit will be reorganized to contain an area consistent with modern transportation and communication, a sociological and geographical entity; it will have a flexible pattern of boundaries consistent with varied functions, and a unit with sufficient size to attract high caliber personnel who can initiate educational innovations and at the same time render needed practical services to local school districts. Anticipating the usual resistance to change, one realizes that the ideally reorganized intermediate unit is still very much in the future, but approaches toward appropriate reorganization are being made.

Regionalism as a concept is replacing rigid county boundaries with larger areas of county–district subunits, attained by legislative action. In

---

[4] Jack Hassinger, "The Intermediate Unit" (Unpublished doctoral dissertation, University of Southern California, 1958).

[5] Gerald A. Rosander, *The Future of the Intermediate Unit in California* (Visalia, Calif.: American Yearbook Company, 1966), p. 10.

the early 1970s, Nebraska had established 17 intermediate units, Pennsylvania converted 66 counties into 29 intermediate units, Michigan reduced to 60, and Iowa designated 16 in place of its 99 counties. In Texas, 254 counties have been combined into 20 regional service centers. The California legislature is demanding county office reorganization with suggestions from the educational profession that as few as 6 geographical areas be established as regional centers. The Ohio plan would convert 88 counties into 40 regional service agencies. Other states have made, or are making, similar regional reorganizations of the inherited county offices.

Education, U.S.A. made a study of the regional offices in Michigan and reported functions pertaining to special education, curriculum development, diagnostic testing, remediation, social work, guidance and pupil personnel services, research, machine test scoring and interpretation, computing services, lending libraries, cooperative purchasing, transportation, training and placing of personnel, instructional materials centers, and data processing. Other state regional centers offer legal advice and interpretation, help with program budgeting, educational television, data storage and retrieval, help with federal programs, and more, including the whole gamut of educational services and problems.

An Example of Intermediate-Unit Reorganization. The trend toward regionalization of the intermediate unit has been exemplified in the state of Washington. The 39 county superintendencies of the state have been reorganized into 14 intermediate school districts.

As early as 1959, Chapter 216 of the state's *Education Code* directed the state board of education to submit a plan for reorganization of county school offices. A statewide committee drew up a plan, and the 1965 legislature provided for the formation of intermediate school districts on a voluntary basis. But only four such districts were established during the succeeding four years. In 1969 the legislature mandated that the state Board of Education create a system of intermediate school districts. This mandate led to the abolishment of the office of county school superintendent and the establishment of 14 intermediate school districts.

Each intermediate school district is governed by a board of seven members elected by the registered voters of the district, one from each of seven board-member subdistricts. The board serves as a policymaking body and selects a superintendent as its executive officer.

The intermediate unit serves as a link between local school districts and the superintendent of public instruction, along with the state board of education. It assists local school districts in improving the scope and quality of education, and it assists the superintendent of public instruction and the state board of education in the administration of a state system of schools.

The mission of the intermediate school district is to work with local school districts and the state superintendent and board to "help all children develop skills, competencies and attitudes fundamental to achieving individual satisfaction as responsible, contributing citizens."[6] In carrying out this mission, the intermediate school district assists the superintendent of public instruction in (1) identification of educational needs; (2) dissemination of information concerning policies and regulations; (3) provision of qualified resource consultants; (4) planning and coordination of educational meetings; and (5) representation of all facets of the state system's program of providing equal and quality education for all students.

The services of the intermediate school district to local districts are voluminous, but some typical ones consist of help with budgets, elections, attendance, transportation, building plans, apportionment of funds, personnel problems, educational meetings, data processing, special and vocational education, cooperative purchasing, psychological service, certification, curriculum development, testing, and program evaluation.

As a link between the local school districts and state authority, the intermediate school district is dependent upon both. It does not have fiscal independence. The superintendent of public instruction has statutory authority to revise and fix the intermediate-unit budget. The local school district superintendents within an intermediate school district, according to the state *Education Code,* serve in an advisory capacity to the board and superintendent in matters pertaining to the budget and program plans. (About 44 percent of the intermediate school district financing in the state comes from federal sources.)

The state of Washington, with its 14 intermediate school districts, represents an example of a growing and necessary trend toward regionalization of intermediate-unit services and control.

Trained Personnel for Intermediate Units

Another problem besetting the intermediate unit is also connected with adequate financing. To perform needed services for school districts, many

---

[6] Louis Bruno, *The Intermediate School District* (Olympia, Washington: Association of Intermediate School District Superintendents, 1972), p. 14.

more better-trained professional personnel are needed. Only higher salaries can attract highly trained specialists to the intermediate superintendent's service. The shortage of personnel can be partially alleviated by focusing professional services toward higher administrative echelons in the local school districts. This is only a partial answer, however, since America still includes small schools in isolated areas. Nearly half of the nation's school districts have fewer than 300 students. In this area there is still a need for direct supervisory help for classroom teachers.

Where trained administrators are unavailable at the local district level, necessary services must be provided by traveling supervisors. County service must be made more attractive through better salaries and better working conditions. When this is accomplished, more young people, particularly teachers now in service, will train themselves as specialists in the several areas needed by intermediate superintendents. The service level of the superintendent's office will never rise above the competency of his staff. More and better-trained personnel are indispensable in order to strengthen the intermediate unit.

Many county superintendents are still elected and subject to various political pressures. The work of the county superintendent is a professional job. It should be undergirded with high qualifications that emphasize training, experience, and personal assets. When county superintendents are chosen on a merit basis and relieved of the necessity of expending their energies to keep their politics in proper shape, they will be free to give more attention to leadership and better professional service to local school districts. Members of county school boards should be elected from district boards; their most important function is the selection of a professionally qualified county or intermediate superintendent.

Political pressures that tend to rob children and youth of needed educational services have no place in the organization of the intermediate unit.

Summary

Traditionally, the intermediate or county educational unit has been supervisory. Most states have this unit today, although its functions have changed to enforcement of laws and upholding minimum standards. It appears that its future role will be as a coordination and service organization.

Essentially, the intermediate unit is a subdivision of state government, carrying out a state function. In this sense, it is not a local governmental unit, and should be financed by the entire state rather than by local political subdivisions. It should perform only those local functions that cannot be performed on the district level.

The county superintendent may be either elected or appointed. His functions fall into two general categories: (1) records and reports and (2) professional services. The first category includes budget approval, control of expenditures, and verification of average daily attendance. The second category includes such services as teacher supervision, inservice training, library and audio-visual aids, and operation of certain federal programs.

The historical development of the county superintendency in California is traced in order to show how it has developed into a service organization, pioneering many educational services.

Problems of the intermediate unit are mainly financial and organizational, the latter hinging upon the vast difference in populations of counties in the same state. The concept of a regional unit transcending political boundaries is discussed, as is the pressing need for well-paid, professionally trained administrators at this level.

Trends

TOWARD INCREASING THE STATUS OF COUNTY SUPERINTENDENT. During the last 150 years the county superintendent has evolved from a bookkeeper, to an educational leader, and to a regional superintendent. This leadership role, which is more and more prevalent upon the part of the intermediate superintendent, results from his participation in community coordination, support of worthwhile legislation, competency as an instructional leader, and spokesman for educational betterment. Many states have raised their requirements with respect to certification, training, and experience. Selection of the superintendent is more often by appointment than by political choice.

The county superintendent is being increasingly recognized in professional conventions and selective associations. The roster of participants for the convention of the American Association of School Administrators contains, annually, a high percentage of county–intermediate superintendents. Many county superintendents have been elected to membership in such selective associations as Phi Delta Kappa. The trend over the last several years has been for the county superintendent of schools to assume a greater leadership role in community affairs and among his professional associates.

TOWARD STRONGER INTERMEDIATE UNITS.   Just as adequate district reorganization is a slow evolutionary process, adequate intermediate-unit reorganization is slow, but nevertheless a trend.   Areas with too few school districts have combined with others to make an adequate intermediate unit. Some counties have combined to jointly finance and administer needed programs over an indefinite period.   Examples of what such a flexible intermediate unit can contribute are educational television, audio-visual service, curriculum guides, and data processing.   Whole states, such as Utah, Texas, and Alaska, have revised their intermediate-unit organization so that the intermediate-unit superintendent has greater coordination and leadership opportunities.   The adequate intermediate unit is becoming one with sufficient population, size, and service facilities to help local school districts in its area.

TOWARD MORE INTERMEDIATE-UNIT EDUCATIONAL SERVICES.   The increase of educational services, as opposed to the bureaucratic functions, is rapidly developing.   A significant study assigned the following functions, most of which are service in nature, as the proper responsibilities of the intermediate unit:

1.   Coordination and leadership.
2.   The provision of transitory or emergency services.
3.   The provision of advisory and consulting services.
4.   Area administration of the state minimum program.
5.   Limited review of specified district action.
6.   Internal organization of the intermediate unit.[7]

TOWARD HIGHER LEVEL SERVICES.   A trend in which the services of the intermediate unit are directed toward a higher level in the district echelon is beginning to take place in some of the states.   The superintendents in the 175 supervisory districts of New York state are giving greater service to the supervisors and administrators.   This trend is apparent in some of the

---

[7] C. C. Trillingham, "A Pattern for School Administration in California," a report from the California Commission of Public School Administration (Pasadena, Calif., 1955), pp. 48–49.

county–district unit states, such as the parish in Louisiana which includes New Orleans, and some of the divisions in Virginia. Riverside County, California, has made noteworthy strides toward coordination at a higher administrative echelon. This trend is to be encouraged, because administrators at the district level want to work with intermediate-unit consultants on their own, or a higher, competency level.

Toward Strengthening of the State Program. The intermediate unit is strengthening the work of the state department. In most states, the state department of education is too remote to have strong impact upon the local school teachers and administrators. There is always a certain amount of suspicion and resentment felt toward officials who are unknown personally and who represent state power. This hesitancy and resentment disappears when local administrators work as a team with members of the county superintendent's office. For a state department to be effective, it must have channels that reach every community. This is the function of the intermediate unit: to furnish those channels of communication and service that strengthen the educational process where the pupils are. States have proved that education can be more effective when their intermediate channels carry on a continuous program of services, interpretation, and reports.

Administrative Problems

In Basket

Problem 1

You are the assistant county superintendent charged with the responsibility of helping school districts with educational planning. Several districts are investigating the possibility of developing alternative schools. The superintendents and boards of education have asked you to help them with their planning.

What research would you use to inform yourself?
How would you proceed in working with the superintendents and boards of education?
What would you recommend that the districts do to help them decide whether or not to develop alternative schools?

Problem 2

You are the county superintendent in a rural county with only eleven elementary schools and one high school. You cannot provide the services that you know are so desperately needed by your schools.

Would you work toward an intermediate unit by combining several counties?
Would you regionalize some services in connection with other counties?
What else could you do?

Selected References

BEEM, H. D., and THOMAS, J. A.   *A Report of the Michigan Committee for the Study of the Intermediate Unit of Administration.*   Chicago: University of Chicago Press, 1956.

"From Rural to Specialized Services: Intermediate School Districts."   *Michigan Education Journal* 44 (May 1967), pp. 8–10.

GRIEDER, CALVIN.   "New Kinds of Intermediate Districts Are Showing Up."   *Nation's Schools* 79 (May 1967).

HOFFMAN, GLENN W.   *The Flexible Intermediate Unit in California: A Study of Regional Educational Activities Performed Cooperatively by County Offices of Education.*   Palo Alto, Calif.: Stanford University, 1966.

LITTLE, ARTHUR D., INC.   *A New Organizational System for State-Level Educational Administration.*   Sacramento: California State Department of Education, 1967.

MILLER, W. W.   "Case History: The County Superintendent's New Job: Interview."   *School Management* 6 (September 1962), pp. 93–97.

MORPHET, EDGAR L., ed.   *Emerging Designs for Education.*   Englewood Cliffs, N.J.: Citation Press, 1968.

MORRISETT, LLOYD N., SR.   *Power Play for Control of Education.*   Denver: Education Commission of the States, 1967.

STOOPS, EMERY.   *Report of the Study Title III, ESEA.*   Sacramento: State Department of Education, 1970.

STOOPS, EMERY, and RAFFERTY, M. L.   *Practices and Trends in School Administration.*   Boston: Ginn & Company, 1961.

WELLS, CHARLES, JR.   "The Dynamics of the Intermediate District."   *Overview* 3 (July 1962).

5

The School District's Role in Education

The local school district is the level at which the education of students takes place. It is influenced by state laws and the will of its electorate. Although districts vary in size and organization, they function under similar policies adopted by the local board of education. An administrative staff is necessary to administer each school district and to carry out the rules and regulations of the school board. Sound, board-adopted policies are needed to help with problems such as teacher militancy, community involvement, and integration.

This chapter includes a discussion of the following topics:

Pros and Cons of Local School District Organization
The Local School Board
Powers of the Local School District
Written Rules and Regulations
Local District Organization Support of the Instructional Program
Organizational Adjustment to Local Conditions
Patterns of Grade Organization
Integration of Public Schools
Summary
Trends

Pros and Cons of Local School District Organization

Nowhere does one find such great divergence of expert opinion in the field of education as over the issue of local district organization. The following quotations illustrate the conflict of opinion:

One of the greatest obstacles to the attainment of good schools . . .
is the pattern of administrative organization in which local school districts
are the dominant feature.[1]

No large centralized system could be as adaptable to individual communities or so quickly responsive to movements toward educational improvement as is the small, semi-autonomous school district.[2]

School districts are defined as local, independent governments "created by the state for the purpose of conducting a system of public
education, within a prescribed geographical area."[3] School districts are
usually politically autonomous and fiscally independent. This independence was originally provided to free the schools from subservience to
partisan governmental bureaus and agencies. It is still treasured by almost
all educators for this reason. It is, in fact, the local character of the
nation's schools which sparks the controversy over the nature of district
organization. However, local initiative has encouraged many of the
advances and innovations that have taken place in education.

School district government is more responsive to the wish of the electorate than any other governmental unit. Pressures of many types are
exerted upon the schools, despite the typically low number of votes cast in
school elections. Such pressures are felt by locally chosen board members
who are remarkably responsive to community wishes, organized parent
groups, individual parents, and sometimes the schoolchildren themselves.
These influences combine to make the school the mirror of the community. Changes in school programs and methods thus often become
difficult to consummate. A new idea or revolutionary concept, brilliant
and long-needed though it may be, must run the gamut of semi-autonomous governmental units, each controlled normally by the most conservative and complacent elements of the population. It has been estimated
that the general acceptance of a new educational practice requires about
twenty years. In other fields of human endeavor, this would have meant
that aircraft would not have come into use until after World War I, that the
Model T Ford would have dominated the nation's highways until 1948,
and that atomic energy would have remained a laboratory exercise until
about 1965.

The local district has certain advantages. It preserves the flavor of

---

[1] Harl R. Douglass and Calvin Grieder, *American Public Education* (New York:
Ronald Press Co., 1948), p. 159.

[2] H. L. Hagman, *Administration of American Public Schools* (New York:
McGraw-Hill Book Co., 1951), p. 81.

[3] Robert E. Wilson, *Educational Administration,* p. 151.

American frontier democracy and sturdy independence. It renders the schools quickly responsive to sudden changes in the manners and morals of the citizenry that supports them. By closely identifying the schools with the community, it compels educators to associate with the lay public more frequently and intimately. By placing control in the hands of lay boards, the local district system theoretically ensures immediate and lasting interest in school affairs by the general public from whose ranks board members are periodically selected. The solution to many problems posed by modern methods of district organization probably lies in the direction of synthesis and compromise between the demands for increasing efficiency and support, and the desire for local independence.

The Local School Board

Legislative groups exercising control over local school districts operate under various titles: board of education, board of trustees, board of school directors, or, simply, school board. These boards have a dual function. Primarily, they represent the people of the school district in the administration of the schools, but they also represent the people of the entire state, inasmuch as education is a delegated state function. The office of school board member differs nationally, but has certain common points. For example, the membership of such boards is composed of laymen who are representative of all classes of the population, rather than only business and professional groups. It was formerly thought that prominent businessmen made the best school board members; indeed, such persons still make up a majority of the membership of school boards. Some people seek election to the school board as a stepping stone to a political career rather than for the more idealistic purpose of improving the education of children.[4] However, the tendency to select board members in accordance with their interest in the schools and their ability to serve intelligently is becoming well established. Wage earners and retired persons from all ranks of life are serving more frequently on America's school boards. Teachers and administrators can serve on school boards not in their own district.

School boards in most states are granted great authority by legislative action. Aside from ascertaining that school operation and personnel meet minimum state requirements, local boards exercise most of the details of

---

[4] Andrew W. Halpin (ed.), *Administrative Theory in Education*, p. 177.

management. These basic requirements usually deal with the teaching of certain subjects, the number of school days per year, standards of teacher certification, and minimum salaries. These are all "floor" requirements; there are no "ceilings" placed on local schools insofar as quality is concerned.

While a school board's legal powers may not be confined to legislative actions, in practice its judicial and executive powers are increasingly falling into disuse. The problem of executing board decisions, formerly tackled directly by the board itself, or, worse yet, by individual board members, is now placed in the hands of the superintendent and his staff. The growing complexity of school affairs makes it unwise and even impossible for the board to attempt to handle all the multitudinous details of administration, supervision, and finance. Most boards today confine the bulk of their activity to legislating, i.e., adopting policies and approving the means by which policies are executed. Examples of this legislative activity are providing for new buildings and equipment, employment of teachers, and adoption of textbooks.

There are still some school boards, however, that try to administer. As a group, or perhaps an individual or two, they may want a voice in every business or administrative procedure. This interference with the superintendent's functions should be discouraged.

Two other functions that closely accompany the legislative process are planning and appraisal. In the former, policies of the school system are carefully studied before being put into effect. This is usually done in close cooperation with the professional personnel employed by the district. Questions such as the legality, wisdom, and practicality of proposed board policies are examined during the planning phase of board legislation. Just as planning is a pre-legislative phase of school board activity, so is appraisal a post-legislative one. Appraisal involves evaluation by the board of the work of the schools and the personnel employed to operate them. Because they are lay people, they may not fully understand how to judge the effectiveness of the programs they have approved. "Under these circumstances, for the sake of the program and to protect his own hide, the educational administrator must become not only the executive but the teacher of the board of education."[5]

In the process of evaluation, the board must examine questions of whether or not the tax dollar is being well spent, whether the schools are

---

[5] Halpin, *Administrative Theory,* pp. 177–178.

turning out adequately educated persons, and whether any changes in any area are desirable. Both planning and appraisal are indispensable supplements to the school board's principal function—legislation.

School board members from all walks of life assume their duties with little conception of the complexity of their jobs, and with little pretraining. Continuing information and guidance are essential. In this connection, an excellent "creed" for school board members has been developed by Phi Delta Kappa, and may be obtained from that fraternity by a request directed to its national headquarters in Bloomington, Indiana.

STANDARDS FOR SCHOOL BOARD ORGANIZATION. The school board should hold an annual organizational meeting between July 1 and July 15 of each school year. At this meeting it should:

1. Elect one member as president, one as vice-president, and one as clerk.
2. Designate the superintendent as its chief administrative officer.
3. Designate who should be the acting superintendent when the superintendent is out of the district.
4. Designate who shall sign all warrants.
5. Readopt all existing policies, publications, rules, and regulations.
6. Adopt the school calendar.
7. Adopt the schedule of regular board meetings.

The superintendent as secretary to the school board should be directed to:

1. Prepare and handle the board agenda.
2. Prepare and handle board minutes.
3. Handle all official district and board correspondence.
4. Attend all board meetings.[6]

The board should act as a united committee on all matters coming before it; i.e., no member is ever given authority to act as an individual on behalf of the board. All actions are taken only in legally called board meetings and board members serve as such only at board meetings. Meetings are presided over by the president, conducting them in accordance with generally accepted rules of order. Newly elected or appointed

---

[6] Irving R. Melbo et al., *Report of the Survey, South San Francisco Unified School District*, p. 94.

members should be oriented to board procedures prior to beginning their term of office.

Board members should be encouraged to attend annual conferences of their state and national school board associations. These conferences enable board members to share ideas, discuss mutual problems with board members from other districts, broaden their outlook, and keep up to date on educational problems and trends.

THE SCHOOL BOARD AND THE INSTITUTIONAL PROGRAM. Governing boards seldom give sufficient time to the instructional program, as discovered by many surveys and research studies. Melbo's report of one survey is presented in Table 5–1.

It is significant to note that only 7 percent of the time of the governing board was given to curriculum and instruction, contrasted with 11 percent for general functions, 25 percent for personnel, and 20 percent for school plant concerns. It is recommended that close to 50 percent of the board's attention be given to matters concerning better instruction and guidance for pupils. At least one board meeting a month should be devoted more or less exclusively to curriculum items.

Powers of the Local School District

With a few exceptions, the local school district is independent of all other branches of government that operate at stratums lower than the state level. It is answerable only to the people of the district and to the state department of education, in that order. In most states, local control is virtually absolute. The local district must rely, of course, on other governmental bodies to perform certain necessary functions (such as tax collection), but its control within its own area is indisputable. Indeed, because the school district is a creature of the state, it may actually take precedence over certain nonstate local governmental bodies whenever a conflict of authority occurs in an uncharted area of the law.

The state has given the local board of education powers necessary to do whatever is needed to conduct the schools, to secure land for school purposes, to enter into contractual obligations, to levy taxes, and to employ personnel. Teachers and administrators are actually exercising board authority in the areas of their assigned duties; this authority is legitimately

TABLE 5-1. *Number of Actions Taken in Functional Areas of Administration by Governing Boards, South San Francisco Unified School District, July 1, 1963 to January 1, 1967**

FISCAL YEAR	GENERAL FUNCTIONS	EMPLOYEES	CURRICULUM AND INSTRUCTION	FINANCE AND BUSINESS	SCHOOL PLANT	STUDENTS	PUBLIC RELATIONS	AUXILIARY SERVICES	ADJOURNMENT	TOTALS	FORMAL MOTIONS**	NON-ACTION**
1965–66	92	186	82	212	142	37	18	13	29	811	581	230
1964–65	96	222	53	208	133	26	15	17	31	801	625	176
1963–64	99	176	29	209	130	40	17	44	32	776	605	171
3-year totals	287	584	164	629	405	103	50	74	92	2388	1811	577
Percent of each type of action	12	25	7	26	17	4	2	3	4	100	76	24
1966–67***	41	96	26	92	75	18	7	11	14	380	265	115
Percent of each type of action	11	25	7	24	20	4	2	3	4	100	70	30

* Irving R. Melbo et al., *Report of the Survey, South San Francisco Unified School District* (Los Angeles: University of Southern California, 1967), p. 98.
** Included in 'Totals' column.
*** July 1, 1966 to January 1, 1967.

91

delegated, unless specifically prohibited by statute. How much they share in the responsibility of operating the public schools is determined by the pleasure of the board.[7] In any proper field of educational activity, school district employees act with full state authority, because powers and duties delegated to them by the local board originally stemmed from the state.

In all but a few states, school districts are immune from suit, although they are liable for tort. The theory behind this immunity is twofold: first, the district, in sharing the authority and responsibility of the state, also shares the state's traditional immunity to suit; second, such immunity guarantees that school funds shall not be diverted to the paying of judgments which, regardless of their equity, would perforce be noneducational in nature. This immunity to suit does not, of course, extend to school employees, who are often proceeded against in court. Even in this case, the authority delegated to teachers stands up against most types of legal action. The teacher, under common law, may do anything with, for, or to a child that the child's own parents may do, including disciplinary action; the courts have ruled this is fair as long as the punishment is not excessive.[8] He stands, in fact, *in loco parentis,* and has such broad powers in this connection that he may exert his authority during hours when school is not in session, and away from school property.

The federal government and state legislatures and boards of education are moving into areas traditionally reserved to local districts. This is due to the hesitancy of local boards in acting on programs that are of state and national interest, such as integration, vocational education, and programs for disadvantaged children. In an attempt to equalize the educational opportunities for all youth, federal and state governments are charting procedures that will accelerate the introduction or implementation of new programs.

The legal structure of the school district may be defined as a school board gifted with both permissive and mandatory authority by the state government, and subject to the state within the framework of legislation setting forth its powers and limitations. The school board is also subject to local community control through the regular election of its members. Its authority is exercised largely through the professional employees of the district, but also by the board itself in legal session. The proper use of these great powers is dependent upon the election of upright and conscien-

---

[7] Halpin, *Administrative Theory,* pp. 176–177.
[8] National Education Association, Research Division, "Corporal Punishment," *NEA Research Bulletin* 36 (October 1958), p. 88.

tious board members, and, in turn, upon their delegation of authority to able and alert teachers and administrators. When one or the other of these two factors is tampered with, the powers of the local district may quickly be perverted to evil or foolish uses, and may do as great harm as they are capable of doing good.

Written Rules and Regulations

School districts and boards that operate within the framework of a written policy handbook are less apt to be accused of abuses of power. Some city districts have written rules and regulations; few rural ones do. A policy handbook, adopted by the board on the basis of recommendations put forth by the superintendent, outlines administrative procedures and relationships in addition to codifying and systematizing previously adopted board policy. It enables each employee to know his functions, thus fixing responsibility. New employees benefit particularly, and the training of inexperienced personnel is facilitated.

Board rules and regulations should be formulated by the board of education and the superintendent with the cooperation of representatives from school employee groups. They should be in meticulous accord with state laws. The general functions of all classifications of employees should be stated clearly, but not so rigidly as to prevent the exercise of individuality. All written rules and regulations should be made available to employees. They should be followed, but if found to be archaic, they should be repealed.[9]

Teachers, in particular, and other personnel are becoming less willing to accept policies promulgated only by the school board. They want and often demand a voice in helping to develop policies that concern them. Teachers want to play a major role in shaping the curriculum. In 1965, five states (California, Connecticut, Oregon, Washington, and Florida) had negotiation legislation applying to school employees. Five other states (Massachusetts, Michigan, Wisconsin, New Hampshire, and Alaska) had collective bargaining legislation with specific provisions for public school employees.

---

[9] By permission of Macmillan Publishing Co., Inc., from *The Fundamentals of Public School Administration,* 4th ed., by Ward G. Reeder. Copyright © 1958 by Macmillan Publishing Co., Inc., p. 72.

TABLE 5–2. Standards for School Board Minutes[a]

STANDARD	PERFECT SCORE
I. CONTENT: BOARD PROCEDURES (150 points)	
The minutes should show:	
1. The date of each meeting	10
2. The place of each meeting	10
3. The type of each meeting: regular adjourned, or special	10
4. Members present, by name	10
5. Members absent, by name	10
6. The call to order	10
7. The arrival of tardy members, by name	10
8. The departure of members, by name, before adjournment	10
9. The date and place of the next meeting	10
10. The adjournment of the meeting	10
11. Record of written notice for special meetings	20
12. Record of all items of business to be considered shown in agenda	20
13. Post agenda as required by law for meetings	10
Subtotal	150
II. CONTENT—BOARD ACTIONS (700 points)	
The minutes should show:	
*1. The approval, or amendment and approval of the minutes of the preceding meeting	30
2. Complete information as to each subject of the Board's deliberations	40
3. Complete information as to the action taken on each subject	30
a. The maker and seconder of the motion	10
b. The vote on the motion	10
c. A roll-call record of the vote on a motion if not unanimous	10
4. All Board resolutions	XX
a. In complete text	30
b. Numbered serially for each fiscal year	10
5. A record of all contracts entered into	40
6. All employments and resignations or terminations of employment	50
7. A record, by number, of all purchase orders approved	50
8. A record of all bid procedures	XX
a. Calls for bids authorized	10
b. Bids received	10
c. Bids let, or other action taken	10
9. A record, by number, of all warrants issued	30
10. Adoption of the annual budget	30
11. Periodic financial reports, as required	20
a. Transfers of funds from one budgetary classification to another	10
b. Collections received and deposited	10
c. Sales of personal property	10

TABLE 5–2 (Continued)

	STANDARD	PERFECT SCORE
12.	The salary schedule for the current year	30
13.	A record of all important correspondence	30
14.	A record of superintendent's reports to the board	30
15.	Approval of all policy documents, such as a course of study, board policies, etc., prepared for district use	50
16.	A record of all delegations appearing before the board	30
17.	Adoption of the annual school calendar	30
18.	Approval of duties of school employees	50
	Subtotal	700

III. FORMAT (100 points)

1.	The minutes should be typewritten on single sheets of durable white paper	10
2.	Pages should be numbered serially for each fiscal year	10
3.	Pages should be entered in a heavy loose-leaf type binder	10
4.	Each item of business in the minutes should have a brief topical heading, preferably in the left-hand margin	10
5.	Each item of business should be entered as a separate paragraph, or a series of paragraphs	10
6.	All motions should be numbered consecutively for each fiscal year; the number of the motions should appear at the left of the first line recording the motion or below the topical heading	10
7.	An index of the minutes should be prepared for each fiscal year	10
8.	All minutes should be signed by the proper officers of the board	10
9.	A duplicate set of minutes should be kept	10
10.	Documents which are made a part of the minutes by Board action should be included in the minute books or Board reports	10
	Subtotal	100

IV. HANDLING OF MINUTES (50 points)

1.	The original minutes book should be secured in a fireproof file, safe or vault in the district offices	10
2.	The duplicate set should be kept in the district office in a designated place where it is readily available for inspection	10
3.	A copy of the minutes should be sent to each board member prior to the next meeting	15
4.	The superintendent should be responsible for recording and preparation of the minutes	15
	Subtotal	50
	Grand total	1,000

a Irving R. Melbo et al., *Report of the Survey, South San Francisco Unified School District* (Los Angeles: University of Southern California, 1967), pp. 101–103.
* Not required at special meetings.

BOARD MEETING AGENDAS.   Written agendas should be prepared by the superintendent's office, distributed to board members prior to the regular meeting date, and followed during the meeting.   They should include all anticipated business, arranged in proper order under such headings as "Reports," "Old Business," or "New Business."   They may also include pertinent enclosures, such as correspondence, financial reports, and lists of outstanding bills, duplicated and attached to the main body of the agenda. In general, there should be *action* items, *study* items, and *information* items.   The distribution of an agenda several days prior to the meeting will afford ample time for consideration by board members, and will save valuable time at the meeting itself.

STANDARDS FOR SCHOOL BOARD MINUTES.   School board minutes are extremely important as the official record of all board proceedings and actions.   They must be meticulously kept as no expenditure can be made unless shown as approved by the board.   Many actions taken by school boards, even though not adopted as official policy, are expected to be followed as if they were policy.

Minutes become official after approval by the board, with corrections, if necessary.   They should then be available to the public and all personnel.

Melbo has developed standards for school board minutes to serve as a guide to superintendents and school boards.   These are shown in Table 5–2.

ADMINISTRATIVE RELATIONSHIPS.   Every school district of any considerable size should prepare an organizational chart showing administrative relationships, school positions, and interrelationships of various parts of the school organization.   Such a chart makes it possible to see in outline the entire school organization, and to detect any weaknesses, such as overlapping authority.

A large district cannot operate effectively without such a chart; a smaller district may improve its efficiency by preparing one.   The chart is a visual supplement to a policy handbook with the added advantage of being instantly intelligible to lay persons interested in the schools.

The illustrated organizational charts should serve only as models. The basic philosophy, size, and amount of money available to employ administrators and support personnel affect the organizational plan.   Figure 5–1 illustrates the main organizational divisions for a large school

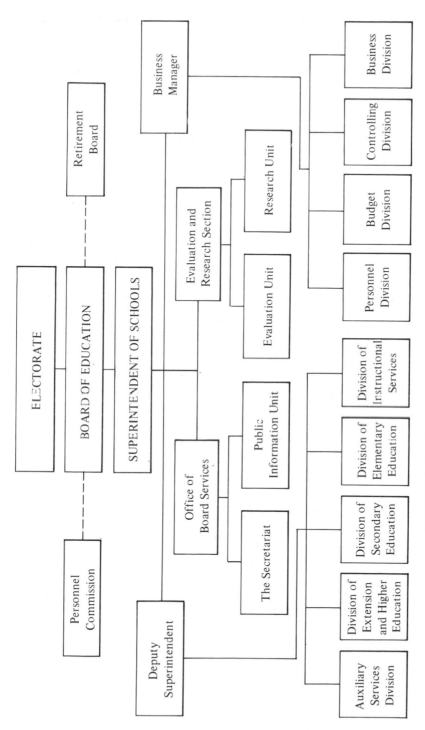

FIGURE 5-1. *Organization of a Very Large School District.*

district. Although only line relationships are shown, each division should have its own organizational pattern showing the breakdown of each position as well as staff relationships. Medium-size districts could be those with 15 to 25 schools. Figure 5–2 is an organizational chart for a medium-size school district. The organizational chart for a small district (with less than 15 schools) is shown in Figure 5–3. Because there are many districts with an enrollment of 1,000 or less, some of the positions shown in the figure may be combined.

Districts that plan to show organizational relationships should involve representatives from every school and department, certificated and non-certificated. Decisions must be made as to whether the chart should be developed on a "position" or a "function" basis or a combination of both. Positions require a title and a name connected with it. Functions are more nebulous and are difficult to chart; they also must have some designation of "who" is responsible for carrying out the function. Examples of categorized functions are: services, assessment and evaluation, research, staff development, curriculum planning, and management. "Lines of authority" are usually indicated by a solid line, and "lines of communication" or "staff relationships" are usually shown by dashed lines. Because there are many communication and staff relationships, it is usually impossible to show all of them without cluttering up a chart.

The organizational plan that is agreed upon should be operable and clearly understood by the personnel and the public. When adopted by the board of education, it should be adhered to until revised.

Local District Support of the Instructional Program

Instruction is the only reason a school district has for existing. It follows, then, that all other school functions of whatever nature are simply supporting and facilitating activities. They are not independent, nor are they justified in their own right; they exist solely to maximize the instructional program. It is desirable that these functions be coordinated under a central administration in such a way that the efforts of the many individuals in the system will be exerted effectively toward a common goal.

Although there are many patterns of organization extant, the following criteria for good school organization can be applied against any or all of them.

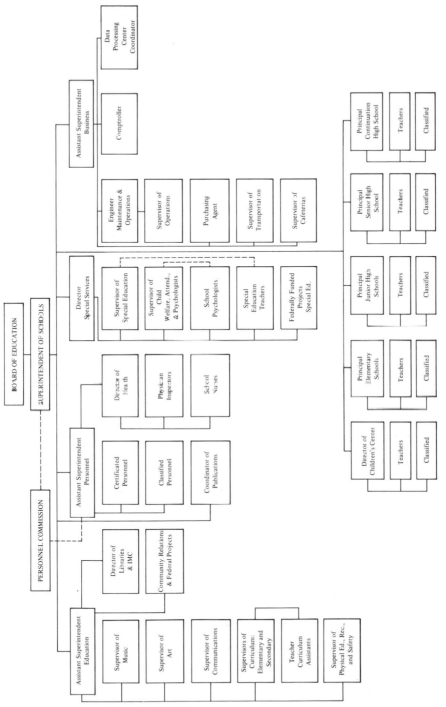

FIGURE 5–2. Organization of a Medium-Size School District.

BOARD OF EDUCATION

SUPERINTENDENT OF SCHOOLS

PERSONNEL COMMISSION

Assistant Superintendent Education

Supervisor of Music

Supervisor of Art

Supervisor of Communications

Supervisors of Curriculum: Elementary and Secondary

Teacher Curriculum Assistants

Supervisor of Physical Ed., Rec., and Safety

Director of Libraries & IMC

Community Relations & Federal Projects

Assistant Superintendent Personnel

Certificated Personnel

Classified Personnel

Coordinator of Publications

Director of Health

Physician Inspectors

School Nurses

Director Special Services

Supervisor of Special Education

Supervisor of Child Welfare, Attend., & Psychologists

School Psychologists

Special Education Teachers

Federally Funded Projects Special Ed.

Assistant Superintendent Business

Comptroller

Data Processing Center Coordinator

Engineer Maintenance & Operations

Supervisor of Operations

Purchasing Agent

Supervisor of Transportation

Supervisor of Cafeterias

Director of Children's Center

Teachers

Classified

Principal Elementary Schools

Teachers

Classified

Principal Junior High Schools

Teachers

Classified

Principal Senior High School

Teachers

Classified

Principal Continuation High School

Teachers

Classified

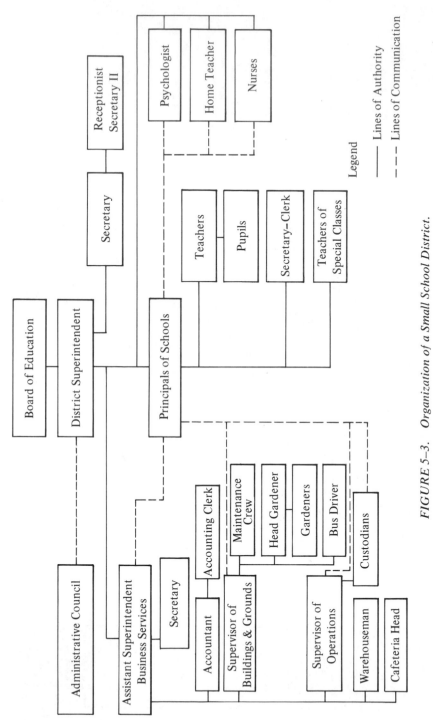

FIGURE 5–3.   Organization of a Small School District.

1. It should be clear. It is essential that its structure be easily understood by those working within it.
2. It should be unobtrusive. Any organizational pattern that attracts attention is poor. It exists as an aid, never as a goal in itself.
3. It should facilitate instruction. Organization is subordinate to instruction, and should never restrict or impede it.
4. It should possess rapid and facile multiple-way communication.
5. It should be flexible. School district organization should be able to accommodate itself to the differing abilities and aptitudes of those who operate the schools.
6. It should be both integrated and composed of semi-autonomous departments. Operating from a central headquarters, insofar as policy and philosophy are concerned, district organization should also feature self-sufficient divisions capable of acting independently if the need arises.
7. It should fix responsibility in terms of each person in the organization.

In most instances, school districts are small. In such districts, it may be expected that the organization will be composed of the superintendent and his clerical staff. The clerical staff, even in small districts, should be large enough to free the superintendent from all office details and enable him to spend his time on policy-level matters. In this type of arrangement, it is necessary to organize the training and supervision of the clerical staff in such a way that the office work will be simple, efficient, and adequate.

In larger districts, the second officer of the administrative structure is an assistant for business affairs; he may be titled business manager, assistant superintendent, or director of business affairs. This position should always be clearly subordinate to that of the superintendent of schools.

The employment of a director of curriculum is usually the next step in the creation of a district's administrative structure. This specialist is employed to direct supervisory activities, advise in the employment of teachers, and work generally toward the improvement of instruction. Large systems also may employ an assistant director or assistant superintendent of instruction. The superintendent, of course, retains his basic responsibility for these phases of the school program; but with the addition of these assistants, he spends more time on supervision and overall coordination.

The third assistant should assume the management of employed personnel, both certificated and classified. Selection, retention, and separation, with all attendant functions, determine his duties and responsibilities.

Districts of considerable size usually employ officers such as guidance director, health officer, library director, audio-visual coordinator, cafeteria supervisor, transportation officer, adult education director, pupil personnel director, and special services director. Research has become so important that it is not unusual for large districts to have an assistant superintendent or director in charge of research. An administrator may also be placed in charge of communication and public relations. School districts participating in many federal programs have found it necessary to employ an administrator to handle them.

A good superintendent attempts to bring his organization together as tightly as possible, and to avoid the necessity of personally managing many varying facets of the educational program. He makes each director or supervisor responsible to one of the assistant superintendents. Coordination does not necessarily mean central control over multitudinous specific functions; rather, it should be a wise combination of all district activities in a common drive toward desired educational objectives. Regular conferences of key personnel and cooperative planning bring about coordination without rigid controls.

Organizational Adjustment to Local Conditions

The neighborhood in which a particular school is located should govern, at least partially, the educational activity of that school. Therefore, sufficient freedom under the organizational plan of the district should be made possible in order that each school may carry on educational activities suited to its individual environment. Such an organizational framework necessitates a building principal who knows how to make decisions and how to lead. Teachers willing to assist in a democratic organizational setup are also a necessity if such flexibility of control is to be a success. Supervision and administration emanating from the central office of each district should be aimed at improving the ability of the individual schools to exercise autonomy effectively.

Small elementary schools are characteristically staffed as follows: a teaching principal, a part-time school nurse, one teacher for each grade, and certain "shared" specialists, such as music teachers or art instructors. Clerical assistance is usually not provided; the principal, unfortunately, spends much of his time doing routine paper work, and teachers are not assisted appreciably in clerical and recordkeeping tasks. Larger elementary schools may have sufficient office personnel to provide such assistance for teachers.

High schools are more often large, and consequently tend to be smaller editions of the district-wide organizational pattern. The high school principal is a nonteaching executive. He often has a vice-principal or similar subordinate assisting him, with boys' and girls' counselors and an adequate clerical staff.

A school principal exists primarily to facilitate the education of children. He should be freed as much as possible from routine tasks and the administration of clerical duties. Some of the many roles he must play are:

The manager of his school.
An agent of educational change.
The educational leader in his school community.
The evaluator, supervisor, and instructional leader of his school.
The school's innovator, expediter, morale builder, facilitator, and organizer.
The provider of specific information for long-range planning and development, implementation of programs, and evaluation.

His instructional role requires refined technical, human, and organizational skills. The principal is in the center of intercommunication between the school board, superintendent, teachers, students, parents, community, other school personnel and administrators, and the curriculum. The Appendix provides a rating instrument to help a principal evaluate himself.

In order to accomplish these multiple demands, the principal must establish priorities that enable him to give direction and emphasis to his activities. Principals and teachers must work cooperatively toward solving problems in all areas of the educational program. Teachers are qualified by professional training to help fashion the learning programs to meet the needs of all students. Those whose lives and work are affected by decisions must have a voice in arriving at those decisions. Along with the school staff, members of the community and students should be involved in developing educational goals and objectives for their schools. The assessment of success is based on the degree to which objectives are met.

In order to work cooperatively together, the principal must schedule meetings and conferences in which all members participate equally. However, the principal should act as the leader to keep discussions under control to achieve the desired.ends of the meeting. He can also establish committees to work on specified projects or problems and to make recommendations regarding their implementation. Each committee should have a faculty member as leader. In large schools, the principal may organize a faculty cabinet to serve as a type of executive board. As representatives of the teachers, they can help make decisions as to what should be brought to the attention of the entire staff and can save time by helping the principal make routine decisions. The cabinet also can act as a sounding board for the principal.

The autonomy of each school should be set forth in written policy statements developed by the board of education together with the staff and faculty. Certain rules and regulations should apply to all schools in the district, such as length of school day, and the selection, assignment, and transfer of teachers. Separate schools should retain considerable freedom of action in areas such as instruction, scheduling, discipline, student government, staff professional growth and development, and faculty meetings. In the field of finance, individual school autonomy does not apply. Central purchasing and deposit of all school monies is a highly efficient practice, and should be conducted on a district-wide basis. The position of each school as a neighborhood agency of education, organized and intended to meet local neighborhood needs as well as the broader district standards of education, should be safeguarded at all costs.

Patterns of School Organization

It is presumed that in each district individual schools will be organized so that the education of the children may be most fruitful and most economically managed. The presumption is somewhat optimistic; no one seems to have discovered the best scheme for school organization. It is unlikely that there is just one best way, for it is possible to have good schools and good schooling under different structures. What is best for one community may not be best for another; and within a single school system, schools with different internal organizations may have comparable achievements.

New organizational plans arise because of dissatisfaction with the concept of the self-contained classroom in which 30 to 35 students are taught by one teacher, with little attention given to individual differences. Any new organizational system should be planned carefully; it should have a goal of meeting educational needs of individuals more completely than the previous organizational structure. Poor planning usually results in the failure of the program. Schools may change the name of their organizational pattern, but make few changes in point of view, program, or structure. The success of any instructional organization will depend upon the extent to which the community, teachers, students, and administrators are involved in the planning, implementation, and evaluation of the program.

Vertical Organization

Vertical organization is based on the idea of promotion or movement upward either by grades or levels. School grade organization from very early times in this country has followed a traditional 8–4 pattern. The 4-year high school originally was superimposed upon the existing 8-year grammar school; today, most small city districts and most town and village school systems are organized on this pattern. Kindergarten is often added at the lower end of the educational ladder to complete the organizational picture.

The introduction of the junior high school to American education prior to World War I served to break the universality of the 8–4 pattern. Larger city school systems are more apt to follow a 6–3–3 plan (the middle number represents a three-year junior high school). The junior high school was originally developed to better serve the children of early adolescence. With this goal in mind, and also to bridge the social and psychological gap existing between elementary and senior high schools, the junior high was set up as an intermediate institution. In many instances, it has become a subject matter-oriented, departmentalized small edition of a typical high school. The 3-year junior high school has not always been satisfactory in meeting the developmental and learning needs of pre-adolescents.[10]

To solve this problem, some districts have moved to a middle-school concept with a 5–3–4 structure. Middle-school advocates reason that because students are now maturing at an earlier age, sixth graders work

---

[10] Wilson, *Educational Administration*, p. 504.

better with seventh and eighth graders, and ninth graders perform better in a four-year high school.   The middle school can be truly transitional.

There are many different plans in effect employing almost every conceivable combination of grades, although it is generally agreed that groups should not be too small.   However, there are a few K–3–3–3–3–2-year junior college plans with the kindergarten and first three grades constituting a primary school and the fourth, fifth, and sixth grades constituting a middle-grade school.

There is evidence of some fairly well-defined practices in grade organization.   A stratified sampling of school districts enrolling 300 or more students was made in January 1966; data from this study are shown in Table 5–3.

The responses show that the size of the school system had some bearing on the type of organization.   In the smaller systems, the 6–6 and 8–4 plans were more frequently found.   In the larger systems, the 6–3–3 plan was used by over three-fourths of the systems.   There is less uniformity today than a few generations ago when most school systems were either of the 8–4, 7–5, or 7–4 type.   Where there are nursery schools, kindergartens, and junior colleges, the vertical organization is expanded at the bottom and the top.

At the upper end of the distribution, only small gains had been made

TABLE 5–3.   *Practices of School Organization by Grade, 1966**

TYPE OF GRADE ORGANIZATION	ESTIMATED TOTAL, SYSTEMS ENROLLING 300 OR MORE PUPILS	SYSTEMS GROUPED BY ENROLLMENT		
		25,000 AND OVER	3,000– 24,999	300– 2,999
6–3–3	21.5%	75.8%	49.1%	12.6%
8–4	21.4	10.1	13.7	23.8
6–6	22.4	0.7	3.8	28.1
6–2–4	11.9	6.7	14.5	11.3
7–5	3.4	2.7	4.7	3.0
5–3–4	3.3	1.3	3.0	3.5
4–4–4	1.1	0.0	0.4	1.3
Other	15.0	2.7	10.7	16.5
Number of systems	12,130	150	234	232

* National Education Association, Research Division, "Public School Programs and Practices," *NEA Research Bulletin* 45 (December 1967), p. 118.

at the junior college level up to 1963 when the number of junior colleges increased to 577.[11]   However, Fretwell states that they are now being established at the rate of about 50 per year.[12]

GRADED PLAN.   In the typical graded plan, each grade is grouped according to age in a self-contained classroom.   The emphasis is on subject-matter achievement.   Other types of vertical organization have been developed because differences in ability and accomplishment within any age group or grade have been recognized.

MULTIGRADING.   Multigrading provides for individual differences by grouping children from two or three sequential grades.   Grade labels are kept, preventing a sharp break with tradition.   Multigrading focuses on the learner's needs rather than on grade-level standards.

NONGRADING.   This is an organizational concept that received its impetus from John Goodlad.[13]   It is based on the premise that every grade has a spread of academic achievement.   It is similar to multigrading except that grade labels are removed and children are grouped for instruction according to their ability or achievement rather than by age.   The nongraded class is usually in a self-contained classroom and is taught by one teacher. However, instruction is individualized and learner centered.   Students progress at their own rate.   Nongrading requires changes in grouping practices, grading practices, curriculum content, methodology, and instructional materials.   For nongrading to be successful, the teacher must diagnose and prescribe for individual students so that they receive instruction directed to their particular needs.[14]

Nongrading has been used in junior and senior high schools.   Melbourne High School and Nova High School in Florida started nongrading early in the 1960s.   Grade lines are eliminated, instruction is based on individual abilities, aptitudes, skills, and interests, and exploration is encouraged.   Classes may be large or small.   There has been some controversy, however, regarding the claims for success of nongrading at the secondary level.

---

11 United States Office of Education, Circular No. 728 (Washington, D.C., 1964).
12 E. K. Fretwell, Jr., "Issues Facing Community Colleges Today," *Today's Education*, p. 46.
13 John I. Goodlad and Robert H. Anderson, *The Nongraded American School*.
14 Marian Pope Franklin, *School Organization: Theory and Practice*, p. 5.

CONTINUOUS PROGRESS.   Continuous progress is a variation of nongrading or multigrading.   Children are neither promoted nor retained and there are no age levels.   Bright pupils move ahead to more difficult tasks, while slower pupils are given more time to learn difficult concepts.   Each pupil may work at different levels in various subjects, moving as rapidly or slowly as his ability permits.   He may remain in a lower block an extra year after conferences with parents and the child.

EDUCATIONAL PARKS.   Educational parks are a total educational facility.[15] Their vertical organizational plan consists of an elementary school, a middle school or a junior high school, a high school, and in some cases, a college, all of which are grouped on a single site.   An educational park can provide for better integration of children from different backgrounds, economy of operation, shared facilities, courses, and personnel, and improved community services.   Shared educational facilities can include auditoriums, language labs, gymnasiums, and instructional materials centers that can be connected to a computerized teaching and information center.   The problem of establishing an educational park is the size of the area needed, the number of buildings and facilities, additional busing, and the large original cost.   Some fear a loss of student identity because of the size of the educational complex.   And logistics can become an administrative headache.

STUDENT PROMOTION.   The vertical organization of a school district requires some method of moving students upward through the various grades. The promotion policy must explain the basis on which a student is promoted to the next higher level.   Several principles concerning promotions that were proposed by the Department of Superintendence of the National Education Association in 1931 are still pertinent today.[16]

1.   Promotion should be decided on the basis of the individual pupil.
2.   Promotion should be on the basis of many factors.   The final decision as to whether a particular pupil should be promoted should rest not merely on academic accomplishments, but on what will result in the greatest good to the all-around development of the individual.

---

[15] Frederick Shaw, "The Educational Park in New York: Archetype of the School of the Future?" *Phi Delta Kappan,* pp. 329–331.

[16] *Five Unifying Factors in American Education,* Ninth Yearbook of the National Education Association, Department of Superintendence (Washington, D.C., 1931), pp. 18–20.

3. In order that promotion procedures may be more or less uniform throughout a particular school system, a definite set of factors should be agreed upon which each teacher will take into consideration in forming his judgment as to whether or not a particular pupil should be promoted.
4. Criteria for promotion must take into consideration the curriculum offerings of the next higher grade or unit and the flexibility of its organization, its courses of study, and its methods.
5. It is the duty of the next higher grade or unit to accept pupils who are properly promoted to it from the lower grade or unit and to adapt its work to fit the needs of those pupils.
6. Promotion procedures demand continuous analysis and study of cumulative pupil case history records in order that refinement of procedure may result and that guesswork and conjecture may be reduced to a minimum.

The school district must make decisions as to whether promotion is based on a grade average, number of subjects passed, chronological age, social maturity, or combinations of these or similar factors. Some of the common types of promotion policies that have been used are:

1. Continuous plan. All students are promoted regardless of achievement.
2. Double promotion. Especially bright or mature students are promoted two grades, skipping one.
3. Trial promotion. Students who have not achieved academically are promoted to the next level on a trial basis. If not successful, they are returned to their former grade.
4. Nonpromotion. Students who fail are not promoted. It is generally agreed that students should be retained only once, usually in the first grade.

Schools have used various plans to help students achieve educational success. Some of these plans are: parallel course of study, nongraded classrooms, homogeneous grouping, ability grouping, cluster grouping, and combination grades. There are some educators who believe that a nongraded organization or an individualized approach offers the best alternative to the concept of retention and promotion because these plans prevent the stigma and discouragement that usually follow retention. However, research has not shown conclusively that any one method is better than another. It is known, however, that students who are retained seldom achieve more and sometimes achieve less in the year of retention. Good teachers will teach a child at his individual level and take him as far as possible, regardless of where he is in relation to the average of a given grade. Students who have been retained in a grade should be given every opportunity to make up their deficiencies and rejoin their normal grade or peer group. When grade adjustments are made, parents should have a conference with the teacher, the counselor, and the principal so that an understanding is reached. The parents' attitude in accepting a grade adjustment must be considered if the change is to be successful. The emotional and psychological attitude of the student is equally important.

Promotion is particularly important in the secondary schools. Colleges and universities are interested in the secondary-level academic achievement of students because they base their prediction of college success on high school success. Employers are more likely to employ those who have been regularly promoted and graduated. Nonpromotion and failure in secondary school is a major cause for dropping out and for delinquency. However, a student who fails to master a subject because of deliberate failure to apply himself leaves the teacher with little recourse.

Horizontal Organization

Horizontal organization divides students into groups and assigns them to classes, subjects, or teachers. The traditional form of horizontal organization is the elementary-level, self-contained classroom wherein about 30 pupils of about the same age are taught by a single teacher, responsible for teaching all subjects. Today, there are few, if any, such classrooms. Subjects such as art, music, physical education, and sometimes science are taught by specialists. Remedial specialists and counselors also help.[17] Modifications may be made in several ways. Individuals, groups, or the entire class may use a wide variety of facilities, equipment, and materials such as the instructional materials center, a multipurpose room, shops, or visit community agencies as the classroom extends beyond its four walls.

OPEN CLASSROOM. The open classroom is based on the philosophy that a child learns in a random way, at his own pace, and through self-moti-

---

[17] Franklin, *School Organization*, p. 189.

vation.[18]   Children work independently or in small groups where they share knowledge and skills.   They have the freedom to move to any one of numerous interest centers in the room, to study, to work on projects, or to read.   Tables in various arrangements replace desks.   There are many objects, games, displays, and learning materials.   Teaching machines, programmed-learning kits, typewriters, and other technological instructional equipment may also be in the room.   Open-classroom programs are not yet numerous, although they have been used in Philadelphia, North Dakota, New York City, and California.   Some secondary schools have developed the open-classroom concept, notably the Philadelphia Parkway Program, the "school without walls" that commenced in February 1969. The school's program goes beyond the school walls and utilizes many community resources.   Chicago and New York are among other cities that have started using a secondary open-classroom program.

DEPARTMENTALIZED ORGANIZATION.   This type is subject matter centered.   Each teacher teaches the subject in which he is most qualified; students go to the class for a class period in that subject.   This is the usual pattern at high schools.   Some junior high schools are completely departmentalized, while others are self-contained or partially self-contained in the seventh and eighth grades, and only departmentalized in the ninth grade. Many elementary schools use departmentalization or semi-departmentalization, usually in the upper grades.

Modifications can be made in both self-contained and departmentalized organizational plans when students are grouped heterogeneously or homogeneously in grades or in subjects.   Homogeneous grouping is based on achievement or ability.   Each type of grouping has its proponents, but research is inconclusive as to which method is best.

TEAM TEACHING.   Team teaching is an organizational arrangement at either the elementary or secondary level in which two or more teachers work together and share their collective skills and expertise in planning the instructional program and in evaluating instruction.   Teams can be of different sizes and be responsible for up to 150 students, depending upon the number of teachers involved.   In some cases, all may receive instruction by a teacher with special skills, and then break into small groups for further exploration.   Each faculty team has a leader and a noncertificated

---

[18] Henry S. Resnik, "The Open Classroom," *Today's Education* 60 (December 1971), pp. 16–17; 60–61.

aide who relieves teachers of clerical duties. Auxiliary or assistant teachers may help the team, particularly at the elementary level. Team teaching requires a different arrangement of space, adaptable rooms, and workrooms. Scheduling is flexible and at the secondary level, varying modules of time may be used instead of class hours.

Modular or flexible scheduling creates a less formal organizational structure.[19] Modules are small periods of time that can be combined to provide various period lengths. Laboratory classes can consist of several modules. The schedule is less regimented, permitting unscheduled time for students to explore their interests, and to participate in mini-courses and seminar classes. The program can be tailored to each student's needs, interests, and abilities.

Vertical and horizontal types of organization may have overlapping characteristics. For example, a nongraded vertical organization may utilize a horizontal team-teaching plan.

SPECIAL TYPES OF SCHOOL ORGANIZATION. Alternative schools are being developed in some areas to meet the needs of disenchanted students who are or have been school dropouts or failures.[20] These schools are non-graded and heterogeneous; instruction is personalized and individualized. The student–adult ratio is kept low. Course titles, curriculum content, and methodology are less traditional. The purpose of an alternative school is to maximize self-motivation and help students develop a desire to learn and to develop self-reliance, initiative, resourcefulness, and creativity. Alternative schools have received much criticism.

Continuation high schools are organized to meet the unique needs of problem students and to furnish adult education.[21] Eligible students are those with discipline problems, excessive suspensions, or constant failure, those who are married or pregnant, or those who must work part time. Instruction is individualized and counseling is intensive. Goals are short term. Each student has his program individually tailored to fit his needs and interests, and teachers encourage students to develop responsibility.

---

[19] Gordon Cawelti, "Does Innovation Make Any Difference?" *Nation's Schools,* pp. 60–63.
[20] Frederick S. Bock and Wanda Gomula, "A Conservative Community Forms an Alternative High School," *Phi Delta Kappan,* pp. 471–472.
[21] Robert E. Botts, "Will J. Reid: Profile of a Continuation High School," *Phi Delta Kappan,* pp. 574–576.

School Size

Differences in school size are caused by population density, land availability, location (rural or urban), and the philosophy of the district. Although opinions differ regarding the optimum size for schools, they should be large enough to offer a rich and varied program to meet the varied needs of youth and to be administered effectively, efficiently, and economically.   Research is inconclusive, but some findings, based on opinions and limited evidence "seem to indicate (1) that extremes in minimum size are uneconomical, inefficient, and do not foster effective educational programs; and (2) that maximums in size do not necessarily guarantee economic efficiency and effective educational programs."[22]

The optimum size recommended for an elementary school is 525 pupils.[23]   A three-year junior high school should have 750 students.[24] There are differing opinions regarding the optimum size for high schools. Conant has recommended a graduating class of at least 100 students.[25] Wright made a survey of eighteen high school research studies concerned with curriculum offerings, extra-class activities, staff qualifications, relationships, and pupil achievement. She found no definitive answer as to how large a high school should be. Favorable responses in regard to the variables ranged from enrollments of 150 to 2,000. Consensus would seem to indicate that the optimum size should be an enrollment somewhere between 500 and 2,000.[26]

Principles of School Organization

There are principles of organization and administration which, while they may not be set down with complete exactness and finality, seem to be logical and justified in business and personnel administration; they should be kept in mind as good general rules to guide in the organization of school administration and supervision.

---

[22] Theodore J. Jenson and David L. Clark, *Educational Administration,* p. 28.

[23] Calvin Grieder and W. E. Rosenstengle, *Public School Administration* (New York: The Ronald Press Co., 1954), p. 14.

[24] James B. Conant, *Recommendations for Education in the Junior High School Years.*

[25] James B. Conant, *The American High School Today* (New York: McGraw-Hill Book Co., 1959), p. 77.

[26] Grace S. Wright, *Enrollment Size and Educational Effectiveness of the High School,* pp. 1–3.

Objectives should be given priority over machinery and personal considerations. There should be coordination of authority and responsibility, and responsibility should be assigned to personnel. Psychological factors need to be recognized.[27]

The following general principles of internal organization can be used as a guide in establishing an educational organizational structure:

1. A sound philosophy should provide the foundation for the structure of organization.
2. Principles of the structure of organization should be established and used in connection with any coordinated group endeavor.
3. No detail of structural organization should be set forth in law.
4. A statement of major aims and objectives should be developed as the basis of the structure of organization.
5. The structure of organization should precede endeavor or operation.
6. Structural organization should be constantly improved.
7. When the number of members exceeds reasonable limits of control and supervision, a new and separate unit of organization should be established, resulting in a multiple organization.[28]

Integration of Public Schools

The Fourteenth Amendment, by implication, guarantees all children equality of education. America's survival is dependent upon this; minorities are not excluded. They are entitled to all rights and privileges—including the education to which all others are entitled. In the 1954 Brown case, the Supreme Court ruled that segregation in the public schools was unconstitutional because it deprived people of equal protection of the laws as guaranteed by the Fourteenth Amendment.[29] This reversed a Court ruling made in 1896 which had established the doctrine of "separate but equal."

Title VI of the Civil Rights Act of 1964 bans racial discrimination in programs and activities receiving federal financial assistance, and author-

---

[27] Harl R. Douglass, *Modern Administration of Secondary Schools* (Boston: Ginn and Co., 1954), p. 12.

[28] Ray W. Johnson, "Principles of Internal Organization for Public School Administration" (Unpublished doctoral dissertation, University of Southern California, 1952).

[29] *Brown* v. *Board of Education,* 347 U.S. 483, 74 Sup. Ct. 686.

izes federal agencies to impose sanctions for noncompliance, including the withholding of federal funds.

School districts must take positive action. They should adopt policies that provide for racial balance among the professional and nonprofessional staff and widen promotional opportunities for minority personnel. Budgets should be adopted that provide for additional staff, educational programs, facilities, and equipment in the inner city and transitional areas. Concentrated effort must be made to attract highly qualified teachers to these areas; incentives need to be provided for them. These teachers should be provided with assistance so that they will have the competence, materials, and equipment to function effectively in disadvantaged areas. Classes should be kept small, and paraprofessional help should be provided. All of these measures have budget implications for the school board and administration to consider. The community, which provides some of the funds, must also be concerned. It, too, must have a voice in the policies and procedures of the school district. Minority members of the community are no longer willing to be dictated to by school boards or administrators.

Summary

Almost all states delegate their powers over the schools to local districts that are largely independent and highly responsive to the wish of the electorate. Such districts, once extremely numerous, are decreasing in number due to consolidation. Yet there are still too many small rural districts, many of them impoverished and incapable of offering an adequate instructional program. Various criteria for a viable school district are cited.

The proper functions of a good school board are set forth, stressing its main job of legislating. A suggested time schedule and agenda for board meetings is also provided. The powers of the local board are described in detail, and the need for detailed written policies and rules is emphasized. Standards for board minutes are provided.

Organizational charts are supplied to illustrate how staffing can be worked out for various size districts. They help to clarify lines of authority and lines of communication. The role of a principal is explained.

The need for sufficient flexibility to meet local needs is very real, including patterns of grade organization. Various types of vertical and horizontal organizational plans are described. Alternative schools and continuation high schools have been developed to meet the special needs of some students who need a more flexible program than is provided in more traditional grade structures. Optimum sizes are recommended for elementary schools, junior high schools, and senior high schools. There are, however, differing opinions regarding the most desirable size.

Districts should establish sound principles of internal organization, based on an agreed-upon philosophy. The structure of the organization should be based upon the established major aims and objectives. The local district should be so organized that it provides adequate materials, supplies, facilities, and personnel. There should be clear lines of communication between all parts of the district organization.

Finally, the school district must eliminate, as much as possible, racial segregation in its schools by adopting policies and budgets designed to provide minority students with increased opportunities for success in school.

Trends

Trends in local districts are more difficult to isolate than are those in federal and state educational affairs. More variable factors are present and the thousands of school districts, each with individual problems, pose a complicated task for the observer. However, the following trends may be suggested.

TOWARD LARGER AND FEWER SCHOOL DISTRICTS. Local school districts are becoming steadily larger. The tendency seems marked, and destined to continue indefinitely, increasing in speed. All the data indicate better results as districts are enlarged, and consistently poor results from smaller districts, which cannot provide the same quality of buildings, materials, equipment, or course offerings that larger or unified school districts can furnish. In addition to the educational logic involved, trends toward increasing centralization on a state level, augmented by federal assistance on a national level, would seem to require larger and more efficient local units of administration as a natural corollary. Except in the most remote geographical areas, the days of the one-room or two-room schoolhouse seem numbered. They will be replaced by well-constructed and adequately equipped consolidated or unified schools to which pupils will be delivered by some form of rapid transportation. Improved highways and modern buses will solve this problem throughout most of the country. The great expanse of mountain and desert country in the Far West may bring helicopter service into the school district picture sooner than most of us think.

TOWARD REDUCED POWERS OF LOCAL DISTRICT. The local district seems fated to lose at least a portion of its present sweeping powers. The abdication of the state from the administration of its educational program, begun in early colonial times, has been transformed into an increasingly active interest in the administration of its long-neglected local units. In the future, it seems likely that state interest will be expressed in the form of higher minimum requirements for school buildings, equipment, teacher certification, and basic curriculum.

TOWARD CONTINUOUS SCHOOLING. The future may see schools without grades or artificial divisions between preschool, elementary school, secondary school, higher education, and adult education. Everyone will be a learner and will be able to start school, move through his school life at his own pace, leave school, and return again throughout his life.

TOWARD LIABILITY OF LOCAL DISTRICTS FOR DAMAGES. There is an increasing tendency to permit local districts to be sued in court for damages. At one time, such suits were automatically barred under the old maxim, "The state can do no wrong." Several states have now waived their immunity to suit and others seem certain to follow their example. The consequences of such enabling legislation are twofold: (1) a great and immediate increase in the amount of time school officials must spend away from their duties sitting in courtrooms and (2) the diversion of tax monies from their proper educational destinations into the pockets of "damaged" individuals. As the concept of governmental responsibility for the welfare of the individual increases, it seems certain that school administration will spend more and more time engaged in litigation.

TOWARD USE OF WRITTEN POLICY STATEMENTS. Only a small percentage of school districts are at present operating under written policy statements. This percentage will steadily increase, until all districts of whatever size have adopted such policies. The advantages are obvious; written policies will relieve the district employees of the necessity of developing policies as they go along, and will discourage casual administration.

TOWARD DIVERSIFIED OPINION ON SCHOOL BOARDS.   The old concept of local school boards serving as repositories for the most unbendingly conservative opinion of the district seems to be waning.   The days when only doctors, lawyers, bankers, and retired army officers filled the ranks of board members are gone forever.   School boards in the future will be composed of many more women and a much higher percentage of men with skilled and unskilled labor backgrounds.   In short, democracy is coming to school boards.

TOWARD OPEN BOARD MEETINGS.   Closely related to the increasing democratization of board membership is the trend toward fewer closed or executive sessions of boards of education.   More open meetings and larger groups of visitors and auditors can be anticipated.   As the schools require more money, and as more and more persons are enrolled in them, it is going to become impossible for any local clique to manipulate the governing board for its own selfish purpose.   The era of open meetings and public transaction of school business is rapidly approaching.

TOWARD COMPLETELY INTEGRATED SCHOOLS.   Integration of students and school staffs will occur.   *De facto* segregation and gerrymandering of school boundaries will be corrected.   Schools in all economic areas will become more nearly equal than at any time in the past in terms of buildings, materials, equipment, and the quality of the teaching staff.

TOWARD DECENTRALIZATION OF LARGE DISTRICTS.   In apparent opposition to another trend, some large school districts, such as Los Angeles, are decentralizing.   They are unwieldy and remote from the people. Areas are being organized within the large district, with an area superintendent as the administrator.   There will also be a trend to establish area boards of education that will be more responsive to the people.   This might counterbalance the consolidation of small districts into larger ones.

TOWARD AN INCREASE IN BUREAUCRACY.   The reduction in the number of small school districts results in an increase in the size of central office administration.   This, in turn, tends to increase the bureaucratic characteristics of the organization.   At the same time, teachers are demanding more of a voice in administrative matters and policy development, thus creating a problem which will intensify and trigger other problems for school boards and superintendents.   The conflict between the desires of the teachers and the bureaucratic administration (as viewed by teachers) will increase.

Administrative Problems

Problem 1

Dr. Dunbar has just become the superintendent of Jefferson Unified School District which has 15 elementary schools, 2 junior high schools, and one senior high school. He discovers that there are numerous conflicts regarding staff responsibilities. For example, the personnel director believes that he has the authority to assign teachers to schools, but the principals think that they should have a voice in selecting their staff. The business manager has developed the budget with little help from others, despite the fact that administrators, department heads, and even teachers want a strong voice in budget preparation. Dr. Dunbar requests an organizational chart showing administrative and department relationships, but finds that the only one available is ten years old and bears little resemblance to the present district structure.

What steps should Dr. Dunbar take to develop an up-to-date, practical chart that shows organizational relationships as they exist today?
What role should the Board of Education play?
When the chart has been developed, how should the superintendent use it to solve the present conflicts?

Problem 2

The Central Springs Board of Education spends most of the time at its meetings on business and administrative affairs. The Board attempts to have the superintendent get its approval before he makes administrative decisions and gives the appearance of not trusting the judgment of school administrators. The superintendent has been unsuccessful in having the Board spend more time on reviewing and adopting policies and approving the means for executing them, thus leaving administrative details to the administrators. He would also like to see the Board become more interested in matters concerning the improvement of instruction.

If you were the superintendent, how would you go about changing the thinking of the Board of Education?

Problem 3

Three new members have been elected to the Central Springs Board of Education on a platform pledging to seek to overhaul the outdated and irrelevant educational program of the district. They outnumber the old Board holdovers three to two.

What procedure should the superintendent use in working with the new Board of Education majority?
How involved should the Board get in district educational reform? In what way?

Selected References

BLANKE, VIRGIL E. *Administrator's Notebook.* Chicago: Midwest Administration Center, The University of Chicago, October 1960.

BOCK, FREDERICK S., and GOMULA, WANDA. "A Conservative Community Forms an Alternative High School." *Phi Delta Kappan* 54 (March 1973).

BOTTS, ROBERT E. "Will J. Reid: Profile of a Continuation High School." *Phi Delta Kappan* (May 1972).

BROWN, B. FRANK. *Nongraded High School.* Englewood Cliffs, N.J.: Prentice-Hall, 1963.

CAWELTI, GORDON. "Does Innovation Make Any Difference?" *Nation's Schools* 82 (November 1968).

CLINCHY, EVANS, ed. *Profiles of Significant Schools: Schools for Team Teaching.* New York: Educational Facilities Laboratories, 1961.

CONANT, JAMES B. *Recommendations for Education in the Junior High School Years.* Princeton, N.J.: Educational Testing Service, 1960.

———. *The American High School Today.* New York: McGraw-Hill Book Co., 1959.

FRANKLIN, MARIAN POPE. *School Organization: Theory and Practice.* Chicago: Rand McNally and Co., 1967.

FRETWELL, E. K., JR. "Issues Facing Community Colleges Today." *Today's Education* 57 (October 1968).

GARBER, LEE D. *Law Governing School Board Members and School Board Meetings.* Danville, Ill.: Interstate Printers, 1963.

GOODLAD, JOHN I., and ANDERSON, ROBERT H. *The Nongraded American School,* rev. ed. New York: Harcourt, Brace, & World, 1963).

HALPIN, ANDREW W., ed. *Administrative Theory in Education.* New York: The Macmillan Co., 1967.

JENSEN, THEODORE J., and CLARK, DAVID L. *Educational Administration.* New York: Center for Applied Research in Education, 1964.

MCLOUGHLIN, WILLIAM P. "Individualization of Instruction vs. Nongrading." *Phi Delta Kappan* 53 (February 1972).

MELBO, IRVING R., et al. *Report of the Survey, South San Francisco Unified School District.* Los Angeles: University of Southern California, 1967.

NATIONAL EDUCATION ASSOCIATION, Research Division. "Departmentalization in Elementary Schools." *NEA Research Bulletin 44* (February 1966).

———, Research Division. "Estimates of School Statistics, 1971–72." Research Report, 1971–R13 (March 1971).

———, Research Division. "Public School Programs and Practices." *NEA Research Bulletin 45* (December 1967).

REEDER, WARD G. *The Fundamentals of Public School Administration,* 4th ed. New York: The Macmillan Co., 1958.

RESNIK, HENRY S. "The Open Classroom." *Today's Education* 60 (December 1971).

SHAW, FREDERICK. "The Educational Park in New York: Archetype of the School of the Future?" *Phi Delta Kappan* 50 (February 1969).

THOMSON, SCOTT D. "Beyond Modular Scheduling." *Phi Delta Kappan* 52 (April 1971).

TUTTLE, E. M. *School Board Leadership in America.* Chicago: Interstate Printers, 1963.

WILSON, ROBERT E. *Educational Administration.* Columbus, Ohio: Charles E. Merrill Publishing Co., 1966.

WRIGHT, GRACE S. *Enrollment Size and Educational Effectiveness of the High School.* Circular No. 732. Washington, D.C.: U.S. Office of Education, 1964.

WYNN, D. RICHARD. *Organization of Public Schools.* New York: Center for Applied Research in Education, 1964.

6

School District Organization and Reorganization

A local school district is an administrative unit governed by a board of education that usually delegates administration to a district superintendent. The district operates as a subdivison of the state from which it receives its power. In the past, many small, isolated school districts were formed rather arbitrarily. In the 20th century, an awareness that some of these school districts could be joined together to offer a better educational program developed. This reorganization and consolidation is continuing, although some extremely large districts in major cities are investigating methods of decentralizing administrative control.

This chapter includes a discussion of the following topics:

Historical Development of School Districts
Framework of School Organization
A Satisfactory Administrative Unit
Reorganization
Inadequacy of Small School Districts
Reorganization Movement
Approach to Reorganization
Criteria for Reorganization
Future of School District Organization
Summary
Trends

Material for this chapter was prepared in collaboration with Dr. David H. Paynter, former Superintendent of Garden Grove Unified School District, Garden Grove, California.

Historical Development of School Districts

A complete review of the development of American education is a study in itself, but a brief description of a few milestones in the development of school districts will help to orient this chapter.

Massachusetts was the first state to take an active leadership role in the development of public education. Its laws of 1642 and of 1647 required every town of fifty or more families to appoint a teacher and to give instruction in reading and writing. A Massachusetts law of 1789 required every town of fifty or more families to furnish six months of schooling during the year. As the frontier was settled, state legislatures required towns with 200 families to support a grammar school.[1] This law also "gave legal recognition to the town school committee as an agency for controlling and supervising schools."[2]

In the early 1800s the control of education changed from the township system to a common school or district type of organization. Communities established schools and school systems, governed by elected boards of education. Several school districts often existed within a single city. This multiplicity of small school districts was a function of a scattered and sparse population with primitive modes of transportation and communication.[3] Consolidation of educational units is a phenomenon of a 20th-century population that is centralized in large urban areas.

Framework of School Organization

The framework of school organization in public education is founded on the basic principle of local autonomy. It is the responsibility of the many school districts throughout the United States to provide an educational program to meet the needs of their local communities. The control of these school districts in most states is carefully outlined in legal statutes. During the past decade, the number and complexity of these statutes have increased appreciably, and the school districts of the United States are

---

[1] R. Freeman Butts and Lawrence H. Cremin, *A History of Education in American Culture,* p. 246.

[2] Butts and Cremin, *A History of Education,* p. 253.

[3] Edgar L. Morphet, Roe L. Johns, and Theodore L. Reller, *Educational Administration: Concepts, Practices, and Issues* © 1959. By permission of Prentice-Hall, Inc., Englewood Cliffs, New Jersey, p. 216.

increasingly placed under the control of the state. A national awareness of the importance of education has accompanied the expansion of statutes. Local autonomy still exists, but the state and federal governments are extending their control and interest.

Recent developments in technical fields have made apparent the need for professional and skilled leadership in local school districts. Educational leaders, guided by sound policy, have a responsibility to meet the needs of their particular communities. Each school district must also bear a responsibility to the demands of state and nation.

Both school boards and educational administrators have recognized the major importance of good school district organization. They are aware that each teacher must be supported by a school district with adequate resources, adequate leadership, and sound district organization in order to provide an acceptable educational program for today's children and youth. The quality of educational opportunity in any school district depends on the adequacy of the local school district. It has the responsibility for providing an educational program commensurate with the needs of the community, state, or nation. At no time in our history has this country looked to the local school districts for leadership as it does today.

It is in the local school districts that the great resources of our youth must be developed. The local school district has been called, quite aptly, the last stronghold of local control in our democracy. This control is carefully guarded by local communities in their desire to maintain their school districts. However, the compelling desire for local control has obscured from intelligent view the responsibility the school district has for the nation's welfare. Such desire for control carries with it a feeling that the school district itself is an end in education, when, in reality, it is only a means to an end. The nation as a whole is aware of the value of good education; we can no longer afford to permit vested interests and selfish desires to retard improvement in school district organization.

Many people, because of their desire for excellence in education and constant improvement in the educational program, have been critical of the elementary and secondary schools. Every school district should be able to meet the changing needs and challenges of the community, state, and nation; to maintain educational homogeneity within its boundaries; and to provide an adequate financial base.

Four specific objectives are proposed here to develop better school district organization. These objectives form the basis for examination of school districts and for progress toward local action that should result in improved school district organization:

1. To produce a more effectively coordinated program of education for all levels of the state's public school system through strong local school district organization, with centralized administrative control over all levels of public education in a given area.
2. To provide a more efficient use of public funds, brought about by the creation of school districts capable of furnishing necessary educational services at a reasonable unit cost.
3. To provide a better and more equalized educational opportunity for all children in the state through the creation of school districts of sufficient size to furnish curricular offerings and other services not possible under existing organization.
4. To effect as great a degree of equalization of financial resources on a local level as circumstances will permit.

A Satisfactory Administrative Unit

It is impossible to classify rigidly the 150 types of legally authorized school districts found in the various states. No state has succeeded in abolishing the district system, although a good many have made considerable progress toward combining and streamlining their districts. In 35 states, so-called "basic" and "intermediate" units are involved in the total picture of district organization. The basic units are operated locally by elected boards, and usually constitute local taxing units as well. An intermediate unit is an agglomerate of basic units exercising supervisory control over certain aspects of the programs operated by the basic units composing it. Intermediate units may be township-inclusive, as in New England, or county-inclusive, as in certain western states. In Hawaii, the entire state is administered as a single district. They generally have in common the provision of certain expert and technical services that the local districts are unable to suppy alone. The basic, or local, units may be of all conceivable shapes and descriptions.

It is generally agreed by educators that the greatest single handicap to educational progress and efficiency is the small, rural administrative unit, a relic of America's past. In addition to being improperly staffed and financed, these units waste millions of dollars annually, largely through inadequate personnel-pupil ratios. The following criteria will help to determine the size of administrative units:

1. They should be large enough to organize a complete system of elementary and secondary schools and an adult education program on an efficient and pedagogical basis. In large population areas, provision should be made for junior colleges and terminal vocational schools.
2. There should be a staff to provide adequate administrative and supervisory assistance.
3. Since schools should be close to the people, units should not be so large that local interest is lost.[4]

Some time ago the Council of State School Governments developed some criteria for the ideal school district that still remain applicable. The Council stated that a properly organized school district should be able to provide the resources to offer a comprehensive program of education from kindergarten through high school, and to make provision for post-high school and adult education at a reasonable unit cost. It should be able to procure capable educational leadership and to maintain a competent, well-balanced staff of teachers, supervisors, and specialists; and it should be able to finance its school program and develop competent instruction at a reasonable cost. School buildings should be located so that minimum time is spent in transportation. The size of the district should be such that the people therein can exercise a knowledgeable vote in choosing the school board, in developing educational programs for all age groups, and in expressing their ideas regarding planning and policymaking.[5]

With these standards in mind, and knowing that a considerable number of the states have a majority of school districts employing nine teachers or less, it is easy to conclude that such standards are far above those of the existing state organizations. Only through a long-range program of extensive district reorganization can modern school services be offered to the majority of American children with any degree of efficiency and economy. The small, local district for many years was an essential part of the nation's educational pattern, but its day has passed. Modern

---

[4] By permission of Macmillan Publishing Co., Inc., from *The Fundamentals of Public School Administration,* 4th ed. by Ward G. Reeder. Copyright © 1958 by Macmillan Publishing Co., Inc., pp. 58–59.

[5] *The Forty-eight State School Systems* (Chicago: The Council of State Governments, 1949), pp. 51–52.

transportation and paved roads, together with telephone and radio, have rendered the rural district's reason for existing obsolete; and, while city conditions are somewhat different, there are probably too many independent city districts as well.

Reorganization

The new interest in district reorganization is especially marked in rural areas. Most rural schools are unable to provide the educational program found in the more populated areas. Rural schools, on the average, pay their teachers a third less than do urban schools. The school year ranges from two to four weeks less than it does in the urban areas. It is difficult to avoid the conclusion that millions of children living in the great rural areas of our nation are being shortchanged educationally. Where pupil population is scattered and the tax base is low, equalization of educational opportunity is impossible without district reorganization. Such reorganization can be justified in two main areas: economy of operation and improved educational services.

ECONOMY OF OPERATION. With reorganization of school districts the taxpayer seldom gets the same education for less money; he usually gets better education for about the same price. On the basis of pupil-per-year costs, however, tremendous reductions in costs can be realized. The cost per pupil in small schools is very high compared with pupil costs in larger schools.

In many places, economies may be effected by reducing the number of unnecessary administrative positions, by better utilizing school buildings, by improving the use of teaching staffs, and by streamlining transportation and other auxiliary services. For example, a school nurse or psychologist, in an adequately sized school district, can provide services for several schools, rather than for one.

One of the major advantages of good school district organization is the resulting equitable distribution of the tax burden.

IMPROVED EDUCATIONAL SERVICES. Unified or consolidated districts make possible a degree of teaching specialization unknown in the smaller districts. In high schools, especially, no one can be expected to teach in more than two subject fields competently. Some of the educational advantages found in the consolidated district include the following:

1. Every year of the child's learning experience in the public schools can be planned in a logical, sequential manner from kindergarten through twelfth grade.
2. Equality of basic educational opportunity may be more easily achieved in a unified district than in another type of organization.
3. A broader and more comprehensive educational program can be effected more easily and more economically. (This is not to say that school taxes will decrease, but rather that a complete program becomes more economically feasible.)
4. A more prudential use of funds is possible through the coordination that can be effected under a unified school district.
5. Community unity can be more easily attained when the citizens are concerned with one group of trustees, a single tax, a single bond issue, and one school system, than when they must be concerned with two or more school systems with separate issues. Community action to achieve the kind of school program desired by the people is also more practical.
6. There can be a much greater flexibility in developing a grade organization designed to meet the community's educational needs. For example, the potential for developing an effective junior high school organization for grades seven through nine is increased.
7. Better personnel policies and procedures are possible. For example, a single salary schedule is more practical in a unified district. Furthermore, teachers can more readily be assigned to the grade level in which they can work most effectively.

Inadequacy of Small School Districts

Small school districts fail not only in meeting the needs of a technological society, but also are a drain on the overall program of education. The Commission on School District Organization of the American Association of School Administrators recommends that small districts be reorganized into effective and efficient administrative units.

The need for examination of district organization is highlighted by the previous two decades of constant increases in enrollment; the present decreases in enrollment in many districts; the increasing costs of school-house construction; higher costs for materials and supplies; increasing salaries; and the lack of revenue sources for the public schools.

There are other factors that must also be considered. The rural farm population has dramatically declined, while the urban population has increased. Rural schools diminished in enrollment, or closed. Remaining school districts established high schools, but they were too small to provide the needed educational experiences for students. Often they were orga-nized separately from the elementary schools and were administered by separate boards of education. This dual administrative structure did not provide educational continuity from kindergarten through the twelfth grade. If secondary school students were sent to a high school in a nearby city, the rural areas had little or no voice in determining the educational program for their children. Rural areas could not attract capable adminis-trators, or even teachers, or pay them the salary they could command in more urbanized areas. In small, rural school districts, it is impossible to provide the specialized services and educational opportunities required by students who need special programs and facilities. These and other prob-lems facing education make the examination of school district organization in each local community an imperative need. Selfishness, mistrust, and an unwillingness to study the facts must no longer restrain education in the United States.

Reorganization Movement

The current status of the movement for improving school district organi-zation has resulted in a marked reduction in the number of school districts. In 1957 the U.S. Department of Health, Education, and Welfare made a study to determine the progress being made in sixteen states toward improving school district organization. The authors have updated this study; Table 6–1 shows the progress made by these sixteen states in reducing the number of school districts.

The most noticeable reduction in the number of school districts occurred in the state of Illinois, where the reorganization program began with 11,955 districts in 1945; by the 1972–73 school year there were only 1,178 districts, a reduction of 10,877 or 91 percent. Progress in school

TABLE 6–1. *Years School District Reorganization Programs Were Started in 16 States and Amount of Reduction in Number of Their School Districts*[a]

STATE	YEAR PROGRAM BEGAN[a]	NUMBER OF DISTRICTS WHEN PROGRAM BEGAN[a]	NUMBER OF DISTRICTS ESTIMATED 1972–73 SCHOOL YEAR[b]	REDUCTION NUMBER	REDUCTION PERCENT
California	1945	2,568	1,135	1,433	55.8
Colorado	1949	1,780[c]	181	1,599	89.8
Idaho	·1947	1,110	115	995	89.6
Illinois	1945	11,955	1,078	10,877	91.0
Iowa	1945	4,891	452	4,439	90.8
Kansas	1945	8,456	311	8,145	96.3
Michigan	1949[d]	5,087	601	4,486	88.2
Minnesota	1947	7,606	437	7,169	94.3
Missouri	1948	8,422	598	7,824	92.9
Nebraska	1949	6,901	1,250	5,651	81.9
New York	1925[e]	9,956	737	9,219	92.6
North Dakota	1947	2,267	338	1,929	85.0
Pennsylvania	1947[f]	2,540	566	1,974	77.7
South Dakota	1951	3,398	227	3,171	93.3
Washington	1941	1,323	316	1,007	76.0
Wisconsin	1947	6,385	441	5,944	93.1

[a] Fitzwater, Charles O. (ed.), *School District Reorganization: Policies and Procedures* (Washington, D.C.: U.S. Department of Health, Education, and Welfare, Office of Education, 1957), p. 11. Updated by the authors.
[b] National Education Association, Research Division, *Estimates of School Statistics, 1972–73,* Research Report 1972–R13 (Washington, D.C.: The Association, 1973), p. 26.
[c] Approximate.
[d] Year that legislation, known as the Area Studies Act, was passed authorizing a program of reorganization studies.
[e] The central school district law was enacted in 1914, but the program was not started until 1925.
[f] Legislation authorizing county reorganization studies was enacted in 1937, but it was not until the law was amended in 1947 that the program became active.

district organization has been found in other states, including complete reorganization in some states where county units were established as school districts. This progress has received impetus from state governments and organizations such as the American Association of School Administrators (AASA) and their Commission on School District Reorganization.

During the last forty years there has been a decline of 87 percent in the number of school districts. From 1931–32 to 1965-66, the total number of school districts in the continental United States dropped from

127,531 to 26,983.[6] The National Education Association reported an estimated record low of 17,036 school districts in 1972–73.[7] Obviously, considerable progress has been made toward reducing the number of inadequate school districts.

The establishment of larger districts does not necessarily assure an improved educational program; but it can be assumed that the larger, more adequate administrative units provide the means for improving the educational program and for more efficient school operation.

Approach to Reorganization

Many different approaches have been made in an effort to improve school district organization. The success of these approaches has depended largely on the amount of community participation in the program. No one approach has proved to be most satisfactory, and in many cases it is necessary to combine various activities into a comprehensive program of study. The following approaches to reorganization represent some that have been used:

1. Permissive statutes that provide for a commission to study district organization.
2. Commissions established legislatures to study on a county-wide or intermediate-unit basis and report back to the legislature.
3. Independent studies by state groups and organizations.
4. Professional survey staffs authorized by state legislatures or educational organizations.
5. Lay county committees established by the legislature.
6. Organizational teamwork between educational organizations and other lay groups.
7. Reorganization by legislative decree abolishing small districts and creating larger ones.
8. Permissive legislation that provides for reorganization by local initiative, with or without ratification by the voters.

---

[6] Clayton D. Hutchins and Richard H. Barr, *Statistics of State School Systems, 1965–66,* U.S. Department of Health, Education, and Welfare, Office of Education, OE–20020–66, p. 23.

[7] National Education Association, Research Division, *Estimates of School Statistics, 1972–73,* Research Report 1972–R12, p. 5.

Following study activities, or in some cases prior to these activities, legislation is necessary to provide for the implementation of recommendations that might be made by the various study groups. This legislation has ranged from a very permissive type of legislation to mandatory reorganization. Many manuals, guides, and helpful booklets have been prepared by study groups and professional organizations in an effort to assist in studies. Much of the work done by these groups has included the gathering of data and statistics. However, in several states the lack of funds has slowed progress and prevented complete studies.

Careful planning is essential in any approach to school district reorganization, especially where legislation provides for a permissive rather than a compulsory program. The U.S. Department of Health, Education, and Welfare, in its booklet entitled "Local Planning for Better School Districts," lists four reasons for good planning:

1. It gives the community an opportunity to evaluate its schools, viewing their strengths and weaknesses objectively.
2. It offers the community an opportunity to decide the kind of school program they believe their children should have.
3. It provides an opportunity to determine what changes in the existing organization will be necessary in order to provide the desired school program at a reasonable cost.
4. It furnishes a means whereby local citizens can work together for better schools.[8]

These study groups must receive the assistance of able leadership if results are to be accomplished. On some occasions, this leadership will develop of itself; in other cases, school boards and community leaders must be responsible for involving others in leading the study activity. Both lay and educational leaders in the local districts have an obligation to children and taxpayers to encourage the organization of study groups among the people and to give serious consideration to the very real advantages of sound, sensible administrative units for their public school systems.

Study groups must be aware of legislation that would effect changes in school district organization. Many state departments of education have prepared school district reorganization guides or manuals of procedure to use in beginning a study. A study group will require a knowledge of

---

[8] U.S. Department of Health, Education, and Welfare, *Local Planning for Better School Districts,* p. 3.

current legislation and of what authority rests with the local school district for changing its boundaries, along with an awareness of the means for implementing change.

CONSULTANTS AID IN STUDY. Professional leadership in the form of consultants has proved helpful in planning and organizing study activities. Their services, when directed by the study group and when maintained in such a way as not to overpower the laity, provide a great impetus to study and are very helpful, especially in the collection of statistical information and its interpretation.

Consultants can give talks to community groups, advise on legal procedures, explain what other communities have successfully accomplished, participate as a resource person in public hearings, see that legal provisions have been met prior to voting on proposals, and serve as a liaison between the state department of education and the local planning group.[9]

Consultants may be obtained through the state department of education, the intermediate units, or colleges and universities.

Resource people from school districts or areas that have accomplished reorganization also may be consulted. They can be helpful in answering questions and providing firsthand information on the success and problems of reorganization.

IMPORTANCE OF STUDY PROCESS. The success of any reorganization of school districts depends on the thoroughness of the study undertaken by a committee or a study group. Relying on professional information and professional study groups is not sufficient. Efforts should be made to work from the "grass roots" to provide statistical information for the people to examine. This activity provides not only an awareness of the need for school district reorganization, but also information concerning the educational program and the problems confronting education.

One of the most difficult problems confronting a study group is implementing the actual change in school district boundaries or district organization. The implementation is facilitated by a thorough understanding of the problem by as many people as possible. Success has been realized by study committees that have incorporated in their organizations smaller substudy groups throughout the area. This has tended to broaden

---

[9] U.S. Department of Health, Education, and Welfare, *Local Planning,* p. 7.

the effect of their activity, as they can feel the community pulse and sense its pride and loyalty toward the proposed organization. Statements such as the following show the justification for organizing school districts around natural communities:

> It is important that school districts be built around communities which have concerns for education and common interests which give them identity. This is so that enthusiasm for schools by the lay citizens may be developed and that schools may make adaptations to meet the needs of a community. School districts should not needlessly divide natural communities.[10]

The value of planning and a complete study program is clearly evident in the following list of reasons for study:

1. Eliminates any necessity of relying upon guesswork or uninformed opinion.
2. Reveals school program weaknesses, inequalities in educational opportunities, and inequities in school costs resulting from the inadequacies of poorly organized districts.
3. Provides information that the planning group must have for a soundly organized district.
4. Shows facts that the planning group will need in explaining to the community why a better school district should be established.[11]

Criteria for Reorganization

STANDARDS FOR REORGANIZATION. It should be stressed that there is a vast difference between standards set up for administrative districts and those established for attendance areas. A modern city has only one administrative office, but operates many schools that are in effect attendance areas. While enlarging administrative districts may bring about some reduction in the number of schools, it will not affect the attendance areas of schools that are purposely large to be efficient.

Because conditions differ greatly throughout the country, each state should set up its own criteria for district reorganization. Such individual

---

[10] Ray W. Johnson, "School District Organization in Riverside County: A Master Plan," Unpublished report, Riverside County Committee on School District Organization, Riverside, Calif., 1959.

[11] U.S. Department of Health, Education, and Welfare, *Local Planning,* p. 13.

standards may well be judged by their conformity to the following general criteria:

1. The tax base of a district must be wide enough to carry whatever local educational load the state may decide is necessary, without unduly burdening local taxpayers.
2. District boundaries should be laid out to coincide wherever possible with natural community lines.
3. Districts should include enough population and pupil enrollment to allow for an adequate school program.
4. Long bus rides should be eliminated by proper reorganization. High school children should never have to ride more than one hour each way and elementary children not more than thirty minutes each way.
5. Districts should be as geographically homogeneous as possible.
6. Boundary locations should consider sociological aspects of the community wherever possible, especially when it is necessary to include within the district more than one community center.

The average size of the districts may range from a few square miles in some states to thousands of square miles in others. The number of districts per state ranges from fewer than twenty to thousands. There is such a variety of school organization that it is difficult to discern any pattern.

It is generally recommended that the ideal district, K–12 or K–14, include a minimum of 10,000 pupils. Exceptions to this size are made for smaller, relatively remote areas to provide for a potential of at least 2,000 K–12 students. The current size of the school district cannot be considered to remain static; every study should include an examination of the potential future enrollment for the area. This potential should include sufficient students for an adequate high school. Larger districts are also able to provide better facilities, administrators, educational specialists, and counselors. And they can provide more effectively an articulated educational program from kindergarten through high school or junior college.

When considering the size and boundaries of school districts, study groups should be urged to examine the curriculum requirements for a good high school, junior high school, and elementary school program. They should consider future changes and requirements that may affect the educational program. Education throughout the country must progress with the society in which it exists. Advances in energy, automation, and social progress should be included in the curriculum to provide the training necessary for modern society.

Rather than consider consolidation as a means of achieving a quality educational program, some small districts, as well as larger ones, have instituted some new educational techniques. Automated learning centers have been developed. Closed-circuit television programs utilize the skills of the most qualified teachers to teach many students at one time. Other programs that are proving successful are: flexible scheduling, open classrooms, mini-courses, and team teaching. Large size, therefore, is not necessarily the criterion for quality education. However, regardless of size, the district should have the means and resources to provide the best possible education for its students.

TYPES OF SCHOOL DISTRICTS. Each state may have several types of school districts, varying in size from the small, one-teacher rural district to the huge city and county district serving hundreds of thousands of pupils and employing thousands of teachers.

Throughout the country there are three basic types of school districts determined by the level of the educational program: the elementary school district, the secondary or high school district, and the junior college or higher education district. There are also many other kinds of school districts within these broad headings. For example, the junior high school program often operates in conjunction with the high school district, thus leaving the elementary district with only grades K–6. In some instances, elementary school districts administer junior high schools. In others, the middle school exists within an elementary school district.

A fourth type of school district, the unified school district, includes kindergarten through the twelfth or fourteenth grades. The unified school district is recommended as the form of district organization that provides the most adequate program of education. The trend in the nation has been definitely toward discontinuing small and separate school districts in favor of a unified school district. This does not mean that the small school will be removed from the scene. Educators are agreed that in some of the far-flung areas, the small school must serve the community, because transportation would consume too much of the students' study time and energy. However, these small schools are best maintained in adequately sized school districts that include K–12 or 14.

Future of School District Organization

Although the improvement in the size of school districts and the reduction of one-teacher schools has been impressive, much still remains to be done. Schools must be able to provide the educational programs necessary for a space-age technology and the multitude of social problems that face the citizens of the next generation. Thus, it behooves all educators to exert their efforts toward better school district organization.

It should be understood that a change in school district organization does not of itself ensure improved education. Opponents of school district reorganization frequently place the blame for poor education in a well-organized school district on the increased size of that school district. The Los Angeles City Unified School District, for example, is so large and cumbersome that it is investigating ways of dividing itself into several smaller districts or components within the larger district. The hope is that these smaller components will be more efficient and accessible to the people that they will serve. However, the well-organized school district provides machinery for an improved educational program with greater economy. The task of bringing about this improvement rests with the educators in these districts.

To enhance the chances of better school district organization, there must be a good working relationship between the school and the community. People in the community must be made to feel that they have a voice in the operation of their school. The chief responsibility for this leadership rests with the principal of the local attendance center.

The schools of our country may succumb to a highly centralized program of education unless an effort is made to provide adequate, sound, self-sufficient local school districts. Districts must be able to offer a program that meets the needs of the local community, the state, and the nation. The adequacy of district organization must be thoroughly examined by educators and laity to provide good educational programs at reasonable cost in each American community. A reaction to extreme centralization can recently be documented in such great educational systems as New York and California.

Summary

The origin of the school district is traced back to colonial Massachusetts, with attention to the change in the early 1800s from the township system to the district system. The local school district is described as a strong-hold of democratic local control, and the need for better district organization is portrayed.

Small, impoverished school districts constitute the major problem in reorganization, although a marked reduction in their number has occurred in recent years. Consolidation of districts can result in many benefits, principally in economy of operation and improved educational services. Several approaches to the problem of district reorganization are listed, ranging from commission studies to legislative fiat.

Reorganization study groups are discussed, and their needs and procedures are analyzed. The desirability of utilizing trained consultants is especially stressed. In addition, it is strongly urged that as many individuals as possible throughout the area studied be involved in the proceedings, so that the changes recommended may stand an optimum chance of eventual implementation.

Criteria for district reorganization are offered, and the future of reorganization is viewed with cautious optimism.

Trends

Several trends are beginning to emerge with respect to school district reorganization. The improvement of roads, the development of trans-portation equipment, the need for educational courses requiring expensive equipment, and the demand for more efficient operation have pointed up these trends. The careful observer can now see definite signs of progress.

TOWARD LARGER ADMINISTRATIVE UNITS. Consolidation and unioniza-tion of school districts have resulted from the ease of pupil transportation and the expansion of community boundaries. Consolidation should con-tinue as long as there are small districts that are unable to provide the services and educational programs that are so necessary to meet the needs of all students. Where administrative units have not grown geographically, they have grown in pupil enrollments because of population increase in urban areas.

TOWARD BETTER ARTICULATION. School districts traditionally organize a horizontal segment of pupils defined by elementary or secondary grade limits. This type of organization impedes articulation of educational offerings from kindergarten through high school or junior college. Reorganization entails delegating to a single administration the responsibility for the entire educational program, resulting in better articulation of subject matter.

Toward Decentralization of the Largest School Districts. Some school districts, such as Los Angeles and New York City, have become large and unwieldy. Dissatisfaction has occurred in school communities because the superintendent and school board are too far removed from the people and do not understand local feelings and problems. Large districts, such as these, will look increasingly at decentralization as a solution. Although the district, itself, will not become smaller, it may organize subdistricts under the administration of an area superintendent and his staff. The school board may meet in the various areas from time to time, rather than in a central location. As administration is decentralized in the very large districts, it will be more democratically responsive.

Toward Community Participation in Reorganization. Less reorganization is being accomplished by fiat and more by popular franchise. Submission of district reorganization to the electorate brings with it the need for study and community participation. Such a process is not only democratic, but increases lay understanding of the place and importance of schools.

Administrative Problem

In Basket

Problem

The Poplar School District has 6 elementary schools and 1 junior–senior high school. Its population is largely black. Across a small river is the adjoining Winfield Unified School District which has 14 elementary schools, 2 junior high schools, and 1 senior high school. Its population is mostly white. The people in Poplar want their children to be integrated and have become very vocal about unifying with Winfield to form one district. They then hope that there will be an interchange of students between the schools in the two former districts. They also expect that there will be a better educational program for their children because the expanded district will be able to provide improved educational services. The Winfield people are opposed to the reorganization of the two districts and are not in favor of integrating their children.

If you were the superintendent of the Winfield Unified School District, what stand would you take?

How would you justify your position?
As superintendent of the Poplar School District, how would you proceed?

Selected References

AMERICAN ASSOCIATION OF SCHOOL ADMINISTRATORS. *School Boards in Action.* Twenty-fourth Yearbook. Washington, D.C.: The Association, 1946.

BUTTS, R. FREEMAN, and CREMIN, LAWRENCE H. *A History of Education in American Culture.* New York: Holt, Rinehart, and Winston, 1953.

CARPENTER, C. C. "Criteria for Determining the Adequacy of School Districts in California." *California Journal of Education Research* 1 (March 1950).

FITZGERALD, CHARLES O. *School District Reorganization: Policies and Procedures.* Washington, D.C.: U.S. Department of Health, Education, and Welfare, 1957.

FITZWATER, C. C. "Educational Changes in Reorganized School Districts." U.S. Office of Education Bulletin, no. 4 (1953).

———. "Selected Characteristics of Reorganized School Districts." U.S. Office of Education Bulletin, no. 3 (1953).

HUTCHINS, CLAYTON D., and BARR, RICHARD H. *Statistics of State School Systems, 1965–66,* OE-20020-66. Washington, D.C.: U.S. Department of Health, Education, and Welfare, Office of Education, 1966.

MELBO, IRVING R. *Transition to Unification: Carlsbad Unified School District.* Los Angeles: Published by the author, 1971.

MORPHET, EDGAR L.; JOHNS, ROE L.; and RELLER, THEODORE L. *Educational Administration: Concepts, Practices, and Issues.* Englewood Cliffs, N.J.: Prentice-Hall, 1959.

NATIONAL EDUCATION ASSOCIATION, Research Division. *Estimates of School Statistics, 1972–73,* Research Report 1972–R12. Washington, D.C.: The Association, 1973.

———, Research Division. "Public-School Statistics, 1970–71 and 1969–70." *NEA Research Bulletin 49* (March 1971).

REEDER, WARD G. *The Fundamentals of Public School Administration.* 4th ed. New York: The Macmillan Co., 1958.

SCHMUCK, RICHARD A., and MILES, MATTHEW B. *Organization Development in Schools.* Palo Alto, Calif.: National Book Press, 1971.

"School District Reorganization." *Phi Delta Kappan* 33 (March 1951).

TOWNSEND, ROBERT. *Up the Organization.* New York: Alfred A. Knopf, 1970.

U.S. DEPARTMENT OF HEALTH, EDUCATION, AND WELFARE. *Local Planning for Better School Districts.* Washington, D.C.: U.S. Government Printing Office, 1957.

Your School District. Washington, D.C.: National Commission on School District Reorganization, National Education Association, 1948.

7

Administering the Urban Schools

Urban schools face many problems that came to the fore in the sixties and have carried over into the seventies. Changes are needed in the urban educational structure. Metropolitan areas contain large segments of minority populations whose educational opportunities are severely limited. Problems of integration and segregation need to be solved, especially in urban areas. Urban districts tend to be large, creating administrative, organizational, community, and communication problems.

This chapter includes a discussion of the following topics:

A Challenge to Urban Schools
Federal Action
Legislative Advocates
Racial Integration
Administrative Organization
Summary
Trends

A Challenge to Urban Schools

The decade of the sixties wrought a challenge to education, a challenge to improve the urban schools. Standardized tests show that reading and number skills have gone down. More minority students with cultural and linguistic problems stay in school longer. Vandalism and drug abuse have

---

Robert N. Rowe, Education Administrative Consultant with the California State Department of Education, collaborated with the authors in preparing this chapter.

increased. Government money and property were wasted, and urban schools faced a crisis in personnel, program, and finance. Urban school districts were buffeted by lay and professional critics.

Most urban schools entered the decade of the seventies plagued by a myriad of unsolvable problems. Financial difficulties caused by a conglomeration of factors—inflation, taxpayer resistance, and an increase in depth and breadth of expectations—resulted in a desperate search for new sources of funds. The surfacing of the aspirations and frustrations of minority groups brought unforeseen demands upon public, private, and parochial schools.

Other public concerns involved war, environmental pollution, poverty, sexual mores, drugs, and the actual structure of the educational system itself. Youthful militancy, teacher strikes, and organizing of teachers and administrators into powerful unions added to the problem. These concerns have produced a protest that portends a cultural revolution as significant as any revolution—political, military, or industrial—of the past, and a revolution that will influence education significantly. As a result, the entire educational system is being scrutinized in varying degrees of intensity from within, and by countless numbers of outside organizations, agencies, and individuals. Before the sixties ended, the urban school rushed, often indiscriminately, to revamp not only its curriculum but procedural, managerial, and organizational aspects as well. The resulting confusion prompted some to observe, "Having long been charged with helping the young discover their identity, education is no longer secure in its own."[1]

Decentralization, increased federal aid, systems analysis, performance contracts, programmed learning, nongraded schools, various types of grouping, ethnic studies, racial integration, and education complexes are examples of the attempts made within the existing structure to alleviate problems of urban schools.

Many recommendations for change have gone far beyond the existing structure—not just heterogeneous grouping versus neighborhood schools, decentralization versus centralization, and ethnic studies versus the traditional curriculum, but a complete restructuring of educational resources versus the further entrenchment of the "education establishment." Paul

---

[1] Fred Hechinger, "This World," *New York Times,* reprinted in the *San Francisco Chronicle* (Feb. 1, 1970), p. 22. © 1970 by the New York Times Company. Reprinted by permission.

Goodman, author and social critic, believes our extremely structured, centralized society needs relief and suggests "decontrol" and decentralization.[2] Bernard Watson has stated that decentralization would bring decision making closer to the people so that educational planning will be more considerate of local needs, interests, and resources.[3] However, Robert Havighurst has questioned the breaking up or decentralization of school districts in large cities such as New York, Detroit, and Los Angeles, and states that results are not yet discernible.[4] He proposes "a metropolitan system that has a coherent set of educational goals and a structure that encourages cooperation among the parts, but permits wide latitude."[5]

Decentralization plans have come about largely because minority and low-income families have protested about discrimination and lack of understanding on the part of school boards, usually composed of people who do not understand their interests and needs. Upper middle-class families have moved to the suburbs. There, they have demanded decentralization to ensure a voice in their child's educational program, and to assure their child's admission to the college of their choice. Decentralization may actually create segregation—economically and ethnically.[6] Peter Schrag questions the idea of separating the rearing of children from the geographical areas in which most of society's business is accomplished, its ideas debated, and its policies determined.[7]

John Holt has advocated "big changes in a hurry," recommending the abolishment of all the requirements for schools and the elimination of the intimidating regime under which too many teachers must work, including: lesson plans, fixed schedules, prescribed texts, censorship, supervision, compulsory testing, and grading. He went so far as to say that parents, and no one else, should decide whether a school is right for their children.[8] The question that loomed large in the sixties still prevails in the seventies: "What can urban school administrators do to engender confidence in urban education?"

---

[2] Paul Goodman, in an address to the National Security Industrial Society, reported in the *Sacramento Union* (Feb. 3, 1970), p. 1.

[3] Bernard C. Watson, "Rebuilding the System: Practical Goal or Impossible Dream?" *Phi Delta Kappan*, p. 353.

[4] Robert J. Havighurst, "The Reorganization of Education in Metropolitan Areas," *Phi Delta Kappan*, p. 354.

[5] Havighurst, "The Reorganization," p. 358.

[6] Havighurst, "The Reorganization," pp. 355–56.

[7] Peter Schrag, "Is Main Street Still There?" *Saturday Review of Literature*, p. 20.

[8] John Holt, "Why We Need New Schooling," *Look Magazine*, p. 53.

ADVANTAGES OF LARGE SCHOOLS.   Along with a careful analysis and sub-sequent modernization of urban school districts, administrators must capi-talize on successful programs of the past.   The product of the urban school has not been limited to vandalism, violence, and failure.   Larger school dis-tricts usually graduate more students per class than smaller school districts. Competition among students is often greater in the larger classes.   Hamilton and Rowe reported the advantages of larger school systems in a 1962 *Phi Delta Kappan* article; they indicated that high school graduates from the largest-class-size category are significantly more likely to obtain advanced degrees than graduates from the smallest-class-size category.[9]

An accentuation of the positive aspects of the larger schools could be useful to the improvement of the urban school and its image.   Not all recommendations developed during the sixties advocated radical change. Changes in educational programs have sometimes been tacked on to what already exists, rather than used to replace dysfunctional programs.   When this happens, new programs tend to be ignored or to be used only until special funds run out.   Every school system has personnel who want to continue as they have always done, as well as those who are willing to experiment and to innovate.   If innovations are to become an integral part of the district's educational program, there must be district-wide, com-munity cooperation and support involving research, planning, and policy-making.[10]

Kingman Brewster, Jr., President of Yale University, in discussing "Impatience versus Objectivity," reported a decline of standards in educa-tion and related much of the decline to disillusionment and impatience. He believes that whether the ideal appears obtainable or not, it must remain as the standard.   He advocates due process to overcome impa-tience, and believes it is as important in academic situations as in legal situations.   The more difficult the judgment, the more important is due process.[11]

Kenneth B. Clark, president of the Metropolitan Research Center in New York, has warned against deviating too far from the existing educa-tional structure, and proposes a revolutionary reappraisal of that which

[9] DeForest Hamilton and Robert N. Rowe, "Academic Achievement of Students in Reorganized Districts," *Phi Delta Kappan,* p. 402.

[10] Watson, "Rebuilding the System," pp. 349–53.

[11] Kingman Brewster, Jr., in a speech "Impatience versus Objectivity," delivered at the annual meeting of the American Association for the Advancement of Science, as reported in the *Wall Street Journal* (Jan. 19, 1970), p. 12.

exists. His observation regarding "ghetto" schools decries the deficiency in the basic academic subjects (reading and mathematics), and suggests an "embarrassingly simple" answer: concentrate on raising reading levels until the objective is reached. He reports that in every case in which ghetto children were exposed to an efficient reading program and taught with sensitivity, their reading performance improved significantly.[12]

Dr. Clark's emphasis on the teaching of reading is not just a characteristic of establishment-oriented educators. Malcolm X, in his autobiography, states, "I have often reflected upon the new vistas opened to me. I knew right there in prison that reading had changed forever the course of my life. As I see it today, the ability to read awoke inside of me some long dormant craving to be mentally alive."[13] Many of the more militant black leaders advocate the total immersion of young people in reading programs to compensate for the neglect of the past.

Seymour Fliegel, writing in the *Phi Delta Kappan,* explains the educational program at P.S. 146 in East Harlem, New York City, which is 45 percent black and 50 percent Puerto Rican. Its program involved teachers and parents in establishing school policy; organized classes on a heterogeneous basis; kept classes small; and individualized instruction. Teachers were reminded that students must "learn" rather than be "taught." He explains that individualization of instruction does not happen automatically. Teachers must have inservice help in utilizing new teaching techniques, planning instruction, grouping, selecting and using materials and new technological equipment, if they are to be successful. P.S. 146 decided to emphasize the improvement of reading performance. Fifth and sixth graders were grouped for reading according to their functional reading levels. In 1964, "fifth and sixth graders were two or more years behind in reading; today, 50 percent are at or above their grade level."[14] Although this is only one school, the implications show what can be accomplished, at least in reading, when controlled experimentation takes place.

---

[12] Kenneth B. Clark, "Slum Schools," excerpted from 1969 Bulletin of the Council for Basic Education, and reported in the *Wall Street Journal* (Dec. 26, 1969), p. 4.

[13] Malcolm X, *The Autobiography of Malcolm X* (New York: Grove Press, 1964), p. 123.

[14] Seymour Fliegel, "Practices that Improved Academic Performance in an Inner City School," *Phi Delta Kappan* 52 (February 1971), pp. 342–43.

FACING THE FUTURE. Urban school districts in the United States are attempting in various ways to build or rebuild their organizational structure. They have the task of educating for an urban society and of changing prejudiced community and ethnic attitudes. They must become less alien to children and parents and more responsive to community needs. Daniel Levine wonders why educators continue to educate basically in the same way as in the past when their methods are no longer working. The problems with any type of urban school are outdated curricula and inappropriate instructional methods. Many urban districts are experimenting with innovative and exciting programs in attempts to meet the needs of students who are dropping out both psychologically and physically. Up to now, however, research and evaluation have not shown conclusively how effective these new developments are.[15]

It should be pointed out that new ideas and new practices may lead to unanticipated consequences. They may succeed or fail, raise doubts and uncertainties, promote tensions, or lead to conflicts. But from these problems, learning takes place. "If education is life and life is the best educator, the school must be alive" as it encourages "the individual's responsible pursuit of new experiences, new challenges, new responses."[16]

Whatever organizational structure or educational program is developed, it should be evident that more people will be involved at the local level—parents, community leaders, teachers, other school personnel, students, and administrators. Their ideas must be considered and acted upon; nothing is so discouraging as spending hours of time in cooperative planning and finding that nothing has changed and the status quo continues. There must be an emphasis on staff development if educational improvements are to be made. The educational program for urban students must become more relevant, more meaningful, more exciting, and more challenging; no school district has yet arrived at a best solution for this difficult task.

In the development of the urban schools, educators must weigh the perceptions of their colleagues and critics to establish a direction that exploits change for the benefit of all children within the urban complex.

---

[15] Daniel U. Levine, "The Reform of Urban Education," *Phi Delta Kappan,* p. 328.

[16] William W. Wayson, "Organizing Urban Schools for Responsible Education," *Phi Delta Kappan,* p. 347.

Federal Action

Urban school critics have proposed changes that vary in degree from no more than subtle alteration to a complete overhaul. Are demands for change in education simply a reflection of the instability of society, or do they represent rational criticisms of an anachronistic system?

Many of the demands are well founded. In March of 1969, Secretary of Health, Education, and Welfare, Robert Finch, appointed a 50-member Urban Education Task Force to help him shape long-range education programs. The task force concluded that big city schools required drastic reform. It proposed an Urban Education Act that would finance a comprehensive plan for improvement of urban school systems. The act suggested that with an additional five to seven billion dollars in federal aid, education for 14½ million inner city young people could be made dramatically superior to education given to children in the suburbs. The method employed to realize their goal would be the bolstering of urban resources with teachers, equipment, counselors, and so forth.

The report claims that education is the only avenue that provides the disadvantaged child a chance to overcome poverty in a single generation. It was negatively critical of past federal programs which, it concluded, had been narrow in scope and effective only with an insignificant portion of the total number of children in need. The proposed Urban Education Act required each district to develop its own plan for community involvement, a requirement designed to make the school board, or whatever policy-determining body was created, more responsive to and representative of the people it serves. Whether such responsiveness is only possible with the decentralization of a system is debatable. But it appears apparent that "involvement" will be the key word in urban change.

The proposed legislation encouraged cities to experiment with alternative programs. Nonschools like the community-oriented Philadelphia Parkway, publicly funded private schools, regional state schools, and educational parks were mentioned by the task force as examples of possible changes. Such alternatives may become the *modus operandi* for education in the future.

Legislative Advocates

Legislation is not easily developed at either the state or the federal level. Large urban school districts in the past have relied on teacher organizations and crisis contact with legislators to promote legislation that administrators felt was important to urban education. During the sixties it became apparent that crisis operation and/or cooperation with education organizations was not sufficient to promote all the legislation crucial to urban school situations. Most urban school districts found it propitious either to employ their own legislative advocates, or lobbyists, or to hire consulting firms to function as advocates.

In 1970, eighty education and allied organizations, including the NEA and AFL–CIO, formed a coalition to push vital legislation past a presidential veto. Although the immediate goal was not reached, significant residual influence was felt which yielded a more lucrative education appropriation than the opponents had originally approved. The machinations of the legislative process undoubtedly will yield increased participation by lobbyists in the promotion of educational legislation. Every large school district will discover that members of its staff or some comparable appendage to administration not only must be fully aware of and conversant with legislation at the local, state, and federal levels but also must be capable of drafting new legislation to meet urban needs.

Racial Integration

In 1964 the Berkeley Unified School District became the largest urban district in the United States to realize complete, planned racial desegregation of its secondary schools. A few years later Berkeley implemented total desegregation of elementary schools as well. Each of its nineteen campuses—elementary, secondary, and continuation—were totally integrated by September of 1968. Other districts smaller in size, such as the Princeton, New Jersey, and the Sausalito, California, elementary school districts desegregated at about the same time. Riverside, also in California, integrated its 18 percent black enrollment. However, Berkeley integration was unique in that the community was part of a vast urban area with a 40 percent black enrollment. It employed new strategies, including busing, to achieve its goal. However, pupil scores on state reading tests declined during this period.

THE BERKELEY PLAN.   Plans for integration of Berkeley schools began in the 1950s when Superintendent Carl Wennerberg planted the seed.   Desegregation was accomplished when an articulate black minister and a forward-thinking patent attorney were appointed members of the board of education to promote the plan developed by Dr. Wennerberg.   In terms of bringing the races together physically to each campus, the plan was a success.   During its first years of operation, the accomplishment appeared worthwhile.   But as time passed, it became apparent that the mere physical deliverance of students of all races to a campus does not accomplish racial integration in its most admirable state.   The turmoil in Berkeley caused by University of California dissidents, advocates of all social and political causes, a high incidence of crime and drug abuse, and the disenchantment of the so-called "silent majority" produced a state of instability in the public schools.   Vandalism increased significantly, student absenteeism rose to an alarming degree, teacher turnover increased, and the educational program became less and less well defined.   Berkeley was not the only urban school district to develop such symptoms.   Few urban districts in the United States were immune.   However, it would be prudent for districts contemplating desegregation to study the successes and failures of the Berkeley integration plan.   Much of it is well documented.

Busing in Berkeley is not a momentous undertaking.   Distances in Berkeley are relatively short, and few students spend more than twenty-five minutes on a bus at one time.   Berkeley has been a university town since the turn of the century; it has always espoused social causes more liberal than those espoused in many other communities.   If planned integration was to succeed in any community, one would suspect that it would succeed in Berkeley.   The degree to which it has succeeded is a matter for individual interpretation.

The original plan for desegregation included a flexible grouping component to replace an archaic tracking system.   Grouping was to be based on the achievement and industry displayed by the student in each subject rather than the IQ and reading scores inherent in the rigidity of tracking.   Within two years after the plan was implemented, a demand for "complete heterogeneity" in the classroom was made and the relatively new and well-conceived grouping system was eliminated.

Berkeley had the determination to forge ahead in an attempt to achieve integration.   It identified integration as the only permanent solution to racial problems.   Whether or not its methods were practical will be revealed in the future.   Busing desegregates school campuses, but the question remains as to whether it integrates the races or whether it encourages an exodus from urban areas and contributes to urban chaos. Although the Berkeley plan is unique to California, it has implications for other cities in the nation.

DESEGREGATION IN THE NORTH.   The first two months of 1970 unveiled a landmark in integration.   A northern Senator, former Secretary of Health, Education, and Welfare, Abraham Ribicoff, challenged his colleagues in relation to their attacks upon segregation in the South.   Senator Ribicoff tried to focus attention upon the "realities of integration, not the theories." He asked why so many northern schools did not desegregate.   He emphasized that wherever one goes across this land when blacks move in, whites move out, and if whites have children, they move far away.   The Senator stressed that it may be futile to chase whites with buses to achieve equitable distribution.   But he felt that America must develop its schools to make sure that its urban children get the best education.   Senator Ribicoff agreed that if we can desegregate, we should do it, but we must recognize that there will be communities across this broad land where it will be physically impossible to desegregate.

As Senator Ribicoff spoke, organized resistance to busing was erupting in major cities not only in the South, but in Los Angeles, San Francisco, Boston, New York, and other northern communities.   Los Angeles busing critics estimated the cost of busing necessary to accomplish total desegregation ranged from $40,000,000 to $100,000,000.   Busing became a symbol to many people not only of political and bureaucratic expediency but also of the end of neighborhood schools.

The Senator was not calling for cessation of the desegregation movement.   He was pleading for immediate alternatives to busing—alternatives that would assure urban minority students an effective education.   In essence, he was stating that where busing is impractical, total desegregation must be postponed and maximum efforts must be devoted toward improving the existing educational program.   Ribicoff was challenging the presumption that in the South, de facto segregation is at all times a guise for de jure segregation.   Instead of being preoccupied with absolute racial balance, the government was being urged to challenge overt obstacles to integration, such as discriminatory laws and demonstrable coercion.   The same federal laws must apply in all states.   However, the Senator felt it would be a far more positive approach if the law became color-blind rather than forcing a specified racial balance.   Good education in urban areas should be the main goal, not a blend of race, religion, or nationality. Increasing evidence was accumulating by 1973 to show that pupil achievement does not improve significantly as the result of forced busing to achieve ethnic balance.

Methods used in the future to correct effects of *de facto* and *de jure* segregation within and outside the immediate school situation probably will vary greatly according to the communities involved. Some communities will use busing; others will forestall the use of buses with improved curricular programs at tremendous financial expense; others will struggle to break down the segregated housing patterns. Some communities will use a combination of methods. Those who wait for an outward movement of the black population to redistribute the races and to solve segregation probably will have an interminably long wait. Smith reports that most urban areas and their schools are becoming increasingly segregated:

> In our study, we checked the patterns of interaction to see how they lined up with the housing patterns. After all, segregated housing wouldn't be so bad if the people were interacting. People don't have to live next door to each other to get together. Here again we found a sad example of Detroit being two communities; the Negro lines of interaction parallel their housing lines, compressed a little more toward the center of the city. The white lines, likewise, parallel their housing lines—a demonstration that Detroit is becoming increasingly segregated in interaction as well as in housing.[17]

There are no standard solutions to problems such as segregation, relevancy of curriculum, school finance, and the political involvement of students and faculty. Each district must determine its needs, goals, and objectives, and then plan activities that can be used to achieve its goals. Goal development and needs development will become more and more important. Plans in education that are hastily conceived or that lack majority consent and minority involvement usually fail. Consequently, urban school districts must develop their plan, whether racial desegregation is involved or not, with the calculated participation of as many representatives of community factions as possible. The procedure for making those who are most affected responsible for development of the plan and its implementation is an important consideration in our society. Administrators and school board members would be prudent to consider their constituents as participants and to provide opportunity for participation. Administrators and board members must find ways to strengthen com-

---

[17] Ralph V. Smith, "Behind the Riots," *American Education* 3, p. 2.

munication with both lower and higher echelons, with professional organizations, and with the lay public.

Administrative Organization

Urban school districts are faced with many challenges and problems that run the risk of being exploited, exaggerated, or overexposed. Exploitation may result from power struggles within or between the various political, social, and professional groups. Such exploitation can be heightened by the inevitability of extended managerial distance between the top and the lower echelons. Often, before a problem is brought to the attention of executive and policymaking personnel, it is exposed to the general public. In smaller suburban or rural districts it is simpler for administrators and trustees who are in control to approach and solve a problem before too many interest groups involve themselves. Managerial distances can only be bridged by effective communication.

Another communication problem in urban districts is the social and psychological distance between school personnel, students, and parents, between divergent school communities within the large district, and between the people and the board of education.[18] When each segment has different values, it is difficult for one to understand or communicate with the other. The district's organizational structure should be rebuilt so that these distances are bridged or eliminated.

Too often in large urban school districts an organizational structure exists that isolates central office administration from personnel of the various campuses within the districts. The typical structure for many urban school systems is one in which only the deputy superintendent talks with the superintendent. As Townsend admonished in *Up the Organization,* the efficiency of the top administrator often decreases as the number of people reporting to him increases; therefore, a vital need exists for thorough communication between the highest and lowest levels of the organization.[19] When a superintendent loses contact with the field, he sacrifices access to sensitive areas which dominate the educational scene.

The typical structure for many urban school systems, illustrated in Figure 7–1, is one in which only deputy superintendents report to the

---

[18] Daniel U. Levine, "Concepts of Bureaucracy in Urban School Reform," *Phi Delta Kappan,* p. 330.

[19] Robert Townsend, *Up the Organization,* p. 46.

superintendent; associate and assistant superintendents, informed by department directors, report to the deputies; and supervisors, curriculum associates, consultants, and others report to the directors. Buried somewhere at the bottom of the structure are building principals and members of the faculties. In a large urban school district, stratification and echelons of authority are unavoidable; they are an organizational inevitability. No matter what diversionary tactic a superintendent employs (*ad hoc* committees, advisory councils, curriculum commissions, resource groups, task forces, and so forth), there always emerge lines of authority which establish, at least temporarily, a stratification. The real challenge lies not in avoiding the echelon effect, but in making the most effective use of echelons.

The structure diagrammed in Figure 7–1 obviously is unwieldy. Various school districts are struggling to reorganize in an attempt to achieve the ultimate goal of effective communication. Los Angeles began the decade of the seventies with a zone plan in which the vast geographical area of the district was to be broken into subareas. Each zone was to be relatively autonomous in terms of administration, but subject to the broad curricular and financial policies of the board of trustees. New York City also implemented an autonomous zone plan of its own. Plans for autonomy are intelligent approaches to the problem of administrative communications, but smaller autonomous units, if lacking in communication, can be as inhibiting as larger units.

Too often, lines of communication are considered to have only a vertical dimension. Horizontal direction, often ignored, is as vital as vertical. Teachers must talk with teachers, principals with principals, assistant superintendents with assistant superintendents, and simultaneously every effort must be made to give the chief administrative officer opportunities to communicate with people other than himself. His little cubicle at the top of the organizational pyramid can condemn him to a state of solitary confinement.

At each level of the organization, a strategy of communication must be developed that enables communicators to exchange information easily and to articulate effectively with members at other steps on the ladder. Face to face encounter after thoughtful preparation is the most effective method, although thoughtfully prepared letters, memoranda, and in-house bulletins comprise reasonable alternatives when time grows short. The more specific, brief, and personally delivered the presentation, the more effectively the message will be communicated. Coffee hours, conference

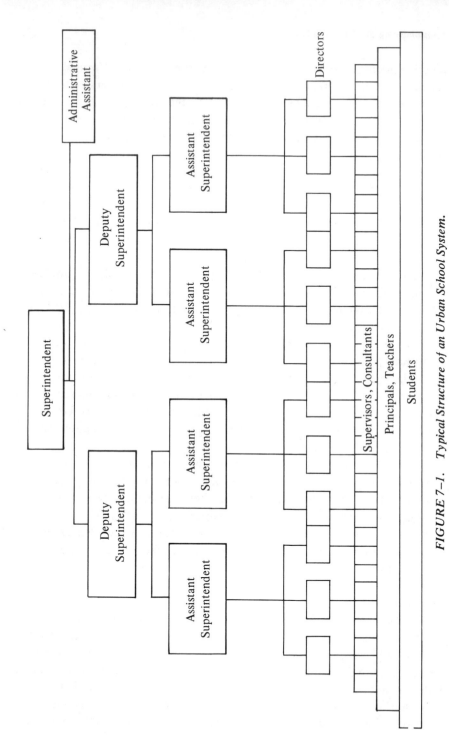

FIGURE 7-1. *Typical Structure of an Urban School System.*

Superintendent

Administrative Assistant

Deputy Superintendent

Deputy Superintendent

Assistant Superintendent

Assistant Superintendent

Assistant Superintendent

Assistant Superintendent

Directors

Supervisors, Consultants

Principals, Teachers

Students

telephone calls, workshops, and symposiums are legitimate ways to communicate when tête-â-tête situations are impractical. Communication in large districts cannot be left to chance meetings, as might be the case in small districts. A strategy can be prepared that incorporates every known medium of communication and systematically ensures that each employee knows how to get his message heard and to whom he may go for information.

Summary

Although rural and suburban schools experienced great problems of growth and change during the sixties, it was in the teeming urban districts that the problems were greatest and most nearly unique. The challenges were many and to a large extent remain so: finances, sexual mores, drugs, student militancy, and teacher strikes, to list but a few.

Attempts to solve the puzzle posed by the big city schools were equally numerous and diverse: decentralization, federal aid, systems analysis, programmed learning, nongraded schools, and educational complexes. Some advocates of even more far-reaching change urged the abolition of textbooks, testing, and even compulsory attendance.

Many neglected the fact that urban school disadvantages are at least partially compensated for by certain advantages, including the productivity of large class sizes and the preponderance of advanced degrees among graduates of larger schools.

One of the main problems in urban schools appears to be deficiency in the basic skills of reading and arithmetic. To furnish answers to this problem as well as to others, the Urban Education Task Force has concluded not only that big city schools require drastic reforms but also that past federal programs have been largely ineffective. State legislation to help big city schools, however, has had difficulty being enacted.

Forced busing has aroused great opposition almost everywhere that it has been initiated or proposed, and has added to the urban school headache. Inner-city areas become increasingly black as whites flee to the suburbs, thus deepening the financial dilemma.

Administrative organization in cities is marked by unwieldy bureaucracies. A trend toward decentralization is noted in at least two major cities, New York and Los Angeles.

Finally, urban teacher unionism and militancy seems to be emerging as one of the significant phenomena of the seventies.

Trends

In the 1950s, the superintendent was emerging as the administrative leader and chief curriculum adviser in most major cities. It had been a long, hard struggle. For decades, boards of education and political considerations had dominated the determination of more than just policy in public schools. Many school boards and local politicians had been usurping the administrative function of the superintendent; however, by 1960 the role of the superintendent became more clearly defined. In the early 1960s, it was predicted that the major concerns of the superintendent in the future would be recruitment and training of competent people to be administrators and teachers, increased consolidation and centralization of districts, and a challenge to the notion of tenure. Although these problems do prevail, they are becoming subordinate to crises in finance, curriculum, and social areas during the latter part of the decade.

Community involvement will become a major emphasis of administration. However, too often the involvement is either subversive to the "system" or violently spontaneous, unanticipated by school administrators. While the trend toward consolidation and centralization continues in the suburbs and rural areas, an almost compulsive interest in decentralization is emerging in the large cities.

TOWARD TWO OVERRIDING CHANGES. Probably the two greatest challenges directly related to education confronting the urban school administrator in the seventies will be: (1) To devise alternative methods to fund urban school education. (2) To interpret what "relevancy" means to a given community and to develop related curricula.

TOWARD AN INCREASING POWER STRUGGLE FOR CONTROL OF URBAN SCHOOLS. New York City points up the nature of this problem. For several years to come, strong teacher unions will be opposing equally strong community groups for more authority over staffing and operation of neighborhood schools.

TOWARD CURRICULUM CHANGE. Curriculum of the urban schools will undergo continuous revision, and significant changes will take place in areas of sociology and vocational education. Professional organizations and lay influences will dictate much of the change.

TOWARD CHANGE IN ATTENDANCE REQUIREMENTS.   Student attendance requirements will be more flexible and administrators will be faced with the task of devising activities other than the traditional ones to involve students outside of the classroom.

TOWARD CHANGE IN ADMINISTRATOR QUALIFICATIONS.   The future portends a need for personnel sociologically, politically, and fiscally astute to fill the position of the urban superintendency.   Administrators will be chosen for reasons other than experience in education.   Men and women from ethnic minorities will fill more top administrative positions than previously.

TOWARD DECENTRALIZATION.   Decentralization of large districts will be implemented to bring policy and administrative decisions closer to the various communities within the districts.

Administrative Problems

In Basket

Problem 1

The San Martin Unified School District has an enrollment of 100,000 students. There have been many complaints about the lack of communication between the district office and the school.   Teachers complain that the district administrators never visit the schools; at least they never see them.   Principals must go through numerous channels to get action and have difficulty in scheduling personal conferences with assistant or deputy superintendents and seldom meet the superintendent in a one-to-one relationship.   Communication at all levels is so bad that morale has deteriorated.   There are few bulletins and those that are received are usually directives.   District policies are out-of-date and many are not adhered to.

If you were the superintendent, what communication strategies would you develop to improve communication?
How would you go about improving the district policies?

Problem 2

The superintendent of a large urban school district faces many problems.   The teacher organizations affiliated with the AFL–CIO and the NEA have joined together in demanding a 12 percent salary raise and have threatened to strike if it is not granted.   However, higher costs have left money for no more than a 2 percent raise.   Taxes are high and there is little chance of the city voting a higher tax rate. Busing for integration has added to transportation costs. The energy crisis has caused additional costs. Further problems have been caused by the gasoline shortage beginning in 1974.

The superintendent thinks that the state legislature moves too slowly in helping urban districts with their problems. The district maintains a legislative advocate or lobbyist at the state capitol who, along with others, has tried to get the legislature to provide legislation that will help the urban districts with their immediate problems. Little success has been achieved.

What are some things that the superintendent can do to help speed up the legislative process?
What can he do in his own district to gain support?
What can he do to help the lobbyist?
What should the state Department of Education do to help urban districts?

Selected References

FLIEGEL, SEYMOUR. "Practices that Improved Academic Performance in an Inner City School." *Phi Delta Kappan* 52 (February 1971).

GOODMAN, PAUL. "A Causerie at the Military Industrial." *New York Review of Books* (November 23, 1967).

HAMILTON, DEFOREST, and ROWE, ROBERT N. "Academic Achievement of Students in Reorganized Districts." *Phi Delta Kappan* 43 (June 1962).

HAVIGHURST, ROBERT J. "The Reorganization of Education in Metropolitan Areas." *Phi Delta Kappan* 52 (February 1971).

HOLT, JOHN. "Why We Need New Schooling." *Look Magazine* (January 13, 1970).

HUMMEL, RAYMOND C., and NAGLE, JOHN M. *Urban Education in America: Problems and Prospects.* New York: Oxford University Press, 1973.

JANOWITZ, MORRIS. *Institution Building in Urban Education.* New York: Russell Sage Foundation, 1969.

LEVINE, DANIEL U. "Concepts of Bureaucracy in Urban School Reform." *Phi Delta Kappan* 52 (February 1971).

———. "The Reform of Urban Education." *Phi Delta Kappan* 52 (February 1971).

MALCOLM X. *The Autobiography of Malcolm X.* New York: Grove Press, 1964.

SCHRAG, PETER. "Is Main Street Still There?" *Saturday Review* 53 (January 17, 1970).

SMITH, RALPH V. "Behind the Riots." *American Education* 3 (November 1967).

TOWNSEND, ROBERT. *Up the Organization.* New York: Alfred A. Knopf, 1970.

WATSON, BERNARD D. "Rebuilding the System: Practical Goal or Impossible Dream?" *Phi Delta Kappan* 52 (February 1971).

WAYSON, WILLIAM W. "Organizing Urban Schools for Responsible Education." *Phi Delta Kappan* 52 (February 1971).

PART THREE

School Finance and Business Administration

8

Financial Support of Public Schools

It takes money to educate children, and the cost keeps going up. The problem of determining the best method of financing education is a major one; up to now no utopian method has been found. Local taxes are so much of a burden that further support must come from increased state or federal aid. Because the educational program is dependent upon available finances, the school budget must be based upon income estimates that are as accurate as possible.

This chapter includes a discussion of the following topics:

The Increasing Need for Additional School Revenue
Main Sources of School Revenue
Dependence on Assessment Rates
The School Budget
Concepts of School Support
The Voucher System
Summary
Trends

The Increasing Need for Additional School Revenue

It would not be realistic to say that every shortcoming of which the public schools are accused can be corrected by simply providing more money; it would be realistic to say that few of them can be corrected without more money.   Excessive class size, poorly qualified teachers, crowded school buildings, antiquated curriculum, insufficient and poorly written textbooks —all of these targets of criticism are casualties of insufficient revenue.

Yet not only do critics refuse to see the need for additional school funds, but they point to the rapid growth of school expenditures in this country as ample reason for retrenchment.   In 1870, for example, we spent 63 million dollars on the public schools; in 1950, this figure had reached 5 billion dollars,[1] and in 1972–73, the total current expenditure for public elementary and secondary schools had climbed to 43.7 billion dollars.[2] Most of this increase was due to the depreciation of the dollar, inflation, and to the steady increase in the length of the school year.   Improvement and expansion of school services have accounted for only about 15 percent of the total increase.

Teachers' salaries, which have more than tripled since the 1930s, actually have had difficulty keeping pace with the rising cost of living; considering the fact that the federal income tax was not deducted from their pay before 1940, the average teacher has experienced little financial improvement.   When one considers that the level of school support before the growth of educational expenditures began was grossly inadequate, it becomes evident that school costs are probably still far below what they ought to be.

Even the most selfish opponents of sufficient money for education should be convinced by the statistics issued by the United States Chamber of Commerce and the National Association of Manufacturers.   These reports demonstrate that the level of economic prosperity is in direct relation to the educational level of the population.   States that have not supported their educational programs adequately are lagging behind the rest of the country economically.   Public education invariably creates increasing demand on the part of consumers, and creates more efficient producers to keep up with the demand.   Money spent on education is therefore money that comes back to private industry a hundredfold.[3]

One of the main problems currently found in the field of educational finance is the inequality in expenditures among the states.   Some states spend approximately one-third less per pupil annually than others.   In 1972–73, for example, New York spent $1,424 per pupil, while Alabama

---

[1] *National Education Association Journal* 37 (February 1948), pp. 86–87.
[2] National Education Association, Research Division, *Estimates of School Statistics, 1972–73,* p. 5.
[3] Emery Stoops and M. L. Rafferty, *About Our Schools,* pp. 26–28.

spent only $556 per pupil.[4]   The educational opportunities for students suffer when states do not support their educational programs with adequate finances.   There are three primary causes for such differences:

1. Inequalities in wealth and income among the states.
2. Environmental differences, such as topography, climate, and population density.
3. Differences in the desire of the people of the several states for good schools.[5]

Those who view with alarm the unevenness of public support of education, together with those who fear the increasing burden of local taxation posed by the deluge of children pouring into the school systems of the nation, unite in urging increased grants of federal funds to the schools. This attitude is sometimes coupled with a proposal for rigid curtailment of educational expenditures, and a concomitant criticism of school officials for indulging in unrestrained spending.   Actually, as the National Education Association has pointed out, we have never spent, nor are we now spending, enough money on education.

America is spending less of its national income on education than it should.   During the 1930s, for instance, annual public school expenditures averaged 3.7 percent of the national income.   Figure 8–1 shows that the average annual percent of the federal budget spent on education was only 4 percent.   The amount that should be spent on education probably could be doubled without putting an excessive drain on the national income. Meanwhile, the amount spent on luxuries is usually considered to be double the amount expended to educate a space-age generation.   The 1964–65 school year was historic because it was the first time that more money was spent on education than on alcohol and cosmetics.[6]

There are some, however, who believe it is useless to speculate upon the percent of money that should be spent on education.   The percent of the national budget that may be considered necessary for defense is a factor.   There is also a question as to whether the gross national product

---

[4] National Education Association, Research Division, *Estimates of School Statistics,* p. 35.

[5] Reprinted with permission of Macmillan Publishing Co., Inc., from *The Fundamentals of Public School Administration,* 4th ed. by Ward G. Reeder.   Copyright © 1958 by Macmillan Publishing Co., Inc., p. 285.

[6] National Education Association, Research Division, "Annual Report on Public-School Financing," *NEA Research Bulletin,* p. 90.

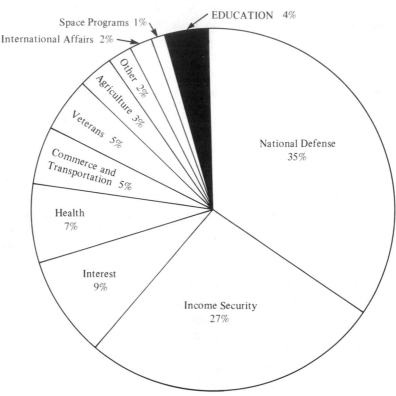

FIGURE 8–1. Average Annual Percent Distribution, By Function, of the Federal Budget: 1970 to 1973. Source: *U.S. Bureau of the Census,* Statistical Abstract of the United 1973 *(Washington, D.C.: U.S. Government Printing Office, 1973), p. 388.*

would continue to increase sufficiently so that a fairly constant percentage would be available for education.[7]

Main Sources of School Revenue

Approximately 95 percent of public school revenue comes from taxation, the remainder accruing from endowments, gifts, and rentals. The four

---

[7] George R. Cressman and Harold W. Benda, *Public Education in America,* Copyright © 1956, 1961 by Appleton–Century–Crofts, Inc. Copyright © 1966 by Meredith Publishing Company, published by Appleton–Century–Crofts, New York, pp. 83–84.

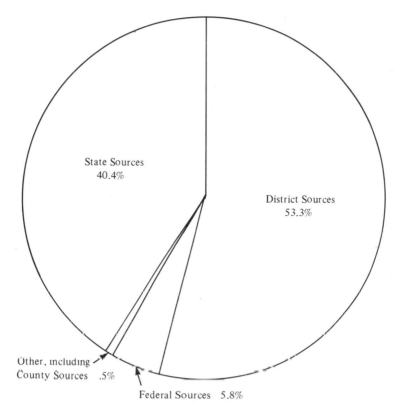

State Sources
40.4%

District Sources
53.3%

Other, including
County Sources   .5%

Federal Sources   5.8%

FIGURE 8–2. The School Dollar: Estimated Income Sources for the School Year 1973–74 for a Typical School District.

units of support for the schools are federal, state, county, and local. Figure 8–2 shows the estimated percentages of income from these sources as budgeted by a typical school district. These percentages vary from state to state and from district to district.

Financial aid may be general or categorical. General aid is financial assistance that is not specifically earmarked for a particular educational program; the funds are available for expenditure at the discretion of the local school district. The general state apportionment is a good example of general aid. Categorical aid is financial assistance specifically earmarked for a particular educational program. The planned program and the budgeted amounts are usually called a project and are subject to the approval of the state or federal granting agency; examples are ESEA–Title I and funds for teaching special education classes.

FEDERAL AID. Regular federal aid to education may be divided into approximately three categories: (1) aid to vocational education; (2) land and money grants to the states; and (3) federal aid under Public Laws 815, 874, and 864, and other educational support acts.

The Smith–Hughes Act of 1917 is the best example of the first, providing as it did federal funds for the teaching of agriculture, industrial education, and home economics. Each state receives funds on the basis of total population and must match the federal funds provided with equal amounts of their own money. The Morrill Act, the George–Deen legislation, and other examples of federal aid, discussed in more detail in chapter 2, represent related varieties of regular federal support for the nation's schools.

The Ordinance of 1787 contained the first example of government grant aid to the schools. One parcel in every township was to be reserved for the maintenance of public schools within the boundaries of the vast western territory, which comprised the present states of Illinois, Indiana, Michigan, Ohio, Wisconsin, and part of Minnesota. As other states came into the Union, the same principle was applied, although many of the later states received more than one parcel of each congressional township, under a liberalization of the original ordinance. A total of more than 98 million acres was thus set aside, an example of massive federal aid to education.

Land grants were not the only type of grant aid made by the government. Lesser money grants were made from time to time, among them the "Surplus Revenue Distribution" of 1837, and the "Five Percentum Fund" of 1803. Today the total value of permanent school funds in the various states exceeds 500 million dollars. Most of this represents land and money grants from the United States government. The states still control over 40 million acres of unsold school land, with an estimated value of about $200,000,000, the income of which amounts to $50,000,000 a year.[8]

Since 1919 the National Education Association has supported bills introduced at almost every session of Congress to increase federal aid for education. After World War II, the federal government recognized that federal activities in certain areas had created increased enrollments without increasing valuations. In order to meet the increasing school cost and decreasing local tax income, Public Law 874 was passed to provide funds for the operation of the educational program. Public Law 815 provided

---

[8] Reeder, *The Fundamentals,* pp. 291–92.

funds for constructing school facilities in federally impacted areas, and Public Law 864 provided funds that strengthened national defense by supporting educational efforts. In the last few years, several educational acts have been passed to assist school districts.

Funds may be distributed as flat grants, special purpose appropriations, or general purpose funds. Some are available for private as well as public schools. The Elementary and Secondary Education Act of 1965 comes as close to being general support as any law yet passed. It is "the largest single commitment by the federal government to strengthen and improve educational quality and opportunities in elementary and secondary schools across the nation."[9]

Most federal aid up to this time has stressed emergency aid or long-range assistance in certain specialized areas. Some federal funds have been provided on a matching basis which in practice permits the rich districts to get richer and the poor to get relatively poorer. This is hardly an equalization. The majority of federal funds for operational expenses should be channeled into needy states and districts on some sort of rough equalization principle. At the present time, federal funds represent the least important source of public school revenue. Federal interest in education is discussed more fully in chapter 2.

STATE AID. In 1929–30, the states furnished only 16.9 percent of public school support. During the past ten years, state support fluctuated between 37.4 and 41 percent. Although, on a national basis, the states were estimated to have 41 percent in 1972–73, the amount ranged from a low of 6.1 percent in New Hampshire to a high of 89 percent in Hawaii. In 1972–73, fourteen states supplied more than 50 percent of school funds.[10] State taxes of various types produce this revenue—income taxes, property taxes, sales taxes, business taxes, and inheritance taxes.

Such state funds come largely from three sources: (1) appropriations made from the general fund of the state; (2) taxes especially earmarked for education; and (3) income from invested school funds. The first source is steadily gaining in favor as the ideal method of financing public education. The general property tax has been largely abandoned by the states as a reliable source of state school revenue. Income from invested funds

---

[9] U.S. Department of Health, Education, and Welfare, *Profile of ESEA, The Elementary and Secondary Education Act of 1965*, p. 1.

[10] National Education Association, Research Division, *Estimates of School Statistics, 1972–73*, Research Report 1972–R12 (Washington, D.C.: The Association, 1973), p. 33.

supplies only a trivial amount, and earmarked taxes are falling into increasing disfavor.

State funds are distributed to schools on two bases: flat grant and equalization. Several states utilize a combination of both methods. The flat-grant aid is granted on a straight per pupil basis, without regard to economic differences among the various school districts of the state. Either enrollment or average daily attendance may be used in figuring the amount to be paid. Equalization aid is distributed in proportion to financial ability, with the poorer districts receiving the larger amounts. Most states have a *foundation program* which is a form of equalization. It guarantees that the state and local district will jointly provide a minimum educational program for all children regardless of the amount of taxes raised in the district. The theoretical amount that the district is able to contribute is determined by multiplying a computational tax times the assessed valuation. In poor districts, the state makes up the difference between the cost of the foundation program and the available money raised by the mandatory local tax rate. The foundation program and its several criteria are predetermined, and it is guaranteed that every child will receive all or parts of the following:

1. Properly qualified teachers.
2. A safe, sanitary, and adequate school building.
3. A minimum school term.
4. Free textbooks and supplies.
5. Free transportation beyond a reasonable distance.[11]

The advantages of equalization are as follows:

1. All pupils are able to take advantage of relatively equal educational opportunities.
2. The real property tax rate in the local districts can be lowered or the program can be enriched.
3. The tax load in the different districts is made more equable.

State aid may be general or special, or both. The former may be used for all educational purposes not specifically prohibited by law. The latter

---

[11] Cressman and Benda, *Public Education,* p. 93.

is earmarked by the state for specific purposes or projects, such as transportation, supervision, libraries, and education of the handicapped. Too often, special aid is limited by the stipulation that the local district must match the state grant. This is a pernicious practice, rendering inevitable the receipt of most money by the districts least in need. Such aid is not equalization in the accepted sense.

Two dangers have been traditionally cited as inherent in any system of state financial aid to local schools. The first danger is the potential stifling of local initiative and a growing tendency among citizens to lose interest in schools they no longer have the responsibility of supporting. The second danger is the possibility of encouraging the wasteful spending of state funds without appropriate controls.

Modifications of these two objections also form the cornerstone of the opposition to federal aid to education. It is safe to say that these dangers, while not entirely imaginary, are unrealistic. For example, if one were a resident of a community in which a state university, which derives its support from the state and federal governments alone, happens to be located, it does not necessarily follow that one will not be vitally interested in its functioning, nor that the community will lose interest in its work. In the case of the second danger, it should be stressed that nearly all public school officials and board members have had more experience with management of strict budgets than have governmental officials; local educators are not apt to change their thrifty habits and waste public funds simply because they are given an increase in state aid.

A certain amount of increased state control most likely will follow in the wake of increased state support. There is no reason, however, why such control should not be exercised in the name of higher standards. Smaller pupil–teacher ratios, cooperative purchasing of supplies, strengthened curriculum—these and other areas of current weakness are surely proper pretexts for state intervention. In addition, the state may properly demand the elimination of small and impoverished districts, amalgamation of all possible districts for the general improvement of administration, and the reorganization of transportation routes to make possible the elimination of unnecessary school busing. The local districts have wrestled unsuccessfully with these problems for generations; it is time they were assisted by higher authority.

The National Education Association has produced a series of recommendations for the organization and objectives of state aid to education which may be summarized as follows:

1. The state should provide at least 60 percent of the total funds needed to support public education.
2. There should be one state fund for school aid, nearly all of which should be raised from sources other than the general property tax.
3. At least half of the state aid should be in the form of equalization.
4. The state should establish and guarantee a "foundation" program for all districts. Districts should be encouraged to supplement the foundation program from their own resources.
5. The state should aid in the construction of school buildings, also on an equalization basis.[12]

COUNTY AID. The county educational unit is often used as an intermediate agency between the local district and the state. In some states, particularly in the South, the county and the local district are identical. These units raise money in the manner of local districts in other parts of the country—i.e., via the property tax. Other states use their county units primarily as an instrument for regulating and aiding local districts. County aid in such cases may be derived entirely from state sources, entirely from county taxation, or from a combination of both.

LOCAL SUPPORT. The chief source of local school revenue has always been the property tax. While this tax at one time may have represented the true wealth of a school district, it is not now the case. The property tax is not suited to an era in which stocks, bonds, and commodities have replaced land and buildings as the main source of taxable wealth. Real estate owners today find themselves bearing the brunt of school support, and quite understandably object. Some states follow the policy of "separation of sources," and reserve almost all general property for local taxation, but in such cases the faults of the property tax outweigh whatever virtues it once may have had. It seems clear that one of the following alternatives must be chosen if a complete breakdown of local school taxation machinery is to be avoided: (1) The state must assume more and more of the financial support burden of the local school districts. (2) The

---

[12] National Education Association, Research Division, "Attainment of Recommended Goals by Present School Finance Systems," *NEA Research Bulletin* 24 (October 1946), pp. 93–96.

state must make available to the local districts additional sources of tax revenue.

The mechanics of raising funds for the support of the schools are in the hands of local school authorities in nearly all states, and follow the procedure outlined below:

1. School authorities calculate the projected costs of the schools within their jurisdiction for the ensuing fiscal year.
2. They estimate the amount of state financial aid to be received.
3. They arrive at an estimate of monies to be received from all sources except state aid and local taxation.
4. The difference between estimated costs and income from sources listed above is then projected.
5. Finally, they levy the necessary tax on local real property in order to raise whatever additional funds are needed.

City school districts often depend upon the approval of municipal authorities for the levying of school taxes, as well as for their collection. Even school districts that are fiscally independent usually depend upon municipal or county tax officers for the assessing, levying, and collecting of taxes, although the districts themselves set their own rates, subject to statutory limitations. Only occasionally does the board of education, through its own agent, do its own assessing, levying, and collecting of taxes. Such practice is probably poor. Economy alone would seem to indicate the desirability of the district employing regular tax officers, available to carry out the actual mechanics of taxation, while the district remains independent of other civil authority in the determination of its tax needs.

Dependence on Assessment Rates

All states fix maximum local tax rates, but simultaneously defeat their own purpose by leaving to local option the rate at which property is assessed. Thus the assessment rate is often more important than the tax rate in determining the amount of school support. The local assessors are usually completely immune from school district control and may nullify the district's financial plans by lowering the assessment. Sometimes it is impossible for a school district to find out what the assessment rate will be, or the expected funds that it will provide, in time to prepare the district budget.

The district, pinned down by statutory tax ceilings, is then completely helpless, unless the state in which it is located permits the overriding of such ceilings by local election. Many states have set up agencies to equalize assessment rates, but they often do not operate very effectively.

Where such agencies do not exist, the variations in the assessment rates are even more glaringly apparent. The solution must be found in one of the following two alternatives: (1) All school assessment rates and valuations shall be arrived at by state action, with such activities taken out of local hands entirely. (2) Each school district through its voters shall adjust its own assessment and tax rates to suit itself, with the state's only concern being that each district shall contribute that portion of its taxable wealth that is fair in relation to its ability.

The problem of decreasing property–assessment rates and increasing district tax rates is strikingly similar in some of its manifestations to the inflationary spiral so notoriously apparent in the world's economy. The only way out of the dilemma now available to the school district is to ask its already heavily burdened taxpayers to vote to exceed the maximum tax rate; many districts have refused to do this. So many tax and bond elections have been defeated that some have described the situation as a "taxpayer's strike." School taxes are normally the only taxes on which voters have a direct voice. Other taxes are determined by city councils, county supervisors, or other governmental agencies.

As the assessment rate slowly declines and the proportion of the district's true wealth, as represented by the property valuation, inexorably diminishes, the tax rate climbs upward. This is an intolerable situation that must be remedied as soon as possible. Not only must there be more rigid state control of the system of assessing property, but the base for school taxes must be broadened. Teacher strikes in various parts of the country are calling attention to the deplorable condition of school finance.

FINANCIAL EQUALIZATION. Financial equalization on both a state and local level must be achieved. The principle that all American children deserve the same minimum educational opportunities is basic to modern educational philosophy. However, at the present time children in various parts of the country, and even in adjoining districts of the same state, are being given schooling of sharply contrasting quality and quantity.

It is all very well to say in rebuttal that the solution lies, not in increased equalization aid from a higher source, but in an increased effort on the part of less favored communities. The truth is that some states, and some school districts, are already making truly staggering efforts to give their children adequate educations, but are failing simply because there is not enough money at their disposal to make their goal a possible one. Some states, for example, have approximately 35 percent more children per 100 adults than others. Table 8–1 indicates the relative position of the several states in this regard.

When one considers that these more prolific states are for the most part those with the lowest per capita wealth, it is obvious that merely mouthing the word "effort" is not going to accomplish much. Local district taxpayers have been so overburdened by property taxes that many are rebelling. In California, for example, approximately half of the elections

TABLE 8–1. Number of School-Age Children (5–17) Per 100 Adults Aged 21–64 in 1970, Listed in Rank Order[a]

1.	New Mexico	64		Kentucky	53
2.	Utah	63		Arkansas	53
3.	Mississippi	62		Ohio	53
4.	South Dakota	61	29.	Kansas	52
5	Louisiana	60		New Hampshire	52
	North Dakota	60		UNITED STATES	51
7.	Idaho	58	31.	Washington	51
	Minnesota	58		North Carolina	51
	Montana	58		West Virginia	51
10.	Wisconsin	57		Maryland	51
11.	Alaska	56		Missouri	51
	South Carolina	56	36.	Hawaii	50
	Arizona	56		Oregon	50
	Michigan	56		Tennessee	50
	Wyoming	56		Illinois	50
16.	Alabama	55		Oklahoma	50
	Iowa	55	41.	Virginia	49
	Vermont	55		Connecticut	49
19.	Maine	54		Massachusetts	49
	Texas	54	44.	Florida	48
	Indiana	54		California	48
	Nebraska	54		Pennsylvania	48
23.	Colorado	53		New Jersey	48
	Delaware	53	48.	Nevada	47
	Georgia	53	49.	Rhode Island	46
				New York	46

[a] National Education Association, Research Division, *Rankings of the States, 1973,* Research Report 1973–R1 (Washington, D.C.: The Association, 1973), p. 10.

that were called in 1969–70 by school districts to raise the local tax rate were defeated.

Equalization operates in this manner: Assume three school systems, A, B, and C, each with the same number of children to educate. The state government guarantees every school district $150 per unit of average daily attendance, provided that each district levies a minimum school tax of $.75 per $100 in assessed valuation. In District A, which is wealthy, this tax yields ample funds to operate without additional state aid, so District A gets no additional state aid. District B is an average district; after levying its tax, it still needs approximately $20 per average daily attendance unit to function at the $150 level guaranteed by the state. Therefore, District B receives $20 per unit in state aid. District C, located in a so-called "bedroom" community, where there is no industry to tax but a large number of school-age children to educate, finds that even after levying the $.75 tax it is still $100 per pupil short of achieving the desirable $150 level. District C thus qualifies for and receives $100 from the state for each attendance unit annually.

All three districts are able in this way to guarantee to their pupils a satisfactory *minimum* educational program. Both District A and District B, of course, and especially A, will be able to tax themselves additionally if they so choose, and thus provide *maximum* programs. This ensures the preservation of local initiative and provides for a constantly rising standard of school support, while at the same time doing away with all educational standards below a certain level of excellence.

The same principle applied above to local districts holds when applied to states. Gross educational and financial inequalities exist *between* states in exactly the same way as they exist *within* the states. Approximately half of America's school-age children live in forty-one (82 percent) of the states and the District of Columbia.[13] Yet these states possess only 43.9 percent of the total personal income.[14] For many years bills have been regularly proposed to Congress that were designed to furnish federal funds on an equalization basis so that poor states would receive more than wealthy states.

There is no reason why the same equalization principle that has

---

[13] National Education Association, Research Division, *Estimates of School Statistics, 1972–73,* Research Report 1972–R16 (Washington, D.C.: The Association, 1973), p. 25.

[14] National Education Association, Research Division, *Rankings of the States, 1973,* Research Report 1973–R1 (Washington, D.C.: The Association, 1973), p. 34.

worked so well when applied to local districts cannot work equally well when applied to the states themselves. It seems certain that the near future will see this type of financial aid made available.

The School Budget

After the funds have been made available from their various sources, they are spent through the medium of the school budget. A good budget is actually a detailed financial program that outlines the educational program to be provided, the plan of spending, and the anticipated receipts. Virtually every policy adopted by the board of education in the course of the school year has some financial implication. Qualifications of teachers, length of school term, class size, capital outlays, upkeep of buildings—all must be planned for in terms of the budget.

Although the largest part of the budget is the plan for spending, income estimating and computation must be incorporated if the expenditure program is to be realistic. This is worked out in considerable detail and includes estimates based on past experience as well as needs for the coming year. A multitude of individual items usually appears, grouped under a number of major heads. School district budgeting is explained in more detail in chapter 9.

Concepts of School Support

Two outstanding changes have taken place in the past century in respect to the public's conception of proper school financing. First, the public has finally decided that education is a public function that must be supported through universal taxation, rather than a private concern of interest only to the parents of the individual child. The philosophical concept underlying this basic change in attitude holds that education, like military defense of one's country, is essential to the continued existence of the nation and the state. It benefits all the state's citizens, directly or indirectly; hence, it must be supported by all alike, whether or not all have children in attendance at the schools.

This concept has been blessed by the courts in hundreds of cases litigated in every state of the Union. The end result has been the establishment of a workable ideal at once simple and sublime: every pupil who is mentally competent shall be given without charge an education extending from the kindergarten through the twelfth grade.

The practice of universal taxation on such a massive scale to support such a wide range of education is unique among the nations of the world. Secondary schools are financed infrequently in foreign lands, and colleges and universities rarely. America embarked upon an experiment in mass education unique in history because it regarded equality of educational opportunity as the birthright of every citizen. Other countries go part way, financing elementary instruction, but weeding out by virtue of intense competition all save a select and brilliant few on the secondary level. Secondary education abroad is thus based on an entirely different principle from our own, and its curriculum and goals are understandably divergent from ours. The future will tell which method works better. Our striking force in World War II and our postwar industrial strength argue strongly for a high level of education for our populace.

The other great change in our conception of school financing—the increasing role of the state in providing educational funds—is still in the process of going on. Figure 8–3 shows the percent of state, county, and local revenues derived from property taxes in the several states for a typical year. Formerly, the entire burden of financing the schools was placed upon the local community. As our society changed from an agrarian to an urban one, local financing became an increasingly unequal burden. At a time when nearly all communities were agricultural, wealth was not concentrated in certain urban portions of each state, as it is today.

As this condition began to change, glaring inequalities in both educational opportunities and tax burdens in the various communities became more and more evident. The state did not volunteer its financial assistance; its influence was brought about by the trend of events. At any rate, the concept of the state's responsibility in setting up minimum educational standards and assisting all communities to comply with these standards has now become a universal one. All states now give financial aid to schools. The amount and degree of this aid is bound to increase.

The Voucher System

The recent concept of the voucher system, in simplified terms, centers on a plan whereby the state or federal government pays a given amount of money, or has the authorization to distribute a given amount of money, to

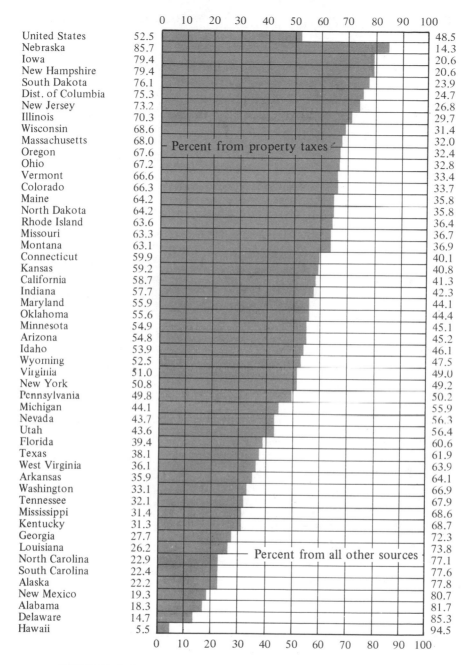

		0	10	20	30	40	50	60	70	80	90	100	
United States	52.5												48.5
Nebraska	85.7												14.3
Iowa	79.4												20.6
New Hampshire	79.4												20.6
South Dakota	76.1												23.9
Dist. of Columbia	75.3												24.7
New Jersey	73.2												26.8
Illinois	70.3												29.7
Wisconsin	68.6												31.4
Massachusetts	68.0												32.0
Oregon	67.6			Percent from property taxes									32.4
Ohio	67.2												32.8
Vermont	66.6												33.4
Colorado	66.3												33.7
Maine	64.2												35.8
North Dakota	64.2												35.8
Rhode Island	63.6												36.4
Missouri	63.3												36.7
Montana	63.1												36.9
Connecticut	59.9												40.1
Kansas	59.2												40.8
California	58.7												41.3
Indiana	57.7												42.3
Maryland	55.9												44.1
Oklahoma	55.6												44.4
Minnesota	54.9												45.1
Arizona	54.8												45.2
Idaho	53.9												46.1
Wyoming	52.5												47.5
Virginia	51.0												49.0
New York	50.8												49.2
Pennsylvania	49.8												50.2
Michigan	44.1												55.9
Nevada	43.7												56.3
Utah	43.6												56.4
Florida	39.4												60.6
Texas	38.1												61.9
West Virginia	36.1												63.9
Arkansas	35.9												64.1
Washington	33.1												66.9
Tennessee	32.1												67.9
Mississippi	31.4												68.6
Kentucky	31.3												68.7
Georgia	27.7												72.3
Louisiana	26.2							Percent from all other sources					73.8
North Carolina	22.9												77.1
South Carolina	22.4												77.6
Alaska	22.2												77.8
New Mexico	19.3												80.7
Alabama	18.3												81.7
Delaware	14.7												85.3
Hawaii	5.5												94.5

FIGURE 8–3. *State, County, and Local Revenues for Public Schools Derived from Property Taxes and Other Sources.* Source: Clayton D. Hutchins and Richard H. Barr, *Statistics of State School Systems, 1965–66* (*Washington, D.C.: U.S. Government Printing Office, 1968*), p. 51.

the parents of children attending public or nonpublic schools. Under this system, parents have the right to "shop around" for the school they consider best for their children. The U.S. Office of Economic Opportunity and several states have proposed in-depth studies and long-range pilot projects to determine the feasibility of the voucher system. Actually, this system, in various forms, has been tried for several years in some states in an attempt to circumvent the Supreme Court's school desegregation decision.

In 1970 the Gallup Poll's "Second Annual Survey of the Public's Attitude Toward the Public Schools" asked: "In some nations, the government allots a certain amount of money for each child for his education. The parents can then send the child to any public, parochial, or private school they choose. Would you like to see this idea adopted in this country?" On a national basis, 46 percent opposed the plan, 43 percent favored it, and 11 percent had no opinion. Although the voucher system is controversial, the Office of Economic Opportunity intended to use $6 million to $8 million a year for the next five to eight years to implement the system.

Some of the questions that have been raised regarding the implementation of a voucher system are:

Will states set up regulations and controls over nonpublic schools that are as extensive and restrictive as those in effect for public schools?

How much money will parents receive each year for supporting each child in the school selected?

Will the same amount of money be allotted for secondary as for elementary children? If there is a difference, on what basis will it be determined?

What will happen to the constitutional guarantee of the separation of the church and the state?

Will increased bureaucracy be necessary to regulate the system?

Will there be enough research to guarantee the effectiveness of the system before it is put into general use?

Is the system more political than educational?

Will the families proposed to be helped really be helped?

Since private schools charge tuition, will public schools be permitted to make such a charge?

How can a school district's budget be predicted if it does not know how many children will be attending or what the income will be?

Can parents move their children from school to school whenever they become disgruntled? If not, what are the controls?

Is it possible that some schools will be overcrowded because too many parents want their children to attend them and other schools will be overstaffed and underpopulated because of lack of attendance?

Will there be safeguards to prohibit segregation or support for religious instruction?

Will schools compete with each other as they attempt to "sell" their particular school and attract students?

These and other questions must be answered before the voucher system is installed on any grand scale. It is too early to predict its future.

Summary

The inflation of the late sixties and the early seventies, coupled with increasing voter resistance to school financial levies, points up the need for additional school revenue. While expenditures for public education have increased markedly during the past decade, with teacher salaries tripling in the last generation, most schools are still underfinanced.

This problem is accentuated by the inequality of expenditures, and hence the unequal educational opportunities for pupils in the fifty states. Increased federal funding is proposed to lessen such inequalities.

When public school revenue sources are examined, it is found that district, state, federal, and county taxes account for virtually all school money, in that order of importance.

Federal aid has a long history of categorical funding dating back to the Ordinance of 1787 and is divided into three main categories: vocational education, land grants, and recent strengthening acts such as Public Laws 815, 874, National Defense Education Act (NDEA), and Elementary and Secondary Education Act (ESEA). The latter comes close to being general aid rather than categorical aid.

State aid may be in the form of flat grants or equalization, or a combination of both; it may also be general or special, or both. State aid is sometimes objected to on the same basis as federal aid: it allegedly would lead to state control and to an end of local school independence.

Local support comes in the form of real property tax receipts, and traditionally has been in most states the mainstay of the schools. One of its weaknesses is the dependence of the school district upon other branches of government to assess, levy, and collect such taxes. County aid to local schools is primarily regulatory and supervisory rather than financial.

The most urgent need in school finance is for statewide equalization to ensure at least the same minimum educational opportunities for all children; this cannot be achieved by increased local effort alone.

Finally, there is the relatively new voucher plan under which parents are reimbursed in one of several ways for sending their children to schools that compete for students. It is too soon to give answers to the many questions surrounding this concept.

Trends

Unlike certain other areas in education, where tendencies are vague and undocumented, the trends in school finance are clear-cut and demonstrable.

TOWARD MORE AND MORE STATE FINANCIAL SUPPORT.   The old American habit of allowing the state to set up numerous local districts, turning over virtually all school responsibility to these small and often impoverished units, and then withdrawing from any further interest in education (barring a few gestures on a state level toward "research" and "leadership"), is destined to become obsolete. It is clear today that improvement of the schools depends upon more money, and that more money must come from the state. The districts, straitjacketed by the antiquated property tax, have reached their financial limits. As has been shown previously, several states today are furnishing more than 50 percent of all district funds. The trend will continue, until within another generation or two, more of the school money will come directly from the state. The school district will be relieved of the necessity of providing a minimum program, but will be permitted to tax itself if it so wishes in order to exceed the minimum. The result will be increased educational opportunities for the nation's children, and relief for the real property owners who are now footing most of the schools' bills.

TOWARD EQUALIZATION OF OPPORTUNITY.   School money in the future will be raised where it exists and spent where it is needed. The wealthy district will receive purely nominal state aid above the basic per-pupil figure, but the poor district will receive massive aid. The goal for all districts will be a "floor" figure set up by the state and guaranteed to all districts, augmented by whatever additional enrichment the local district will feel itself financially able to provide. The equalization will thus extend to a minimum figure which represents an adequate level of education; the districts will still be able to differentiate above this figure if they wish to make the necessary effort.

TOWARD MORE MONEY FOR EDUCATION. The nation's schools should receive immediately a substantial increase in operational funds, from whatever source. When it is remembered that a larger proportion of the national income went for education during the depression, when schools were far below today's standards, it becomes apparent that massive amounts of additional revenue must be made available for education in this country.

No educator should be satisfied with the schools' share of the national wealth until education at least receives the equivalent of what is being spent in the United States each year on liquor, tobacco, and gambling. The trend is in this direction, and probably will bring in its train wholesale modification of present tax and assessment restrictions which now shackle the schools' spending. It is necessary that educators stop thinking in terms of pin money, and start thinking about educational financing in terms of between 5 and 10 percent of the gross national income.

TOWARD MORE FEDERAL MONEY FOR EDUCATION. The long history of federal nonintervention in school financing soon may be over. Everything points to an eventual program of government aid to states; it will start out modestly and gradually expand until a substantial portion of each school dollar will be furnished by the national government. Much of the federal assistance will be of the categorical type, granted on a project-approval basis for a particular purpose. Congress will give more approval to the principle of equalization; that is, the states with the least ability to finance their educational systems will receive the most federal money. However, states must show evidence that they have desegregated their schools in order to receive federal funds.

An alternative device would be to have government deal directly with the individual school districts instead of the states. However, this would require the creation of a tremendous and complex management agency, nullifying the qualities of speed and simplicity that should be an integral part of any national aid program. The distribution of federal money through the state departments of education would preserve the legal principle that education is a state function, and would largely eliminate the onus of federal control. Federal money that is turned over to the states and immediately deposited in the general educational fund can hardly retain any strings. The mere distribution of federal funds upon an enrollment basis would carry an element of equalization.

TOWARD A MORE DIVERSIFIED TAX BASE.   Little progress can be made toward improving the educational standards of the nation as long as the real property tax remains the basis for school financial support. Fortunately, the trend is toward increased diversification in this field. As increasing percentages of school funds come from the state instead of the local district, the proportionate importance of the property tax is bound to diminish.

More and more of the money needed for school expenditures seems destined to come from such sources as income, inheritance, excise, and sales taxes. The progressive decline of the property tax will probably be linked by future historians with the upgrading of school financing.

TOWARD FINANCING FROM GENERAL STATE FUNDS.   The principle that education should be supported financially on as broad a tax base as possible is a sound one. It is the responsibility of all the people. Therefore, the earmarking of specific tax revenues for education is philosophically unsound. In addition, any attempt to divert certain taxes for the sole support of schools potentially endangers the schools because specific tax sources eventually may diminish their returns. The trend is clearly away from the earmarking of taxes for education and toward the supplying of the schools' financial needs out of the general state fund.

TOWARD INCREASING STATE AID IN THE CONSTRUCTION OF SCHOOL BUILDINGS.   Once thought of as local enterprises, school plants are now increasingly recognized as capital investments of the entire state. The acceptance of such a theory makes inevitable the growth of state aid for schoolhouse construction. Most states now offering such aid are doing so on a loan basis, with the money obtained from state bond issues, doled out to the local districts on a basis of need, and repayable over a twenty-year period from local tax revenues. The future doubtless will see the acceptance by the state of its responsibility of supplying such building funds without demanding eventual repayment. The need for more schools is preeminently the concern of the whole state, not merely of individual school districts.

TOWARD COMPLETELY FREE SCHOOLS.   The schools are not yet all free. Many states still do not furnish free textbooks to elementary school children; only half furnish them to secondary schools.   Three-fourths of the states still require pupils to pay for their own school supplies.   Some states still charge for tuition of rural pupils in high school, and some are still sending bills for transportation.   All these hangovers from the past are negations of the worthy principle that the schools of America should be completely free to all.   The trend, happily, is strongly toward completely free education in a free country.

TOWARD INCREASED VOTER RESISTANCE TO BOND ISSUES AND MAXIMUM TAX RATE INCREASES FOR EDUCATIONAL PURPOSES.   This increasing resistance is due partly to the overtaxed property owner, anger over violence, vandalism, and student rebellion at schools (including colleges), and teacher strikes.   People take out their resentment in the only way they feel they can by refusing to grant schools the support they so desperately need. There is also a public belief that the tax base needs to be broadened.

TOWARD INCREASED USE OF DATA PROCESSING.   Electronic computers will be used more and more to perform clerical and accounting tasks related to school business management.   School districts are so overwhelmed with the increasing multiplicity of reports to state and federal governmental agencies that there is not enough clerical assistance to handle them.   Computers permit the storing of the vast amounts of information that are necessary if intelligent financial decisions are to be made.

TOWARD COMBINING COUNTIES WITH SMALL POPULATIONS.   In the twin areas of educational finance and administration, more states will do what California is already doing: combine small counties into larger, more viable units.

Administrative Problems

In Basket

Problem 1

The Modoc School District is situated in a rural community spread over a large area.   There are four elementary schools and one small junior–senior high school. Because of the long distances students must travel, transportation has always been necessary. School costs have risen continuously, yet the district is operating on a tax rate approved seven years ago. Tax elections were defeated overwhelmingly four years ago and again two years ago.

The district has diminished services, raised class loads, and eliminated some personnel. The breaking point has been reached; it appears impossible to balance the budget for the coming year. The Board of Education has decided to go to the people again and ask for a $.75 tax rate increase. This is the minimum that will be necessary over the next two or three years, even with tightened belts. It does not allow for the restoration of any of the reduced services or personnel but would permit the continuation of the bus services.

As the superintendent, how would you propose to gain community support?
In what capacity would you involve various school personnel?
What campaign strategy would you plan?

Problem 2

Assume the same situation exists as in Problem 1. The superintendent has asked each building principal to develop a plan for gaining support in his attendance area for the tax rate increase, an issue in the upcoming election.

If you were the junior–senior high school principal, how would you proceed?
What are the possible plans you would propose to the superintendent for your school?
As one of the elementary school principals, how would you proceed and what plans would you propose?
If you were the superintendent, how would you handle the problem if one of the principals drags his feet and does almost nothing?

Selected References

BENSON, CHARLES S. *The Economics of Public Education.* Boston: Houghton Mifflin Co., 1968.

CRESSMAN, GEORGE R., and BENDA, HAROLD W. *Public Education in America.* 3rd ed. New York: Appleton-Century-Crofts, 1966.

Education Vouchers. *A Report on Financing Education by Grants to Parents.* Cambridge, Mass.: Center for the Study of Public Policy, 1970.

HANDLER, BENJAMIN. *Economic Planning for Better Schools.* Ann Arbor: University of Michigan, 1960.

HUTCHINS, CLAYTON D., and BARR, RICHARD H. *Statistics of State School Systems, 1965–66.* Washington, D.C.: U.S. Department of Health, Education, and Welfare, U.S. Government Printing Office, 1968.

LINN, HENRY H. *School Business Administration.* New York: Ronald Press Co., 1956.

MORT, PAUL R., and REUSSER, W. C. *Public School Finance.* New York: McGraw-Hill Book Co., 1941.

MUSHKIN, S., and CROWTHER, B. *Federal Taxes and the Measurement of State Capacity.* Washington, D.C.: U.S. Public Health Service, 1954.

NATIONAL CITIZENS COMMISSION FOR THE PUBLIC SCHOOLS. *How Do We Pay for Our Public Schools?* New York: The Commission, 1954.

NATIONAL EDUCATION ASSOCIATION, Research Division. *Estimates of School Statistics, 1972–73.* Research Report 1972–R13. Washington, D.C.: The Association, 1973.

———, Research Division. "Rankings of the States, 1973." Research Report 1973–R1. Washington, D.C.: The Association, 1973.

———, Research Division. "Annual Report on Public-School Financing." *NEA Research Bulletin* 43 (October 1965).

NUNNERY, MICHAEL Y., and KIMBROUGH, RALPH B. *Politics, Power, Polls, and School Elections.* Berkeley, Calif.: McCutcheon Publishing Corp., 1971.

REEDER, WARD G. *The Fundamentals of Public School Administration.* 4th ed. New York: Macmillan Publishing Co., 1958.

STOOPS, EMERY, and RAFFERTY, M. L. *About Our Schools.* Los Angeles: California Education Press, 1955.

U.S. DEPARTMENT OF HEALTH, EDUCATION, AND WELFARE. *Profile of ESEA, The Elementary and Secondary Education Act of 1965.* OE 20088A. Washington, D.C.: U.S. Government Printing Office, 1967.

9

School District Budgeting

A school district budget is an organized, written plan representing the financial picture of the district. It should be based on past experience but should look ahead to the future. Careful, continuous planning is necessary if the budget is to meet the needs of the district. In the last few years, some school districts have utilized the systems approach of planning–programming–budgeting (PPBS) in their approach to budget development.

This chapter includes a discussion of the following topics:

The Budget and Overall School Planning
Proper Budgetary Procedures
Planning–Programming–Budgeting Systems (PPBS)
Summary
Trends

The Budget and Overall School Planning

It is a mistake to think of a school budget in terms of a balance between revenue and expenditures only; more important, it is an educational forecast drawn up a year in advance that reduces school planning to a systematized form. The school budget is different from the budget in business or industry; it has as its goal the securing, not of financial profit, but of the greatest possible educational dividends from the investment of the taxpayers' money.

Educational benefit is the measure of good school business management, not monies saved or records accumulated. Effective management in the public interest will require the wise expenditure of money for educational purposes and the avoidance of any waste. The principle that must be kept in mind while working with a budget is that business administration is merely one of several facilitating services in the advancement of the educational program; it is subordinate to educational administration, but should be integrated with it. The business office should never dominate the school program. Sometimes it appears that the budget determines the educational program. Should this situation ever develop, the educational program may easily degenerate into a succession of inventories and tightened economies. There is little point in running a school system that is financially prosperous but educationally poor.

On the other hand, intelligent business management is absolutely necessary if the educational program is to prosper. Poor administration of the district's financial affairs can result in spending money in ineffective areas and in diverting administrators' attention from the educational problems of the district to tasks that could be carried on by clerical personnel under the proper direction. The channeling of business affairs into the appropriate areas of the district-wide educational picture can best be charted through the medium of a properly constructed budget.

The school budget states in dollars and cents the policies and philosophy of the school district. It "is one way of expressing a set of purposes translated into a plan of action for a stated period of time."[1] It exercises decisive control over the aspects of the school program that are to be emphasized or de-emphasized. The budget also serves the purposes of public relations by bringing the public into closer contact with the schools through published figures, public hearings, and joint committees. It enables the people to judge the cost of the educational program in terms of educational services provided. Finally, the budget should be the expression of the will of the people of the district.

Proper Budgetary Procedures

School budgetary procedures may be divided into three main parts: preparation, consideration and adoption, and administration. A fourth step, often considered as part of the budget administration, is appraisal.

---

[1] Stephen J. Knezevich (ed.), *Administrative Technology and the School Executive*, p. 65.

PREPARATION OF THE BUDGET.   Too much importance cannot be attached to the proper preparation of the school budget.   Its advantages are summarized as follows:

1.   It makes for better educational planning.
2.   It gives an overview of the school program.
3.   It aids in the analysis of details.
4.   It develops cooperation within the school.
5.   It stimulates confidence among the taxpayers.
6.   It contains a balanced estimate of receipts.
7.   It provides a legal basis for the proper authorities to levy the necessary local taxes.
8.   It authorizes expenditures.
9.   It aids in the economical administration of the school.
10.   It improves financial accounting procedures.
11.   It aids in administering extra-curricular activities.
12.   It projects the school into the future and thus stimulates long-range planning and forecasting.[2]

Despite the lack of standardization in budgeting among the various states, there is a growing area of agreement centering about the classifications of expenditures.   The United States Department of Health, Education, and Welfare lists the headings commonly employed as follows:[3]

ADMINISTRATION
100 Series

110.   Salaries
      110-a.   Board of Education
      110-b.   Board Secretary's Office
      110-c.   Treasurer's Office
      110-d.   School Elections
      110-e.   Tax Collection
      110-f.   Legal Services
      110-g.   Superintendent's Office

---

[2] C. A. DeYoung, *Budgeting in Public Schools*, pp. 9–14.
[3] U.S. Department of Health, Education, and Welfare, *Financial Accounting for Local and State School Systems*, pp. 27–35.

110-h.   Personnel Office
110-i.   Public Relations
110-j.   Centralized Research
110-k.   Census Enumeration
110-l.   Office of Business Administration
110-m.   Fiscal Control
110-n.   Administration of Buildings and Grounds
110-o.   Purchasing Office
110-p.   Printing and Publishing
110-q.   Other Salaries for Administration
120.   Contracted Services
130.   Other Expenses
130-a.   Board of Education
130-b.   Board Secretary's Office
130-c.   Treasurer's Office
130-d.   School Elections
130-e.   Tax Collection
130-f.   Legal Services
130-g.   Superintendent's Office
130-h.   Personnel Office
130-i.   Public Relations
130-j.   Centralized Research
130-k.   Census Enumeration
130-l.   Office of Business Administration
130-m.   Fiscal Control
130-n.   Administration of Buildings and Grounds
130-o.   Purchasing Office
130-p.   Printing and Publishing
130-q.   Miscellaneous Expenses for Administration

INSTRUCTION
200 Series

210.   Salaries
211.   Principals
212.   Consultants or Supervisors
213.   Teachers
214.   Other Instructional Staff
214-a.   School Librarians
214-b.   Audiovisual Personnel
214-c.   Guidance Personnel
214-d.   Psychological Personnel
214-e.   Television Instructional Personnel

      215.   Secretarial and Clerical Assistants
          215-a.   Principal's Office
          215-b.   Consultants or Supervisors
          215-c.   Teachers
          215-d.   Other Instructional Staff
      216.   Other Salaries for Instruction
220.   Textbooks
230.   School Libraries and Audiovisual Materials
      230-a.   School Library Books
      230-b.   Periodicals and Newspapers
      230-c.   Audiovisual Materials
      230-d.   Other School Library Expenses
240.   Teaching Supplies
250.   Other Expenses
      250-a.   Supplies
      250-b.   Travel
      250-c.   Miscellaneous Expenses

ATTENDANCE AND HEALTH SERVICES
300–400 Series

300.   Attendance Services
      310.   Salaries
          310-a.   Attendance Personnel
          310-b.   Secretarial and Clerical Personnel
          310-c.   Other Salaries
      320.   Other Expenses
          320-a.   Supplies
          320-b.   Travel
          320-c.   Miscellaneous Expenses
400.   Health Services
      410.   Salaries
          410-a.   Professional and Technical Health Personnel
              410-a-1.   School physicians, including psychiatrists
              410-a-2.   School dentists
              410-a-3.   School nurses
              410-a-4.   School dental hygienists
              410-a-5.   Other professional and technical health
                        personnel
          410-b.   Nonprofessional and Nontechnical Health Personnel
      420.   Other Expenses
          420-a.   Supplies

420-b.   Travel
420-c.   Miscellaneous Expenses

PUPIL TRANSPORTATION SERVICES
500 Series

510.   Salaries
     510-a.   Supervisors
     510-b.   Drivers
     510-c.   Mechanics and Other Garage Employees
     510-d.   Clerks and Other Employees
520.   Contracted Services and Public Carriers
530.   Replacements of Vehicles
     530-a.   Cash Purchase
     530-b.   Lease-Purchase and Installment-Purchase
540.   Pupil Transportation Insurance
550.   Expenditures in Lieu of Transportation
560.   Other Expenses for Operation and Maintenance
     560-a.   Gasoline
     560-b.   Lubricants
     560-c.   Tires and Tubes
     560-d.   Repair Parts
     560-e.   Supplies and Expenses for Garage Operation
     560-f.   Garage and Garage Equipment Repairs
     560-g.   Maintenance of Vehicles by Private Garages
     560-h.   Rent
     560-i.   Miscellaneous Expenses

OPERATION OF PLANT
600 Series

610.   Salaries
     610-a.   Plant Engineers
     610-b.   Custodial Services
     610-c.   Care of Grounds
     610-d.   Other Salaries for Operation of Plant
620.   Contracted Services
630.   Heat for Buildings
640.   Utilities, Except Heat for Buildings
     640-a.   Water and Sewerage
     640-b.   Electricity
     640-c.   Gas
     640-d.   Telephone and Telegraph
     640-e.   Other Utilities

650. Supplies, Except Utilities
    650-a. Custodial Supplies
    650-b. Supplies for Operation of Vehicles
    650-c. Supplies for Care of Grounds
    650-d. Other Supplies for Operation of Plant
660. Other Expenses

MAINTENANCE OF PLANT
700 Series

710. Salaries
    710-a. Grounds
    710-b. Buildings
    710-c. Repair of Equipment
    710-d. Manufacture of Replacements of Equipment
720. Contracted Services
    720-a. Grounds
    720-b. Buildings
    720-c. Repair of Equipment
730. Replacements of Equipment
    730-a. Instructional Equipment
    730-b. Noninstructional Equipment
740. Other Expenses
    740-a. Grounds
    740-b. Buildings
    740-c. Repair of Equipment
    740-d. Manufacture of Replacements of Equipment

FIXED CHARGES
800 Series

810. School District Contributions to Employee Retirement
    810-a. State, County, or Local Retirement Funds
    810-b. Social Security
    810-c. Pension Payments
820. Insurance and Judgments
    820-a. Property Insurance
    820-b. Employee Insurance
    820-c. Liability Insurance
    820-d. Fidelity Bond Premiums
    820-e. Judgments
830. Rental of Land and Buildings
    830-a. Land and Buildings for Instructional Purposes
    830-b. Land and Buildings for Noninstructional Purposes

840. Interest on Current Loans
850. Other Fixed Charges

FOOD SERVICES AND STUDENT BODY ACTIVITIES
900–1000 Series

900. Food Services
    910. Salaries
    920. Other Expenses
    930. Expenditures to Cover Deficit of a Separate Food Services Fund or Account
1000. Student Body Activities
    1010. Salaries
    1020. Other Expenses
    1030. Expenditures to Cover Deficits of Student Body Activities Funds or Accounts

COMMUNITY SERVICES
1100 Series

1110. Recreation
    1110-a. Salaries
    1110-b. Other Expenses
1120. Civic Activities
    1120-a. Salaries
    1120-b. Other Expenses
1130. Public Libraries
    1130-a. Salaries
    1130-b. Books, Periodicals, and Newspapers
    1130-c. Other Expenses
1140. Custodial and Detention Care of Children
    1140-a. Salaries
    1140-b. Other Expenses
1150. Welfare Activities
    1150-a. Salaries
    1150-b. Other Expenses
1160. Nonpublic School Pupils
    1161. Instructional Services
        1161-a. Textbooks
        1161-b. Other Expenses
    1162. Attendance and Health Services
        1162-a. Attendance
        1162-b. Health
    1163. Transportation Services

CAPITAL OUTLAY
1200 Series

1210.   Sites
     1210-a.   Professional Services
     1210-b.   Sites and Site Additions
     1210-c.   Improvement to Sites
1220.   Buildings
     1220-a.   Professional Services
     1220-b.   New Buildings and Building Additions
     1220-c.   Remodeling
1230.   Equipment
     1230-a.   Professional Services
     1230-b.   Administration
     1230-c.   Instruction
     1230-d.   Attendance and Health
     1230-e.   Pupil Transportation
     1230-f.   Operation of Plant
     1230-g.   Maintenance of Plant
     1230-h.   Food Services and Student Body Activities
     1230-i.   Community Services
     1230-j.   Investment Property

DEBT SERVICE FROM CURRENT FUNDS
1300 Series

1310.   Principal of Debt
     1310-a.   Bonds
     1310-b.   Short-term Loans
     1310-c.   Long-term Loans
     1310-d.   Warrants or Bills of Preceding Years
1320.   Interest on Debt
     1320-a.   Bonds
     1320-b.   Short-term Loans
     1320-c.   Long-term Loans
1330.   Amounts Paid into Sinking Funds
1340.   Expenditures to Schoolhousing Authority or Similar Agency
     1340-a.   Principal
     1340-b.   Interest
1350.   Other Debt Service

OUTGOING TRANSFER ACCOUNTS
1400 Series

1410.   Expenditures to Other School Districts or Administrative Units in the State
     1410-a.   Tuition

1410-b.   Transportation
1410-c.   Miscellaneous
1420.   Expenditures to School Districts or Administrative Units in Another
State
1420-a.   Tuition
1420-b.   Transportation
1420-c.   Miscellaneous
1430.   Tuition to Other than Public Schools
1430-a.   Private Nonsectarian Schools
1430-b.   Individuals

In the three steps of budgetary development listed by DeYoung, the first is educational planning, and it centers in its financial aspect around the expenditure categories described and listed above.[4] Before figures are placed in the budget, important decisions must be made. Planning should not only be concerned with the coming year but look ahead for several years. It is not wise to start a program that cannot be supported financially for more than the year ahead. However, fragmentation occurs when planning is only short range. Continuity is essential if improvements are to be made.

Long range policy decisions should be made regarding many factors. A determination should be made as to who should be educated; whether the program will include kindergarten, junior college, and adult education opportunities. Enrollments should be projected five to ten years. Additional sites, buildings, equipment, and personnel should be projected. The length of the school year must be established. Decisions must be made regarding teacher load, provisions for educating exceptional children, guidance services, transportation services, lunch programs, special teachers for special subjects, health services, the education of the culturally different, maintenance and operation services, summer school programs, salary schedules, and fringe benefits for personnel. Policies should be developed regarding the type of secondary schools to be provided and the grade organization: comprehensive or vocational high schools, junior high schools, or intermediate schools. There should be decisions regarding the educational program, the subject matter to be taught, and the electives to be offered.[5]

All school policies adopted by the school board contribute to the size and content of the budget in the sense that the material expression of these

---

[4] DeYoung, *Budgeting*, p. 30.
[5] Edgar L. Morphet, Roe L. Johns, and Theodore L. Reller, *Educational Organization and Administration*, pp. 467–68.

policies is found primarily in the budget. All problems of curriculum and personnel must be attacked first through budgetary provision. Grose compares the budget to a funnel through which must pass, at the time of its adoption, the whole accumulation of policy changes and developments of the entire year.[6]

The second step in budgetary development consists of planning the program of expenditures. When this step is allowed to come first, and to assume priority over educational planning, it may constitute the entire budget. It is a common mistake to start budget figuring from the standpoint of an assured income, and to compel the various expenditure categories to accommodate themselves to the fixed revenue. This second step in budgeting should be directly dependent upon the first step—educational planning—and should in turn govern the third step—income planning—instead of being determined by it.

The interpretation of plans into costs is one of the outstanding contributions that the business office performs.

Planning the income constitutes the third step. When the educational program for the coming year has been decided upon, and when the expenditures needed to finance that program have been determined, then the final step in budgeting is to determine whether the expected income will support the program, and if not, how to augment it. When a discrepancy between projected income and proposed expenditure is found, the productivity of each source of income should then be examined with an eye to a possible increase in revenue production. Other possible sources then should be sought out and scrutinized and eventually used in an attempt to finance the planned program.

The superintendent of schools is the chief executive officer of the district. He should therefore be given the primary responsibility for the performance of the task that is basic to the efficiency of the school system, the preparation of the budget.

In line with policies previously adopted by the board of education, the board approves and amends the budget as it is presented by the superintendent. Whereas the superintendent knows more about the educational needs of the system than anyone else, the board members, by virtue of their residence in the community for many years, know more about the financial

---

[6] C. H. Grose, "Educational Plan of the School Budget," *American School Board Journal,* pp. 23–24.

capabilities and desires of the community than do the school personnel. Cooperation between the board and its superintendent is therefore essential.

Such cooperation extends beyond board–superintendent relations; it involves other school employees as well. All school principals and department heads should be consulted as to needs and requirements, but democratic budgeting should go still further. It should attempt to secure the cooperation of teachers, custodians, and clerical employees in making the school budget an expression of the needs of the whole school system. Consulting his staff will not only assure the superintendent of the securing of much needed information but also contribute to employee morale and status.

Forms such as those illustrated in Tables 9–1 to 9–7 can be used to gather specific budget information and recommendations from schools and departments. These should be compiled after consultations with all members of the staff. The business office or administrative council can meet with those who completed the forms and analyze them. At this time priorities should also be established. If the total for the budget is not approved, items with highest priority would then be included.

Budget making should be considered a year-long activity. Definite deadlines should be adopted for the completion of the several phases of budgeting in order to avoid last-minute improvisation. The following Budget Calendar is an example of a schedule for planning and adopting a budget:

Oct. 22, 1973	Presentation of Classified Salary Proposals to the District Superintendent.
Nov. 1–30	Conferences of Classified Employees Negotiating Council with Superintendent and selected staff regarding salaries.
Dec. 3	District Superintendent presents Classified Salary recommendation to the Board of Education at the first meeting in December.
Dec. 13	Budget Request Forms for ensuing year's budget in the hands of Division Heads, Principals, and Department Heads.

TABLE 9–1. Certificated Personnel Needs

School or
Department: Washington Elementary School
Note: Personnel needs are to be requested and set forth on the basis of *existing* facilities or known additions. Please explain fully in "justification" column the reason for any additional personnel requested.

JOB TITLE	GRADE OR CLASS	CURRENT STAFF	STAFF REQUESTED	INCREASE OR DECREASE	JUSTIFICATION
Principal		1	1	0	
Teacher	Primary	10	10	0	
Teacher	Upper Grade	7	8	+1	Expected increase in enrollment
Teacher	Kdg.	2	4	+2	To establish single-session kindergartens instead of double-session ones
Teacher	Educ. Handicap.	0	1	+1	To establish program for educationally handicapped pupils
Counselor	1–6	0	½	+½	To provide needed counseling services
Speech Therapist	1–6	0	½	+½	Many children have speech problems that should be corrected
Teacher	EMR	2	2	0	
Reading Specialist	1–3	2	3	+1	Reading scores show need for additional teacher

200

TABLE 9–2. Classified Personnel Needs

School or
Department: Washington Elementary School
Note: Personnel needs are to be requested and set forth on the basis of *existing* facilities or known additions. Please explain fully in "justification" column the reason for any additional personnel requested.

JOB TITLE	CURRENT STAFF	STAFF REQUESTED	INCREASE OR DECREASE	JUSTIFICATION
Secretary	1	1	0	
Clerk	0	½	+½	Increased enrollment entitles school to additional part-time clerk
Noon Duty Assistants	3	4	+1	Due to increased enrollment
Teacher Assistants	0	8	+8	To enhance the educational program by relieving teachers of "chores" to do their professional job
Custodian	2	2½	+½	To return to previous year's custodial service which was cut this year
Cafeteria Manager	1	1	0	
Cook-helpers	3	4	−1	Due to increased enrollment and cafeteria usage

TABLE 9–3. *Budgetary Requests for Conferences*

School or
Department: Washington Elementary School

NAME OF CONFERENCE	DATES	LOCATION OF CONFERENCE	JUSTIFICATION	NUMBER ATTENDING	ESTIMATED COST PER PERSON
CESAA	Mar. 22–25	Los Angeles	Professional growth	1	$ 40.00
Claremont Reading Conference	Spring	Claremont	To update information on reading programs	2	$ 35.00 each
ASCD	Mar. 15–19	San Francisco	To gain information on new programs and curriculum trends	1	$150.00

TABLE 9–4. Budgetary Request for Printing and Forms

School or
Department: Washington Elementary School
Note: Include report cards, diplomas, attendance forms or any other printing to be done at district expense. If allowance is made for unforeseen items, please indicate as such. Quantities of printed materials should be requested on the basis of a one-year supply.

DESCRIPTION	TYPE OF FORM	QUANTITY REQUIRED	ESTIMATED COST	LENGTH OF TIME QUANTITY WILL LAST	DATE NEEDED
Promotion Certificates	Standard form for 6th graders	120	?	1 year	5/1
Bulletin	Summer school announcements to send home	1,000	?	1 year	3/1
Cards	Summer school enrollment cards	500	?	1 year	5/1
Report cards	Standard summer school form	500	?	1 year	5/1

TABLE 9–5. Budgetary Request for Replacement of Equipment

School or
Department: Washington Elementary School

QUANTITY	TYPE OF EQUIPMENT (BRAND, MODEL, YEAR PURCHASED)	PRESENT CONDITION	CAN ITEM BE REPAIRED?	COST OF REPAIR	ESTIMATED CURRENT VALUE	ESTIMATED COST OF REPLACEMENT
1	Primary electric typewriter (1955)	Fair	No		$50.00	$250.00
4	Basketball goals and poles (1948)	Poor	No			150.00
2	Tape recorders: Webcor BP 7340-1 (1955) Brush (1950)	Poor	Doubtful			140.00 ea.
1	16 mm Victor 65-10 Movie pro-jector (1955)	Poor	No			650.00
1	Desk, Secretary (1950)	Fair	Maybe	$25.00	20.00	200.00
1	Desk, Principal (1950)	Fair	Maybe	25.00	20.00	200.00
3	Chairs, visitors (1952)	Fair	Yes	10.00 ea.	5.00 ea.	50.00 ea.
4	Record players	Poor	No		5.00 ea.	85.00 ea.

TABLE 9-6. *Budgetary Request for Buildings, Needed Repairs and Rehabilitation*

School or
Department: Washington Elementary School

ROOM OR BUILDING	DESCRIPTION	ESTIMATED COST	JUSTIFICATION
Rooms 1–12	Replace classroom light fixtures	$1,500.00	Present lighting is below acceptable standard
All rooms	Replace gas heaters	5,000.00	Present heaters are outdated and illegal
All rooms	Paint interior of all classrooms	3,000.00	They have not been painted for 10 years and are in poor condition
Playground	Replace all playground equipment	1,000.00	Present equipment is worn out and dangerous
All rooms	Add electric outlets	?	Rooms now have only one or two outlets which is not adequate for equipment in regular use
A & B	Replace clocks	50.00	Present clocks do not work well and need constant adjustment

TABLE 9–7. Budgetary Requests for New Equipment

School or
Department: Washington Elementary School

QUANTITY	DESCRIPTION OF EQUIPMENT	ESTIMATED COST	JUSTIFICATION
18	Independent study carrels	$ 50.00 ea.	To allow pupils independent work space when using taped or filmed materials
1	Controlled Reader—EDL	275.00	To develop reading skills in upper grades
1 set	Controlled Reader programs	600.00	To use with Controlled Reader in upper grades
1	Tachistoscope, EDL, Tach-X	200.00	To develop visual discrimination skills and visual memory—upper grades
1	Tach-X program	250.00	For use with Tach-X in upper grades
1	Planetarium, Ken-A-Vision	79.50	For teaching elementary astronomy
10	Globes—Readiness, Beginner	25.00 ea.	None available. Needed to introduce geography concepts
4	Maps, simplified political, U.S. & World	25.00 ea.	No usable maps for lower grades
5	Projectors, film strip	50.00 ea.	These are compact, low-voltage projectors and are needed for individual or small-group instruction

Dec. 10–Jan. 14	Division Heads, Principals, and Department Heads meet with their staff to develop a division and school budget. Expenditure estimates due in Business Office by January 15.
Jan. 7, 1974	Enrollment projections for 1974–1975 from Principals to the Assistant Superintendent, Instructional Services, with copy to the District Superintendent.
Jan. 14–Feb. 4	Business Manager and Director of Maintenance and Operations will meet with school principals and review major items of maintenance for buildings, grounds, and equipment.
Jan. 14–April 8	Planning meetings with the Board of Education, District Superintendent, Cabinet, Administrative Staff, and Negotiating Council.
Jan. 16	Principals and staff members to submit two copies of personnel needs for 1974–1975 (one to the Superintendent and one to Business Office). This would include both certificated and classified personnel.
Feb. 11	Principals and department heads will submit requests for major repairs to buildings, grounds, and equipment.
Feb. 15	School principals and staff members submit estimate of needs for ensuing year for Capital Outlay items, replacement of equipment, maintenance needs.
Feb. 18–March 22	Preparation and assembly by Business Office of first draft of working budget by detailed classification.
March 1	Presentation of Certificated Salary Proposals to District Superintendent.
March 11–April 1	Conferences by Negotiating Council, District Superintendent, and selected staff regarding salaries.
March 18	Copy of Tentative Budget given to District Superintendent for study.
March 31–April 10	Tentative Budget referred to Division Heads, principals, and staff for review. Conference scheduled with Superintendent and Business Manager for appropriate revision.

April 8–10	District Superintendent recommends salaries to Board of Education (provided state support has been determined as needed for salary determination).
April 22–26	Adoption by Board of Education of Certificated Salary Schedules for the ensuing year (provided state apportionment needed and known).
May 6	Contracts issued.
May 6–10	Presentation to Board of Education by District Superintendent of Preliminary Budget.
May 6–31	Revision and readjustment as required. Meetings with the Board of Education, principals, and department heads on budgetary questions as necessary.
June 3	Tentative Budget presented to the District Superintendent by the Business Manager.
June 10–14	Tentative Budget presented to Board of Education by the District Superintendent at the first regular meeting in June. Board adopts resolution permitting Board to increase annual salaries during school year for certificated and/or classified personnel.
June 24–28	Second regular meeting of the Board of Education in June to adopt the Tentative Budget to be filed with the County Superintendent of Schools.
*July 1	Tentative Budget filed with County Superintendent of Schools.
*July 15	Tentative Budget returned by County Superintendent of Schools.
*July 15	Meeting of Board of Education to adopt Publication Budget.
*July 19	File Publication Budget with County Superintendent of Schools.
*July 24–31	Publication Budget in the local newspaper by County Superintendent of Schools.

*Aug. 2   Meeting of the Board of Education—Public Hearing and
                Adoption of Budget.

*Aug. 5–9   Adopted Budget filed with County Superintendent of
                Schools.

---

* Mandatory dates set by Education Code.

The Budget Calendar should be adopted by the board of education, and regular reports should be made to the board showing the progress that is being made.

The final budget should present a complete picture of the school district's financial plans. Each proposed appropriation should be followed by supporting explanation and detail. There should be no "padding" and no money "hidden" in the various categories. If this occurs, people lose confidence in the administration and investigations may be requested. Because every expense cannot be predicted precisely, it is legitimate to budget contingency funds to provide for possible changes in enrollment, repairs, programs, or emergencies.

Many states prescribe rules governing the development of the budget and prescribe a standard budget form. In states that have no such requirement, the superintendent should prepare the budget according to the classifications recommended by the United States Department of Health, Education, and Welfare (see pages 190–197). Subheadings can be developed within the recommended categories to fit the needs of each district. For example:

213   Teachers
213.1   Salaries, Regular Teachers
213.2   Salaries, Special Training Teachers
213.3   Salaries, Speech Teachers
213.4   Salaries, Home Teachers
213.5   Salaries, Dental Health Teachers
213.6   Salaries, Guidance Teachers
213.7   Salaries, Substitute Teachers

To keep various categories within reason, expenditure percentages should be allotted according to general practice. As an example, thirty-

eight unified school districts in California allotted the following percentages
to the main categories of their school budgets:

| | | PERCENT OF CURRENT |
SERIES	CATEGORY	EXPENSE OF EDUCATION
100	Administration	3.28
200	Instruction	75.40
300	Attendance Services	.05
400	Health Services	1.36
500	Transportation Services	1.24
600	Operation	7.93
700	Maintenance	4.65
800	Fixed Charges	6.09
Total current expenses, classifications 100–800		100.00

New budgets are generally compared with previous budgets. To help
with this comparative analysis, a budget should show the previous year's
expenditures, the current budget, and the estimate of expenditures for the
year ahead. To be realistic, every item should be justified.

Most budgets show only what the expenditure buys. The performance budget is coming into use and supplements the figures by explaining,
after each item, what is to be achieved by the expenditures. This creates a
longer budget but business, too, has found this useful.[7] Table 9–8 is an
example of such a budget.

CONSIDERATION AND ADOPTION OF THE BUDGET. The duty of the superintendent of schools is to prepare as clear and concise a budget as possible,
and to present it to the school board in a manner designed to secure its
adoption with as few changes as possible. Reciprocally, it is the duty of
the board to refuse to approve any elimination or decrease of a budgetary
item without consulting the superintendent. In the presentation of the
budget, two principles should be followed:

(1) The public should be informed. Ample publicity is a necessity
in modern administration. Many states now require public budget hearings, on the sound grounds that the manner in which the budget is prepared

---

[7] Henry H. Linn (ed.), *School Business Administration*, pp. 169–70.

TABLE 9–8. *Example of a Performance Budget*

CLASSI-FICATION NUMBER	ITEM	EXPLANATION		1968–69 ACTUAL PREVIOUS YEAR BUDGET	1969–70 CURRENT YEAR BUDGET	1970–71 PROPOSED YEAR BUDGET
230	*Textbooks*					
231	Elementary Supplementary Texts	2,982 Pupils @ $ 1.00		$2,268	$2,400	$2,982
232	Junior High Supplementary Texts	788 Pupils @ $ 2.00		833	597	1,576
233	High School Texts	1,340 Pupils @ $10.00 = $13,400				
233.1	English Dept.	Dictionaries	100 copies	1,694	2,134	2,840
		9 Grammar Basic	350			
		9 LMCL	40			
		10 LMCL	40			
		10 LBLA	30			
		Replacement	50			
233.2	Homemaking Dept.	Clothing	40 copies	729	40	840
		Home Management	40			
		Home Ec. I	40			
		Replacement	20			
233.3	Foreign Language Dept.	Spanish I	85 copies	821	1,439	1,020
		Grammar I	55			
		Replacement	30			
233.4	Mathematics Dept.	Replacement		593	1,276	300
233.5	Science Dept.	Life Science	325 copies	1,837	—	2,250
		Replacement	50			

and adopted has a direct relation to the public pocketbook.   Despite its tax implications, however, the average budget hearing is not noted for its heavy attendance.   It is necessary, therefore, to see that the public is informed about this vital feature of school planning.   This can be accomplished by giving information to the newspapers, holding public hearings, publishing and disseminating bulletins, and giving addresses before educational and civic groups.[8]

(2) All requests should be justified.   The budget is not a mere statement of intent; whenever an increased appropriation is requested for a certain item, an explanation and justification for the increase should be given.   In order to do this successfully, detailed information should be provided by all departments and individuals working to formulate the budget, so that every request can be justified.

The budget as it is finally presented by the superintendent to the board of education should be either in typewritten or mimeographed form.   Each board member should be presented with a copy, labeled and placed in individual loose-leaf folders.   Although not necessarily in this order, the following subjects should be presented:

Title page.
Table of contents showing series numbers, budget categories, and page
    numbers.
List of charts, graphs, figures.
Letter of transmittal from the superintendent to the board of education.
A statement of the educational philosophy from which the budget is
    developed.
A statement regarding proposed programs.
A statement regarding population growth trends.
Budget summary.
Definitions of special terms.
Supporting data.
Index.

Usually, the use of pictorial and graphic representations in connection with the budget is for the benefit of the general lay public, rather than for

---

8 By permission of Macmillan Publishing Co., Inc., from *The Fundamentals of Public School Administration,* 4th ed. by Ward G. Reeder.   Copyright © 1958 by Macmillan Publishing Co., Inc., pp. 308–309.

school personnel or board members. The picture of the tax dollar, with wedges representing the proportionate expenditures in each of the budgetary categories, is a common device and is often reproduced in leaflets and brochures for public distribution. Figure 9–1 is an example of an expenditure dollar.

After the tentative budget has passed through the various departments and has been developed to the superintendent's satisfaction, the presentation is then made to the school board. Following preliminary discussions of various sections and incorporation of whatever changes may be deemed necessary, a public hearing should be held. The budget is then adopted by the board, and, under most state laws, presented to the necessary municipal, county, or state authorities for approval. After final adoption and approval, it then becomes the legal instrument governing the school district's finances for the next fiscal year. The entire budget should

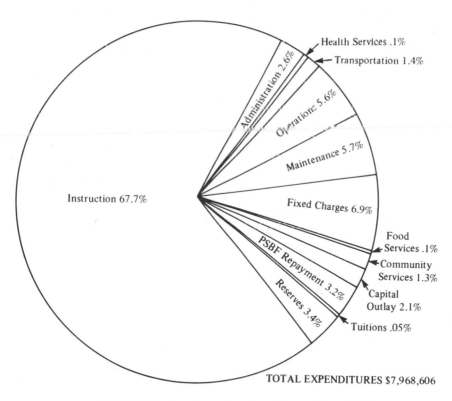

FIGURE 9–1. Example of an Expenditure Dollar.

be open to all people because it is a public record; copies should be readily available.

ADMINISTRATION OF THE BUDGET. Either the superintendent or the business manager, depending upon the internal organization of the school system, administers the budget as an executive function. Expenditures that remain within the amounts authorized by the budget are made as the need arises and without further action by the school board. Should the occasion arise when an emergency appears to necessitate the spending of sums over and above existing amounts in specific budgetary categories, board approval for the transfer of funds from the reserve will be necessary. Reserves usually should be maintained at a figure totaling not more than 10 percent of the entire budget. Some states require a "general reserve" for carry-over purposes during tax-scarce months; this normally cannot be touched for inter-budgetary transfer purposes. All states permit an "undistributed reserve" which can be tapped to meet unexpected expenditures or similar emergencies.

It should be remembered that, while a budget should be followed as closely as possible, it should not always be followed blindly and slavishly, regardless of school needs. A budget, even in its most efficient form, is only an estimate; it is never a perfect projection of the future. There is always an "x," an unknown quantity which necessitates a budgetary revision sometime within the subsequent year, however slight. The variance may be due to unexpectedly large school enrollment, requiring an unexpected expenditure of funds for a particular item. It may result from heightened expenditures due to a flood, fire, earthquake, or other natural calamity. An inflexible interpretation of the budget will result in scrimping and perhaps cutting back on priority categories in order to avoid a deficit. A more liberal interpretation will meet the emergency in one of two ways: either by borrowing money or by transferring funds from one budgetary category to another.

Every board of education should strive for a balanced budget. To say that a budget should not be interpreted inflexibly is not to say that it should be interpreted loosely. Every school district should operate within its income limits. It should be remembered that borrowing money to pay current operating expenses is as risky as an individual borrowing in order to pay for food and rent. However, deficit financing over a period much in excess of a year should be discouraged.

In connection with good budget administration, it goes without saying that a financial accounting system should be established that makes it possible for school officials to know from month to month how much money is available in any appropriation item. Such a system should be closely allied in form and structure to the budget forms themselves, and should show not only amounts actually expended from each appropriation item, but also all encumbrances upon each appropriation item. Nelson's encumbered bookkeeping system[9] includes control of both encumbrances and actual expenditure, as illustrated in Table 9–9. Monthly budget reports showing a detailed breakdown of the school finances are essential to good practice.

Planning–Programming–Budgeting Systems (PPBS)

CONCEPTS BEHIND PPBS. A planning–programming–budgeting system (commonly referred to as PPBS) is a systems-analysis approach to budget development based on goal setting, analysis and review, long-term projections, and selection of alternatives. It assumes that goals and objectives will be predetermined. Goals are "statements of purpose unconcerned with accomplishments in a given specific period of time, while objectives are quantified achievements accomplished within a specified time period."[10]

The function of the system is to (1) provide a planning framework; (2) place facts in programmed arrays so that decision making is based upon a complete knowledge of the situation; and (3) provide opportunity for systems-analysis readjustment and evaluation.

The AASA Commission on Administrative Technology has listed four major dimensions to PPBS:

1. Structure. A particular kind of classification for budget items, exhibit arrangements, or report formats. Structure is also concerned with the output-oriented categories of budget accounts.
2. Generation and analysis of alternative courses of action.
3. Facilitation of prudent decision making.

---

[9] D. Lloyd Nelson, *School Finance* (syllabus), published by the author (Los Angeles: University of Southern California, 1957–58), p. 32.

[10] Stephenson Parker, "PPBS," *CTA Journal,* p. 10.

TABLE 9–9. Suggested Encumbered Bookkeeping Plan[a]

APPROPRIATION RECORD

Remarks   Amount
Budget July 1972   655.

APPROPRIATION LEDGER

Sheet No. 1

Classification 4
Operation of School Plant   Supplies
Fiscal Year 1972–73

DATE	REFERENCE	ENCUMBRANCES		EXPENDITURES		APPROPRIATION	UNENCUMBERED BALANCE
		ISSUED (+) LIQUIDATED (−)	BALANCE OUTSTANDING	AMOUNT	TOTAL TO DATE		
July 1, 1972	Budget					655.00	655.00
Sept. 3	Purchase Order 1	+100	100				555.00
Sept. 20	Purchase Order 2	+207	307				348.00
Oct. 1	Wt. 20—Purchase Order 1	−100	207	100	100		348.00
Nov. 1	Wt. 50—Purchase Order 2	−207	0.0	205	305		350.00
Dec. 5	Purchase Order 40	+300	300				50.00
Jan. 1	Purchase Order 47	+ 45	345				5.00

[a] D. Lloyd Nelson, "School Finance" (syllabus), published by the author, Los Angeles, 1957–58.

4. Time. Multi-year planning and programming is an important element of PPBS.[11]

The following is an example of a budget arranged with reference to program structure.[12]

Program No.	Program
1	Learning intellectual skills.
2	Learning about the world.
3	Developing the individual.
4	Preparation for employment.
5	Preparation for higher education.
6	Assessment, guidance and counseling.
7	Development and evaluation.
8	Instructional resource and media services.
9	Auxiliary services.
10	Community services.
11	Operations and maintenance.
12	Capital outlay.
13	Administration.

HISTORICAL IMPETUS. Program budgeting in one form or another has been used by several major industries for approximately 40 years. The Department of Defense introduced a program based on systems technology in 1961 to improve planning functions. Because of the success of PPBS in the Department of Defense, President Johnson in 1965 called for the introduction of this system in all federal agencies and departments. Twenty-one non-defense departments, including the Department of Health, Education, and Welfare, were instructed to institute similar planing techniques by 1966. Since then, state and local governments have employed some aspects of PPBS.

In the past few years, school districts have begun to utilize PPBS principles, although the program is difficult to implement in the more abstract area of public education. Some school districts purporting to use PPBS are not doing so in actual practice. They may change the name of line-item functions, use only the unit-cost analysis part of program budget-

---

[11] Knezevich (ed.), *Administrative Technology*, pp. 69–70.
[12] Sue A. Haggart (ed.), *Program Budgeting for School District Planning* (Englewood Cliffs, N.J.: Educational Technology Publications. Copyright 1972, The Rand Corporation), p. 239.

ing, or apply the concept only to the functions of the business administrator without involving others, such as curriculum specialists.

In 1969, California created a State Commission on School District Budgeting and Accounting. It involved fifteen school districts for the 1969–70 school year in instituting a PPBS program. The purpose was to provide a statewide system for efficient planning and effective budgeting.

Pilot programs in PPBS have been conducted in Clark County, Nevada; Montgomery County Schools in Maryland; Milwaukee, Wisconsin; Peoria, Illinois; Memphis, Tennessee; Long Island, New York; Westport, Connecticut; and Douglas County, Colorado. It appears that PPBS is here to stay in one form or another since approximately 75 percent of the states have mandated or are considering the mandation of a PPBS program.[13]

CHARACTERISTICS OF PPBS. Traditionally, budgets have been developed by assembling costs by types of resource inputs, line items, or organizational categories. There is often no plan and the status quo is projected on the basis of current experience.

PPBS is output oriented, looks at the end product, and is based on the idea that goals and objectives can be planned and predetermined. Goals should be not only immediate but long range as well. For example, a program may have the immediate objective of being instituted in the district's kindergarten classes for the following year; however, planning for its institution in all grades might take five or more years. Within each program, often there will be several subcategories.

PPBS is a total planning process, not merely a budget preparation. It utilizes analytical techniques and forms of systems analysis. "The output of systems analysis is a set of alternatives which have its performance or benefits listed and its costs shown. The alternatives are evaluated, ranked, and presented to the decision maker who can then select a preferred set."[14]

In selecting alternatives, the organizational objectives and the necessary resources must be considered. Resources include not only finances but people, materials, and environment. The community is a major resource. A resource team composed of staff members, community

---

[13] "Program Budgeting Design for Schools Unveiled, with Much More Work Still to Go," *Nation's Schools,* pp. 42–43.

[14] Gustave J. Rath, "PPBS Is More Than a Budget: It's a Total Planning Process," *Nation's Schools,* p. 53.

people, and students should be utilized in the planning stage and again in the final evaluation of the program.[15]   Parents who are involved will be able to understand where their taxes are spent if the budget is written in layman's language.   Better administrative decisions can be made when all areas of the school and community are involved in establishing a PPBS program.

ADMINISTRATIVE CONSIDERATIONS.   No district should jump into a PPBS program without thorough planning.   The new program should be integrated carefully into the present program without destroying it, and probably should be started on a small scale or only in one area.   It can be established on a decentralized basis with each program handled by an autonomous administrator, or on a centralized plan with one administrator totally responsible.   Because few administrators have the technical skill to handle the transition from traditional budget preparation to PPBS, it is necessary for them to become knowledgeable; or it may require the creation of a new position and the employment of a trained specialist.   The specialist must have the ability to work in both curriculum and fiscal areas and to influence the responsible personnel.   His duties would include the establishment of a resource team, the training and orienting of PPBS personnel, and the establishment of clear lines of communication and authority.

Part of the administrative problem of implementing a PPBS program is the lack of an effective organizational structure and specific technical skills to handle the transition.   In order to institute a PPBS program, the AASA has stated that:

> At least four conditions must be satisfied to move into a state of readiness —a restatement of educational objectives in a program format that facilitates the use of indicators and more precise output measurement devices in education; the generation of a supply of alternatives for reaching an objective; a reclassification of budget accounts now used in individual states or recommended nationally to reflect program- and output-oriented classifications; and employment of specialized personnel with systems analysis capability.[16]

Figure 9–2 diagrams the method used by one school district to implement PPBS.

---

[15] "Program Budgeting," *Nation's Schools,* pp. 40–43.
[16] Knezevich, *Administrative Technology,* pp. 87–88.

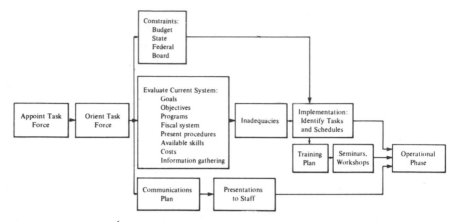

FIGURE 9–2.   Implementation Phase for PPBS.

EDUCATIONAL PLANNING.   Educational planning is often frustrating.   The demands on the available money come from many directions.   Federal and state fiscal policies may influence the shape of the educational program, or there may be no plan except the continuation of the status quo.   Programs desired or developed by the staff may never be budgeted.   Too often the budget determines the educational programs.   PPBS is an attempt to solve problems like these because it presumes that educational planning will be part of the budgeting procedure.

Goals and objectives need to be predetermined and established. Objectives must be organized into programs that are concerned with the end product, the emphasis on output rather than input.   Personnel, materials, and resources must be allocated, costs analyzed, and priorities established.   An essential ingredient of PPBS is continual evaluation and analysis which is often difficult and subjective, but does encourage the revision of objectives, the reallocation of personnel and materials, and the changing of goals whenever the need arises.

BENEFITS OF PPBS.   Some of the benefits that may stem from PPBS are:

1.   Information is directly aligned to educational needs.
2.   Information arrives at the top level more quickly, efficiently, and in a coordinated fashion.

3. Program costs are directly related to program objectives.
4. A framework to analyze costs and benefits of alternative programs is provided. The decision process in program selection is strengthened.
5. The comparison of actual and planned performance is facilitated through systems analysis.
6. A method for revising goals, changing plans, or reallocating resources is provided.
7. A framework for staff planning is provided.
8. It provides an evaluation procedure, cost-benefit analysis, and a method for comparing actual with planned performance.

PROBLEMS OF PROGRAM BUDGETING. As with all programs, there are problems in the use of PPBS. These should be pointed out even though the advantages outweigh them. By understanding some of the shortcomings, a careful administrative planner can make them negligible. Some of these problems are listed below:

1. It is difficult to decide what is a meaningful program. Many people will be involved and all agreements will be made on the basis of consensus. Decision sharing will be done by some personnel who do not have all the information.
2. PPBS requires highly trained personnel, and there is still a paucity of such people. Specific technical skills are necessary, and few districts have the staffs to handle the transition to PPBS.
3. Few districts have access to electronic data processing equipment that is so essential to the proper use of PPBS.
4. The effectiveness of program budgeting is difficult to measure. Standardized tests are usually used, but they are based on objective measurement. PPBS involves subjectivity. Subjective evaluation instruments are rare, but they can and must be developed.
5. PPBS will add to a school district's costs, both in time and money. It will probably require an additional administrator to implement the program, and additional accounting equipment and procedures will be needed. Many highly paid hours will be spent to put PPBS into action, and it will probably take several years before a school district can design and implement a PPBS for its own use.
6. It is difficult to translate general terms into operational terms.

Summary

A school budget is a planned forecast and a systematized form of educational planning. In addition, it states in dollars and cents the philosophy of the school district.

Proper budgeting procedures furnish a test of school administration; hence, the preparation of the budget is extremely important. The three steps of budgetary development are (1) educational planning; (2) expenditure program planning; and (3) income planning. This should be done under the supervision of the school superintendent, but should also involve other school employees and should be a continuing year-round activity during which a detailed budget calendar should be followed.

The final budget should be a complete picture of the district's financial plans, with each item accompanied by an explanation; this constitutes a "performance budget." Two basic principles to be observed in budget presentation are to inform the public and to justify all requests.

After its adoption, the budget should be administered as approved, with any changes due to unforeseen circumstances requiring action by the school board. To facilitate such administration, an encumbered book-keeping system should be used.

Many districts are now moving to some form of a planning–programming–budgeting system, or a systems-analysis approach based on goal setting and long-term projections. It is output oriented, and divides its objectives into short-term and long-term categories. It can be administered either horizontally by autonomous administrators or vertically by one person. Usually a specially trained administrator must be employed when PPBS is installed.

Trends

The outworn conception of the budget as a static and unchanging device for balancing income with outgo is passing swiftly from the educational scene. Although still primarily an instrument of financial planning, the budget is undergoing a series of changes that seem certain to transform it into a tool of far greater educational value than it has ever been in the past.

TOWARD INCREASED PARTICIPATION IN BUDGET PLANNING. Democratic participation in all phases of school administration extends to the budget also. The more teachers, maintenance men, board members, and lay citizens who can be enticed into the complicated routine of budget preparation, the better the finished product is apt to be and the more firmly based the district's financial support is certain to become.

The era when the superintendent and the business manager put their heads together and produced an arbitrary budget based wholly on their particular concepts of good planning is gone in most parts of the country. Instead, a situation is prevailing in more and more school systems in which the superintendent and business manager act as leaders and coordinators of a district-wide program of budget planning. A budget prepared in this fashion is far more likely to embody a consensus of district thought and personnel needs than the older authoritarian document.

TOWARD CONTINUOUS BUDGET DEVELOPMENT. A budget should not be a spasmodic enterprise, suddenly activated as a result of the approach of a deadline. It should be a continuous activity. As soon as the board of education has placed its stamp of approval upon one budget, the committee on budgeting should immediately begin to lay the groundwork and to accumulate data needed for the next budget. Rather than having special budget meetings of the board a few weeks before the legal time limit expires, it is advisable to devote some time at each board meeting throughout the year to budgetary matters.

TOWARD GREATER EMPHASIS ON EDUCATIONAL PLANNING IN THE BUDGET. The trend here is definitely toward revamping the budget with a view toward making it an educational rather than a financial document. The goals and objectives of the district's policy should be set forth as justification for various expenditure items. The budget as an instrument of long-range planning is also an important tool in the modern educational arsenal. The implications attaching to this concept of the budget are profound, ranging from the positive need for wide participation in budget planning to the use of the annual budget as merely one in a series of building blocks toward the district's objectives.

TOWARD MORE DETAILED BUDGETING. Budgets of the future will be longer and more fully developed than is the case today. There is a trend toward justifying each item of expenditure that differs substantially from the previous year's, and toward providing space in the written budget for this to be done in writing. A breakdown of expenditure items in extreme detail is another trend in this general area, although one of doubtful value.

TOWARD PLANNING–PROGRAMMING–BUDGETING SYSTEMS. Budgets will be output oriented, based on systems analysis, consider continuous, multiyear planning, and aim at perceptible goals and objectives. Many people will be involved, and alternative plans will be developed. Evaluation of progress toward goals and objectives will be an integral part of the system. School boards and administrators will be held accountable for pre-set goals.

TOWARD COMPUTER-ASSISTED BUDGET TECHNOLOGY. As **PPBS** is adopted by school districts, computers must be utilized to perform the necessary tasks and analyses. Districts that cannot afford the luxury of their own computers will join with other districts and share in the use of common computers. Computer-assisted programs, whether for educational or business planning, will evolve slowly due to the cost of the necessary hardware and software.

TOWARD LENGTHENING OF THE TIME INVOLVED IN BUDGET PREPARATION. During the years ahead, more time and effort will be expended on some form of collective bargaining. Together with increasing voter resistance to higher school taxes, this will be one of the most important elements in the budgeting process.

Administrative Problems   In Basket

Problem 1

Mr. Richards is the principal of John Adams High School which has an enrollment of 1,800 students. In December, the business manager sent all department heads and principals forms on which to list their budget requests for the following school year in the areas of personnel needs, conference attendance, equipment replacement or repair, new equipment, new books and supplies, printed forms of all types, and building and ground repairs and replacement.

It was explained that because each department head and principal would probably not be able to get everything he wanted, he should list the requested items in priority order.

What procedure should Principal Richards use to determine his budget requests?
How should he go about setting his priorities?
*If conflicts arise between departments (athletic, foreign language, business
education, and vocational education) in establishing priorities, how might Mr.
Richards solve them?*

Problem 2

The Big Valley School District consists of 20 elementary schools, 4 junior high
schools, and 2 senior high schools, and has an enrollment of 25,000. After
lengthy consideration, the Board of Education and the Superintendent have
decided to institute a planning–programming–budgeting system (PPBS). Mr.
Murdock, the business manager, has been given the task of developing the system and of bringing his tentative plans to the Board of Education for discussion.

How should Mr. Murdock start?
What information will he need?
How should he suggest that the plan be integrated into the present system?
What time schedule should he recommend?

Selected References

DeYoung, C. A. *Budgeting in Public Schools.* New York: Doubleday and
Co., 1936.

Grose, C. H. "Educational Plan of the School Budget." *American School
Board Journal* 108 (February 1944).

Haggart, Sue A., ed. *Program Budgeting for School District Planning.* Englewood Cliffs, N.J.: Educational Technology Publications. Copyright 1972,
The Rand Corporation.

Hagman, H. L. *Administration of American Public Schools.* New York:
McGraw-Hill Book Co., 1951.

Hartley, Harry J. *Educational Planning–Programming–Budgeting: A Systems Approach.* Englewood Cliffs, N.J.: Prentice-Hall, 1968.

Kidd, J. R. *Financing Continuing Education.* New York: Scarecrow Press,
1962.

Knezevich, Stephen J., ed. *Administrative Technology and the School Executive.* Washington, D.C.: American Association of School Administrators,
1969.

Linn, Henry H., ed. *School Business Administration.* New York: The Ronald
Press Co., 1956.

Morphet, Edgar L.; Johns, Roe L.; and Reller, Theodore L. *Educational
Organization and Administration.* Englewood Cliffs, N.J.: Prentice-Hall,
1967.

MORT, PAUL R., and REUSSER, WALTER C. *Public School Finance.* New York: McGraw-Hill Book Co., 1941.

NELSON, D. LLOYD, and PURDY, WILLIAM M. *School Business Administration.* Lexington, Mass.: D.C. Heath and Co., 1971.

PARKER, STEPHENSON, "PPBS." *CTA Journal* 65 (May 1969).

"Program Budgeting Design for Schools Unveiled, with Much More Work Still to Go." *Nation's Schools* 84 (November 1969).

RATH, GUSTAVE J. "PPBS Is More Than a Budget: It's a Total Planning Process." *Nation's Schools* 82 (November 1968).

REEDER, WARD G. *The Fundamentals of Public School Administration.* New York: The Macmillan Co., 1958.

U.S. DEPARTMENT OF HEALTH, EDUCATION, AND WELFARE. *Financial Accounting for Local and State School Systems.* Washington, D.C.: U.S. Government Printing Office, 1960.

WILSON, ROBERT E. *The Modern School Superintendent.* New York: Harper & Row, 1960.

10

School Accounting Procedures

Accounting provides statistical information and data regarding the educational program, personnel, finances, and business procedures of a school district. It expresses the actual functioning of the budget throughout the school year. Good accounting practices furnish the means for appraisal and evaluation and help to build trust and confidence in the school district's programs and procedures. There are several essential parts to an accounting system and many records must be kept. The system should be kept as simple as possible, yet be adequate and well organized.

This chapter includes a discussion of the following topics:

Accurate Organization of Data
Controlling the Administration of the Budget
Adequacy, Simplicity, and Standardization in Accounting
Essential Parts of an Accounting System
Three Main Bases of an Accounting System
Receipts
Periodic Financial Statements
Cost Accounting
Internal Accounting
Food Services Accounting
Accounting Technology
Summary
Trends

Accurate Organization of Data

An accurate supply of information is essential to any business or profession, and education is no exception. There should be no place in thoughtful policymaking for vague guesses and estimates. Statistics, accurate and ample, are the building blocks of school administration; they provide the underlying skeleton upon which the remainder of the school program must depend. Administrators must rely upon accounting to provide such data.

In policymaking, for example, the selection and implementation of guiding principles based upon any information other than the most complete and reliable will be apt to result in confusion and internal conflict. Assuming that sound policies have been arrived at, any attempt to execute them without using statistics as a guide will result in confusion. In the area of appraisal, the use of accurate and detailed data is absolutely essential, unless the many phases of the school system are to be allowed to run themselves. Records should never be accumulated for their own sake, but as a measure of the efficiency of every material, every employee, and every process concerned with the running of the school system.

The following areas are largely dependent for smooth functioning on the keeping of complete records:

1. Certificated personnel: teachers, supervisors, administrators, nurses, attendance officers, counselors.
2. Classified personnel: maintenance men, custodians, transportation personnel, cooks and helpers, clerks, secretaries, lay helpers and aides, groundsmen.
3. Students.
4. Budgets.
5. Insurance.
6. Expenditures and receipts.
7. Internal accounts.
8. Books, supplies, equipment.
9. School property.
10. School bonds.[1]

---

[1] By permission of Macmillan Publishing Co., Inc., from *The Fundamentals of Public School Administration*, 4th ed. by Ward G. Reeder. Copyright © 1958 by Macmillan Publishing Co., Inc., p. 554.

Good accounting practices accomplish a number of purposes. They provide an accurate historical record of all the business procedures of a school district and information for board of education decisions. Because of annual audits, they assure that legal prescriptions have been met and public funds are safeguarded properly. They form a sound basis for improved administrative decisions because data is available for budget preparation and revision. Accounting procedures provide a public record of the stewardship charged with handling public funds. They provide the financial records for administering the educational program.

Controlling the Administration of the Budget

A central system of financial accounting should always be associated with the central budget for the annual operation of a school district. Accounting practices have differed widely from district to district, and good procedures have been nonexistent in many. It was not until 1957 that the first acceptable plan for standardizing accounting practices was developed when the U.S. Office of Education published *Handbook II, Financial Accounting for Local and State School Systems*. Many states have adopted variations of this standard form and provide them for the use of local school districts. More emphasis has been given to developing good accounting practices during the last few years. This has been brought about in part by the public demand that school districts be held accountable and publicize and justify their financial needs.

Because all accounting depends upon the accumulation and preservation of adequate records, it should be kept in mind that red tape for its own sake should be stringently avoided. Record keeping should be made as easy and simple as possible for all employees; in particular, reports should be regularly used and examined, so that employees will not have the feeling that no use is being made of their work. The collection of statistical data from school employees should be conducted in line with the following principles:

1. Make certain that the employees who make the reports know what use is being made of the reports.
2. Set and maintain reasonable deadlines for filing reports.
3. Do not ask for superfluous or unnecessary information.

4. Impress upon all persons concerned the importance of the reports and the need for accuracy.
5. Avoid the use of ambiguous report blanks.
6. Design report blanks so that they can be filled out in as brief a time and with as little effort as possible.
7. Endeavor to delegate all purely clerical work to a clerk.
8. Design reports and forms so that they can be adapted to the existing business office machines or computers.

Adequacy, Simplicity, and Standardization in Accounting

Adequacy in accounting implies a survey of all the necessary elements of a good system, and the inclusion of all these elements in the actual system adopted by the school business office. Simplicity becomes necessary in school accounting because of the frequent lack of professional accountants among the personnel who work with the books, and also because of the chronic shortage of time available to perform such work. Standardization is effected when the classification of the accounts achieves a wide degree of uniformity throughout all school systems and a similar degree of continuity from year to year.

In the past, such uniformity has been theoretical with some practical application. In accounting forms, definitions, and nomenclature, school financial-accounting systems have been widely and justly criticized for their lack of standardization. Although school accounting is similar to the practices used by government and business, it is not identical to either. Following New York's adoption of a uniform accounting system in 1916, most states have adopted similar systems that prescribe regulations for record keeping, official reports, auditing, purchasing, and payment procedures. More recently, state accounting manuals for school district use have been based on the standards developed in the U.S. Office of Education Handbook. Such uniformity gives rise to the following advantages:

1. Easier auditing of accounts, because auditors have to contend with only one kind of financial-accounting system.
2. Easier reporting by school officials to federal, state, and county authorities.

3. Easier comparison of financial practices in one district with those in others.
4. Easier training of school clerks and business personnel in financial-accounting methods.

Melbo lists standards for financial accounting, bookkeeping procedures, and handling of cash. These standards can be adapted for use in any school district.[2]

Recommended Standards for Financial Accounting

1. Financial statement regarding expenditures presented to board each month.
2. Unencumbered balance shown for each major account in financial statement.
3. Budgeted receipts, receipts, receipts to date, and revised estimated receipts for year included in financial statement.
4. Annual financial report provided board.
5. Financial statements provided for each fund.
6. Financial statements posted on bulletin board of each school.
7. Monthly collection report made to board.
8. Bank accounts (student body and cafeteria) reconciled monthly.
9. District books balanced with county offices monthly.
10. Principals informed each month regarding status of supply budgets.
11. Head of food services and school board informed each month regarding status of cafeteria account.
12. Cost-analysis reports provided for major functions.

Recommended Standards for Bookkeeping Procedures

1. Machine bookkeeping should be used. Larger districts are moving toward the use of computers that will make "double entry" bookkeeping a must.
2. All contracts and purchase orders should be encumbered as issued.
3. Utilities should be encumbered for each month at beginning of the year.
4. Appropriation accounts should be correlated with budget classifications.

---

[2] Irving R. Melbo et al., *Report of the Survey, Paramount Unified School District*, p. 80, 82, and 84.

5. All warrants should be posted immediately after receipt from county offices.
6. A receipt ledger should be maintained for each source of revenue.
7. Prior years' expenses should be recorded on separate ledger form.
8. The bookkeeper should be allowed sufficient time to post books daily without frequent interruptions.
9. The bookkeeping machine should be operated in a separate, sound-proof room adjacent to the other business offices.
10. Payment for materials should be charged to year in which they are received.
11. Double entry bookkeeping revealing cost of food, labor, etc., and showing exact financial condition each month should be used for the food service programs.
12. An appropriation ledger, a receipts ledger, and a general ledger should be maintained.

Recommended Standards for Handling Cash

1. Printed prenumbered receipts supplied in triplicate should be provided.
2. One person in each school designated to make all collections for school.
3. Record maintained by business office of all receipt books issued.
4. Collections turned into business office daily with duplicate copies of receipts.
5. Master receipt given by business office to schools for collections.
6. Original receipt given to person from whom collection is made; duplicate sent to business office with money; and triplicate kept in receipt book to be checked in to business office at end of fiscal year.
7. All collections deposited with county treasurer at least once a month.
8. All deposits made with county treasurer noted in board minutes.
9. No illegal collections.
10. All persons bonded who handle money.
11. Procedure established to differentiate between revenue receipts and abatements.
12. Procedure established to make sure all money due district is collected.
13. All sales authorized by board.
14. Bids obtained for sales in excess of $200.

15. Money collected for lost or damaged state textbooks sent to state department of education.
16. Securities deposited with county treasurer.

Essential Parts of an Accounting System

ORIGINAL RECORDS. First, original records must be preserved of all financial transactions, embracing two major types of data: those showing assets and liabilities, and those showing income and expenditures. To allow these two sets of data to be available at all times, the original documents should be filed by category and should include receipts, requisitions, purchase orders, invoices, cancelled checks, payroll lists, and any other evidence that will support financial transactions. Receipts should be given and copies retained for all monies received just as records are kept for all expenditures. Auditors find such original records indispensable to the proper performance of their annual duties.

VOUCHER RECORD. Some schools still utilize the daybook or journal for the retention of records. A more modern practice is the use of the voucher record, in the form of a book or sometimes an envelope wherein are filed the records to be kept, and on which is recorded the distribution of expenditures for later copying into the ledger.

LEDGER. This is the classified record of expenditures. It should be itemized in exact correspondence with the budget, only in vertical columns where the budget items are listed on horizontal lines. This is the portion of the system most prominently in need of the uniformity in accounting procedures which previously has been stressed as of the utmost importance. The standardized system of accounting described earlier in this chapter centers about the ledger, and is usually called the "National System." Its classifications should be synchronized completely with those of the district budget. A separate ledger form should be provided for each of the major classifications of the National System: administration, instruction, attendance and health services, pupil transportation services, operation of plant, maintenance of plant, fixed charges, food service and student body activities, community services, capital outlay, and debt service from current funds. Figures 10–1 and 10–2 show examples of actual school revenue and appropriation ledger forms.

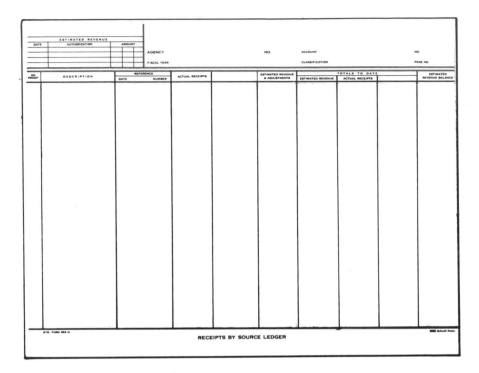

FIGURE 10–1. Example of a School Revenue Form. Courtesy of the Paramount Unified School District, Paramount, California.

Studies of unit costs are facilitated by the use of code numbers or letters as follows: elementary school expenditures are coded "E" and expenditures for high schools are coded "H." Similarly, coded numbers or letters can be applied to each of the many services, departments, or buildings of the school district. A more detailed coding system is the system originally developed by Engelhardt and Engelhardt, which provides a four-digit system from 1,000–2,000 for all receipts and revenues. In addition, the character classes of expenditures are subdivided and coded on the ledger sheets. General control is subdivided into two categories—business administration and educational administration. Under the former come columns headed "school elections," "school census," "board of education," and the like. Educational administration subdivides into "superintendent's salary," "superintendent's clerical help," "superintendent's supplies," and other expenses.

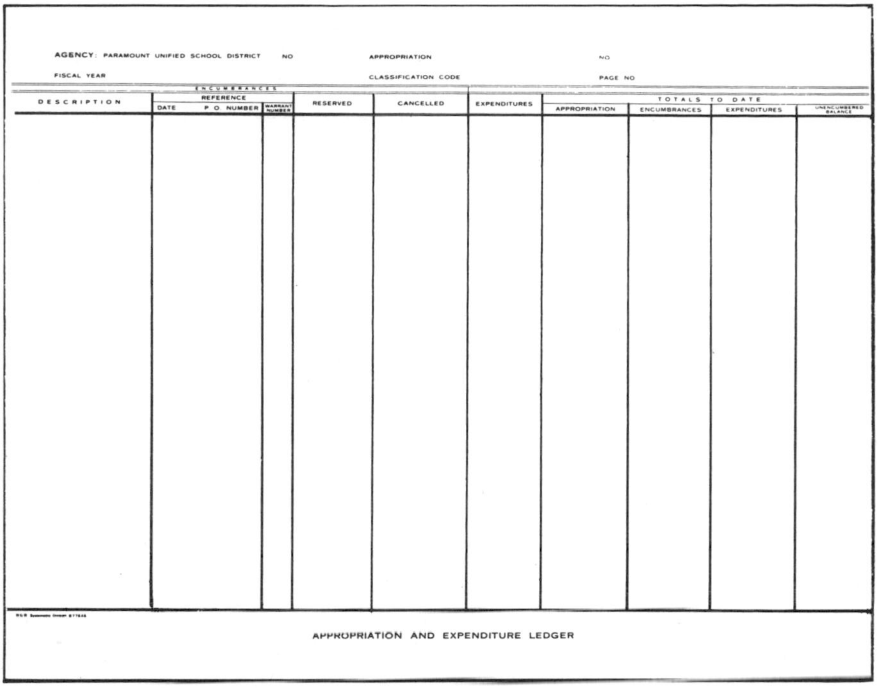

AGENCY: PARAMOUNT UNIFIED SCHOOL DISTRICT NO APPROPRIATION NO
FISCAL YEAR CLASSIFICATION CODE PAGE NO

DESCRIPTION	ENCUMBRANCES						TOTALS TO DATE			
	REFERENCE			RESERVED	CANCELLED	EXPENDITURES				
	DATE	P. O. NUMBER	WARRANT NUMBER				APPROPRIATION	ENCUMBRANCES	EXPENDITURES	UNENCUMBERED BALANCE

APPROPRIATION AND EXPENDITURE LEDGER

FIGURE 10–2. Example of an Appropriation and Expenditure Ledger Form. Courtesy of the Paramount Unified School District, Paramount, California.

Cash–Receipts Book. All revenues as they are made available to the district should be listed in a cash–receipts book. All entries should be made on a monthly basis, thus enabling the monthly financial statements to be at least partially based on the data contained in the cash–receipts book. Prenumbered receipts should be issued in triplicate: the original to the person from whom the collection was made, the second to the business office, and the third should remain in the receipt book. Figure 10–3 shows a sample page from a cash–receipts book.

Three Main Bases of an Accounting System

The Cash–Disbursements Basis. In a system organized upon this principle, only actual income and payments are considered and no account is taken of deferred payments, uncollected receipts, and short-term loans.

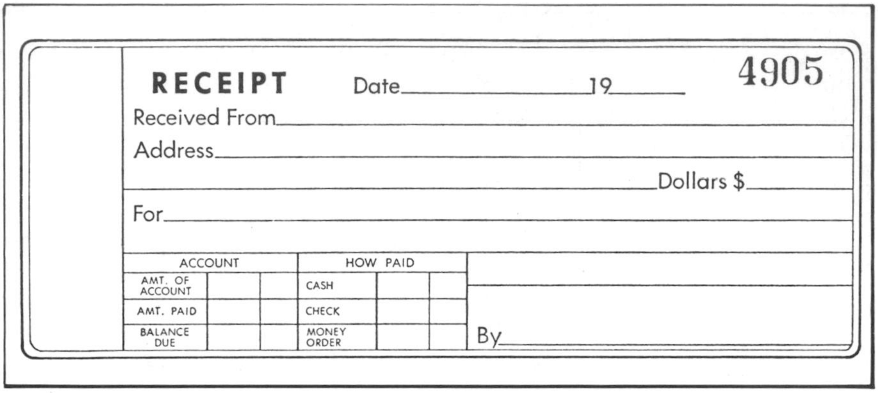

RECEIPT Date__________ 19____ 4905

Received From__________

Address__________

__________ Dollars $__________

For__________

ACCOUNT			HOW PAID			
AMT. OF ACCOUNT			CASH			
AMT. PAID			CHECK			
BALANCE DUE			MONEY ORDER			By__________

FIGURE 10–3. Sample Page from a Cash–Receipts Book. Courtesy of the Paramount Unified School District, Paramount, California.

Cost figures in this type of accounting include current costs plus cash payments for plant increase (such as site purchasing, equipment, and buildings, and the payment of interest on necessary loans). The cash basis is limited by many factors which combine to complicate obtaining a true picture of the district's financial condition. Wehn lists these unaccounted-for items as follows: state aid not yet received; tax collections still in arrears; collection of tuition from other school districts; payment of bills in a year subsequent to that in which they were incurred; underwriting costs of financing bonds; and others.[3]

THE ACCRUED–ECONOMIC–COST BASIS. This system takes into consideration everything that has worth or value, including all assets, accounts payable, and deferred payments. Cost reckoned on this basis includes current expense plus the interest on all capital invested and the annual depreciation on equipment and buildings. This method is the basis of business accounting, and enables one to know the true account chargeable to each year on account of operation and maintenance of the schools, together with the interest on the value of the plant in use.[4]

---

3 W. C. Wehn, "School Accounting on the Basis of Income and Expenditure," *American School Board Journal,* pp. 29–30.

4 G. D. Strayer and R. M. Haig, *The Financing of Education in the State of New York* (New York: The Educational Finance Inquiry Commission, 1923), pp. 36–38.

THE INCOME–AND–EXPENDITURE BASIS. This is the principle adopted by most of the standard school accounting methods. It represents a compromise between the cash-disbursement and the accrued-economic-cost basis; and it accounts for all actual and potential assets and liabilities, but does not usually attempt to estimate depreciation as an accounting factor.

In any discussion of desirable school accounting principles, it should be kept in mind that school accounts differ widely from business accounts in that proprietary interest does not apply. According to Mort and Reusser, it is desirable not to use the balance sheet, but rather to replace it by a statement of assets and liabilities. This statement is not in balance when such items as land, buildings, plant equipment, and educational equipment are added to the assets, while bonded indebtedness is added to the liabilities. The operating statement presents a picture of the financial status of the schools at any time.[5]

Receipts

In addition to listing receipts by the sources from which money has been received, it has been found useful to group them under the threefold classification of revenue receipts, non-revenue receipts, and revolving-fund receipts. Revenue receipts are those that do not result in increasing school indebtedness or in decreasing school assets; taxes are an example. Non-revenue receipts create an obligation which must be met at some future date. Insurance adjustment receipts and sale of property are examples of this kind of income. Revolving-fund receipts are so called because they include money received from services that the board renders as an agent. They may relate to cash that has already been obligated or expended for which an accounting must be made and for which a return is anticipated. Examples are the sale of textbooks or shop supplies by the district to pupils at cost.

Periodic Financial Statements

There are two types of financial statements that take stock periodically of the fiscal condition prevailing within the school district.

---

[5] P. R. Mort and W. C. Reusser, *Public School Finance,* pp. 211–12.

THE ANNUAL STATEMENT. A yearly financial statement, showing an itemization of the income and expenditures during the year just closed, is a legal requirement in most states. Usually published in a local newspaper or as a bulletin, this document interprets the financial condition of the school district to the general public. Accompanying it should be an auditor's statement to the effect that the accounts have been audited and that they are legally in order.

THE MONTHLY STATEMENT. This statement is a comparative device, showing appropriations compared with expenditures. It should be made either by the superintendent or the financial officer to the board of education, and should list the sources of income, the budget amount, and the budget available. Contractual and other planned expenditures should be handled on an encumbrance rather than on an actual disbursement basis. The encumbered column shows the amount expected to be paid when a contract or purchase order is made out. The expenditure column shows the amount actually expended after the bill is received. The unencumbered balance shows the amount that has no encumbrance against it. All existing liabilities are accounted for, thus serving to prevent the year's expenditures from exceeding appropriations. This type of statement enables school officials to keep informed of the status of school funds, and simultaneously to make comparisons of the finances with those of the preceding year or with earlier months of the current fiscal year. Examples of monthly district financial statements are given in Tables 10–1 and 10–2.

It is recommended, in addition to the financial statements described above, that the school district should prepare an annual balance statement at the end of each year. This would be merely a statement of assets compared with liabilities, contrasting positive factors—such as school sites, buildings, permanent equipment, taxes, and appropriations receivable—with such liabilities as accounts payable, bonded indebtedness, short-term loans, and interest payable. This has the inestimable advantage of confronting the taxpayer with a simple balance sheet instead of a bewildering array of figures and peculiar bookkeeping techniques wherein operating expenses are confused with capital expenditures, and the like.

AUDITING. Auditing of school funds is essential because it inspires public confidence, renders an account of stewardship, and improves procedures.[6]

---

[6] Melbo, *Report of the Survey, Paramount,* p. 85.

TABLE 10–1.   Monthly Income Statement Form

	BUDGETED INCOME	REVISED BUDGETED INCOME	RECEIPTS TO DATE	BALANCE
State Aid				
ADA				
Physically Handicapped				
Transportation				
Driver Education				
Current Growth				
Federal Money Received through State				
Federal Aid				
PL 874				
Vocational				
Other				
Tuition				
Regular Day Schools				
Adult Education				
Other				
District Taxes				
Secured Roll				
Unsecured Roll				
Prior Year				
In Lieu of Taxes				
Other Income				
Trailer Coach Fees				
Investment Earnings				
Rent from School Facilities				
Gifts and Bequests				
Miscellaneous Revenue				
Non-revenue Receipts				
Sale of Bonds				
Loans				
Sale of School Property				
Insurance Adjustments				
Totals				

The Association of School Business Officials has stated the following objectives for an audit program:

1.   To safeguard money, property, and employees.
2.   To determine the adequacy of the methods of internal check.

TABLE 10–2.   Monthly Budget Control Statement Form

	BUDGETED	ENCUMBERED	EXPENDED	UNENCUM-BERED BALANCE
Administration				
Certificated Salaries				
Other Salaries				
Other Expense				
Instruction				
Certificated Salaries				
Other Salaries				
Other Expense				
Auxiliary Services				
Certificated Salaries				
Abate from Elementary				
Other Salaries				
Other Expense				
Operation of School Plant				
Salaries and Wages				
Other Expense				
Maintenance of School Plant				
Salaries and Wages				
Other Expense				
Fixed Charges				
Transportation				
Salaries				
Other Expense				
Food Service				
Salaries and Wages				
Other Expense				
Community Services				
Salaries and Wages				
Other Expense				
Capital Outlay				
Land				
Improvement of Grounds				
Salaries and Wages				
Other Expense				
Buildings				
Salaries and Wages				
Other Expense				
Equipment				
Undistributed Reserve				
Totals				

3. To maintain adherence to the established standards, policies, and procedures—financial, accounting, and operating.
4. To check condition and use of property and equipment, particularly from the standpoint of adequate return.
5. To maintain and coordinate internal auditing procedures with those of the public accountant.
6. To present accurate, complete, and unbiased statistics with respect to the operation of the educational system.[7]

There are two types of audits: continuous and annual. In the case of the former, usually the school's regular business and financial officers conduct the audit, which goes on constantly as monthly and other short-term financial statements are made ready and tentative balances are arrived at.

The annual, or periodic, audit is preferably conducted by an agency independent of the school business office. A special agency appointed by the state department of education to audit all school district accounts would be the best solution to the problem of periodic auditing. Failing this, the use of the services of a certified public accountant is to be preferred. This has the disadvantage of being a paid service, with a resulting drain of district funds better spent on educational needs, and also of involving an accountant in a highly specialized area, namely school finance, where he may not have had any previous experience. A wise school district will select an auditing firm that is experienced and competent in auditing school accounting records.

Occasionally audits are performed by committees of school board members or by committees of laymen appointed by the board for that specific purpose. This method is pregnant with potential blunders and scarcely better than no audit at all.

In dealing with an auditor it is important to convince him of the necessity of confining his attentions to the functions of an audit. He is being paid to discover errors in the accounts, if any, and to expose any misuse of funds from a legal standpoint. He is not to succumb to the urge to deplore the wisdom of the board's judgment in spending funds. An auditor may also be employed successfully as a consultant in business practices and methods. School funds that are kept in a county treasury are already subject to at least one and frequently two audits. However, school

---

[7] Thor W. Bruce, "The Why and Where of Auditing," *Proceedings, the Association of School Business Officials,* p. 236.

district accounts that are maintained in banks should be audited more frequently than the funds mentioned above.

Cost Accounting

A school system bears sufficient resemblance to a well-administered private industry to render advisable periodic studies of the cost of its product and of the several processes which go to make up its internal functioning. The practical value of such studies to the school administrator lies in judging the adequacy of the financial support enjoyed by his district and in evaluating the distribution of expenditures among the various budgetary items.

UNIT COSTS.   The basis of cost accounting is unit costs.   Unit costs are determined by dividing the total cost of education, or any part of it, by the total units of school, classroom, child, etc.   According to Morphet, Johns, and Reller,

> Cost analysis is the process of studying total costs of public education for a given community, state, or district for a given year, trends in total school costs, the costs of specific services or subjects, the cost of education by grades or levels, cost of nonattendance, costs and ability, cost and size of school, reasons for increased costs, reasons for decreased costs, need for increased school costs, and need for decrease in school cost.[8]

Unit costs may be compared with corresponding costs for similar services at previous times and in different school districts.   One of the most popularly compared cost units is cost per child.   It may be compared, for instance, to similar cost units in other schools of the same general area, or, internally, cost per elementary child may be compared to cost per secondary child in the same system.   Such information will often make it possible for a school district to lower its costs without decreasing the quality of the service provided.   Costs, of course, should not be calculated for trivial items; only where the expenditure is large enough to make possible an economy that outweighs the expense of making the cost calculation should the operation be performed.

Several different types of unit-cost studies might be made.   As an

---

[8] Edgar L. Morphet, Roe L. Johns, and Theodore L. Reller, *Educational Administration: Concepts, Practices, and Issues* © 1959.   Reprinted by permission of Prentice-Hall Inc., Englewood Cliffs, New Jersey, p. 457.

example, a study might be made comparing cost per pupil for a certain kind of service with that for another kind of service in the district—e.g., teacher cost per pupil *v.* educational supply cost per pupil. Studies of the cost of furnishing particular supplies on a per-classroom basis are also common. Proportion of expenditures going for maintenance and operation within individual schools of a given system may also be of value, and may often be studied through some type of unit-cost approach. Cost analysis provides information for the school board, school administrators, the staff, and the public to evaluate the efficiency of various types of programs and operations.

There are two main problems to be solved in making a unit-cost study: (1) securing comparable and accurate data, and (2) determining the best cost unit for computing the cost of the particular item upon which information is desired.

COMPARATIVE COSTS. The evaluation of local levels of financial support usually can be conducted objectively only with the aid of comparative data from other school systems with similar characteristics and problems. Only with such information can a school administrator decide whether the amount spent upon a school system is sufficient, compared with the amounts spent upon other systems, and whether the amounts spent on different areas of the instructional program are properly proportioned.

The reliability of intersystem studies is sometimes difficult to establish because several items are not always reported in exactly the same way. It is generally better to attach more significance to comparative costs of different subjects in the same system than to comparisons between systems.

It is never wise for an administrator to attach too much importance to comparative cost data. Allocation of expenditures to the several classes may differ from district to district; school accountants may be inexperienced and make mistakes. The conditions that determine the appropriateness of any school expenditure differ from one part of the country to another, and often from one part of the same state to another. A district cannot be allowed to straitjacket itself within cost table norms when, in relation to local needs, its action may be completely wrong. However, comparative costs do make it easy for an administrator to identify quickly and accurately expenditures that are conspicuously too high or too low. This is all comparative cost accounting can do; it can never say by itself which expenditures are justified and which are not.

Internal Accounting

Certain extra-curricular activities are conducted by most secondary schools; virtually all such activities, in addition to those nonclassroom services provided by the schools, are revenue producing and revenue spending. Activities and activity centers such as lunchrooms, bookstores, athletics, school clubs, and publications create a problem of the management of nonpublic funds within the framework of district accounting. The need for the governing board to establish rules and regulations controlling the finances of these activities is obvious. Although the funds involved are not strictly public in nature, they necessarily fall within the purview of public interest. Inexperienced administrators have experienced difficulties in accounting for such funds, probably because the monies expended for these purposes are not commonly considered to be in the same category as district funds. Difficulties can be avoided by having such funds audited annually by the district auditor. This is a legal requirement in some states. The auditor can be of invaluable assistance in helping to establish proper controls that will prevent inadvertent or intentional misuse of such funds. Several methods have been developed to account for internal revenues and expenditures.

The traditional way was for boards of education to include such funds in the regular accounting systems by providing for a revolving-fund account; such an approach to the problem is not now recommended. It assumes that there is no distinction between these funds and those used by the school district for operational purposes and makes no provision for student participation in the handling of student money.

Many schools have elected to set up mechanisms to account for these funds separately. In many cases, they are placed under the supervision of the principal or a staff member who reports regularly to the board of education through the superintendent. Although this method distinguishes properly between "activity" and "general" funds, it does not encourage pupil participation.

A separate bank account is used by some schools. Receipts from all high school activities are deposited in the bank to the credit of the organizations raising the money. The student treasurer authorizes expenditures by means of vouchers signed by the faculty sponsor of the particular activity, and a complete accounting is required of all monies received and of all expenditures. The principal's office in such a plan usually is the central clearinghouse for all receipts and expenditures.

Probably the best plan centralizes all student activity funds in the central office, into which receipts from each activity are paid and a receipt form filled out and given to the treasurer of the organization. Activity vouchers, issued by the treasurer and adviser of each organization and countersigned by the treasurer of the activity fund, are used to authorize expenditures. A central office clerk can serve as treasurer for the funds of all activities from each school in the system. These are kept in a single bank account. A special ledger designed to keep track of the various school activities should be used. Monthly financial statements showing the status of the schools' student body funds should be made to the school board for their approval since ultimately they should be responsible for the supervision of these funds. Each student body organization should prepare a budget at the start of the fiscal year forecasting its expected receipts, needs, and expenditures.

Student body funds, which come primarily from students, should be used for the benefit of those students and not be permitted to accumulate for an indefinite future, which is often the case. They should not be used to purchase materials or equipment which the school district legally should provide. Because these are student body funds, students should have a strong voice in how they are collected, invested, banked, and dispersed. The principal or faculty sponsor serves as adviser, however, so that mismanagement does not occur.

Food Services Accounting

The school lunch program is monumental in size. Over three billion meals are served annually in the schools, providing over a billion dollar market for the nation's food industry.[9] Because of the scope of food services, more detailed accounting records usually are required than are necessary for ordinary internal accounting systems. The business management of the program should be centralized in the district office. All purchasing, fiscal accounting, property accounting, construction, maintenance, and employment of cafeteria personnel should be handled centrally to effect savings.[10]

---

[9] Robert E. Wilson, *Educational Administration,* p. 676.

[10] Wilson, *Educational Administration,* p. 676.

Accounting records consist of kitchen and service records, purchase orders, cash-record vouchers, and requisitions. Records and purchases of federal allocations of money and purchases of surplus foods also should be kept. Although cost accounts should be kept for each school's lunch program,

TABLE 10–3. *Food Service Statement of Operations*[a]

	NOVEMBER 1971 AMOUNT	YEAR TO DATE AMOUNT
Income		
Sales–Student Lunches		
Adult Lunches		
Milk		
Miscellaneous		
Banquets		
Total Food Sales		
Cost of Food Sales		
Food		
Disposables		
Total Cost of Food Sales		
Operating Expenses		
Payroll–Food Services		
Office		
Laundry		
Cleaning Supplies		
Pest Control		
Equipment Replacement		
Cash Over or Short		
Mileage		
Equipment Repair		
Equipment Rental		
Office Expense		
Theft and Vandalism		
Total Operating Expense		
Net Income from Operation		
Other Income		
National Lunch Program		
National Milk Program		
Head Start		
Free Lunches		
Total Other Income		
Net Income or Loss		

TABLE 10–3. *(Continued)*

	AMOUNTS
Assets	
Current Assets	
Change Fund	
Security Pacific Bank	
Accounts Receivable	
Inventory: Food	
Disposable Utensils	
Cleaning Supplies	
Due from National Lunch	
Due from National Milk	
Due from Head Start	
Due from Free Lunches	
Total Assets	
Liabilities	
Current Liabilities	
Accounts Payable	
Accrued Payroll	
Accrued Sales Tax	
Total Liabilities	
Fund Balance	
Cafeteria Fund July 1, 1971	
Net Income or Loss to Date	
Fund Balance	
Total Liabilities and Fund Balance	

[a] Melbo, *Report of the Survey, Paramount,* pp. 105–106.

the total program should be financed as one district account. Food services accounting is based more on a profit-and-loss basis than on a revenue-and-expenditure basis (more frequently characteristic of school finances). The governing criterion is the ability of the food services program to be self-supporting.[11]

The board of education should receive monthly and annual reports showing income, expenses, profit, and loss of the food services program. Table 10–3 is an example of such a report.

---

[11] Melbo, *Report of the Survey, Paramount,* p. 104.

Accounting Technology

Accounting practice has progressed toward automation. Few, if any, business offices do all their work by hand. In order of sophistication, accounting is handled mechanically, electromechanically, or electronically. The more sophisticated office machines become, the more they cost. This, as well as the lack of electronic "know-how" on the part of business managers, is a deterrent to the improvement of accounting procedures. Chapter 13 explains technological progress in more detail.

Summary

Accounting provides and organizes the statistical data needed for the administration of any school district. In addition, it provides the only device for controlling the administration of the budget. Problems involve avoiding unnecessary red tape while still keeping adequate records and reporting regularly.

Adequacy, simplicity, and standardization are the keys to good accounting, which is composed of several essential parts: original records, voucher record, ledger, and cash–receipts books. The accounting system should be founded on any one of three bases: cash disbursement, accrued economic cost, or income and expenditure.

Receipts should be classified by revenue sources, and periodic financial statements made to the school board by the administration, either annually or monthly. In either case, such statements should be audited.

Whatever accounting system is used, it should lend itself both to the determination of unit costs and comparative costs. Internal accounting should be careful and well organized, with special attention paid to the so-called extra-curricular programs that are so often poorly accounted for. The food service program, too, needs more detailed accounting records than are often kept.

Trends

The historical tendency of school accounting has long been in the direction of greater standardization and detail. As more and more money is poured into education, the demands on the bookkeeping and accounting departments of the myriad districts are bound to increase.

TOWARD ENCUMBRANCE BOOKKEEPING. Encumbrance bookkeeping deducts from the unspent balance column all committed and approved expenditures, as well as cash actually paid out. The advantage of this system is that it reveals at a glance the actual funds available for unplanned expenditures; these figures remain in the balance column. If approved expenditures are not encumbered and deducted, the balance column shows a misleading figure because part of the balance has already been committed and will be expended when the actual bill is received. School districts, many of which are able to employ only inexperienced accountants, are finding the practical advantages of this system sufficient to warrant the extra time involved in keeping the accounts. Under an encumbrance system, it is difficult if not impossible to end the fiscal year overdrawn in any budgetary category, unless knowingly intended.

TOWARD INCREASED CONTROL OVER EXTRA-CURRICULAR AND SPECIAL SERVICE FUNDS. The days of informal pupil–teacher administration of athletic, student store, and related funds are almost over. The trend is definitely toward the inclusion of such funds in the district-wide accounting system, but with combined organizational and school district control.

TOWARD INCREASED STANDARDIZATION OF SCHOOL DISTRICT ACCOUNTING SYSTEMS. The day seems to be approaching when most if not all American school districts will adopt some form of the so-called "National System" of school accounting. Under such a nationwide system, identical budget categories would be used, and unit-cost studies will be infinitely facilitated. Accountants changing positions and moving from one school district to another will have no trouble in taking over the books of the new district. Many economies and efficiencies will be made possible.

TOWARD THE INCOME-AND-EXPENDITURE BASIS FOR SCHOOL ACCOUNTING. The few school districts still using the cash–disbursement basis for their systems of school accounting will become even fewer in the years to come.

TOWARD COMPULSORY AUDITING OF SCHOOL ACCOUNTS BY IMPARTIAL EXPERTS. The trend is away from the informal board audits of the past, and in the direction of the use of certified public accountants for legally mandatory annual audits of all school district accounts.

TOWARD INCREASED USE OF ELECTRONIC ACCOUNTING EQUIPMENT. Sophisticated electronic equipment is becoming more readily available for accounting practices. Its use will be more widespread as business managers become more knowledgeable and school boards allot the necessary finances. Because of the cost, there will be cooperative arrangements made with other school districts, business firms, or regional agencies to purchase and share computer time.

Administrative Problem

Problem

Two small districts have just merged, forming the Lincoln Unified School District with 14 elementary schools, 2 junior high schools, and 1 senior high school. Previously, neither district had done any cost analysis, making it impossible for the new district to evaluate the distribution of expenditures among the various budgetary items.

Clifford Jacobson has been employed as the new accountant. The morning after one of the first Board of Education meetings, he found a note from the business manager on his desk. It stated that the Board wanted to commence a cost-analysis program to determine whether expenditures were being allotted wisely. The accountant was asked to develop a cost-analysis plan. As a first step, the note asked that he determine the unit cost of all instructional supplies and give the business manager a preliminary report in four weeks.

How should Clifford proceed?
What information will he need?
What new accounting machines and systems should Mr. Jacobson recommend for use in the merged district?

Selected References

BRUCE, THOR W. "The Why and Where of Auditing." *Proceedings, The Association of School Business Officials.* Chicago: Association of School Business Officials of United States and Canada, 1950.

GARVUE, RONERT J. *Modern Public School Finance.* New York: Macmillan Co., 1969.

HOLLEY, E. R. "Discussion of Accounting for Attendance and Health Services, Pupil Transportation, Food Services, and Student Body Activities." *Proceed-*

ings, The Association of School Business Officials. Chicago: Association of School Business Officials of United States and Canada, 1955.

HUMBLE, JOHN W. *Improving Business Results.* New York: McGraw-Hill Publishing Co., 1966.

IRVINE, W. H. "Extra-Curricular Funds Accounting in the Various States: Preliminary Report." *Principals' Bulletin,* National Association of Secondary Schools, 38 (March 1954).

MCLACHLAN, E. M. "Designing Your Accounting System to Fit Your Needs." *Proceedings, The Association of School Business Officials.* Chicago: Association of School Business Officials of United States and Canada, 1954.

MELBO, IRVING R., et al. *Report of the Survey, Paramount Unified School District.* Los Angeles: University of Southern California, 1970.

MORPHET, EDGAR L.; JOHNS, ROE L.; and RELLER, THEODORE L. *Educational Administration: Concepts, Practices, and Issues.* Englewood Cliffs, N.J.: Prentice-Hall, 1959.

MORT, PAUL R., and REUSSER, W. C. *Public School Finance.* New York: McGraw-Hill Book Co., 1941.

NELSON, D. LLOYD, and PURDY, WILLIAM M. *School Business Administration.* Lexington, Mass.: D. C. Heath and Co., 1971.

REASON, P. L. "New Financial Accounting Handbook." *Proceedings, The Association of School Business Officials.* Chicago: Association of School Business Officials of United States and Canada, 1956.

REEDER, WARD G. *The Fundamentals of Public School Administration.* 4th ed. New York: The Macmillan Co., 1958.

WILSON, ROBERT E. *Educational Administration.* Columbus, Ohio: Charles E. Merrill Publishing Co., 1966.

11

School Supply and Equipment Administration

Due to the proliferation of software and hardware and the increasing demands of teachers and administrators, modern supply and equipment management is a complex task. Logical, simple procedures should be cooperatively developed for selecting, purchasing, and handling supplies and equipment. Purchasing should be centralized and handled according to school board-adopted policies.

This chapter includes a discussion of the following topics:

Supply and Equipment Management
Selection of Supplies and Equipment
Centralized Supply Purchasing
School Board Purchasing Policies
Receiving Supplies
Supply Storage
Supply Requisitioning
Summary
Trends

Supply and Equipment Management

As is the case in most other school service areas, supply administration is moving rapidly from simplicity to complexity. Formerly, the methods followed in purchasing supplies and equipment were few and simple. Books, fuel, and furniture constituted the materials needed in a rural school, and in many instances some of these items were provided free of charge by the parents and citizens of the district.

Today, hundreds of different supply items may be discovered in the warehouses of a modern city school system, proof that the increasing specialization and size of education is being reflected in the complexity of supply administration. A sizable percentage of the annual expenditure of school systems is being spent for supplies and equipment.

Supplies may be defined as those items that are consumed or that enjoy a relatively short life, usually less than a year. Supplies may be divided into two categories, consumable and nonconsumable. Examples of consumable supplies are paper, pencils, and paints. Nonconsumable supplies are those that cost less than $10 and are not used up. Examples are small tools, scissors, staplers, and the like.[1]

Equipment refers to nonexpendable items which are more or less permanent, have a long life, and qualify as a capital expenditure. There are two categories of equipment, fixed and movable. Examples of fixed equipment are built-in clock systems, counters, cabinets, and communication systems. Movable equipment includes such items as large tools, office machines, and furniture.[2]

The importance of this area of school administration cannot be overemphasized. Such supplies and equipment are employed for the most part directly by the teacher, and their proper procurement and use are essential to the schools' primary function. Constant attention and study are needed to get such supply items delivered on schedule and to determine what types and brands of supplies and equipment are most effective and economical. In order to promote such study, the administrator should remember that the employees using these items in their daily work have a tremendous practical incentive to evaluate their effectiveness. He should promote in this area, as in all others, the principle of democratic participation in administrative activity. Here again the budget plays an important role in expressing a school district's educational program. Democratic staff participation in supply and equipment purchasing can be related to budget development.

TYPES OF SUPPLIES AND EQUIPMENT. There are numerous types of supplies and equipment which may be categorized as follows:

---

[1] Emery Stoops and Russell E. Johnson, *Elementary School Administration*, p. 176.

[2] Stoops and Johnson, *Elementary School*, p. 177.

General instructional, such as the various kinds and sizes of paper, paints, pencils, crayons, clips and fasteners, folders, and other similar items.

Audio-visual, including all types of projectors, maps, globes, charts, films, tape recorders and tapes, and pictures.

Science.

Music, art, and dramatics.

Books and periodicals.

Specialized supplies and equipment for special classes for the mentally retarded, the educationally handicapped, and the orthopedically handicapped.

Vocational education.

Business education.

Homemaking education.

Physical education and playground.

Health and nursing services.

Cafeteria.

Custodial.

Maintenance.

Gardening.

Transportation.

Lounges and faculty rooms.

Gymnasiums, auditoriums, and multipurpose rooms.

Libraries.

District office.

Other offices.

OPERATIONS FROM NEED TO RECEIPT OF AN ARTICLE.   Except for emergencies, supplies and equipment are ordered at specified intervals, either weekly or monthly.   This assists the principal, department head, and central office in combining the individual orders into one large, coordinated order.   The specific steps involved in ordering supplies and equipment are as follows:

1.   The individual schools, departments, and offices compile their list of needs.
2.   Requisitions are filled out and sent to the central business office.
3.   Centralized purchase orders are prepared and sent to the various vendors.   Budget control must be maintained.   Board of education authorization is needed before purchase—or ratification afterwards.

4. The articles are delivered to the district warehouse and thence to the various schools or departments. Upon receipt, they should be inventoried and checked against the purchase order.
5. Finally, distribution is made to the person ordering the article.

Melbo sets forth fifteen recommended standards for requisitioning and warehousing.[3] These standards apply to a district large enough to have a central warehouse:

1. District operates central warehouse.
2. Warehouse contains approximately one year's needs.
3. Perpetual inventory maintained in business office.
4. Requisitions issued by principals for all needs of each school.
5. One person responsible for warehouse receipts and deliveries.
6. Requisitioner informed of disposition of each requisition.
7. Separate requisition forms provided for warehouse items and "buy out" items.
8. Each school placed on budget basis for supplies.
9. Proper budget control exercised by business office.
10. Requisitioner provides helpful descriptive data but does not contact vendors.
11. Requisition forms printed, prenumbered, and supplied in quadruplicate.
12. Priced requisitions used.
13. Standard school supply list provided.
14. Daily deliveries provided.
15. Adequate supplies on hand for opening of school.

Selection of Supplies and Equipment

Many school systems today use teacher committees to study needs and to make specific recommendations for the purchase of particular items. Often such committees originally are designed to study curriculum problems, but find that their supply needs evolve naturally out of that study. A committee on textbooks will certainly select preferable texts as a result of

---

[3] Irving R. Melbo et al., *Report of the Survey, Paramount Unified School District,* published by authority of the Board of Trustees, Paramount Unified School District (Los Angeles: University of Southern California, 1970), p. 69.

its deliberations; one on audio-visual education will no doubt recommend certain films and slides. Large custodial staffs lend themselves to committee conferences that may be held as frequently as is found necessary to help in the selection of maintenance equipment and supplies. Even a small district can use consulting methods as a means of determining the kind of materials best suited to the needs of the schools.

The result of such cooperative action should be the preparation of standard supply lists that contain specifications for all items commonly used in schools. A school system should use as few kinds of supplies for a particular need as possible. Vendors customarily quote prices on a basis of quantity rather than on an individual item basis; it follows that the adoption of any policy that enables a school district to purchase items in greater quantity will result in considerable savings. Buying in this manner also simplifies warehousing and record keeping. Such standardization makes supply administration much easier, but carrying the process too far results in crippling needed educational services. For example, a supply item that may be suitable for a given subject or grade may be inappropriate for another.

Such standard supply lists call for careful appraisal of items and needs and for periodic revision. The teacher and classified employee committees who developed the lists originally should be asked to study them and to suggest revisions as they become desirable. The standard supply list should include the name of each supply item used in the school district and the grades or subjects for which the item is being ordered. A valuable aspect of the mimeographed list of standard supply items is its ability to function as a requisition form when checked by personnel and returned to the purchasing officer. Standard supply lists thus marked become the basis for the eventual reorder of supplies. It is helpful to have a supply list for each elementary school grade, and other lists for such special departments as custodial, clerical, and library.

Large districts find it profitable to conduct continuous experimentation to ascertain the quality of supply items. Most supplies are intended to be used only once; these supplies are usually the least expensive, capable of providing good service for a very brief period of time. Inasmuch as little research has been done in the area of quality and adequacy of an item, except by supply houses whose motives are biased, it behooves a school district spending thousands of dollars a year to put its own employee force to work evaluating this factor.

Consultation with employees who use certain supplies and equipment is necessary. Teachers should be asked about supplies which are to be used by them in the performance of their duties; custodians should be consulted about the type of supplies and equipment furnished them. Clerical employees should have a voice in the selection of stationery and carbon paper; bus drivers may be able to make valuable contributions in the area of motor oil and gasoline. As in all phases of school administration, the ultimate goal of cooperative supply selection is improvement of instruction. Improvement in methods of selection is based upon the following issues:

1. Determination of the relation of selection of equipment and supplies to the aims of education.
2. Determination of responsibility for selection.
3. Determination of the particular equipment and supplies needed.
4. Determination of the importance of the job analysis in the procedure of selection.
5. Determination of the characterisics of written specifications.
6. Determination of the quantity of equipment and supplies necessary per unit.[4]

A committee of teachers working with the purchasing agent or business manager should select classroom supplies with reference to the following criteria:

1. The curriculum offerings.
2. The methods used in presenting information.
3. Specialized usage.
4. Simplicity and practicality of usage.
5. Quality.
6. Economy.
7. Availability.

Such criteria should make possible a dual efficiency because they facilitate selections that can be used widely throughout the school system, and at the same time serve the purpose of the particular department that made the order. In order to ensure uniformity in the quality of equipment,

---

[4] R. W. Hibbert, "Improved Methods of Selecting Equipment and Supplies," *American School Board Journal* 95 (September 1937), p. 44.

it is necessary to set up specifications for each item. Such specifications are the definitions of the standards of quality desired for the particular items. In modern school districts, as we have stated, specifications are commonly developed by personnel committees working in conjunction with the business office. Specifications should be complete, especially when more than one firm is asked to bid on supplies or equipment. The construction, composition, and nature of the items ordered must be specified in such a situation. Supply and equipment committees may find it valuable to visit places where similar items are being used, survey catalogs from the various supply companies, schedule demonstrations, and talk to those who have used such supplies and equipment.

After supply criteria and standards are developed, the superintendent should submit them to the governing board for policy development and formation.

Requisition forms should be provided by the district so that employees can file requests for individual items of equipment or supplies. The following information should be included on all requisition forms:

1. Date of request.
2. Approval or disapproval.
3. Name of person making request.
4. School, room, or department for which item is ordered.
5. Source of supply.
6. Name and description of item.
7. Unit price.[5]

Usually, requisition forms are filled out in duplicate; one copy is returned to the originator following approval or disapproval, and the second sheet is kept by the business office until delivery of the item ordered.

Centralized Supply Purchasing

There is an advantage in giving one person the responsibility for purchasing all school district supplies and equipment: it provides for up-to-date budgetary accounting, economy, purchasing in accord with instructional needs, and maintenance of balance in supply provision to various school areas.

---

[5] H. L. Hagman, *Administration of American Public Schools,* p. 275.

The purchasing administrator has an exceedingly responsible position since he is held accountable for the expenditure of large sums of money. He should organize in a systematic way so that he can compile many requisitions into one purchase order, handle the purchasing, place bids as needed, inventory upon delivery, store and distribute many kinds of articles, and keep accurate records. "The purchasing officer needs to understand commercial transportation facilities and regulations, freight rates, shipping hazards, and packaging."[6] He must also have a knowledge of state laws regarding purchasing, contracts, and bids. He should understand how to purchase economically.[7]

School Board Purchasing Policies

Supply and equipment administration requires a well-planned purchasing program that has been approved by the board of education. Purchasing policies should be cooperatively adopted, but the purchasing administrator should initiate or approve all policies before they are presented to the school board because he will be responsible for carrying them out. Policies should spell out purchasing priorities in terms of educational objectives; the budgeting of supplies and equipment; the handling of local purchasing and vendors; how specifications are to be developed; and who is to make the final approval of requisitions before purchase. For example, should the assistant superintendent for instruction approve all educational requisitions before they are purchased? Procedures must be developed to carry out these policies. Finally, all policies and procedures must be communicated to all people so that there is no misunderstanding. Despite the fact that most authorities recommend board of education-approved policies, Pasnik found (1970) that only half of the 224 districts responding to a survey prescribed board of education regulations for purchasing procedures.[8]

One of the problems often overlooked in the development of standard procedures is the need for additional supplies and equipment when new rooms, new programs, and new schools are added. These contingencies should be planned far enough ahead for allowance to be made in the

---

[6] Edwin A. Fensch and Robert E. Wilson, *The Superintendency Team*, p. 219.

[7] Fensch and Wilson, *The Superintendency Team*, p. 219.

[8] Marion Pasnik, "Survey Evaluation of Purchasing Procedures," *School Management*, p. 20.

budget. There should also be a clear understanding of why these additional costs are needed.

Melbo recommends the following standards for purchasing which should be considered by boards of education and administrators:

1. All purchases approved or ratified by board and shown in minutes.
2. Printed, prenumbered purchase orders supplied in quadruplicate.
3. Preference to local merchants only when all factors are equal.
4. Purchasing centralized in business office.
5. Open charge accounts not used.
6. Blanket monthly purchase order used for frequent purchases with single vendor.
7. Purchasing needs consolidated.
8. Bids obtained when required by law.
9. Estimates obtained to justify minor purchasing when bids not necessary.
10. County purchasing used when advantageous.
11. Detailed specifications used when bids are taken.
12. Bids authorized by board, accepted by board, awarded by board, and shown in board minutes.
13. Cafeteria purchases meet spirit of legal requirements.
14. Standard school supply committee used.
15. Wise and efficient purchasing effected.
16. No improper interest in purchasing by board or employees.
17. Proper ethics observed.
18 Purchase orders should be issued for all purchases.
19. With only rare exception, purchase orders should be issued for known amounts.
20. Board policies established for purchasing.
21. Purchasing calendar used.
22. Purchasing accomplished in time to meet educational needs.
23. Purchase order forms should be designed to permit use of window envelopes.[9]

DETERMINATION OF QUANTITY. The best way to determine the amount of supplies to be purchased for a given year is to base the order on accurate information supplied by the various schools and departments. This infor-

_____
[9] Melbo, *Report of the Survey, Paramount*, p. 71.

mation should be gathered annually on the basis of a broad policy adopted by the board of education and administered by the superintendent or business manager. Policy should set forth who shall purchase; what amount of money shall be spent in any single transaction; what kind of supplies and equipment shall be purchased by the purchasing officer; what kind of reports shall be filed on purchases; and what the basis shall be for opening purchasing to bids. As a matter of course, board policy should remove board members.from any active purchasing, delegating such duties to the superintendent, who usually delegates these duties to a purchasing administrator.

If the proper supply inventory form has been used throughout the district, the supplies and equipment needed for the next fiscal year will be made known at the time of the annual inventory, usually in the spring. One form should be used; it will include a column on the left listing supplies currently on hand and another on the right indicating supplies that will be needed for the coming year. In estimating needs, the quantity used in preceding years should be kept in mind, together with such pertinent factors as projected enrollment and curriculum changes which may be contemplated. Such a form makes possible the correct appraisal of both current needs and available supplies, without the necessity of resorting to diverse reports or stapling inventories to estimate blanks.

In chapter 10, the importance of a plan of encumbering accounts is stressed. The purchasing officer should always enter the amount of money anticipated to be involved in the purchase in the encumbrance column of the account ledger. This should be done immediately after the expenditure has been authorized via the purchase order. As a result of this anticipatory procedure, sufficient funds will always remain in the budget allocation to pay the bill when it has been presented subsequent to the delivery of the purchase. It is difficult if not impossible to overdraw an account during the period between filling out the purchase order and paying the presented bill, if proper encumbrance procedures have been followed. The amount of the encumbrance involved in an uncompleted transaction is always deducted from the last entry in the balance column, thus enabling the state of the account to be seen at a glance.

It is probably unwise to purchase for more than a year ahead of current need, and uneconomical to purchase for less than that period. Should purchasing involve overly long time spans, deterioration of stored supplies may occur; an inability to take advantage of innovations and improvements in a supply category would also result. On the other hand, larger orders secure cheaper prices. A prudent solution to this dilemma would be to order all standard supplies one year in advance of current needs. This is especially advisable when, in addition to the price savings made possible by mass ordering, the saving of school officials' time in ordering, receiving, and checking is taken into consideration. Such annual ordering is particularly valuable for the smaller school districts, whereas the very large districts often can order semiannually and still effect considerable savings owing to the mass nature of such orders.

With respect to supplies and equipment, the superintendent should develop legal forms, approved by the county counsel.

Transactions involving large amounts of one kind of item are commonly arranged on the basis of bids submitted by the supply dealers to the school district. After lists of supplies and equipment have been drawn up and after quality and quantity standards have been set up, the district business manager submits the lists to supply houses and dealers for bids. He selects his contacts from a file of suppliers previously compiled and carefully screened for reliability and prompt service. The cooperation of vendors will be assumed if the purchasing administrator has established cordial relationships with them. Bids are called for to ensure competitive figures for exactly comparable items, thus gaining the advantage of the lowest possible cost for the district. Steps in calling for and receiving bids include:

1. Drawing of exact specifications as to quality and description of the item desired.
2. Publication of notice that sealed bids will be received.
3. Publication of the time and place at which bids will be opened.
4. Examination of the bids.
5. Awarding of the purchase contract to the bidder deemed by the board to be most likely to meet the specifications at the lowest price.[10]

A sample request for bid with instructions and conditions is found in Figure 11–1.

COOPERATIVE PLANNING. Neighboring school districts may legally cooperate in the purchasing of supplies. It is especially practical for small districts that have no occasion to order for themselves great amounts of

---

[10] Hagman, *Administration,* p. 277.

supplies at any one time to join together in such purchasing in order to take advantage of the large savings to be effected by volume purchasing. Some states actually compel the rural schools of a county to purchase their supplies cooperatively through the office of the county superintendent of schools or through the county purchasing agent. In Massachusetts, nine school districts combined their purchases and saved 75 percent over the cost of buying separately.[11] Others have reported savings of from 17 to 43.5 percent.[12] Districts that are contiguous to one another can cooperate not only with each other but with municipal and county governments in purchasing certain supplies, thus saving money for each of them.

PURCHASING AT PROPER TIMES. School systems are well advised to follow the example of industrial concerns in studying the supply market and placing orders during months when prices in certain areas are lowest. It is well known, for example, that staple school supply items such as pencils, paper, and ink are most expensive during the summer and fall and cost less during the spring. The following time schedule for the purchasing of supplies was recommended many years ago but is still applicable:

January 2. Start preparation of annual requisition for supplies.
January 3. Submit annual requisition estimate to principals for correction or approval.
February 5. Annual requisition to be returned to the assistant superintendent in charge of business affairs or to the business manager.
February 5–March 15. Preparation of bid forms.
March 15. Bid forms mailed to bidders.
April 15. Bids must be submitted by this date.
April 15–May 15. Tabulation of bids and examination of samples.
May 15. Recommendation to purchase submitted to board of education.
June 1. All purchase orders to be mailed before this date.[13]

School districts should allow for delays in delivery after purchase if factors such as the energy and fuel crisis and paper shortages of the early 1970s continue or return.

---

[11] Allan S. Hartman, "Saving Money Through Better Business Practices," *School Management,* p. 25.

[12] Aldan F. O'Hearn, "Cooperative Purchasing Pros and Cons," *48th Annual Volume of Proceedings,* p. 207.

[13] R. B. Taylor, *Principles of School Supply Management* (New York: Teachers College, Columbia University, 1926), pp. 90–91.

REQUEST FOR BID

ADDRESS ALL COMMUNICATIONS TO

BUSINESS OFFICE

SANTA MONICA UNIFIED SCHOOL DISTRICT

1723 Fourth Street
Santa Monica, California 90401

THIS IS NOT AN ORDER

GENTLEMEN: PLEASE QUOTE US YOUR LOWEST PRICE ON THE ITEMS BELOW

Bid No..............................

Page.................................

Date.................................

Firm Name and Mailing Address:

Delivered To:...

....

....

....

Bid Due ....

A check or bid bond must accompany this bid if your proposal totals $2500 or over.

Enclosed is Bidder's Check No.................................. Amount..................................

If you are not bidding or bidding on only a few items see Number 1 on reverse side.

Prices quoted must be net or discount must be based on payment within 30 days. No other discount will be considered in determining the net price.

Quantity More or Less	Description	Brand or Trade No.	Unit Price	Total Price

When bidding on electrical items, all regulations of the California Electrical Safety Orders 1965, must be fulfilled. (3-wire cord with a grounding plug)

WE AGREE TO FURNISH ABOVE ITEMS DELIVERED AS DESIGNATED, SUBJECT TO INSTRUCTIONS AND CONDITIONS ON REVERSE SIDE OF SHEET AND TERMS AND CONDITIONS BELOW:

Signature of Bidder...

Terms....................Delivery Date..................................

FIGURE 11–1.   Bidder's Agreement with Instructions and Conditions. Courtesy of the Santa Monica Unified School District, Santa Monica, California.

264

INSTRUCTIONS AND CONDITIONS

1. **BID PREPARATION:** This bid is sent to you in duplicate. Retain for your files the copy that does not have a flap attached and return the copy with the flap attached filling in completely the information called for on both the flap and bid form proper. Return only those pages on which you have bid. **Bid must be signed by a responsible officer or employee.** If not bidding on any items, return first sheet and state reason for not bidding; otherwise your name may be removed from our mailing list.

2. **PRICES:** All prices should be filled in (preferably typed) in duplicate according to instructions on the bid form. Quote each item separately on units specified in the bid form or on trade standards. Both unit price and extensions must be shown. In case of a discrepancy between the unit price and the extension, the unit price will be considered correct. Each item must be considered separately by the bidder and not in combination with other items, unless otherwise specified on bid form. Cash discounts may be taken into consideration in determining the lowest responsible bid.

3. **ERRORS AND CORRECTIONS:** No erasures permitted. Mistakes may be crossed out and corrections inserted adjacent and must be initialed in ink by person signing the bid. Verify your bids before submission as they cannot be withdrawn or corrected after being opened. The Board of Education will not be responsible for errors or omissions on the part of bidders in making up their bids.

4. **TAXES:** Do not include California State Sales or Use Tax in unit prices, said tax will be added and paid by the District. The Federal Excise Tax is not applicable as school districts are exempt therefrom.

5. **BRAND NAME AND NUMBER:** Brands of equal make or type which are substantially the same as specified are acceptable. Brands as listed on the bid form are given for descriptive purposes only. The bidder shall state the brand name and number in the column provided. If none is indicated, it shall be understood that the bidder is quoting on the exact brand name and number specified in the bid form. When bidding on brands or models other than specified, bidder must state on bid, brand, catalog number, and other trade designation, and submit brochures or information complete enough to fully describe the alternate item. Burden of proof as to equality of article shall rest with the bidder. Bids submitted without complete descriptive information may be rejected. The District reserves the right to determine the acceptability of alternate items offered.

6. **SAMPLES:** Samples, when required, must be furnished free of cost to the District. The District reserves the right to reject the bid of any bidder failing to submit samples as requested. Samples should be plainly marked with name of bidder, bid number, item number and description. The return of samples (if not destroyed in testing) shall be arranged by the bidder, at no cost to the District.

7. **CALIFORNIA ORIGIN:** In compliance with State of California Gov. Code Sections 4330 to 4334 inclusive, price, fitness, and quality being equal, preference shall be given to items produced wholly or partially within California, when such origin is stated by bidder.

8. **ACCEPTANCE OR REJECTION OF BIDS:** Bids shall remain open and valid and subject to acceptance anytime within 90 days after the bid opening date unless otherwise stipulated. The District may issue a purchase order for an individual item or combination of items whichever is to the best interest of the District; may reject any or all bids or any part of a bid; or may waive any informality in a bid.

9. **DELIVERY:** The supplier shall be responsible for delivery and shall pay all costs, including drayage, freight, and packing, **for delivery F.O.B. the District warehouse or to other points in the Santa Monica School District as may be specified in this bid form.** Each item shall be securely packed and clearly marked as to contents. All materials furnished must be assembled and ready for use, unless otherwise specified. All shipments shall be accompanied by a packing slip and the District purchase order number shall appear on all cases and packages. The right is reserved to reject and return at the risk and expense of the vendor such portion of any shipment which may be defective or fail to comply with specifications, without invalidating the remainder of the order.

10. **INVOICES AND PAYMENT:** Invoices shall be submitted in duplicate under the same firm name as shown on the purchase order. The District shall make payment for materials, supplies, or services furnished under the purchase order within a reasonable and proper time after acceptance thereof and approval of the invoices by the authorized District representative. Cash Discounts: All cash discounts shall be taken and computed from the date of delivery of acceptable material or the date of the receipt of invoices, whichever is the later. If corrections or replacements are required, cash discounts will be figured from the date of satisfactory delivery.

11. **HOLD HARMLESS CLAUSE:** The supplier shall hold harmless and indemnify the School District and the Santa Monica Board of Education, its officers and employees, from every claim or demand which may be made by reason of:

    (a) Any injury to person or property sustained by the supplier or by any person, firm, or corporation employed directly or indirectly by him upon or in connection with his performance under the purchase order, however caused.

    (b) Any injury to person or property sustained by any person, firm, or corporation, caused by any act, neglect, default, or omission of the supplier or of any person, firm, or corporation, directly or indirectly employed by him upon or in connection with his performance under the purchase order.

    (c) Any liability that may arise from the furnishing or use of any copyrighted or uncopyrighted composition, secret process, or patented or unpatented invention, under the purchase order.

12. **DEFAULT BY SUPPLIER:** If the supplier fails or neglects to furnish or deliver any of the materials, supplies, or services at the prices stated and in accordance with the terms and conditions of the bid and purchase order, the District may cancel the entire purchase order or any items affected by such default; may procure the articles or services from other sources and may deduct from any unpaid balance due the supplier or collect against the security, excess costs so paid. The prices paid by the District at the time such purchases are made shall be considered the prevailing market prices.

FIGURE 11–1. (Continued)

265

TAX EXEMPTIONS.   Although not all states provide for the same type of sales tax exemption, most school districts in the United States enjoy certain exemptions.   Since the payment of unnecessary taxes by school districts is not only illegal, but is a useless dilution of school wealth, it is very important that school administrators be aware of and exercise their districts' rightful exemptions.   Figure 11–2 is a standard form for Federal Excise Tax exemption and may be employed nationwide.

Receiving Supplies

One of the most important areas of supply administration is the establishment of proper machinery to ensure that the items received are those that were ordered originally, and that the amounts received match amounts ordered.   Large districts handling hundreds of thousands of dollars worth of supplies usually employ special checking clerks.   In smaller districts, the superintendent or business manager must perform this task.   There should be central receiving facilities available to ensure prompt delivery, inspection, and verification of the orders.   The best procedure to follow is to check the supplies received against the accompanying invoice to be sure of agreement, then to check the invoice against the copy of the purchase order retained by the school district, and finally against the requisitions that were combined to form the order. Delivery of the items ordered to the appropriate classroom or storeroom is made after these checking procedures.   When satisfied with the delivery, a copy of the purchase order should be signed by the warehouseman or clerk and returned to the district business office.

Payment for supplies after delivery should be conducted as follows:

1.   After billing is received on a given order, the total order is broken down by account categories in the distribution ledger, and each expenditure recorded in the proper category.
2.   The exact expenditure is entered next to the amount of the encumbrance in each affected budgetary category, and a new balance is then arrived at.
3.   A warrant is then made out to the supply house for the correct amount and submitted to the school board for approval before mailing.   The warrant number also should be indicated on the purchase order.
4.   At least two signatures should be required on each warrant.   Such a

PARAMOUNT UNIFIED SCHOOL DISTRICT

MEtcalf 0-3131

NEvada 6-8361

15110 South California

Paramount, California

EXEMPTION CERTIFICATE

(For Use by States, Territories, or Political Subdivision thereof, or the District of Columbia.)

...., 19........
DATE

The undersigned hereby certifies that he is ....
(TITLE OF OFFICER)

of PARAMOUNT UNIFIED SCHOOL DISTRICT and that he is authorized to execute this certificate and

that the article or articles specified in the accompanying order or on the reverse side hereof, are purchased from

....
(NAME OF COMPANY)

for the exclusive use of PARAMOUNT UNIFIED SCHOOL DISTRICT, STATE OF CALIFORNIA.
(GOVERNMENT UNIT)

It is understood that the exemption from tax in the case of sales of articles under this exemption certificate to States, etc., is limited to the sale of articles purchased for their exclusive use, and it is agreed that if articles purchased tax free under this exemption certificate are used otherwise or are sold to employee or others, such fact will be reported by me to the manufacturer of the article or articles covered by this certificate and/or items covered by retailers' excise tax should be reported and tax paid direct to the Collector of Internal Revenue for the district in which the sale was made. It is also understood that the fraudulent use of this certificate to secure exemption will subject the undersigned and all guilty parties to a fine of not more than $10,000, or to imprisonment for not more than five years, or both, together with costs of prosecution.

(Signature)..

....
PARAMOUNT UNIFIED SCHOOL DISTRICT

FIGURE 11–2.   *Federal Excise Tax Exemption Certificate for Use by States or Political Subdivisions Thereof. Courtesy of Paramount Unified School District, Paramount, California.*

267

precaution, added to monthly board approval, guards against double payment of a bill and all other incorrect disbursements.

Supply Storage

Frequency of use is the only significant criterion for measuring the effectiveness of a district's supply administration. The possession in sufficient quantities of instructional and operational supplies is no indication in itself of adequacy. The supplies must be quickly available to the teacher in the proper amounts and with as little effort as possible. Parsimony in supply matters results in hoarding by personnel; prodigality, on the other hand, inevitably produces extravagance.

There are two storage practices generally in use throughout the school districts of the nation; the central warehouse system, wherein the supplies for the entire school system are stored; and the system of storing the supplies in the school where they are to be used.

The central warehouse should be located near a railroad or major truck highway, and in fairly close proximity to the administration building or the main offices of the school district. It should be easily accessible to the firefighting equipment of the neighborhood, and in addition, should be equipped with an automatic sprinkler system of its own. Adequate shelving should be supplied, with proper indexing, and a shop or garage should be provided as an adjunct for the repair of district equipment and rolling stock. Supply stockrooms in the various schools are kept replenished by trucks operating out of the warehouse, and several weeks' supply of each standard item is customarily kept on hand in the smaller stockrooms of the individual schools. Usable equipment should at all times be stored in the places where it is needed, and only such items as replacement parts and equipment needing repair should concern the central warehouse. The records of a central warehouse should be set up in such a manner as to account both for the receipt of supplies and the issuance of them.

There are a number of advantages to centralized storage: deliveries are checked more easily; financial accounting and bill payments are facilitated; storage is more economical for quantity purchasing; inventories and record control are more efficient; and time and money are saved by reducing the need for many small purchases.[14]

---

[14] Edgar L. Morphet, Roe L. Johns, and Theodore L. Reller, *Educational Administration: Concepts, Practices, and Issues* © 1959. By permission of Prentice-Hall, Inc., Englewood Cliffs, New Jersey, p. 463.

Inventory on an annual basis is the most practical method to employ. A continuous inventory can be kept of all supplies on hand in the district warehouse, but this may take too much time and money to be worthwhile. An annual inventory can be kept in the warehouse or the business office on a card with columns for the date, the quantity received, the quantity delivered on requisition, and the balance in stock. Such an inventory makes it possible to anticipate needs well in advance.[15] Districts that use computers can handle inventory information more quickly and efficiently.

Formerly, in-school storage meant storage in the principal's office, from which supplies were sent as needed to the teachers' rooms. Today, most in-school storage is in stockrooms and custodial supply rooms, provided by the individual schools, where supplies are stored for a period of several weeks or months in advance of actual use. However, these rooms are not to be thought of as long-term reservoirs of supply materials. Teachers usually have supply cupboards in which to store supplies for daily use. Supplies kept in storage areas should be handled with the following general rules in mind:

1. Supplies should be stored uniformly and neatly on shelves or in bins in order to be issued and inventoried easily and to lessen the possibility of damage.
2. Old supplies and those with defective wrapping or containers should be placed on top or in front so that they can be issued first.
3. Each supply item should be perpetually inventoried.
4. The location of each supply item should be shown on a diagram in every storeroom or warehouse.[16]

Supply Requisitioning

A carefully formulated supply requisitioning system is needed in every school district. A few districts have utilized so-called automatic issuance of supplies to all teachers, custodians, and other employees at stated intervals, and the employee is expected to gauge his usage accordingly. This is a somewhat inflexible method, however; most districts utilize some sort of requisitioning plan.

---

[15] Morphet, Johns, and Reller, *Educational Administration,* p. 464.

[16] By permission of Macmillan Publishing Co., Inc., from *The Fundamentals of Public School Administration,* 4th ed. by Ward G. Reeder. Copyright © 1958 by Macmillan Publishing Co., Inc., p. 325.

The old philosophy of supply requisitioning held that material should never be allowed to leave either the general storehouse or the school supply room unless a properly signed and approved document had been exchanged for the item in question. Such a regulation is properly applied to a central warehousing situation, where supplies are issued in bulk to different schools in the district. However, the tendency in individual school stockrooms is toward the use of the "open" stockroom. In the latter case, teachers are relied upon to behave in a cooperative and professional manner, and to check out only supplies that they need for the proper functioning of their classes. In schools with open stockrooms, teachers are free to enter the supply headquarters of the school at any time and remove the items that they need, without being obliged to fill out any requisitions or reports of any kind.

In order to obtain nonstandard supplies, or items that are not customarily kept in the school supply room, a requisition of some kind is needed. Such a requisition is shown in Figure 11–3.

Supplies should be allocated to individual schools on the basis of the per-pupil share in the overall cost of the supplies. It is difficult and unfair to try to determine a common factor in the varying demands of teachers using the supplies. One teacher may use certain items more than another; or, one may rely more heavily upon the lavish use of various materials than another. Both may be excellent teachers, presenting above average class programs. The best basis on which to allocate school supplies appears to be the construction of a supply budget based on number of pupils rather than on teacher idiosyncrasies.

Summary

The increasing specialization in education is reflected in the complexity of supply administration. Since supplies and equipment are essential to the teacher and to the school's instruction program, the principle of democratic participation especially should apply to this field.

Efficient supply administration decreases the frequency of individual "emergency" orders and favors large, coordinated orders, thus achieving economy through volume purchasing. Any sizable school district can save money by establishing and maintaining its own central warehouse.

The selection of supplies and equipment should be a cooperative process, with maximum standardization of commonly used items being one

Stockroom Requisition

Business Office No.

School No.

Date

School..Dept. Head or Teacher................................
Signature

Department.. (Whenever possible use separate request for each account)

Quantity Requested		Quantity Issued	Stock Number	DESCRIPTION
Number	Unit of Issue			

K17 PF-6202540

Material Issued:

APPROVED:

Rec'd..

....
Principal or Supervisor

Date..

....
Department Director or Supervisor

ACCOUNT NUMBER

FIGURE 11–3. Standard Stock Requisition. Courtesy of the
Santa Monica Unified School District, Santa Monica, California.

271

of the main goals. Committees of both certificated and noncertificated employees should participate in this process of selecting and evaluating.

Unlike selection, purchasing should be centralized, with one person delegated the responsibility. He should operate within the scope of a well-planned purchasing program which has been approved by the local board of education, and should follow definite standards of purchasing.

Determination of the quantity of supplies to be purchased for a given year should be based on information supplied by the individual schools and departments. For any large purchases, competitive bids should be sought.

Neighboring school districts should cooperate in supply purchasing, and should place orders during months when prices in certain areas are lowest. In addition, setting up proper machinery to receive supplies and to match them with the original purchase orders is essential. In districts of any size, supplies should be stored in a central warehouse where a continuous inventory can be kept. Finally, an efficient supply requisitioning system should be established and adhered to.

Trends

The trends in school supply administration are generally in the direction of increased efficiency and flexibility, particularly in the impact of the supply system on the teaching program.

TOWARD INCREASED VARIETY IN SUPPLY AND EQUIPMENT ITEMS. The number of different items required in today's classrooms has multiplied greatly in the last few years, and there is no indication that this trend will not continue. The increasing complexity of the modern world makes it imperative that the schools reflect that complexity in their offerings and in their tools.

TOWARD MORE FREE SUPPLIES FOR PUPILS. Supply items such as pencils, ballpoint pens, and notebooks, which not too long ago were considered the personal property of the pupils and were expected to be furnished by them, are becoming suitable supplies for the schools to furnish without charge. The trend toward equalization in education extends to the issuance of supplies, and will become more marked. Eventually, everything the pupil needs in order to do successful school work will be furnished by the school at no charge to the pupil.

TOWARD COOPERATIVE EMPLOYEE SELECTION OF SUPPLIES AND EQUIP-
MENT. While actual purchasing will continue to be centralized, the selection of the items to be purchased will move inevitably in the direction of
group planning. It is only common sense to let custodial groups experiment and select their own supplies, and to allow teachers to evaluate the
many items used by them in the performance of their duties. The
recommendation to purchase supplies should emanate from appropriate
employee committees.

TOWARD THE USE OF STANDARD SUPPLY LISTS. The result of the planning of employee groups will be the formulation of standard lists of
supplies, evaluated and selected as optimum for the schools concerned.
These lists will be used for all ordering of standard items.

TOWARD THE USE OF A COMBINED ANNUAL INVENTORY AND SUPPLY
ESTIMATE LIST. The teacher's convenience in taking an annual inventory
of his classroom supplies and on the same form indicating his future needs
in each category is obvious. The same advantage in ordering supplies
accrues to other employees, such as clerks and custodians.

TOWARD ORDERING SUPPLIES ON AN ANNUAL BASIS. The waste involved
by small school districts in ordering supplies more often than once a year
will become increasingly apparent. All that is needed to make annual
ordering possible is more efficient planning on the part of the employees
and the administration.

TOWARD COOPERATIVE VOLUME PURCHASING BY NEIGHBORING SCHOOL
DISTRICTS. Economies implicit in cooperative purchasing, either through
a county purchasing office or through voluntary associations of districts,
will tend to become important enough to overcome the provincialism
inherent in many school districts.

TOWARD THE USE OF THE OPEN STOCKROOM IN INDIVIDUAL SCHOOLS.
The trend toward the establishment of open stockrooms eliminates much
paper work and a lot of wasted time. Professional persons should be
trusted to take freely only such supply items as their children need to do
the job at hand; teachers who abuse the open stockroom privilege should
be educated to its advantages. This same principle applies to other school
employees.

Toward the Increasing Use of Computers in Supply and Equipment Administration. The amount of bookkeeping and records that is so essential to the administration of supplies and equipment usually requires an inordinate amount of time from those who are responsible; it also requires costly clerical assistance. As more and more districts purchase computers or share computer time with other districts or agencies, supply and equipment administration will be computerized. This will make requisitioning, purchasing, inventorying, and record keeping more efficient and more accurate. Information will become more readily available for budgeting and for anticipating needs.

Administrative Problems

In Basket

Problem 1

Assume that you are a junior high school principal in a small unified school district that has never used standard supply lists. Your new superintendent believes that such lists have many benefits and will lead to quality control. At a weekly administrative council meeting, he has asked you to form a committee and develop standard supply lists for educational supplies, secretarial and clerical supplies, and custodial supplies.

How would you organize your committee?
Which personnel would you select?
How would you proceed?
What criteria would you develop?
What problems do you foresee?

Problem 2

As the new principal of Truman Elementary School, you find that your school has always had a "closed" stockroom for supplies. Every other Friday, teachers fill out a supply requisition and turn it in to the school office. Henry Robinson, a sixth grade teacher, has charge of filling the requisitions and seeing that they are delivered to each classroom. He uses students to help him and to deliver the supplies. Sometimes, he is so busy that he has another teacher, the school secretary, or a custodian help.

In case of emergency, a teacher can place a special order for Henry to fill. Since he never complains, teachers take advantage of him; nearly every day he has one or more "emergency" orders to fill. This takes time after school hours and interferes with pupil conferences, lesson planning, and grading papers. Sometimes he gives his class an assignment and takes one or two of his best pupils to the stockroom during school hours to fill requisitions.

As the new principal, you see many problems in the present system and decide to have an open stockroom.

What procedure will you use in setting up an open stockroom?
What information would you give your teachers?
What problems might arise when you change from a "closed" to an "open" stockroom? How would you solve them?
How would you keep an up-to-date inventory?

Selected References

ALLASINA, T. A. "Open Door Policy on Instructional Materials." *National Elementary Principal* 36 (September 1957): 167–169.

CROSBY, R. "Centralized Purchasing Improves Control." *Association of School Business Officials of the United States and Canada, Research Bulletin* 22 (August 1954): 112–114.

FENSCH, EDWIN A., and WILSON, ROBERT E. *The Superintendency Team.* Columbus, Ohio: Charles E. Merrill Publishing Co., 1964.

HAGMAN, H. L. *Administration of American Public Schools.* New York: McGraw-Hill Book Co., 1951.

HARTMAN, ALLAN S. "Saving Money Through Better Business Practices." *School Management* 14 (December 1970).

MELBO, IRVING R., et al. *Report of the Survey, Paramount Unified School District.* Los Angeles: University of Southern California, 1970.

MORPHET, EDGAR L.; JOHNS, ROE L.; and RELLER, THEODORE L. *Educational Administration: Concepts, Practices, and Issues.* Englewood Cliffs, N.J.: Prentice-Hall, 1959.

NELSON, D. LLOYD, and PURDY, WILLIAM M. *School Business Administration.* Lexington, Mass.: D. C. Heath and Co., 1971.

O'HEARN, ALDAN F. "Cooperative Purchasing Pros and Cons." *48th Annual Volume of Proceedings.* Chicago: Association of School Business Officials, International, 1962.

PASNIK, MARION. "Survey Evaluation of Purchasing Procedures." *School Management* 14 (December 1970).

REEDER, WARD G. *The Fundamentals of Public School Administration.* 4th ed. New York: The Macmillan Co., 1958.

RICKETTS, R. S. "New Treatments, Supplies, Equipment, and Replacements." *Association of School Business Officials of the United States and Canada, Research Bulletin* 26 (1955): 88–91.

"Standardization of School Materials." *Association of School Business Officials of the United States and Canada, Research Bulletin* 22 (August 1954): 109–136.

STOOPS, EMERY, and JOHNSON, RUSSELL E. *Elementary School Administration.* New York: McGraw-Hill Book Co., 1967.

12

School Insurance

Insurance has become a major financial burden of school districts, and its cost is continuously rising. Employees are demanding more and more insurance protection of all types. Vandalism and arson have become more prevalent, causing a rise in insurance rates and needs.

This chapter includes a discussion of the following topics:

The Need for School Insurance
Protection of School Property
Fire Insurance Program
Types of Fire Insurance
Local Conditions and Fire Insurance Policy
Steps to Reduce Fire Insurance Costs
Comprehensive Liability and Property Damage Insurance
Workmen's Compensation Insurance
Fidelity Bond Coverage
Optional Insurance
Liability of School Districts
Insuring Public Property in a Common Fund
Insuring Employee Welfare
Summary
Trends

Material for this chapter was prepared in collaboration with Lewis Weldon, President of Employee Security Plans, Inc., Encino, California.

The Need for School Insurance

There are two main types of school insurance: (1) policies having to do with casualty, property, or liability insurance and (2) policies dealing with the wide spectrum of the health and welfare of school employees. The purchase of insurance by school districts is taken as a matter of course today, but in the past, particularly in the property, casualty, and liability fields, it was considered by many to be a dubious expenditure of public funds. A liberalization of court opinion and public sentiment has brought about a general desire to soften the blow occasioned by accidents involving innocent people. And a prudent desire to safeguard the tremendous capital investment represented by school plants has completed the acceptance of the insurance principle, particularly in the field of liability insurance. Likewise, the universal practice of inviting insurance companies and underwriters to participate in plant safety programs and in plans for new construction has resulted in the lowering of fire insurance premiums; better construction has similarly decreased the number of serious school fires and other calamities.

Policies of insurance involving the protection of school plants and equipment have become an integral part of the budgeting and financing of school districts. While the need for this type of insurance is readily discernible, there is dispute over the legitimacy of a need for policy coverage of the health and welfare needs of school employees, the premiums of which are paid by the school district. Nevertheless, policies of insurance covering employees have become a major part of the school insurance portfolio. The expansion of health and welfare insurance programs has been brought about by employee negotiation.

The only alternative to insuring school property is the creation and maintenance of a cash reserve fund by the district. Formerly, some large city districts avoided heavy insurance commitments on the grounds that their replacement program was a continuous one, and that it was actually cheaper to replace buildings damaged or destroyed than to pay many thousands of dollars in annual insurance premiums. Such an argument is seldom heard today except in the largest districts of the nation.

There are, of course, disadvantages to the insurance reserve fund in that it serves to put the school district into the banking business, takes large numbers of tax dollars out of circulation and immobilizes them against the possibility of future emergency need. A more serious objection is based on the tendency for the reserve fund to penalize the current generation of taxpayers for the benefit of their successors. The reliance upon insurance, with its annual premium, spreads insurance costs more equally among its beneficiaries.

The same arguments as those against insurance reserve funds hold true for policies covering the health and welfare of employees.

Protection of School Property

The various kinds of insurance that may be carried by school districts are dependent primarily upon the laws of the state. Assuming that permissive legislation exists, it is wise to carry certain types of insurance whenever the risk of loss is too large for the district to assume. A logical corollary to this rule is that small districts are in much greater need of insurance than are their larger neighbors.

NECESSARY INSURANCE. The following types of insurance should be carried by most school districts:

1. Fire insurance and extended coverage on buildings and contents. Replacement insurance should be considered.
2. Comprehensive liability and property damage insurance.
3. Workmen's compensation insurance.
4. Broad form monies and securities.
5. Vehicle insurance.[1]

OPTIONAL INSURANCE. Under certain circumstances, it is advisable for school districts to carry one or more of the following types of insurance:

1. All risk coverage, on specified items.
2. All risk coverage, such as musical instrument floater policy.
3. Plate glass policy.
4. Open stock burglary with theft endorsement.
5. Vandalism coverage as a part of the fire insurance program.
6. Boiler insurance.
7. Fidelity bond.

---

[1] Irving R. Melbo et al., *Report of the Survey, Antelope Valley Joint Union High School District,* p. 110.

Fire Insurance Program

Every school district needs fire insurance. In order to secure proper and economical coverage, the following steps should be taken in the order listed:

1. Place responsibility for handling the school district's insurance.
2. Secure a reliable appraisal of property to determine insurable values.
3. Determine the method to be used in insuring the building and contents.
4. Develop a school form.
5. Obtain all possible rate deductions.
6. Maintain adequate records.
7. Establish an equitable plan for distributing insurance to companies and agents.
8. Obtain maximum adjustments on fire losses.[2]

Types of Fire Insurance

In deciding what type of fire insurance to procure for a given school district, the administrator should consider the following varieties.

FULL-VALUE, OR FLAT, INSURANCE. Before deciding whether or not to obtain full-value insurance, it is necessary to clarify what is meant by "full value" in the particular district. Factors such as the distribution of school property, the peculiar hazards involved, and the size and wealth of the district affect the amount of insurance which should prudently be carried. "Full value" would be the ideal goal, but for several reasons it may be difficult to achieve. The formula often used is that obtained by subtracting from a carefully determined estimate of the costs of replacement an equally carefully determined estimate of actual depreciation. A simpler method is to base real value upon an appraisal of the probable cost of replacement only. In most cases, considerable savings in premiums can be effected by insuring property for somewhat less than the "full value."

COINSURANCE. There is a common misunderstanding about coinsurance, to the effect that, in any loss, the insured must automatically pay a certain

---

[2] H. H. Linn and S. C. Joyner, *Insurance Practices in School Administration,* p. 76.

percent, with the remainder shouldered by the insurance company. As Joyner points out, this concept is erroneous; insurance companies will meet the loss up to the amount of the policy, if the insured has followed the requirement that the amount of insurance actually carried corresponds with the amount required to be carried.[3] Actually, coinsurance simply provides that the greater the amount of insurance carried on a risk relative to its full insurable value, the lower the insurance rate per unit of value. Except in the rare event of a 100 percent loss, coinsurance is by far the best bargain. The following formula[4] shows how coinsurance operates in case of a loss:

$$\frac{\text{Amount of insurance carried}}{\text{Amount required by form}} \times \text{Loss} = \text{Recovery up to face of policy}$$

"PROBABLE LOSS" INSURANCE. A relatively small number of school districts insure without reference to full value. Some insure only their most hazardous risks, while others try to estimate "probable loss" and carry a small amount on each property. This is, of course, an imprudent method of insuring. Small premium savings may be effected, but the danger of a major loss which would be inadequately covered by insurance is so preponderant, it renders this course of action unwise.

Local Conditions and Fire Insurance Policy

The particular situation in which a school district finds itself often determines the kind of insurance that should be purchased. For example, non-fireproof buildings need to be insured at a higher percentage of full value than do steel and concrete structures. The more buildings owned by the school district, the more justified would be the purchase of some type of coinsurance policy. The nature of the community enters into the picture, also. A city with ultra-modern fire equipment and safety devices lends itself to coinsurance; a rural school, isolated and remote from firefighting apparatus, requires coverage by a flat policy.

---

[3] Linn and Joyner, *Insurance Practices,* pp. 88–89.
[4] Linn and Joyner, *Insurance Practices,* p. 90.

Steps to Reduce Fire Insurance Costs

Although insurance rates are tending more and more to become standardized and fixed by statute, it is possible for well-managed school districts to keep their insurance costs at a reasonable level.

REGULAR APPRAISALS. Insurance values should be determined by a reputable appraisal firm and kept up to date on an annual basis. A good plan provides for a complete appraisal once every five years, with annual appraisal checks on a revolving basis. It has been shown that it is a common practice for school boards to pay insurance premiums on amounts greater than those that could be collected in case the property were destroyed.[5] Frequent and accurate appraisals on the school property would assist in eliminating this source of waste.

The first step in appraisal is to fix the replacement cost of the property. Unit costs must be determined by establishing values for the different materials used in the building under consideration; from such costs, values for such portions of the structure as roof, floors, walls, and stairs are established. The cost of labor in the community in question enters into the final figure arrived at. After figuring the replacement value of the different building parts, it is then necessary to establish similar figures for fixtures and equipment in much the same manner. After these replacement values have been established, the depreciation is then deducted from the amounts decided upon. Serviceability as foreseen in the future may be as important a factor in such calculations as are age and obsolescence.

The figure reached by subtracting depreciation from the replacement value is termed the *sound value* of the property. To arrive at the *insurable value,* the cost of excavations and foundation work must then be deducted from the sound value.

REMOVAL OF FIRE HAZARDS. While it is true that school buildings are relatively free from fire hazards compared with other structures, school fires do continue to occur, illustrating the need for active and increasing fire prevention techniques. Virtually all fires are preventable; even those caused by lightning may be avoided by correctly installed and maintained

---

[5] Warren S. Holmes, "How the Cost of Insurance of Public School Property Can Be Reduced," *American School Board Journal* 87 (August 1933), pp. 23–24.

lightning rods. The first step in any campaign to reduce insurance costs by eliminating fires must be diagnosis. A generation ago, defective heating plants, poorly installed and maintained chimneys, and bad flues accounted for 25 percent of all fires, with defective electrical wiring as another major cause.[6] There is no reason to believe that these causes of school fires have changed in order of importance during the intervening years. Since electrical wiring and the heating system are leaders in causing school fires, the installation of these items should be carefully inspected, and their later maintenance scrupulously conducted. District employees can take an active part in the following additional fire precautions:

1. Eliminate the accumulation of rubbish in any area of the school plant.
2. Provide fireproof receptacles for all matches, paper, and other combustible materials.
3. Provide safe storage facilities for materials used in laboratories, shops, and home economics classrooms.
4. Provide each department and corridor with chemical extinguishers.
5. Sponsor regular "cleanup weeks," when all above precautions are especially stressed.
6. Strictly enforce fire prevention regulations applying to both the adult and pupil personnel of a school.

PERIODIC INSPECTIONS. The National Board of Fire Underwriters has prepared a form to be used for self-inspection by school districts to check on elimination of fire hazards (*see* Figure 12–1). While such inspections are often made by the director of maintenance and operations, or someone in a similar capacity from the district's business office, it is better from every standpoint that the inspector be an employee of the local fire department.

TRAINING IN USE OF FIREFIGHTING EQUIPMENT. The first three minutes of a fire are by far the most important from a control standpoint. It is important that all school employees are trained in the use of whatever firefighting apparatus may be at hand. No longer can the maintenance and custodial employees be relied upon to be in the proper spot when a fire

---

[6] W. T. Melchior, *Insuring Public School Property* (New York: Teachers College, Columbia University, 1925), p. 122.

occurs. It is far more likely that the employee nearest to a nascent blaze will be a teacher, a secretary, or a cafeteria cook. Once this is acknowledged, it becomes obvious that all district employees should be properly instructed in firefighting techniques.

FIRE DRILLS. Fires occurring in school buildings that result in loss of life fortunately have been rare. Nevertheless, they have happened, usually as the result of gas or boiler explosions. It is essential, therefore, that pupils and school employees be properly instructed in a routine to be followed in case of fire. Most states now require such drills in all schools on an average of once a month. Fire drills should be completely standardized throughout the district, and should be as parallel as possible to the standard procedure followed elsewhere in the state.

Each teacher should be held responsible for imparting fire drill instructions to all children in his charge. Fire drill instructions in brief form should be posted permanently in each room. They should be called to the children's attention frequently and mastered by them. Drills should be arranged so that they will ensure orderly, rapid evacuation of the building under any condition of the school day. It is advisable for the principal to keep a record of the date and time of every drill as well as a comment regarding its effectiveness. The following is an example of an evacuation order which can be used, not only for fire drills, but also for bomb threats.[7]

Example of an Evacuation Order

EVACUATION ORDER FOR ROBERT E. LEE HIGH SCHOOL

A. Explanation of Evacuation Signals
   1. A rapid ringing of bell is the signal to evacuate the building.
   2. *One* long ring of the bell is the signal to stop.
   3. *Two* long rings of the bell is the signal to move forward.
   4. *Three* long rings of the bell is the signal to return to classrooms.

B. Evacuation Procedure
   1. Close all outside windows.
   2. Close transom windows.
   3. Close door after room has been emptied.

---

[7] Clinton Carter, *Evacuation Order* (Montgomery, Ala.: Robert E. Lee High School, 1971).

Prepared by **ENGINEERING & SAFETY DEPARTMENT**
AMERICAN INSURANCE ASSOCIATION
New York   Chicago   San Francisco
Approved and Adopted by
The Association of School Business Officials of the
     United States and Canada
Endorsed by the
International Association of Fire Chiefs

INSPECTION BLANK FOR SCHOOLS

> If precautions are taken to minimize the danger of fire and to provide for safety in case fire occurs, real progress will be made in safeguarding life and protecting property. Intelligent thought and care in practice can eliminate practically all fires within schools.

INSTRUCTIONS

Inspection to be made each month by the custodian and a member of the faculty at which inspection only Items 1 to 21 need be reported. At the quarterly inspection, a member of the fire department should accompany the above inspectors, and the complete blank should be filled out. The report of each inspection (monthly and quarterly) is to be filed with the Board of Education or School Commissioners.

Questions are so worded that a negative answer will indicate an unsatisfactory condition.

Date . . . .

Name of School . . . . Address . . . .

Class: Elementary . . . . Junior High . . . . Senior High . . . .

Capacity of School . . . . Number now enrolled . . . .

1. Are all exterior exit doors equipped with approved panic locks? . . . .
   Are these locks tested each week? . . . . Are they readily operable? . . . .
2. Are all outside fire escapes free from obstructions and in good working order? . . . . Are they used
   for fire drills? . . . .
3. Is all heating equipment, including flues, pipes, ducts and steam lines:-
   (a) in good serviceable condition and well maintained? . . . .
   (b) properly insulated and separated from all combustible material by a safe distance? . . . .
4. Is coal pile inspected periodically for evidence of heating? . . . .
5. Are ashes placed in metal containers used for that purpose only? . . . .
6. Is remote control provided whereby oil supply line may be shut off in emergency and is it readily
   accessible? . . . .
7. Is outside shut-off valve on gas supply line provided? . . . . Is it readily accessible? . . . .
8. Has automatic heating and air-conditioning equipment been serviced by a qualified service man within
   the past year? . . . .
9. Are the following locations free of accumulations of waste paper, rubbish, old furniture, stage scenery, etc?
   attic? . . . . basement . . . . furnace room? . . . . stage? . . . . dressing
   rooms in connection with stage? . . . . other locations? . . . . (explain "No" answers under Remarks.)
10. Are spaces beneath stairs free from accumulations or storage of any materials? . . . .
11. If hazardous material or preparation is used for cleaning or polishing floors: Is the quantity limited as much
    as practicable? . . . . Is it safely stored? . . . .
12. Are approved metal cans, with self-closing covers or lids, used for the storage of all oily waste, polishing
    cloths, etc? . . . .
13. Are approved safety cans with vapor-tight covers used for all kerosene, gasoline, etc., on the premises and are
    they stored away from sources of heat or ignition? . . . .
    Is it essential that such materials be kept on the premises? . . . .
14. Are premises free from electrical wiring or equipment which is defective? . . . .
    (If answer is No, explain under Remarks.)
15. Are only approved extension or portable cords used? . . . .
16. Are all fuses on lighting or small appliance circuits of 15 amperes or less capacity? . . . .
17. Are electric pressing irons equipped with automatic heat control or signal and provided with metal stand? . . . .
    . . . .

FIGURE 12–1. Inspection Blank for Schools. Courtesy of the American Fire Insurance Association.

18. Are sufficient proper type fire extinguishers provided on each floor so that not over 75 feet travel is required to reach the nearest unit? . . . .
In manual training shops and on stage, 50 feet? . . . .

19. Have fire extinguishers been inspected or recharged within a year? . . . .
Is date of inspection or recharge shown on tag attached to extinguisher? . . . .

20. Is building equipped with standpipe and hose with nozzle attached? . . . .
Is hose in good serviceable condition? . . . .

21. Where sprinklers are installed: Are all sprinklers clean and unobstructed? . . . .
Are all sprinkler valves open? . . . . Has the system been thoroughly
inspected within the past year? . . . .

22. Are large woolen blankets readily available in kitchens and science laboratories for use in case clothing is ignited? . . . .

Remarks (Note any changes since last inspection)

The following items to be included in each quarterly inspection:-

23. Building construction: Walls . . . . Floors . . . . Roof . . . .
No: stories . . . . No. classrooms . . . .

24. State sections of buildings equipped with automatic sprinklers . . . .

25. Are there at least two means of egress from each floor of the building? . . . .
Are these so located that the distance measured along the line of travel does not exceed:-
From the door of any classroom, 100 feet?
From any point in auditorium, assembly hall or gymnasium, 100 feet? . . . .

26. Are all windows free from heavy screens or bars? . . . .

27. Do all exit doors open in direction of exit travel? . . . .

28. Are all interior stairways enclosed? . . . .
Are doors to these enclosures of automatic or self-closing type? . . . . Are they unobstructed
and in operable condition? . . . .
If automatic closing type, are they closed as routine part of fire exit drill? . . . .

29. Are windows within 10 feet of fire escapes glazed with wire glass? . . . .

30. Are manual training, domestic science, other laboratories and the cafeteria so located that a fire in one will not cut off any exit from the building? . . . .

31. Are heating plant and fuel supply rooms cut off from the main corridors and other parts of the building by fire-resistant walls, floor and ceiling assemblies and doors? . . . .

32. Do all ventilating ducts terminate outside of building? . . . .

33. State type of construction of any temporary buildings in school yard . . . .

34. Is nearest temporary building at least 50 feet from main building? . . . .

35. State frequency of fire drills. . . . . State average time of exit. . . . .

36. Are provisions made for sounding alarm of fire from any floor of building? . . . .
Is sounding device accessible? . . . . Plainly marked? . . . .

37. Give location of nearest city fire alarm box . . . .
Give distance from the premises to box . . . .

Inspector . . . . Title . . . .

Inspector . . . . Title . . . .

Fire Chief and/or Building Inspector . . . .

ATTACH COPY OF ANY "REMARKS" DEALING WITH INSPECTION FINDINGS

FIGURE 12–1. (Continued)

4. Maintain order during drill. No talking, shoving, or horseplay of any kind.
5. Stay in line.
6. If exit route is blocked it is the teacher's responsibility to find an alternate route.
7. *Every person must leave the building during a drill.*

C. Routes (Circle your room number in red)
Rooms 2–4–6–8–10–14–16 are to use the door at the extreme south end of the building to the playground.
Do not cross the track.

Room 12 exit at the outside door of 12 and move to the playground. Do not cross the track.

Rooms 116–118 (Home Ec Dept.) and gym are to use the south end stairs to the basement on to the playground. Do not cross the track.

Rooms 100–101–102–103–104–105–106–110 are to use the steps to the lobby and out the front door. Library and Guidance use the front door. Move to grass plot between parking lot and Ann Street. Even numbers right. Odd numbers left.

Rooms 200–201–202–203–204–205–206 use the north stairs and out north door.

. . . .

. . . .

. . . .

Band rooms exit rear of auditorium into parking. Do not block driveway.

Choral room exit rear of auditorium into parking lot. Do not block driveway.

THIS ORDER IS TO BE *POSTED PERMANENTLY* AND IN A CONSPICUOUS PLACE IN EACH CLASSROOM. TEACHERS KNOW EVACUATION ROUTE FOR EACH ROOM YOU USE.

Individual differences in drill patterns will of course exist even within a school district. Characteristics of the school plant, such as number of pupils, single-level or multi-level construction, width of corridors, and location of exits will largely determine the particular routine for conducting a fire drill. However, the main principles of a standard list of instructions should be observed on as broad a basis as possible in order that children transferring from one school to another in a given district, county, or state may be familiar with procedure.

INSTRUCTION IN FIRE PREVENTION.   The average city or village fire department will willingly cooperate with a school system that requests special assistance in setting up some type of instruction in fire prevention for its students.   Most local fire authorities will detach equipment and personnel to dramatize Fire Prevention Week, and will supply speakers to demonstrate fire hazards at school assemblies.   Many states now require a certain amount of such instruction.

Comprehensive Liability and Property Damage Insurance

Under these headings are found two main types: property damage and bodily injury.   Legal liability for property damage and bodily injury must be established by court action.   Accidents that do not result from negligence are not legally actionable.   But when negligence contributes to property damage or bodily injury, the school district (in certain states) or the individual becomes liable, and the insurance company is obligated to pay damages specified in the policy coverage.

Although liability must be established by court action, companies that write property damage and bodily injury policies often seek out-of-court settlements and hold the insured free from suit or damages to the extent of policy coverage.   In recent years, courts have awarded increasingly higher claims to successful plaintiffs.   For this reason, school districts periodically should re-examine their property damage and bodily injury coverage.

A school survey by a team of experts recommends the use of comprehensive liability insurance as required by the laws of the state.   It should cover the liability of the district, the board of education, and district members, officers, and employees when acting within the scope of their employment.[8]   The amount of coverage should depend upon the number of employees and the value of the school district's property.

---

[8] Irving R. Melbo et al., *Report of the Survey, Paramount Unified School District*, p. 115.

Workmen's Compensation Insurance

Many states require that district employees be protected by workmen's compensation insurance. In most cases, however, coverage is not provided for all classifications of employment. Wherever compensation insurance is compulsory, a required form is issued by the state and the rates are set by a central agency. In states where compensation statutes are either nonexistent or optional, school employees must then depend upon some liability system for reimbursement. Since compensation insurance favors employees by doing away with the need to prove or disprove negligence, and by furnishing definite reimbursement for industrial or occupational injuries, it is strongly to be preferred to ordinary employer liability insurance.

Fidelity Bond Coverage

Whether or not state law requires school districts to bond all employees who handle school funds, the coverage is of such self-evident importance that every district should acquire this protection as a matter of course. For the average school district, the best and most economical way to accomplish this is to use the blanket commercial fidelity bond. Individual bonds tend to be too specific and to result in possible heavy losses as a result of embezzlement on the part of employees not included in the categories covered by the bonds.

Optional Insurance

It is impossible to specify the need of any particular district for the several types of special insurance which may be required under certain individual circumstances. Insurance should be provided only after a careful analysis of the district's needs.

BROAD FORM MONEY AND SECURITIES POLICIES. A policy of this type insures not only money and securities, but also other merchandise. It may be written to cover loss both inside and outside the premises. Money and securities are covered against risks of any kind, including fire, but other property is usually insured only against burglary. The amount of coverage, of course, is dependent upon the district's individual needs.

ALL-RISK COVERAGE. Many districts carry all-risk insurance, such as a floater policy on musical instruments and audio-visual equipment. Articles thus insured are protected both on and off the premises against various types of loss, such as theft, burglary, fire, and accidental damage.

PLATE GLASS POLICY. Modern schools with large areas of plate glass are well advised to insure this highly expensive feature by means of a policy that will replace all glass damaged in any way.

OPEN STOCK BURGLARY WITH THEFT ENDORSEMENT. Such insurance should be maintained as a matter of course by all districts that have valuables or expensive equipment that are kept in the school plant and that are not covered by one of the policies previously described.

VANDALISM COVERAGE. Vandalism damage should be taken care of as a part of the extended coverage–comprehensive portion of the district's fire insurance program.

WIND AND STORM COVERAGE. Protection against windstorms and other natural calamities should also be a part of the fire insurance coverage of the district.

BOILER INSURANCE. In many districts the chief value of a boiler insurance policy may be the inspection service furnished by the insuring company, rather than payment for possible loss. All districts that use high pressure boilers should by all means carry adequate boiler insurance. Those that have only low pressure plants will find such insurance highly desirable but not essential.

Liability of School Districts

In states where school districts are not legally liable for accidents and damage caused by their negligence, they share such immunity with other governmental agencies. The theory behind school district immunity from liability relates to the historical concept of the common law rule of non-liability, based, in turn, upon the ancient concept that "the king can do no wrong." In this country, it has been assumed that the state is sovereign and cannot be sued without its consent. A further justification exists in the legal concept which holds that a school district, in performing a purely public and nonprofit function imposed upon it by law and for the benefit of society, is not subject to liability.

A number of states have recently modified and in some cases eliminated this immunity by enacting legislation. Legislation has been enacted in Alaska, California, Connecticut, Maryland, Minnesota, New Jersey, New York, North Carolina, Oregon, Washington, and Wisconsin which materially modifies the immunity of a school district from liability. Illinois has completely abolished the immunity of the school district. Even in those states where school immunity still exists, the courts have recognized certain exceptions such as: summer recreational programs and renting school facilities to other organizations; active or positive wrong; injuries arising as a result of the creation or maintenance of a nuisance; and taking or damaging private property for public use without offering adequate compensation.

A great variety exists among the states with respect to the liability of school districts for injuries arising out of its negligence; hence, each district should be aware of the extent to which it might be held liable. Generally, school board members, trustees, and similar persons are not held personally liable for negligence for their official actions. However, teachers and other school personnel may be sued for negligent supervision and other causes. Negligence, however, must be proven.

Once the exposure to liability has been determined in the school district, appropriate insurance should be carried as a matter of course.

Insuring Public Property in a Common Fund

South Carolina and Wisconsin were two of the first states to enact laws specifying that public property, including school buildings, shall be insured in a common fund by the state. North Carolina and Alabama later authorized such insurance. Insurance rates in these states vary from one-half to three-fourths of those charged by private companies, and losses are apparently made good with promptness and efficiency. Transportation insurance is provided to all North Carolina schoolchildren by the state; in most other states the local districts purchase such insurance. Apparently the opposition by private companies to such state or community insurance has been the main reason for the failure of such practices to spread widely.

Insuring Employee Welfare

INSURANCE FRINGE BENEFITS. The rapid increase in benefits for school employees in the late 1960s and early 1970s is a carbon copy of the development of these benefits for industry during and following World War II. When prices and wages were frozen during that time, employers utilized fringe benefits to attract workers from a sparse labor market. Following World War II, unions bargained for and won broader and more comprehensive benefits. Once established, such benefits became a permanent part of the employment package.

As the population expanded, the need for more teachers and other employees also expanded and created an "employee market." Again, fringe benefits were used to attract qualified employees into the school systems. These benefits then became a permanent part of the employment package. In many cases, salary increases were bypassed in order to provide broader and more comprehensive benefits. It was easier for many districts to raise revenue for such benefits than to increase salaries. Competition for employees became more intense as wages increased in industry and schools found themselves in a spiral of increasing salaries and fringe benefits. The evolution of these benefits for school employees followed the same pattern as industry, although it lagged behind by some fifteen to twenty years.

Fringe benefits are those forms of insurance for which premiums are paid by, or which are made available to the employee by, the school system. These benefits include:

1. Life Insurance
2. Health Insurance
3. Income Protection
4. Dental Insurance
5. Retirement Plans
6. Tax Sheltered Plans

Do Fringe Benefits Improve the Quality of Education? There are as many people who claim that fringe benefits do improve education as there are those who disagree. The fact remains that these benefits have become an integral part of the employment package and it is doubtful that they will be removed. In fact, they will probably be increased as school employees become more militant and demanding in their negotiations with local boards of education. Employment in a school district includes protection against monetary loss as a result of ill health and, in many cases, as a result of death. The effect on the school system has been similar to that imposed upon industry. Administrations now have to adjust their management capabilities, accounting, bookkeeping, and personnel practices to accommodate these benefits.

Types of Coverage Afforded by Fringe Benefits. Most fringe benefits are provided under group insurance policies, with the school district as the policyowner and its employees considered as the insureds. It is important to note that the employee is not a party to the contract. The policyowner is responsible for the timely payment of the premium and for the collection of any premium paid for by its employees. The employee receives a certificate of insurance which contains the important details of coverage but is not a contract in and of itself.

Group life insurance provides that in the event of the death of the insured employee, the amount for which he was insured will be paid to his designated beneficiary. These designations are made upon enrollment into the plan and can be changed by the employee by proper notification to the insurance company. Most group life policies also contain benefits for accidental death and dismemberment; these provide an additional amount usually equal to the amount payable under the life insurance (which would be paid in the event that the death were due to an accident).

Group health insurance provides for the payment of charges incurred as a result of the disability of the insured. While this is the intent of this type of coverage, it is a gross oversimplification to stop at this point. Charges that a disabled person can incur are varied and in some cases abstruse. In general, charges may be incurred as a result of hospitalization, surgery, physician's visits, medications, nursing, and medical supplies and appliances such as wheelchairs. Group health policies can be written to provide coverage for each source of charges or can be all-inclusive. The latter is generally referred to as Major Medical or Comprehensive Medical coverage.

The amounts that will be paid by the policy for charges incurred also vary and have a major impact on the premium that will be charged. For example, a policy that provides full coverage for charges made by a hospital would obviously cost more than one that limits the amount payable for room and board and ancillary services. Likewise, a policy with a smaller deductible would be more expensive than one with a larger deductible. Major Medical and Comprehensive Medical plans are typified by three features—a deductible, coinsurance, and high maximum benefits. The deductible is used to reduce the impact of the higher frequency of smaller claims which can be budgeted by the insured. Coinsurance causes the claimant to participate in the overall cost of the disability and, theoretically, reduces the overuse and abuse of medical facilities. The high maximum provides the coverage necessary for the serious disability which could lead to financial chaos.

Service-type plans such as Blue Cross and Blue Shield provide full benefits for charges incurred when their approved hospitals or physicians are used. In the case of Blue Cross, those charges for which benefits are paid would be incurred in a hospital that is a member of the Blue Cross organization. It is not necessarily true that full benefits would be paid for charges incurred in a nonmember hospital. Similarly, Blue Shield arranges for service-type benefits through its member–physicians.

The basic approach to rating varies between service-type organizations and private insurance companies. Service-type organizations tend to gear their rates to the experience which they sustain on a community-wide basis, while insurance companies tend to base their rates on the experience of the group itself. Competition has been very keen in the group health field; hence, the district should obtain a good cross section of bids prior to selecting their insurer. Staff members should participate in such a survey.

Income protection is a form of coverage that reimburses the insured employee for a portion of his lost income due to a disability. There are two categories of plans based on the length of time for which benefits may be payable. Short-term disability benefits usually will afford payments to the claimant up to twenty-six weeks and some up to fifty-two weeks. Long-term disability benefits can run up to lifetime benefits for disabilities due to an accident and up to age 65 for disabilities due to sickness. In either case, the plan generally will contain a waiting period before benefits commence. As in the use of a deductible, the longer the waiting period, the lower the rates.

Four states (Rhode Island, New York, New Jersey, and California) have compulsory disability benefits laws. These short-term disability benefits may be obtained from either the state fund or private insurers in each of these states, with the exception of Rhode Island, where benefits must be purchased from the state fund. A typical short-term plan might provide that benefits shall begin on the eighth day of covered disability and would be payable up to twenty-six weeks of continuous total disability. Long-term disability plans usually vary their definition of disability. They require that the insured be unable to perform the duties of his regular occupation for the first two years of disability, and thereafter be unable to perform the duties of any occupation for wage or profit for which he is suited by virtue of his education, training, and experience. Such a plan can be abused by employees and result in increased rates; the school system may find that it cannot bear the cost or, in some cases, find a suitable carrier for their plan. Plans are designed to avoid malingering and consequently should not afford more in the way of benefits to the disabled employee than he would have received had he not been disabled. Most long-term disability plans will limit benefits payable to 66⅔ percent of the employee's weekly or monthly salary and will integrate this maximum amount with benefits payable from other plans, such as state compulsory disability benefits; benefits payable under the disability provisions in retirement plans; benefits payable under Social Security; and other similar benefits payable under plans afforded by the employer. When an employee becomes disabled for an extended period of time, the idea of disability in itself is disabling, and if an adequate income is not guaranteed, recovery tends to be delayed. Premium rates will reflect loss experience under any group program, and increased costs for these plans could very well be transferred to the taxpayer. Selection of the plan and the insurer is an essential responsibility of school administration.

Dental insurance is a form of insurance that reimburses the insured employee for charges he might incur as a result of dental services performed by a qualified dentist. This is a more recently developed form of insurance, having become popular during the 1960s. Many school administrators have questioned its importance in the fringe benefit portfolio since it involves an expense that is more budgetable than severe illness and disability. Since most people need some dental work, and since premium rates tend to reflect the loss experience sustained by the insurer, some experts have raised the question of whether the future rates for this coverage might not be so high as to negate the value of insuring these charges.

Administrators should evaluate their portfolios of fringe benefits carefully and set priorities for coverage. The highest priorities should be placed on coverages for which the school employee is least able to budget. Dental costs are more readily budgeted than the cost of a severe heart attack or a disabling injury.

There are a number of other insurance plans (vision care, accident coverages, nursing home coverage, etc.) which could be classified as a fringe benefit if adopted by the school system. These have not been adopted by many systems and are merely mentioned to point out the potential complexities faced by school administrators in the age of fringe benefits.

FINANCING THE COST OF FRINGE BENEFITS. Raising funds through taxation to provide fringe benefits for school employees traditionally has received little publicity since it is usually included as a part of a salary package. However, some systems find themselves affording fringe benefits amounting to 10 percent or more of the average employee's salary. The question then arises: should the school system pay the entire cost of these fringe benefits or should the employee share in some of the cost? Should the school system pay the cost of providing health insurance for dependents of its employees? Systems that have decided to provide dependent coverage then face the problem of equal benefits for single employees. Who pays the increased cost for existing plans when sizable rate increases are requested by the insurer? Can benefits be reduced or eliminated if taxes cannot be raised to pay for them? How much will it cost to expand an existing plan? What will it cost next year? School administrators are faced with these questions, the answers to which are often difficult to resolve.

SELECTION OF A PLAN OF BENEFITS. Every insurance plan is based upon some need, but all needs are not insurable. Some needs lend themselves to the solution of insurance while others are best solved in other ways. The uncertainty of death and the financial loss created generates a need which can best be solved by insurance. The financial loss associated with lack of good health is not as clearly solved by insurance as in the event of death. For example, the medical profession has some difficulty in distinguishing between superannuation and disability. The aging process itself fosters lack of good health for which medical attention usually is required.

Insurance is based on events that are fortuitous in nature; it is not operating efficiently when selection of insured events can be controlled by those who would benefit by it. If maternity coverage were to be written only on the lives of pregnant women, then the cost of such coverage would tend to negate its value because the premiums needed by the insurer to cover all expenses would exceed the actual cost of maternity services.

Many knowledgeable insurance people have referred to group health insurance as a mechanism for the prepayment of medical and hospital bills. The insurance element is still apparent, but it can be overshadowed by the high frequency of expected usage of medical and often hospital facilities. Many of the benefits that are included in group health plans today are of a budgetable nature, and their inclusion tends to reduce the efficiency of the insurance mechanism. Insurance companies, as well as service-type plans, find themselves "trading dollars"—from premium income to claims payments.

The group approach makes it possible for the employer to participate in the cost of disability of its employees. The insureds under a group plan feel that the plan is a good one if they have had an opportunity to collect under it; their chances of collecting benefits increases with the increase of budgetable items in the plan. The first group major medical plan, written for the Elfun Society of the General Electric Company in 1949, was an attempt to utilize the insurance mechanism in its most efficient manner by providing protection against financial loss as a result of a severe or catastrophic disability. Deductibles, coinsurance, and high maximum limits were the three cornerstones of the plan. Present-day plans combine these features with the full payment coverage of service-type hospital and surgical plans.

Selection of a life insurance program can be based upon the lowest premium rate obtainable. Very little service is required of the insurer, and the event which precipitates the payment of benefits is quite definite and final.

Selection of a health insurance program is contingent upon the ability of the school system to pay the premiums. If only a nominal amount of money is available, then the most efficient use of it would be in the purchase of a benefit plan covering the more catastrophic types of disabilities, thus taking advantage of the reduced premiums afforded for higher deductibles and coinsurance. Certainly, a smaller number of employees would be able to collect benefits under such a plan, but those that really needed financial assistance for a severe health situation would be the benefactors. As larger sums of money are made available for health coverage, deductibles can be reduced and even eliminated for hospitalization and surgery; coinsurance can be eliminated for hospitalization and surgery; maximums can be increased; and limitations and exclusions can be reduced and, in some cases, eliminated. The plan should be designed to fit the pocketbook of the school system, rather than to fit the pocketbook to the plan.

Selection of a dental insurance plan may depend upon who will pay the premiums and how much they are willing to pay. In most instances, such plans involve the "trading" of premium dollars into claims dollars. If the school system is paying the entire premium, then employees would feel cheated if the plan had a deductible, coinsurance, and limitations for cleanings and x-rays. On the other hand, if the plan were to provide broad, full, first-dollar coverage, the cost of it could well exceed the actual cost of the dental services rendered; this would soon be recognized by employees if they were required to pay the premium. Again, by starting with a plan weighted in favor of the unexpected and serious dental conditions and then expanding toward more full coverage as funds become available, serious financial and personnel problems could be avoided.

SELECTION OF THE INSURER. Differences in rates as well as service exist among insurance companies. It is to the advantage of the school system to select the insurer with the best plan of benefits at the best rates, who can also provide the most efficient and effective service. Several approaches to the selection of an insurer are available. Specifications of benefits can be put out under sealed bid. The hazard in this approach is that the carrier presenting the lowest bid might not have the most efficient and effective service, particularly important in the handling of claims. The advantage to this approach is that it relieves the school system of lengthy interviews with insurance company sales representatives. The specifications can be sent to a selected list of insurers who then come in individually to present their quotation. This approach allows the school system to look into the service qualifications of the insurers, although it can take considerable time. Both approaches require that the person or persons reviewing the bids be knowledgeable about insurance.

The broker-of-record approach has been quite popular throughout the country and has the advantage of placing an insurance expert between the insurance companies and the school system as a buffer; as a broker, his interests should lie with the school system. A disadvantage arising from this method can occur in the selection of the broker. If a broker is selected on a subjective basis (because he is popular in the area or for some other personal reason), then the hazard of lack of competence might arise. Some agents and brokers represent only one or a few insurers; this might not provide the school system with the exposure to the best insurer for the particular plan desired. An alternative might be to select an expert consultant for a fee or on salary to act in the best interests of the school system in designing plans and selecting the insurer. This could add cost on the one hand, but it could save premiums on the other. Whatever system is used will require some expertise in the field of insurance in order to produce the best results. If that expertise does not exist within the system, then it should be sought from outside.

Summary

One kind of school insurance covers district property; the other deals with employee health and welfare. Only the very largest school districts can avoid insuring property by maintaining a cash reserve fund; the others must insure.

Given the assumption that insurance should be carried whenever the risk is too large for the district to assume, it follows that small districts need insurance the most. Necessary insurance includes fire, liability, and workmen's compensation. Optional insurance is typified by all-risk coverage, plate glass, and vandalism policies.

Fire insurance is offered in various forms: full value, coinsurance, and "probable loss." The appropriate type is often determined by local conditions. A district can reduce fire insurance costs by regular appraisals, removal of fire hazards, periodic inspections, training in use of firefighting equipment, fire drills, and instruction in fire prevention.

Liability and property damage insurance is of two kinds: property damage and bodily injury. Negligence in many states is actionable, thus making such insurance necessary, while in others, school districts enjoy relative immunity from suit.

A blanket commercial fidelity bond should always be taken out on employees who handle school funds. Other optional insurance includes monies and security policy, all-risk coverage, open-stock burglary, and boiler insurance.

Tomorrow's employee contracts will increasingly include fringe benefits through insurance such as life and health insurance, retirement plans, and tax-sheltered annuities. Most fringe benefits are provided under group insurance policies with the school district as the policyholder and the employees as the insureds. Income protection is a recent addition to employee fringe-benefit packages, and may be either short-term or long-term.

Administrators are cautioned that such fringe benefit plans can constitute either a decided asset for the district or a perennial headache. Financing the cost is a continuing challenge, involving complicated questions such as maternity coverage, the difference between superannuation and disability, and the rapidly rising costs in any health insurance plan.

Since selection of the insurer is important, districts are advised to hire an expert consultant to act in the best interests of the district in designing plans and selecting the insurer.

Trends

The increase in capital investment represented by school plants today has brought about a corresponding increase in the importance of insurance. Fringe benefits have become an integral part of the employment picture for school employees and are a major expenditure for the school system.

TOWARD INCREASED INSURANCE COVERAGE. The major discernible trend is in the direction of increased coverage. As building replacement costs mount, and as the volume and diversity of school equipment increase, more and more school districts are seeking to approximate either full or majority coverage under the terms of their insurance policies. There will also be more comprehensive and all-inclusive coverage for life, health, and disability income. The national trend is toward security on all levels. No administrator in the future will be able to gamble very much in the area of insurance.

TOWARD BROAD-FORM, MULTIPLE-LINE PACKAGE POLICIES AND BLANKET COVERAGE. There is little question but that the era of multiple policies is passing. The trend is toward a few comprehensive policies, and we may live to see the day when all school insurance of every type is provided for by one company under a single policy.

TOWARD THE ABROGATION OF SCHOOL DISTRICT IMMUNITY FROM SUIT. The trend here is toward making it possible for an injured person to sue a school district.   The legal concept of immunity that so long interposed itself between the district and the law court was a safeguard against the pouring out of public funds for noneducational purposes; but it is on its way out.   As the public conscience becomes everywhere more sensitive, states will tend more and more to pass enabling legislation similar to that already existing in several states, and judges will tend to liberalize interpretations involving the right to sue school districts.   The result will be inevitable; the nonproductive portion of the budget dedicated to insurance will mushroom percentage-wise, and school administrators will find more and more of their time occupied by appearances in court.

TOWARD THE INCREASING USE OF LIABILITY INSURANCE.   This trend will be a natural corollary of the preceding one.   No district will be able to afford the luxury of dispensing with liability insurance.

TOWARD THE USE OF PRIVATE INSURANCE COMPANIES.   With the exception of variations on the theme of workmen's compensation, most school insurance will be purchased in the future from private companies. Decreasing costs and increasing efficiency in the servicing of claims are putting the private companies in a more and more favorable light.   Except in the very largest districts, public or "community" insurance faces a losing battle with the well-organized and progressive private companies.

TOWARD COINSURANCE.   School architectural trends are developing in a manner that will benefit the coinsurance principle.   Architects are favoring a more dispersed, ground-level structure which is much less of a fire hazard.   It will become increasingly economical to insure for only a percentage of the true value of a school plant as the danger of a total loss diminishes.

TOWARD INCREASED COST FOR INSURANCE.   As the programs of benefits become more comprehensive and employees more demanding, the overall cost will also increase.   Greater utilization of medical and hospital facilities will also tend to increase cost of the programs.   Overuse and abuse of programs will lead to controls and plans which will include benefits for preventative medicine.

TOWARD INVOLVEMENT OF GOVERNMENT IN HEALTH INSURANCE.   Increased cost without control of the charges will tend to involve both the federal and state governments in legislation of benefits and precipitate controls of costs.

Administrative Problems

Problem 1

There are 350 teachers in the Palomba Unified School District. The local teacher's association has become increasingly strong and demanding. Its newly elected president, Jim Brower, is a forceful and vocal young teacher. A membership drive has resulted in over 90 percent of the teachers joining the association.

Jim has appointed an insurance committee to look into increasing fringe benefits. Up to now, the school district has paid only part of the health and medical insurance which is handled through Blue Cross. The committee's objective is to have the district pay all the Blue Cross insurance premiums for teachers and part of the premium for dependents. It is also planning to request fully paid dental insurance and is looking into the possibility of the district paying income protection, life insurance, and tax-sheltered plans.

The superintendent has not been consulted by the teacher's association or the insurance committee, but has heard reports that they are planning to ask the Board of Education to authorize the payment of many additional insurance premiums. He does not believe that the district can afford to do this, especially because of the high salaries paid to teachers.

If you were the superintendent, what would you do when you heard about the teacher's association proposals?
What would you tell the Board of Education?
What stand would you take? Why?

Problem 2

Assume the same situation as in Problem 1. At this point, insurance committee has met with you and asked for your advice.

What kind of unified insurance package would you recommend to them?

Selected References

ANGELL, FRANK JOSEPH. *Health Insurance.* New York: The Ronald Press, 1963.

EILENS, ROBERT D., and CROW, ROBERT M. *Group Insurance Handbook.* Homewood, Ill.: Richard D. Irwin, Inc., 1965.

GREGG, DAVIS W. *Group Life Insurance.* Homewood, Ill.: Richard D. Irwin, Inc., 1962.

HUEBNER, S. S., and BLACK, KENNETH, JR. *Life Insurance.* New York: Appleton–Century–Crofts, 1969.

KING, FRANCIS P. *Benefit Plans in Junior Colleges.* Washington, D.C.: American Association of Junior Colleges, 1971.

LINN, H. H., and JOYNER, S. C. *Insurance Practices in School Administration.* New York: The Ronald Press, 1952.

LONG, JOHN D., and GREGG, DAVIS W. *Property and Liability Insurance Handbook.* Homewood, Ill.: Richard D. Irwin, Inc., 1965.

MAGEE, JOHN H., and SERBEIN, OSCAR N. *Property and Liability Insurance.* Homewood, Ill.: Richard D. Irwin, Inc., 1967.

MELBO, IRVING R., et al. *Report of the Survey, Antelope Valley Joint Union High School District.* Los Angeles: University of Southern California, 1956.

————. *Report of the Survey, Paramount Unified School District.* Published by the authority of the Board of Trustees, Paramount Unified School District. Los Angeles: University of Southern California, 1970.

NATIONAL EDUCATION ASSOCIATION. *Guidelines to Fringe Benefits for Members of the Teaching Profession.* Washington, D.C.: The Association, 1969.

NELSON, D. LLOYD, and PURDY, WILLIAM M. *School Business Administration.* Lexington, Mass.: D. C. Heath and Co., 1971.

PICKRELL, JESSE F. *Group Health Insurance.* Homewood, Ill.: Richard D. Irwin, Inc., 1965.

TURNBULL, J. G.; WILLIAMS, C. A.; and CHEIT, E. F. *Economic and Social Security.* New York: The Ronald Press, 1968.

13

Technology in School Practice

As in business and industry, technology is exerting an impact on education and is accelerating due to innovations and demands for accountability. Educators must become more knowledgeable regarding automation and systems analysis; they need to become familiar with a new terminology. The reader should be cautioned that changes in technology are taking place at such a rapid rate that the contents of this chapter are outdated quickly.

The purposes of this chapter are to make the reader conversant with machines available for school use, to suggest many applications of the machines, and to present a systems framework that should help establish guidelines for their employment.

This chapter includes a discussion of the following topics:

The Move toward Technology in Education
The Systems Approach in Education
An Educational Information System
Available Machines
Copying and Duplicating Processes
Applications of Educational Data Processing
Instructional Technology
Access to EDP Systems
Automation in an Educational Organization
Instructional Materials Center (IMC)
Summary
Trends

This chapter was written by Dr. Richard H. Strand, Professor of Education, Azusa Pacific College, Azusa, California.

The Move Toward Technology in Education

What has been termed the "second industrial revolution," the movement toward automation in business, industry, and the armed services, is making inroads in education. Many concurrent trends are ushering in the era of educational data processing in school offices and instructional technology in classrooms. The primary causes of the movement are great progress in technology, accompanied and stimulated by the application of the systems approach to many man–machine enterprises; a climate of opinion demanding new kinds of accountability for all money expended; and major reforms in curriculum, instruction, and school organization.

TECHNOLOGICAL PROGRESS. Machines have been perfected that function largely under their own power and direction. A new theory referred to as the systems approach has matured. Source data automation, which captures original data by machine in a language that machines can read and act upon without any further manual intervention, is being perfected as the capstone of automation. The culmination of these developments is typified by computers that guide missiles to interplanetary moving targets.

THE SYSTEMS APPROACH TO INFORMATION MANAGEMENT. The application of technology to business, industry, and military projects has evolved a separate field called systems analysis or systems design. It is a cross-disciplinary field of knowledge and procedures that draws upon new technical areas such as management science, contract engineering, logistics, value engineering, human factors engineering, and behavioral engineering.

Systems concepts began appearing regularly in educational literature in the 1960s. Now it is becoming commonplace to see flow charts and to discuss inputs, outputs, feedback, needs assessment, objectives, alternative procedures, choice of final procedures, simulation, trial runs, evaluation, and modification within a systems framework.

In the systems approach, an organization, such as a school or school system, is viewed as a kind of biological organism composed of interdependent subsystems that must function as an organic whole.[1] For effective operation such an organization needs an intercommunication network so that, whenever needed, it can internally exchange all information that

---

[1] Robert W. Sims, "Systems Concepts and Practices in Education," in *Automated Educational Systems,* Enoch J. Haga (ed.), p. 4.

any part of the system receives from external or internal sources. Norbert Weiner coined the word "cybernetics" to cover the field of controlling and communicating such information. *The concept of an organization as an organic whole, controlling itself toward a goal by its information system, is the crux of cybernetics.* This is the key concept in the systems approach, in developing the controlling mechanisms in all automated equipment, and in establishing guidelines for the wise application of technology to any organization.

ACCOUNTABILITY. The money squeeze of recent years has increased the clamor for fiscal accountability for all public ventures. In education, the stress on accountability is not only of fiscal but of philosophical origin. The public and many educators are seeking ways to improve the quality of education. In the late 1960s, the measure of a good educational program switched from the amount of money that was being expended on the program to the performance of the students—i.e., to how much they were learning and what they could do after the money had been spent on their education. Measurable educational outcomes were being sought, to which the cost of education could be meaningfully related.

"Accountability is the coming *sine qua non* for education in the 1970s. How to engineer accountability for results in public education is the central problem for the education profession."[2] There are many possible responses to this demand for accountability. Performance contracting, educational audits, national assessment, merit pay, incentive plans, and educational voucher plans are a few of the variations. Competition or cooperation of public schools with private, public, or government agencies is involved in many of these proposals.

Applying the Systems Approach to Education

The net impact of technological progress, the movement toward accountability, and educational innovation is to push education into the front lines of the "Second Industrial Revolution." Educators should not now retreat or run for cover. It should be possible to weave all the threads into a new educational fabric by applying the systems approach. A systematic ("system"atic) application of technology can develop and support innova-

---

[2] Leon Lessinger, "Engineering Accountability for Results in Public Education," *Phi Delta Kappan*, p. 21.

tions that can stand the test of accountability, resulting in a stronger educational fabric.

EDUCATIONAL ENGINEERING.   Applying the systems approach to education can appropriately be termed "educational engineering."[3]   The wise application of technology is not the mere adoption of business machines, computers, and ready-made programs.   Rather, it means turning an educational system into an effectively functioning information system.   Information, flowing to and from everyone, including the students, is the heart of the educational operation.   The greatest need is to systematize the flow and handling of all the necessary kinds of information.   Engineering all the parts of an educational information system will involve the best of what is known in the fields of educational data processing and instructional technology.

A NEW "PEDAGUESE."   The approach necessitates not only a new way of thinking but, since thinking is done primarily in words and symbols, also a new vocabulary, phraseology, and symbol system that is very different from the old "pedaguese" familiar to educators.   The language of the "new mathematics" or the "new linguistics" was only a foretaste.   When the language of systems—of technology and computers, of accountability, of the new curriculum projects and administrative innovations—are all combined, the linguistic burden is formidable indeed.   Educators—especially administrators—need to be familiar with many terms and concepts that did not exist, say, in 1955.

Resistance to any unnecessary language change is understandable.   It is easy to empathize with reactions such as Nash's:

> We are rapidly approaching the point where we are speaking a quasi-mystical language which bears little resemblance to the real world.   Thus we hear of modules, entry and re-entry, tandem and chained schedules, differentiated staffing, mands, and tacts.   Such mystogogy—the inevitable result of fetishistic thinking—would be laughable, if it were not for the legitimacy it is getting . . .[4]

However, it is not possible to simply turn back the clock and try to ignore all the new language.   For purposes of this chapter the language burden

---

[3] Lessinger, "Engineering Accountability," p. 218.
[4] Robert Nash, "Commitment to Competency: The New Fetishism in Teacher Education," *Phi Delta Kappan,* p. 241.

will be minimized, but administrators are advised to continue to learn to communicate in the new areas.

An Educational Information System

GENERAL DESCRIPTION AND PURPOSE. An information system collects, stores, and makes readily available all important information needed by all segments of the organization at all levels of management. Data collected by any subsystem become available to any other subsystem as needed. The collection, storage, processing, and distribution are planned so as to avoid as much duplication of effort as possible. The system provides succinct and timely reports for purposes of successful present operation and future planning.

Under the systems approach an individual or subdivision of an organization need not do independent research to discover things already known by others in the organization. In school operations outside of a systems framework, administrators are continually accumulating information pertinent to their individual needs in relative isolation from the whole district. A total systems concept would provide a common data bank and data processing center that can furnish the basic data needed by all administrators and other authorized personnel in the system. Each administrator would add to the bank and draw from the bank information that is useful for the management of the system.

SPECIFIC FUNCTIONS. An information system performs all the functions included in the field of data processing:

1. Originating records, which involves data reduction.
2. Classifying, coding, indexing, and the like.
3. Sorting.
4. Comparing and analyzing.
5. Calculating, in the sense of computing or finding mathematical solutions.
6. Storing and retrieving.
7. Summarizing and reporting—by listing, recording, tabulating, printing, graphing, or other means.
8. Communicating—by transmitting, transporting, disseminating, displaying, or in other ways making information available to users.

KINDS OF INFORMATION. A school system needs information about the community, pupils, staff, program, property, and finance. Alcorn's list of "Categories of Educational Data" is a very useful classification scheme from the systems standpoint.[5] Other classification schemes such as those analyzing the kinds of data needed by various school divisions are often more complex, less comprehensive, and subject to much overlapping and ambiguity.

A TOTAL OR INTEGRATED SYSTEM. The words "total" and "integrated" apply to an ideal conception of an information system—one in which the system operates as a unified whole, like a living organism. The information flow has been analyzed and planned to make the best conceivable use of human and machine resources in relation to the goals of the enterprise and within the limits of the available funds and other restricting conditions.

Not many educational agencies or organizations have yet attempted a total or integrated systems approach. It is initially costly; few experts are available to perform the necessary systems analysis and design; and not many educators have caught the vision of what this might do for education.

However, the fact that one cannot institute an integrated system overnight does not mean that one needs to be satisfied with a disintegrated one. Systems concepts can be applied to areas and subdivisions within a total organization. Some can be applied, for instance, to the principal's desk, where information is originated, accumulated, processed, stored, retrieved, and communicated to other parts of the organization.

TWO MAJOR SUBSYSTEMS: INSTRUCTIONAL AND ADMINISTRATIVE. Within a school system or other educational organization, two subsystems can be identified: an instructional system and an administrative support system. The first is concerned primarily with the specific management of pupil learning, the second with the overall management of the organization. Both subsystems are information systems employing all aspects of educational data processing (EDP)—collecting, processing, retaining, and distributing information.

Providing and distributing educational information for teachers and pupils is the aspect of EDP that is predominantly stressed by instructional technology (IT). The broad meaning of IT includes the application of a

---

[5] Bruce Keith Alcorn, "The Concept of Total Systems in Education," in *Automated Educational Systems,* Enoch J. Haga (ed.), p. 12.

systems approach to instruction. The systems approach, as has been stated, is a major part of technology today. Consequently, the term "instructional technology" has replaced terms such as "audio-visual aids."

There should be a close partnership between the instructional and administrative information systems. In the data bank on community, pupils, staff, program, property, and finance is much information that has relevance to the teaching–learning situation. Upon short notice, teachers, counselors, and administrators should have access to all program information; property and financial information pertaining to educational resources and equipment; pupil personnel data that might affect pupil learning; data on community background and community resources; and staff assignments and schedules. It is highly desirable for authorized users to have such information available without having to do laborious research.

Other kinds of information useful for business, personnel, special services, or public relations would be useless to instructional personnel; thus it should be inaccessible to them. Still other information should remain as privileged communication, available only to those having legal jurisdiction.

Available Machines

Automation is not requisite to a dynamic information system. Varying degrees of automation are possible or desirable, depending upon the local situation. Systems range, theoretically, from purely manual to completely automated. Heyel lists the following six:

1. Hand system.
2. Electromechanical system.
3. Service bureau system.
4. Tab card system (EAM—electric accounting machine).
5. Basic computer system.
6. Source data automation system.[6]

Other systems are also conceivable by combining elements of these categories.

---

[6] Carl Heyel, *Computers, Office Machines, and the New Information Technology*, p. 235.

The average organization ranges between the extremes of manual and automated operation, using machines to handle the operations most in need of mechanical assistance. The operations that machines can assist are word processing, data processing, information storage and retrieval, communicating, and miscellaneous office operations chiefly related to paper handling.[7] "Data processing" in this context implies specific operations such as tabulating, sorting, computing, and accounting. Paper operations capable of being handled by machines include cutting, punching, folding, collating, stapling, and others.

A true system is a planned one; it does not grow haphazardly, and it is not a mere aggregation of subsystems supported by a conglomeration of machines. Machines should not be added at the whims of personnel or under the pressure of machine company representatives.

CLASSIFICATION OF OFFICE MACHINES. From Heyel's list it is evident that progress toward automation utilizes increasingly sophisticated equipment. Machines are usually classified as mechanical, electromechanical, or electronic, in order of increasing sophistication. Some equipment in these three categories will be itemized. The equipment presented in this chapter is illustrative only; mention of a machine does not constitute a recommendation for its purchase.

Mechanical Equipment

Mechanical equipment is operated by hand (Heyel's "hand system"). It uses physical and chemical principles to make man's work easier. Simple tools such as pens and pencils are mechanical in this sense, although they are not usually thought of as machines. A hand system of operation in a school office would include many items purchased from office equipment and supply stores, such as various types of paper, forms, sorting equipment, files, mail and coin handling devices, microfilm equipment, and various types of machines.

Electromechanical Equipment

When mechanical equipment is powered or controlled wholly or partially by electricity, it is called electromechanical. A large number of items listed

---

[7] Heyel, *Computers, Office Machines*, pp. 13–54.

as mechanical equipment have their electromechanical counterparts. Electric adding machines, calculators, typewriters, and duplicators have largely supplanted the manual types. Increased speed, convenience, and quality of production have resulted.

PUNCH CARD EQUIPMENT. High on the scale of electromechanical equipment is the automatic punch card or "tab card" equipment. It is also called unit record equipment because each card records only one type of transaction and cards are acted upon one at a time by a processing machine. Directions controlling the operation of each machine in the system are wired into changeable control panels called plugboards. Punch card machines are described in detail by Levy[8] and by Arnold, Hill, and Nichols.[9]

The data originating machine is the keypunch that has an operator, or, with electrical and electronic refinements, can punch automatically from mark-sense cards. Input to all other machines is provided by standard-sized cards that have been keypunched in 80 columns (IBM cards) or 90 columns (UNIVAC cards). Each punched column represents an alphabetic, numeric, or special character which can be read electrically by the other machines.

Data on punched cards can be verified, reproduced, summarized, or interpreted by machines that are named to match these processes. The interpreter, for instance, prints the punched code in English letters, numerals, or symbols. Other machines called the collator and the sorter work in combination to sort decks of cards alphabetically, numerically, or in other manners; to check sequences, compare or match cards, merge decks, select specific classification of cards, find particular cards; and to perform other similar classifying, filing, and retrieving operations.

Two major types of output machines are the electric accounting machines (called EAMs or tabulating machines) and the calculating machines. The accounting machines prepare journals, ledgers, statements, financial reports, and other records automatically, printing both numbers and verbal explanations. They can add, subtract, and be adapted to do multiplication and division by repeated addition and subtraction like an adding machine. The calculating machines, or multiplying punches, can do all four basic arithmetic operations at high speed.

---

[8] Joseph Levy, *Punched Card Equipment—Principles and Applications*.
[9] Robert R. Arnold, Harold C. Hill, and Aylmer V. Nichols, *Introduction to Data Processing*.

OTHER ELECTROMECHANICAL EQUIPMENT.   The punched card is a common machine language medium; another is punched paper tape in a continuous roll.   Perforations are made on the tape as a by-product of the first machine-made record of the data; the tape is then used to control the operations of electromechanical machines.   Examples of other electromechanical equipment operating with these machine languages are automatic type-writers·such as the Flexowriter, automatic calculating typewriters, punched tape adding machines, and address plate embossing machines.

Heyel aptly summarizes the mechanical and electromechanical equipment situation that is applicable to the average school system:

> The office machines industry continues to fill a growing demand for unsophisticated, easy-to-use devices for semi-manual operations in small companies and in decentralized locations of large organizations.   The office machines industry, likewise, has developed and continues to improve versatile, high-speed electromechanical machines in self-contained configurations independent of computers, for data tabulating, sorting, accounting, printing and copying, mail handling, filing and retrieving, timekeeping, intercommunication, and the like . . . in all areas of public and private administration.[10]

Electronic Equipment

In the field of data processing, the highest grade of equipment is electronic. Schools, however, are more familiar with electronic equipment in the field of communication.   Radios, television sets, tape recorders, videotape systems, dictaphones, and wireless intercoms are examples.

The distinguishing feature of electronic equipment is the circuitry that amplifies signals by using vacuum tubes, transistors, resistors, capacitors, inductors, and diodes; or the thin-film integration of some of these components.   Thin-film integrated circuitry is responsible for miniaturized devices such as hand-sized calculators, as well as for the remarkable central storage capacity of some of the powerful "fourth generation" computers.

The input/output media for automatic operation of electronic data processing (EDP) equipment may be punched cards or perforated tape, but a faster language medium is magnetic tape.   This is also a convenient storage medium to supplement the main memory of computers or electronic

---

[10] Heyel, *Computers, Office Machines,* p. 14.

calculators. For storage, however, magnetic tape is rivaled by magnetic drums and, especially, disks which provide more rapid access to stored material.

There are now electronically controlled typewriters, calculators, accounting machines, and various-sized computers. Because of developments in electronic equipment, inspired largely by computer technology, there is an ever-widening circle of office machines that approach computer capabilities in certain regards, but that are less expensive to acquire, operate, and maintain. They also have the advantage of being less threatening to some personnel and clientele.

As a case in point, the new electronic accounting machines may be classified as desk-model computers.[11] They are no longer restricted by plugboards to either billing, posting, bookkeeping, or accounting, but are general purpose machines with rapid computational and processing speed. Accordingly, the Business and Equipment Manufacturer's Association has suggested that full-scale computers should be reserved for processing kinds of data other than accounting types of information.[12]

In like manner, programmable electronic calculators are available that might also be called desk-top computers. The Wang 700 series, for example, can be programmed from its own keyboard, storing the program in a usable core memory of 8,000 bits and on cassette tapes for later automatic reprogramming. A program can be 960 steps in length; one standard tape can hold ten such programs which can be loaded and executed automatically by the calculator. An electric typewriter can serve as an output printer, recording each step of the program or writing out the results of calculations upon command. The user merely selects the program and inserts the new variable data on the keyboard. Such calculators are designed for scientific or engineering uses, but could easily handle the majority of statistical problems for a school district's research department.

COMPUTERS. Regardless of its rivals, the king of electronic data processing and computing equipment is the digital computer. Electronic data processing often signifies a computer center. The computer is a general purpose

---

[11] Business Equipment Manufacturers Association, *New Techniques in Office Operations: Machines, Forms, Systems*, p. 84.
[12] Business Equipment Manufacturers Association, *New Techniques*, p. 86.

machine, performing virtually alone all kinds of tasks that would otherwise require several kinds of machines and much human effort.

On the other hand, a computer is, in itself, a system composed of separate units or machines. The heart of the computer is its central processing unit (CPU), containing a memory unit (storage unit), an arithmetic and logic unit, and a control unit. The control unit receives coded instructions from storage, interprets them, and signals the proper circuits to carry out instructions in the necessary sequence. A control panel (console) is part of the control unit that allows a human operator to monitor the computer operation.

Input and output units provide the means of communication for computer users. Various types of units are employed at the input/output terminals. The most common is the electric typewriter, or a similar keyboard, often connected with the computer by a telephone in a time-sharing system. Other means of input/output, in ascending order in relation to speed, are punched cards, perforated tape, and magnetic tape. High-speed printed output uses line printers, some of which can print an entire page in less than two seconds.

Optical scanners or magnetic character readers are making it possible for printed copy to be used as an input to the computer. These pieces of equipment convert the printing into punched cards, or "read" the printed data directly onto magnetic tapes or disks. This represents a form of source data automation.

The cathode ray tube (CRT) is a special means of output that is increasing in popularity. Similar to a television tube, a CRT can display data in the form of printing, curves, graphs, schematics, and pictures. It can even serve as input to a computer in an interactive mode. The computer receives communication by means of a light pen with which the viewer directs a beam of light so as to "draw" or "mark" on the cathode ray screen.

The major feature distinguishing a computer from a calculator is its basic memory or storage unit. This unit stores all the instructions that guide the computer's operations and all kinds of reference information in addition to the input data, intermediate results, and final solutions. It releases any part of this mass of information as requested by the program. The size or power of a computer is measured chiefly by the storage capacity of this basic memory (barring auxiliary or peripheral storage units).

Several measures of size are used, often making comparisons difficult for the layman. Units of measure may be characters, bits, bytes, or words. Characters are letters, numerals, and symbols, as on a typewriter. A character requires a minimum of six bits of storage space. Bits are binary digits, the numerals in the base two system that are directly stored in the computer memory. Bytes vary with companies; an IBM byte is eight bits. Of all the various possible measures, the total number of bits of core storage available is the most direct and meaningful one. This probably will have to be calculated from the number of characters, words, word lengths, or other units customarily advertised. The symbol "K" in computer technology stands for 1,000 of anything, e.g., 4K bits equals 4,000 bits.

It is rather futile to try to define size classifications of computers precisely in relation to words like mini, small, medium, or large because there is little uniformity among companies and because medium-scale computers today may be small-scale tomorrow. IBM Corporation presently classifies 8K bytes (64,000 bits) as small, 512K bytes as medium, and 4 million bytes as large.

The basic size of a computer does not consider the auxiliary memories that are added as peripheral equipment in the form of magnetic tapes, drums or disks, which increase memory capacity astronomically. New types of auxiliary memories are being developed. A laser memory can store up to a trillion bits. A holographic memory developed by Nippon Telephone and Telegraph reportedly can store 10,000 times as much information in the same space as magnetic tapes and at about one-hundredth the cost.

A school administrator should study computers to learn of their potential and to acquire some grasp of data processing and information systems. The computer has had a direct application in about 10 percent of the school districts in the United States and has indirectly exercised a strong influence on others, particularly in the development of systems concepts.

Copying and Duplicating Processes

Copying and reproducing the contents of all kinds of documents is a special aspect of data processing that is a vital part of modern school practice.

Decisions regarding the acquisition of copying or duplicating equipment are not simple. Each machine must be evaluated in relation to its special uses. Many questions should be asked. What kinds of data will be handled: single sheets, pages in bound volumes, small and extra-large sheets, cardstock originals, or whatever? How fast should the machine produce single or multiple copies? How many copies may be needed frequently? On what kind of material should the copy be printed for purposes of later handling, writing upon, or storing? What kind of stencils, masters, or transparencies will the machine make for use on machines such as the offset press, mimeograph, duplicator, or overhead projector? How will employees probably handle this copier, and what guidelines will be necessary to avoid its abuse? Finally, how do all the proposed uses relate to the original and continuing costs?

A description of various copying processes follows.

Facsimile copy machines employ various kinds of chemical, thermal, photographic, and electrostatic processes. They use either a dry or wet process and make prints from direct contact or projection. Examples are: the diazo process, the thermal process (Thermofax machine or the like), the dye-transfer process, and the diffusion transfer.

Electrostatic or Xerography copying is an electrical dry process. Ordinary paper or other materials can be used as the copy material.

Microfilming is a truly photographic copying process. High-speed rotary cameras, microfilm cards that are key-punched for automatic filing and retrieving (aperture cards), cartridge microfilm, electronic beam recorders, cathode-ray tubes, and a 3M printer that can make hard copy from a CRT transmission are exciting new developments facilitating the mechanized or computerized retrieval and transmission of microfilmed information.[13]

Spirit duplicating (dittoing) is a familiar process in schools.

Azograph duplicating is a liquid process machine that avoids the mess and stain of spirit duplicating.

Mimeographing is another familiar process. A recent development is a copying machine that electronically scans original copies that are typed, printed, or hand-drawn. Halftone pictures are also reproducible.

Offset duplicating or printing is being used more by school districts each year, especially where the enrollment approximates 10,000 students. School districts can save up to 40 percent of their printing costs by owning their own offset press. Only the photographic metal plate process-

---

[13] Business Equipment Manufacturers Association, *New Techniques,* pp. 29–32.

ing or some occasional special effects need to be farmed out to the local print shop.

Other types of duplication are needed for special purposes. Automatic typewriters, operating by commands from various kinds of machine language media, have been mentioned previously. Addressing and listing machines are often useful for large mailing lists. They use either metal plates that have to be embossed on a special machine, or fiber or tissue stencils that can be typed on a typewriter that has a special platen.

The computer itself can be applied to purposes such as these. It can be programmed to control automatic typewriters in the same manner as a Flexowriter. Conceivably, almost any word-duplicating operation could be computerized, but the volume of business determines the practical utility or cost benefits of this procedure.

Applications of Educational Data Processing

The initials EDP signify either "electronic data processing" or "educational data processing." This chapter will use the term "educational data processing" because it restricts the meaning neither to the use of electronic equipment nor to the use of computers in particular, as some of the literature does. In educational data processing, whatever equipment is most appropriate for a given purpose should be utilized. This could be computers, but it could also be many other kinds of equipment, electronic or electromechanical.

In this section a large number of previously successful and promising school uses of semi-automatic or completely automatic EDP equipment are itemized. For semantic reasons, school work is classified under five headings: (1) business, (2) student personnel and guidance, (3) research and decision making, (4) personnel, and (5) classroom instruction. Since there are so many uses for educational data processing in the first four areas, they are only outlined. The uses in classroom instruction are handled more descriptively, but still briefly.

The reader should keep in mind that the outlines have been compiled eclectically from many sources; they were not developed from a logical analysis of any complete or ideal data processing system. This has several implications. The classification scheme does not constitute a recommendation for structuring a school system, and it is not really comprehensive of all school functions. By the same token, there is some overlapping of ideas in the outlines and the items are not presented as a complete list of possibilities in this changing world.

The purposes of the lists are to suggest to a school administrator many possibilities that might be adaptable to his needs and also to stimulate his creative thinking of other applications. The potential uses of automatic and semi-automatic equipment are nearly infinite.

BUSINESS APPLICATIONS OF EDP. Automation in office routines was pioneered and largely perfected in business and commercial enterprises, so it is natural to find schools adopting similar procedures initially in the area of business services. The design of the available data processing equipment makes it applicable to school business with little, if any, required modification.

Schools are finding that they can produce significant improvements in their business operations by taking advantage of what business has learned about data processing. Time and money can be saved while the accuracy and timeliness of all reports can be improved. It has been repeatedly found that business services can be made more efficient and can be expanded appreciably without hiring additional personnel. Business administrators can keep up with their ever-increasing load of paper work and still have more office time for studying important problems and making decisions.

The following outline suggests uses for electronic or electromechanical data processing equipment in the area generally defined as business services.

Business Applications of EDP

I. Budgeting and budgetary control.
   A. Planning budgets: requests, worksheets, cost projections for new salaries or new programs.
   B. Guiding expenditure patterns with periodic pro rata reports to schools and departments.
   C. Cost accounting and cost analyzing.

II. Purchasing and appropriations accounting.
   A. Assessing needs, products, vendors, and developing bid specifications.
   B. Writing and posting purchase orders.
   C. Writing warrants and posting expenditures.
   D. Compiling financial reports for departments, schools, school board, or state.

III. Equipment, materials, and supply accounting.
   A. Maintaining an inventory of equipment and furniture that includes records of maintenance.
   B. Maintaining textbook and instructional material inventories and reporting annual needs in relation to enrollments and proposed programs.
   C. Scheduling the use of equipment, instructional media, and materials.
   D. Adjusting warehouse supply inventory continuously to show ordered, received, distributed, and on-hand material.
   E. Reporting the requisition and distribution of supplies, materials, and equipment according to schools, classrooms, and departments.

IV. Payroll and employee benefits.
   A. Writing and posting warrants for payroll.
   B. Keeping employee earning records and making written reports and statements of earnings, withholdings, and retirement contributions.
   C. Informing individual employees of the present and long-range value of their own employee benefits.

V. Cafeteria accounting.
   A. Keeping the records on cafeteria sales, purchases, and other expenses.
   B. Billing cafeteria users automatically when users eat on credit with a charge-plate system (college level).
   C. Making financial reports to the board on cafeteria operation.

STUDENT PERSONNEL AND GUIDANCE APPLICATIONS OF EDP. The many needs for information relative to student personnel have offered a broad field for the application of the new technology. Most schools employing automatic data processing equipment use it for many applications in this field. This relieves teachers of many clerical chores and also aids the clerical staff in accomplishing their tasks expeditiously. If data on pupil personnel are accumulated, processed, stored, and made accessible by a systems approach, it becomes available to counselors, teachers, and administrators when they need it.

Student personnel and guidance applications may not be easily justified by the concept of money saved, but if time and effort are not wasted in unnecessary duplication of tasks, all personnel and resources can be used to greater advantage.

An example of the use of computer technology in the area of counseling is the design, by Systems Development Corporation, of a man–machine counseling system which includes the following major elements: (1) an information retrieval system for information on students; (2) a tracking and monitoring system that will alert the counselor when critical situations occur; (3) an automated report generation for preparing cumulative records, report cards, and other reports or lists; and (4) a prediction system that does not require the counselor to have a technical knowledge of statistics.[14]

The following is an outline illustrative of some applications in the student personnel area.

Student Personnel and Guidance Applications of EDP

I. School census records.
  - **A.** Making population analyses of children ready for school by grades.
  - **B.** Recording background information on parents and guardians with all the data necessary for later communications and reports.
  - **C.** Making the master cumulative record file for each student which will later be expanded and updated.
  - **D.** Reporting school census findings to the state and federal governments as requested or as needed for project and grant requests.
  - **E.** Making the school mailing lists and the address labels for mailing.
  - **F.** Making PTA calling lists.
  - **G.** Listing students with various handicaps or special needs by grade.
  - **H.** Listing nonresident students under inter-district agreements.
  - **I.** Scheduling and routing buses and other means of transportation and issuing bus passes.
  - **J.** Coordinating family vacations in schools operating on a twelve-month school year.

II. Registration and scheduling.
  - **A.** Constructing the master class schedule.
  - **B.** Registering pupils by mark sense cards.
  - **C.** Scheduling pupils into classes.
    1. Balancing class loads and sections and distributing classes and students fairly.
    2. Making class lists, homeroom lists, study hall lists.
    3. Making program schedules for individuals that avoid course conflict in individual programs.

III. Attendance accounting.
  - **A.** Preprinting documents for recording attendance.
  - **B.** Recording and summarizing attendance daily, monthly, annually.
  - **C.** Computing statistics on attendance—ADA, percent of attendance, etc.

---

[14] H. F. Silberman and R. T. Filep, "Information Systems Applications in Education," *Annual Review of Information Science and Technology*, pp. 367–68.

      D.   Listing new pupils, pupils whose attendance is spotty or shows signs of developing trouble, pupils who drop out and the reasons for leaving school, etc.

IV. Cumulative records.
      A.   Collecting pupil personnel data in machine readable form at the time of enrollment (using mark sense cards or forms).
      B.   Storing data for machine transmittal later (on punch cards or magnetic tape, etc.).
      C.   Updating machine records from new source data collected and transmitted from schools.
      D.   Updating cumulative record folders or cards in schools by pasting gummed labels made by the data center from results of test scoring or student report cards.
      E.   Printing cumulative record data in part or whole upon request from authorized persons.

V. Testing, scoring, and statistical handling of test data.
      A.   Test constructing and evaluating (*see* Research and Decision-Making Applications outline).
      B.   Test preprinting.
      C.   Testing by use of mark sense answer sheets or cards.
      D.   Scoring tests and recording scores.
      E.   Producing gummed labels for scores on standardized tests to update pupil cumulative records.
      F.   Computing statistics and reporting test results by preparing rank-in-class lists, reports by subject and school, etc.

VI. Mark reporting and recording.
      A.   Preprinting personalized report cards (IBM cards) from pupil file data for each subject on pupil's class list; teachers have only to record a grade on the cards.
      B.   Making gummed labels of student grades for pasting on permanent records in the schools.
      C.   Computing individual and group statistics on pupil grades.
      D.   Preparing lists of student grades.
          1.   Rank-in-class lists.
          2.   Honor rolls of various kinds.
          3.   Scholarship award candidates.
          4.   Lists of failures, probable failures, underachievers, and pupils receiving incompletes.

VII. Making district reports of class and school progress.

RESEARCH AND DECISION-MAKING APPLICATIONS OF EDP.   Turning machines toward the accomplishment of routine tasks that would require endless repetition of the same operations and procedures by human "slaves" is a liberating operation; but, at a higher level, using machines to help make analyses, predictions, and surveys, all of which may involve massive amounts of data, makes the use of sophisticated equipment most worthwhile.   For example, business is calling for nearly instantaneous operating reports, from which decisions can be made at the time they are needed.   Without data processing equipment and good communication, business operations are slowed down considerably.   Schools can utilize data processing equipment in much the same manner, as the accompanying list of potentialities will indicate.

Research and Decision-Making Applications of EDP

I.   Stimulation of research and facilitation of decision making in general.
    A.   Freeing teachers and administrators to do research by reducing their routine paper load.
    B.   Improving the quality of research through machine-processing capabilities.
    C.   Providing operating reports almost on demand to facilitate administrative decision making to control current plans and conditions.
    D.   Providing planning reports covering a three-year or longer period from which trends and predictions may be extrapolated.

II.   Surveys of community and schools.
    A.   Recording and reporting census information related to the school community.
        1.   Children's ages.
        2.   Mobility patterns.
        3.   Housing conditions and patterns.
        4.   Economic conditions.
        5.   Racial patterns.
        6.   Police records.
        7.   Parental background factors.
        8.   Sibling status.
    B.   Polling or surveying students and teachers.
    C.   Making class size and teacher-load studies.
    D.   Making plant utilization studies that include simulation studies of proposed plans.
    E.   Making college and educational opportunity surveys.

III.   Attendance studies.
    A.   Studying attendance by school, class, race, sex, etc.
    B.   Discovering attendance patterns of pupils—pinpointing situations that merit attention before they get worse.

IV. Grade (marking) studies.
    A. Making grade distribution studies.
    B. Analyzing course-marking standards and teacher-marking practices.
    C. Computing rank-in-class statistics by different formulas for different purposes.

V. Test development and the use of tests in research.
    A. Perfecting tests by item analysis, correlations, reliability checks, etc.
    B. Scoring of standardized and teacher-made tests—with any kind of score desired: raw score, percentile, stanine, standard score, etc.
    C. Finding statistical significance of test results wherever tests are used.
    D. Making score distribution studies of classes, schools, and district.
    E. Producing local norms, expectancy tables, and expected grade curves for a teacher based on pupil ability and achievement tests.

VI. Salary administration.
    A. Designing salary schedules and employee benefit programs on the basis of research and simulation.
        1. Projecting costs that would accrue if contemplated salary schedules were inaugurated.

PERSONNEL APPLICATIONS OF EDP. The application of data processing equipment in the personnel field is relatively recent, both in industry and in education. In this analysis, personnel applications deal with both certificated and noncertificated employees, involving both the business and personnel offices. Items pertaining to personnel may be found in all the preceding lists of EDP applications, including the one on research and decision making. Therefore, only those functions not already suggested elsewhere are itemized in the accompanying short outline.

Personnel Applications of EDP

I. Employee records.
    A. Keeping the master personnel file up to date.
    B. Informing employees of needed X rays, credential renewals, leave expirations, next evaluation, unexpired sick leave days, units needed by a certain date to attain next salary hurdle, etc.
    C. Reporting reasons for termination of employment as determined by exit interviews or questionnaires.

II. Staff selection and assignment.
    A. Aiding in screening applications and interview records according to established job needs and criteria.
    B. Assigning teachers on the basis of known background, skills, and abilities in relation to specified classroom and school needs.

    C.   Writing teacher contract documents including salary, method of payment, contract dates, and conditions of employment.

    D.   Assigning day-to-day substitute teachers by (1) matching first requests with first available substitutes or (2) matching skills possessed by substitutes with skills requested by regular teachers.

One of the most interesting potentials of a computerized, or otherwise systematized, personnel program is the possibility of assessing skills, abilities, and interests of teachers during the hiring stage and during their continued employment so that differentiated assignments can be made. Greene recommends a skills inventory such as that developed by Systems Development Corporation of Santa Monica, California, in their package called "General Purpose Data Management System."[15]

Instructional Technology

Since instructional technology is a major part of the picture of technology in education, some discussion of it must be included. However, because much literature is readily available in this field, this chapter will only highlight certain new trends and practices.

Technology has been slow to come to the classroom and still meets with considerable resistance. The broadened meaning of instructional technology (to include the systems approach applied from within an educational establishment) is an encouraging development. The new concept is not the imposition of technologies and systems *on* education, nor the application of existing technologies *to* education, but each teacher's conscious participation in developing "a growing, indigenous technology within education."[16]

THE SYSTEMS APPROACH. In 1965, in his concluding summary of the New Media Workshop held in Tahoe City, California, Tom A. Shell-

---

[15] Robert Edward Greene, "Application of Electronic Data Processing to the Functions of Personnel Administration" (Unpublished doctoral dissertation, University of Southern California, 1970), p. 105.

[16] P. Kenneth Komoski, "The Continuing Confusion About Technology and Education; or the Myth-ing Link in Educational Technology," *Educational Technology: Educational Technology Around the World*, p. 74.

hammer stated that "we are ready for a technological approach. The hard look, the bold look, the youthful eager look—is developing as a systems approach to education."[17] Current thinking about curriculum, instruction, school organization, school buildings, and new models of staffing—all of which are designed to improve the quality of education—make it feasible to implement a systems approach to instruction such as that outlined by Popham and Baker.[18]

Applying such an approach means at least (1) preassessing (diagnosing) needs in relation to pupil learning modes, abilities, and curricular objectives; (2) prescribing individual and group learning experiences; (3) having students actively participate in instructional activities; and (4) evaluating pupil performance in relation to behavioral objectives. Choosing the best means from among alternatives available to accomplish each of these four objectives is the key to the systematic instructional process. The many instructional means available include all kinds of pupil learning activities: the traditional instructional approaches such as books, lectures, demonstrations, and discussions; all the conventional audio-visual media that were in common use in the 1950s; and the new technological media.

NEW MEDIA. There is nothing new about the use of "new media," or audio-visual aids (materials that appeal directly to the senses of sight and hearing). Probably since the beginnings of formal education, certain types of audio-visual materials have been used in the classroom. Great advances have been made since the introduction of phonographs, radios, and movie projectors.

The so-called "new media" are not simply more hardware, although some is included. The hardware may be television and closed-circuit television systems; videotape recorders and cameras; listening centers; cassette recorders; cartridge projectors; individual carrels equipped with communication devices; electronic language laboratories; electronic testing machines; learning laboratories with partially or completely automated retrieval of instructional programs; and computerized programs with various kinds of student response systems. The trends in the hardware are toward miniaturization, simplicity of use, the use of media in combination, and classrooms planned for the use of all kinds of media.

---

[17] James W. Brown and Ruth H. Aubrey, compilers, *New Media and Changing Educational Patterns*, p. 72.

[18] *See* James W. Popham and Eva L. Baker, *Systematic Instruction*.

New media that might be called "software" include the programs for all the above hardware; also, programmed or individualized learning materials packaged as texts, cross-media packets, or self-selection kits. Many new kits and packages are called "systems," which may sometimes stretch the definition beyond its customary flexibility, but confirms the trend that has been discussed.

Industries, such as the Systems Development Corporation of Santa Monica, California, are cooperating with schools in developing new types of hardware and software.

INDIVIDUALIZED INSTRUCTION. The chief new emphasis in the use of the new media is to personalize instruction. The classroom conceived of as a learning laboratory exemplifies this idea. Individual pupils or groups are dispersed among learning centers which students select or to which they are assigned on the basis of needs and interests. Various activities are scheduled to be done by different people at different times.

Individual study carrels are provided for self-pacing instruction and completely individualized and concentrated work. This multimedia facility can be equipped with a cassette tape player, a super 8-mm film projector, slides, film strips, a screen, a headset jack for earphones, a television receiver, switches for operation, and dials to select videotape lectures and demonstrations. An electronic communication system can connect the study carrel to the library or the Instructional Media Center for data and information retrieval.

SUPPORTING THE TEACHER. A major reason for resistance to technology in the classroom has been the idea that the media will replace the teacher. Some resistance by professional teachers has been justified as a reaction to some of the propaganda of media enthusiasts. Programmed learning has been proposed as an economy measure or as a means of importing new curricula into classes where the teacher, it is assumed, lacks competence in the subject. If the use of media proposes to ignore the teacher, compete with the teacher, or supplant the teacher in order to presumably keep up with the changing times, such use is very questionable. There is real reason to fear dehumanization in the age of cybernation.

It is more sensible to provide media as an auxiliary aid in support of the teacher and under his direct control. Smith and Smith term this "adjunctive programming."[19]   Earl McGrath recommends using media as teacher "extenders," rather than teacher "replacers."[20]

COMPUTERIZED INSTRUCTION.   Certainly media should do direct teaching at times.   At the teacher's discretion this is often the most desirable way to stimulate learning of some concepts.   Direct instruction, in a programmed learning format, is one of the areas in which the computer has been applied experimentally with some success.   Bundy has stated:

> Essentially, this technology seeks to provide an individualized learning environment for each student.   Instructional programs are stored in the computer and the student interacts with these programs by means of electronic interface devices.   The instructional programs may include a broad range of subject matter content and extend across a spectrum from simple drill and practice routines to complex tutorial-type learning experiences.[21]

There are several kinds of tutelage that the computer may be able to provide under the label of computer-assisted instruction (CAI).   It can stimulate and simulate.   To stimulate, "the machine is capable of presenting material to children, requiring them to respond to the material, evaluating these responses, and providing the children with additional information depending on the nature of their performance."[22]   Instruction can be individualized so that slower students are given remedial instruction and faster students are given more difficult material.   Systems can be installed that permit students to dial the computer for additional information from a retrieval center.

A computer can be used to simulate learning situations on a hypothetical basis.   The teacher's decisions can be programmed into the computer which can then predict how a decision will affect a student or the class.

In some places, all the schools in a district are tied together electronically by co-axial cable and/or telephone lines in order to handle data or telelectures.   Statewide and regional educational television networks also

19 Karl U. Smith and Margaret Foltz Smith, *Cybernetic Principles of Learning and Educational Design,* p. 298.

20 Earl J. McGrath, "What Are We Learning About Learning Centers?"   A symposium, Oklahoma Christian College, Oklahoma City, March 3, 1971.   (Unpublished.)

21 Robert F. Bundy, "Computer-Assisted Instruction—Where Are We?"   *Phi Delta Kappan,* p. 424.

22 Harry F. Silberman, "The Digital Computer in Education," *Phi Delta Kappan* 43 (May 1962), p. 346.

are being used.[23]   The public schools of Philadelphia have the most comprehensive system of computer utilization in operation.   Computers are used as a medium of instruction, and students in vocational programs are taught to maintain and repair them.

CAI is still in its infancy, with many problems to be resolved to make it practical for widespread implementation in public schools.[24]   One of its major problems is simply program cost, whether figured in hours or dollars. To serve 43,000 students, it costs $1.5 million annually and requires a special computer-oriented professional staff of 42 people.[25]   A 1971 survey by the National Education Association showed that less than one percent of the teachers reported that they themselves had used computers in their classes, although it appeared that perhaps 10 percent of the districts were experimenting with instructional uses to some degree.[26]

Decisions must be made regarding the objectives of CAI.   Educators must decide whether education is to be computer oriented and directed or humanly oriented.   Questions must be raised and answered.   For example: Are theoretical and intellectual considerations to be neglected?   If not, how will they be coordinated with the use of CAI?   Will computers get in the way of general education and academic proficiency?   In what way will CAI be used?   Will the development of the personal attributes that are so necessary to effective teaching be obscured?

When a computer is available, its use as a powerful calculator is an indirect aid to the instructional program.   In mathematics and science, the computer can quickly solve problems that students know how to solve, but that would consume excessive amounts of time better spent in learning new concepts.   It is an ideal aid to problem solving and operates as a check on problem-solving abilities.   Secondary school students would be fortunate to have some exposure to this use of the computer.

COMPUTER-MANAGED INSTRUCTION.   Another use of computers that is very promising and may be closer to implementation than CAI is computer-managed instruction (CMI).   As an aid to instructional management, the computer helps the teacher in the diagnostic, prescriptive, and evaluative

---

[23] Philip Lewis, "Instructional Technology: Revolution on the Horizon," *Nation's Schools* 82 (December 1968), p. 60.

[24] James L. Rogers, "Current Problems in CAI," *Datamation,* pp. 28–33.

[25] Stephen J. Knezevich and Glen G. Eye (eds.), *Instructional Technology and the School Administrator,* p. 58.

[26] National Education Association, Research Division, "The Use of Computers for Instruction," *Research Bulletin,* pp. 3–4.

phases of the instructional cycle. Examples of experimental projects in CMI are becoming quite numerous. Some of the first were the Instructional Management System (IMS), the Individualized Prescribed Instruction (IPI) program, the Program for Learning in Accordance with Needs (PLAN), and the Teacher's Automated Guide (TAG)—all briefly described by Silberman and Filep.[27]

Computer-managed instruction is much less expensive than CAI and is not so threatening to existing classroom procedures. It de-emphasizes the author-programmed learning sequence, the extremely costly aspect of CAI. It fits conveniently into the administrative uses of a computer as a data processor; for instance, it utilizes student census and cumulative record data. Theoretically, CMI can make individualized instruction possible by aiding in the diagnosis of individual needs; by suggesting available original sources of data, media, materials, other resources, and activities most suitable to the accomplishment of the objectives established for each student; by directly scoring the pupil work or by providing the teacher or pupils with specific criteria and means by which they can evaluate progress.

In other words, the computer can function as a highly sophisticated resource unit. Tape, disk, or drum file storage can provide quick access to resources limited only by the creative imagination of the educators. This does not place the computer in the role of the final authority on all questions, but uses it as a handy library to pinpoint sources, means, and procedures that might aid the instructional process. CMI is considered by some to be a good, intermediate step to more complete computer use in the instructional program; by others it is considered the best, the ultimate, use.

OVERDEPENDENCE ON COMPUTERS AND MACHINES. Common errors are being promulgated in relation to this world of the future. There is a growing overdependence on gadgetry and a corresponding underemphasis on the role of human intellect and teacher–pupil relationships. To illustrate, teachers frequently hear the question: "Why do we need to learn to do arithmetic when soon all we will have to do is push buttons and get the answers?" The needs for understanding mathematical processes and learning multiplication and addition facts are being shortchanged. Many similar errors are part of what Barrett[28] terms "The Computer Mentality."

Predictions for the new machines are frequently presented as though

---

[27] Silberman and Filep, "Information Systems," pp. 363–64.
[28] Richard S. Barrett, "The Computer Mentality," *Phi Delta Kappan*, pp. 430–34.

they were existing realities. Many unresolved problems are thereby concealed. Computer hardware itself needs considerable improvement for educational use. Some things that are clearly needed are better communication between the user and the machine; better, more standardized human–machine languages; more hard-copy output devices; and, above all, lower costs for the whole procedure. A skilled technician is needed to keep the equipment in working order.

The gross lack of software presents more serious problems. There are few persons with the expertise to produce it, and the time required for its production is exorbitant. Perhaps even more crucial are the major gaps in knowledge within the educational establishment in relation to the learning process, diagnostic testing, other critical educational questions, and in relation to technology itself.

Even the application of central data processing systems to administrative areas has dangers that should be mentioned: the problem of oversimplifying data in the data reduction and coding phases, the problem of storing and safeguarding confidential information, the lack of standardized meanings for data stored in different data processing systems, and many other problems. Another problem is the physical construction of schools. Older schools are not built for the electronic age. Electrical circuits and panels may be so inadequate that if too much equipment is used at one time, electrical breakers are thrown or fuses are blown. The cost of rewiring to carry the extra load and the installation of intercommunication systems is costly. Fortunately, many newer schools are being built with an awareness of the future.

Man has developed an immense and complicated technology which may create physical, psychological, and educational dangers. The problems can be overcome, but they must be considered before a district decides whether to involve itself deeply with the new instructional media.

Access to EDP Systems

Schools and other educational agencies may obtain access to computers or other educational data processing facilities in many ways. Equipment can be possessed locally or cooperatively with other schools or even with other public agencies such as a city government. Possession is attainable by purchasing, renting, or leasing (often with an option to buy) equipment. Even without cooperative possession, cooperative use, which implies time-sharing, is a growing trend. Schools share equipment with other, perhaps noneducational, users. The equipment may be possessed by either public or private agencies. Public agencies may be within or outside of the educational hierarchy. Private agencies may include local business concerns who will rent computer time or commercial data processing service bureaus.

Public data processing systems are being conceived and established at all levels of the educational establishment. Local schools or districts alone or in collaboration with one another, city schools, county or intermediate units, intrastate regional agencies, state agencies, state universities and colleges, and even interstate and national educational agencies have data processing centers in various stages of planning and operation.

Most of the public data processing centers operate on a batch-processing program utilizing a relatively small computer. Others use electromechanical equipment. Their function has been primarily the processing of administrative information.

An example of a regional computer center is the Minnesota Total Information for Educational Systems (TIES). It was developed as a regional information center to respond to the needs of individual school districts for management, research, and instructional capabilities. TIES is an established, on-line information system utilizing telecommunications, an integrated data base, and advanced information systems concepts. It recognizes and establishes the interdependence of all data—descriptive, instructional, fiscal, etc. It has been described as the most complex and sophisticated educational computer system in the country, serving 31 Minnesota school districts and over 325 schools in Minnesota and Illinois. Districts of any size can utilize the services. The TIES districts vary from 800 students to over 32,000 students. Although two districts are 120 to 125 miles from the computer location, they have a 5- to 7-second turnaround in inquiry and update of their data file. The system is flexible so that districts retain their own decision functions and assume responsibility for in-district communication and data processing related activity. The following services are available as part of the daily activities of teachers: computer instruction, computer-assisted instruction, computer-managed instruction, and computer guidance programs. TIES can also provide statistical analysis, enrollment projections, and personnel services. The system can provide periodic and special reports such as: census information, student information, personnel and payroll preparation and reports, and finance and budget information and reports.

Examples of other large projects are the California State master plan for integrated data processing;[29] the state of Oregon's OTIS (Oregon Total Information System);[30] the New York State system under the Board of Cooperative Educational Services;[31] the New England Educational Data Systems (NEEDS);[32] and the national program BEDS (Basic Educational Data System), sponsored by the United States Office of Education and the Council of Chief State School Administrators.[33]

The national system is designed to be used in conjunction with several handbooks prepared by the U.S. Office of Education that identify and define educational items of information in an attempt to produce a common data base in order to produce comparable data in various parts of the country. The handbooks are useful to local and state school administrators whether or not their operation is to be automated. The available handbooks discuss a common core of state educational information, financial accounting, property accounting, and staff accounting. Additional handbooks are in preparation.

Paralleling the developments in the public sector, there is a proliferation of commercial service bureaus that furnish batch-processing or on-line time-sharing service to schools and other customers. There are some companies specializing in service to education or with divisions dedicated to such service. Commercial service agencies, like public ones, cover a wide variety of territorial ranges. Some commercial enterprises are engaged in developing what may properly be called a "computer utility," comparable to a telephone company. The General Electric Company has invested millions of dollars in a data-processing network that will span the United States and later be extended to Europe.

With the ever-increasing access potential represented by the development of minicomputers, cooperative possession or use, commercial service bureaus, and regional data-processing centers, computers are certainly becoming available to serve any purpose that cannot be adequately served by other means. In 1970, it was estimated that 4,300 school districts in

---

[29] Robert L. Howe, "The Concepts of Regional Educational Data Processing Centers," in *Automated Educational Systems*, chap. 7.

[30] Jesse W. Tonks, "Wake the Dead: Project O.T.I.S.," *Data Processing for Education Administration*, p. 88.

[31] Justus A. Prentice, "Multi-School Educational Data Processing Via Central Computer," *Data Processing for Education Administration*, p. 167.

[32] John I. Goodlad, John F. O'Toole, Jr., and Louise L. Tyler, *Computers and Information Systems in Education*, pp. 69–70.

[33] Lorne H. Woollatt, "An Automated Statewide Information System," in *Automated Educational Systems*, p. 67.

the United States were using computers. The majority leased or rented the equipment. The larger part of the minority subscribed to time-sharing programs, and fewer than 10 percent owned their computer.[34]

Automation in an Educational Organization

In the new systems approach, local schools and districts must be considered as parts of a larger network. The implication is clear that a school superintendent must be knowledgeable about the systems approach and must avoid taking an insular stand that will put the entire burden of accountability upon himself and his local staff. He must consider means of involving his school district with other districts and agencies in whatever manner would improve its capacity to educate its students. This means he should become well acquainted with all public and private agencies who are in the business of planning communication and data-processing systems in his area.

A principal, likewise, must consider his school as part of a system of schools and agencies that should coordinate their efforts. He should make his school a true information system in its own right, and also as an integral part of a larger network with good lines of communication. All administrators should plan not only to develop and operate a good system of their own, but also to cooperate with programs designed to exchange information. This will give new life to the education process.[35]

Technological progress will require school districts, especially large ones, to employ an administrator with the training and skill to coordinate and supervise the use of the latest electronic equipment that the district is using or planning to use. He might be called a communications specialist, educational technician, or technological coordinator. He must provide for all eventualities in selection, purchasing, storage, allocation, scheduling, maintenance, and repairs of valuable equipment. He should also serve as the communication link between schools, the district, and the computer center.

One of the coordinator's most important functions should be the continuous inservice training of teachers and administrators. Workshops give teachers an opportunity to become proficient in operating all types of sophisticated machines and the necessary software. The coordinator can

---

[34] "How Computers Are Changing Education," *School Management,* p. 13.
[35] Woollatt, "An Automated Statewide Information System," p. 79.

help teachers and administrators evaluate the use of electronic equipment and interpret findings and data.

A SYSTEMS STUDY.   An educational unit must follow an orderly procedure in converting from a semi-manual system to machine processes in any of the areas of educational service.   Before any major changes are made, there should be a systems study of the organization that is broader in scope than what was once termed a feasibility study, aimed primarily at the decision to employ hardware.   A systems study aims at determining how a system can be designed or improved.

A systems analyst or consultant firm should be retained to help make the study.   The analysis will identify the sources of information (inputs) and the uses of information (outputs) demanded by the organization.   The most efficient manner of recording initial data, handling the flow of information, and producing all the necessary outputs will be recommended.

The analysis must be made with the close cooperation of all personnel affected by the operations studies.   An administrator with understanding of the systems approach and power to make decisions must be an active participant in the study.   This administrator will probably be the person who would have overall charge of the data-processing center if one were to be established within the system.   The works of Fairbanks[36] and Grossman and Howe[37] are good references for a background to understanding systems analysis.

THE DECISION TO EMPLOY HARDWARE AND SOFTWARE.   The decision to employ certain kinds of hardware and software comes as an outgrowth of the study; it is not a foregone conclusion.   By an analysis of need and comparative costs of alternatives (the feasibility aspect of the study), such decisions will be made.   Blanket recommendations cannot be made in advance, and statistics of use in other districts are not relevant to local needs.

The purchase of equipment will take into consideration many things, for example, the availability of software or programming for equipment requiring it.   Whether it is an 8-mm motion picture projector or a large-scale computer, the same principle applies.   Neither is of any use without a reasonable potential for software acquisition or production.   Films or

---

[36] *See* Ralph W. Fairbanks, *Successful Office Automation.*
[37] Alvin Grossman and Robert L. Howe, *Data Processing for Educators* (Chicago: Educational Methods, 1965).

filming are needed for the projector; programs or programming are needed for the computer. The latter, especially for programmed instruction, can be excessively costly—$5,000 to $30,000 per program hour, for example.

The software must meet local needs. This can be accomplished only by involving the users in its production and its evaluation. Imposing an entire system produced outside the organization is simply unwise if the staff will not use it.

PERSONNEL CONSIDERATIONS. A chief concern is whether the new system or equipment will improve employee morale or be threatening to some personnel. Some specific suggestions in this regard may be offered. Spend adequate time in planning and designing the new process. Make certain that persons directly involved understand the reasons for the changeover and have some voice in the design of the new system. Create a teamwork approach. Use every possible means to make the new system seem desirable. Attempt in every way to eliminate skepticism and to promote a willingness to try new things objectively. Implement the changeover gradually. One technique is to have employees produce required new data manually, prior to the changeover to a machine operation, to give them a practical appreciation of its usefulness. When the new system is installed, train all users, taking enough time to develop reasonable competence and respect for the system.

PLANNING FOR LONG-RANGE USE. The procurement of major equipment items should also plan for long-range use and ask questions related to expansion possibilities, obsolescence, compatibility with other machines with which information might be exchanged, and availability of service, training, and advice. The question of whether a school is being tied into a closed system that is wholly dependent upon a particular company may be pertinent. In this age of rapid change, the more open-ended a product or service is, the better.

COMMON ERRORS TO AVOID. Besides the above guidelines, there are several common pitfalls that careful planning should avoid. Do not purchase equipment to meet a particular need without considering its impending effect on other needs and operations. The equipment could easily prove more disruptive than helpful. Do not purchase equipment to improve personal or institutional status instead of job performance. Do not acquire more equipment, or more powerful equipment, than is practical.

The Instructional Materials Center (IMC)

Historically, a school library was a room containing books, periodicals, newspapers, and pamphlets. The student went there to study quietly. It was supervised by a librarian who enforced silence, helped students locate material, and checked books out and in.

Technology, however, has changed the old, traditional concept of a school library. No longer is it a mere repository for printed materials, valuable as they are. The term Instructional Materials Center, sometimes called Instructional Media Center (IMC) or Learning Resource Center, is more appropriate today in many school districts. The center should include individual study carrels, small reading rooms, areas for listening and viewing, work areas for producing software, storage areas, and a typing room. When adequately furnished, supplied, and equipped, it is the educational heart of a school. It is interesting to note that *School Libraries,* the journal of the American Association of School Librarians, has been changed to *School Media Quarterly.*

FUNCTIONS OF AN IMC.   The chief purpose of an IMC is to provide resources that are not available in classrooms. In the library section, students should be encouraged to read that which is worthwhile, to supplement their studies with literature other than textbooks, to use reference books effectively, and to develop and use research techniques.

There should be an adequate collection of books selected to meet the reading ability needs of students in all subjects and for all grade levels. For example, a high school student with a sixth grade reading ability should be able to find low level, high interest books for subject matter research or pleasure reading. The American Library Association has recommended that there should be 6,000 to 10,000 books for schools with less than a thousand students. If the school is larger, it should provide 10 books per student.[38]

There should be periodicals appropriate to the age and grade levels of the students using the facilities, as well as local and national newspapers,

---

[38] *Standards for School Library Programs* (Chicago: American Library Association, 1960), p. 25.

pamphlets, bulletins, and monographs from many sources. Governmental agencies supply free materials which are usually accurate and free from bias. Industries and private agencies also supply free materials, but they should be screened carefully since they may be distorted, present propaganda, or have objectionable advertising. There should be a balance between recreational and subject matter books and periodicals to encourage students to read for pleasure as well as for academic knowledge. The carry-over value to later life is important.

Study carrels, as explained previously, can be used by individual students to gather information from tapes, films, film strips, slides, videotapes, and microfilms. They can be the communicating link between the student and libraries of information recorded on tapes or disks in computer centers. Telephonic communication can connect the student with specialized libraries, people, or teachers having specialized information. Students who have been absent can use the carrel as a place to make up work that they have missed. The future of the individual study carrel is unlimited.

The IMC should be open during after-school hours such as late afternoons, evenings, weekends, and vacations. Too often it is closed and deprives students of extra opportunities for research, study, or pleasure. During school hours, schools that have not done so should break down the traditional lock-step classroom procedure that requires students to receive permission to leave a class and go to the IMC. Students should be given the freedom and trust to go freely to the IMC when they find the need to do research or to use the electronic machines.

In order for an IMC to function properly, students need to know how to use it. They should have pre-visitation preparation from the teacher, followed by visits to the center for further instruction. If properly oriented in the use of facilities and equipment of the IMC, students will realize the educational opportunities that are afforded there.

The IMC also provides professional materials for teacher use. There also should be some provision for teachers to review the books, films, and other software that their students will be using.

Although technology is reshaping libraries and enlarging their functions as instructional media centers, much still remains to be accomplished. Rowell and Heidbreder, in an extensive study of educational media selection centers, found that:[39]

---

[39] John Rowell and M. Ann Heidbreder, *Educational Media Selection Centers; Identification and Analysis of Current Practices* (Chicago: American Library Association, 1971), pp. 89–92.

1. No one model approximates the ideal.
2. Functions and evaluation of media are performed at a wide variety of levels and with varying degrees of effectiveness.
3. There is a need for an accepted definition of a center.
4. Differences among the centers were greater than similarities.
5. There were differences in the levels of effectiveness.
6. High potential programs appeared to be characterized by flexibility and fluidity of services.
7. There is a great diversity of needs to be met.
8. There is a schism between audio-visual interests and print-oriented interests.
9. There is a need for improved communications.
10. There appears to be a duplication of effort among the centers in evaluating and selecting media.
11. Media evaluation files were not kept by one-third of the centers and half of them needed improvement.

At this time, data-processing techniques have been used mainly for distribution of materials and circulation control. Retrieval systems are not used extensively at this date.[40]

FINANCING AN IMC. In addition to school district funds, two sources of federal funds are available to help school districts purchase library resources and instructional materials. Title II of the Elementary and Secondary Education Act (ESEA) aims to increase the quantity, quality, and availability of library books, textbooks, and audio-visual teaching materials in the schools. Eligible materials include: books, periodicals, documents, pamphlets, photographs, reproductions, pictorial or graphic works, musical pieces, maps, globes, sound recordings, slides, transparencies, kinescopes, and videotapes. Matching district funds are not required.

The second federal source has been Title III of the National Defense Education Act (NDEA) which authorized matching grants to public schools (and loans to private schools) for the purchase of equipment and materials for instruction in "critical subjects." It should be emphasized that federal aid of this kind is apt to be transient, depending upon the joint mood of Congress and the administration.

---

[40] Knezevich and Eye, *Instructional Technology,* p. 45.

STAFFING THE IMC. Formerly, the library was staffed by a librarian assisted by a clerk and student help; this staff is no longer sufficient. Technology is changing the library into a multimedia instructional center and an integral part of the school's educational program. The person in charge of the IMC must have training, not only in library science, but also in the use of the sophisticated IMC equipment. Universities are recognizing this need and are granting degrees (e.g., University of Minnesota) for media specialists.

The American Association of School Librarians, a division of the American Library Association, initiated a School Library Manpower Project in 1968 which was designed to investigate the problem of using school library manpower. The NEA Research Division was asked to make a Task Analysis Survey as part of the project. The survey of sample schools with outstanding programs of unified library–audio-visual services showed that all responding elementary and secondary schools had heads of library media centers or IMC centers.[41] More elementary than secondary schools had paid clerks or aides. More secondary schools employed assistant librarians, audio-visual specialists, and technicians.

The major responsibilities of the heads of library media or IMC centers are: administration, selection of materials and equipment, development of educational programs, instruction, and special services to faculty and students. With the expansion of the library into a media center, schools must expect to employ more specialized personnel, such as audio-visual specialists and technicians, who can help in selecting hardware and software, maintaining it, and producing materials, as well as helping students and teachers with their educational program. A qualified, enthusiastic media specialist can make the IMC one of the most popular rooms in a school—a learning laboratory that whets the curiosity and interests of students. The future of the media center is unlimited. See chapter 29 for a discussion of a multimedia learning resource center.

Summary

As in business and industry, automation is increasing in education. Systems analysis and design view a school district as an organic whole. Together with goal-directed programming, it provides an intercommuni-

---

[41] National Education Association, Research Division, "School Library Staff Duties," *Research Bulletin* 47 (December 1969), pp. 121–124.

cation network that includes all parts of the school system. Its acceptance is being accelerated by the growing demand for school accountability and the current trend toward innovations such as nongraded and open schools.

The systems approach to education requires both educational engineering and a new terminology derived from the concept of cybernetics. The information system implicit in the approach originates records, classifies and sorts data, and reports results. The ideal system is the "total" or "integrated" one. However, this is very expensive and the supply of experts needed to operate it is still so inadequate that most districts settle for a "partial" system. The ones most widely used are (1) an instructional system and (2) an administrative support system.

Machines utilized include mechanical, electromechanical, and electronic. Copying and duplicating processes, especially important to modern school practice, include microfilming, diazo, thermal, dye-transfer, and electrostatic copying devices.

Educational data processing (EDP) can be useful in five areas of school administration: business, student personnel and guidance, research and decision making, personnel, and classroom instruction. Access to EDP systems can be gained by purchasing, renting, leasing, or by cooperative possession by several school districts or counties.

In moving toward a systems approach, school administrators must first become knowledgeable in this new field. Then, a systems study should be conducted by the district using a systems analyst or consultant firm. Hardware and software will need to be acquired. Finally, school personnel must be fully involved in the new approach in order to eliminate skepticism and to promote a willingness to try new things.

The old concept of a library has changed; its modern counterpart is an Instructional Materials Center or IMC. It includes study carrels for individualized study and research and is linked with computer centers for data retrieval on any subject. The IMC should be in the hands of a trained media specialist.

Trends

An increased use of machines and systems is necessary in school organizations as in all other kinds of enterprises. The endless battle with school budgets requires a continual reassessment of systems, procedures, and methods of operation. The best possible means should be selected to implement the educational program.

The amount of paper work and the flow of forms and reports will not diminish. Improved records, more exchange of information, and better ways of individualizing programs are needed in order to improve the educational process. Advancing technology in data processing and systems approaches can help. Under the new circumstances, schools cannot remain static without facing obsolescence. They will be held accountable.

Several major trends pertaining to the application of educational engineering and technology to school management are itemized below.

TOWARD SYSTEMS CONCEPTS. Systems concepts are being applied from within school systems to both administration and instruction even without dependence on machines.

TOWARD AUTOMATION. It is becoming feasible to automate many routine tasks and avoid much duplication of labor.

TOWARD MICROFILM AND MACHINE RECORDS. The storage of all permanent school records may be on microfilm, microfiche, and/or in machine-readable forms in auxiliary computer memories. Any record will become rapidly accessible to authorized persons.

TOWARD STANDARDIZED REPORT FORMS. Forms may be standardized on a state or even national basis to facilitate data processing and exchange.

TOWARD MORE COMMERCIAL INVOLVEMENT. Business is becoming more involved in education in competitive, cooperative, and consultative ways.

TOWARD DATA BANKS AND DATA-PROCESSING CENTERS. Banks and data-processing centers, some within school districts but many in remote centers, will provide rapid information retrieval and data processing.

TOWARD STATEWIDE AND REGIONAL ETV OR ITV NETWORKS. These networks will mean that all schools from the smallest to the largest will have access to library, reference, and research data that only large systems have afforded previously. The ultimate achievement will be the linking of state and regional networks into a national network for education.   International coverage may be attained in the more distant future via satellites, allowing all classrooms of the world to communicate with each other.

TOWARD MORE COMPUTER-ASSISTED INSTRUCTION.   As computers become less expensive and more readily available to schools, education will change from a man to a man-machine system of school organization.   This does not mean that man will become less important.   He will become even more necessary since he will be freed from nonessential duties and can devote more time to actual instruction.   Computers, as a type of instructional equipment, make a mass of information available at the touch of a button.   Changes will be made in the preparation of instructional materials and methods of teaching; greater individualization of instruction will result. No aspect of instruction is more pregnant with possibilities for the future than this.

TOWARD COMPUTERIZED RESEARCH.   An exciting educational application of the computer in the future is its use for research in any discipline.   A computerized research system can do a whole series of computations that otherwise would take hours or days to do, such as analyzing, comparing, refining, and interpreting evidence.   It is very expensive to build a computerized data bank that will be able to suggest answers to almost any question, but technology is still advancing.   There is still a need for more research on the quality or effectiveness of learning.   Auditory and visual dialogue with the computer are in prospect to augment the typed and printed communication now common.   The world of information may someday become almost instantaneously available to teachers, students, and researchers.

TOWARD MORE TECHNOLOGICAL UNDERSTANDING.   There is a great need for educators and students to understand machine processes, computers, and the potential applications of technology to school practices and to daily life.

TOWARD AN INCREASING DEVELOPMENT OF INSTRUCTIONAL MEDIA CENTERS.   The advantages of changing the traditional library into an instructional media learning center will be seen by more educators.   The impact of technology on the educational system will become less fearful to teachers and administrators, especially those who are growing up with it.

The IMC of the future will have not only printed materials, but data retrieval hardware and intercommunicating computers which will make it possible to have unlimited access to information wherever it is located.

Administrative Problems

In Basket

Problem 1

The Levering Unified School District, with an average daily attendance of 22,000, has used manual and semi-manual processes for handling all of its services. The Board of Education has decided to convert to a computer system, but neither the Board nor the Superintendent has specialized knowledge of computers. Therefore, the employment of a systems coordinator was authorized. The Board has asked him to make a systems study of the school district and make recommendations on the best way to convert to a computer system.

How should the systems coordinator proceed?
What information does he need?
What recommendations might he make?

Problem 2

In the problem above, assume that the Board of Education has accepted the recommendations and has agreed to install a computer system utilizing the rental services of a nearby school district.

What procedures can the systems coordinator use as the district converts to a computer system?
What problems might he foresee?
How might these problems be solved?

Selected References

ALCORN, BRUCE KEITH. "The Concept of Total Systems in Education." In *Automated Educational Systems,* Enoch Haga, ed. Elmhurst, Ill.: The Business Press, 1967.

ARNOLD, ROBERT R.; HILL, HAROLD C.; and NICHOLS, AYLMER V. *Introduction to Data Processing.* New York: John Wiley and Sons, 1966.

BARRETT, RICHARD S. "The Computer Mentality." *Phi Delta Kappan* 49 (April 1966).

BROWN, JAMES W., and AUBREY, RUTH H., compilers. *New Media and Changing Educational Patterns.* Sacramento, Calif.: State Department of Education, 1965.

————; NORBERG, KENNETH D.; and SRYGLEY, SARA K. *Administering Educational Media: Instructional Technology and Library Services.* New York: McGraw-Hill Book Co., 1972.

BUNDY, ROBERT F. "Computer-Assisted Instruction: Where Are We?" *Phi Delta Kappan* 49 (April 1968).

BUSINESS EQUIPMENT MANUFACTURERS ASSOCIATION. *New Techniques in Office Operation: Machines, Forms, Systems.* Elmhurst, Ill.: The Business Press, 1968.

DAVIES, RUTH A. *The School Library: A Force for Educational Excellence.* New York: R. R. Bowker Co., 1969.

DYER, CHRISTOPHER; BROWN, R.; and GOLDSTEIN, E. D. *The Role of School Libraries in Education.* Hamden, Conn.: Archon Books, 1970.

FAIRBANKS, RALPH W. *Successful Office Automation.* Englewood Cliffs, N.J.: Prentice-Hall, 1965.

GOODLAD, JOHN I.; O'TOOLE, JOHN F., JR.; and TYLER, LOUISE L. *Computers and Information Systems in Education.* New York: Harcourt, Brace, & World, 1966.

HEYEL, CARL. *Computers, Office Machines, and the New Information Technology.* London: The Macmillan Co., Collier-Macmillan Ltd., 1969.

"How Computers Are Changing Education." *School Management* 14 (October 1970).

HOWE, ROBERT L. "The Concepts of Regional Educational Data Processing Centers." In *Automated Educational Systems,* Enoch Haga, ed. Elmhurst, Ill.: The Business Press, 1967.

KNEZEVICH, STEPHEN J., and EYE, GLEN G., eds. *Instructional Technology and the School Administrator.* Washington, D.C.: American Association of School Administrators, 1970.

KOMOSKI, P. KENNETH. "The Continuing Confusion About Technology and Education; or the Myth-ing Link in Educational Technology." *Educational Technology: Educational Technology Around the World* 9 (November 1969).

LESSINGER, LEON. "Engineering Accountability for Results in Public Education." *Phi Delta Kappan* 52 (December 1970).

LEVY, JOSEPH. *Punched Card Equipment: Principles and Applications.* New York: McGraw-Hill Book Co., 1967.

LEWIS, PHILIP. "Instructional Technology: Revolution on the Horizon." *Nation's Schools* 82 (December 1968).

NASH, ROBERT. "Commitment to Competency: The New Fetishism in Teacher Education." *Phi Delta Kappan* 52 (December 1970).

NATIONAL EDUCATION ASSOCIATION, RESEARCH DIVISION. "The Use of Computers for Instruction." *NEA Research Bulletin* 49 (March 1971).

PALOVIC, LORA, and GOODMAN, ELIZABETH B. *The Elementary School Library in Action.* West Nyack, N.Y.: Parker Publishing Co., 1968.

POPHAM, W. JAMES, and BAKER, EVA L. *Systematic Instruction.* Englewood Cliffs, N.J.: Prentice-Hall, 1970.

PRENTICE, JUSTUS A. "Multi-School Educational Data Processing via Central Computer." *Data Processing for Education Administration.* Detroit: American Data Processing, 1968.

ROGERS, JAMES L. "Current Problems in CAI." *Datamation* 14 (September 1968).

ROSSOFF, MARTIN. *The School Library and Educational Change.* Littleton, Colo.: Libraries Unlimited, 1971.

ROWELL, JOHN, and HEIDBREDER, M. Ann. *Educational Media Selection Centers: Identification and Analysis of Current Practices.* Chicago: American Library Association, 1971.

SILBERMAN, H. F., and FILEP, R. T. "Information Systems Applications in Education." *Annual Review of Information Science and Technology,* vol. 3, Carlos Cuadra, ed. Chicago: Encyclopaedia Britannica, Wm. Benton, publisher, 1968.

SIMS, ROBERT W. "Systems Concepts and Practices in Education." In *Automated Educational Systems,* Enoch Haga, ed. Elmhurst, Ill.: The Business Press, 1967.

SMITH, KARL U., and SMITH, MARGARET FOLTZ. *Cybernetic Principles of Learning and Educational Design.* New York: Holt, Rinehart and Winston, 1966.

TONKS, JESSE W. "Wake the Dead: Project O.T.I.S." *Data Processing for Education Administration.* Detroit: American Data Processing, 1968.

WOOLLATT, LORNE H. "An Automated Statewide Information System." In *Automated Educational Systems,* Enoch Haga, ed. Elmhurst, Ill.: The Business Press, 1967.

PART FOUR

Administration of the School Plant

14

Financing, Planning, and Constructing Educational Facilities

School buildings represent the culmination of carefully coordinated planning by personnel in education, architecture, governmental agencies, and, in varying degrees, the lay public. Because good planning takes time and financing and the construction of school buildings throughout the United States costs millions of dollars annually, expert management is required. Since this is only one chapter on a topic about which volumes have been written, it cannot go into minute detail on how to achieve various objectives that are part of the total plan.

This chapter includes a discussion of the following topics:

Financing School Construction Programs
Planning for School Construction
New Concepts in School Construction
Critical Path Method
Summary
Trends

Financing School Construction Programs

Construction costs have to be met if school building programs are to be accommodated. Situations vary from district to district and from state to

This chapter was prepared in collaboration with Dr. Robert E. Hummel, Superintendent of Hemet Unified School District, Hemet, California.

state.   This section deals with the systems of financing construction that are most frequently applied and considerations that must precede gaining approval for the programs.

TAXES OR PAY-AS-YOU-GO.   Current financing is generally reserved for school districts that are able to secure voter approval to provide enough revenue to meet the building needs of the school district.   The success of the pay-as-you-go method is dependent upon comprehensive public information campaigns.

BONDS.   Approximately two-thirds of all school construction is financed by voter approval of bonds.[1]   There are four types of bonds:

1.   Serial bonds are numbered serially and are retired in numerical order, either annually or semiannually to reduce interest costs.   This type of bond is usually used by school districts.
2.   Straight-term bonds provide for the entire amount to be repaid at some future date.
3.   The sinking-fund type of bond may require a separately earmarked tax which is deposited in a sinking fund to build up the amount needed for repayment.   Interest may be earned during the interim.
4.   A *callable bond* may have a higher rate of interest, but since it can be repaid at any time, it may save the district interest in the long run.

Whatever type of bond is used, a competent counsel should be employed and the type of loan to be requested should be determined.   When the type of bond has been determined, the amount and the date of sale should be advertised and should include the deadline date for bids.[2]

Generally, bonds are voted for a specific project or series of projects, depending upon the laws of the state in which the school district is located. Bonds are paid off from taxes levied over a period of time ranging as long as twenty-five to thirty years.   The repayment plan, or the schedule for retiring the bond, is dependent upon state and local regulations.   Because bonds are generally paid off over a longer period of time, some people believe they are more equitable, reasoning that many people who use the

---

[1] Clyde Bunnell, "Fiscal Planning," *Guidelines for School Planning and Construction, A Handbook for School Business Officials,* Research Bulletin No. 8 (Chicago: Research Corporation of the Association of School Business Officials, 1968), p. 7.

[2] Bunnell, "Fiscal Planning," pp. 10–11.

facilities over the years will assist in repaying the loan. High interest rates, however, cause this program to be expensive when total interest costs are added to the principal of the bond issue.

FEDERAL FUNDS. Congress has made possible, in specific situations, the appropriation of funds to school districts that find themselves "impacted" with pupils from families of federally employed parents. Public Law 815 allows school districts near federal installations to apply for such funds. There is some doubt, however, that this "impacted" aid will continue much longer.

PRIVATE GRANTS OR BEQUESTS. Parochial and private schools are more often the recipients of private grants or bequests that may be used to provide much needed facilities. Such funds generally are made available for a specific building project.

LEGAL ELEMENTS TO BE CONSIDERED. Because school finance is a complex program, and because the laws differ in each state, the administrator must work closely with the legal adviser for his school district. Legal deadlines must be maintained. Sufficient time should be scheduled into the plan to allow for contingencies. The key to success is knowing legal requirements and planning accordingly.

IDENTIFYING THE NEED. If any plan to obtain financing for school construction is to achieve success, it must be based upon a demonstrated need for the facilities. How the need is developed and justified to the voters is dependent upon local conditions. Nationwide reports of voter rejection of bond proposals portends that any proposal that does not adequately justify the need in the minds of the voters is doomed to failure. Some techniques for identifying and assessing the needs for school construction are explained as master plan saturation studies for school district construction, pupil population studies, and a systematic examination of existing facilities related to building safety and projected pupil populations.

SATURATION STUDY. The saturation study is a projection of maximum land use in the district based upon present zoning requirements and geographical conditions. This study develops the ultimate pupil and adult population for the particular school district, and may also project future school sites. It may be prepared by the school district, an architectural firm, a planning consultant, or a governmental agency. The district should choose and employ its own consultant wherever possible. It must be predicated upon the district's determination of class size, grade level organization, and school size. The saturation study becomes a valuable tool for planning building needs; thus, it is frequently known as a District Master Plan.

PUPIL POPULATION PROJECTIONS. Projecting pupil population is a method that may be the most useful in projecting future building needs. Many variables can influence the data. People in the United States today are highly mobile. Industrial cutbacks, governmental spending, international crises, modern technology, the "pill," and other factors influence population projections. Some districts have migratory pupil populations, while others are stable; some are located where people seem to be "pouring in," while other communities are losing population.

Pupil population projections should be developed after a careful examination of data drawn from pupil enrollments of the past five years. Samples drawn from data covering fewer years can be subject to greater error.

Demographic studies are sometimes available from banking institutions, chambers of commerce, planning commissions, or other governmental agencies. A study of births recorded at local hospitals may reveal trends in pupil population at the preschool level. A review of permits for new construction, the record of water and gas meters set, or telephones installed may provide information useful in projecting pupil populations. Recent declines in the birth-rate level already have had their effect on the number of pupils entering kindergarten and the lower grades in some school districts. The babies born in the boom following World War II will soon have their own children in school. How large their families become will have a direct influence on future waves of pupils in the schools during the 1980s and 1990s.

When pupil populations are projected against available classroom spaces, they provide valuable data for assessing present space as related to future needs. Caution should be exercised in any straight line projection of data, and pupil population figures should be reviewed annually.

SCHOOL PLANT ASSESSMENT. Physically obsolete school buildings should be studied to determine whether cost of modernization is greater than the cost of building a completely new structure. Several variables influence the decision. Cities have changed due to zoning requirements. Schools that were in a neighborhood setting fifty years ago may now be surrounded by industry. Changes in the birth rate and in life expectancy also affect school populations.

Geological conditions affect schools. School districts in quake, tornado, or flood areas have employed licensed structural engineers or architects to make studies and recommendations. These recommendations become need assessments for planning future buildings.

New construction should be modifiable so that rooms can be altered easily as educational programs are changed. Movable structures may prove useful because they can be relocated on other sites as student population changes. Seven-year maintenance plans should be given consideration. In various suburban districts, community changes have caused school buildings to become vacant; long-range planning should take into account the possibility of converting them into community spaces or factories.

SCHOOL BOARD APPROVAL. The proposed building program must be approved by action of the governing board of the school district. The school board must authorize the calling of the election to provide the building funds, generally approve the plan for public information on the proposal, and may participate with either the administrative team or citizens committee developed to carry the campaign to the people.

COMMUNITY. The success or failure of any tax levy or bond election lies with the electorate. The people decide the issues. Therefore, strategy should be designed to create a positive impression of the building project in the mind of the voter. Each building project has to be justified as reasonable, necessary, and proper from the voter's point of view. A study of the people who influence voter opinions is vital. Who are the people who believe in the merits of the building project and can win voter support? This question becomes the key to the information campaign of the election. Planning the election program requires time and personnel skilled in communicating with people.

THE CAMPAIGN. The organization of successful elections is hard work. It requires hours of preparation, organization, and management of the systems of information and action to get out the "yes" votes. The plan should be organized to permit feedback as it develops so that corrections or modifications may be made. A program planning chart with detailed subcharts is helpful in keeping all phases of the total campaign in mind. Informed and dedicated workers are indispensable in executing a well-designed election campaign plan. Success is based upon a people-to-people kind of contact. Victories in tax and bond elections do not just happen; they are the result of careful planning and hard work by a variety of people, all dedicated to the task of getting the voters' approval on the issue.

Planning for School Construction

In planning educational specifications for buildings, the school district should use the services of educational specialists. The Council of Educational Facility Planners in Columbus, Ohio, for example, has evaluated and abstracted school plant research; planning information of national relevance has been released to Council membership. It has also supplied the Educational Research Information Center (ERIC–USDE) with planning resumes and documents.

Other excellent sources of school building information are the School Planning Laboratory at Stanford University, The American Institute of Architects in Washington, D.C., the National Academy of Science in Washington, D.C., the Educational Facilities Laboratories, Inc., in New York, the Association of School Business Officials of the United States and Canada in Chicago, and the National Council on Schoolhouse Construction at Michigan State University.

SELECTING AN ARCHITECT. The responsibility for the actual design of the building lies most frequently with licensed architects who are responsible for the preparation of the working drawings, the written specifications, and the supervision of building construction. The architectural firm is employed by the school district to provide this technical service in the development of a building design that will meet the educational space requirements of the school district.

Research varies on when it is best to select the architect. However, it is generally best to select the most qualified architect early and to utilize his services during the educational planning phase of the design as well as to enlist his aid in site selection, if this has not already been accomplished.

Some architectural firms are available to provide service during the campaigns for securing voter approval of the building tax or bond issues.

Several criteria are helpful in considering architectural firms:

1. Is the firm familiar with the legal elements of the particular state and county in which the building is to be constructed?
2. Is the firm near enough to the school district to provide the necessary personnel as needed both for design as well as for construction?
3. Have they had previous experience in school construction of the grade level and quantity of pupils to be housed?
4. Do they have a staff of professionals large enough to successfully accomplish the design tasks?
5. Are former clients satisfied with the work of the architectural firm?
6. Does inspection of school plants designed by the architectural firm reveal that the buildings function properly for the educational program utilizing them?
7. How do those who use the buildings feel about the design qualities which the architect has put into the building?
8. Did the architect stay within the project budget?
9. Does the firm design a high quality, low maintenance building for the lowest dollar cost?
10. Does the architect employ capable, consulting professional engineers to provide the necessary electrical, structural, mechanical, and other design support staff personnel?
11. Does the architect provide the services required of the district at a fee suitable for the services rendered?
12. Does the architect employ fresh designs that add to the educational needs without becoming purely architectural monuments?
13. Is the architectural firm able to provide imaginative and creative solutions for the space requirements of the educational problems presented?
14. Does the firm employ the necessary consultant personnel for specialized needs, i.e., color, acoustics, landscape, and similar specialized needs?
15. Does the firm have personnel who will be easy to work with in the design and construction stage?
16. Does the firm have a selection of competent personnel at all levels of responsibility?

17.   Can the firm deliver what it proposes to do for the agreed price and on schedule?

18.   What is the firm's philosophy concerning change orders?

Current practice among school districts includes visitation to the offices of a selected group of architects who are considered as finalists in the selection process. Sometimes several finalists may be asked to interview the board of education and display some of their designs. School board members may wish to visit some of the buildings designed by various architectural firms. The final decision or selection lies with the board of education, which hopefully follows valid criteria.

ARCHITECT'S TEAM.   The architect may employ certain specialized personnel as a part of the office staff or contract with firms who provide specialized services to many different architectural firms. The architect should have access to design specialists, color consultants, draftsmen, field inspectors, specification writers, and related clerical and support personnel. The office may include or contract for the services of civil engineers, acoustical engineers, landscape architects, and other specialized personnel.

ARCHITECT'S CONTRACT.   The architect's contract is a legal document that should clearly answer the following questions:

1.   Which buildings are to be designed (specific project or projects)?

2.   What are the limitations on cost of project—i.e., if project bid exceeds architect's estimate by 10 percent, does he redesign at no cost to the district?

3.   What fee is the architect to charge for his services?   (An 8 percent fee has been the AIA standard.)

4.   What fee will be charged for small special jobs which normally do not fall within the standard percent fee?

5.   What added services will the architect provide beside normal preliminary and finished drawings and specifications? Will he also provide a landscape plan, a master plan for the school project? Will he provide a sequential schedule of building plan, time lines, and educational planning responsibility? What are his responsibilities in the educational planning phase?

6.   Is the architect liable for errors in design which cost money in change orders?

7. What responsibility does the architect have for inspection during construction?
8. What will be the fee for extras, i.e., copies of blueprints and specifications?
9. Who owns the design drawings and specifications when the job is completed?
10. How may the contract be terminated?

DEVELOPING EDUCATIONAL SPECIFICATIONS. Educational specifications have been defined as "the direct product of educational planning activity by the school district or an educational consultant. They incorporate an explanation of educational methodology or teaching techniques employed and an explanation of space requirements in terms of educational activities, materials, areas, and affinities. They form a list of specifics or directives to enable the architect to design the needed facilities. Educational specifications serve the architect as the building plans and specifications serve the contractor. Educational specifications are best presented in the form of written statements of the educational requirements of the school district."[3]

PLANNING TAKES TIME. The single factor most often mentioned by personnel engaged in planning for school construction is time. Good planning for finance, educational needs, design, bidding, and construction all take time. A minimum of from two to three years will be required for the educational planning, design, and construction of good schools. The larger and more complex the facility, the greater the time necessary to complete the task.

THE PLANNING COMMITTEE. Research findings indicate that planning committees function best if limited to six or eight persons. Larger committees may be used, but it is desirable to establish a smaller executive steering committee to synthesize reports and translate the work of the larger committee into written directives to the architect.

The educational planning committee is generally composed of the following people: principal, superintendent of schools, teachers, assistant superintendent in charge of educational services, and business manager. Frequently, department chairmen or grade level teachers are selected to

---

[3] Robert E. Hummel, "Educational Planning Procedures for School Building Construction" (Unpublished doctoral dissertation, University of Southern California, 1961), p. 11.

work on the larger committee under the direction of the superintendent or building planning specialist. One or two interested community persons may be invited to serve on the planning committee. After all, the school is a community institution.

CONTENT OF EDUCATIONAL SPECIFICATIONS. The actual educational specification document, which should be written by specialists, may be structured in several ways: (1) a narrative document that follows the general content outlined below or an outline with paragraphs filled in as needed (to convey to the architect what particular requirements are desired in a specific learning space or area in the school).

The following outline includes educational specifications for a typical secondary school plant.

I.   Introduction.
   A.   Description of grade levels to be served.
   B.   Statement of the philosophy of school district regarding this age group of pupils or district's philosophy for all grades.
   C.   Description of courses offered and grade levels to be served.
   D.   Number of pupils who will participate in each of the various courses offered.

II. General architectural requirements.
   A.   Basic design considerations.
   B.   Lighting requirements.
   C.   Heating, air conditioning, ventilation, and acoustics.
   D.   Treatment of inside wall surfaces (e.g., chalk and tackboards).
   E.   Intercommunication and electronic equipment, closed circuit television or cable TV capabilities.
   F.   Community service (park concept).
   G.   Building orientation.
   H.   Cabinet work.
   I.   Furniture.
   J.   Carpet or other type of floor finish.

III. Recommendations for general instructional spaces.
   A.   General classrooms.
      1.   Total number of rooms required.
      2.   Approximate room size.
      3.   Number of students to be accommodated.
      4.   Activities to take place in these rooms.
      5.   Location requirement in relation to other parts of the plant and other departments.

      6. Cabinet and storage requirements.

      7. Furniture and equipment.

      8. Other requirements and recommendations.

   B. Arts and Crafts. *See* details in this outline as under "A."

   C. Business Education.

   D. Foreign Language.

   E. Homemaking.

   F. Industrial Arts.

   G. Instrumental Music.

   H. Physical Education facilities.

      1. Interior.

      2. Exterior.

   I. Science.

   J. Special classrooms.

   K. Vocational Education.

IV. Recommendations for auxiliary spaces.

   A. Multipurpose.

   B. Curriculum materials area.

      1. Library.

      2. Textbook room.

      3. Audio-visual and multimedia space.

      4. Curriculum materials laboratory.

   C. Office area.

   D. Student health services.

   E. Faculty lounge.

   F. Other building areas including restrooms and storage area.

   G. Community services.

      1. Access to grounds and buildings.

      2. Storage.

      3. Restrooms.

   H. Maintenance and operation considerations.

      1. Landscaping.

      2. Mechanical systems.

      3. Hardware.

      4. Power and lighting.

      5. Site development.

After the specifications have been developed, they should be reviewed and agreed upon by a planning committee composed of administrators, teachers, and interested community people.

SITE SELECTION.   Determining the best location for a future school is a complex process.   Final determination of the most suitable location should be based upon careful research by authorities responsible for preparing the recommendation to the board of education. An architect may be helpful in the selection of a suitable site. Factors to be considered in site selection are presented below.

EDUCATIONAL CRITERIA. The educational criteria determine to a great degree the location, size, soil conditions, and topography of the school site. A given parcel that is of sufficient size and shape for an elementary school would be totally inadequate for a high school that requires a larger area. The educational philosophy of the school district regarding grade-level organization, educational program, and desired recreational and physical education facilities must be considered.[4] What grade levels will be assigned to the particular site? How many pupils will expect to be housed according to the master plan on this site?

LOCATION. The location of the school plant must be carefully planned. If land is not available, condemnation proceedings must be instituted; this takes time and is costly. Factors such as initial cost, size, access, and attorney's fees need to be considered. Questions such as the following must be answered:

1. How does the site relate to the proposed pupil population—i.e., will most pupils walk to the school or ride a bus?
2. How is the site oriented in relation to the prevailing winds?
3. Will the extremes of winter and summer weather adversely affect the building on the site?
4. What is the location of the site in relation to industrial noise, odors, traffic, and related distracting elements?
5. What zoning surrounds the proposed site, and will the school be compatible with the zoning in this area?
6. What utilities serve the proposed location?
7. Will the necessary service be provided without excessive cost to the school district?
8. What other factors should be considered in locating the school on the site?

---

[4] Lester E. Andrews, "Site," *Guidelines for School Planning and Construction, A Handbook for School Business Officials*, Research Bulletin No. 8 (Chicago: Research Corporation of the Association of School Business Officials, 1968), p. 14.

SOIL CONDITIONS AND TOPOGRAPHY.

1. Does the location contain any geological qualities that would make it unsuitable for the school, e.g., earthquake fault lines?
2. What drainage qualities does the soil contain?
3. Does the soil provide adequate strength to support the proposed structure?
4. Will the topography permit development without extensive site development costs, e.g., grading, expense of trenching in rocky soil, problems of recompacting soil which is unstable, requires excessive fill, or is extremely sandy?
5. What other factors should be considered?

A SITE SELECTION CHECKLIST. To provide some means of evaluating the relative merits of several sites, it is well to identify various criteria that are to be used to measure the relative merits of several sites. Several considerations that must be made in site selection may be assigned a numerical value, permitting comparison of several sites which might at first glance appear to be equal. Suggested criteria for evaluating proposed school sites are presented in Table 14-1.

Through the use of such a site evaluation device, a comparison of the relative strengths and weaknesses of several sites can be made.

PLANNING FOR CONSTRUCTION. Architectural firms can be of immense help with the multitude of paper work and detail associated with the design, bidding, and construction of school buildings. An architect who has had experience with school construction knows the procedures to be followed and can frequently anticipate problems which could otherwise delay the project.

Preliminary plans may need to be reviewed and approved by designated officials at the county and/or state level. It is well to know in advance who should be involved and make certain that the planning and design program includes the necessary review and approvals required according to state or local practice.

A district-hired architectural consultant is almost a necessity if the district's long-range interests are to be protected.

FIRE HAZARDS. Fires in schools across the nation have affected the design of buildings. It may be mandated that the state fire marshal

TABLE 14–1. Site Selection Checklist

CONSIDERATIONS	WT. RATING SCORE
Location	
A. Proximity to pupils	20
B. Zoning in area	10
C. Kind of neighborhood	10
D. Accessibility to pedestrians	15
E. Available utilities	10
F. Width and condition of streets	5
G. Weather factors	5
H. Freedom from industrial smoke and noise	10
I. Relationship to existing and future freeways	10
J. Available highways	5
K. Public transportation	5
L. Hazards	10
M. Police and fire protection	5
N. Community recreation value	10
Size	
A. Size of parcel	75
B. Shape of parcel	15
C. Expansion features	10
Topography and Soil	
A. Drainage	10
B. Terrain	10
C. Soil conditions	10
D. Special natural features	5
E. Special geological conditions	15
Cost	
A. Availability	10
B. Initial cost of site	25
C. Development	20
D. Available utilities	15
E. Available streets	15
F. Other factors that could increase costs	10
	Total Score

approve school construction plans.   These and other regulations, although desirable, result in higher costs for school construction compared with commercial designs.   The cost comparisons sometimes result in public criticism of "overdesigned" schools, when, in fact, laws passed by the people's representatives have mandated the more expensive and safer designs.

The design of the school should be carefully monitored by various elements of the administrative staff to determine that the educational requirements have been met in the most efficient manner and that the design does not exceed the budget. All conditions present in the design must assure maximum educational benefits for the dollars spent.

BIDDING. The announced building project is advertised in trade papers as well as in local newspapers. The announcement advises bidders of the nature of the project, where plans and specifications may be obtained, and other details of the building project. It may also list a schedule of wage rates.

Competitive bidding by qualified contractors on the building plans and specifications is the most common method used to determine which firm will be assigned the job of constructing the building. Sealed bids submitted at a designated time and place are then opened by authorized personnel. The bids submitted by the various builders are analyzed. Some states require that a bond be submitted to assure the owner that the contractor will faithfully complete the project; these are called faithful performance bonds. The lowest qualified bidder is generally awarded the contract by action of the board of education.

PLANNING AND INSPECTION. A pre-construction conference may be held involving the architect, school district officials, all principals from the construction firm, and consulting engineers. The meeting should clarify procedures of communication and working relationships for the duration of the project.

The law may require the school district to employ a qualified building inspector to assure that the building is built in accordance with the de-signed building plans and specifications. Consulting engineers, architect's representatives, and state representatives from the Office of Architecture and Construction may also, from time to time, visit the site and inspect the progress of the construction.

The school district will have various other personnel, other than the inspector, who will visit the construction site to monitor the progress. The district building inspector generally works through the architect to effect any changes or to resolve any problems.

The completion of the new physical structure is only part of the solution. Orders for the necessary furniture and equipment must be placed far enough in advance to allow for availability of the items upon the completion of the plant.   Advance planning is absolutely essential if all phases of the building program are to be successful.

It is recommended that those who have had little or no experience with building programs arrange to visit districts where successful building programs are in progress.   Periodic contacts with school administrators experienced in school planning and building will also be helpful.

New Concepts in School Construction

In the continuing effort to improve teaching, there have been many changes in basic classroom concepts.   A brief listing of the major classroom plans that have developed over the years shows the following evolution:

1.   Lancastrian classroom
2.   Quincy box plan
3.   Modified Quincy plan
4.   Rectangular classroom plan with double-loaded corridors
5.   Finger plan with single-loaded corridors
6.   Back-to-back plan

Each of these plans has come about because of changes in the educational philosophy of the times, new developments in construction, and to achieve construction economies.

More recent trends in design and construction have produced classrooms with movable walls, artificial lighting, air conditioning, carpeted floors, and highly controlled environments.   Figure 14–1 is an example of modular shell construction that offers degrees of flexibility never before equalled; ability to vary interior spaces is the most common illustration of flexibility.   Construction techniques using modular construction provide buildings with long-span shells and few permanent interior walls.   The mechanical and electrical systems are integrated with the structure (i.e., they are fairly easy to move).   Flexibility of spaces has recently captured the imagination of many educators and school architects and appears to be highly desirable for the newer techniques of instruction.

The latest concept in designing instructional spaces is to provide variously shaped classrooms.   These include hexagonal, wedged, circular, squared, and triangular shapes, all in a clustered arrangement (*see* Figure 14–2).   These rooms have all the latest components in modular-shell

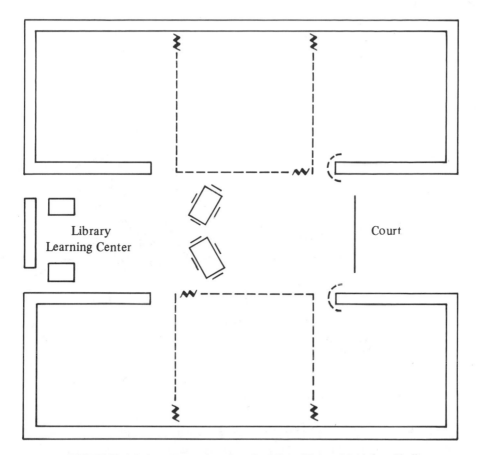

FIGURE 14–1. Example of a Building Using Modular Shell Construction with Flexible and Open Spaces.

designs; the spaces are purported to stimulate innovative and experimental teaching methods, including team teaching, large- or small-group instruction, use of audio-visual and electronic equipment, and independent or exploratory study. (*See* chapter 29 for further comments regarding innovations in school construction.) These more imaginative designs are found in school districts experimenting with newer approaches, stressing cooperative teaching programs and various sizes of learning groups.

Some of the new educational techniques and media that must be planned for are: science, reading, and language laboratories, overhead and opaque projectors, microfilm readers, tape recorders, teaching machines, videotape equipment, and closed-circuit television. These are in addition

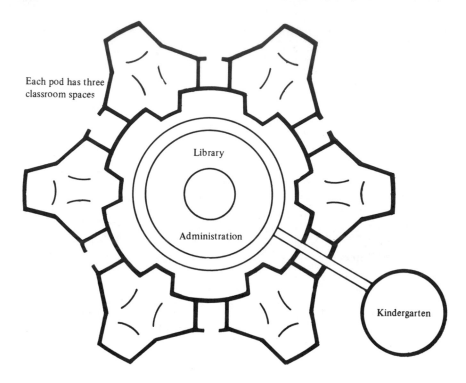

Each pod has three classroom spaces

Library

Administration

Kindergarten

FIGURE 14–2. Example of a Building Using Cluster Plan Construction with Flexible and Open Spaces.

to the usual movie projectors, film-strip projectors, and record players. New planning may include the installation of computers for data processing, class scheduling, and information retrieval. New schools must be constructed with sufficient wiring, electrical panels, breakers, and electric outlets to handle the extra load imposed by the use of newer instructional media. Older schools will need to be completely rewired.

Improvements are continuously being made in sound proofing, lighting, heating, flooring materials, and construction materials. Air conditioning is no longer a luxury; in some sections of the country it is almost mandatory. Experiments are being made in constructing schools without windows so that lighting is controlled better, outside distractions are minimized, and vandalism is reduced. All of these improvements help to create a better environment for learning that ultimately benefits the students.

One of the problems facing many school districts is the existence of many old schools that are neither built nor equipped to handle these innovations. Remodeling and modernizing can be accomplished, but this is a costly process. However, if a school district is concerned with improvements in its educational program, any cost should be considered worthwhile.

Critical Path Method

Since its initiation in 1957, the Critical Path Method (CPM) has been used for planning and scheduling building programs by private industry and some forward-looking school systems. It is adaptable for computers where they are available but is also effective where they are not. CPM is:

> based entirely on the detailed logical analysis of a project into the component separate activities which make up the total project, and the arrangement of each activity in its proper sequence with respect to the other activities . . . The basic working tools of C.P.M. are the arrow diagram, sometimes called the network, and the printout or listing of tasks in their sequential order.

> The arrow diagram is the graphic model of a project from start to finish. Each activity is represented by an arrow in which the tail represents the beginning point of the activity, and the head the finish of that activity. The logical arrangement of arrows in sequence and groups will show for each which arrows proceed it, which run concurrently, and which must follow.

> The arrow is given a title which describes the activity in simple terms. The beginning or tail of the arrow is given a number, depending on its proper position in the total sequence, and the head of the arrow is given the next higher number. The time duration of the activity is estimated either empirically or with direct assistance from the contractor or other specially qualified person.[5]

When this method is used, construction can be speeded up, unnecessary steps removed, staffs adjusted for the work needed, activities run concurrently, inconsistencies eliminated, and performance improved.[6]

School districts planning to use CPM should contact its consulting service, discuss the possibilities of utilizing this type of service, and determine the fees. The services that can be rendered by the consultant are:

---

[5] Henry F. Daum, "The Use of the Critical Path Method in Schoolhouse Construction," *Guidelines for School Planning and Construction, A Handbook for School Business Officials,* Research Bulletin No. 8 (Chicago: Research Corporation of the Association of School Business Officials, 1968), pp. 34–35.

[6] Daum, "The Use of the Critical Path Method," p. 35.

1. Development of a project schedule.
2. Development of a design schedule.
3. Maintenance of the design schedule in a current condition.
4. Development of a preliminary construction schedule.
5. Preparation of CPM specifications.
6. Development of a complete project schedule.
7. Maintenance of construction schedules in a current condition.[7]

The success of CPM depends upon the administrator's understanding of its use. Many people should be involved: the school board, the superintendent, the business manager, principals, teachers, citizens, and contractors. The forward-looking school administrator should look into CPM or some similar program before he commences a building program.

Summary

The most common sources of revenue for financing school construction are current taxation, long-term bonding, or federal funds. Planning should include legal research, identifying the need, projection of maximum land use in the district, pupil population projections, and school plant assessment. After approval by the school board, the funding proposal must be presented to the electorate in such a way as to secure the maximum turnout of favorable voters.

In planning for construction, the first step is to select an architect in accordance with predetermined criteria. He will then choose his team of specialized consultants and in due course will present his contract for board approval. The next step is to develop educational specifications to guide the architect in his planning, a process that will be aided by the appointment of a planning committee. The specifications should include the general architectural requirements, recommendations for instructional spaces, and suggestions for auxiliary spaces.

Site selection is a major consideration, embracing educational criteria and locating the new plant by using a site selection checklist.

In addition to seeking assistance from designated officials at the county and state levels, the district should employ its own consultant to protect its interests. He should monitor such problems as elimination of

[7] Daum, "The Use of the Critical Path Method," pp. 37–39.

fire hazards, competitive bidding, planning, and inspection of actual construction.

New concepts of movable walls, modular-shell construction, and cluster plans should be considered in the light of foreseeable needs. The Critical Path Method (CPM) analyzes the component activities making up the total project and arranges each activity in its proper sequence with respect to the other activities.

Trends

Flexibility has been and will continue to be a key word in school planning and design for the future. The knowledge explosion will produce more technological changes, permitting a variety of changes in educational practice.

TOWARD MORE FLEXIBLE SCHOOL BUILDINGS. The advent of more innovations in teaching methods, such as team teaching, the use of paraprofessionals, and learning laboratories, requires schools to be flexible enough to provide space for learning—for large and small groups and individuals working in a one-to-one relationship. These types of educational programs will increase and will require many changes in school building construction.

TOWARD MORE SYSTEMATIC PLANNING METHODS TO PROVIDE FOR THE EDUCATIONAL NEEDS OF CHILDREN. This will be partly related to the degree of population control. School building needs will diminish, but structures will require modernization to meet new instructional needs.

TOWARD MORE AUTOMATED DEVICES FOR EDUCATION. Technological advances may make it possible for many children to obtain their education through more automated devices. Video cassettes, individual study carrels, electronic equipment of all types, and prepared programs for computer terminals in schools will become more common in the next decade. Several schools and the district office may be programmed into a central computer for a multitude of uses. Schools must be built with the facilities to handle these new media.

TOWARD MORE STUDENT INVOLVEMENT IN COMMUNITY EDUCATIONAL PROJECTS. Secondary and higher education will see more students involved in community education projects. Classes will be held on the job in an industrial, technical, social service, business, governmental, or other setting. A school district coordinator will work with these agencies to arrange for student involvement, supervision, and credit. Industrial education students, for example, can receive on-the-job training in an industrial plant using equipment they would seldom or never see in a school. Thus, the school program can be broadened without the necessity of building more rooms or buying extra equipment.

TOWARD THE EXPANSION OF FACILITIES TO CARE FOR INCREASED ADULT EDUCATION. Adult education will expand, requiring schools to operate longer hours and more days per year. Changes in technology will require retraining of personnel. The school building must be constructed so that rooms and facilities are available for such programs.

TOWARD CONTROLLED SCHOOL ENVIRONMENTS. Air conditioning and rugs on classroom floors are not yet in common use. Schools of the future will have a completely controlled environment. All rooms will be air-conditioned so that air will be continuously purified and maintained at a constant temperature and humidity level. Sound will be controlled by acoustical materials and rugs. Artificial illumination will be automatically adjusted so that, regardless of outside light, a constant intensity of lighting will be maintained everywhere in the room.

TOWARD REGIONAL EDUCATIONAL CENTERS. Regional educational centers will provide specialized personnel and spaces for certain kinds of educational programs. School buildings that may be constructed to serve wide areas will be paid for from state monies rather than from local bond levies.

TOWARD CLUSTERS AND "OPEN-SPACE" ENVIRONMENTS. There is a conditional and somewhat tentative trend toward a less formal and more unstructured internal space arrangement. Since architectural innovations freeze into steel and concrete what may prove to be transient educational theories, they should always be analyzed in the planning stage with an eye toward long-range goals, as well as economy of construction and operation.

Administrative Problems

Problem 1

The Lancaster Unified School District is located in a rapidly growing area. Because several elementary schools need to be built, the Board of Education has voted to call a bond election to provide the funds for capital outlay. The superintendent also foresees the need for additions to the secondary schools.

As superintendent, how would you organize the bond election campaign?
Whom would you involve?
What information would you need, and how would you disseminate it to the public?

Problem 2

Assume that the bond election in Lancaster was successful. The superintendent has asked Mr. Hertel, the business manager, to select an architect and recommend his employment to the Board of Education.

What criteria should Mr. Hertel use in selecting the architect?
If employed, what conditions should be explained in his contract?
At what stage should he be employed? Why?

Problem 3

Assume the same situation as in Problem 2. Bill Bixby, an elementary principal, has been asked by the superintendent to select a committee to make recommendations regarding the type of buildings and educational facilities they would like.

Whom should Bill select for his committee?
What research should they do?
What are some of the educational specifications they might recommend?
What furniture and equipment should be recommended?

Selected References

AMERICAN ASSOCIATION OF SCHOOL ADMINISTRATORS. *Planning America's School Buildings.* Washington, D.C.: The Association, 1960.

CALIFORNIA DEPARTMENT OF EDUCATION. *Forty Years of School Planning.* Sacramento: State Printing Office, 1969.

———. *School Site Analysis and Development.* Sacramento: State Printing Office, 1966.

EDUCATIONAL FACILITIES LABORATORIES. *Air Structures for School Sports.* New York: Educational Facilities Laboratories, Inc., 1964.

————. *Educational Change and Architectural Consequences.* New York: Educational Facilities Laboratories, Inc., 1968.

————. *Relocatable School Facilities.* New York: Educational Facilities Laboratories, Inc., 1964.

————. *The Cost of a Schoolhouse.* New York: Educational Facilities Laboratories, Inc., 1960.

ENGELHARDT, NICKOLAUS LOUIS, et al. *School Planning and Building Handbook.* New York: F. W. Dodge Corp., 1956.

FROST, FREDRICK G. "The New Secondary School Environment." *American School & University* 41 (June 1969).

GILLILAND, J. W. "How Environment Affects Learning." *American School & University* 42 (December 1969).

GOODLAD, JOHN I. *The Non-graded Elementary School.* New York: Harcourt, Brace & World, 1963.

HANDLER, BENJAMIN. *Economic Planning for Better Schools.* Ann Arbor: University of Michigan, 1960.

HANSON, CARROLL B. "How to Pass a Bond Issue." *School Management* 13 (July 1969).

HERRICK, JOHN HENRY, et al. *From School Program to School Plant.* New York: Henry Holt and Co., 1956.

"How 16 Award-Winning Schools Compare." *Nation's Schools* 85 (January 1970).

"How 18 Award-Winning Schools Compare." *Nation's Schools* 85 (January 1970).

KOERNER, THOMAS F., and PARKER, CLYDE. "Happiness Isn't Necessarily When a Board Gets the Kind of a School It Deserves." *American School Board Journal* 157 (January 1970).

NATIONAL COUNCIL ON SCHOOLHOUSE CONSTRUCTION. *Guide for Planning School Plants.* East Lansing, Mich.: The Council, 1964.

NORDRUM, GARFIELD B. "Selection and Development of the School Site." *American School Board Journal* (January 1957).

SAMMARTINO, PETER. *Multiple Campuses.* Rutherford, N.J.: Fairleigh Dickinson University Press, 1964.

SCHOOL PLANNING LABORATORY. *Shaping Schools to Change.* Palo Alto, Calif.: School of Education, Stanford University, 1967.

ZELIP, FRANK F. *Guidelines for School Planning and Construction, A Handbook for School Business Officials.* Research Bulletin No. 8. Chicago: Research Corporation of the Association of School Business Officials, 1968.

15

Administering the Operation of School Buildings

The primary purpose of a school building is the maintenance of a good educational program. The building in itself may be an architectural masterpiece, it may represent the largest capital investment of the entire community, and it may be the only cultural and recreational facility in the surrounding area. Meetings, operettas, dramatic clubs, and civic gatherings may depend upon the availability of the school building's auditorium and classrooms. However, it is the educational program that should determine the utilization of the building and its administration. This chapter describes the administration of the use and operation of the school plant and provides operational charts and checklists for the use of the building administrator.

This chapter includes a discussion of the following topics:

Maximum Use of School Building
Proper Care of School Buildings
Regular Operation of the School Plant
Custodial Time Schedules
Custodial Workloads
Summary
Trends

Maximum Use of a School Building

The efficiency of school plant utilization depends largely upon the degree to which the various rooms can be used during all hours of the day. In most schools, ordinary classrooms can be scheduled with an eye toward maximum utilization, but special areas such as cafeterias, auditoriums, and gymnasiums pose difficult and sometimes insoluble problems.

CIRCULAR USE OF THE SCHOOL BUILDING. It is customary in most large school districts to study the problems involved in maximum utilization of the school plant by means of "room-use" charts which show at a glance the rooms that are in use and empty rooms for each period of the school day. They may also include the number of pupil stations occupied or unoccupied during the several periods. A room-use chart should demonstrate maximum utilization potentialities such as multi-purpose rooms, furnishing of classrooms for dual use, and use of specialized areas for more than one purpose. There is no reason, for example, why a lunchroom or library cannot double as a student lounge or organizational meeting room. Similarly, a chemistry laboratory may, with a minimum expenditure, be equipped to qualify as a physics classroom or even a natural science room. Without such economy of utilization, even the most overcrowded schools may achieve only a very low degree of room utilization. Morphet, for example, in a pioneer study of this problem, was the first to point out that room utilization in the schools he studied was only 75.4 percent.[1] This is probably still true.

Another factor in any consideration of building utilization is the "pupil station," referring simply to any sitting or standing pupil location in any room of the school. Needless to say, a room that is usually operated with about half its pupil capacity is only using the same percentage of its pupil station potential. In the study previously referred to, the average percentage of pupil station utilization was found to be only 41.1.[2] To be economically sound, there should be at least 75 percent pupil station utilization.

By industrial standards, school building utilization is grossly inadequate. As an example, a typical factory will use its plant six or seven days a week, twelve months of the year, and twenty-four hours a day. Even the most streamlined school programs will not permit the use of their buildings anywhere near this potential. While building utilization has improved since Morphet's day, with buildings used at night as well as by day and multi-purpose rooms becoming more and more common, no one will seriously

[1] E. L. Morphet, *The Measurement and Interpretation of School Building Utilization* (New York: Teachers College, Columbia University, 1927), p. 83.
[2] Morphet, *The Measurement and Interpretation,* p. 83.

propose that schools should imitate industry in all-out utilization of plant space. It is certain that more serious attempts than have been made in the past to provide the "twelve-month school year" will be a part of future developments in this field of school utilization; but the few experiences in implementing such a program have not been encouraging to date. Elementary schools are usually able to utilize their space to more complete advantage during the school hours; high schools, handicapped by scheduling problems during the day, make up for this by a more complete utilization program during post-school hours. If there is circular use of school buildings, custodial cleaning cannot start when students are dismissed. It may have to be scheduled between 11:00 PM and 7:00 AM.

The problem is twofold: first, the avoidance of waste in utilization of building space, and, second, the avoidance of setting up maximum utilization as an end in itself. Engelhardt and Engelhardt have recommended a range in room utilization of between 68 and 80 percent.[3] This is probably the optimum range. Any school program that utilizes its room facilities to a noticeably lesser degree is running the risk of being criticized for wasting the taxpayer's dollar. A school administration, on the other hand, that sets its goal at a much higher percentage of utilization is apt to be making a fetish out of utilization for its own sake, without due regard for its curriculum or personnel. "Normal maximum capacity is defined as the maximum number of students that may be assigned to a particular instructional unit under conditions which allow an effective instructional program to take place."[4]

In determining the degree of utilization of a school building, a "building use" chart should be resorted to. Such a chart, or tabular representation of existing capacity as compared with actual use, should list the rooms by number and kind, and give the following information:

1. Number of pupil stations in each room.
2. Daily and weekly pupil-station capacity of each room.
3. Daily and weekly utilization of each room.
4. Percentage of utilization determined by dividing item 3 by item 2 (above) for each room.
5. Total percentage of utilization for entire building, determined by dividing room percentages.

---

[3] N. L. Engelhardt and F. Engelhardt, *Planning School Building Programs*, p. 263.
[4] Irving R. Melbo and others, *Report of the Survey, Laguna Beach Unified School District*, p. 339.

The combination of such a building-use chart with a room-use chart will provide the type of information needed to assure maximum utilization.

The largest non-utilization factor is found to exist in such special rooms as gymnasiums and cafeterias. Most such special areas, but not all, are found in high school plants. Such facilities often bring down the wrath of businessmen and taxpayers' groups, on the grounds that they constitute an uneconomical capital investment. The logic behind such complaints is that any room that is in use only a small percentage of the school day, or that possesses a very large ratio of square feet to pupil stations, must be proportionately less useful or efficient than the more orthodox classroom. Such reasoning is, of course, pernicious. Nevertheless, it is important that maximum ingenuity be brought to bear upon the problem of scheduling in the special rooms in order to meet whatever justice there may be in these accusations.

Auditoriums may be used for drama, speech, and debating classes, as well as for assemblies; cafeterias may be combined with libraries and used as reading and study halls by judicious use of movable partitions; and laboratories may be used for classes in subjects other than science. Such devices inevitably result in more complete utilization of existing facilities.

NONCURRICULAR USE OF THE SCHOOL BUILDING. No trend is more clear-cut than that which indicates an ever-increasing community use of the school plant. With the exception of certain restrictions involving subversive and religious use of school facilities, most states now permit and even encourage the use of the school as a community center. All sorts of lodge meetings, fraternal gatherings, public forums, and social get-togethers are making use of school rooms, cafeterias, gymnasiums, and auditoriums. This is far from a new development in American education; rather, it is a rebirth of the bygone pioneer use of the schoolhouse as a public gathering-place. Together with the village church, the schoolhouse in the 18th and 19th centuries served as a rallying-point for community social and recreational life. Quilting parties, spelling bees, musicales, and political meetings were all held in the "little red schoolhouse"; it was public property, and therefore a fitting rendezvous for all public and quasi-public functions.

Non-school utilization of buildings and rooms will greatly increase the percentage of use of such facilities; therefore, it is to be desired, if only from the standpoint of the taxpayer. Adult education falls into a somewhat different category of community use, but is essentially an example of it. Most high school buildings are now being used for some sort of adult classes almost every evening of the week. Some industrial concerns in large cities are utilizing school facilities for vocational and apprentice training. Some colleges are decentralizing their graduate courses for teachers and are scheduling them, if the enrollment warrants, at a district school. Community recreation commissions and directors usually work closely with the schools, and multiply their available playgrounds, gymnasiums, and auditoriums by entering into agreements with the local school districts for the after-school and evening use of their facilities. The bettering of school-use ratios, however, is only one advantage to be gained by encouraging such community–school cooperation. It is a well-worn axiom that every citizen who can be induced to visit the schools with any degree of regularity thereafter will become a supporter of those same schools. It follows, then, that the use of the school buildings for civic and community activities will bring many into the schools who would not otherwise come; to that extent, it should be warmly supported by intelligent administrators.

Another type of noncurricular use of school plant facilities is to be found in the growing field of student extra-curricular activities. The use of the gymnasium for junior proms and student dances has long been common. More and more auditoriums are being used for class plays and student operettas. Football banquets and class potlucks are keeping large numbers of high school cafeterias open on many evenings of the school year. Such utilization of school areas also assists in increasing the ultimate percentage of classroom use, and in the end makes for more economical administration of school buildings.

Four main types of community use of school buildings may be cited:

1. Use by local groups upon application.
2. Use for school-sponsored activities.
3. Use for extra-curricular and related activities.
4. Use by self-supported organizations.

Desirable as such community use of school property may be, it must not in any way conflict with the use of the same areas by the regular pupils of the school.

Certain other problems remain to be resolved. The matter of proper supervision of school property during periods of community use poses several problems, such as, who is to pay for cleaning and heating, lighting, and other utilities. The presence of adults in large numbers at evening

Education Code

SECTION 16551. The governing board of any school district may grant the use of school buildings or grounds for public, literary, scientific, recreational or educational meetings, or for the discussions of matters of general or public interest upon such terms and conditions as the board deems proper, and subject to the limitations, requirements, and restrictions set forth in this chapter.

SECTION 16552. No use shall be inconsistent with the use of the buildings or grounds for school purposes, or interfere with the regular conduct of school work.

SECTION 16553. No use shall be granted in such a manner as to constitute a monopoly for the benefit of any person or organization.

SECTION 16554. No privilege of using buildings or grounds shall be granted for a period exceeding one year. The privilege is renewable and revocable in the discretion of the board at any time.

SECTION 16564. Any use, by any individual, society, group, or organization for the commission of any act intended to further any program or movement the purposes of which is to accomplish the overthrow of the government of the United States or of the state by force, violence, or other unlawful means shall not be permitted or suffered.

Any individual, society, group, or organization which commits any act intended to further any program or movement the purpose of which is to accomplish the overthrow of the government by force, violence or other unlawful means while using school property pursuant to the provisions of this chapter, is guilty of a misdemeanor.

SECTION 16565. No governing board of a school district shall grant the use of any school property to any person or organization for any use in violation of section 16564.

For the purpose of determination by such governing board whether or not any person or organization applying for the use of such school property intends to violate section 16564, the governing board may require the making and delivery to such governing board, by such person or organization, of affidavits in form prescribed by such governing board, stating facts showing that such school property is not to be used for the commission of any act intended to further any program or movement the purpose of which is to accomplish the overthrow of the government by force, violence or other unlawful means.

Rules and Regulations for Use of School Property for Public Purposes and as a Civic Center

1. Use and occupancy of school property shall be primarily for public school purposes. Any authorized use or occupancy of the property for other than public school purposes shall be secondary and subordinate to this primary purpose.

2. Pursuant to Article IV, Sections 30 and 31, and Article IX, Section 8 of the California constitution and Sections 8453 and 7102 education code, no use or occupancy of school property will be permitted for or in aid of any religious purpose, nor shall any sectarian or denominational doctrine be taught, or instruction thereon be permitted, directly or indirectly, at any meeting in school property.

3. Pursuant to Section 8451 education code no public meeting or entertainment held on the school property will be permitted to reflect in any way upon citizens of the United States because of their race, color, or creed.

4. No use or occupancy of any school property will be permitted if the governing board in the exercise of its discretion determines that such use or occupancy is prohibited by law, or that such use or occupancy will interfere with the use of the property for school purposes, or that it will result in picketing, rioting, or other disturbance of the peace, or in damage to the property which will render it unfit for or will interfere with its proper use for school purposes.

5. The governing board may inquire into the facts and may hold hearings at which all interested citizens may appear and present facts in support of, or in opposition to any proposed use of any school property.

6. The governing board may require that it be furnished reasonably in advance with a complete program, with copies of all speeches and addresses and script of any entertainment proposed to be given in school property. If such copy reasonably demonstrates that the program will be in violation of law or of these rules, the proposed use shall not be permitted.

7. All individuals, groups or organizations in their use or occupancy of school property shall comply with all applicable laws, rules and regulations. Any use contrary to or in violation of any law, rule or regulation shall be ground for cancellation of the permit and removing the users from the property and shall bar such individual group or organization from further use thereof.

8. The principal assigned to a school has full responsibility for supervision and management of all property of that school during school hours, which extend generally from early morning to late afternoon. He is authorized to assign use and occupancy of the property without charge during these hours for meetings of the following organizations: girl scouts, boy scouts, campfire girls, cub scouts, Hi-Y, girl reserves, coordinating council, and parent-teacher association, provided that such meetings are not inconsistent with and in no wise interfere with the use of the property for school purposes.

9. The business manager of the school district or his designated representative is authorized to issue all permits for the use and occupancy of school property by authorized individuals, groups, or organizations during non-school hours; and by all individuals, groups or organizations other than those named in rule 8 during school hours. Such permits will be issued only at the office of the business manager. If the district employee who receives any application shall have any question as to the availability of the building or the propriety of the requested or proposed use, he shall not issue any permit but shall refer the application to the board of education for its consideration and action. The applicant in his application shall state the date of use requested, the hour of opening and closing, the names of the speaker or speakers, the topic of discussion, the title and nature of the entertainment if an entertainment, the name of the organization for which the application is made and the name of the owner, producer, or controlling agency if other than the applicant.

10. Permission to use school facilities will be granted in accordance with a schedule of charges adopted by the board of education from time to time. Copies of the same may be obtained on application. Charges, if any, must be paid in full before a permit will be issued.

11. Service or sale of food or refreshments will be permitted in auditoriums with fixed seats.

12. Vending or sale of any article will not be permitted at any use or occupancy of the school property for civic center purposes.

13. Smoking is not permitted in any school building, except in approved places at the City College.

14. Social dancing by non-school groups on the school property will be permitted only when such dancing is incidental to a function held for members of an organization with a known and established membership and the purpose of the organization is other than that of providing opportunity for dancing. Permission for dancing must be obtained for each such event.

15. Any individual group or organization using school property for civic center or other purposes shall hold the Santa Monica Unified School District, its governing board, the individual members thereof, and all district officers, agents and employees free and harmless from any loss, damage, liability, cost or expense that may arise during or be caused in any way by such use of occupancy of school property.

16. School furniture or apparatus may not be removed or displaced by any permittee without permission from and under the supervision of the school district employee in charge.

17. School property shall be protected from any damage or mistreatment and permittees shall be responsible for the condition in which they leave the school building. In case school property is damaged, the cost thereof shall be paid by the permittee.

18. Upon receipt of notice that a permit has been issued to a non-school agency for use, the principal in charge of the school shall designate a regular employee to open the building, be in charge during the use, and to close the building after the use. The school district employee in charge of the building or grounds, within or upon which any meeting may be held, is empowered to take all necessary means to enforce these rules.

19. Any permit may be revoked without previous notice where conflicting dates have resulted or where need of the property for public school purposes has subsequently developed. For other cause permits may be revoked at any time upon reasonable notice.

20. For all groups of minors using school facilities, an adult supervisor must be present at all times and such groups will not be admitted to the buildings until the supervisor who has signed the application arrives to take charge.

21. In cases where any fees or charges are waived under the provisions of education code, section 16562, the Board of Education may require a report showing the disposition of the net receipts derived from the meeting or entertainment.

L27

FIGURE 15–1. Rules, Regulations, and Policies Regarding the Use of School Premises. Courtesy of the Santa Monica Unified School District, Santa Monica, California.

activities poses additional problems of policing and sanitation. There is little question that operational budgets go up proportionately with community utilization of school facilities. Despite these considerations, the school district, from a standpoint of public relations, will be well advised to assume all reasonable expenses in order to ensure maximum utilization of school buildings, and to induce lay citizens to come freely into the schools. As long as the instructional program is not interfered with, it is entirely to the schools' advantage to make their facilities available to the public on as broad a basis as required.

A prudent school policy dealing with community use of the school plant will always include a mimeographed or printed set of rules governing such use. This should set forth the legal obligations of the user, and should embody the local school district regulations insofar as they affect both parties. Regulations of this sort are included in the sample set of school use rules contained in Figure 15–1. References to the Education Code are peculiar to California law.

Every applicant for permission to use portions of the school building or grounds for community or related purposes should be handed a set of these rules at the time of application. In addition, he should be requested to fill out an application form, setting forth his reasons for seeking permission for use and making certain guarantees as to conduct of participants, care of building facilities, and type of activity to be carried on. Should the board of education have a policy on rental charges for profit performances in the school auditorium or multi-purpose room, for example, rates should be clearly set forth in the application form, and the applicant, in signing the form, agrees to pay such charges. The form will usually oblige the applicant to take whatever steps may be necessary to prevent the use of liquor or tobacco on the school premises during the time an outside organization is using them. It should also include a written affirmation that the use of the school building will not involve dissemination of sectarian religious precepts. Such an affidavit is necessary for the school district to ensure legal use of school property. An example of a school-use application is reproduced in Figure 15–2.

Proper Care of School Buildings

In any district employing a trained and experienced director of maintenance and operations, the chief administrator will be freed from personal

TABLE 15–1. *Schedule of Fees for Civic Center Use of Buildings (When Fee Is Required)*

BUILDING OR FACILITY	MINIMUM FEE	HRS. ALLOWED BY MINIMUM	HR. RATE FOR TIME USED OVER MINIMUM	MAXIMUM FEE
Classroom	3.00	2	1.50	7.50
Cafetorium	5.00	1	3.50	15.50
Kitchen Facilities	6.00	1	4.00	18.00
Jr. High Auditorium	25.00	3	10.00	50.00
Gymnasium	20.00	2	10.00	45.00
Additional Chgs., Aud.:				
Hourly Rate Over Min.	5.00 per hr.	Stage Equip., Including Spotlights		6.00 per hr.
Stage Crews ea.	1.10 per hr.	Arc Projector		4.50 per hr.
Sound Equip.	2.00 per hr.	Piano		1.00 per hr.

Santa Monica Unified School District
1723 Fourth Street
Santa Monica, California 90401

APPLICATION AND AGREEMENT FOR USE OF SCHOOL PROPERTY

Date of Application...

School...

Facility Desired

☐ Auditorium

☐ Multipurpose room only

☐ Multipurpose room with kitchen

☐ Cafeteria

☐ Cafeteria with kitchen

☐ Gymnasium with showers

☐ Gymnasium without showers

☐ Swim pool

☐ Class room

☐ Football field

☐ Football field with lights

☐ Baseball field

☐ Tennis courts

☐ Track

☐ Other...

Equipment Needed

☐ Piano

☐ Folding chairs

☐ Sound System

☐ Stage lighting with district electrician

☐ Other...

☐ Other...

☐ Other...

Type of Food Service

☐ Banquet

☐ Potluck

☐ Coffee and cookies

Contact must be made with the
Supervisor of Cafeterias for kitchen use.

Facilities are available ☐

Facilities are unavailable ☐

On the date and time requested

....
Principal

OFFICE COPY

Purpose of the meeting...

Expected attendance...

Is meeting open to the public?...............................

Will admission, solicitation or collection be made?........

If yes, for what purpose will net proceeds be used?.......

Indicate day, date and time of use below:

DAY	DATE	HOUR
		........M to............M
		........M to............M
		........M to............M
		........M to............M
		........M to............M
		........M to............M

We hereby certify that we shall be personally responsible, on behalf of our organization for any damage or unnecessary abuse of school buildings, grounds or equipment growing out of the occupancy of said premises by our organization. We agree to abide by and enforce the rules and regulations of the Santa Monica Unified School District governing the non school use of buildings, grounds and equipment and hereby acknowledge receipt of a copy of said rules and regulations.

Name of organization..

....
Name and Title of Authorized Agent

Address...

Business Phone.......................Residence Phone.........

Fee Charged $...........................

Payment $............ Receipt No............ Date...........

Payment $............ Receipt No............ Date...........

Payment $............ Receipt No............ Date...........

Application granted this............day of............19......

SANTA MONICA UNIFIED SCHOOL DISTRICT

By...

FIGURE 15–2. *Example of an Application for Use of School Facilities. Courtesy of the Santa Monica Unified School District, Santa Monica, California.*

supervision of school building care. Since most school districts, however, do not yet boast such an officer, the typical superintendent must take whatever steps may be necessary to ensure that buildings and grounds are kept neat and clean, and that natural deterioration does not exceed the bounds of normalcy. In such a situation, the chief administrator should set up a system that will include two main types of maintenance.

INDIVIDUAL BUILDING MAINTENANCE. The maintenance of the individual school plant should properly be the administrative province of the building principal. Here, the primary factor will be the relationship between the principal and the school custodians. The former will necessarily chart the latter's work assignment and regular daily routine, supervise the work, and evaluate the results. The principal should meet with his custodial staff at the beginning of each school year, and cooperatively set up the master plan for building maintenance at that time. Since misunderstanding and friction between classroom teachers and custodians are unfortunately so common that they often interfere with the proper performance of maintenance duties, the principal should take whatever steps may be necessary to see that the views of his faculty are taken into account in planning the year's maintenance schedule.

Once the work schedule has been decided upon, the principal should plan on regular inspections of the physical plant. An inspection checklist should be prepared by the principal and the custodians, or a standard form supplied by the district business office. Such a form, even when it originates on a level higher than the individual school, should be the product of group thinking, and various component factors should be agreed upon in advance by all concerned. The checklist should be used whenever inspections are made, and should be marked by both the principal and the custodian whose work is being checked. It should never be used as a rating scale, but rather as a guide to improvement. A checklist of this type is shown in Figure 15–3.

The principal should be particularly alert to detect internal building flaws such as broken windows, inadequate lighting fixtures, defective wiring, and roof or wall leaks. Teachers should be asked to help identify similar maintenance needs and report them promptly to the office. Particularly because these needs tend to be of a classroom nature, such as broken desks, burned-out light fixtures, or damaged blackboards, they should be reported to the principal by means of a form asking for special maintenance service. A form of this type is shown in Figure 15–4.

DISTRICT-WIDE MAINTENANCE. Maintenance is defined as "those activities designed to repair or restore the plant and equipment to their original condition."[5] Modern schools with new facilities and a great variety of technical teaching equipment such as television, teaching machines, language laboratories, electronic installations, and vocational equipment increase the demands for maintenance.[6]

Each district possessing more than two school plants should organize some system of district-wide maintenance. An annual inspection of all school property should be a part of this system. School districts that are not large enough to have qualified experts on their staff should employ them from their own or nearby communities to conduct inspections, preferably at some time immediately prior to the consideration and adoption of the budget for the following fiscal year. The annual inspection should produce recommendations for district-wide maintenance measures to be reflected in budgetary items. Particular attention should be given to the following needs:

1. Roof and chimney repairs
2. Window and door trim
3. Guttering and drainage systems
4. Plumbing and electrical service
5. Heating systems
6. Condition of stairways
7. Condition of flooring

A school district with more than three or four separate school plants should consider establishing a separate maintenance department, with a crew of trained men who move from school to school in accordance with a definite schedule. Such a mobile force, under the direction of an expert maintenance foreman, can follow up regular inspections with a comprehensive program of repairs and replacement which will closely follow the recommendations of the inspector. They can also complement the cleaning and maintenance staff. A maintenance center should be established at one of the centrally located school plants, or at a separate maintenance facility, with the maintenance crew operating out of that headquarters. This center should include office space, storage facilities, and a well-equipped repair shop. Except for unexpected emergencies, maintenance

---

[5] Melbo, *Report of the Survey, Laguna Beach*, p. 329.
[6] Robert E. Wilson, *Educational Administration*, p. 671.

	Condition	Remarks
School _____ Date _____		
Building _____		
Custodians _____		
Roofs		
Roofing		
Flushing and Coping		
Skylights		
Gutters		
Vents		
Exterior Wood Trim		
Rakes and Facia		
Soffits		
Window Frames, Sash		
Louvres and Vents		
Ceilings		
Doors		
Exterior Plaster and Concrete		
Walls		
Ceilings		
Arcade Slabs		
Platforms		
Splash Blocks		
Exterior Plumbing and Electrical Fixtures		
Hose Bibbs		
Fire Hose Cabinet		
Fire Extinguishers		
Break Glass Alarms		
Water S O Valves		
Gas S O Valves		
Switches and Plates		
Exterior Lights		
Yard Horns and Bells		
Electrical Panels		
Drinking Fountains		
Exterior Metal		
Down Spouts and S Blocks		
Columns		
Louvres		
Grease Traps		
Doors		
Screens		
Sumps, Gratings		

FIGURE 15–3.   Checklist for Regular Inspections of Individual Maintenance.

384

Exterior Concrete, Brickwork, A.C. and D.G.

Curbs and Gutters	
Drive-ins	
Sidewalks	
Incinerators	
Water-Meter Boxes	
Gas-Meter Boxes	
Electrical Vaults	
Asphalt-Concrete Areas	
Decomposed Granite Areas	
Fences and Gates	
Bicycle Stands	
Flag Pole	
Parking Lots	
Splash Blocks	
Playground Equipment	

Exterior Areas

Turf	
Lawns	
Sprinkler Systems	
Trees	
Shrubs	

	Condition	Remarks		Condition	Remarks
Room No. _____			Room No. _____		
Floor			Intercom Amplifier System		
Walls					
Ceiling					
Wood Trim, Venetian Blinds			Metal Partitions		
			Tile		
Cabinets			Plumbin & Fixtures		
Drain Boards & Splashes			Kitchen Equipment		
Furniture					
Heating & Controls			Stage Equipment		
Hardware			Towel & Toilet Tissue Cab.		
Electrical Fixtures					
Educational Equipment			Mirrors		

FIGURE 15–3. (*Continued*)

PARAMOUNT UNIFIED SCHOOL DISTRICT

MAINTENANCE WORK REQUEST
Via Business Office—Retain Last Copy for Your Files

School or Department_____ Building No._____ Room No._____ Date_____ 19____

WORK REQUESTED: List single item or group of like items (Type—Single Space)

For unusual or non-budgeted requests add justification statement. (Use separate sheet if necessary.)

Requested By:_____ Approved By:_____

Principal or Department Head

Accounting Classification_____

Do Not Write Below This Line

MAINTENANCE DEPARTMENT INFORMATION

Assigned To: _____ Section

New Construction ☐   Maintenance ☐   Vandalism ☐   Crew: _____   _____

_____   _____

Estimated Man Hours _____

Signature of Workman: _____

Scheduled Completion Date _____

Remarks: _____

Actual Completion Date _____

_____

Approved _____

Ass't Supt. Business Services

MATERIAL AND LABOR COST DATA (Attach extra sheet if required)

UNIT	MATERIAL USED	COST	DATE	LABOR USED	HRS.	RATE	COST
	TOTAL MATERIAL			TOTAL LABOR			
	Remarks or Instructions of Maintenance Manager			TOTAL MATERIAL			
				TOTAL COST OF COMPLETED REQUEST			

FIGURE 15–4.   Maintenance Work Request. Courtesy of the
Paramount Unified School District, Paramount, California.

386

should be scheduled for individual schools approximately one month in advance. Building principals should be informed of impending visits of the maintenance crew and of the areas in which they plan to operate. In fact, such scheduling should be the result of prior programming with the administrators and custodians of the separate schools affected.

Small districts may not be able to afford the luxury of employing their own skilled tradesmen. They may find it more advantageous to contract for specialized services. Larger districts, on the other hand, usually employ their own plumbers, electricians, carpenters, painters, audio-visual repairmen, and other special technicians. Some districts find it more economical to contract for larger services, while allowing their own maintenance staff to perform smaller services.

The principal goal of school maintenance should be the maximum retardation of depreciation. Reeder cites four cases of such depreciation: wear and tear of normal usage, physical decay, obsolescence, and accidents resulting from negligence or defects in materials or construction.[7] All causes, barring obsolescence, can be successfully combatted by informed and effective maintenance procedures. Priority listings should be made to include all areas of school maintenance in the order of their probable deterioration; items of top priority should receive proportionately more frequent attention.

The essential element in all maintenance is speed, both in reporting and identifying deterioration, and in effecting prompt repairs. There is an almost perfect corollary between delay in making repairs in cases of minor damage, and the multiplication of such cases. Thus, one knife nick on a desk breeds a whole series of similar nicks, whereas gleaming, intact facilities seem to discourage both conscious and unconscious vandalism. Effective building administration, then, will establish a routine especially designed to identify, report, and repair promptly all instances of damage or deterioration.

Regular Operation of the School Plant

Plant operation has been defined as "those activities necessary to keep the plant in condition for use, such as cleaning, disinfecting, heating, care of

---

[7] By permission of Macmillan Publishing Co., Inc., from *The Fundamentals of Public School Administration*, 4th ed. by Ward G. Reeder. Copyright © 1958 by Macmillan Publishing Co., Inc., p. 270.

lawns and shrubs and other similar work."[8]   It includes the following activities:

1. Regular cleaning of building and grounds.
2. Regulation and operation of heating, lighting, plumbing, and ventilating facilities.
3. Selection, purchase, use, and care of operational equipment.

ORGANIZATION OF CUSTODIAL SERVICES.   Perhaps the greatest single factor militating against operational efficiency is the lack of liaison between the custodial staff and the faculty of the school.   Because the primary purpose of the former is to facilitate the work of the latter, such a breakdown in common understanding must be avoided at all cost.   The best way to accomplish this is to establish an operational pattern based on the following principles:

1. Each building principal shall be directly in charge of the duties and scheduling of the custodians and matrons working in his building.
2. The district director of operations and maintenance shall serve as expert adviser to the principal on matters of technique and materials, and shall instruct the individual custodians as to the best and most economical ways of performing their duties.
3. During the weeks or months when school is not in session, the building operational personnel shall be under the supervision and control of the director of maintenance and operation, and may be used to augment the maintenance force of the district.

Such an organizational design helps to solve the problem of dual control.   The operational services remain subordinate and responsive to educational needs; and the temptation of individual custodial workers to "pass the buck" by playing off one "boss" against the other is greatly minimized.   The perennial complaint of the custodian that he has too many people giving him orders is eliminated; during the school year, only the building principal issues his orders, and in the summer, only the director of maintenance and operations.   Such an organizational plan presupposes the possession by the principal of the necessary knowledge and planning skills in the field of operation.   Such knowledge should be a part of the preparation of every administrator.

---

[8] Melbo, *Report of the Survey, Laguna Beach*, p. 329.

Evaluation of every operational program should be the function of the building principal, but he should perform this duty in close cooperation with the district director of operations.   Regular meetings should be scheduled with the operations personnel by the principal, in the same manner that regular faculty meetings are held and for much the same reason.   A job analysis that examines custodial duties and responsibilities should be used as a basis for developing a comprehensive description of each custodian's duties.   During the custodian–principal conference, mutually agreed-upon decisions should be made about the custodian's duties and hourly working schedule.   Each job analysis should be reviewed periodically and updated to take advantage of new products, new materials, and new techniques and procedures.   For example, new facilities such as acoustic flooring (carpeting) require vacuuming rather than sweeping.

Although building custodians are to have their duties assigned and their time scheduled by the principals, the technical details of their work are to be supervised by the chief maintenance and operations officer of the school district.   He will decide on the precise nature of the supplies and equipment that are needed for the rapid and efficient performance of the custodian's duties.   He also will instruct the custodian in the most effective ways to carry out the many types of work which combine to form his job, such as floor polishing, window cleaning, and grounds policing.

It is clear that such an organizational plan will call for the utmost in democratic cooperation on the part of all concerned.   Indeed, this is one of the crucial areas of modern school administration.   The administrator must solve the difficult problem of keeping the teacher sympathetically aware of the custodian's duties and problems, and vice versa.   If this is successfully accomplished, the school plant will operate harmoniously, and by combining utility and aesthetic appeal, will be a public relations asset also.   The average citizen may judge his neighborhood school largely by the neatness and beauty of its external appearance, rather than by the excellence of its instruction or the quality of its curriculum.   Since this is often true, the machinery set up to operate the school plant assumes an importance over and beyond its value to the school program as such.   It becomes a symbol of the efficiency and "know-how" of the entire school system in the eyes of the public.

IMPORTANCE OF THE SCHOOL CUSTODIAN.   Second to no one in the importance of his school position is the building custodian.   Years ago, the accepted practice was to award "janitor" jobs to old men, disabled veterans, or politically "deserving" individuals.   Fortunately, there is a marked trend away from this practice, in the direction of professionalizing the position of school custodian.   People selected for custodial positions should meet certain qualifications.   They should be:

1.   Physically able to do the work.
2.   Of good character.
3.   Mentally alert so as to read, report, and keep records.
4.   Dependable and prompt in handling duties.
5.   Able to get along with students, teachers, administrators, and visitors.
6.   Willing to grow on the job and assume responsibility.
7.   Orderly, and show care for tools and equipment.
8.   Economical, and guard against waste.[9]

Regular inservice training courses are commonly provided in most large school systems for "classified" employees.   The avowed purpose of such programs is to increase the competence and dignity of the position of custodian.   The custodian should be considered a regular member of the total school staff, not a lower level person to be looked down upon.   He should not have to jump at the beck and call of teachers, thus neglecting his assigned tasks.   Too often this is the case unless the building administrator stops the practice.

Custodians should be chosen carefully and standards for their selection should be devised and adhered to.   Physical examinations may be desirable.   Examinations to determine mental aptitude and knowledge of custodial work should be given.   Those who pass the physical and written examination should be given a practical examination.   Small school districts without sufficient administrative personnel may have to cut short the desirable testing program.

No custodial employee should ever be nominated or appointed by anyone except the duly designated school administrator, who may be the superintendent of schools, the business manager, the personnel administrator, or the director of buildings and grounds.   School boards are no more qualified to appoint custodians directly than they are to decide on teacher applications.   Any attempt to introduce favoritism or nepotism in the classified hiring system is bound to react unfavorably to the district.

The custodian's functions are more important than most people

---

[9] John David Engman, *School Plant Management for School Administrators*, pp. 29–30.

realize.   It is his responsibility to see that valuable school property is kept repaired and operable.   Often, he is deputized by the civil authorities to enable him to preserve the peace at public functions held on the school grounds.   Since he is a major user of expensive supplies and equipment, he should help in their selection.   The housekeeping standards that the custodian maintains set the tone for judging the entire school program. Typical custodial responsibilities include:

1.   Safety, health, and comfort of students and school staff.
2.   Condition of buildings and equipment.
3.   Cleanliness of buildings and grounds.
4.   Sanitation.
5.   Proper storage of materials and supplies.
6.   Prevention of damage by wear and abuse or by any external means.
7.   Keeping adequate records as required.[10]

SCHEDULE OF OPERATIONS.   Pittenger recommends the following schedule of operations for a typical elementary school to maintain proper standards in custodial service:

1.   Twice daily: sweep kindergarten floor, clean entrance corridors, pick up paper in toilets, clean drinking fountains.
2.   Daily: unlock and lock up the building; open and close windows; raise and lower flag; clean toilets; empty pencil sharpeners and waste baskets; clean erasers and chalk gutters; sweep corridors; sweep classrooms, offices, and special rooms; sweep lunchroom; sweep boiler room; carry out ashes; turn off lights; check supply of toilet paper and towels; set clocks; bank fires; clean boiler flues.
3.   Weekly: wash blackboards, make minor repairs, bale paper, mop untreated floors, clean light fixtures.
4.   Monthly: wash glass in rooms inside and out, clean bulletin boards, dust pictures, polish brass, read meters.
5.   Periodically: fire boiler, clean boiler, repair furniture, clean walks, scrub floors, trim shrubs, mow lawn, provide other necessary care for school yard, refinish seats and furniture, paint, preserve floors, renew preservative treatment, make out necessary records and reports, wash windows on outside, make inventory, receive and check supplies.[11]

---

[10] Engman, *School Plant Management,* pp. 30–31.
[11] B. F. Pittenger, *Local Public School Administration,* p. 368.

This work schedule should be supplemented by a daily time schedule, allotting certain routine duties to each hour of the custodian's work day. This schedule should be adhered to as strictly as possible, barring emergencies. Nothing is more frustrating to a building principal than to attempt to locate a custodian for some unexpected need and to be unable to find him. A code signal should be assigned to each custodian, and he should always be within earshot of the school's buzzer system so that he may be promptly available in times of emergency. A custodial schedule combining both work and time factors is shown in Table 15–2.

EQUIPMENT AND SUPPLIES. Great strides have been made in recent years in the field of operational supplies and equipment. Formerly, school equipment was purchased on the basis of cost, with very little attention given to quality. Second-hand tools and refinished furniture were common; rickety "contributions" from board members and public-spirited citizens often made up the bulk of the school custodian's equipment. Most items today are purchased on the open market from legitimate supply houses, and qualify for most standards of efficiency and safety. However, many schools with expensive plants and elaborate teaching tools are still using antiquated and makeshift custodial supplies and equipment. Comparatively little research has been done in this particular field, and as a result, many schools are simply following the line of least resistance. School districts that fail to provide the proper tools and supplies are not receiving their money's worth from their custodial employees.

TABLE 15–2. Daily Custodial Work Schedule

7:00 AM to 12:00 AM (5-hour worker)	
7:00–8:00 AM	Check heating temperatures. Inspect school premises—pick up trash as you enter. Put out hose for watering. Open administration unit at 7:30 AM.
8:00–9:00 AM	Report to office at 8:00 AM—Do this every day! Open front gate at 8:15 AM. Open vehicle gate at 8:15 AM. Put up flags at 8:30 AM. Burn trash.
9:00–10:00 AM	Sweep corridors and pick up paper blown and thrown on yard as you water lawns. Water lawns. Sweep patio with sweeper.
10:00–12:00 AM	Help set up cafetorium for lunch or special assembly. Do any odd jobs requested by principal.

TABLE 15–2. (*Continued*)

10:00 AM to 6:30 PM (8-hour worker—30 min. for lunch)

10:00–10:30 AM	Report to office at 10:00 AM. Dust administration unit. Inspect women's and men's toilets for paper, soap, towels, etc.
10:30–11:00 AM	Inspect girls' toilets for supplies. Set up cafetorium for lunch —morning custodian helping.
11:00–11:30 AM	Spot, wash windows, weed flowers, and do any small cleaning jobs needed.
11:30–12:00 AM	Eat lunch.
12:00–1:00 PM	Spot, wash windows, weed flowers, and do any small cleaning jobs needed.
1:00–3:00 PM	Work in cafetorium. This includes teachers' dining room and setting up for any afternoon or evening cafetorium use.
3:00–4:00 PM	Sweep, dust, clean toilets, clean drinking fountains, empty wastebaskets in rooms 21 and 22. Sweeping takes 20 to 30 minutes per room, depending upon the primary furniture in the rooms and including cleaning toilets and drinking fountains.
4:00–6:00 PM	Sweep, dust, clean toilets, clean drinking fountains, empty wastebaskets in rooms 1, 2, 3, 4, and 5.
6:00–6:30 PM	Clean administration unit.

2:00 PM to 10:30 PM (8-hour worker—30 min. for supper)

2:00–2:30 PM	Report to office at 2:00 PM Empty garbage cans, clean, scald, let drip—replace. Help with cafetorium set-up when needed.
2:30–3:00 PM	Sweep rooms in primary dept. Dust, close windows, turn out lights, etc.
3:00–6:00 PM	Sweep, dust, clean toilets, drinking fountains in primary dept. rooms.
6:00–6:30 PM	Supper.
6:30–9:30 PM	Sweep, dust, clean toilets, drinking fountains in upper grade rooms. Finish by dusting all cleared surfaces in all rooms.
9:30–10:30 PM	Check all doors and windows throughout the plant even though you locked them as you finished in each unit. Check all gates as you lock up.

Dusty and unsanitary brushes and brooms are still the standard tools used for school cleaning, although vacuum cleaners of various sizes and types are now available for school use at reasonable prices. Clumsy and dirt-collecting mops are used to remove excess water and soap from scrubbed classroom floors, although the wet-process vacuum is infinitely preferable from the standpoint of ease, speed, and sanitation. Power mowers equipped with sulky seats enable a school custodian or gardener to mow an expanse of lawn in an hour; the job might easily have taken him all day if he had used the small, hand-operated lawnmower still so common in many school districts. There is no economy in shackling a custodian with outmoded equipment. This invariably results in hiring more personnel or in accepting inferior standards of work.

Custodial Time Schedules

It is economical to stagger the working time schedules for custodians. Since the custodian's chief task is sweeping and cleaning, he can be more efficient on a working schedule that follows the dismissal of pupils.

Many school districts could profit by assigning more custodial positions to after-school hours. Assignment of a few custodians at night provides a minimum of night watch service. When custodians are assigned to late evening or night hours, they should receive a one-step higher increment on the salary schedule than custodians of similar classification who work the more favorable day shift.

If there is enough overlapping of duties, all custodians can meet together for a short time to discuss mutual problems. They can also help each other if some major task needs to be done. It is also a good idea to allow time for the head custodian at each facility to supervise or inspect the work of other custodians.

Many districts have had to reduce custodial services due to budgetary problems. Because of this, custodial schedules may be different from day to day. For example, classrooms may be swept only on alternate days. Needless to say, lavatories and drinking fountains should be cleaned every day.

Table 15–3 shows one district's attempt to stagger working time. It is likely that more late afternoon assignments would have resulted in greater efficiency for this district.

TABLE 15–3. Working Hours for Custodians

Custodial Positions	6	7	8	9	10	11	12	1	2	3	4	5	6	7	8	9	10	11	12	1	2
	AM																				PM
4	6:00								2:30												
33		7:00								3:30											
1		7:15									3:45										
1		7:45			10:45			1:00					6:00								
18			8:00									5:00	6:00								
8									2:30									11:00			
1											4:30				8:15 (3¾ hrs.)						
1													6:00								2:00
	AM																				PM

395

Custodial Workloads

Many formulas have been developed for the measurement of reasonable custodial workloads, e.g.: "one custodian per 20,000 square feet of building; one custodian per 250 students; one custodian per 10 teachers; one custodian per 11 rooms to be cleaned; and combinations of the preceding."[12]   The chief ingredients of these formulas are square footage, rooms, students, or teachers.   The type of construction, texture of surfaces, adjacency to dust or fumes, building usage, nature of cleaning equipment, and other factors must be considered as a supplement to any formula that is adopted.   Local conditions cause many variables.

Melbo and his survey staff have developed custodial workload standards as a result of more than 60 major school surveys.   Their criteria have been standardized on more than 500 schools in several states.   During the Pomona Survey, the Melbo staff prepared many tables upon the measurements and conditions of 1,157,567 square feet of varied areas and compared the available custodial hours of time available to the time needed.   Data from the many tables, measurements, and corrections are summarized in Table 15–4.

This type of objective calculation takes the guesswork out of custodial workload assignments.   As a result, greater economy accrues to the district and custodians maintain a higher level of morale in the belief that their workload assignments are impartial and fair.   All districts should justify workload assignments by the use of cooperatively formulated and objective standards.   Whatever method is finally agreed upon, it should consider the task itself and the frequency and quality of performance expected.[13]

Summary

Maximum utilization of the school plant is the goal; it may be approached by circular use of the buildings and use for noncurricular purposes.   In order to achieve this goal, proper care of the buildings is necessary, requiring the cooperation of all school personnel.   A trained director of maintenance and operation can do much in this connection, but in the absence of such a person, the superintendent should establish a system which provides both for individual building maintenance and district-wide maintenance.

---

12 Joseph J. Baker and Jon S. Peters, *School Maintenance and Operation*, p. 141.
13 Baker and Peters, *School Maintenance*, p. 141.

TABLE 15–4. *Application of Custodial Performance Standards to the Buildings and Grounds of Pomona Unified School District, June 1957*[a]

BUILDINGS AND GROUND AREA	SQUARE FOOTAGE OF AREAS	RECOMMENDED HOURS PER DAY
Classrooms	329,050	137.0
Shops	26,287	13.2
Administrative offices	41,244	20.5
Auditoriums	23,410	6.6
Gymnasiums	16,252	5.4
Auditorium–cafeteria	35,637	10.2
Auditorium–gymnasium	10,254	2.9
Kitchens and snack bar	13,571	9.7
Restrooms and locker area	50,576	21.0
Stairs and landings	12,967	9.2
Outside corridors	166,511	3.3
Inside halls	2,470	.8
Sidewalks	23,642	3.0
Surfaced playgrounds	144,020	2.9
Dirt playgrounds	149,210	1.9
Lawn and turf (by custodians)	10,191	.3
Shrubs and flowers (by custodians)	4,382	2.3
Parking lots	48,130	1.0
Paved areas between buildings	10,118	.2
Libraries	6,438	2.7
Patios	3,024	.4
Surfaced eating pavilions	8,184	1.6
Teacher rooms	1,647	.8
Stages	1,232	.4
Workroom and bookroom	648	.3
Art workroom	1,152	.6
Music laboratory	576	.2
Teachers' laboratory and band	2,688	1.3
Miscellaneous areas	556	.3
Double-session classrooms	13,400	5.6
Totals	1,157,567	165.6
Custodial supervision		10.0
Purchasing, inspecting, and reporting		3.0
Emergency assignments		2.0
Total hours needed		280.6[b]

[a] Irving R. Melbo, et al., *Report of the Survey, Pomona Unified School District*, vol. 2 (Los Angeles: University of Southern California, 1957), p. 433.
[b] Total hours needed, 280.6; total hours available, 273.

Regular operation of the school plant should combine efficiency and economy. Custodial services should be under the direction of the building principal, with the director of operation and maintenance serving as expert adviser to the principal except during the summer, when the director should assume control.

Operational charts and custodial checklists occupy much of this chapter, which is intended to be a very practical guide to school plant operation.

Trends

The basic trend in school building administration is toward modernization and streamlining both of organization and equipment. For generations, the most archaic area of public school services has been that of building maintenance and operation. To the same degree that it has lagged behind other phases of school administration, building administration offers the most fertile field for rapid improvement. It seems probable, therefore, that the next twenty years will see a complete transformation in this area of educational administration.

TOWARD INCREASED EFFICIENCY IN BOTH CLASSROOM AND PUPIL STATION UTILIZATION. The coming upon the educational scene of the multi-purpose room has been the signal for a marked rise in building utilization efficiency. As more and more auditorium–cafeteria, cafeteria–library, or gymnasium–auditorium combinations are built, the utilization ratio will continue to climb. In addition, the use of school plants for community and extra-curricular activities will cut down markedly on the total number of hours per day during which great areas of the plant stand idle and unoccupied. The combination of flexibility in architectural planning and extension of school services to a community-wide level is bound to make for far greater utilization of plant facilities.

TOWARD MORE USE OF THE SCHOOL PLANT AS A COMMUNITY CENTER. The modern school, with its electronic aids to speech and hearing, its athletic facilities, and its recreational equipment, is the natural choice of most communities for a social and civic center. The decline of the church and the home, insofar as their roles in social and recreational life are concerned, presages the vast enlargement of the school's role in such vital areas of community living.

TOWARD THE CENTRALIZATION OF SCHOOL MAINTENANCE.   Every school district of any size will soon support the position of director of maintenance and operation.   This position will be an important executive one, requiring extensive experience in construction, maintenance, and personnel management.   The result will be the centralization of the maintenance program on a district-wide level, with maintenance workers being hired on the basis of individual skills in fields such as plumbing, carpentry, and electricity.

TOWARD THE PROFESSIONALIZATION OF THE SCHOOL CUSTODIAN.   As more of modern science enters into the maintenance and operation of a school plant, the position of custodian will be revolutionized.   The custodian will become an educated, scientifically trained, well-paid professional.   The trend is in the direction of more careful screening and inservice training of custodial and maintenance employees.   Much more attention will be given to proper time scheduling and to objectification of assignments of workloads.

TOWARD INCREASED AUTOMATION IN SCHOOL MAINTENANCE.   The use of wet-process cleaning, high-power vacuum cleaners, and other mechanical aids to the custodian will continue to grow, as machines increasingly assume the functions formerly assigned to muscle power.

Administrative Problems

In Basket

Problem 1

As principal of an elementary school, you have instructed your teachers to have their pupils put away books, clear their desks, pick up papers, crayons, and pencils from the floor, and leave the room neat at the end of the school day. Windows are to be closed and latched and doors locked.   The purpose is to make it easier for the custodian to clean and dust each room in his allotted time.

Miss Perkins, a new fifth grade teacher, has paid little attention to your instructions and usually leaves her classroom in a mess.   You have talked to her several times about this problem; after each conference, the room is left in better condition for several days but gradually returns to its former slovenliness.

Sam Jones, the custodian, has complained to you numerous times about the difficulty of cleaning Miss Perkins' room. This afternoon, he storms into your office and states that he is refusing to clean her room whenever he finds it too messy.

What will you tell Sam?
What action will you take with Miss Perkins?

Problem 2

The Toyon Junior High School of which you are principal has many civic center activities scheduled. Cub Scout Pack 83 uses the multi-purpose room the third Wednesday of each month for its Pack meeting. Refreshments are served at the end of each meeting—coffee for adults and punch and cookies for the boys. Adults are permitted to smoke and ash trays are furnished. After each meeting, however, punch is left spilled on the floor, crumbs are everywhere, and cigarette stubs have been ground into the floor.

How should the principal handle this situation?

Problem 3

At a recent district administrative council meeting, several principals complained about their maintenance service. A summary of their complaints showed:

1. Two men are sometimes sent to do a one-man job.
2. Maintenance men spend too much time drinking coffee and chatting with the school custodian.
3. Requests for repairs are not taken care of promptly and unsafe conditions exist for days.
4. Repairs are often slipshod.
5. Phone calls to the maintenance and operations manager have resulted in promises to remedy the problems; but the problems remain, according to the principals.

The superintendent asks the business manager to investigate the complaints and to try to remedy the situation.

How should the business manager proceed?

Selected References

BAKER, JOSEPH J., and PETERS, JON S. *School Maintenance and Operation.* Danville, Ill.: Interstate, 1963.

ENGELHARDT, N. L., and ENGELHARDT, F. *Planning School Building Programs.* New York: Teachers College, Columbia University, 1930.

ENGMAN, JOHN DAVID. *School Plant Management for School Administrators.* Houston, Texas: Gulf School Research Development Association, 1962.

FELDMAN, EDWIN B. *Housekeeping Handbook for Institutions, Business & Industry.* New York: Frederick Fell, 1969.

GEORGE, N. L. *Effective School Maintenance.* West Nyack, N.Y.: Parker Publishing Co., 1969.

HILL, FREDERICH W., and COLMEY, JAMES W. *School Custodial Services.* Minneapolis: T. S. Denison & Co., 1968.

MELBO, IRVING R., et al. *Report of the Survey, Laguna Beach Unified School District.* Los Angeles: University of Southern California, 1961.

————. *Report of the Survey, Pomona Unified School District,* vol. 2. Los Angeles: University of Southern California, 1957.

PITTENGER, B. F. *Local Public School Administration.* New York: McGraw-Hill Book Co., 1951.

REEDER, WARD G. *The Fundamentals of Public School Administration.* 4th ed. New York: Macmillan Publishing Co., 1958.

SACK, THOMAS F. *A Complete Guide to Building and Plant Maintenance.* 2nd ed. Englewood Cliffs, N.J.: Prentice-Hall, 1971.

SCHOEFELD, CLARENCE A. *Year-round Education.* Madison, Wis.: Dembar Educational Research Services, 1964.

WALTON, JOHN. *The Discipline of Education.* Madison, Wis.: University of Wisconsin Press, 1963.

WATERS, JAMES E., and STOOPS, EMERY. *Administration of Maintenance and Operations in California School Districts: A Handbook for Administrators and Governing Boards.* Sacramento: California State Department of Education, 1969.

WILSON, ROBERT E. *Educational Administration.* Columbus, Ohio: Charles E. Merrill Publishing Co., 1966.

PART FIVE

Administration of Special Services

16

Transportation Services

Transportation services have greatly expanded over the years. Today transportation is costly and creates financial problems for many districts, forcing some of them to eliminate or curtail their bus services. Rigid controls are necessary, requiring rules and regulations for the safety of the students and for the maintenance and efficient operation of the equipment. Because of their great responsibility, bus drivers should be selected carefully and trained to maintain the district's standards. Field trips by school bus are an important supplement to the educational program.

This chapter includes a discussion of the following topics:

Expansion of Transportation Services
Growth of Pupil Transportation
Types of Pupil Transportation
Purposes of School Transportation
Busing for Racial Balance
District Policies for Pupil Transportation
Administration of Transportation Services
Cooperative Determination of Bus Routes
State Financing and Regulation of Pupil Transportation
Selection and Training of Bus Drivers
Bus Identification and Equipment
District Transportation Directors
Care and Maintenance of Transportation Equipment
Bus Behavior
Bus Safety
Field Trips

Accidents
Summary
Trends

Expansion of Transportation Services

The schools of today reflect the impact of 20th-century America's changing mores and standards. Nowhere, perhaps, are these marks so evident and the impact so manifest as in the area of special services. Barely a generation ago, schools offering door-to-door bus service were in a very small minority. Such functions were deemed the proper prerogatives of the home.

Today, the lessening of the ties binding the home and church to the personal life of the individual has brought about an amazing transformation in the overall role of the school. Education, in the older sense of the word, is no longer the only concern of the schools. Classroom instruction competes for the tax dollar and the time and energy of the administrator with such highly essential noneducational portions of the school program as mass transportation.

A substantial portion of the general public believes that the revolutionary expansion of school functions stems directly from a concerted attempt by educators to aggrandize their responsibilities. However, the apparently insatiable demand of the American people during the past few decades for increased comforts, a rising standard of living, and luxury services of all kinds has been the prime factor in the growth of school programs. In most cases, the schools were reluctant to add services that were educational in nature only secondarily, if at all. However, the schools are run by the representatives of the people; therefore they must be governed by the majority opinion as to what constitutes their proper sphere of activity.

Buses are used when there are hazards involved in walking—such as the necessity of crossing main boulevards or the lack of sidewalks on busy streets. Children may be transported for even a few blocks, and parents expect and often demand this service though they may dislike paying taxes to provide such door-to-door transportation.

A steadily increasing growth in the sheer number and complexity of functions the school is expected by its supporters to perform has resulted. It is no longer sufficient for the administrator to be an educator; he must be trained and experienced in a diversity of skills formerly thought to be the proper province of the business or industrial world. No trend in education is more pronounced than this, and there is no sign of its imminent diminution.

Growth of Pupil Transportation

The earliest record of transporting students to school was in 1840 at private expense. In 1869, schoolchildren in Massachusetts were brought to school in horsedrawn carts and carriages paid for by school funds. This represented the first form of subsidized pupil transportation, but did not become either popular or prevalent until about 1920. The first motorized bus, called a "school truck," came on the scene in Pennsylvania in 1909. Laws were enacted in 1925 to regulate the speed at 25 miles per hour and to establish the rights of students on the highway. In 1966, over fifteen million school pupils were driven to and from school each day, and more than $787,000,000 was spent for this purpose.[1]

CONSOLIDATION OF SCHOOL DISTRICTS. A main factor in the growth of pupil transportation services has been the movement toward the unification or consolidation of school districts. The larger the area served by the single school, the greater the amount of bus transportation required. Some states make cash payments to parents living in remote regions, allowing them to bring their children to school, or to room and board them in the vicinity of the school. Such arrangements, however, are so patently undesirable that they should be resorted to only when bus transportation is clearly out of the question.

INCREASED STATE AID FOR TRANSPORTATION. The majority of states now provide financial aid for school transportation through special funds or through provisions in foundation programs. States may also reimburse local school districts for transporting handicapped children.

IMPROVEMENT OF ROADS AND BUSES. Pupils are now driven to and from schools for distances inconceivable only a generation ago. Paved high-

---

[1] Clayton D. Hutchins and Richard H. Barr, *Statistics of State School Systems, 1965–66,* U.S. Department of Health, Education, and Welfare (Washington, D.C.: U.S. Government Printing Office, 1968), p. 62.

ways have supplanted the rutty, mud-filled back roads of the past, and modern multi-horsepower motors reduce fifty miles to barely an hour's trip. The American people are geared to an age of high-speed travel, and look with equanimity upon school bus routes whose length would have called forth a storm of protest in the not-too-distant past. For example, children in union high school districts in Lancaster, Barstow, and Coachella, California, travel as far as 70 miles one way each day.

THE DECLINE OF THE SMALL COMMUNITY. Although there remain many exceptions to this generalization, small community boundaries are no longer universally regarded as necessarily coterminous with school attendance areas. The jealously guarded role of the small community as the center of civic, cultural, and social life has begun to be discarded under the growing impact of motion pictures, rapid transportation, and radio and television. Under such shifting conditions, people are increasingly willing to allow their children to be driven for many miles, if necessary, outside the community limits to enjoy increased educational opportunities.

UNIVERSAL COMPULSORY SCHOOL ATTENDANCE LAWS. Once a state enacts a statute compelling all children to attend school, it is compelled by the force of logic to remove whatever obstacles may stand in the way of such attendance. Since enforcement in an isolated or sparsely settled region would be virtually impossible if walking or private transportation were solely depended upon, it follows that the state or its creature, the school district, must supply the means of getting to the nearest school.

Types of Pupil Transportation

There are two main varieties of pupil transportation: school owned and operated, and privately owned and operated. Public ownership, used by most school districts, is strongly preferred. However, quite a wide variety of practices exists.

SCHOOL OWNERSHIP AND OPERATION. In small districts operating only one or two buses, public ownership may represent a financial drain because buses require a high capital investment. In such a situation, public ownership, however, is preferable to private; in all larger districts, it becomes economical as well as educationally desirable. For example, the profit factor is eliminated from the operational costs, thus effecting considerable savings. Schools do not have to pay taxes on the purchase of buses and other related equipment, another point operating in favor of public ownership. Aside from the economic point of view, there is the overriding factor of school control and administration. Once it is granted that pupil transportation is an integral and important part of the school program, it follows that it should be as much under school control and operation as the instructional program or the maintenance and operation of the school buildings. There is no excuse for divided control and unclear lines of authority when one is dealing with children's lives. Some of the other advantages of school district ownership are:

1. The school district can be more selective in employing capable drivers.
2. Buses can be more easily scheduled for educational and co-curricular activity trips.
3. It is easier to route the school district buses than privately owned buses; changes in routes can be made more quickly.
4. The supervision of drivers, other transportation employees, and students is easier to accomplish because the school district has direct control.

PRIVATE OWNERSHIP AND SCHOOL OPERATION. Some school districts are forced by initial lack of funds to begin a pupil transportation program by leasing buses from private companies, operated by school employees. The long-term expense is so great under this arrangement that it can serve only as a temporary stopgap for districts that are short of capital funds.

SCHOOL OWNERSHIP AND PRIVATE OPERATION. This arrangement is rare. Occasionally, a school district will purchase a bus or several buses, and find itself unwilling or unable to employ and train temporarily the necessary number of drivers. Therefore, the district turns to private companies or individuals and contracts with them to operate the buses until such time as the district is able to assume the responsibility. This method of arranging for pupil transportation has most of the disadvantages implicit in any program involving school funds and schoolchildren that is not under the complete control of the school.

Purposes of School Transportation

The major purposes of transportation services are to transport children to and from school; to provide the means for educational field trips; and to transport students for co-curricular activities such as athletics, music, and dramatics. Physically handicapped or severely mentally retarded children should be transported regardless of the distance.

Each time a child rides a school bus he has an opportunity to add to his social and educational growth provided time and effort are used to promote these values. The teaching of safety and courtesy has direct application to bus riders. Field trips offer a rare opportunity to extend the classroom and to give children firsthand knowledge of the world around them—far better than the best picture or the most interestingly written explanation.

Busing for Racial Balance

The concept of the neighborhood school has created problems in many parts of the country. American neighborhoods and communities are composed of black, Mexican-American, white, and Oriental children who may never have the opportunity to go to school with someone of a different ethnic background and culture. Many schools in lower economic areas, usually attended by minority children, are not as well built, maintained, equipped, or supplied as other more fortunate schools; and teachers are often not as well prepared or qualified. The opposite should be the case. Minority children need the best-trained teachers and the most up-to-date equipment and supplies.

One of the proposed methods for solving the problem of racial balance is to transport children from a minority area to a school in a predominately white community. In turn, white children would be transported to a minority neighborhood school. Administrators in the seventies are faced with this additional transportation problem.

There are pros and cons regarding compulsory versus voluntary busing to achieve integration. The American Association of School Administrators and the National Education Association have resolved to support busing of students to implement desegregation plans. In 1973, a federal district court ordered the Department of Health, Education, and Welfare to enforce desegregation in 17 states and directed the department to cut off federal funds to districts that failed to comply. The department is expected to appeal the decision. In 1973, the Massachusetts Supreme

Court ruled that a state law that would have prohibited busing students without their parents' written permission was unconstitutional.

On the other hand, President Nixon asked Congress to place a moratorium on court orders that required school busing for racial balance and he pledged to work with Congress to enact legislation to end involuntary busing. Numerous school districts have appealed to the courts about busing to achieve racial balance. State court rulings have differed, others are pending, and still others are on appeal to higher courts. Consensus seems to favor voluntary busing. As of 1974, there was no forced busing to any extent and the legal situation was confused and undecided.

There is no assurance that a student will learn as much or more if he is forced to be transported to another school. Attitudes must be changed first.

Administrators must be aware of the attempt to achieve racial balance by busing. They must develop realistic guidelines and policies so that integration pressures can be met on a practical, moral, fair, and educationally sound basis. The cost to a school district for adding this type of busing can be enormous, whether it is compulsory or voluntary. It may mean the purchase of more buses, the hiring of more drivers, and the extension of bus routes. Budget considerations become important. Whether or not busing for racial balance is a solution has not yet been determined. What has been determined is that forced busing adds enormously to the problems inherent in administering a school district.

BUSING FOR DIFFERENT TYPES OF SCHOOLS. In addition to busing for racial integration, additional busing may be required for special types of schools. The alternative school, with an open, free type of curriculum and attended on a voluntary basis, may exist within a school system, requiring an interchange of students between it and other schools. A continuation high school for students who cannot adjust to the regular curriculum for various reasons may require extra busing. Special classes for atypical children in selected schools may also require extra busing.

District Policies for Pupil Transportation

In order to provide the best transportation service for pupils and to keep the service fair and impartial for all patrons, the governing board of the school district should set forth policies in writing.

Many problems will arise regarding the bus services, and parental and community pressures may become exasperating. Decisions should be made only according to established policies. School boards or administrators who make decisions without regard to policy expose themselves to increasing demands from others, and they cannot justify their actions. Community relations and staff and student morale may suffer. Transportation policies should be developed by the cooperative action of administrators, parents, teachers, bus drivers, and students. They should be made available, not only to school personnel, but also to the citizens of the community. School policies can be developed from the checklist shown in Table 16–1.

Administration of Transportation Services

The administration of school district transportation must be in conformity with "Highway Safety Program Standard No. 17," issued by the National Highway Traffic Safety Administration in 1972.[2] It says, "Each state, in cooperation with its school districts and its political subdivisions, shall have a comprehensive pupil transportation safety program to assure that school vehicles are operated and maintained so as to achieve the highest possible level of safety." The standard "established minimum requirements for a state highway safety program for pupil transportation safety, including the identification, operation, and maintenance of school buses; training of personnel; and administration." The standard's purpose "is to reduce, to the greatest extent possible, the danger of death or injury to school children while they are being transported to and from school." There will be a number of references to Standard No. 17 in the remainder of this chapter.

In larger school districts, transportation services are usually handled by a transportation manager working under the direct supervision of the administrator in charge of business services. In small school districts, the principal may manage these services and, in some cases, may even drive the school bus. The principal, regardless of district size, should have

---

[2] *Highway Safety Program Standard No. 17* was issued on May 2, 1972 by Douglas W. Toms, Administrator, U.S. Department of Transportation, National Highway Traffic Safety Administration. Published in the Federal Register, vol. 37, no. 89, May 6, 1972, it became effective 30 days after the publishing date.

administrative and supervisory responsibility for bus service at the school level.

Featherston and Culp describe three criteria that should be applied in evaluating transportation services:[3] (1) Safety. This involves an understanding of the number of accidents and injuries; bus miles per accident; responsibility; safety training for drivers and students; and the maintenance of buses. (2) Economy. This pertains to the cost per pupil per bus mile; cost comparison with other districts and state averages; informing drivers and maintenance personnel of costs; the selection and purchase of equipment; a survey of instances where savings can be made; and the adjustment of schedules to eliminate unnecessary driving. (3) Adequacy. This relates to the written transportation policies; the difference between state and district regulations regarding eligibility to ride and walking distances; load limits that are prescribed; service to isolated areas; and the provision for sufficient seating.

The principal of each school and district administration has the immediate administrative responsibility for determining:

1. The number of children who need to be transported.
2. Where children live in relation to bus routes.
3. The location of the bus stops or stations for pickup and delivery.
4. The method of loading and unloading the bus at school or at the bus stations.
5. Transportation safety.
6. The control of discipline.
7. The extent of supervision on the part of teachers.
8. The compiling of records and reports that are required by law and by school district policy.

EVALUATION OF TRANSPORTATION SERVICES. Melbo has developed a checklist for the evaluation of school transportation services (see Table 16–1). It can be used to help in the development of transportation policies and in the administration of the services. Standard No. 17 requires each state to evaluate the pupil transportation program at least annually and to report to the National Highway Traffic Safety Administration.

---

[3] E. Glenn Featherston and D. P. Culp, *Pupil Transportation: State and Local Programs,* pp. 139–141.

TABLE 16–1. *Checklist for the Evaluation of Transportation Services*[a]

ITEM	SUPERIOR	AVERAGE	POOR
1. The district should operate its own transportation system rather than contract for major services.			
2. The transportation program should be directed by an employee who has the ability, and who is allowed sufficient time to supervise adequately all operations.			
3. Only modern equipment in excellent mechanical condition should be used.			
4. Inspections by the State Highway Patrol should be welcomed and all recommendations should be followed.			
5. Under no conditions should anyone other than a properly licensed bus driver operate the vehicle while transporting children.			
6. Classified employees rather than teachers should be used as bus drivers.			
7. Classified employees not regularly used as bus drivers should be licensed as substitutes when necessary.			
8. A utility bus or buses should be available for use in case of emergency and for special field trips.			
9. An adequate plan for doing the repair work and servicing the buses should be followed.			
10. The district should try to standardize its transportation equipment. This simplifies repair work and other procedures. It is then possible to carry a minimum stock of needed parts.			
11. The district should provide safe and adequate storage facilities for gasoline and oil, and should purchase these items according to specifications on open bid.			
12. Adequate insurance protection should be carried.			
13. Controls regarding the dispensing of gasoline should be exercised the same as if cash were involved.			

TABLE 16-1. (*Continued*)

ITEM	SUPERIOR	AVERAGE	POOR
14. Adequate cost records should be maintained.			
15. Definite regulations regarding pupil transportation should be adopted by the board and made available in writing to certificated and classified employees.			
16. Bus drivers should wear uniforms. The district should provide caps equipped with bus drivers' badges. The use of uniforms increases the dignity and authority of the bus driver in dealing with pupils as well as with the general public.			
17. No person other than public school pupils, or adults assigned for supervision, should be permitted to ride on school buses.			
18. The bus capacity should never be exceeded by even one pupil.			
19. Loading of buses at school should be done at established safety zones under proper supervision.			
20. Buses should not be backed up on school grounds.			
21. Cost of transportation should compare favorably with transportation costs in other similar districts.			
22. All state regulations and all laws enacted by the state legislature should be adhered to rigidly.			
23. All bus routes should be approved by board action.			
24. Constant study should be given to bus routes to make sure that changes are made as needed, and routes laid out in the most efficient manner possible.			
25. Each bus driver should make daily written reports and weekly or monthly reports showing the condition of his bus and recommending any necessary repairs.			

TABLE 16–1.   (*Continued*)

ITEM	SUPERIOR	AVERAGE	POOR

26.   Each bus driver should possess a valid first aid certificate issued by the American Red Cross or United States Bureau of Mines.

27.   No bus driver should require any pupil to leave the bus before the pupil has reached his destination as a disciplinary measure.

28.   No person should be permitted to serve as a bus driver for more than ten hours in any twenty-four hour period.   Neither should bus drivers be permitted to do more than fifteen total hours of work in a twenty-four hour period when driving a bus with children is included.

29.   Each school bus should be kept clean at all times and should be thoroughly cleaned after each day's use.

30.   No smoking in a school bus should be permitted when pupils are aboard.

31.   No animals should be transported in a school bus.

32.   The bus driver should escort school pupils across the street or highway at any dangerous point.

33.   No school bus stop along the highway should be approved unless a clear view, when the bus is stopped, is available from a distance of 400 feet in each direction.

34.   The driver should bring the bus to a full stop at all railway crossings not closer than 10 feet and not more than 40 feet from the nearest rail.   He should not proceed until he has opened and closed the entrance door of the bus and has, by hearing and by sight, ascertained that the tracks are clear in both directions.

35.   No bus stop should be approved that is closer than 200 feet from the nearest railroad grade crossing except at regular railroad stations or on highways which parallel the railroad.

36.   In general, large and heavy transportation equipment should be used rather than small, light equipment.   This is recommended in the interest of efficiency and economy.

TABLE 16–1. (*Continued*)

ITEM	SUPERIOR	AVERAGE	POOR
37. Unless unusual traffic hazards exist, school districts should transport only those pupils for whom state-aid reimbursements will be received. On the other hand, all pupils who qualify for state-aid reimbursement should be transported.			
Total overall rating			

ᵃ Irving R. Melbo, et al., *Report of the Survey, Taft City School District* (Los Angeles: University of Southern California, 1960), pp. 270–272.

Cooperative Determination of Bus Routes

Administrators, drivers, and business office representatives should meet early in the summer to map out the bus routes for the coming school year. Normally, the first step in this process is to list all eligible pupils by place of residence. In most states, eligibility for free transportation to and from school is determined by law. Distance from school is usually the governing factor; children living less than one to two miles from school are expected to walk in most cases. Despite statutory provisions, most states allow wide latitude to the local districts in determining bus runs and stops. Hazardous traffic conditions, especially in large cities, may require the transportation of children over much shorter distances than would be the case in smaller communities or rural areas. Standard No. 17 requires states to minimize highway hazards by an annual review of routes for safety hazards.

MAPPING THE ROUTES. No bus route should be taken for granted simply because it has been in use for a long period of time. Any shift in pupil population or minor adjustment of school boundary lines may make a vast difference in a given bus route. Alterations may become necessary during a school year, and should certainly be seriously considered annually, preferably before the start of school in the fall. The best single tool for planning is a transportation map of the district, prepared and kept up to date by the school administration; the map will be based upon the data on eligible children. The data should include the name, age, grade, and house number of each child living within the area to be served, and should be collected for preschool children as well as for those already enrolled in school, so that plans may be made several years in advance. Reeder makes the following suggestions for the construction of transportation maps:

1. Outline the boundaries of the school district on the map. Locate the school or schools of the district.
2. Draw in streams, railroads, and similar barriers.
3. Draw in (to scale) the roads, designating their condition as paved, improved, graded, and dirt.
4. Mark bridges, fords, grade crossings and other hazards with appropriate symbols.
5. Locate homes with such symbols as the following: Mark those homes that have children with a square ☐ . Where homes have pupils to be transported, put the number of pupils inside the square, thus 1 . If the children are not to be transported, put the figure at the right side of the square, thus ☐ 1. If children are under school age, put the number at the left side of the square, thus 3 ☐ .
6. Total the number of pupils to be transported. Using the scale of the map, determine the total mileage of the shortest routes by which all pupils may be reached.
7. Lay out tentative routes. Avoid retraces wherever possible. Unless the buses are kept in the school garage at night, the starting points of the routes will be the homes of the drivers, which cannot be known until the drivers are selected.
8. Total the number of pupils on each route. This total will show the capacity required for each bus. Compare it with the capacities of the buses on hand. If necessary, make adjustments to avoid overcrowding or consider the advisability of getting busses of larger capacity. Although it is not ideal, an unused seat is more to be condoned than standing and sitting in aisles.
9. Check each route, adjusting if necessary to keep its length within the time limit.
10. Check the proposed routes by going over them, preferably with the driver; then lay out the routes on a new map; this master map to be placed in the superintendent's office for reference.
11. From the master map, lay out separate route cards for each driver, marking the exact route to be followed both morning and evening, and all stops in the order in which they are to be made.

12. Revise the routes during the year to take account of any shift in population, changes in condition of roads, bridges, etc.[4]

A string-and-colored-tack route map can be used in conjunction with or superimposed on the pupil-residence map. An overlay route-and-stop designation map drawn on clear plastic may also be used, superimposing it on the school attendance area map. It should show the route covered and the direction traveled by each bus.

Once the map has been developed, the principal, the district transportation department, and the bus drivers should develop a time schedule for pickup and delivery of the pupils. Parents, too, may be invited to offer their suggestions since they are personally interested in the transportation of their children.

Schools having access to computers can use them to design school bus routes. The following variables must be considered when preparing the input data for the computer:

Adequacy.	Railroad crossings.
Backtracking.	Road conditions.
Boarding location.	Road gradient.
Bus miles.	Salary of driver.
Bus time.	Safety.
Economy.	School starting time.
Efficiency.	Size of buses.
Grade level of children.	Student miles.
Location of driver's residence.	Student time.
Location of garage.	Turnarounds.

Using this data, the school system is partitioned into individual bus routes. The computer then generates all feasible routes for each partition. The computer printout gives information on the best route for each bus. A breakdown on cost analysis can also be determined by using the computer.[5]

Pupils should never be picked up earlier than one hour before the opening of school; no child should ride longer than one hour at a time. The scheduling of more buses or larger buses will eliminate the necessity

---

[4] By permission of Macmillan Publishing Co., Inc. from *The Fundamentals of Public School Administration,* 4th ed. by Ward G. Reeder. Copyright © 1958 by Macmillan Publishing Co., Inc., pp. 334–335.

[5] R. A. Boyer, *The Use of a Computer to Design School Bus Routes,* pp. 8–10.

of pupils riding too long. However, in rural areas where children live far from school or are widely scattered, scheduling can create a problem.

TYPES OF ROUTES. The use of one bus to travel more than one route is called "multiple routing." Such a route is cheaper than a "single" one, because it enables one bus to perform the functions of several. In practice, the multiple route is much less desirable than the single one. For example, groups of children arrive at the school several minutes in advance of others. In addition, dismissal times have to be staggered, or supervision provided during lengthy intervals of waiting for pickups. Both daily programs and pupil discipline tend to break down under such conditions. Wherever the financial condition of the district will permit, the use of one bus per route is always to be preferred. Where the need for financial economy is too great to permit the single route policy, it is sometimes possible, where two schools are located relatively close to one another, to arrange opening and closing hours in such a way as to permit the same buses to serve both schools without the disadvantages mentioned here.

SCHEDULING BUS STOPS. Buses at each school should be loaded at an established safe-loading zone, off main highways; this is required by Standard No. 17. The neighborhood loading zones should be located away from hazards and busy corners; children should not cross a busy street or highway, and no child should have to walk too far. It is impractical, however, to stop at every house, although some parents desire this. The bus should not make so many stops that it delays covering the route within a reasonable time. Children should not have to wait so long at their loading zone that they cause discipline problems.

Parents should be instructed to have their children at the bus stop from five to ten minutes ahead of time. They should also be told that sometimes the return to the stop may be delayed, since weather and traffic conditions, as well as the number of children who may be absent and not riding, may speed up or delay the time listed in the printed schedule. If parents understand this, they are less likely to worry or to call the school to find out where their children are.

DISTRIBUTION OF SCHEDULES. When the bus schedule has been developed, it should be duplicated and distributed to the teachers, the homes where children are to be transported, and the local newspapers. The printed schedule should include:

1. The location of the bus stops.
2. The bus number.
3. The name of the driver.
4. The time the bus will pick up the children at each stop.
5. The time at which children will arrive back at the stop after school is dismissed.

State Financing and Regulation of Pupil Transportation

There is no sphere of school financing in which the state has taken a more active interest than in pupil transportation. More than three-fourths of the states now provide some form of aid, and all states authorize the expenditure of local funds by the districts for this purpose. Many states that do not provide specific aid for transportation nevertheless include transportation costs in the formulas for basic and equalization aid to local districts. Transportation costs (in 1965 66) as a percent of current expenditures for education in elementary and secondary schools varied from 0.4 percent in the District of Columbia to 9.3 percent in North Dakota. The United States average was 3.7 percent.[6] Transportation is so vital in some rural areas that as much as 25 percent of the school budget may need to be spent for transportation.[7]

TRANSPORTATION COST ACCOUNTING. The main purpose of cost accounting is usually the establishment of standard unit costs. In administering pupil transportation, accurate information on both total and unit costs is needed. Although innumerable studies of pupil transportation cost have been made, unit costs have proved impossible to determine because of the large number of variable factors involved. However, the only way to evaluate the efficiency and economy of a transportation program is through cost accounting, using standard unit costs. The following cost units are usually used: (1) cost per pupil, (2) cost per mile, and (3) cost per bus.

Cost estimates are usually made shortly before the beginning of each

---

[6] Hutchins and Barr, *Statistics of State School Systems,* p. 62.

[7] Roald F. Campbell, John E. Corbally, Jr., and John A. Ramseyer, *Introduction to Educational Administration,* 3rd ed. (Boston: Allyn & Bacon, 1966), p. 124.

fiscal year, and are designed to assist in making out the transportation budget.   They are based upon the following factors:

1.   Number of passengers involved.
2.   Aggregate home–school distances.
3.   Number of buses.
4.   Length of routes.
5.   Road conditions.
6.   Price of bus supplies.
7.   Wages of drivers.
8.   Costs of maintenance and repairs.

   Except when a new district transportation program is inaugurated, cost estimates are arrived at on the basis of previous experience.   Where a new program is involved, it is advisable to secure comparable data from the state office or from nearby school districts that have been operating buses for some time and that have accumulated sufficient cost data to be of help.   Table 16–2 is an example of transportation cost accounting.

BUS DRIVER'S MONTHLY REPORT.   In any state that gives financial aid to transportation on any direct basis, the bus driver's monthly report is of paramount importance.   It is customarily kept up to date every day, or at least every week, and is turned into the business office once a month. From it are derived all data on costs, as well as data required by the state as a basis for financial reimbursement.   It must be signed by the driver, and should be as complete as possible.   Table 16–3 shows a sample Daily Bus Report form from which weekly and monthly reports can be compiled.

VARIABLE FACTORS IN TRANSPORTATION COSTS.   The most important factors in determining transportation costs are density of population, number of stops, and condition of roads.   Other factors combine to produce marked variability in transportation costs from state to state, and even from district to district: legal speed limits, traffic conditions, capacity of buses, and weather.   Topography can be very important in determining bus expenses.   Obviously, it will cost less over a period of years to operate a given bus in a dry, flat desert than in a rugged, stormy mountain region. As a result of these variable factors, it has proved difficult to develop reliable unit cost figures to use as standards against which a given operational program can be measured.   In comparing district costs to state averages, allowances must be made for varying local conditions.

TABLE 16–2. *Comparison of School Bus Transportation Costs over a Five-year Period, Laguna Beach Unified School District, 1955–60*[a]

ITEM	1955–56	1956–57	1957–58	1958–59	1959–60	FIVE-YEAR AVERAGE
Cost of operation	$ 34,768.85	$ 30,235.50	$ 31,074.36	$ 32,074.40	$ 35,255.65	$ 32,681.75
Miles traveled	72,203	60,758	61,561	62,045	61,814	63,676.20
Pupils carried	334,690	330,649	315,288	330,472	340,794	330,378.6
Bus days	1,307	1,173	1,328	1,372	1,414	1,318.8
Average miles per bus day	55.24	51.80	46.36	45.22	43.72	48.47
Average pupils per bus day	256.07	284.44	237.40	240.90	241.01	255.96
Average cost per bus mile	48.105¢	49.76¢	50.5¢	51.69¢	57.04¢	51.42¢
Average cost per bus trip	10.39¢	9.14¢	9.8¢	9.7¢	10.3¢	9.87¢
Average cost per bus day	26.60	25.78	23.40	23.38	24.93	24.82
Average cost per bus day in California	16.33	16.92	17.81	18.00	18.93	17.60

[a] Irving R. Melbo, et al., *Report of the Survey, Laguna Beach Unified School District* (Los Angeles: University of Southern California, 1961), p. 282.

423

TABLE 16–3.   Daily Bus Report

Bus No. Report No.	Signature of Driver Date		
EQUIPMENT	**COMPLY WITH SAFETY STANDARDS**		**REMARKS**
	YES	NO	
Steps			
Entrance & Exit Doors			
Speedometer			
Capacity Card			
Driver's View: Front, Side and Rear			
Windshield			
Windshield Wipers			
Steering Device			
Driver's Seat			
Rear Vision Mirrors			
Signal Systems			
Horn			
Brakes			
Flares			
First Aid Kit			
Fire Extinguisher			
Heating System			
Defroster			
Lights			
Interior Lighting			
Fog Lamps			
Reflectors			
Windows, Glass			
Ventilation System			
Skid Chains			
Gasoline Gauge			
Tires			
Engine: Mechanical			
Costs	*Dollars*	*Cents*	
Gasoline			
Oil			
Repairs (itemize)			
Servicing & Cleaning			
Other Costs			
Totals			

Much of the tremendous improvement in the typical school bus of today compared with its prototype of a decade or more ago is the result of increasing state interest. The area of choice enjoyed by a school district in selecting a new bus has been steadily narrowed by state regulations that have evolved over a lengthy period of time with beneficial results. Today's school bus is powerful and comfortable, with all the safety devices and equipment that the ingenuity of modern science can provide.

Each state should set up specific standards of bus construction based upon the following general standards in conformity with Standard No. 17: safety, comfort, economy, durability, and possibility of repair.

Selection and Training of Bus Drivers

The role of the bus driver has changed; formerly, he transported children, most of whom he knew, over rural, traffic-free roads to school. Instead of a few children on a small bus, today a bus driver may make several trips carrying over 70 students per trip. He must be skilled in safety and public relations; possess an understanding of students and be able to discipline them; and be skilled in mechanical ability.[8]

In one essential respect, the bus driver is the most important employee of the school district. At times he is the actual arbiter of life and death in his relations with the students; this is true of no other school employee. Too often not enough care is taken in selecting drivers. Previous experience and training should be considered when drivers are employed. The ability to drive an automobile does not mean necessarily that a man or a woman can drive a school bus. To ensure the competency of school bus drivers, Standard No. 17 requires each state to "develop a plan for selecting, training, and supervising persons whose primary duties involve transporting school pupils, in order to assure that such persons will attain a high degree of competence in, and knowledge of, their duties."

CRITERIA FOR SELECTION. All bus drivers must be certified by the state and of legal age, preferably twenty-one. A doctor's examination should be required, certifying physical fitness. But drivers should have a knowledge of state and local laws and regulations pertaining to school bus transportation; this should be determined by written and oral tests and an actual

---

8 Lester C. Winder, "Qualifications for Pupil Transportation Personnel," *47th Annual Volume of Proceedings, 1961,* pp. 191–93.

driving test. The necessary qualities for a bus driver are: driving skills, good attitude, good personality, emotional stability, and a good relationship with students to help in controlling discipline.[9] Drivers should refrain from the use of alcohol or narcotics before or while driving. They must possess a valid state driver's license to operate a school bus, a good safety record, and no prior conviction for a felony. The certificate or license should be valid for one year only, renewable on the basis of an annual physical examination and recommendation by the employing district.

When psychiatric examinations become a recognized part of school-hiring practices, they should be given first of all to the bus drivers. No one else in the district's employ is more in need of strong nerves, healthy attitudes, and a sense of humor. The bus driver must be much more than a chauffeur or mechanic. He or she must be a lover of children, a leader, and an effective but unobtrusive disciplinarian. To persuade men and women of such qualities to become school bus drivers necessitates paying much higher wages than is presently the case. The alternative, however, is to continue to place children, in all too many cases, in the hands of un-qualified drivers.

METHODS OF SELECTION. The business administrator or the director of the transportation services (assuming the school district employs such an officer) should recommend candidates for bus driver positions through the superintendent's office to the board of education for final appointment. Candidates should make out application forms, submit personal histories and qualifications, supply references and recommendations, and in general undergo the same rigid screening as an applicant for a teaching, secretarial, or administrative position. The old dishonorable practice of hiring bus drivers on the basis of financial competition and low bids is fortunately disappearing. It is time that all school districts stop looking at transpor-tation services as a necessary evil and the employment of bus drivers as a haphazard practice.

It is not necessary for professional bus drivers to have been previously employed, of course. The techniques of safe and effective school bus operation can be and have been learned by such diverse occupational representatives as ministers, housewives, farmers, mechanics, and clerks. Teachers, custodians, and principals are sometimes used; however, this is not recommended because of the possible loss of efficiency in their regular

---

[9] Featherston and Culp, *Pupil Transportation,* pp. 74–75.

jobs. Women are good bus drivers and have an ability to control pupils with ease and maintain good relations with them.[10]   Student drivers, usually college students, are almost always hired because of district inability to pay better wages to adults, and also because of their availability for part-time work.   Some believe that this process is wasteful, that tenure is impossible to establish, and that students lack maturity and are often reckless.   Statistics do not support the fear that students are too immature. The solution is to select good, steady applicants from any category and give them adequate training and supervision.[11]

DUTIES AND RESPONSIBILITIES OF BUS DRIVERS.   The chief duties of bus drivers are to transport children safely and efficiently, to keep their buses clean and in good running condition, and to make minor bus repairs according to district policy.   They should also maintain respect and order on the bus, assign seats to pupils, and escort pupils across the street where dangerous situations exist.   Behavior that is out of the ordinary should be reported to the principal.   After receiving the approval of the principal, the driver may refuse transportation to pupils when their conduct is detrimental to other passengers.   No child should ever be put off the bus for disciplinary reasons except at his own bus stop.   Drivers who pass the school bus when red lights are blinking should be cited by the bus driver.

In addition to driving the bus, which usually takes only three or four hours a day, full-time drivers may be assigned to other duties such as bus maintenance, transportation of supplies, custodial or gardening work, or school-yard and cafeteria supervision.   In no case should such activities interfere with scheduled driving duties; promptness in picking up and delivering children at the scheduled time is extremely important.

INSERVICE TRAINING.   Upon employment, drivers should be properly inducted and oriented to their jobs.   They should be given a copy of district policies pertaining to the transportation services, and the district "transportation manual."   Uniforms, if required, should be purchased before actually commencing regular driving.   It is good policy to have the new driver accompany a regular bus driver on a route to familiarize him with district bus procedures.

With increasing traffic problems, mounting horsepower, and multiplying statutes and traffic laws, the need for comprehensive inservice

---

[10] Featherston and Culp, *Pupil Transportation,* p. 73.
[11] Featherston and Culp, *Pupil Transportation,* p. 74.

training for bus personnel should be obvious. Students pose more disciplinary problems than in the past, and special understanding of how to cope with them is necessary. Today drivers need instruction in how to recognize students who may be under the influence of drugs when they board the bus and what to do if such is the case.

Preservice and inservice training programs and workshops should be established. Standard No. 17 requires each state to develop a training program for school bus drivers. Periodic meetings can be scheduled for veteran drivers to exchange problems and opinions. Bi-monthly meetings may be necesary for new drivers. The goal of the training program is to promote safety, economy, and efficiency in the total transportation effort. The iollowing outline illustrates topics for discussion in a school bus driver workshop:[12]

   I.   Driving Skills.
        a.   Driving fundamentals.
        b.   Driving discourtesies.
        c.   Hazardous and adverse driving situations.
        d.   Driver errors.
        e.   Defensive driving.
        f.   Railroad crossing procedures.

  II.   Human Relations.
        a.   Importance of the school bus driver.
        b.   Pupil behavior and control.
        c.   Driver relationships to supervisors and other school officials.
        d.   The driver and parents.
        e.   The driver and the community.

 III.   Accident and Emergency Preparedness.
        a.   Contingency plans.
        b.   Accident procedures.
        c.   Vehicle evacuation.
        d.   Reasons for emergency evacuation.
        e.   Emergency equipment.
        f.   Emergency medical care—first aid procedures.

  IV.   Vehicle Maintenance.
        a.   Inspection and maintenance.
        b.   Daily road check.
        c.   Use of sense.
        d.   Common driving abuses.

---

[12] Furnished through the courtesy of Independent School District No. 624, White Bear Lake, Minnesota.

V. Laws and Regulations.
   a. State highway laws and regulations.
   b. Highway traffic regulations.
   c. Examinations.
   d. Qualifications of school bus drivers.
   e. School bus driver license laws.
   f. Rules for operation of school buses.
   g. District administrative policies regarding transportation.
   h. State and district requirements for reports. (State financial aid for transportation may hinge upon the accuracy of these reports.)

Bus Identification and Equipment

As a result of the requirements of Standard No. 17, states have adopted standardized regulations for bus identification and equipment. The main purpose of standardization is to provide safe equipment that is easily identifiable. Clear identification of school buses provides a safety alert for other drivers.

There are two classes of school vehicles: Type I refers to any motor vehicle used to carry more than 16 pupils to and from school exclusively. Type II refers to any motor vehicle used to carry 16 or fewer pupils to or from school; it does not include private motor vehicles. Type II vehicles must either comply with *all* of the requirements for Type I vehicles or be of a different color and have *none* of the identification or equipment required for Type I vehicles. States shall determine which of the specifications apply to Type II vehicles.

The following identification requirements and equipment are specified in Standard No. 17 for Type I school vehicles:

1. Identification lettering.
2. Color: national school bus glossy yellow.
3. Bumper color: glossy black.
4. Signal lamps.
5. Mirrors.
6. Stop arms: according to state option.
7. Seating: no auxiliary seating is to be used.
8. Lap belts—required to be worn if so equipped.

Individual states may also prescribe equipment regulations regarding the type of body, width of aisle, window guards, heaters, fire extinguishers, and other special equipment.

District Transportation Director

Whenever possible, a school district should employ a full-time transportation director or supervisor whose major duties should be supervisory and administrative. If the district is small, the director may also serve as a mechanic or part-time driver. He should be the key man in selecting bus drivers and training them. His other responsibilities include: scheduling of buses, inservice training, recordkeeping, making reports, bus maintenance, and ordering supplies and equipment. He must maintain a close working relationship with the business office since purchases and reports must be made through that office.

Large districts employ a dispatcher. His responsibilities are:

1. To see that the required number of buses are serviced and ready to roll each day.
2. To have stand-by buses available in case there is a breakdown.
3. To determine that all drivers are on duty on time.
4. To call substitutes as needed.
5. To see that buses leave on time and follow their prescribed schedules.
6. To handle problems and complaints regarding pick-up and delivery of students.

School districts will find it advantageous to install two-way radios in all school buses. They allow for more efficient scheduling and reduction of route mileage, and can advise of delays and road conditions. Two-way radios permit the driver to keep in constant communication with the dispatcher regarding:

1. Breakdowns
2. Traffic tieups
3. Discipline problems
4. Late-run situations
5. Civil disturbance
6. Sudden illness
7. Accidents
8. Storm conditions
9. Road conditions

Radios also permit drivers to talk to each other about road conditions and blockages, lights that are not working, or problems where a nearby driver can assist.

Care and Maintenance of Transportation Equipment

Unless there is only one school in a district, the central transportation department, operating under the district business office, maintains the school buses. Some school districts maintain their own repair shops while others contract out this work. When the district does its own work, major repairs are usually made at the transportation shops. Minor repairs may be made by the driver who should have some skill as a mechanic.

The bus maintenance facility should be large enough to house a bus being repaired and to provide enough working space for the mechanic. There should be equipment on hand to make any needed repairs. A well-supplied stockroom should be readily accessible and a checkout system set up to keep track of the items used. An office with a desk, telephone, and filing cabinet should be provided for the transportation supervisor.

Standard No. 17 requires that school vehicles "shall be maintained in safe operating condition through a systematic preventive maintenance program." Each bus should be thoroughly checked, greased, and oiled at monthly intervals or more often if trouble is suspected. Buses, according to the standard, must be inspected at least semiannually. If properly serviced and maintained, they should last at least ten years and costly repairs should be minimized.

Each driver should see that his bus is swept, washed, and kept clean, whether he does it himself or the district provides this service at the maintenance facility. A clean bus indicates to the public that the school is interested in taking care of its equipment. Children, too, deserve to ride on clean buses, especially since cleanliness is one of the habits taught at school and at home.

Bus Behavior

Discipline is often a serious problem on the school bus. Children sometimes seem to feel that they can do as they please as soon as they leave home or school; it may tax the ingenuity of the driver to handle the situation. Problems should be reported to the principal. The driver may give a student a citation and a copy to the principal if the problem is a serious one. Pupils should be impressed with the fact that they are in school while they are on the bus or at the bus stop. Bus problems are actually school problems and must be dealt with as such.

TYPICAL BUS RULES.   Some typical bus rules that might be adopted by the school and the transportation department are:

1.   All children must obey the driver.
2.   There should be no loud talking.
3.   Children must stay seated at all times when the bus is moving.
4.   There must be no talking to the driver while the bus is in motion.
5.   Children are not to eat on the bus.
6.   All parts of the body must be kept inside the bus.·
7.   Pets and animals are not to be transported on the school bus.
8.   There is to be no playing, pushing, poking, or doing other things that bother others or the driver.
9.   Children are not to scratch, write on, or mar the seats or the paint.

Although some of these rules may appear self-evident, children need many reminders about good conduct and safety. Standard No. 17 requires that "twice during each school year, each pupil who is transported in a school vehicle shall be instructed in safe riding practices, and participate in emergency evacuation drills."

Bus Safety

The transporting of up to 75 or more children on a bus is a tremendous responsibility; the bus driver must do everything in his power to provide for their safety. One of his most important concerns is to keep his bus in perfect operating condition, particularly the brakes, lights, door mechanism, and tires. Standard No. 17 requires bus drivers to make daily pre-trip inspections of the vital functions of the school bus and to make a prompt, written report regarding any defect, which should be repaired immediately. Each bus should carry a fresh and well-supplied first aid kit and the driver must know how to administer first aid.

MAXIMUM LOAD. All school buses are built for maximum loads; the maximum number of children permitted to be carried is listed inside the bus. At no time should a driver exceed the maximum number of passengers by even one child.

TRAFFIC PRECAUTIONS. Traffic laws, and particularly those that apply to school buses, should be obeyed at all times. Children should always be let out on the curb side of the bus, never on the traffic side. Route stops should be established so that few children need to cross a street; careful scheduling may eliminate all such crossings. At no time should a bus be backed up on the school grounds because of the danger of running over someone. Doors should never be left open, even in hot weather.

A SCHOOL PRINCIPAL'S RESPONSIBILITY. To gain firsthand information about the conduct of the pupils and the safety precautions being used, as well as the driving habits of the driver, a principal may want to ride the bus on occasion. He might follow the bus in his car to see how the children act after the bus has gone on or to see how they act when they load the bus. He can also check on discipline at the bus stops.

Bus safety is a part of school safety and should be a regular part of classroom instruction. Teachers can dramatize safety situations in the classroom or hold periodic discussions about bus safety. Occasional bulletins from the principal will help to impress the idea of bus safety.

PUBLIC MOTORISTS. One hazard to bus transportation is the public motorist. Too many do not follow safety rules or obey traffic laws. Many do not know the rules for passing buses that are loading or unloading children and do not realize what the blinking red lights mean. Although the school can do little about this, school administrators and the PTA may have some influence on the driving habits of the school community by holding public meetings and securing newspaper publicity on the responsibility of motorists for the safety of schoolchildren. The police or sheriff departments are usually happy to assist schools with their safety programs.

CONSISTENT RIDING. Children who ride the bus should do so every time. If they ride part of the time and walk part of the time, the driver will never know whether or not he has left a pupil. Each child should get on and off at his regular bus stop, unless he has a note signed by his parent requesting otherwise. Unless the parent has requested a change, he has every right to expect that his child will be on a certain bus at a regular time and will get off at a designated stop on schedule. Children should understand that these regulations for regular riding are for their protection. Some school districts require student riders to carry a bus pass, issued by the principal and shown to the driver when boarding the bus. He then knows that the student is authorized to ride his bus.

Field Trips

School districts that provide their own transportation services have a rare opportunity to supplement the classroom educational program without too much added cost by utilizing their own buses and drivers for field trips. With careful planning, most field trips can be scheduled between the regular bus runs. When this cannot be worked out, substitute or stand-by drivers may need to be employed or other buses contracted. If the transportation services are handled by contract with transportation companies, special arrangements must be made for field trips.

EDUCATIONAL VALUES OF FIELD TRIPS. Most field trips are taken for educational reasons. Some schools, however, permit school buses to be used for picnics, swimming parties, social activities, and various recreational activities; this occurs mostly at the secondary level.

Field trips for instruction should be carefully planned, fit logically into the instructional program, and grow out of a need to supplement available textbooks. Firsthand information always leaves a more indelible impression than secondary sources. Follow-up activities enhance the value of a field trip.

SCHEDULING FIELD TRIPS. Arrangements for field trips should be made at least one week in advance of the desired date; no trip should be taken without a definite reservation. Parents should be informed of the trip by the teacher and supply a signed permission slip indicating that their child has approval to take the trip. Requests for field trips, whether for educational or co-curricular purposes, should be forwarded by the principal to the transportation department through the district business office. Figure 16–1 shows a sample form which might be used to request bus transportation.

PARAMOUNT UNIFIED SCHOOL DISTRICT

REQUEST FOR BUS TRANSPORTATION
FIELD TRIPS, ATHLETIC TRIPS AND OTHER SPECIAL TRIPS

SCHOOL REQUESTING:_____ DATE OF REQUEST:_____

DATE OF TRIP:_____ Leaving School Time:_____(AM) (PM)

 Day of Week   Month and Date   , 19 ___ Return to School:_____(AM) (PM)

DESTINATION:_____ ADDRESS:_____

                                                          NUMBER OF TEACHERS:_____

TEACHER:_____GRADE_____ NUMBER OF PUPILS:_____ NUMBER OF PARENTS:_____

REMARKS, DIRECTIONS, ETC.:_____

FOR TRANSPORTATION DEPARTMENT USE ONLY   FIELD TRIP #_____OF YOUR SCHOOL ALLOCATION

	TIME	TOTAL HOURS	SPEEDOMETER READING	MILEAGE
Leave Bus Garage	AM PM	XXXX		XXXX
Arrived at Destination	AM PM			
Leave Destination	AM PM	Lay-Over Time	XXXXXX	XXXX
Returned to Bus Garage	AM PM			
TOTAL HOURS AND MILEAGE	XXXX		XXXXXX	

THIS SECTION FOR USE ONLY WHEN SECOND ROUND TRIP IS REQUIRED

	TIME	TOTAL HOURS	SPEEDOMETER READING	MILEAGE
Leave Bus Garage	AM PM	XXXX		XXXX
Arrived at Destination	AM PM			
Leave Destination	AM PM	Lay-Over Time	XXXXXX	XXXX
Returned to Bus Garage	AM PM			
TOTAL HOURS AND MILEAGE	XXXX		XXXXXX	

APPROVALS

	Signature	Approved	Not Approved
Principal			
Transportation			
Business Manager			

DRIVERS INSTRUCTIONS

All copies must be submitted to the Transportation Department a minimum of five (5) days prior to previously approved trips and eight (8) days for an unapproved trip. Following proper authorization you will receive a copy for your records.

COPIES TO: Transportation
           Principal
           Business Office

FOR ACCOUNTING USE ONLY

Charge to:_____

Driver Time:_____Hours @ $_____ $_____

Mileage Costs:_____Miles @ $_____ $_____

Other Costs— Itemize:_____ $_____

_____ $_____

TOTAL AMOUNT CHARGED: $_____

Entered by:_____ Date:_____

FIGURE 16–1. Example of a Request for Bus Transportation. Courtesy of the Paramount Unified School District, Paramount, California.

Accidents

If accidents do occur, the bus driver must make out an accident report giving the date, the name of the injured persons, the cause of the accident, the names of at least two witnesses, the first aid rendered, and the disposition of the case. This form should be forwarded to the central business office within twenty-four hours. If a child is involved, the principal, who may wish to make a personal contact with the parents, should also be informed.

Summary

School bus transportation has been stimulated by parental demand, consolidation of districts, increased state aid for transportation, improvement of roads and buses, decline of the importance of the small community, and compulsory attendance laws.

Several different types of pupil transportation exist, among them school ownership and operation, private ownership with school operation, and school ownership with private operation.

The public generally opposes forced busing to achieve ethnic balance, although a few systems have bused voluntarily. In either case, busing to achieve integration has budget implications, as the cost can be enormous.

District busing policies should be established by cooperative action on the part of administrators, parents, teachers, bus drivers, and pupils. Busing should be administered whenever possible by a trained transportation manager who should stress safety, economy, adequacy, and efficiency. Similarly, bus routes should be determined cooperatively and mapped extensively, with "multiple routes" favored over "single" ones, bus stops carefully scheduled, and bus schedules distributed publicly.

Financing pupil transportation increasingly is becoming a state function, although in both district and state financing, cost accounting and bus drivers' monthly reports are customarily required.

School buses rightly are subject to strict regulations because of the serious safety implications. A federal law, Highway Safety Program Standard No. 17 (June 1972), requires states to implement many controls over school district transportation systems. The selection and training of bus drivers should be two of the school administration's most important concerns. Transportation employees should be screened carefully, and should have their duties and responsibilities fully delineated, with inservice training required at regular intervals.

All states must have bus equipment that meets the requirements of Standard No. 17. Most districts have some person in charge of transportation who maintains a regular program of bus care and maintenance. Bus behavior and safety are rightly under his direction, with maximum loads and traffic precautions carefully supervised. He should see that drivers understand exactly what to do in case of accidents.

The principal has the responsibility at the school level to see that students who ride the bus are given instruction in safety and bus behavior. Buses can be used for field trips to expand education beyond the confines of a school.

Trends

The major discernible trend in school bus transportation over the past generation has been the vast increase in the percentage of pupils transported, and the number of school districts adopting bus transportation for their pupils. Within this general pattern, several indicative trends may be identified.

TOWARD DOOR-TO-DOOR BUS TRANSPORTATION. Parental demands are leading school districts in the direction of more complete bus service. Door-to-door transportation may never quite eventuate, but the trend is in that direction. Increasing traffic congestion and traffic accident rates trigger more imperative requests on the part of worried parents for increased school bus service.

TOWARD INCREASED STATE FINANCIAL AID TO TRANSPORTATION. The recognition of the state's paramount role in encouraging school districts to furnish bus transportation to their students will result in the state's shouldering more and more of the bill. The trend seems to be in the direction of smaller proportionate district contributions, with the difference coming from the state treasury.

TOWARD INCREASING STATE REGULATION OF SCHOOL BUSES AND DRIVERS. On the theory that the state more and more pays for school bus transportation, we may expect more state regulation of standards governing transportation equipment and drivers. Standards of safety and performance are going to rise steadily due to state pressure in this direction, including increasingly rigid licensing regulations for drivers.

TOWARD MORE RAPID BUS SERVICE OVER LONGER ROUTES. The tremendous advances in horsepower and bus design, coupled with better and safer highways, will encourage the trend toward longer bus routes. This dovetails with the trend toward unification and consolidation of school districts.

TOWARD DISTRICT OWNERSHIP AND OPERATION. As more federal, state, and local money becomes available to the local school district, the trend toward district ownership and operation of school buses will become more pronounced. The only possible excuse for private ownership and operation is lack of money.

TOWARD MORE EFFECTIVE INSERVICE TRAINING FOR BUS DRIVERS. The position of school bus driver will become more professionalized in the next decade. The chief factor in this process will be the development by the local districts of inservice training techniques comparable in thoroughness to those used for teachers.

Administrative Problems

In Basket

Problem 1

The Bellwood Unified School District maintains a fleet of 15 buses to transport students to its 2 high schools, 3 junior high schools, and 18 elementary schools. It has used buses to achieve integration on a voluntary basis because of community pressure. Over the years students have also been bused shorter distances than required by the state law. Parents have insisted on this because of the lack of sidewalks and unsafe walking conditions, and the Board of Education has authorized this extra busing.

Because of increased expenses, the district has cut back many services. Bus service has not been reduced because of the emotional impact it was expected to have on community feeling. However, in preparing the budget for the next year, it appears that bus service must be curtailed if the budget is to be balanced. The superintendent has asked the business manager to prepare a plan for reducing or even eliminating bus service.

If you were the business manager, what would you propose?
What type of information would you include in your report?

Problem 2

Assume the same situation as in Problem 1. The decision was made to drastically reduce bus services, especially the "extra" busing which is more than the law requires.

As superintendent, how would you explain it to the public?
How would you handle the reduction of transportation personnel?
What would you do with the buses that are no longer needed?

Problem 3

Assume the same situation as in Problem 2. The parents rise up in arms and pack the next Board of Education meeting demanding to be heard. During the day, the district administrative office has been picketed by angry parents.

What should the superintendent do about the pickets?
How should he handle the Board meeting?
If you were the superintendent, what would you do about the transportation services in the months ahead?

Selected References

"ABC's of Running a Safe Transportation Program: From Buying a Bus to Training Personnel." *American School Board Journal* 158 (November 1970).

BOYER, R. A. *The Use of a Computer to Design School Bus Routes.* Project No. 1605. Washington, D.C.: U.S. Department of Health, Education, and Welfare, Office of Education, 1964.

BRONSON, J. D. "Busing Between Classes: Shuttle Bus System Between High School Classes." *School and Community* 60 (October 1973).

"Computer Router: Program for School Bus Routes." *Saturday Review of Education* 1 (May 1973).

DEMONT, ROGER, ed. *Busing, Taxes, and Desegregation.* Special Monograph No. 4, Management Series. Danville, Ill.: Interstate Printers and Publishers, 1973.

FEATHERSTON, E. GLENN, and CULP, D. P. *Pupil Transportation: State and Local Programs.* New York: Harper & Row, 1965.

GUANIOLO, JOHN. *Transportation Law.* 2nd ed. Dubuque, Iowa: William C. Brown, 1973.

Highway Safety Program Standard No. 17. Washington, D.C.: U.S. Department of Transportation, National Highway Traffic Safety Administration. Published in the Federal Register, vol. 37, no. 89 (May 6, 1972).

MELBO, IRVING R., et al. *Report of the Survey, Taft City School.* Los Angeles: University of Southern California, 1960.

————. *Report of the Survey, Laguna Beach Unified School District.* Los Angeles: University of Southern California, 1961.

OZMAN, HOWARD, and CRAVER, SAM. *Busing: A Moral Issue.* Fastback Series, no. 7. Bloomington, Ind.: Phi Delta Kappa, 1972.

PIELE, PHILLIP K. *Computer Applications in Class and Transportation Scheduling.* Educational Management Review Series, no. 1. Washington, D.C.: National Center for Educational Research and Development, 1971.

POWELL, THEODORE. *School Bus Law: A Case Study in Education, Religion, and Politics.* Middletown, Conn.: Wesleyan University Press, 1960.

RUBIN, LILLIAN B. *Busing and Blacklash.* Berkeley: University of California Press, 1972.

SCHOOL BUS TASK FORCE. *Pupil Transportation Safety Program Plan.* Washington, D.C.: U.S. Department of Transportation, 1973.

School Transportation: A Guide for Supervisors. Chicago: National Safety Council, 1967.

SNELLING, W. R. "Day School Busing: Dilemma and Solution." *Indiana School Bulletin* 16 (November 1972).

SUMMERS, J. B. "How to Get More Mileage from Your Transportation Spending." *American School Board Journal* 159 (November 1971).

"Transportation: Problems and Prospects for 1973." *School Management* 16 (November 1972).

UNITED STATES DEPARTMENT OF TRANSPORTATION. *Selection and Training of School Bus Drivers.* Washington, D.C.: National Highway Traffic Safety Administration, 1971.

WINDER, LESTER C. "Qualifications for Pupil Transportation Personnel." *47th Annual Volume of Proceedings, 1961.* Chicago: Association of School Business Officials, International, 1961.

WONNACOTT, PAUL. *Transportation Legislation.* Washington, D.C.: American Enterprise, 1972.

17

School Health and Nutrition Programs

The school health program is closely allied to the nutrition program. Although both have profound educational implications, they are commonly considered auxiliary services. In a well-coordinated school district, the school nurse and the cafeteria director work cooperatively in developing menus and childhood eating habits based on accepted nutritional principles. Diet is intimately related to the broader field of general health; it is only logical that it should take an important but subordinate place in the framework of general health. Physical education and safety instruction are other aspects of the school health program.

This chapter includes a discussion of the following topics:

Responsibility for Health and Nutrition Programs
The Goal of Health Education
Governmental Concern with School Health Programs
Administration of Health Education
Optimum Staffing of Health Services
The School Nurse
Teachers and Classroom Health
The Health of Teachers and Administrators
Health Supplies and Equipment
Administration of the School Health Program
School Nutritional Programs
Summary
Trends

Responsibility for Health and Nutrition Programs

In the past generation the school has assumed responsibilities for health and nutrition on a larger scale. The reasoning has been as follows:

Major premise. The school exists to assist the child in developing his maximum potentialities.

Minor premise. The child cannot develop to his maximum potential if he is undernourished or if his medical needs are neglected.

Conclusion. Therefore, the school must correct undernourishment and provide for the child's medical needs, if necessary.

School intervention in the feeding and medical treatment of America's youth is well entrenched and gives every indication of expanding its scope in the decades to come. This intervention came, in part, as the direct result of public demand arising from the erosion of the American family.

Goals of Health Education

The immediate justification of the school's interest in child health is educational. From a long-range viewpoint, however, its goal may be said to be the ultimate improvement of the health of society. Its short-range objective is to achieve pupil understanding of the basic facts of health, disease, nutrition, physical fitness, and environment, and to develop a sense of responsibility for improving his or her own health. If the student accomplishes this, his physical and mental condition should improve so that he may be able to receive the education he needs to become a contributing member of society. Optimum conduct and the ability to concentrate and think clearly are impossible without good health. If health habits are constantly improved by successive generations, there can be a profound effect upon the evolution of the human race; it is this goal that particularly excites the protagonists of health education.

GENERAL GOALS OF HEALTH EDUCATION. In 1934 a joint committee of the National Education Association and the American Medical Association drew up the following aims, still valid today, and recommended them as guides to school health education programs:

1. To instruct children and youth so that they may conserve and improve their own health.

2. To establish in them the habits and principles of living which through-out their school life, and in later years, will assure that abundant vigor and vitality which provide the basis for the greatest possible happiness and service in personal, family, and community life.
3. To influence parents and other adults, through the health education program for children, to better habits and attitudes, so that the school may become an effective agency for the promotion of the social aspects of health education in the family and community as well as in the school itself.
4. To improve the individual and community life of the future; to insure a better second generation, and a still better third generation, and a healthier and fitter nation . . .[1]

The American Association of School Administrators out of concern for health and family life education adopted a resolution at its annual con-ference in 1970 stating that "the only effective way in which the school can fulfill its responsibility for meeting the health needs of youth is through a comprehensive program of health education in all grades at all levels" so that they are prepared "for their role as future parents and citizens."[2] There should be a sound, interrelated, and sequential program which includes sex and family life education as well as the other health topics. The program should be long-range, covering specific areas appropriate to the stage of the student's development.[3]

SPECIFIC GOALS OF HEALTH EDUCATION. The health program of a school district should strive toward achievement of the following objec-tives. There should be a health examination and follow-up program for all students which includes counseling for them, their parents, and teachers. Individualized programs of health instruction should be established. The environment of a school can be raised by improving safety and hygiene standards and by serving better food. Students in both elementary and secondary schools should follow a program of health instruction and physi-cal conditioning. Instruction in the avoidance of accidents and communi-

---

[1] National Education Association and American Medical Association, *Health Education,* Report of the Joint Committee on Health Problems in Education, pp. 1–251.
[2] American Association of School Administrators, *Your AASA in Nineteen Sixty-Nine–Seventy,* Official Report of the American Association of School Administrators (Washington, D.C.: The Association, 1970), p. 131.
[3] American Association of School Administrators, *Your AASA,* p. 131.

cable diseases should be intensified. Qualified medical advisers and nurses should be employed to make examinations and to help in planning and carrying out the total health program. Handicapped children should be identified as early as possible and optimum facilities provided for their education. Teachers should have inservice training in health and safety. Plans should be developed for extending physical education and recreational activities outward into the community and onward into the years of adult life. Provision must be made to handle emergencies, injuries, and serious illness.

Three major problems have been recognized recently; goals should be established to help solve them. Our youth no longer live in a Victorian age. Social change has occurred rapidly in the previous decades, reflected in changing mores and sexual attitudes. Abortions are increasing since their legalization; the pill is making sexual intercourse "safe"; and family planning now regulates the number of children desired. Young people have recognized the problems posed by these changes and in many schools students are demanding courses in family life and sex education; at the same time, organized parent groups are fighting against such courses. Whatever the arguments, it is essential that schools confront the social reality and provide such instruction on a voluntary basis with parental approval.

Another problem of national concern is the prevalent use of drugs by young people. At first, drug abuse was noted in the high schools, then the junior high schools, and now, in the '70s, it has spread to the elementary schools. School administrators cannot close their eyes and hope the problem will go away.

How should a teacher handle a student taking drugs? Should he be reported? Or ignored? Or sent out of class to sleep it off? Should parents be notified? What is the influence on other students? It is imperative that the problem be responded to. Administrators must recognize that it exists and see that policies are developed to handle it. Health education courses should describe various drugs and explain their effects because their use affects both mental and physical health and social relationships. Teachers should be informed about the drug problem, how to recognize the symptoms, and how to handle students who are obviously under the influence of drugs. Emergency service should be available for students with acute drug reactions at school. The American Association of School Administrators, because of its concern with the increasing incidence of drug abuse, adopted a resolution in 1970, stating that, "Educational programs stressing the serious effects of drug abuse are an imperative responsibility of every school district."[4]

Ecology, a sociological science, is also of concern in health education. Manmade pollution caused by chemicals, garbage, sewage, fumes, noise, and urban overcrowding affects the water we drink, the food we eat, the air we breathe, and the environment we live in. Although man has been contaminating himself for years, it has been recognized only recently as a real problem, and our youth are probably most concerned about it. They will inherit the environment created by past generations—in the name of progress—and will live in this contaminated world after the present generation is gone. Time is running out; something must be done immediately to save our environment and protect the health of everyone. Students must be educated as to what is involved in protecting and purifying our air, our soil, our water, and our food. This is a health problem of the greatest magnitude.

Governmental Concern with School Health Programs

Every White House Conference on youth has found cause for alarm in the physical condition of American youth. Their various reports have consistently stressed that between 30 and 40 percent of our children and adolescents are operating with limited effectiveness as the result of bad teeth, damaged hearts, impaired hearing, mental retardation, deafness, blindness, or some type of limb disability. A great deal of this waste of human resources could have been prevented by physical examinations and competent medical advice in early childhood.

United States Selective Service authorities have pointed out that the rate of rejections for physical and mental disabilities soared after World War I until it reached approximately 50 percent—despite an increased emphasis on physical education and health. Although this may have been caused by a rise in standards, the fact remains that virtually all experts in the field agree that American youth should be in much better condition, physically and mentally.

In 1956 the President's Conference on Fitness for American Youth pointed out that fitness of our youth could not be taken for granted in an age of automation. Physical debilitation that results from lack of partici-

---

[4] American Association of School Administrators, *Your AASA*, p. 131.

pation in energetic activities causes erosion of health; and physical fitness goes hand in hand with moral, mental, and emotional fitness.[5]   The 1970 White House Conference for Children called for massive expansion of health services and health insurance for children.

In 1961, President Kennedy urged the adoption of the following recommendations made by his Council on Youth Fitness:

1.   Identify the physically underdeveloped pupil and work with him to improve his physical capacity.
2.   Provide a minimum of fifteen minutes of vigorous activity every day for all pupils.
3.   Use valid fitness tests to determine pupils' physical abilities and evaluate their progress.[6]

There are certain puzzling factors, however, that seem to run counter to the conclusion that our youth are not physically fit.   One is the constantly increasing efficiency of athletes who establish records that seemed out of reach a decade or two ago.   Another is the apparent trend, attested to by selective service records, toward increasing height and weight in young men.   Despite these conflicting statistics, it seems apparent that mechanized personal transportation, spectator sports, and sedentary entertainment have combined to create a major problem in health and physical condition.   Only the schools are in daily mass contact with children; they are in a position to apply the massive therapy which appears to be needed.

Administration of Health Education

The school health program, like most other matters with which the schools have had to interest themselves, has included several phases that range from simple to complex.   The three major stages in the history of school health programs are summarized in the following discussion.

PROPHYLAXIS.   The first attempts made by schools to deal with problems of pupil health probably go back to antiquity; they dealt with protection of the pupil against contagious diseases and with unsafe factors in the physi-

---

[5] President's Conference on Fitness of American Youth, *Fitness of American Youth,* A report to the President of the United States, pp. 3–4.

[6] John F. Kennedy, "A Presidential Message," *CTA Journal* 57 (October 1961), p. 5.

cal environment. The early manifestation of the school's interest in pupil health was largely and by necessity negative in nature, and designed to stave off certain obvious dangers. This facet of the health program has been supplemented by other, more modern practices, but it still remains essential today.

REHABILITATION. Second in the evolutionary progression of the health program came work designed to ascertain the degree of damage to physical and mental conditions already existing, and to correct problems as far as possible. Remedial physical education classes were instituted during this phase, as were follow-up home conferences by the school nurse.

PREVENTIVE HYGIENE. Most recent in this progression is the development of techniques that aim at prevention of health problems. Courses in dietetics and hygiene, supplying balanced school lunches, and emphasis in science and home economics classes on how to avoid contagion and deficiency diseases are features of this phase of the health program.

In carrying out these three principal stages, the administrator must consider them in relation to the whole school program. Health relates intimately to so many aspects of the curriculum and the environment afforded by the school that it must be considered in relation to them.

THE PLACE OF THE SCHOOL PLANT IN HEALTH EDUCATION. The location of the school plant is paramount in importance. If its site is in proximity to one or more dangerous traffic arteries, safety education will be of great significance. A building situated near a contaminated city dump or sewer outfall is of course a constant menace to pupil health. Dust and odors emanating from the grounds or from the surrounding neighborhood may pose health problems not susceptible to easy solutions. Fire protection will necessitate instruction in both prevention and survival drills. In the plant itself, the following physical conditions should be the subject of constant inspection and improvement wherever needed:

1. Lighting
2. Heating
3. Ventilation
4. Water supply
5. Cleanliness of lavatories
6. Condition of seating
7. Food storage

Simple cleanliness and basic sanitation are more important in the maintenance of school plant hygiene than expensive and pseudoscientific installations. Innovations such as ultraviolet radiation projectors to eliminate disease germs have not proved their worth. Money wasted on such gadgets would be better spent on vacuum cleaners and custodial salaries, insofar as pupil health is concerned.

THE CURRICULUM AND HEALTH EDUCATION. The core of the health program is the curriculum. Health education, guidance and counseling, the germ theory of disease, the principles of diet and sanitation—all are taught in relation to the overall curriculum. Apart from theory, the emphasis placed by school personnel upon health in relation to school experiences will have a profound effect upon children exposed to such experiences. In large districts, certain curricular blocs may be set up to deal specifically with health problems:

1. Sight-conservation classes.
2. Speech therapy classes.
3. Lip-reading classes.
4. Remedial physical education classes.
5. Special education for the mentally retarded.
6. Classes for the physically handicapped.
7. Classes in which family life and sex education are taught with parental consent required.
8. Classes in which knowledge of drugs is taught.

SCHOOL PERSONNEL AND THE HEALTH PROGRAM. It is necessary to "sell" the health program to the district employees most directly concerned with its implementation before the program can be presented to the pupils. Unless those who are to carry on the program are convinced of its importance and advised as to its goals, little can be achieved. Key persons involved in the health program would include: the classroom teacher, the school nurse, the school physician, the school psychologist, the school counselor, the cafeteria manager, and the health service aide.

These school employees, in addition to the administrators most directly concerned, should be entrusted with the organization and implementation of the health program. Often they will work as a team. The program should be cooperatively constructed, with the appropriate areas democratically assigned to the proper personnel. Too often, without consulting others, the school principal and the nurse decide what the health program will be. Teachers should also welcome the services and knowledge of the school nurse in helping them with health education. And the school custodian is often overlooked in health education, but he can be an important asset; he is responsible for the cleanliness of lavatories and drinking fountains and for keeping dust and dirt from accumulating. An explanation by him to the children could recruit their assistance in helping to maintain the cleanliness of the school plant.

Optimum Staffing of Health Services

A study made in 1956 produced data indicating a decided discrepancy between recommended procedures in health education and actual practice in this field. In contrasting the recommendations of literature with actual statistics, the personnel–pupil ratio in each of four health service categories was found to be decidedly inferior.[7]

THE SCHOOL NURSE. Most experts in this area recommend one nurse to every 1,000 pupils in elementary school districts, and a slightly higher ratio for secondary schools. Actual practice, even in the most wealthy states, involves a ratio of 1 to 1,500. However, the idea of using a health team is coming into vogue. It consists of one public health nurse and two or three aides and provides services at a secondary school and several elementary schools.

THE SCHOOL PHYSICIAN. The recommended ratio for this health position is one school physician for every 4,000 elementary pupils. The California ratio in 1955 was one for every 23,000, or almost six times the recommended figure.

THE SCHOOL PSYCHOLOGIST. Here the existing personnel–pupil ratio exceeds the recommended ratio by more than 500 percent. Actually, California schools employ one psychologist for every 8,000 pupils, while the literature urges one for every 1,500.

---

[7] M. L. Rafferty, "Personnel–Pupil Ratios in Certain California Elementary School Districts" (Unpublished doctoral dissertation, University of Southern California, 1956).

THE DENTAL HYGIENIST.   This is a relatively new health position, and as yet is included in few school district personnel organizations.   Whereas one dental technician is recommended for every 15,000 children, the actual ratio is 1 to 53,000.

Larger districts may employ nutrition specialists, eye, ear, nose, and throat specialists, dentists, sanitation experts, and environmental experts for lighting and heating.   Social workers may be employed to work with parents and schools on a cooperative basis.   School health problems are often related to the home environment; the social worker can promote home–school relationships as they affect the child.

In smaller districts, health personnel may be secured on a part-time, a fee, or a contract basis when wealth and pupil population do not warrant full-time employment.   It is also possible for adjoining districts to share the cost and services.   County health departments sometimes provide health services on a cooperative, jointly financed basis.

The School Nurse

Whenever a school's size and income preclude the employment of a full staff of health personnel, it is generally conceded that at least a school nurse should be hired.   Some states require a registered nurse.   There is a trend toward updating the position to "School Public Health Nurse" or "School Nurse Practitioner."   The nurse's role in the new concept will be expanded and she will have more decision-making power.   Her functions would include:

1.   Inspecting the school and recommending health and safety improvements.
2.   Assessing the school's health needs.
3.   Informing administrators about the problems, needs, and accomplishments of the health program.
4.   Developing and implementing a health care plan.
5.   Administering or supervising screening tests: vision, hearing, weight, height, dental, cardiac, and communicable disease.
6.   Responsibility for maintaining a system of current health records and data for each student.
7.   Identifying and assessing factors that could contribute to learning disorders.

8. Working with students to help them understand emotional problems and to function under emotional stress.
9. Supervising the health service aide.

Since education now emphasizes evaluation and needs assessment, nurses, as well as teachers and administrators, should develop goals and measurable objectives. Goal-directed school nursing will provide an effective measuring tool for determining the effectiveness of the nursing services and health programs.

The administrator should remember that the school nurse does not nurse. Except in cases of minor first aid, she performs no medical services of any kind. She does not diagnose; she does not prescribe; she does not treat. Her function is to advise, to evaluate, to organize, and to integrate. She works closely with classroom teachers in subject fields of science, homemaking, and physical education. Her relations with the cafeteria director are necessarily close; the maintenance and operation personnel will be guided by her recommendations in anything bearing directly upon the health and safety of the children.

Health service aides are being employed in many school districts to carry out assigned routines and technical tasks related to the school health services program. This frees the school nurse to give more attention to the coordination of the total health program. It also makes it possible to provide team services to several schools without the nurse running back and forth for emergencies or problems.

The aide works as an unlicensed, non-certificated paraprofessional employee with special training skills. He or she should have preservice and inservice training, along with clerical skills to perform duties such as the following: typing, preparing and maintaining records and reports, making appointments and handling communications, arranging health displays and exhibits, helping teachers with duplicating and distributing health materials, and ordering, inventorying, and distributing health and first-aid supplies and equipment. The health aide can also perform clerical duties for the building principal, providing these duties do not interfere with health service duties.

In addition, the health service aide can perform the following direct health services:

1. Appraisal services through screening of vision, hearing, and other areas.

2. Reports to the school nurse of names of children requiring further physical evaluations.
3. Interpreting first-aid emergency procedures and school health policies to the school staff.
4. Seeing that teachers and others submit necessary reports.
5. Taking care of emergency illness or accidents.
6. Organizing and participating in health activities as directed by the school nurse (testing and immunization programs, preschool orientation, etc.).
7. Checking absentee records and following up on students with frequent absences.

Table 17–1 shows the nursing services provided in school systems with a 12,000 or more enrollment in 1965–66. It is probable that nursing services may be further depleted in the seventies as school districts cut back on budgets; some may eliminate nurses entirely. This is a completely unsatisfactory situation, penalizing the schools and their children. A district-wide health team provides an answer to schools with small budgets.

A large school system should have a head nurse or health supervisor at the district level, who should also be an experienced nurse or a physician. This officer would be in charge of employing, discharging, and coordinating the activities of all school nurses and other health personnel.

TABLE 17–1. *Nurse Services Provided in School Systems with 12,000 or More Enrollment, 1965–66*[a]

	PERCENT OF SYSTEMS	
NURSE SERVICE PROVIDED	ELEMENTARY	SECONDARY
Full-time nurse in each school	2.6%	24.6%
Part-time nurse in each school	62.0	33.3
Full-time nurse in some schools, part-time in others	17.8	23.8
Nurses provided on call	9.2	9.6
Other arrangements	1.6	2.2
No nurse provided	6.8	6.5
Number of systems reporting[b]	382	366

[a] National Education Association, Research Division, "School Health and Nurse Services," *Research Bulletin* 44 (December 1966), p. 108.
[b] The number of replies for both elementary and secondary schools falls below the total of 396 replies to this question since some of the responding school systems included only elementary or only secondary grades.

The position would involve coordination between the health department and the other departments of the school district.

Teachers and Classroom Health

The teacher is often the key person in screening health problems in the classroom. Teachers are well qualified to observe pupils' physical conditions, to note personal health habits and attitudes, social health habits, and emotional reactions or problems. Their skill is due to their training, knowledge, and experience in working with children every day. The school nurse seldom sees individual children unless they are referred to her or she calls a group to her office for examinations or consultation. Whenever a teacher observes a condition in need of remediation, he should consult with the principal or the nurse to determine what steps to take.

The Health of Teachers and Administrators

Too often teacher and administrators are only concerned with the health of children and neglect their own health. Teaching and administrating are demanding work that saps physical energy and mental sharpness if not controlled. School workdays do not end at 3:30 PM or 5:00 PM. Teachers and administrators cannot go home and forget their job until tomorrow because there are plans to make, papers to grade, and PTA meetings to attend. Most teachers and administrators work for advanced degrees. Many work at "moonlighting" jobs to increase their earnings. Others participate actively and assume leadership roles in teacher organizations, service clubs, churches, or work as youth leaders. If these extra activities are not controlled, teachers and administrators become overly tired and run down mentally, physically, and emotionally. For teachers, this is not fair to their students; for administrators, it is not fair to their staffs.

Educators should set an example of health by scheduling regular physical and dental examinations. A program of regular daily physical exercise should be followed, including recreational activities and hobbies. Regular hours for rest and sleep should be kept. If teachers and administrators control their health, they will avoid extreme weariness, mental and emotional stress, and job inefficiency.[8]

Health Supplies and Equipment

Certain items of health equipment should be distributed throughout every school district so that every school, and preferably every classroom, has them available. Standard items include: a first-aid kit, weight scales, eye-test card, tongue depressors, height and weight charts, thermometer, and height-measuring device.

An audiometer and a light meter should be supplied each individual school, though not necessarily each classroom. Teachers should be instructed in the proper use of such equipment, and encouraged to operate various items with the help and guidance of the school nurse.

The older system located health offices centrally in the main administration building of a school district, and the health personnel operated out of the central office. Recent developments have pointed out the advantages of providing a nurse's office or health room in each of the larger schools of a system. It is far easier and less expensive for the school nurse or physician to travel from one office to another throughout the district than to arrange for children requiring health attention or advice to be transported to one central headquarters.

The school health center should be large enough to accommodate a 20-foot clear space to test visual acuity and soundproofed for hearing examinations. At least one cot in a screened-off space should be provided to isolate children with communicable diseases. There should be a sink and counter for the nurse's use, a lavatory room, and a shower room if cleanliness is a problem in the community. In schools that use the services of doctors and dentists, it will be necessary to provide an examining room and possibly a dentist's chair. Locked cupboards should be provided for the storage of health supplies. Minimum equipment and supplies include:

A scale with a nonspring platform and a measuring device to determine height.
An instrument and dressing table.
Chairs.

---

8 Roald F. Campbell, John E. Corbally, Jr., and John A. Ramseyer, *Introduction to Educational Administration*, pp. 321–22; 328–29.

Cots.
Sanitary disposal cans.
First-aid cabinet.
Enclosed cabinet for medicines and small supplies.
Bedding with washable mattress cover.
Plastic cover for bed and pillow.
Paper towel and cup dispensers.
Nurse's desk, chair, telephone.
File cabinet for records.
Portable screen to keep cots from the view of others.
Open shelves for storing large items.
First-aid supplies of all types.
Blankets.[9]

Health records should be kept in every school so that teachers and guidance personnel have easy and immediate access to the information they contain. Records should be kept up to date by the school nurse as a part of her regular duties. They should contain pertinent data on pupil height, weight, dental care, immunizations, childhood diseases, psychological test results, and any serious physical disorders or conditions that might inhibit the child's success in school. The health card should be cumulative and should follow the child from grade to grade, and from school district to school district if necessary.

All schools should keep daily reports of referrals to the nurse's office, stating the name of the pupil, the symptoms, the first aid administered, any contact with parents, the final disposition of the case, and the person handling it. In addition, injuries to the head, back, teeth, bones, or anything that might be construed as of major significance usually call for reports to the district office. They should also be reported to the school's insurance company if accident insurance is carried on pupils. A written report should be made of all accidents whether they involve students or staff members.

Administration of the School Health Program

The health program should be considered an integral part of the educational program as a whole. It is properly described as a special service,

---

[9] Emery Stoops and Russell E. Johnson, *Elementary School Administration,* pp. 373–74.

but should not be thought of as an auxiliary or subordinate service. In the sense that the health program deals with elements generally considered foreign to the educational program, such as scientific equipment, medically trained personnel, local physicians and dentists, and health offices and clinics, it is special. However, once it is granted that education deals with all aspects of growth of a child, health education becomes coequal with the academic curriculum.

BOARD OF HEALTH ADMINISTRATION. In the past, many cities have permitted the local board of health to exercise control of the health program in the schools; some larger cities still countenance this practice. This arrangement assumes that the health work of the school district is part and parcel of the community health program, and, therefore, all health services should be administered by one directive body, assumed to be the local board of health. In the past and in some areas presently, many school districts are receiving fine service at no expense with this method. There is little question, however, that the trend during the past decade has been in the direction of school control and direction of school health programs. For the same reasons that private ownership and operation of school transportation is less desirable than school ownership, the relegation of school health problems to a non-school entity is to be avoided. The necessity of maintaining close contact with home and parents indicates that the school be the initiating agent for health education, rather than a civic board of health.

HEALTH INSTRUCTION. In the elementary grades, the creation of beneficial health habits is the principal goal of the health program; other areas that assume great importance later are not emphasized here. Principal stress is placed upon the following factors at the elementary level:

1. Personal cleanliness
2. Posture
3. Safety
4. Diet
5. Sleep and rest habits
6. Care of teeth and eyes
7. Prevention of environmental pollution

The secondary school health education program sometimes features special classes in health or hygiene, but more often depends upon health units covered in the subject matter of courses in science, physical education, and home economics. Many secondary schools include special optional courses in family life and sex education and drug problems. Health instruction should include information not only about drugs but about alcohol and tobacco as well.

PHYSICAL EDUCATION AND HEALTH.   Separate periods are set aside in elementary schools for instruction in physical education.   The classroom teacher is trained to instruct children in this type of educational activity; large districts and county education offices usually supply supervisors who assist teachers with such instruction.   Between thirty and forty minutes a day are commonly allotted to elementary physical education.   Attention should be given to exercises and group games, with rhythm an important emphasis of the instruction.

Physical education in high school is a much more expensive and technical proposition than it is on the elementary level.   Gymnasiums, athletic fields, and trained personnel are necessary.   Both interscholastic and intramural sports are customary, with proper balance allotted to each of these important phases of the athletic program.   A vital part of the physical education design should be the development of lifelong interest in individual and group recreation of a type enjoyable and practical in post-school life.[10]

SAFETY EDUCATION.   The rising accident rate in the United States points up the growing need for adequate instruction in the principles of safety. The American Association of School Administrators listed the following objectives of safety education:

I.   To prevent accidents.
   A.   By developing safety habits.
   B.   By imparting knowledge of health.
   C.   By developing habits and skills that help in safeguarding oneself and others.

---

[10] American Association of School Administrators, *Health in Schools,* Twentieth Yearbook (Washington, D.C.: The Association, 1942), Chapter VI.

II. To fuse these elements into a discipline important in itself as a means toward effective citizenship.[11]

Except in the area of driver training and education, safety education
is largely the province of the classroom teacher. Inservice training for
teachers in safety problems is probably the most effective way to promote
safety instruction on a scientific basis. Outside experts, from industry and
government as well as from education, can be called upon to provide such
training. The following methods may be used:

1.   Regular classwork
2.   Special classes
3.   Safety councils
4.   Pupil safety patrols
5.   First-aid groups
6.   Safety campaigns [12]

In the field of accident prevention, primary emphasis should properly
be placed on freedom from school-related accidents. There is very little to
be gained by giving theoretical instruction in safety education on a broad
scale unless it is supported by specific training in avoiding accidents in the
school area itself. Areas where school-related accidents most commonly
occur, in order of their frequency, are as follows: streets and highways
adjacent to the school, playgrounds, gymnasiums, laboratories, and shops.
Instruction in school accident prevention usually follows the pattern outlined below:

1.   Close supervision of pupils on their way to and from school.
2.   Academic instruction in safety and accident prevention.
3.   Safety engineering to ensure maximum safeguarding of school sites,
     buildings, and facilities.
4.   Cooperation between the school and other agencies for the promotion
     of accident control.

---

[11] American Association of School Administrators, *Safety Education,* Eighteenth
Yearbook (Washington, D.C.: The Association, 1949).

[12] W. A. Yeager, *Administration and the Pupil* (New York: Harper & Brothers,
1949), pp. 275–78.

SCHOOL SAFETY. In addition to teaching safety, the school buildings themselves must be safe. Ayars lists the following considerations for making schools safe and reducing risk:

1. When new buildings are to be erected, plan for fire safety by locating them at a reasonable distance from frame buildings and other fire hazards, and by locating the heating plant in a separate structure.
2. Use non-inflammable floor seals, varnish removers, and paints. Store oily cleaning cloths, mops, unsealed paint cans, gasoline, and other inflammable materials carefully, preferably in fireproof rooms or rooms outside the main building.
3. Pick up papers, rubbish, and trash regularly. Eliminate broken glass, pointed sticks, loose floor boards, slivery stair railings, and other safety hazards.
4. Make safety a prime consideration in purchasing playground equipment, transportation equipment, furniture, and other items.
5. Keep firefighting and first-aid equipment easily accessible and in working order.
6. Define carefully each person's responsibilities in reducing risk. Check regularly to see that regulations are complied with.[13]

All buildings, furniture, and equipment must be kept repaired. Regular checkups should be made of hardware, fire escapes, fire alarm systems, fuse boxes and electrical wiring, boilers, hinges, locks, window casings, and exit signs.[14]

School buses not only must be regularly serviced but should be inspected daily for safety, the lives of many children depending on their careful maintenance. Inspection and maintenance records should be kept by the transportation department. All laws must be obeyed by drivers also trained in first aid. Bus riders should be instructed in bus safety and must be required to obey all safety regulations, at the bus stops as well as when riding.

---

[13] Albert L. Ayars, *Administering the People's Schools* (New York: McGraw-Hill Book Co., 1957), p. 207.

[14] Ayars, *Administering,* p. 42.

School Nutrition Programs

Most of our larger school districts, and many smaller ones, now provide cafeteria facilities and services for their pupils. The Department of Agriculture has reported that 3 billion meals are served annually in the schools. These daily hot lunches result in an improvement in nutritional standards that cannot be underestimated. The same reasoning that justifies the modern school's interest in health and safety underlies its concern with nutrition.

OBJECTIVES OF THE SCHOOL LUNCH PROGRAM. The main objective of the school lunch program is to provide sufficient attractive, nutritious, and palatable food at the lowest possible cost. In a larger sense, however, the goal is that of the entire school health program: the creation and maintenance of a healthy pupil capable of profiting to the optimum degree from the educational instruction offered. Malnourished children are "more likely to be apathetic, irritable, and lack a long attention span."[15] More and more, food is also being made available to pupils at intervals throughout the school day. Early morning nutrition for children who come to school with little or no breakfast is increasing, as is the custom of offering mid-morning snacks, especially for children in the primary grades. Experimental studies have indicated the positive value of good nutrition on learning ability and high pupil morale.[16]

ORGANIZATION. A high degree of cooperative effort exists between a variety of government agencies in the nutrition program. By a singular set of coincidences, almost every level of American government has interested itself in the problem of pupil nutrition in the past two decades.

The federal government during the sixties found itself faced with great surpluses of grain, meat, and dairy products. A solution to this chronic

---

[15] Rita Bakan, "Malnutrition and Learning," *Phi Delta Kappan* 51 (June 1970), p. 529.

[16] The reader is referred to the following publications for further information on the relationship between nutrition and learning: M. Winick, "Malnutrition and Brain Development," *Journal of Pediatrics* (May 1969), p. 667; R. H. Barnes, A. U. Moore, I. M. Read, and W. G. Pond, "Effect of Food Deprivation on Behavioral Patterns," in N. S. Scrimshaw and J. E. Gordon (eds.), *Malnutrition, Learning, and Behavior* (Cambridge, Mass.: MIT Press, 1968), p. ·168; H. F. Eichenwald and P. C. Fry, "Nutrition and Learning," *Science* (February 1969), p. 664; and Margaret Mead, "The Changing Significance of Food," *American Scientist* (March–April 1970), p. 176.

problem of oversupply was the allocation of much of the surplus to the nation's schools, at nominal prices.   At the cost of a few reports and a minimum of red tape, schools have been able to translate such aid into enriched lunch menus at reduced prices.   The federal government entered food service programs for schools with the National School Lunch Act of 1946 and the School Milk Act of 1954.   More recently, Title I of the Elementary and Secondary Education Act provided funds for food service for disadvantaged children.   The Child Nutrition Act makes a breakfast program available for children who travel long distances from homes with little food.   In the near future, school lunches may be provided for summer school programs.

States maintain nutritional offices and expert consultants whose duty it is to improve on existing menus and to advise schools on proper techniques of feeding large numbers of children at different age levels.   Some states follow the example of the national government in giving food subsidies and financial aid.   Most state departments of education publish minimum requirements for school menus, establishing proper amounts of fats, carbohydrates, proteins, and vitamins to be included in the weekly lunch program.

Counties often give supervisory assistance in the establishment and improvement of nutritional programs.   In its commonly assumed function of supervising the accounts and records of school districts, the office of county superintendent of schools often renders valuable service in placing the financial portion of the school lunch program on a sound basis.

Local school districts actually operate the nutrition programs.   They organize the distribution of food, hire and pay the personnel who administer it, and evaluate the success of the system after it has been in operation for a sufficient length of time.   The building and equipping of the cafeteria are functions of the local district alone.   Often, the meals are subsidized in part from the district's general fund; this subsidy most often is applied to the cafeteria director's salary.

Private community organizations may contribute funds for nutrition. Meals for needy children are often pledged by such groups and PTA organizations often finance mid-morning snacks for kindergarten and first-grade children.   In small schools, mothers and other interested women frequently volunteer their services to serve and prepare meals, enabling districts to offer lunches to pupils which otherwise would have been impossible financially.

ADMINISTRATION OF THE NUTRITION PROGRAM.   It is important to realize
that the nutrition program involves more than the preparation and serving
of food.   Modern schools consider the lunch period an important part of
the educational program and stress instructional aspects such as menu
preparation, principles of sound diet, and good table manners.   Standard
meals are advisable, with the menu being changed each day.   Menus can
be cooperatively planned by pupils, teachers, and cafeteria personnel
within the framework of state standards.   In all but very small districts, a
cafeteria director should be placed in charge of the program, and should
work under the general supervision of the business manager or superintendent of schools.   The cafeteria director should be a person of wide
experience in mass feeding, and preferably should be especially acquainted
with the nutritional needs and habits of children.   Larger districts may
employ a dietician to plan the meals.

Usually school district cafeterias attempt to be self-supporting, except
for the cafeteria director's salary, which is normally subsidized by the
school district.   No attempt should be made to show a profit of any kind
from serving meals to pupils and teachers.   Semi-annual balances should
be struck, and any monetary surplus should be applied to lower the cost of
meals.   The object of the program should always be to serve the largest
possible number of pupils, and to this end the cost of meals should be kept
as low as possible.

A cafeteria clerk may also be employed by large districts.   He should
keep necessary accounts, order and receive supplies, and conduct the
annual inventorying and budgeting necessitated by a sizable operation.   He
would work under the direction of the cafeteria director, and in close
cooperation with the district business office.

There must be communication and coordination between:

1.   The superintendent, who has overall responsibility for the cafeteria pro-
     gram, establishing policies and procedures, and organizing central ad-
     ministration.
2.   The business administrator, who has responsibility for food-service
     financial management, the purchase, storage, and distribution of food
     supplies, the purchase and maintenance of kitchen equipment and
     facilities, and cafeteria personnel.
3.   The cafeteria director, who has responsibility for the menus, food
     preparation, and the supervision and training of cafeteria personnel.
     He works closely with the school principal, school cafeteria manager,

and with the district business administrator in handling food supply, equipment purchases, storage, and distribution.

4.   The school principal, who has responsibility for the management of the cafeteria within his school, the scheduling and supervising of students for lunch and snack hours, the collection and handling of money within his school, adherence to district policies and compliance with health laws, and the working relationships of his staff with cafeteria personnel and the district office.

Teachers are not as fortunate as people working in business or industry who usually receive not only a duty-free lunch hour, but a morning and afternoon coffee break. The NEA Research Division made a study in 1966 of school systems enrolling 300 or more pupils and found that only one-fifth of the elementary school teachers and slightly over one-fourth of the secondary school teachers had duty-free lunch periods. "Approximately half of all systems reported teachers having some type of lunch period responsibility on a rotating basis while one-fifth of the systems reported elementary school teachers and one-twentieth of the systems reported secondary school teachers with lunch time supervision of pupils every day."[17] Because of pressure from teacher organizations and enlightened administration, many schools are freeing teachers from lunch hour supervision and employing teacher aides or lunch hour supervisors for this duty. These people are usually lay persons, parents, or PTA members paid on an hourly basis. This trend is encouraging because it allows teachers to have a relaxing lunch period and to be more capable of teaching effectively in the afternoon.

Because of the expense involved, many school districts are experimenting with centralized cooking rather than having food prepared in each school. The cooked food is delivered in special, heated containers to each school from a central kitchen. Other districts are utilizing food-dispensing machines. When such changes are made, the organizational pattern for handling the nutrition program must be revised. Students, school personnel, and parents must be involved and informed if radical changes in the traditional program are to be accepted.

REASONS FOR PUPIL PARTICIPATION IN SCHOOL LUNCH PROGRAMS. If school cafeterias are to be run successfully, they must attract from one-

---

[17] National Education Association, Research Division, "Teacher Supervision of Lunch Periods," *Research Bulletin,* p. 72.

third to one-half of the pupil population. Administrators and pupils do not always agree upon the reasons for participation or non-participation. Practical administrators should rely more heavily upon pupil judgment, rather than following their own hunches as to why the participation level rises or falls.

Administrators and cafeteria managers generally believe that a balanced lunch, well-prepared and tastefully served, will attract students. They believe in a more or less quiet atmosphere in the lunch room with good supervision. Parents want a reasonable cost, especially if there are several children in the family. Students, on the other hand, prefer simple food and do not care whether the lunch is nutritionally balanced. They often prefer to bring their own lunches unless urged by their parents or teachers to eat the school-prepared lunches. They dislike long lines and slow handling of the trays and cash registers, and like to talk and socialize while eating. High school students prefer snack-type lunches with freedom of choice. Some schools have moved to this type of service and have found it more successful than the traditional tray lunch. Students differ from administrators in regard to the time allowed for eating. Whatever an administrator thinks, student use of the cafeteria is dependent upon the students' attitude and desire to eat there.

DESIRABLE STANDARDS FOR FOOD SERVICES. The following standards will assist a school district in developing an adequate food-service program:[18]

    I. Organization.
        A. Every school should provide cafeteria service for pupils.
        B. The district should operate its own food service.
        C. When three or more cafeterias are in operation, the program should be headed by a trained and experienced district cafeteria director.
        D. Cafeteria facilities should serve 50 percent or more of the pupils enrolled.
        E. The food service should be related to the health program of the school.
        F. The district should take advantage of federal food-surplus commodities to reduce costs for pupils.
        G. The food-service program should be on a nonprofit but self-supporting basis.

[18] Irving R. Melbo et al., *Report of the Survey of the Bear Valley Unified School District*, pp. 230–33.

    H. Food service for pupils should be the primary aim of the program, rather than primarily service for community groups or employed personnel.

    I. The food-service program should be operated on a school board-approved policy basis, subject to review as conditions change.

II. Personnel.

    A. The employment and termination of food-service personnel should be recommended by the superintendent and approved by the school board.

    B. The district should make provision for an adequate inservice training program and an impartial appraisal of food-service personnel performance.

    C. Prior to service, all those who handle food should be given a general health examination by a district physician at district expense.

    D. Food-service personnel should be provided with equitable benefits, including salary, leaves, vacations, health insurance, etc.

    E. Student help should be shielded from the operation of machines with moving parts or other dangers. Student work in cafeterias should be a learning experience and should not interfere with study programs. Such work should be paid for at an hourly rate, not by provision of free meals.

    F. Cafeteria workers should wear appropriate white uniforms.

    G. Food-service personnel should be given priority to earn overtime pay when the facilities are used by school-related associations.

    H. Food-service personnel play an important role in the nourishment and well-being of pupils and faculty and should receive appropriate recognition by administrators.

III. Operation.

    A. All disbursal of funds and payment of bills should be made through the business office.

    B. Cash registers with tapes and totalizers should be used to collect money at cafeterias and snack bars.

    C. All receipts should be double checked and deposited in the local bank each day.

    D. A financial report of food-service operations should be submitted to the school board at the close of each month and at the close of each fiscal year.

    E. Charge accounts should not be permitted; free meals should be provided by tax overrides or by welfare agencies.

    F. The cafeteria account should be audited at the close of each fiscal year.

    G. Central purchasing and warehousing of staple food and supplies is recommended.

H. A standard replacement policy for equipment should be approved by the school board.

I. Dishes, utensils, and equipment should be kept clean and hygienic by cafeteria workers. Floors, windows, and the like should be cleaned by custodians.

J. Periodic inspections by the county health department and other agencies should be welcomed.

K. Every effort should be made to decrease the length of lines and other delays at the cafeteria and snack bars.

Summary

The goal of health education is the gradual improvement of the health of society. In order to do this, health programs are set up in schools to improve health habits, provide knowledge about health, influence parents and other adults indirectly, and to ensure that each successive generation is healthier than its predecessor.

Recently recognized areas of interest and concern in this field are sex information, drug information, ecological measures, and general improvement of physical activity in a highly automated society. To deal with these problems, most school health programs stress the triple approach of prophylaxis, rehabilitation, and preventive hygiene. The location of the school plant itself is of paramount importance to health, especially in relation to traffic hazards, pollution, and ventilation.

The health program curriculum should include sight conservation, speech therapy, remedial physical education, and the dangers of drug abuse. The program should involve all school personnel and should be cooperatively constructed.

The school nurse is indispensable in any health program, as is the classroom teacher who does most of the screening of health problems. Both teachers and administrators should set an example of health habits.

Health supplies should be widely available throughout the district, the health program being considered an integral part of the district-wide instructional picture. The school district, however, should control and direct it, not the local health authorities. Health education should occur in both elementary and secondary health units, as well as in physical education classes.

Safety education, in addition to its part in driver education, should be taught in regular classes and in connection with safety councils, pupil safety patrols, and first-aid groups. The school itself should be safe, with fire prevention and safe wiring of first priority.

School nutritional programs have become an important part of the overall health program. Their objectives include not only the provision of good meals at low cost, but more particularly the creation and maintenance of a healthy pupil capable of profiting optimally from the instruction offered. In the last twenty years, all levels of American government—federal, state, county, and local—have been involved in the problem of pupil nutrition.

Most school cafeterias are self-supporting, although the director's salary is paid from school budget sources. Large districts employ an accounting clerk, in addition to cooks and other personnel. Centralized cooking is becoming more common.

The chapter lists desirable standards for organization, personnel, and operation of the nutrition program.

Trends

Like transportation, health is an area of responsibility that has been delegated to schools by the citizenry at large.

TOWARD A GENERAL EXPANSION OF SCHOOL HEALTH AND NUTRITION PROGRAMS. If the current trend continues without great modification, the future may see the principle of free nutrition for all schoolchildren during the school day as universally accepted as free tuition. If it is unfair to penalize pupils economically by compelling them to purchase textbooks, it is equally unfair to compel them to buy school lunches. Eventually, supplying free food to all schoolchildren will become part and parcel of free public education, a proper charge against the tax dollar. Free immunizations and medical care also seem to be possible within a measurable period of time. The result of this trend is bound to be a tremendous expansion in the extent and cost of these services and in the number of experts working in and with the schools to further these ends.

TOWARD THE CONTROL AND OPERATION OF SCHOOL HEALTH SERVICES BY SCHOOL OFFICIALS. The practice of entrusting pupil health and safety programs to outside agencies, still lingering in some areas, is archaic. The future will inevitably see the concentration of all school-connected activities under the direct control and operation of the school administrators.

Toward More Emphasis on Health and Nutrition Instruction. Broader and more rigorous instruction in health helps to maintain and improve the health of society. There will be an increasing number of schools adding family life and sex education instruction to meet the needs of our earlier maturing youth. The harmful effects of drugs, narcotics, and tobacco usage will be universally taught. The use of outside consultants, doctors, scientists, and researchers will increase and less experienced teachers will not be expected to handle all health instruction.

Toward Improved Methods of Handling the Food Services. An increasing number of schools will utilize centralized cooking facilities or catered lunches. The use of infrared stoves and electronically controlled equipment will simplify food preparation procedures. Food-dispensing machines will come into more common usage and cut down on personnel and expenses.

Toward Use of Technology to Increase the Capacity of Personnel. The latest findings of science in the field of health and nutrition should be used to improve the condition and working efficiency of the school staff as well as the pupils. We now know much more about diet, food preparation, food supplements, vitamins, and how to maintain good health. The technology acquired from space programs is being utilized to improve the health and well-being of all mankind.

Administrative Problems

In Basket

Problem 1

The principal of the Lakewood Elementary School has asked his school nurse, Mrs. Simpkins, to go into classrooms to give health instruction. He believes that this aspect of her services is as important as weighing and measuring pupils and giving first aid. However, several teachers have refused to let her talk to their pupils. They do not like the way she talks to students and have told her that they do not want her interfering with their class schedules, insisting they will teach health courses. Mrs. Simpkins has gone to the principal and explained that she is not permitted to give health talks to some of the classes.

What should the principal do?
How might he have arranged the health program to prevent this problem?

Problem 2

Danville High School is having a problem with school cafeteria usage. Fewer and fewer students are eating in the cafeteria, claiming that they do not like the food. The cafeteria is losing money, which perturbs the business manager. The district cafeteria director is also upset because he has been planning menus that are balanced and of good quality. The problem is aggravated because every noon students leave the school grounds in droves and patronize a nearby taco and hamburger lunch stand.

What can the principal do to alleviate the situation?
What can the cafeteria director do?
What can the business manager do?
What can the teachers do?

Selected References

BAKAN, RITA. "Malnutrition and Learning." *Phi Delta Kappan* 51 (June 1970).

BRION, HELEN H. "School Nurse to the Rescue." *Today's Education* 59 (November 1970).

CAMPBELL, ROALD F.; CORBALLY, JOHN E., JR.; and RAMSEYER, JOHN A. *Introduction to Educational Administration.* 3rd ed. Boston: Allyn and Bacon, 1966.

EDDY, REGINA. "Changing Trends in School Health Services." *Thrust for Education Leadership* 2 (February 1973).

MELBO, IRVING R., et al. *Report of the Survey of the Bear Valley Unified School District.* Los Angeles: University of Southern California, 1962.

NATIONAL EDUCATION ASSOCIATION, RESEARCH DIVISION. "School Health and Nurse Services." *Research Bulletin* 44 (December 1966).

————, Research Division. "Teacher Supervision of Lunch Periods." *Research Bulletin* 45 (October 1967).

OBERTEUFFER, DELBERT. *School Health Education.* New York: Harper & Row, 1960.

President's Conference of American Fitness on Youth. *Fitness of American Youth.* A report to the President of the United States. Washington, D.C.: U.S. Government Printing Office, 1956.

SLIEPCEVICH, ELENA M. *School Health Education Study.* Washington, D.C.: Samuel Bronfman Foundation of New York, 1964.

STOOPS, EMERY, and JOHNSON, RUSSELL E. *Elementary School Administration.* New York: McGraw-Hill Book Co., 1967.

TURNER, CLAIR. *School Health and Health Education.* St. Louis: Mosby, Inc., 1957.

U.S. Office of Education, Department of Health, Education, and Welfare. *Better Health for School-Age Children.* Children's Bureau, Office of Education and the U.S. Public Health Service. Washington, D.C.: U.S. Government Printing Office, 1951.

18

Administration of Co-curricular Activities

Co-curricular activities have become an integral part of the total educational program of a school and are considered by many to be as important as the academic curriculum. They require coordination and personnel with specialized interests and skills. They should complement the education of all students, rather than cater to a few. Co-curricular activities have grown rapidly in scope and importance and have been demonstrated to be of major educational value.

This chapter includes a discussion of the following topics:

Role of Co-curricular Activities
Criticisms of Co-curricular Activities
Elementary School Activities
Secondary School Activities
Organization and Supervision
School and Community Cooperation
Summary
Trends
Administrative Problems

Role of Co-curricular Activities

Modern schools, especially secondary schools, devote a great deal of time and effort to the development of student activities outside regular classroom hours. This area of the school program has traditionally been referred to as "extra-curricular activities," because it covered areas not included in the academic curriculum. The recent growth of the concept that all school-directed activities should be considered part of the curriculum has brought the term "extra-curricular" into disuse, and has popularized an alternate term, "co-curricular." Whatever its name, the importance of this phase of the school program is not to be underestimated. In terms of totality of experience, student activities are essential. Many times, they are scheduled as regular class periods with credit granted.

In analyzing the value of such experiences, it is important to justify them in terms of their contributions to the overall objectives of the school. Unless they produce a measurable contribution to the program as a whole, they should be eliminated as non-educational. Often certain activities proliferate with little thought given to their basic value. The school calendar often becomes overcrowded. A student demand is not sufficient for allowing an activity; it must also be demonstrated to have positive educational value.

CRITERIA. Within the framework of educational value, the following questions should be used to judge a school activity:

1. Is it conducive to democratic citizenship?
2. Does it meet a recognized need of a sufficient number of students?
3. Has it arisen in response to a permanent rather than a transient need?
4. Has it sprung from a broadly based demand, rather than from a small group?
5. Is the activity allowed to interfere in any way with the classroom program?
6. Are the students who benefit from the activity willing to spend enough time and energy to carry the main burden of its operation?

For the co-curricular program as a whole, the following opportunities should be provided for all students if the program is to be considered a success: opportunities in athletics and physical development; speech and drama; journalistic and creative writing; music; recreation; hobbies; social development; and academic and other interests not covered in a regular curriculum, clubs, and student government.

Broadness and scope characterize a good activity program. Often a tendency exists to sanction certain popular and glamorous activities, such as interscholastic athletics, and to play down areas of the co-curricular program such as language clubs and literary societies. Each is of equal educational importance if it meets a real need for a sufficient number of students. At least 85 percent of the student body should participate; the program becomes dubious if under 70 percent participate.[1]

EDUCATIONAL GOALS. Some educational goals that may be achieved by co-curricular participation are:

1. Leadership development
2. Improvement of school morale
3. Practice in democratic processes
4. Social development
5. Growth in student responsibility

Criticisms of Co-curricular Activities

When anything is superimposed on a regular program, criticisms and problems may arise; this is especially true with co-curricular activities. One criticism is the added cost for the average student for participating in co-curricular activities. Special clothes, uniforms, or athletic shoes often are required, making some activities prohibitive for some students. Subscriptions, admission fees, and student activity tickets add to the cost of student participation. Too often, students feel exploited, public events become spectacles, and students become preoccupied with raising money. Certain activities sometimes accumulate thousands of dollars, some of which may be banked to draw interest. If fees and admissions are collected, they should be used for the students who handled the activity and not held for some indefinite future use. Ideally, fees should be reduced or eliminated altogether. If co-curricular activities have the educational values that are claimed for them, perhaps it is time that they are financed totally at public expense.

Another criticism is that too few students participate and receive all the benefits, financial and educational. Or, others are active in so many activities that their school work suffers. The school staff should strive to

---

[1] George R. Cressman and Harold W. Benda, *Public Education in America,* 3rd ed., p. 251. Copyright © 1956, 1961 by Appleton-Century-Crofts, Inc. Copyright © 1966 by Meredith Publishing Company. Published by Appleton-Century-Crofts, New York, 1966.

engage as many students as possible in some worthwhile activity without jeopardizing their total educational development.

The overemphasis on social aspects of co-curricular activities is another criticism. Decisions must be made as to how these activities are scheduled to fit into the total school educational environment. Social life, valuable as it is, should be balanced with academic expectations.

Criticisms and problems can be minimized if the district administrators, teachers, and students work together to plan the co-curricular program carefully. Plans should be made at the beginning of the year for the total program. Each activity should be required to justify its existence or it should be abolished.

OVEREMPHASIS ON ATHLETICS. Interscholastic athletics often dominates the co-curricular program, receiving the most publicity and support. Community enthusiasm and pressure often create problems as the demands for a winning team become so great that the school loses control over its own athletic program. Many coaches, especially in small towns, can testify to this.

Winning puts financial pressure on the school district for equipment, high-salaried coaches, stadiums, lights, and well-manicured athletic fields. There is also pressure on the coach, who may be overzealous for fear of losing his job, and on the players who may spend too much time in practice. Inordinate pressure is placed on star athletes by college recruiters. A high-pressured atmosphere for school athletics can be damaging to the school's major goal of education. There does appear to be a slight trend toward de-emphasis of athletics. Students are questioning the emphasis on competitive athletics and are looking at the world around them in a different light.

ATHLETIC DISCRIMINATION. Traditionally, most after-school athletic programs have been for boys. Girls participate in play days, intramural sports, and some interschool competition in sports such as swimming, volleyball, tennis, or badminton. Boys, on the other hand, have a full program of competitive interschool athletics as well as intramural ones. Because of this, male teams have more coaches who receive higher remuneration than coaches of girls or women. An unbalanced allotment of money has been spent on athletic uniforms, supplies, and equipment for boys.

The women's liberation movement of the seventies has spotlighted the inequality of sports programs in the schools. Girls and women are showing more interest in sports than in the past, and they are asking for equal funding and equal opportunity. Women coaches are asking for equal pay. This movement complicates the budget picture for many schools.

Girls are asking for the right to be included on boys' teams and in some high schools have made a team. Some boys have not accepted this and have refused to play; others have agreed to play on the same team with girls or against them. The future will probably see a change in male attitudes as the idea becomes accepted. The courts may force the issue; a court in New Jersey has held that girls are eligible to play baseball on Little League teams.

Some educators, as well as parents and doctors, are concerned about girls competing with or against boys in sports. They wonder whether girls have the physical makeup and stamina to handle physical contact in such games as football, basketball, or even baseball. Others feel that girls have the right to find out. Although no one knows the answer, it is evident that discrimination between what boys and girls are permitted to do athletically will be lessened, and perhaps eliminated. Athletic opportunities that have been withheld from girls probably will be open to them in the future. A 1974 decision of the Department of Health, Education, and Welfare on equal athletic opportunity supports this prediction.

Elementary School Activities

The elementary school curriculum, normally less subject centered than the secondary, provides many opportunities for extra activities. Some of these are: hobby clubs, science clubs, square dancing, chess and checkers, sports, and student government. They can be carried on before school, after school, during the noon hour or recess, and possibly during class time.

Student government can start in the classroom at any elementary grade level. First grade is not too early to explore the democratic process by electing monitors. Class officers can be elected, perhaps monthly, so that many pupils have the opportunity to develop leadership skills. A teacher should sponsor the student government and develop rules with students to determine the officers needed, the term of office, the method of conducting elections, and what official duties will be. The elected officers can meet with class representatives and plan assemblies. Since these pupils are young, they will need a great deal of help from the sponsor, not only in planning but in developing leadership.

At the elementary level, student government should be less structured and less formal than at the secondary level. There are some educators who believe that elementary schools should not have school-wide student government because the pupils do not have the maturity to carry out the program; they prefer it to remain at the classroom level.

Elementary school music (band, orchestra, or chorus) is usually taught by music specialists or a musically talented teacher. It may be scheduled during class time, with pupils excused from their regular class for the special music period. Sometimes music practices are scheduled as an extra class period.

It is possible to organize intramural games, an extension of the physical education program, for out-of-school hours. Some schools schedule games during part of the noon hour, although most believe that free play is more important. Interschool competition takes place in some districts although it is less prevalent today. At the elementary level, participation in athletics should be less structured and less competitive than in secondary schools. The desire to win at all costs, intensive coaching, and the possibility of injury have no place in the elementary co-curricular program.

With the increasing amount of leisure time available in modern society, elementary school is not too early to begin preparation for it. Recognizing this, many elementary schools have organized "Lifetime Sport Activities" in their after-school programs. Examples of these activities are: archery, tennis, table tennis, bowling, badminton, swimming, and chess and checkers. Some do depend on the existence of proper facilities.

In summary, most elementary co-curricular activities usually can be left to individual teachers and conducted in the classroom, with a minimum of organizational regulations. Certain basic rules should be understood by all concerned, but these should relate to safety, conduct, and time schedules.

Secondary School Activities

A well-organized high school co-curricular program provides various types of activities to meet the needs and interests of many students. Typical activities are the following:

Subject-matter clubs: art, foreign language, literary, and science
Assemblies
Athletics
Cheerleading and drill teams
Class organizations
Speech-arts groups: debating, dramatic, and oratorical clubs
Honor societies
Student newspapers and yearbooks
Musical organizations: band, orchestra, glee club
Dances and other social functions
Photography
Student government
Hobbies

Extra-class activities often grow unchecked and complicate scheduling and supervision problems.

The principal, in consultation with his school staff and student leadership, must determine what activities should be permitted and how they are to be scheduled. Faculty members must be assigned as coaches, directors, supervisors, or sponsors. These assignments are critical since the success of any activity depends upon its leadership, which should be enthusiastic and supportive. Teachers should encourage each activity group to be self-motivating.[2]

Many teachers are needed to furnish leadership for co-curricular activities. In the past, they either volunteered or were assigned to sponsor or supervise a club or activity. Such assignments are now part of the teacher organization's annually negotiated package. The package includes the extent of the extra duties and the amount of extra pay to be received. Written, agreed-upon policies help to minimize personnel problems with extra assignments. Those who do take on co-curricular responsibilities find that it is rewarding to see the closer understanding that develops between students and teachers when they work together in student activities.

A great and continuing effort should be made to spread the benefits of the co-curricular program to as large a percentage of the student body as possible. Otherwise, a relatively small percentage of student leaders find

---

[2] Muriel Karlin and Regina Berger, *The Effective Student Activities Program,* p. 189.

themselves involved in a disproportionate number of activities, and a large minority or a majority of their classmates will never participate.

THE INTRAMURAL ATHLETIC PROGRAM.   Lifetime, carry-over sports grow out of the intramural program, not from interscholastic games.   "Intramural" refers to activities that take place *within* the school.   The intramural athletic program provides the best opportunity for any or all students to participate in sports, and at less expense than interscholastic sports.   Every type of sport or game can be scheduled.   The advantages afforded by the intramural program are:

1.   Less expense is involved than in interscholastic sports.
2.   Uniforms are not needed, although some type of identification should be worn.
3.   Participation is open to everyone, not just those who qualify for the school team.
4.   It is less commercialized.
5.   Although rivalry is high, there is less emphasis on winning and more on participation.
6.   There is more variety of sports than in interscholastic sports.

Activities are usually scheduled for after school hours and sometimes on weekends.   Sports may be team or individual ones, such as handball, tennis, or squash.

Teams can be organized by classes, homerooms, clubs, or created without regard to organizational identity.   The intramural program might prove a good place to initiate coeducational competition.

A faculty director should be responsible for working with student leadership to plan the intramural program.   He should:

1.   Draw up schedules.
2.   Arrange for the school areas and equipment to be used.
3.   Establish agreement on rules.
4.   Assign umpires and referees.
5.   Arrange for reporting results and determining winners.
6.   Arrange for winner recognition.
7.   Work with the student council to see that these functions are carried out.

Intramural activities are particularly important in junior high schools. The emphasis should be on a broad scope of activities without the competitiveness of interschool rivalry. Athletic skills and sportsmanship can be developed by more students, helping them to prepare for high school.

REQUIREMENTS FOR CO-CURRICULAR PARTICIPATION. There is a difference of opinion on the requirements for participating in co-curricular activities. Some believe that students with poor behavior or poor grades should be prevented from taking part in co-curricular activities, particularly student government or athletics. Coaches often exclude from playing those who violate team rules. Students are often not permitted to run for a school office unless they demonstrate "good behavior" or are "good students." There are those who believe a student should "earn" the right to participate; others believe that this deprives a student of the right to do something in which he might achieve success. The achievement of success in a co-curricular activity might be the incentive a student needs to become a better student or citizen. Some schools are reducing or removing academic and behavior restrictions on participation in co-curricular activities.

STUDENT GOVERNMENT IN SECONDARY SCHOOLS. Student government provides an excellent opportunity for secondary school students to develop leadership and to learn how democracy functions. Students, with the guidance of teachers, should cooperatively develop policies that establish and control student government and are approved by the principal. The council should operate under a constitution and bylaws, with committees to carry out the various functions. Students should be given as much responsibility as they can handle for conducting elections, running meetings, and planning activities. The council should be composed of the elected and appointed student body officers, class representatives, and possibly club representatives. Each class should elect its own officers, hold its own meetings, and schedule its own activities.

Some of the activities that the student government can plan are: assemblies, festivals, exhibits, hobby displays, play days, special-event days, event of the year, weekend trips, and interschool exchange of officers. In many of these activities, parents and the community can be invited to help or to participate—a good public relations gesture.

The council can perform many services for the school, such as: planning and conducting assemblies, supervising school areas, serving as visitor guide, preventing vandalism, planning social and recreational activities, and helping with the intramural program. It can be instrumental in promoting school spirit. In some schools, the student council forms a leadership class for credit and meets under the direction of a teacher-sponsor.

Organization and Supervision

The expansion of the services rendered America by its public schools is reflected in the area of co-curricular activities. As the extra-class program grows from year to year in complexity and size, the administrator must of necessity devote more time and attention to its organization and supervision. The administrator's task will be easier if he follows principles such as the following:

1. The school should supervise all co-curricular activities, including control and discipline.
2. The principal or some other school administrator should approve activities before they are launched.
3. Every co-curricular activity should have worthwhile values, rather than being purely leisure time enjoyment.
4. The principal, as the responsible school administrator, should have veto power over proposals made by any school organization. (This is being challenged by some student organizations.)
5. School size and school needs should determine the number and type of activities to be developed.
6. The individual needs of a student should determine the number of activities in which he is permitted to participate.
7. A good counseling and educational guidance program will help each student to plan a program of curricular and co-curricular activities leading to his well-rounded development.
8. All co-curricular activities should be democratic in nature so that as many students as possible may participate without being excluded by social or economic snobbery. Secret societies should be taboo.
9. Co-curricular organizations should not be permitted to enroll members unless they are students or employees of the school.
10. School buildings should be used for the school's co-curricular meetings and functions.

11. All activities should be scheduled in advance to avoid conflict in dates and to facilitate administration.
12. Activity expenses should be kept as low as possible.[3]
13. The school should closely supervise all co-curricular funds and accounts.
14. Activities should be developed by the cooperative planning of students, teachers, and building administrators.
15. Sponsors should be selected carefully and should have enough interest and experience to make each activity a successful one.

It should be explained that the word "student" refers to both sexes, although "he" or "his" is used in the statements.

Although co-curricular activities should be under the autonomous direction of the school principal, the school district should exercise some control. The activities should be supervised by the assistant superintendent for instruction because of their educational values. All school activities and clubs should have their funds under the direct supervision of the school district business office in order to minimize the dangers of strict student control of finances. Reports on student activity income, expenditures, and balances should be given periodically to the board of education and should be audited annually. The district personnel administrator should also be involved. Because of the multiplicity of co-curricular activities, especially in the secondary schools, he must see that newly employed teachers can fill any co-curricular vacancies.

It is customarily left up to the building principal to handle the coordination and direction of co-curricular assignments at the individual school level. He may delegate this task to an assistant principal or a faculty chairman, but larger schools should have a director of co-curricular activities. This arrangement has the advantage of centralizing the responsibility and helping to assure a standardization of organization and control to promote ease of operation. The director of activities should be responsible for:

1. Approving activities.
2. Scheduling and coordination.
3. Assigning faculty sponsors.

---

[3] By permission of Macmillan Publishing Co., Inc., from *The Fundamentals of Public School Administration* by Ward G. Reeder, 4th ed. Copyright © 1958 by Macmillan Publishing Co., Inc., New York, pp. 505–510.

4.   Supervision.
5.   Scheduling transportation as needed.
6.   Arranging for credit.
7.   Inservice for sponsors.
8.   Finances.
9.   Adherence to the constitution, bylaws, and policies of the student government.

If athletics is a major program, the director of athletics supervises sports activities in cooperation with the director of activities.   Coordination is often difficult and the principal may have to advise.

Schools that collect funds and charge admission for activities should assign a clerk to collect money, prepare financial reports, and bank funds, subject to the approval of the person assigned to supervise all co-curricular activities.   The clerk should work directly with the district business office.

SALARY SUPPLEMENTS FOR EXTRA DUTIES.   It is common practice for a school district to pay salary supplements for extra duties.   This practice is based on the premise that teachers deserve to be rewarded if they supervise co-curricular activities beneficial to the mental, physical, and social growth of students.[4]   Extra work takes time, ability, and a dedication to youth.[5]

The State College Area School District in Pennsylvania lists over 60 job descriptions related to co-curricular activities.   Extra duties involve activities beyond the normal contractual obligations, e.g., Parent Teacher Association meetings and American Education Week activities.   Activities are rated for extra-duty pay according to the following criteria:[6]

1.   Total out-of-school hours.
2.   Weekend and vacation hours.
3.   Number of students involved.
4.   Experience and training necessary.
5.   Injury risk to students.
6.   Pressures from spectators, community, faculty, or administration.
7.   Amount of responsibility for equipment, facility, and funds.
8.   Environmental influences.
9.   Supervision on trips.

---

[4] Solley, Paul M., "Extra Pay for Extra Duty," *Today's Education,* p. 54.
[5] Karlin and Berger, *The Effective Student,* p. 193.
[6] Solley, "Extra Pay," p. 54.

The rating favors activities conducted in after-school time; it is lower for class-related activities because there is less overall responsibility.

A study made by the National Education Association of 489 supplementary salary schedules for 1969–70 showed that 82.6 percent of schools made supplementary payments for both athletic and non-athletic activities, 13.3 percent paid for sports activities only, and 3.9 percent paid for non-athletic activities only. Payments for athletic activities ranged from $25 for softball to $5,500 for football while those for non-athletic activities ranged from $25 for directing the publication of the school newspaper to $2,000 for directing the school band.[7] Table 18–1 shows the median-maximum extra-duty supplements reported in this survey.

School and Community Cooperation

The co-curricular program can be extended into the community. If the concept of a community school is fully developed, the school will be in continuous use six or seven days a week. The community school concept assumes that everyone who uses the school at any time is a member of the student body. The "core" student body consists of children and youth who attend school according to the laws requiring attendance. The curriculum of a community school includes recreational, social, academic, personal interest, and cultural activities.[8] Elementary children may have a sports program on a Saturday or after school. Adults and young people may attend evening classes in stitchery, woodwork, clothing, food preparation, English for the foreign born, or hobby clubs. Senior citizens may have a dinner and social evening. Families may participate in dancing, games, or enjoy movies, lectures, plays, or concerts. Thus the co-curricular program can extend into the community, its activities helping to bridge the generation gap.

Schools that become community centered should employ a person with the title of Community School Program Director.[9] He would start work in the afternoon and remain on duty until evening activities are completed; he would also work all day on weekends, during vacation, and throughout the summer. His responsibilities would be to establish com-

---

[7] National Education Association, Research Division, "Salary Supplements for Extra Duties," *Research Bulletin,* pp. 42–45.

[8] Robert G. Pickering, "Accountability + Search for Consensus = Community Education," *The School Administrator,* p. 10.

[9] Pickering, "Accountability," p. 10.

TABLE 18–1. *Median–Maximum Supplements to Teacher's Schedules, 1969–70 in Systems with Enrollments of 6,000 or more*[a]

| | NUMBER OF SYSTEMS REPORT-ING[c] | SCHEDULED MAXIMUM ANNUAL SUPPLEMENTS | | |
| | | MEDIAN MAXIMUM SUPPLE-MENT | RANGE | |
ACTIVITY[b]			LOW	HIGH
PUPIL-PARTICIPATING COMPETITIVE SPORTS				
Head coach (or only coach)	76	$1,012	$225	$3,500
Football	418	1,050	111	5,500
Athletic director	208	1,000	150	3,200
Basketball	419	950	108	3,865
Hockey	51	920	135	2,200
Track	398	725	105	2,500
Wrestling	329	712	100	1,929
Baseball	378	660	105	2,100
Equipment manager	56	615	100	1,876
Soccer	106	650	75	1,553
Swimming	252	643	50	1,617
Gymnastics	145	594	92	1,430
Intramural sports	200	475	100	1,800
Cross country	321	460	25	1,800
Water polo	31	374	200	1,617
Tennis	374	442	50	1,350
Rifle	33	370	150	900
Golf	360	396	50	1,158
Bowling	41	350	82	791
Cheerleader	168	300	75	1,080
Softball	24	268	25	550
PUPIL-PARTICIPATING NONATHLETIC ACTIVITIES				
School band	305	600	100	2,000
Director of music[d]	42	497	120	1,540
Instrumental music	181	450	92	1,800
Vocal music	256	419	100	1,829
Director of dramatics	259	400	50	1,800
Debating	209	384	92	1,906
Yearbook	260	400	50	1,200
Newspaper	225	350	25	1,055
Production of school play(s)	126	309	100	1,375
Magazine	36	278	100	600

[a] National Education Association, Research Division, "Salary Supplements for Extra Duties," p. 43.
[b] Activities listed are the most frequently occurring; other activities are mentioned but not in sufficient numbers to justify summary data.
[c] A total of 489 schedules provide supplements for one or more of the activities shown here. Many schedules provide supplements for several of the categories shown.
[d] Vocal and instrumental combined, or not specified.

munication between the school and the community, people and organizations, and to coordinate and schedule programs and activities to satisfy predetermined interests. He should establish committees, seek group leaders, supply teachers, and furnish officials. The community use of school facilities is explained more fully in chapter 15.

Summary

Co-curricular activities are an important part of the total educational program of a school that should meet set criteria for appropriateness in a school situation, and ideally should provide opportunities for every student. Objections such as commercialization, excessive cost, and overemphasis should be considered and eliminated. Interscholastic athletics, which have dominated the co-curricular program, should be de-emphasized. The women's liberation movement is causing schools to reevaluate their athletic program and equalize opportunities and funding, although debate over whether girls should compete in physical contact sports still goes on.

Elementary schools, although they need to offer far fewer co-curricular experiences than secondary schools, should provide opportunities such as bands, hobby clubs, and science groups. Lifetime sport activities can be commenced in elementary schools. The typical secondary school, on the other hand, offers everything from football to photography, necessitating a highly structured co-curricular program. The intramural program provides the best arrangement for promoting broad student participation. Requirements for co-curricular participation should not be so stringent that they prevent some students from taking part. Student government provides an outlet for students to develop leadership and to experience the democratic process at work. Co-curricular activities should be organized so that they meet the needs of as many students as possible without interfering with their academic program. The principal should have the final power to approve or veto any activity. Many teachers are needed to furnish leadership. It is common practice for extra pay to be given to teachers who sponsor and supervise co-curricular activities; this is becoming part of the negotiated employment contract.

School and community can work together to make the school a community school, permitting co-curricular activities to flow into the community, developing closer relationships, and helping to bridge the generation gap.

Trends

Co-curricular activities are becoming more and more an integral part of the school's educational program. Educators are increasingly aware that strong academic achievement, balanced by physical, social, and leadership development, creates a better citizen. Sportsmanship, fair play, and learning to win and lose are valuable assets that grow out of a co-curricular program.

TOWARD THE PROVISION OF MORE LIFETIME ACTIVITIES. Regardless of whether it is called "co-curricular" or "life experience," the portion of the school program that deals with educational experiences outside the classroom is due to increase in importance. As leisure time increases, schools must stress increasingly areas that afford opportunities for the student to engage in activities designed to train him in the art of living for today and for the future. These areas will become less haphazardly organized and more of a planned part of the school program. The intramural program will become more important because it provides the best means of promoting lifetime sports activities.

TOWARD THE EQUALIZATION OF ATHLETIC ACTIVITIES FOR GIRLS. The women's liberation movement will not lessen its influence; it will continue to promote equalization of athletic opportunities for girls. Funding will equalize, with women coaches paid as well as men coaches. Girls will be permitted to compete on boys' teams under circumstances that will be clarified in the future.

TOWARD LESS EMPHASIS ON COMPETITIVE INTERSCHOOL SPORTS. Educators will finally recognize the harm that comes from producing a winning team at any cost. As communities and schools develop educational goals and objectives and assess the lifelong needs of students, they will realize that interschool sports are too commercialized, too costly, and meet the needs of too few students.

Administrative Problems

Problem 1

You are the principal of a high school with a full interschool athletic program for boys. Girls have only competed in tennis and volleyball. The parents, encouraged by a local women's liberation group, are demanding that girls have an athletic program equal to that of the boys, and including at least basketball, baseball, and track. Furthermore, some girls are asking to try out for the boys' teams. Your school district has no policy regarding this.

How would you proceed?
What would you tell the parents?
How would you handle the girls' request?

Problem 2

Stanley Abel is the faculty sponsor for the student council at El Dorado High School. The council meets as a leadership class during the third period. The council members do not take their job seriously and spend class time joking and laughing. Few activities are planned and those that are conducted are haphazardly carried out. Mr. Abel has tried without success to improve the council and to encourage the students to approach it seriously. The annual spring carnival, a big event at El Dorado, is scheduled to take place in two months but Mr. Abel has not been able to get the council started on its plans. Its president shows no interest, and the student body is upset because nothing is being done. Mr. Abel finds out that several students are circulating a petition calling for the impeachment of the student body president. He is shocked and reports this to his principal, Mrs. Jackson.

How should Mrs. Jackson proceed?
What should she do about the petition?
What should she do about the attitude of the student council?

Problem 3

The North Woods High School is in a little town of about 10,000 people. It has had three disastrous football seasons and the townspeople are up in arms. The high school football games have been popular community events for years. There is increasing demand for the coach, Benny Rodriguez, to be fired. Mr. Jenson, the principal, knows that his small school does not have enough good football players to compete with larger schools in the league. He also knows that the players respect Benny. At the end of the last football season, a delegation of prominent townspeople called on Mr. Jenson and demanded that he fire Benny and hire a coach who can produce a winning team. Benny is not tenured.

If you were Mr. Jenson, what would you tell the delegation?
What action would you suggest that the Board of Education take?

Selected References

CRESSMAN, GEORGE R., and BENDA, HAROLD W. *Public Education in America.* 3rd ed. New York: Appleton-Century-Crofts, 1966.

GORDON, TED, et al. "The Community Education View of Health, Physical Education, and Recreation," *Phi Delta Kappan* 54 (November 1972).

HORN, GUNNAR. "Extracurricular Activities: Right or Privilege?" *Today's Education* 61 (May 1972).

KARLIN, MURIEL, and BERGER, REGINA. *The Effective Student Activities Program.* West Nyack, N.Y.: Parker Publishing Co., 1971.

National Education Association, Research Division. "Salary Supplements for Extra Duties." *Research Bulletin* 48 (May 1970).

PICKERING, ROBERT G. "Accountability + Search for Consensus = Community Education." *The School Administrator* (September 1972).

REEDER, WARD G. *The Fundamentals of Public School Administration.* New York: Macmillan Co., 1958.

SOLLEY, PAUL M. "Extra Pay for Extra Duty." *Today's Education* 58 (May 1969).

19

Administering
Special Education Programs

Students differ from each other in a variety of ways—physically, socially, intellectually, and emotionally. When differences exist to a degree such that the student cannot profit fully from regular school instructional offerings, special education programs should be developed. The term "exceptional children" is used to describe pupils whose educational needs are very different from those of the majority of schoolchildren. Special education programs require specially trained teachers who have an interest in and an empathy for handicapped children. Others on the school staff should have an understanding of the special education programs so that children can be integrated into as many regular school activities as possible.

This chapter includes a discussion of the following topics:

History of Special Education
Administration of Special Education
Special Education Terminology
Placement of Students
The Principal's Role in Special Education
Assisting Special Education Teachers
Staff Understanding of Special Education
New Instructional Methods for Special Education
Well-staffed Special Education Programs
Working with Parents of Exceptional Children

Material for this chapter was prepared in collaboration with Dr. Hugh Pendleton, Principal, Hermosa Beach City School District, Hermosa Beach, California.

History of Special Education

The recognition of the exceptional or handicapped child and his need for special education programs is not new in America.   As school systems have grown, so has the education of the exceptional child.   Changes in attitudes toward the handicapped have shown improvement in recent years.   The history of the development of special education has followed a pattern of establishing programs for the most visible and handicapping exceptionalities.   Because giftedness is perhaps the least visible and handicapping, programs for gifted children have been slow to develop.   Some key events in the development of education of the handicapped are outlined by Cruickshank and Johnson:[1]

1817   Parish school education for deaf created in Connecticut
1829   Massachusetts School for the Blind
1829   Perkins School for the Blind
1832   New York Institute for the Education of the Blind
1842   Syracuse State School for Retarded Children
1896   Providence, Rhode Island, day school programs for mentally handicapped
1908   Providence, Rhode Island, open-air school for health problems
1914   Binet Intelligence Test introduced to the United States
1914   Lapeer State Home and Training School in Michigan began teacher-training program for teachers of the mentally retarded.

At the beginning of the century, there were few special education programs in local school districts.   Since then, there has been a significant increase in the educational opportunities provided for handicapped children.   It is estimated that at the present time nearly two million children are receiving special education in all fifty states.   Much still remains to be

---

[1] William M. Cruickshank and G. Orville Johnson, *Education of Exceptional Children and Youth,* pp. 11, 13, 14, 24.

done; it has been estimated that there are approximately six million school-aged children who need special education.[2]

Because of increasing interest in and knowledge of exceptional children, special education classes are becoming more common as the years progress. Many schools all over the country are experimenting with programs for exceptional children.

Administration of Special Education

It is necessary for the administrator to be aware of the needs and means of providing a program for the education and development of the exceptional child. School administrators have a responsibility to provide leadership and apply in practice the following principles:

1. The American promise of equality of opportunity extends to every child within the borders of this country, whatever his gifts, his capacity, or his handicaps.
2. The school is responsible for the "normalization" of the child's school experiences to the greatest possible extent. Thus, placement in a regular, ongoing program is preferable to placement in a special class; and placement in a special class is preferred to leaving the child at home.
3. The school must interpret the exceptional child, his needs, and his abilities to form an attitude favorable to his acceptance and development in the community.
4. Every resource of the community must be utilized to aid in maintaining the exceptional child's family life and in furnishing guidance and encouragement to his parents.
5. The school should strive to educate and train the exceptional child, utilizing his strengths of learning rather than concentrating on his disabilities.
6. Teachers of exceptional children must possess the personality and develop or acquire the understanding, knowledge, skill, and special preparation that will enable them to inspire, motivate, and teach the arts of living and enjoying life.

---

[2] Romaine P. Mackie, "Special Education Reaches Nearly 2 Million Children," *School Life,* p. 8.

7. The home of the exceptional child, the schools, the churches, and the health and social agencies in his community must work together in his behalf.

Efforts must be made by school districts to keep educators, parents, and citizens of the community informed of the philosophy and goals of the special education program. Handbooks describing the special education program are frequently developed for this purpose by larger school districts. In such a handbook developed by Los Angeles City Schools, Leonard Mayo states that:

> We believe in the exceptional child himself; in his capacity for development so frequently retarded by the limits of present knowledge; in his right to a full life too often denied him through lack of imagination and ingenuity on the part of his elders; in his passion for freedom and independence that can be his only when those who guide and teach him have learned the lessons of humility, and in whom there resides an effective confluence of the trained mind and the warm heart.[3]

Special Education Terminology

The term "special education" is difficult to define because its meaning has changed and is still redefining itself. Currently used, the term identifies a program of education or training provided for children or young adults with exceptional educational needs that cannot be adequately met in regular school programs.

The term "exceptional child" essentially is used for a student who deviates physically, intellectually, socially, or emotionally from what is considered to be normal growth and development and who cannot satisfactorily benefit from a regular school program. Special or supplementary class services and instruction are required by such a student.

Within the field of special education, many terms have rather flexible definitions. The practicing administrator may work with very precise legal definitions required by state funding regulations, and these often vary from state to state. This situation is especially true in relation to the intellectually exceptional child. The most common groups of intellectually exceptional children for whom school administrators are frequently responsible at the building level are the gifted and the mentally retarded child.

---

[3] Leonard Mayo, *We Serve the Exceptional Child*, p. 7.

The "gifted child" encompasses children characterized by high mental ability. Defined statistically, these children perform beyond two standard deviations from the mean in the typical normal distribution of intelligence on an IQ test. In order to qualify for gifted programs, many states and school districts require that the child's intellect measure above a 130 IQ on a standardized, individual mental abilities test. Frequently, requirements state that the gifted child be performing within the top 2 percent of the normal pupil population. Some schools use other performance criteria that take into consideration creative abilities and talents for admission to gifted programs.

Frequently, exceptional children's programs are thought to provide education to help compensate only for handicaps of students. This concept is correct, but limiting as it overlooks the gifted child whose exceptionality is in terms of superior capabilities. Organized programs for the gifted have developed slowly and have been limited in support and scope because of the frequent failure on the part of the public to identify these students as exceptional.

At the other end of the spectrum of intellectual exceptionality are the "mentally handicapped" or "mentally retarded" students. Again, working definitions and legal definitions may vary from state to state and from school district to district. Statistically, these children perform below two standard deviations from the mean in the typical normal distribution, with IQs below approximately 70 on individually administered mental abilities tests. Frequently, for class grouping purposes a further division is made; students whose intelligence quotient falls below 55 or 60 are classed as *trainable*. The lower limits of this group may be 30 and occasionally lower, depending on local policy. In contrast, the "educable" child is one with an intelligence quotient between 50 or 60 and 70 plus. Many school systems are recognizing that difficulties exist in accurate and appropriate identification of intellectually exceptional students by a single criterion. This recognition especially applies to the evaluation and placement of children from different cultural or social backgrounds. Further discussion of the criteria that help to identify and place the mentally exceptional child will be given later in this chapter.

A second major grouping consists of "physically handicapped" children. Within this large category are a number of separate and distinct groups of children, each of which requires special educational assistance. Included in this category are children with orthopedic, vision, hearing, speech, and neurological impairments.

The third group of exceptionalities requiring special educational assistance includes those children who are emotionally, educationally, or socially handicapped. Frequently, such youngsters function fairly well in regular class settings as their handicap is not as visible. Currently, educational programs for this group are less available than for children with more visible handicaps. The sixties and seventies have seen a continuing recognition of these children's needs, and the creation of many new classes and programs for those with "invisible" handicaps.

This term, "educationally handicapped," is a broad one that operationally identifies the children described above. Recognizing that agreement on a common term to describe these learning handicaps has not yet been reached, and realizing that the existing literature uses a variety of terms, Cruickshank lists eighteen terms currently used to describe brain-injured children (referring to the educationally handicapped).[4] Clements isolated thirty-eight terms used in the professional literature to identify them.[5] Clearly, there is a lack of a commonly accepted term to apply to these children.

Finally, the individual child who has more than one type of exceptionality is frequently referred to as "multi-handicapped." In some cases, such a child may have more than two conditions, each disabling. According to Cruickshank and Johnson, the largest group of multi-handicapped youngsters is characterized by mental retardation in conjunction with a physical disability.[6] Emotional problems frequently tend to accompany these disabilities. Much thought is currently being given to the education of multi-handicapped children, but the creation of programs, research, and understanding as to the best teaching approaches is more limited than for any other group of exceptional children.

Placement of Students

The determination of the most appropriate placement for the exceptional child requires teamwork. Frequently, the principal or the director of special education heads this effort. Utilizing the expertise of the child's teacher, a school psychologist, a physician or school nurse, plus the prin-

---

[4] William M. Cruickshank, *The Teacher of Brain-Injured Children*, p. 11.

[5] United States Department of Health, Education and Welfare, Office of Education, *Minimal Brain Dysfunction in Children*, prepared by Sam D. Clements, p. 27.

[6] Cruickshank and Johnson, *Education of Exceptional Children*, p. 7.

cipal and director of special education, an admissions and discharge committee should be formed to consider placement for the special student. The committee will make use of all available information compiled by its members concerning the strengths and handicaps of the student in selecting the most appropriate placement. The committee will need to consider placement alternatives in light of available options. Few exceptional children precisely fit the legal classifications that are used for funding the programs.

The same committee may meet to review the progress of special students in relation to their continuance, transfer, or discharge from special programs. In this review, current information and test results should be considered to determine the continuing needs, shifting needs, and progress in the program of the handicapped student. Only by thorough and accurate reappraisal can the school fulfill its responsibility for returning children to the mainstream of the school program as soon as the student is able to successfully cope with the regular classroom.

Inherent in the placement of a pupil in a special program is the danger of labeling, classifying, and categorizing a handicapped child or youth. Frequently, the label may further handicap the student by becoming a self-fulfilling prophecy that limits the expectations of the student, parents, and teachers. Rosenthal and Jacobson indicate the unintentional aspect of the self-fulfilling prophecy even when an effort is made to avoid using labels that affect the student's performance.[7]

There appears to be a current developing trend for removing labels from handicapped children in the school system. Dean suggests that there is a movement to stress the child's ability rather than his disability.[8] Most handicapped pupils have the same needs, desires, and expectations as do so-called normal children. Schools can avoid stigmatizing labels by placing children who have special needs in regular classes (mainstreaming) and by providing special assistance to the teacher and student.

The Principal's Role in Special Education

The success of special education programs depends upon many people, especially the school administrator and his staff. The school principal has

---

[7] Robert Rosenthal and Lenore Jacobson, *Pygmalion in the Classroom,* p. 35.

[8] Martin J. Dean, "Some Major Issues in Special Education in Large Cities," *Thrust for Education Leadership,* p. 32.

a vital role in the functioning of any special education program. Because exceptional children differ from their normal peers, special educational programs and services should differ from those for regular pupils. The school administrator responsible for special education programs should be well prepared for the task. A broad knowledge and understanding of the principles of child growth and development is essential. The principal should have the ability to plan and execute the policies and practices of both regular and special education and have a full knowledge of the laws concerning special education. He should be aware of the services of public and private agencies in assisting the handicapped. Since parents of exceptional children have many concerns and special responsibilities, the principal should be skilled in counseling and assisting them. He should be able to utilize information from professional literature and research concerning the instruction of the handicapped.

ORGANIZATION OF SPECIAL EDUCATION PROGRAMS. The building administrator's special responsibilities vary according to the way classes for the handicapped are organized within his school system. In large school systems, classes for the severely handicapped are located in schools designed solely for special education. The more frequent pattern of special education is to locate one or two special classes at an existing elementary or secondary school. In rural areas and in small school districts where there are insufficient numbers of children to warrant specialized programs, classes are frequently maintained cooperatively by several districts or by the intermediate school unit. In such a situation, handicapped pupils are bused to the school maintaining the special class or classes.

For the most severely handicapped youngsters, residential schools are maintained by the state. The current trend is toward phasing out state institutions and returning children to their local communities, although the need will likely continue for such state-maintained residential school programs.

SUPERVISION OF STUDENT MEDICATION. In recent years, there has been increasing use of medication to assist youngsters in learning and behavior problems. Frequently, stimulant medication is prescribed in the treatment of specific behavioral disturbances. In certain situations, these medications have the paradoxical effect of calming and assisting the child in controlling his behavioral impulses and in aiding him in gaining ability to attend to a learning task for a longer period of time.

The physician prescribing medication is frequently assisted by information on the child's success in school. Occasionally, the school is contacted for such information, but more frequently comments on school success are related to the doctor by the child's parents. Once the medication is begun, information on the child's performance in school will be needed by the physician. The teacher can assist by relaying his observations to the parent or directly to the physician.

Nationwide concern has been expressed over medication of school-aged children, placing the school in a delicate position. Clarification of the school's role in regard to the medication of students was made in a letter to all California district and county superintendents of schools by Wilson Riles, Superintendent of Public Instruction in California:

> I wish to emphasize that under no circumstances should any attempt be made to coerce parents to accept any particular mode of treatment or therapy for any condition. It is proper for school personnel to inform parents of a child's behavior problems, but members of the school staff should not diagnose or prescribe treatment. Every district superintendent should take appropriate measures to inform his staff of their limitations and responsibilities in this regard.[9]

Each school administrator has the responsibility of identifying children under medication, of establishing safety rules for the administration of such drugs during school time, and of setting school policy on teacher communication with parents regarding observations of pupils under medication.

THE PRINCIPAL'S ROLE IN "INTEGRATION" AND "MAINSTREAMING." A frequently stated objective of special education programs is to assist a child to develop, to the greatest potential, his academic, physical, and social abilities, in order to function as satisfactorily as possible as an independent adult. Special education classes serving youngsters by legally defined categories are able to concentrate on development and remediation of academic and physical skills. In so doing, the task of developing social skills with normal children is often difficult to accomplish. The building administrator can be the key person in seeing that social developmental experiences are provided for special children.

---

[9] Wilson Riles, Letter to California District and County Superintendents, March 2, 1973.

"Integration" refers to the provision for regular scheduling of special pupils or classes in all-school instructional activities, where success can be achieved. Many opportunities for integration exist when one or several special classes are located at the campus of a regular school. The degree of integration accomplished depends upon the emphasis given to it by the school's principal and the special class teachers.

The term "mainstreaming" is applied to the practice of placing special children in regular classes who are ready to cope with a regular class. Again, the principal is the key person in the success of mainstreaming the special youngster. Through his leadership by example, other staff members and the community will treat handicapped youngsters with understanding. Murphy suggests that every special child cannot be mainstreamed, and some children have to be segregated because of the nature of their handicap.[10] The key criterion for mainstreaming is the ability of the handicapped student to achieve success in a regular class.

The benefits of integration and mainstreaming apply both to the special student and to his classmates. The development of appreciation of the handicapped as individuals is dependent to a large degree upon the care taken in class placement, the skill of the teachers, and the support of the school's administrators.

Assisting Special Education Teachers

Teachers of special classes often work more independently than the regular class teacher. Instruction must be individualized according to the special needs of the pupil. Special instructional materials must be located or created by the teacher. Transportation to and from school needs frequent teacher supervision. The readiness of students for integration into regular programs is determined by the special class teacher. Counseling and conferring with children and their parents is an ongoing need.

DIRECTOR OF SPECIAL EDUCATION. Depending on the size of the school system and the organization of special programs, several individuals will be the major sources of help for the special education teacher. The director or coordinator of special education should be a member of the district office staff, assigned to direct the program of special education. Generally,

---

[10] Betty A. Murphy, *NAESP Convention Reporter*, "You Can't Mainstream Them All," p. 25.

he is selected for this position on the basis of his experience and knowledge in special education as well as his ability to administrate. He should be able to see the global picture of all aspects of the school system's special programs and must keep informed of the newest developments in all phases of the system's program for exceptional children. Provision of teaching materials, facilities, staffing, placement of pupils, and inservice training for all special teachers is handled by the director.

SUPERVISORS OF SPECIAL EDUCATION. The role of the supervisor in special education is primarily that of a consultant, contributing to the improvement of instruction and the growth of teachers. He is available to give assistance to beginning teachers, particularly to those who have special education assignments without complete training in this field. Most teachers of special education appreciate a frequent visit from someone who is interested, understands their problems, and provides continual reassurance.

In large school systems with sizable special education enrollments, one or several supervisors of special classes and programs are employed. The supervisor also assists school principals in the management of many extra administrative responsibilities which are always present in special education programs.

RESPONSIBILITIES OF THE BUILDING PRINCIPAL. With few exceptions, the building principal should be the one to render daily assistance to the special teacher. It is his responsibility to see that the special teacher receives materials and services to meet the needs of his special pupils. If the special education program is to be a success, the principal should fulfill his dual role as instructional leader and administrator. He should plan inservice experiences that will result in the teacher's professional growth, such as expediting the special teacher's observation of teaching demonstrations, attendance at conferences, and visitation to observe other special schools and classrooms.

School systems throughout the nation are recognizing the need of exceptional children for a number of services to compensate for their disabilities, including: extra guidance and counseling, regular psychometric evaluation, physical and speech therapy, and small pupil-to-staff ratios. To give effective assistance to the special education teacher, the principal must be able to organize such services so that they are readily available when the need arises.

Understanding Special Education Programs

The interpretation of special education is a continuous, ongoing phase of its programs. All public school programs require some communication with several publics. This is especially true for special education which represents a minority requiring an expensive education.

The location of two or more special education classes at a regular school has several distinct advantages. Special teachers can discuss problems and share successes with their colleagues. Regular class students also are given the opportunity to share school experiences with handicapped children. Special classes are provided with special equipment and teaching materials which are not in continuous use. These materials can be shared with other teachers in the school.

Teachers of special classes are perhaps the principal interpreters of special education programs to their fellow teachers. They usually have a wealth of training and experience in helping children over basic learning hurdles; this skill can be used to assist a regular teacher in selecting teaching materials and strategies to help a child in a regular class. Providing opportunities for teachers and students of regular classes to visit the special class is helpful to all, as are visits at recess, noon hours, or after school. Some special teachers develop a buddy system whereby each special child chooses a friend from another class to visit the special classroom.

Teachers of special classes frequently are admired by those around them for teaching exceptional children. Mays asks, "Why is there a general feeling that a teacher of the retarded should be tremendously admired (or even pitied) for working with 'those' children?"[11] She suggests some generalizations and misconceptions that contribute to this situation: (1) Despite the efforts of teachers, parents, and volunteer organizations, the general public seems to regard the retarded child as an unattractive oddity. (2) As special teachers talk about their work, the impression is conveyed that they work harder than other teachers and that their children require patience beyond human limits.

A careful and successful integration of a special child into a regular class, in addition to increasing the child's feeling of accomplishment, has a side effect of interpreting the special education program to the regular class

---

[11] Maxine Mays, "No Stars Please, for Teaching the Retarded," *Today's Education,* pp. 50–51.

teacher. By regular teacher observation of a child's progress and by teacher conferences with the special teacher, a ripple effect on many staff members is often created.

PARTICIPATION IN REGULAR SCHOOL ACTIVITIES. The inclusion of exceptional children in as many regular school functions as possible, depending upon their handicaps, should be the goal of each special education teacher and administrator. Assembly programs, recess, lunch time, play days, open houses, and school contests are a few activities in which all students should be encouraged to participate. An understanding and willing attitude exhibited by the building principal will set the tone for the staff's attitude. There are always some school days when some exceptional children may not be able to handle school-wide activities successfully. Their teacher can determine when it would be inadvisable for certain pupils or for the whole class to participate.

New Instructional Methods for Special Education

During the decade of the 1960s, special education programs expanded rapidly both in scope and size with the development of more sophisticated methods of identification and with increasing public awareness, demands, and support for the education of handicapped children. A number of promising techniques have been developed in the behavioral sciences, in technology, and in general education. Many are in general use and others are in the final stages of research or implementation. Jones states that special education is at a stage of continually evolving developments and directions. Among these developments, he suggests:

New models for assessment of exceptional children.
Promising approaches to the training of special education personnel.
New forms of community organization to provide comprehensive services for exceptional children.
New programs directed to the development of cognitive skills.
Preventive approaches through infant stimulation and preschool programs.[12]

---

[12] Reginald L. Jones, ed., *New Directions in Special Education*, p. 441.

Included in the following sections are several methods currently in use which are proving to have great potential in the education of exceptional children.

THE ENGINEERED CLASSROOM. Techniques of behavior modification have been implemented by Hewett with emotionally disturbed children in an engineered classroom.[13] This approach concentrates on bringing the overt behavior of the child into line with standards required for learning. The emotionally disturbed child exhibits behaviors that handicap learning. Such behaviors often include: poor concentration, hyperactivity, acting out, defiance, avoidance, and withdrawal. The teacher takes on the role of a behavioral engineer by controlling the learning environment to maximize the probability of student success. Three essential ingredients for effective teaching are built into the structure of the engineered classroom:

1. Selection of a suitable educational task for the child.
2. Provision of a meaningful reward following accomplishment of that task.
3. Maintenance of a degree of structure controlled by the teacher.

The engineered classroom technique includes a range of rewards offered to the child for completion of tasks from a hierarchy of seven task levels. The range of earned rewards include: tangible rewards, social attention, sensory stimulation, and social approval. At the beginning of the school day, each student is given a student record card ruled into squares. During the day, checkmarks are given every fifteen minutes for starting the assignment, following through, and for accomplishment. Students save completed record cards and exchange them on a weekly basis for candy, small toys, and trinkets. Preliminary observations suggest that changes in work efficiency and adaptive behavior occur quickly in the engineered classroom, and a purposeful, productive attitude toward work develops within the student.

PROGRAMMED INSTRUCTION. The use of programmed instructional techniques for teaching the exceptional child holds promise as an aid to the teacher. Characteristics of programmed instruction to be considered in

---

[13] Frank M. Hewett, "Educational Engineering with Emotionally Disturbed Children," *Exceptional Children*, pp. 457–467.

determining whether this technique will meet the child's particular needs include:

1. Highly directive step by step guidance.
2. Individual pacing of the learner at his own rate.
3. Systematic ordering of material for efficient learning.
4. Depersonalization of the learning experience.
5. Provision for immediate feedback to the learner.

Rudimentary concepts of programming are used by all teachers. What differentiates informal teacher programming from more formal programmed instruction is the emphasis on systematic ordering of material and provision for immediate feedback. Although teaching machines use programmed material, programmed instruction can be used easily without teaching machines.

Programmed instruction is often considered inappropriate for dealing with creative thought and the more complex cognitive functions. Covington's work, however, on the use of programmed instruction to teach productive thinking to the intellectually gifted has shown that this technique is not limited to mentally handicapped pupils.[14] Although the gifted child usually does not need the assistance of step-by-step guidance in assimilation and retention of factual content, Covington's study shows that the capacity to make imaginative use of these facts can be efficiently developed when gifted children use programmed materials.

TEACHING MACHINES. Exceptional children learn many skills in the same way that normal youngsters do, but the pace and the amount of practice to master a task often varies from the norms for regular pupils. The special teacher often searches for ways to increase his efficiency while giving each student the necessary individual practice. Many have explored the use of teaching machines to aid in special education instruction.

Characteristics of teaching machines that apply to special education instruction have been enumerated by Jones:

1. A teaching machine interacts directly with the individual learner.
2. The learner has immediate knowledge of results.
3. Machines, unlike teachers, have infinite patience.

---

[14] *See* Jones, *New Directions,* pp. 72–84 for a discussion of Covington's work.

4. The machine is unprejudiced, giving the same service to every student.
5. A demand is made on the learner to eventually make the correct response.[15]

Concern is sometimes expressed that teaching machines are likely to replace the teacher. However, the teaching machine rather will lead to a redefinition of some of the teacher's tasks, and in so doing will make his job less clerical and less routine. The teacher will be freed from some of the frustrations and repetitious aspects of his job, gaining more time for innovative teaching.

Well-Staffed Special Education Programs

The success of a special education program depends to a large degree on the quality of the teaching staff. Administrators of the special education program should provide each handicapped child with the opportunity to be instructed by a capable teacher. If this task is to be achieved, considerable attention must be given to recruitment, selection, and inservice professional growth of those who serve handicapped children.

RECRUITMENT OF SPECIAL TEACHERS. As new special classes or programs are launched and as staff attrition occurs, the director of special education becomes responsible for establishing the personal and professional qualifications required of special teachers. A number of studies have investigated the personal traits believed to be necessary for teachers of the exceptional child. In a study conducted by the U.S. Office of Education regarding the qualifications of special teachers, Mackie, Dunn, and Cain found the traits that characterize the successful special class teacher.[16] Special teachers particularly exhibit:

1. Extra patience
2. Mental alertness
3. Flexibility
4. Resourcefulness

---

[15] Jones, *New Directions,* p. 4.
[16] Romaine P. Mackie, Lloyd M. Dunn, and Leo F. Cain, *Professional Preparation for Teachers of Exceptional Children: An Overview,* U.S. Office of Education, Bulletin No. 6, p. 16.

5. Enthusiasm
6. Emotional stability
7. Personal warmth
8. Friendliness
9. Understanding
10. Sympathy
11. Objectivity
12. Sensitivity

SELECTION OF SPECIAL EDUCATION TEACHERS. Certification requirements for teaching handicapped children vary from state to state and from program to program. For some exceptionalities, credential requirements frequently require undergraduate or graduate training and practice teaching experience in the field of preparation. For other exceptionalities, the frequent pattern of certification requirements places less emphasis on formal training and experience and more emphasis on personality characteristics. School systems often require regular class teaching experience before entry into special education teaching. In any case, the possession of strong professional preparation and outstanding personality characteristics are valuable assets for a teacher of handicapped students.

Recruitment sources for teachers of special education are: colleges and universities, teachers currently serving in other assignments in the school system, and experienced special education teachers from other systems. Each of these sources has different assets.

Recent college-trained teachers bring in new instructional techniques and methods. A beginning teacher often will have had practice teaching experience in the area of exceptionality in which he is hired to teach. Through orientation and inservice programs, the school district can train the beginning teacher in the special education philosophy used by the system.

Teachers selected from other assignments in the school system will be familiar with general district philosophy and instructional goals. Those who volunteer for transfer to a special education assignment are somewhat familiar with the district's program and the requirements of the job. Assignment to special education teaching should always be done with the teacher's agreement to the transfer.

Recruitment of special education teachers from other school districts will have the benefit of adding an experienced person to the special education staff. Such a veteran teacher will often bring worthwhile new ideas to the program.

INSERVICE EDUCATION FOR SPECIAL TEACHERS. During periods of teacher shortage, selection requirements have often been modified to allow recruitment of strong teachers who have not completed full certification requirements. Additional responsibility for encouraging teachers to complete academic training and meet credential requirements falls on the administrator of special education, as does the responsibility for providing additional inservice training opportunities. Periodic inservice training is valuable for all teachers of special education, including the veterans. As stated earlier, many new programs and methods are being investigated and tried. Teachers must be familiar with these programs in order to adopt new ideas to improve their methods.

Working with Parents of Exceptional Children

Parents of special children carry a heavy and exceptional burden of responsibility from the moment they become fully aware of their child's handicap. If the child is to realize his maximum growth and development, complete cooperation and understanding between home and school are essential. Special educators have been particularly sensitive to this need and have developed many methods to increase respect and understanding between parents and teachers. Acceptance by parents of their child's handicap and adjustment to its responsibilities is a difficult task which can be eased by suitable guidance services at the school.

GUIDANCE PROGRAMS FOR PARENTS. When a child is enrolled in a special education program, the teacher and the administrator must provide leadership in the guidance process. Cooperation between home and school can be achieved through parent–teacher conferences, parent visits to class, telephone calls to the parent, and home visits by the teacher. These contacts help parents gain a true appreciation of the strengths and weaknesses of their child.

A complete school guidance program for parents of the handicapped might involve the teacher, school psychologist, nurse, principal, and director of special education. In addition, community members of the guidance team often include doctors, ministers, and social workers.

Ideally, parents should have the opportunity to be counseled by a trained professional leader. Unfortunately, this seldom occurs and parents receive guidance through a series of experiences with unrelated agencies or individuals. The school can provide some uniformity of guidance by establishing channels of communication between all persons involved and by working as a team to counsel the parent.

PARENT GROUPS. Parents of exceptional children sometimes join together because of their common interest. Because they share similar problems, parents are able to assist each other in gaining insights not possible through other means. A second related purpose of parent groups is to develop broader community understanding and acceptance of their children and to sponsor legislation on their behalf.

Parent groups often are organized by parents of children with a specific disability to share and exchange sources of information, medical services, and recreational opportunities for their children. Parent and teacher workshops can be sponsored to share the latest information. These groups can create their own libraries dealing with literature on the exceptionality of their interest. Frequently, parents raise money through various projects to supplement the school's instructional equipment and supplies. They may sponsor the gift of books for public and professional libraries.

Volunteer parent groups have repeatedly shown their value in articulating needs for special services and obtaining public monies and legislative support. As new programs are created, these groups publicize needs and influence legislators to support needed programs. When the need arises, statewide organizations have quickly mobilized their membership for letter-writing campaigns or marches on the state capitol to assure passage of legislation and funding for special education programs.

The director of special education will frequently be called on by parent groups for counsel and advice. He should eagerly accept this invitation to use his knowledge and experience in helping these organizations develop worthwhile programs for the handicapped.

Financing Special Education Programs

The education of exceptional children requires added services, smaller classes, specially trained teachers, and often, specially built classrooms.

Additional supplies and equipment are needed, some of which are quite different from those required in regular classrooms. For these reasons, school systems find that educating a special youngster is more expensive than educating an average child. This situation has retarded the full development of special education programs.

The concept of support of public education at the state level has been universally accepted in the United States; the expansion of state financing to include the increased costs of educating exceptional children has been much more recent, however. State school systems have attempted to encourage the creation of classes for the exceptional child by what is known as "the excess cost principle." The local district continues its responsibility for educating all children but the state reimburses expenses incurred for special class pupils.

Several methods are used by states to reimburse school districts for excess costs. Some reimburse according to actual pupil attendance, others by classroom units, and still others by numbers of teachers and special personnel. Extra responsibilities for the school administrator result from receiving such reimbursement. Included are reports of programs, pupils, and teaching activities which must be filed regularly with the state department of education.

To a limited degree both state and federal governments have supported and promoted research in special education by providing funds for (1) local pilot projects, (2) studies leading to the improvement of services, and (3) studies on the prevention and correction of disabling conditions. It is the responsibility of the local school administrator to keep abreast of new research. As effective new methods and programs are found, he should seek the necessary support to make the appropriate ones available.

Costs for special education on a per pupil basis appear high until the possible benefits to the exceptional child are considered. Often the individual handicapped child, his family, and the community reap benefits far in excess of the costs as the individual becomes self-sufficient and self-supporting. State legislators have encouraged state support of special education in order to reduce costs to welfare departments. Keeping some handicapped children at home and providing the supplements they need in school is not only best for the child and family, but markedly less expensive to the state.

Summary

There has been increasing interest in educating children with handicaps. Until recently, those with visible handicaps have received more attention than those with less visible handicaps.

Successful administration of special education requires skill in providing programs for all types of exceptionality, placing pupils advantageously, using all resources, counseling pupils, parents, and teachers, interpreting the programs, and providing special materials and facilities.

A willingness to take the extra time and make the extra effort for children with special needs is a minimum requisite for the administrator responsible for special education. Increasing knowledge, skills, and interest on the part of citizens and legislators in recent years have resulted in accelerating support for special education.

This chapter defines many terms used in special education programs. Children with special needs are being recognized as possessing the needs of normal youngsters, in addition to a need for special assistance to overcome and to compensate for their handicaps. These children can frequently meet with success if they can be "integrated" into many of the school's instructional activities or "mainstreamed" into regular classes.

The principal has a key role in organizing his school's special education program, supervising student medication, placing exceptional students, assisting teachers, and cooperating with parents and community.

Special education class teachers have a difficult task and face many problems. They should be selected carefully, have special training, and participate in inservice programs. They need the support of their principal and understanding from others on the staff, as well as from the district director of special education and district supervisors. The entire staff can help exceptional children by including them in as many regular school functions and activities as possible.

In recent years, there has been much research in special education, and new methods, programs, and teaching techniques have been developed, such as the engineered classroom, programmed instruction, and teaching machines.

The school should involve the parents in special education programs.

Parents need help in understanding their child's problems and in assisting and cooperating with the school so that their child receives the maximum benefit from his education. The community also needs to develop an understanding of exceptional children to help them adjust, not only during their school years, but after they leave school.

Trends

TOWARD THE INDIVIDUALIZATION OF INSTRUCTION. Schools are becoming increasingly conscious of the need to provide special education services according to individual needs of the pupil rather than on the basis of rigid categories. In the past, grouping by categories has brought about limited progress and learning.

TOWARD INDEPENDENCE FOR THE HANDICAPPED. Utilization of special instruction in the home community for all but the most severely handicapped prepares the student for a degree of independence greater than that developed in residential schools.

TOWARD THE DEVELOPMENT OF REGIONAL CENTERS FOR SPECIAL EDUCATION PROGRAMS. Parents of severely handicapped children tend to migrate to large cities where special education programs are offered. Large cities with state support will become, in effect, regional centers where all types of special programs can be offered.

TOWARD EARLIER ADMITTANCE TO SPECIAL EDUCATION PROGRAMS FOR THE SEVERELY HANDICAPPED. There are now more definitive ways of identifying handicaps in children three years old or younger. Promising results have also occurred in remedying severe handicaps before a child starts academic instruction. Severely handicapped children will be admitted to special education programs at a younger age.

TOWARD THE ESTABLISHMENT OF DEVELOPMENTAL CENTERS FOR THE MULTI-HANDICAPPED. Multi-handicapped children will be provided with developmental centers designed to relieve the schools and provide better educational programs for the multi-handicapped. The centers will also permit training to start in very early childhood.

TOWARD THE CREATION OF SPECIAL EDUCATION CLASSES IN ALL SCHOOL SYSTEMS. Children who are emotionally handicapped, learning disabled, brain-injured, or socially maladjusted are increasingly being recognized as requiring special classes and programs to provide better learning opportunities for them.

Administrative Problems

Problem 1

The Saugus Unified School District has identified enough educable mentally retarded children to form another class. These children are in three different elementary schools so the decision has been made to place the class at the Lincoln Elementary School which is centrally located, and to transport children by school buses.

What should the principal do to prepare his staff and pupils for the addition of this class?
How should he integrate them into the school program?
What difficulties might arise and how can they be remedied?

Problem 2

Mr. Peterson has been employed as the new director of special education. The district has ten classes for educable mentally retarded children, two classes for the trainable mentally retarded, and two classes for the physically handicapped. There are limited programs for those who have been identified as gifted in several elementary schools, a junior high school, and the high school. Teachers have repeatedly requested that the district provide programs for so-called emotionally disturbed children, but have met with no success. There are no supervisors for special education and little coordination of the district's special education programs exists.

What priorities should Mr. Peterson consider as he assumes his new position?
How should teacher demands for establishing programs for the emotionally disturbed be handled?
What should Mr. Peterson do about the current programs for the gifted?

Problem 3

Assume the same situation as Problem 2. The director of special education has now been in the district for 6 months and has found that several of the special education teachers are inadequate. He has also identified enough children to add two classes for the educable mentally retarded and one for the trainable mentally retarded. District policy is not clear as to who has the responsibility for evaluating special education teachers. The addition of the new classes will make it important to keep as many effective teachers as possible in the program.

What policy should Mr. Peterson develop for the evaluation of special education teachers?
How can the poorer teachers be helped?
What should be done if these do not show improvement but are tenured teachers?
What qualifications should Mr. Peterson look for as he selects new special education teachers?

Problem 4

The regular classroom teachers in two of the elementary schools in the Garvey School District are upset because the district has proposed a new concept in special education. Their schools have been selected for a pilot program in which all but the most seriously handicapped children will be assigned to regular classes. The teachers claim that they do not have the technical knowledge, training, or experience to teach special education pupils and fear their class will be disrupted.

The new proposal is based partly on the idea that segregating and labeling special education pupils is detrimental to their achievement in school. The director of special education has stated that when handicapped and non-handicapped children are mingled, they learn from each other. He has also explained that teachers will be given help in modifying their regular program so that all children will benefit educationally.

Another problem has been created by uninformed parents who claim that they do not want handicapped children in their children's classroom.

What can be done to help regular teachers prepare for teaching handicapped pupils?
What extra help and resource programs will be needed?
How can the parents be involved in establishing the pilot program?
How should the program be evaluated?

Selected References

CRUICKSHANK, WILLIAM M. *The Teacher of Brain-Injured Children.* Syracuse: Syracuse University Press, 1968.

CRUICKSHANK, WILLIAM M., and JOHNSON, G. ORVILLE. *Education of Exceptional Children and Youth.* Englewood Cliffs, N.J.: Prentice-Hall, 1958.

DEAN, MARTIN J. "Some Major Issues in Special Education in Large Cities." *Thrust for Education Leadership* 2 (May 1973).

HEWETT, FRANK M. "Educational Engineering with Emotionally Disturbed Children." *Exceptional Children* (January 1967).

JONES, REGINALD L., ed. *New Directions in Special Education.* Boston: Allyn and Bacon, 1970.

MACKIE, ROMAINE P. "Special Education Reaches Nearly 2 Million Children." *School Life* 47 (December 1964).

MACKIE, ROMAINE P.; DUNN, LLOYD M.; and CAIN, LEO F. *Professional Preparation for Teachers of Exceptional Children: An Overview.* U.S. Office of Education, Bulletin No. 6. Washington, D.C.: U.S. Government Printing Office, 1959.

MAYO, LEONARD. *We Serve the Exceptional Child.* Los Angeles: Los Angeles City Schools, Special Education Branch.

MAYS, MAXINE. "No Stars Please, for Teaching the Retarded." *Today's Education* 61 (March 1972).

MURPHY, BETTY A. "You Can't Mainstream Them All." *NAESP Convention Reporter.* Detroit: April 1973.

ROSENTHAL, ROBERT, and JACOBSON, LENORE. *Pygmalion in the Classroom.* New York: Holt, Rinehart, and Winston, 1968.

UNITED STATES DEPARTMENT OF HEALTH, EDUCATION, AND WELFARE, OFFICE OF EDUCATION. *Minimal Brain Dysfunction in Children.* Prepared by Sam D. Clements. Monograph No. 3. Washington, D.C.: National Institute of Neurological Diseases and Blindness, 1966.

20

Early Childhood Education

"Early childhood education" is a term increasingly utilized by schools and parent groups, despite a great deal of confusion concerning its clear definition. James L. Hymes characterizes early childhood as a period of high dependency when the child himself feels young, when he feels small, and when he feels like a child. Usually, it is described as that period from birth to the onset of preadolescence around age eight or nine.[1]

With the advent of Head Start in 1965 came a new focus on early childhood education programs involving nursery schools, day care centers, and parent participation programs, many of which had been in existence for decades. Now, as we look toward the mid-1970s, early childhood education programs are still in demand, but many are experiencing financial difficulties that threaten their existence or expansion.

Hundreds of early childhood education programs are in existence under the auspices of diverse funding agencies and groups. It is hoped that those that are described in this chapter will provide insight into the profession of early childhood education.

This chapter includes a discussion of the following topics:

Goals for Early Childhood Education
Major Early Childhood Education Programs
Administration of Early Childhood Education Programs
Early Childhood Education Research and Evaluation
Summary
Trends

Material for this chapter was prepared in collaboration with Othella E. Daniels, Administrator, Children's Center and Pre-School Education, Los Angeles Unified School District.
[1] James L. Hymes, Jr., *Early Childhood Education*, p. 5.

Goals for Early Childhood Education

Early childhood education programs that are more than merely custodial in purpose embrace goals such as the following:

1. Enhancing each child's physical, psychosocial, and cognitive development by:
   a. Facilitating the child's development of communication skills
   b. Promoting the development of a sense of self-worth and well-being within each child
   c. Encouraging the child to experience a varied social environment

2. Involving parents in the education process by:
   a. Enumerating ways parents can help their children
   b. Suggesting alternative ways of rearing children and coping with problems
   c. Reassuring parents that they can understand and facilitate the physical, psychosocial, and cognitive development of their children
   d. Forming parent advisory committees as vehicles for parent participation in planning, development, operation, and evaluation of programs
   e. Assisting parents in the continuation of their self-development and education
   f. Providing opportunities for parents to develop appropriate ways and means of improving existing institutions

3. Demonstrating methods for developing similar programs by:
   a. Setting up model programs
   b. Training and utilizing volunteer personnel
   c. Developing effective articulation of early childhood education programs with other educational and community agencies[2]

Major Early Childhood Education Programs

A clear picture of early childhood education is produced by beginning with a look at preschool programs, progressing in sequence as the child moves through kindergarten and the primary grades. Many programs overlap, adding to the complexity of describing a logical sequence based on age. Nevertheless, an attempt will be made to discuss programs on a chronological basis.

---

[2] California State Department of Education, *Guidelines for Compensatory Preschool Educational Programs*, pp. 1–3.

Although the span in a child's life from birth through age eight or nine is commonly considered to be the early childhood period, attention given to infant programs in this discussion will be minimal for two reasons. First, the number of programs for infants is very limited; and second, from the standpoint of school administration, provision of programs and services for infants is not a major consideration. The American Academy of Pediatrics Committee on Infant and Preschool Children has published a set of day care standards for children younger than three. This pamphlet states that the primary purpose of such programs for infants and very young children is to provide a sound basis for learning and to encourage the mother in her efforts to care for her child.[3] Most programs for infants and children younger than three are sponsored by health or social service agencies.

HEAD START.   Project Head Start began as a summer project in July 1965 primarily funded by the U.S. Office of Economic Opportunity as a part of the war on poverty. Its purpose was to give a "head start" to poor children to ensure their success, instead of failure, when they entered school. (It is permissible for ten percent of the children in Head Start to come from families with incomes above the poverty line, however.)

Head Start programs are administered at the local level by public school systems, private schools, churches, Community Action Agencies, or local private organizations. Local communities are required to contribute ten percent of the cost, usually accomplished by means of in-kind services in lieu of cash.

When Head Start began in July of 1965, it was a summer program that operated six to eight weeks prior to the opening of regular school. Eligible children about to enter school enrolled in Head Start at age four if school began with kindergarten and at age five if school began with first grade. About half a million children were enrolled each summer in 1965, 1966, and 1967, totaling approximately 1,500,000 youngsters.

Summer Head Start proved to be too short a period to achieve desired results. It was determined, therefore, that in addition to the summer program a year-round program should be added. Funding constraints required a reduction in the number of children served in the summer program to accommodate the extended period of operation. With more

---

[3] American Academy of Pediatrics, Committee on Infant and Preschool Child, *Standards for Day Care Centers for Infants and Children Under 3 Years of Age,* preface.

money available for the year-round program, the enrollment increased from 20,000 children in 1965–66 to 190,000 children in 1967–68. Fifteen children comprise the maximum Head Start group size. A trained head teacher, a paid aide, and volunteers work together as a team providing a multi-disciplinary approach and at least a one-to-five adult–child ratio.

What is the philosophy of Head Start? Head Start groups are designated Child Development Centers symbolizing commitment to the development of the whole child—to his physical, emotional, social, and intellectual growth. The well-being of the family is also a part of this comprehensive goal because of the realization that a child's success cannot be isolated from his family relationships. Parent involvement is an important aspect of the program. Parents meet, observe their children, and assist in the program in meaningful ways. Teachers visit parents at home with a view toward making home and school supplement each other for the child's benefit.[4]

TITLE I PRESCHOOL. Title I of the Elementary and Secondary Education Act of 1965 (Public Law 89–10) made funds available to public school districts and permitted the financing of compensatory preschool education as a part of a comprehensive plan for compensatory education. It requires that programs serve children from families meeting established criteria relating to economic deprivation; it also applies to children from families of low incomes where English is not the primary language spoken. An essential difference between Head Start and ESEA Title I preschool programs is that Title I funds are available only to public school districts.

With regard to class size, there must be one qualified teacher for every fifteen children. Assistants and volunteers, including parents of the children enrolled, reduce the adult–child ratio to one to five as is the case in Head Start programs. Eligible children must have passed their third birthday and not be chronologically eligible to enter regular school.

The major components of Title I preschools and Head Start groups are very similar. Activities and experiences are designed to facilitate development of the whole child. The curriculum usually emphasizes language development, perceptual training and cognitive learning, creative exploration and enrichment activities, social development, and physical development. Health and nutrition services and parent involvement and participation are also considered essential.

---

4 Hymes, *Early Childhood,* p. 11.

Higher certification standards for teachers are often required in Title I (ESEA) preschools, or pre-kindergartens as they are often called. Such classes operated by school districts are usually housed in elementary school classrooms.

CALIFORNIA STATE PRESCHOOL PROGRAM. By authority of the California Legislature in 1965, the State Department of Social Welfare and the State Department of Education entered into a contract to provide preschool education for children of former, current, or potential welfare recipients. This law is peculiar to California but provides an example of what a state can do.

Although funding sources may differ, the required components for most preschool programs are very similar in nature, emphasizing a comprehensive approach that focuses on the development of the whole child.

KINDERGARTEN PROGRAMS. Kindergartens, both public and private, have been in existence in the United States for more than 100 years. Of the fifty states, however, twenty-nine provide full or partial state aid for kindergarten and twenty-one do not. Only sixty percent of our five-year-olds are in school.

Preschool programs have had and are continuing to have a significant impact upon kindergarten programs. The encouragement of articulation of preschools and kindergartens often has necessitated revisions of kindergarten program content and development of provisions for appropriate learning environments for children with a preschool experience.

Contrasted with preschool groups of fifteen, the kindergarten class size in most states is twenty and in some cases close to thirty children per teacher. Paraprofessionals assist teachers in some kindergarten classrooms, usually in schools where federal funding is available.

KINDERGARTEN–PRIMARY PROGRAMS. Children in the 5- to 8- or 9-age range are participating in programs utilizing various teaching strategies, including but not limited to the self-contained classroom, team teaching arrangements, or multi-age grouping situations.

Perhaps the California Early Childhood Education Plan proposed by the State Superintendent of Public Instruction of California, Dr. Wilson C. Riles, passed by the state legislature, and signed into law in 1972, can best describe a fresh approach to kindergarten–primary education. The purpose of the proposal was to redesign and revitalize early childhood education in

California. For the first year (1973–74), 12 percent of the kinder-garten–primary children in the state participated. The California State Leg-islature appropriated $25,000,000 for the first year and $40,000,000 for the second year. This state aid will make it possible for school districts to provide a personalized approach to primary education by effecting changes such as:

1. Providing small-group and individual instruction.
2. Encouraging greater parent participation in the educational process.
3. Strengthening the family through a closer home–school partnership.
4. Utilizing more adults in the classroom (paid aides, parents, grandpar-ents, other volunteers) to reduce adult–child ratios and to assist the teacher in providing personal help for each child.
5. Affording opportunities for children at various age levels to engage in learning activities together.
6. Encouraging bi-lingual children to strengthen their primary language while developing competency in English.

Participating school districts, in cooperation with parent and com-munity groups, develop a master plan for early childhood education designed to meet the unique needs of the communities involved. Nine factors considered by the California State Department of Education in approving a district's plan are:

1. Needs assessment
2. Goals and objectives
3. Individualization of instruction
4. Staff development
5. Parent–community involvement
6. Auxiliary services
7. Evaluation
8. Coordination and continuity of resources
9. Initiation of program

It is expected that all public schools in the state of California will be phased into the Early Childhood Education Plan over a five-year period.

FOLLOW THROUGH. The Follow Through program is funded by the U.S. Office of Economic Opportunity and administered by the U.S. Office of

Education.   It began in 1967–68 in thirty pilot school systems throughout the country.   The program was designed to continue the enriching learning experiences preschool children in first grade had received in Head Start and other preschools.   Follow Through spans kindergarten through third grade. Adult–pupil ratios of about 1 to 7 are achieved with a maximum of 20 children to a class and utilization of paid aides and volunteers to assist the certificated teacher.[5]

The Follow Through program emphasizes instruction, nutrition, health, social work, psychological services, and staff development.   Serving children from low-income families, this program allocates additional funding to school districts enabling them to provide:

1.   Counseling for both children and their parents.
2.   Services to meet the medical, dental, psychosocial and nutritional needs of the children.
3.   Instruction by teachers and aides trained in accordance with the approach to child learning and development selected by the community.
4.   Involvement and participation of the parents of children enrolled in development, operation, and overall direction of the program.

Under the Follow Through design, maximum effort is expended in bringing together the school, the family, the neighborhood, and the community.

Since 1967, Follow Through has served over 78,000 children, eighty percent from low-income families.   In approximately 4,000 Follow Through classrooms about 7,400 paraprofessionals are employed as classroom aides, most of whom are parents of children enrolled in the program.[6]

DAY CARE CENTERS.   Day care center education is one of the most important but least understood facets of early childhood education.   Child care centers, day nurseries, or day care centers are terms often used interchangeably to describe a program that has been in existence to some degree for a long time.[7]   In recent decades the employment of mothers, like the employment of all women, has been steadily rising, underscoring the need for expansion of child care services.   Statistics from the U.S. Department

        [5] Hymes, *Early Childhood*, pp. 15–16.
        [6] U.S. Department of Health, Education and Welfare, Office of Education, *A Mini-Guide to Follow Through.*
        [7] Hymes, *Early Childhood*, p. 22.

of Health, Education and Welfare reveal the following significant facts: In 1940, the number of women in the labor force was 13.8 million; in 1972, it rose to 32.9 million. The number of working mothers with children under 18 years of age in 1940 was 1.5 million; it was 12.7 million in 1972.[8] From 1940 to 1972, the number of women in the labor force more than doubled and the number of working mothers increased more than eightfold. According to projections, the number of mothers between the ages of 20 and 44 with young children under age 5 who will be working will increase from 4.4 million in 1972 to 6.6 million in 1985. Although several million children need child care services, it is estimated that care in licensed centers and family homes is available for only about 905,000 children.

Although various kinds of facilities and groupings exist for child care purposes, the group day care center arrangement will serve to describe the nature of the program. In contrast to Head Start, kindergartens, and nursery schools, day care centers are usually open a full day rather than a half day. Most of the children in the centers are from families with working mothers, requiring the day care center to be open while the mother is at work. In most cases, this would necessitate centers to be operating from six or seven o'clock in the morning to about six o'clock in the evening.

The quality of the day care center program varies widely with its source of funding which is, as might be expected, the major variable. For the most part, children served in day care centers are from poor families with mothers working because they must. Private or public subsidies are essential to supplement fees paid by parents for the operation of a good program. Day care centers forced to operate without benefit of subsidies can offer little more than custodial care. The child in this situation obviously suffers from a lack of individual attention and stimulation.

Tax support for day care education appears to be the only viable solution to the serious problem of lack of adequate funds to operate existing programs or to expand facilities and programs to meet the growing need.

During World War II, over 100,000 children of mothers working in essential, war-related jobs attended federally subsidized child care centers.

---

[8] Women's Bureau, Employment Standards Administration, *Day Care Facts,* pp. v; 1–2.

These centers, known as the Lanham Child Care Centers, were discontinued after the war.

CALIFORNIA'S CHILDREN'S CENTERS. In California, the state legislature voted to continue funds for child care centers although federal funds previously had been withdrawn. Although this description is peculiar to California, it explains how a state can handle children's center programs. California law specified that the centers were to be administered and operated by the governing boards of school districts. Centers were opened on or near school sites. In 1965, the California Legislature changed the name "Child Care Centers" to "Children's Centers." The intent of the centers was also changed from "provision of care and supervision" to "provision of supervision and instruction." More than 24,000 children between two and fourteen years of age are enrolled in approximately 400 such centers operated by about 80 California school districts.

As an example of what a large city can do, the Los Angeles Unified School District established seventy-six Children's Centers in 1973 for children of parents who must be out of the home all or part of every day. Financial support comes from local taxes and parent fees, in addition to state and federal-through-state funding. Federal funds are available pursuant to the 1967 amendments to Title IV of the Social Security Act.

All of the Los Angeles Children's Centers are located on or near elementary school sites. Most of the centers have a combined program for preschool and school-aged children. The school-aged program is usually referred to as the "Extended-Day Program," meaning that children are in school during regular school hours and attend the Children's Center before and/or after school.

Curriculum has been developed for multi-age grouping with open-ended learning tailored to the individual abilities of the children. Equipment and learning materials are provided to develop self-direction and self-reliance in learning centers. Nutritious meals, excursions, and opportunities for rest or sleep also are important parts of the program.

PRIVATE NURSERY SCHOOLS. The first nursery schools were started in this country around 1918 or 1919. For more than half a century, parents who could afford it wanted nursery education for their three- and four-year-old children.

Private nursery schools may be categorized generally as:

Private-for-profit nursery schools
Private nonprofit nursery schools
University schools
Church-sponsored weekday nursery schools
Cooperative nursery schools

COOPERATIVE NURSERY SCHOOLS.   The Cooperative Nursery School (often called a "co-op") is an interesting type of school for discussion purposes. It represents a plan for keeping tuition reasonable, and at the same time provides additional benefits.   One trained teacher is paid from tuition fees collected from parents who pay with services as well as cash.   Parents as staff members work as assistant teachers, secretaries, nurses, equipment repair people, grounds keepers, bus drivers, and purchasing agents.

In addition to reducing tuition fees, total parent participation and involvement encourages support and reinforcement for the program and for the children.   Use of parent skills promotes enriched classes, individualized education, and exciting programs.

Not only do parents give, but they benefit through a better understanding of their own children and the processes of learning in which their children are involved.   Parent–teacher education becomes mutually beneficial as parents and teachers observe, plan, confer, and discuss the ongoing program.   A good cooperative nursery school helps parents gain a great deal of insight into their children's development.

PUBLIC NURSERY SCHOOLS.   Public funds are available in a number of states to provide nursery schools for cerebral-palsied children, crippled children, hard-of-hearing youngsters, children with a vision loss, and mentally retarded or emotionally disturbed children.

State funds for special education in California schools, for example, can be supplemented by local taxes to construct facilities known as Development Centers for Handicapped Pupils, serving children at least three years of age with special problems.

Nursery schools for exceptional children emphasize social living, exploration of the world around, freedom to explore, and the value of allowing youngsters to do as much for themselves as possible.[9]

----

[9] Hymes, *Early Childhood*, pp. 28–37.

Administration of
Early Childhood Education Programs

A discussion of the administration of early childhood education programs must of necessity be general in nature and broad in scope. The myriad of programs, both public and private and operating under the all-inclusive term, "early childhood education," precludes an in-depth review of legal mandates, funding sources, and other considerations related to a specific program. An effort will be made to delineate certain important steps that should be taken to administer effectively any early childhood education program.

LEGAL REQUIREMENTS. Most states have a licensing law administered by the state health, welfare, or educational agency. The purpose of such a law is to ensure the health and safety of children. Covered in its requirements are standards relating to the type and location of building used, the amount of space required for indoor and outdoor activities, the provision of a safe staff–pupil ratio, training and certification of teachers, nutritious meals, and health and safety regulations. It is not unusual for federal, state, and local requirements to apply particularly to programs with multiple funding.

SITES AND FACILITIES. Local zoning ordinances often have an impact upon the location of facilities. It is advantageous to consider selecting sites and facilities near homes of the children served unless transportation is provided. Locating facilities on streets where public transportation is available is another important consideration. It is advisable when considering placement of facilities to study the geography of the community, transportation patterns, locations of schools, business, and industry, and the places of residence of the children to be enrolled. In some cases churches, vacant stores, or large vacant houses are altered to meet requirements; in other cases, land is purchased and new facilities are constructed or elementary school classrooms are used. Some program sponsors rent or lease facilities. All facilities must be in compliance with applicable state and local laws, regulations, and ordinances, including those pertaining to zoning, fire protection and fire safety, building safety, and health.

FUNDING SOURCES. Sources of financial support for early childhood education programs vary. Some programs operate with one funding source and others have many. It is very important to determine which sources of funding are available and how each may be used to assure long-term financing. Some programs are supported totally from tuition or fees. When in-kind services such as facilities, utilities, equipment, and maintenance services are obtained free of charge, parents' fees are reduced. However, adequate financing is necessary if a quality program is to be provided.

Other programs receive some financial support from private donors through United Way, Community Chest, United Givers Fund, or individual donations. Programs that receive more community support serve more families who would otherwise be unable to pay the full cost of the program.

Local, state, and federal funds are sometimes available to finance early childhood education programs. Usually when such funds are granted, low-income families receive priority for enrolling their children. California's Early Childhood Education Program is unique in providing additional state funding for all children participating, regardless of income levels of their parents.

ORGANIZATIONAL STRUCTURE. Early childhood education programs operating within school districts are directed by the board of education through administrative structure approved by the board. Some programs operate under the supervision of a project director for special programs in cooperation with a parent advisory council whose members participate in the planning, organization, and evaluation of the program. Other programs operated by school districts are part of the elementary school and are under the administrative direction of the elementary school principal. The teacher of the early childhood education class is a member of the school staff as are any assigned paraprofessional aides. The parent advisory council for the school should be involved with the early childhood class as well, but the final authority should reside in the board of education.

A community program is usually directed by a group of citizens interested in early childhood education. Membership on the board of directors, in most cases, includes parent representation of the children enrolled. The board has responsibility to the community, the parents of children participating in the program, the staff, and the children themselves. The community expects the board to provide early childhood programs for families and children who need them. Funds are entrusted to the board so that beneficial programs can be provided.

The parents look to the board for needed services. When they enroll their youngsters in the programs, they expect health, educational, and social needs of their children to be met. The staff members expect the board to create sound and workable policies through which they can operate good programs. Most of all, the board is expected to provide for the children the kinds of persons, buildings, equipment, and philosophy that will make their days happy, stimulating, and creative.

STAFFING PRACTICES.   Staff selection and development are, perhaps, the most important elements in a good early childhood education program. The staff creates the environment in which learning takes place and in which each child's needs are identified and, hopefully, fulfilled. It is the staff that develops a partnership with parents to promote the well-being of the children and to make it possible for parents to express their concerns, with the hope of receiving support and assistance in alleviating them.

Staff members should have such personal attributes as dedication, sensitivity, warmth, good health, emotional stability and maturity, patience, and the ability to develop trusting relationships with children and adults. In addition, they should have the knowledge, training, and experience to assume the responsibilities of their positions. The teacher, the aide, the nurse, or any other staff member must observe numerous regulations, policies, and procedures.

Employment conditions have a direct relationship to staff morale, stability, and effectiveness. Effective personnel practices such as the following protect the staff from unnecessary pressures.

1.   Written personnel policies.
2.   Up-to-date job descriptions and staff organizational chart.
3.   Objective hiring practices.
4.   Fair and equitable wages and salaries.
5.   Continuing staff development.
6.   Objective supervision.
7.   Regular, periodic staff evaluation.
8.   Fair resignation and termination procedures.[10]

HEALTH AND MEDICAL SERVICES.   Early childhood education programs must provide for the health of the children enrolled. Practices and

---

[10] U.S. Department of Health, Education and Welfare, Office of Child Development, *Day Care Administration*, pp. 19–23.

procedures must be established to detect illness and physical impairment; to protect children from communicable diseases; to assist parents in arranging for the elimination of correctable impairments; to emphasize positive health practices and preventative medicine; and to provide for immediate medical attention when accidents occur.

Although health programs in the field of early childhood education vary widely, improvement in this area is a dire need in far too many cases. Exemplary health programs go beyond compliance with legal requirements for health and safety. They include parent health education and some provision for assistance to parents of children with health or medical problems. Additionally, they make provisions for staff health and well-being.

As a pre-enrollment requirement, good health programs provide for an assessment of the child's health status which includes:

Report by a licensed physician of a medical history and a physical examination of the child certifying that he is free of communicable disease.
Description of abnormal conditions.
Instructions for staff and a record of immunization against the common childhood diseases.
Report of a dental examination.
Routine blood studies and a urinalysis.

Desirable components in the health curriculum are:

Screening tests to identify hearing, sight, and motor coordination.
A continual immunization program.
Daily health inspections.
Nutritionally balanced meals and snacks.
Nutrition education as a part of the curriculum.
Isolation of ill children.
Dental treatment.
Procedure for coping with accidents and injuries.
Medical insurance plans.

Each staff member should receive copies of health and safety policies and procedures and should be thoroughly familiar with his responsibilities.

It is advisable for all staff members to receive basic training in administering first aid.[11]

PARENT INVOLVEMENT.   Parent involvement begins with parent education, usually conducted within the framework of a parents' group affiliated with the early childhood education program.   As parents are encouraged, they will increase their participation in the planning, organization, and evaluation of the program.

Teachers, supervisors, and administrators should examine every aspect of their work to create opportunities for parent involvement and to incorporate parents' views and recommendations into their plans and practices.   Timing, selection of experiences, and a genuine desire to have parents participate are essential elements of meaningful parent involvement.   Each group of parents has requirements uniquely their own.   With patience, skill, attention to detail, hard work, and wisdom the desired results of a partnership between program personnel and parents will be achieved.

Staff members who really want parent involvement are willing to work, struggle, and wait.   When genuine parent involvement develops, children benefit from the reinforcement at home and school of new, exciting concepts of early childhood education.[12]

Early Childhood Education
Research and Evaluation

The evaluation of early childhood education programs appears to be in a state of transition.   A prevalent tendency to examine and evaluate the process, rather than the product, is beginning to disappear as advanced management and systems technologies become better understood.

An approach to program evaluation gaining recognition and acceptance is one of assessing and measuring results.   This approach looks at the program and attempts to determine its effectiveness and its efficiency. Effectiveness is assessed both quantitatively and qualitatively by determining whether or not the program achieved the results it committed itself to

---

[11] U.S. Department of Health, Education and Welfare, *Day Care Administration,* pp. 69–72.
[12] U.S. Department of Health, Education and Welfare, *Day Care Administration,* pp. 103–105.

achieve within a given period of time. The evaluation determines whether the program achieved few, many, or all of its objectives for the period.

Hundreds of studies and research projects regarding early childhood and the implications for later instruction and schooling have proliferated in the last decade. Shane comments that research is "beginning to form a mosaic of data suggesting that these years of early childhood are more critical than any other stage of human development."[13]

It is not possible in this chapter to do more than mention some of the research that attempts to evaluate early childhood schooling. The interested reader should make a more thorough review of the many studies before making a definite decision as to the effectiveness of any preschool educational program.

RESEARCH SHOWING POSITIVE EFFECTS OF EARLY SCHOOLING. The following paragraphs reveal some of the positive effects of early schooling which have been reported in the research.

A study made by Skeels and Dye in 1939,[14] and completed by Skeels in 1966,[15] followed thirteen experimental children, diagnosed as mentally retarded, who were removed from an overcrowded and unstimulating orphanage and placed in an institution for the mentally retarded where they received "mothering" from older mentally retarded girls. After one and a half years, they had gained 27.5 points in IQ and were placed in foster homes. In 1966, they were functioning as typical middle-class adults, demonstrating the lasting effects of the initial cognitive gains. A contrast group of twelve children with normal intelligence was placed in an orphanage. After two years they showed a drop of 26 points in IQ. Thirty years later, they had long histories of mental institution enrollment, poor employment habits, and poor social adjustment records. The advantage of special attention is clearly indicated in this study.

Hodges and Spicker reviewed selected research in an attempt to determine how successful preschool intervention programs were in ameliorating deficits reported for severely disadvantaged preschoolers. They

---

[13] Harold G. Shane, "The Renaissance of Early Childhood Education," in Robert H. Anderson and Harold G. Shane, *As the Twig Is Bent: Readings in Early Childhood Education*, p. 6.

[14] H. M. Skeels and H. B. Dye, "A Study of the Effects of Differential Stimulation of Children," *Procedures, American Association for the Mentally Deficient* 44 (1939), pp. 114–136.

[15] H. M. Skeels, "Adult Status of Children with Contrasting Early Life Experiences," *Society for Research in Child Development* 31 (1966).

concluded that intellectual functioning can be substantially raised; that language development occurred more readily during preschool years; that fine motor proficiency can be improved; and that "intervention programs especially designed to remedy cognitive deficits during the preschool years and to prevent progressive school failures during the later school years have been relatively effective to date."[16]

Deutsch's experiments indicate that preschool, kindergarten, day-care experience, or a combination of these were associated with higher scores on intelligence tests (in contrast to scores of children without these experiences).[17]

Kirk's study in 1958, in which some children living in the community and in institutions were given one to three years of preschool experience, showed positive effects.[18] The group averaged gains of about 10 points on various intelligence and social maturity measures. Some of them maintained these gains for as long as five years.

Stanley states "that early intervention probably prevents a cumulative deficit—that even keeping children achieving up to [their] initial IQ is a victory for such programs."[19]

Robinson and Robinson draw three tentative conclusions from a study of research which assessed the effects of preschool intervention on culturally deprived children: (1) During the first year, there are relatively large gains on intelligence test scores. (2) The spurt is not maintained in the second year. (3) Control groups tend to gain intelligence points when exposed to stimulating school experiences, reducing the difference between experimental and control subjects.[20] They add that extensive and perhaps irreparable damage to developing cognitive apparatus may be caused by prolonged deprivation of stimulation during the early years. Evidence shows that individuals are proven to be clearly superior in achievement if they have had the benefit of special education programs

---

16 Walter L. Hodges and Howard H. Spicker, "The Effects of Preschool Experiences on Culturally Deprived Children" in Willard W. Hartup and Nancy L. Smothergill (eds.), *The Young Child, Reviews of Research,* pp. 275–287.

17 Martin Deutsch, "The Disadvantaged Child and the Learning Process," in A. H. Passow (ed.), *Education in Depressed Areas,* pp. 163–181.

18 *See* S. A. Kirk, *Early Education of the Mentally Retarded,* pp. 175–202.

19 Julian C. Stanley, "Introduction and Critique," in Julian C. Stanley (ed.), *Compensatory Education for Children, Ages 2 to 8, Recent Studies of Educational Intervention: Proceedings,* p. 6.

20 Halbert B. Robinson and Nancy M. Robinson, "The Problem of Timing in Pre-School Education," in Robert D. Hess and Roberta Meyer Bear (eds.), *Early Education: Current Theory, Research, and Practice,* pp. 42–44.

when they were very young, with the programs continued through their formative years. Some of the studies they reviewed support the idea that the very early years are most important in the development of intelligent behavior.

RESEARCH CLAIMING NEGATIVE ASPECTS OF EARLY SCHOOLING. Moore, Moon, and Moore have made an exhaustive study of research on early schooling covering early and late school entry, neurophysiology and cognition, visual maturity, auditory maturity, maternal deprivation, the mother's attitude, school versus home, parent education, and home schools.[21] Their findings indicate that schooling initiated as early as the age of four or three may have a negative effect and cause possible damage to young children. They conclude that "research and comparisons of school entry ages clearly point to the need (1) to delay any type of educational program that proposes or permits sustained high cortical effort, or strain on the visual or auditory systems, before the child is seven or eight, and for (2) a warm, continuous mother or mother-surrogate relationship (without a succession of different people) until the child is at least seven or eight."[22] They also note that evidence clearly favors the home rather than the school as an early childhood environment.

Stanley reports that careful research by several people has not shown permanent elevation of IQs of disadvantaged children, even after great expenditures of time and effort.[23] Although large gains were common in the first year, they did not persist through the primary grades. He believes that there are limits to the effectiveness of current preschool intervention programs, and that preschool programs cost more per child than more effective teaching (assuming the school system should be restructured).

Numerous problems have been pointed out by various writers regarding research projects on early childhood:

1. The control and experimental groups are not always demonstrably comparable.
2. The Hawthorne effect may influence the results of testing.
3. Some researchers develop tentative hypotheses rather than firm conclusions.
4. Enhanced rapport at the time of testing may give false high scores.

---

[21] Raymond S. Moore, Robert D. Moon, and Dennis R. Moore, "The California Report: Early Schooling for All?" *Phi Delta Kappan,* pp. 615–621.

[22] Moore, Moon, and Moore, "The California Report," pp. 620–621.

[23] Stanley, "Introduction and Critique," pp. 7–8.

5. Errors of measurement may lead to statistical regression toward the mean of the group.
6. The results may lack reliability.
7. The practice effects on testing may influence the results and lead to false conclusions.
8. Test results are sometimes ambiguous.

Despite problems, research does provide suggestions for improved programs and raises questions for further research.

TENTATIVENESS OF RESEARCH ON EARLY CHILDHOOD EDUCATION. Research is inconclusive at the present time on the effectiveness of early childhood education. According to Glick, it is a false premise to interpret IQ changes due to preschool intervention as being fundamental changes in cognitive structure.[24] One must be critical of interpreting the beneficial effects of achievement as a result of preschool intervention until the basic processes underlying achievement are uncovered. Achievement may occur, for example, without any substantive change in the process.

Many questions have been raised by research which still need to be answered. Are we preparing children for immediate progress or ultimate adult success? What is the cause of the progressive drop in IQ points observed in lower-class children when there has been no intervention? What is basically important during the later preschool years? Have children benefited to the greatest possible extent from programs designed to remedy deficiencies?

Since most research has focused on specific behavioral areas, assessment of creative adaptability is still needed. A vast amount of information about early childhood and the effects of experience and schooling is still outstanding, indicating that more basic research is needed. Research needs to be more coordinated and its efforts and findings shared.

Evaluation and research should not overlook or diminish human values. It is incumbent upon those involved in early childhood education programs to begin to prepare for the more precise, product-oriented evaluation systems that are rapidly becoming a part of management practice for programs designed for young children.[25]

---

24 Joseph Glick, "Some Problems in the Evaluation of Pre-School Intervention Programs," in Robert D. Hess and Roberta Meyer Bear (eds.), *Early Education: Current Theory, Research, and Practice*, pp. 217–219.

25 U.S. Department of Health, Education and Welfare, *Day Care Administration*, p. 49.

Summary

Early childhood education applies to that period in a child's life spanning birth to about age eight or nine. Goals for early childhood education programs focus upon enhancing total development, facilitating communication skills, promoting the development of self-worth, encouraging social experiences, and involving parents in the education process.

The following major early childhood education programs operating in the United States are described in this chapter.

HEAD START. This program began in the summer of 1965 as a part of the war on poverty and was designed to give a "head start" to poor children in kindergarten or first grade before entry into regular school programs. Head Start is characterized by a 15-to-1 pupil–teacher ratio and the use of aides and volunteers.

TITLE I PRESCHOOL. ESEA Title I preschool programs are distinguished from Head Start primarily on the basis of funding differences, Title I funds being available only to public school districts. A review of the program components highlighted similarities of public preschool programs despite differences in funding sources.

CALIFORNIA STATE PRESCHOOL PROGRAM. Mentioned briefly because of its unique arrangement, this program requires a contract between the State Department of Social Welfare and the State Department of Education for the purpose of providing preschool education for children of welfare recipients.

KINDERGARTEN PROGRAMS. These programs are described as either public or private. Although kindergartens began over 100 years ago, only twenty-nine of the fifty states provide full or partial funding to support them. The impact of preschool programs upon kindergartens and the encouragement of program articulation between the two levels are recent developments.

KINDERGARTEN–PRIMARY PROGRAMS. Discussed primarily in terms of a description of the Early Childhood Education Plan in California, the purpose of this program is to redesign and revitalize early childhood education, with emphasis upon smaller class size, a personalized approach to primary education, use of more adults in the classroom, and the encouragement of bi-lingual, bi-cultural education.

FOLLOW THROUGH.   Funded by the U.S. Office of Economic Opportunity, this program is designed to build upon experiences preschool children have received in Head Start programs.

DAY CARE CENTERS.   These centers are the result of the growing need for child care services due to the increasing number of working mothers.   A description of the California Children's Center program reveals that multiple sources of funding—federal, state, and local—improve program quality and enable communities to build needed facilities.   Lack of funding is a major problem for this program.

PRIVATE NURSERY SCHOOLS.   These schools include private-for-profit, private nonprofit, university, church-sponsored, and cooperative nursery schools.   Parents are involved in the cooperative nursery school.

PUBLIC NURSERY SCHOOLS.   These schools were developed for exceptional children—the blind, hard-of-hearing, cerebral-palsied, and emotionally disturbed.
     The administration of early childhood education focuses upon the significant areas of: legal requirements, sites and facilities, funding sources, organizational structure, staffing practices, health and medical services, parent involvement, and evaluation.   Each area serves to delineate important steps that should be taken in order to administer effectively any early childhood education program. Tentative research is reviewed, showing both positive and negative effects of early childhood education.

Trends

This chapter attempts to present an overview of the major early childhood education programs and to offer some ideas for the effective administration of such programs.   Although early childhood education is not new, new directions seem to be emerging.

TOWARD LESS FEDERAL AND MORE STATE AND LOCAL FUNDING.
Changes in federal regulations will require states and cities to set priorities
for funding programs utilizing general rather than categorical aid.

TOWARD MORE INVOLVEMENT OF ADULTS IN THE EDUCATION PROCESS.
There will be an increase in the involvement of aides and volunteers who
will assist in reducing adult–child ratios. In some cases, older children will
assist.

TOWARD PROFESSIONALIZATION OF EARLY CHILDHOOD EDUCATION.
There will be an upgrading of professional requirements for early childhood teachers and maintenance of the concept of upward mobility. This
will promote a higher regard for this field of education.

TOWARD THE PROVISION OF DAY CARE CENTERS BY INDUSTRIES. Business and industry will provide day care centers for children of employees.
Absenteeism will be reduced when parents know that their children are
being taken care of properly.

TOWARD DAY CARE CENTERS IN TRACT HOUSING DEVELOPMENTS. It
may become a legal requirement for a tract contractor to include day care
centers before he is given the authority to develop a tract. Day care
centers should be an incentive for people to purchase homes in the tract.

TOWARD MORE INVOLVEMENT OF SCHOOL DISTRICTS IN EARLY CHILD-
HOOD EDUCATION PROGRAMS. California's Early Childhood Education
plan is giving impetus to the idea of providing pre-kindergarten classes on
an optional basis. Other states may pattern their programs after this plan.
As the idea spreads, all pre-kindergarten children will benefit.

Administrative Problems   In Basket

Problem 1

The rural Fort Tejon School District has kindergarten classes in each of its six
elementary schools, but no preschool program. Many of the families are
Mexican-American who speak little or no English in the home. Children entering school have bi-lingual problems, complicating their education. Because of

low incomes, many mothers work in the fields. The Board of Education is concerned and has heard that several kinds of preschool programs are available that could help prepare children for formal schooling. The superintendent has asked the assistant superintendent for educational services to investigate preschool programs and prepare a recommendation for the Board.

How should the assistant superintendent proceed?
What recommendation should he make?
What control should the school district exercise over the preschool program if it is approved?

Problem 2

Assume the same situation as in Problem 1. A decision has been made to commence a preschool program under Title I of the Elementary and Secondary Education Act.

How should the assistant superintendent proceed in seeking the federal funds?
How can he go about locating teachers and volunteer aides in his rural area?
What paraprofessional qualifications should he look for?
What preservice and inservice programs should he provide?
Where might the assistant superintendent establish the classes? What information would he need?
What equipment, facilities, and supplies will be needed?
What procedure can he use to enroll the children?
What should be the essentials of the curriculum?

Selected References

ALMY, MILLIE. "Spontaneous Play: An Avenue for Intellectual Development." In J. L. Frost, ed. *Early Childhood Education Rediscovered*. New York: Holt, Rinehart and Winston, 1968.

American Academy of Pediatrics, Committee on Infant and Preschool Child. *Standards for Day Care Centers for Infants and Children Under 3 Years of Age*. Evanston, Ill., 1971.

BISSELL, JOAN. *Implementation of Planned Variation in Head Start*. Washington, D.C.: National Institute of Child Health and Human Development, April 1971.

DEUTSCH, MARTIN. "The Disadvantaged Child and the Learning Process." In A. H. Passow, ed. *Education in Depressed Areas*. New York: Teachers College, Columbia University, 1963.

DUCKWORTH, ELEANOR. "Piaget Rediscovered." In Ronald G. Good, ed. *Science Children: Readings in Elementary Science Education*. Dubuque, Iowa: Wm. C. Brown, 1972.

EVANS, ELLIS. *Contemporary Influences in Early Childhood Education.* New York: Holt, Rinehart and Winston, 1971.

GLICK, JOSEPH. "Some Problems in the Evaluation of Pre-School Intervention Programs." In Robert D. Hess and Roberta Meyer Bear, eds. *Early Education: Current Theory, Research, and Practice.* Chicago: Social Science Research Council, 1968.

HODGES, WALTER L., and SPICKER, HOWARD H. "The Effects of Preschool Experiences on Culturally Deprived Children." In Willard W. Hartup and Nancy L. Smothergill, eds. *The Young Child, Reviews of Research.* Washington, D.C.: National Association for the Education of Young Children, 1970.

HOOPER, FRANK. "An Evaluation of Logical Operation Instruction in the Preschool." In Ronald K. Parker, ed. *The Preschool in Action: Exploring Early Childhood.* Boston: Allyn and Bacon, 1972.

HYMES, JAMES L., JR. *Early Childhood Education.* Washington, D.C.: National Association for the Education of Young Children, 1968.

KIRK, S. A. *Early Education of the Mentally Retarded.* Urbana, Illinois: University of Illinois Press, 1958.

KOHLBERG, LAWRENCE. "Early Education: A Cognitive-Developmental View." *Child Development* 39 (December 1968).

LAVATELLI, CELIA STENDLER. "A Piaget-Derived Model for Compensatory Pre-School Education." In J. L. Frost, ed. *Early Childhood Education Rediscovered.* New York: Holt, Rinehart and Winston, 1968.

MAYER, ROCHELLE S. "A Comparative Analysis of Preschool Curriculum." In R. H. Anderson and H. G. Shane, eds. *As the Twig Is Bent: Readings in Early Childhood Education.* Boston: Houghton Mifflin Co., 1971.

MOORE, RAYMOND S., MOON, ROBERT D., and MOORE, DENNIS R. "The California Report: Early Schooling for All?" *Phi Delta Kappan* 53 (June 1972).

ROBINSON, HALBERT B., and ROBINSON, NANCY M. "The Problem of Timing in Pre-School Education." In Robert D. Hess and Roberta Meyer Bear, eds. *Early Education: Current Theory, Research, and Practice.* Chicago: Social Science Research Council, 1968.

SHANE, HAROLD G. "The Rennaissance of Early Childhood Education." In Robert H. Anderson and Harold G. Shane, eds. *As the Twig Is Bent: Readings in Early Childhood Education.* Boston: Houghton Mifflin Co., 1971.

SMART, MARGARET. "What Piaget Suggests to Classroom Teachers." *Childhood Education* 44 (January 1968).

SONQUIST, H., and KAMII, C. "Applying Some Piagetian Concepts in the Classroom for the Disadvantaged." In J. L. Frost, ed. *Early Childhood Education Rediscovered.* New York: Holt, Rinehart, and Winston, 1968.

STANLEY, JULIAN C. "Introduction and Critique." In Stanley, Julian C., ed. *Compensatory Education for Children, Ages 2 to 8, Recent Studies of Edu-*

cational Intervention: Proceedings. 2nd ed. Hyman Blumberg Symposium on Research in Early Childhood Education. Baltimore: Johns Hopkins University Press, 1973.

State Department of Education. *Guidelines for Compensatory Pre-school Educational Programs.* Sacramento, California: State Printing Office, 1972.

U.S. Department of Health, Education, and Welfare, Office of Education. *A Mini-Guide to Follow Through.* Washington, D.C.: U.S. Government Printing Office, June 1972.

U.S. Department of Health, Education, and Welfare, Office of Child Development. *Day Care Administration.* Washington, D.C.: U.S. Government Printing Office, 1971.

WADSWORTH, BARRY. *Piaget's Theory of Cognitive Development.* New York: David McKay, 1971.

Women's Bureau, Employment Standards Administration. *Day Care Facts.* U.S. Department of Labor Pamphlet 16, rev. Washington, D.C.: U.S. Government Printing Office, 1973.

PART SIX

School Personnel Administration

21

Administration of Pupil Personnel

Pupil personnel services encompass non-instructional activities that affect the school lives of students. They supplement regular classroom instruction and assist the teacher in understanding and helping students. Services such as the following should be provided by school districts: guidance and counseling, health, psychological, pupil welfare, testing, social work, exceptional child or special education, clinical, child study or case study, and speech, hearing, and visual therapy. Large districts are able to provide more of these services than small districts.

This chapter includes a discussion of the following topics:

Organization of Pupil Personnel Services
Enrollment of Students
Administering Child Welfare and Attendance
Guidance Services
Control of Behavior
Progress Reporting
Pupil Personnel Reports and Records
Summary
Trends

Organization of Pupil Personnel Services

Most school districts provide pupil personnel services. However, they often have been uncoordinated or distributed among several departments or individual schools. A recent trend toward centralizing these services in a single pupil personnel department, headed by an administrator responsible for their coordination, is discerned.

Teachers for too long have been expected to help the atypical student alone. Two or three such students take an inordinate amount of the teacher's time, depriving the rest of the class of the instruction. If a teacher wants extra help, he might have to contact several different district departments. But when the district has a centralized pupil personnel division, a single referral can provide the assistance of several specialists working together to solve a problem.

Figure 21–1 shows a type of organization for a pupil personnel department appropriate in a large school district. It is recommended that the department be administered by an assistant superintendent responsible solely to the superintendent. Various department functions should be considered services and should be headed up by lower level administrators or directors.[1] All services would have the purpose of helping to solve student problems, and maximizing benefits of the educational program. Although most districts provide these types of services, their organization varies and they may even function independently.

Especially large schools (usually secondary) may have specialists assigned to them. Even then, they may need assistance from central office personnel. Smaller districts may not be able to afford the separate services indicated in Figure 21–1; it may be necessary for them to combine or rearrange them. A head counselor, for example, may be given responsibility for guidance and counseling. Counselors, nurses, or other specialists may be assigned on a roving basis to serve several schools. Psychologists may be employed on a per case basis. An assistant principal may handle attendance functions. County health departments often provide needed health services. Several small districts may cooperatively employ specialists to work with student personnel on a shared basis or to utilize the services of governmental agencies or intermediate (county) offices of education.

Whatever arrangement is developed, it is necessary to have one district administrator, possibly the superintendent in a very small district, responsible for all pupil personnel services. No plan will work unless clearly understood policies and administrative procedures are developed. These should explain lines of communication and levels of responsibility. Counselors and other specialists may be assigned to a specific school, work on a roving basis, or be scheduled from the central office. A principal is considered responsible for all activities that go on in his school.

---

[1] Emery Stoops (ed.), *Guidance Services: Organization and Administration.*

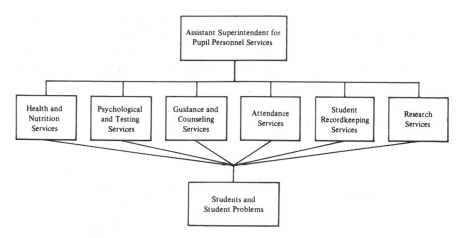

FIGURE 21–1. Organization of a Pupil Personnel Department in a Large District.

On the other hand, districts that have centralized pupil personnel services may assign specialists to schools and be responsible for them. It is absolutely necessary that policies cover these situations or conflicts, or confusion and disagreements will result. The best policy would delegate responsibility to the principal for all people assigned to his school for services rendered in his school, even though they are scheduled from the central office. However, procedures, reports, coordination, inservice training, and district meetings can be handled by the central office. If understanding, rapport, and cooperation are properly established, there should be fewer problems.

HEAD OF PUPIL PERSONNEL SERVICES. If districts are large enough, the administrator in charge of pupil personnel services should be an assistant superintendent. This is both a line and a staff position. It is a line position in organization because the administrator must make decisions and be responsible for specialists who work out of his office; he himself is responsible to the superintendent. It is a staff position in that he must work cooperatively with teachers and school administrators and share his decision making with others. He also should work closely with the head of the instructional services in a staff relationship.

The pupil personnel administrator has many responsibilities and functions aimed at the well-being of students. Some of these are:

1. Maintaining student records: student progress, test data, family histories, psychological studies, educational histories, etc.
2. Dispensing information to colleges and universities, other school districts, welfare agencies, governmental agencies, military services, employment offices, courts, and corrective institutions.
3. Supervising and coordinating the work of specialists.
4. Administering the testing program.
5. Supervising health services.
6. Supervising psychological services.
7. Coordinating guidance and counseling services.
8. Administering procedures for enrolling and transferring students and establishing boundaries for attendance areas.
9. Supervising attendance.
10. Administering assignment to special classes, such as: mentally retarded, physically handicapped, emotionally handicapped, and continuation classes.
11. Conducting research and compiling research reports.
12. Advising school administrators, teachers, and parents.[2]

There is no definite pattern in the number of functions handled by pupil personnel offices. The philosophy of the district administration and the school board, and the district size, determine the organizational pattern. A single administrator cannot handle these numerous functions without the help of others. However, an assistant superintendent could have responsibility for supervising necessary specialists, services, and clerks, and for coordinating their activities. Although many of the functions may be carried out within individual schools, it is wise to have the district administrator unify and coordinate these functions and activities to promote similarity among district schools. Records should be forwarded to the central office when a student leaves the district. They should be microfilmed there to ensure a permanent record of all students. There are numerous occasions, often years later, when requests are made for information about a student and the district record may be the only legal or official information available.

QUALIFICATIONS OF THE PUPIL PERSONNEL ADMINISTRATOR. The pupil personnel administrator's office is responsible for aiding students in their

---

[2] Edwin A. Fensch and Robert E. Wilson, *The Superintendency Team,* pp. 184–200.

personal, social, and academic development and for "providing a sound basis on which to build learning skills and to absorb and retain facts and understandings."[3]

States vary in their requirements for a pupil personnel administrator. Some have special pupil personnel credentials while others require administration and supervisory credentials and experience.[4] Specific course work is sometimes required.

Pupil personnel administrators should be, first of all, administrators rather than specialists in psychology, counseling, or guidance. They should be well grounded in classroom procedures and understand the learning obstacles facing many students; possess the personality to relate successfully with teachers, administrators, and parents; have a knowledge of community social, welfare, and health agencies and the ability to work cooperatively with them. Since the administrator will often be called upon to speak before community organizations, he should have the ability to speak effectively and to interpret the school's program.

Many districts lack the personnel and finances to provide all needed services, requiring an ability to plan programs carefully with limited resources. The ability to make decisions is also essential because the future educational achievement of students is dependent upon the right decision.

The ability to coordinate is one of the most important qualifications of the pupil personnel administrator. The administrator must have the respect of specialists and skill in human relations. The American Association of School Administrators has stated that "the coordinating function involves not only bringing into appropriate relationships the people who comprise the pupil personnel departments, but also, and more importantly, fostering relationships between these pupil service workers and other personnel in the school system."[5]

Another major qualification for the pupil personnel administrator is the ability to evaluate programs, services, and personnel in the pupil personnel department. Administrators should be able to change their course of action, revise programs, or eliminate inefficient personnel. The value of pupil personnel services is determined when the administrator demonstrates that the education of students with problems or handicaps is being

---

[3] Fensch and Wilson, *The Superintendency Team,* p. 184.

[4] American Association of School Administrators, *Profiles of the Administrative Team,* pp. 114–115.

[5] American Association of School Administrators, *Profiles,* pp. 105–106.

improved. His emphasis should be on prevention rather than remediation; this is dependent upon identifying problems before they become acute.

The pupil personnel administrator should study areas such as psychology, methods of evaluating pupil progress, the dynamics of behavior, educational statistics, theory of measurement, research design, education of exceptional children, education of handicapped children, and guidance and counseling techniques. Courses should be taken in school law, school finance, administration, supervision, and public relations. Actual experience in some area of pupil personnel such as teaching the handicapped, guidance, counseling, or testing is desirable. It should be reiterated, however, that the ability to administer, plan, make decisions, and coordinate are the most important qualifications.

Enrollment of Students

Prior to actual enrollment, it is necessary for the school district to estimate the number of students it will be educating. This is often difficult to do and there is no method that is completely accurate. The office responsible for attendance accounting should also be responsible for maintaining the census.

SCHOOL CENSUS. The school census developed historically as a basis for pupil accounting and in the early days of public schools was used as a basis for apportioning state monies. An annual census is essential. Long-range estimates are always helpful but are essential in districts with increasing or declining patterns of growth. Age limits for census coverage range from birth to twenty-one years, although the most common ranges are from six to twenty-one years, six to eighteen years, and five to fifteen years.

A commonly used method of analyzing census results is the grade progression method which projects ahead the number of students in each grade. Other types of census techniques are: the periodic, the city directory, and the registration type, which are all maintained on an annual basis. These methods are administratively expensive to operate and inadequate statistically because they use only annually reported information. They are being abandoned in many localities in favor of a more accurate accounting, the continuous census. A continuous census is claimed to be up-to-date throughout the year and from year to year.

Grieder and Rosenstengel believe that certain basic requirements are required for the installation and maintenance of a continuous census program. A master census card should be completed for each child, including those just born. Cards should be so designed that they can be used from birth until the child reaches the legal age limit for schooling. Methods should be established for locating children by contacting registration authorities about births and deaths; contacting utility and other agencies to determine those who move in or out; keeping track of pupils who transfer in and out, and of student promotions and failures. A continual census requires a house-to-house canvass at the time of installation and periodically to ensure accuracy.[6]

Whatever method is used, it is necessary to determine the number of people of child-bearing age, housing developments, economic and social trends, private school developments and drawing power, secondary school holding power, and community mobility.[7]

The school census has a number of functions:

1. It determines future enrollment by grade level and school attendance areas.
2. It determines the amount of materials and supplies.
3. It provides information for establishing necessary transportation services.
4. It helps to determine educational services, courses, and programs.
5. It determines personnel needs by grade level, subject matter, or school.
6. It analyzes the characteristics of students to determine the need for special classes or programs.
7. It helps in enforcing compulsory attendance laws.
8. It analyzes the mobility of the school population.
9. It helps to determine school plant use and new construction needs.[8]

Unless there is some discussion or cooperation with parents at the time of the census, it may not be possible to determine the number of children with special problems or needs.

---

[6] Calvin Grieder and William Rosenstengel, *Public School Administration,* p. 334.

[7] Edgar L. Morphet, Roe L. Johns, and Theodore L. Reller, *Educational Administration: Concepts, Practices, and Issues* © 1959. By permission of Prentice-Hall, Inc. Englewood Cliffs, New Jersey, p. 431.

[8] Adapted from Roald F. Campbell, John B. Corbally, Jr., and John A. Ramseyer, *Introduction to Educational Administration,* p. 109; Grieder and Rosenstengel, *Public School Administration,* p. 332; and Morphet, Johns, and Reller, *Educational Administration,* pp. 372–373.

ENROLLMENT PROCEDURES.   Confusion at the beginning of each school year will be minimized if the district has an effective pre-registration program.   This can be accomplished before the school year ends and during summer vacation.   Presently enrolled elementary pupils can be assigned to their grade and room for the following school year.   Secondary students can make out their new programs and consult with their counselors to work out conflicts.

Dates can be set for the pre-enrollment of new students with wide publicity by the local press and radio.   Parents should be encouraged to accompany their children when they enroll; this helps establish a good working relationship with school personnel, and they can help verify required information for younger children.

State or local laws establish entrance age and method of verification for kindergarten or first grade.   Health information is often required, such as immunization records for smallpox, poliomyelitis, and measles.   An example of an enrollment form is shown in Figure 21–2.   The primary purpose of an enrollment blank is to supply data for school records and to learn enough about a student to help him in school.

Students entering from other schools should present a transfer, report card, or some evidence of grade placement.   After enrollment, the school should request the cumulative record from the other school.   Students should be assigned to classrooms on a tentative basis until official verification of their status is confirmed.   Counselors should help secondary students work out their new class schedules.

ORIENTATION OF NEW STUDENTS.   All new students should be properly oriented to their new surroundings to put them at ease.   Orientation should include:

1. A tour of the buildings and grounds, preferably conducted by another student.
2. Explanation of school rules and regulations.
3. Introduction to the office staff, school nurse, school administrators, and counselors.
4. Explanation of the school's class schedules, lunch hour, and bus schedule.
5. What to do if sick or injured at school.
6. How and where to report after an absence.

PARAMOUNT UNIFIED SCHOOL DISTRICT
15110 South California Avenue
Paramount, California

Date _____
    Mo.   Day   Year

ENROLLMENT BLANK FOR ALL PUPILS

Pupil's Name _____ □ □   Telephone _____
      Last   *First*   *Middle* *Boy* *Girl*

Birthdate _____ Birth _____ Age as of _____ Grade _____
     Mo.   *Day*   *Year* Place   *City*   *State*   September 1

Father's or
Guardian's Name _____

Home
Address _____
        Number   *Street*   *City*

Mother's or
Guardian's Name _____

Home
Address _____
      (If different from above)

Father's or
Guardian's Occupation _____

Mother's or
Guardian's Occupation _____

Last School attended by pupil _____
            Name   *City*   *State*

Has the pupil ever attended a Paramount school before? Yes ____   School _____ Year _____
                                       No ____

Please list brothers and sisters:

        Boys   Age   Girls   Age

_____ _____   _____ _____
_____ _____   _____ _____
_____ _____   _____ _____

Please list and explain any pertinent HEALTH problems such as heart defects, abnormalities, poor vision, deafness:
_____
_____
_____

FOR PUPILS NEW TO PARAMOUNT SCHOOLS, PLEASE COMPLETE CERTIFICATION OF IMMUNIZATION:

I certify my child has been immunized on the following
dates:

Immunization is contrary to my
belief.

□ Polio dates: 1_____ 2_____ 3_____   □ Polio

□ Measles date: _____   □ Measles

Date _____   Signature of Parent or Guardian _____
                   Exemption statements are available at the school office

            DO NOT WRITE BELOW THIS LINE - - - - OFFICE USE ONLY

Verification of Birthdate:

  Birth Certificate [   ]

  Affidavit   [   ]

Date Entered _____ School _____
         Mo.   *Day*   *Year*

  Baptismal   [   ]   E 1   E 2   E 3   E 4   Grade _____

  Passport   [   ]

                                 Teacher _____

Initials of Person   Permit _____
Verifying Birthdate _____   *(District)*

FIGURE 21–2. *Example of an Enrollment Form. Courtesy of the Paramount Unified School District, Paramount, California.*

7. Explanation of the school's co-curricular program such as clubs, student government, and athletic program.
8. Explanation of the academic expectancy and grading system of the school.
9. Whom to see with questions or problems.

It is helpful to all parties to invite parents of children enrolling in a public school for the first time to an orientation meeting conducted by the principal. An explanation should be made of what is expected of their children; what the school's rules and regulations are; what parents can do to help their child; and how to verify absences. A Parent Teacher Association officer can explain how their organization functions and invite the new parents to join. If the school has a *Parent's Handbook,* it should be given out at this time.

Administering Attendance and Child Welfare

One of the important functions of the pupil personnel department is that of administering child welfare and attendance. Absences, whatever the reason, must be investigated because they affect the welfare and educational progress of a student. Students who need to work should be granted work permits.

A PHILOSOPHY OF ATTENDANCE. Historically, compulsory education is almost as old as this country. Thirty-five years after the first permanent English settlement was established in Jamestown, Virginia, the Massachusetts Colony in 1642 enacted the first compulsory education law in America. The law was colony-wide and provided that "the selectmen in every town shall have the power to take account of all parents and masters as to their children's education and employment." The law of 1642 left the responsibility of education to the parents but did not provide for a school. It simply required the parents to see that their children were educated. Five years later the "Old Deluder Satan Law" was passed, making education the responsibility of the community. This law provided that every township with fifty householders must appoint a master within the town to teach all children to read and write. If the town had one hundred householders, it had to establish a grammar school. The law provided for the assessment of a five pound fee if the act was not complied with, a large fine at that time.

Historically, compulsory attendance laws have been the chief factor in the establishment of attendance departments in the public schools. Although these laws have been challenged, the courts have affirmed their constitutionality.

The first type of attendance officer found in public schools was an officer of the law. His sole job was to obtain reports of pupils who were absent an undue amount of time and then proceed to bring these children back to school.

A major problem of the school is to convince parents and students that the attitudes toward school attendance "truant officer" have changed; that attendance is not only compliance with the law *per se,* but an opportunity, a privilege, and a responsibility. The main purpose, then, of a child welfare and attendance supervisor should be to *help* the pupil, rather than to *control* the pupil.

The child welfare and attendance supervisor is concerned with the reasons behind pupil non-attendance. An actual count of heads is a mechanical process; discovering why the child is not in school and attempting to remove the causes are the real challenges. "Problem children" should be considered as "children with problems." There must be an attempt to understand the child in relation to his home, his community, and his school program. A modern teacher accepts the child where he is and attempts to develop a program to fit his needs. The child welfare and attendance person must also attempt to find out where the child is with respect to his family, his environment, his peers, his school life, and, if possible, himself. To effect a return to a normal school life for a child with problems may involve extensive use of resources within the school and community and a considerable cost in effort, time, and money. This cost is justifiable as a means of developing productive members of society.

A philosophy of attendance and child welfare must often be tempered in practice. When confronted with parents who feel that compulsory education is an invasion of parental rights or with recalcitrant teenagers who are immune to any form of guidance, the administrator may find that recourse to laws governing attendance becomes the only alternative.

A BASIC CONCEPT IN CHILD WELFARE AND ATTENDANCE. A child welfare and attendance worker should consider differences in responses by children. Many school problems arise because of the difficulty of recognizing individual pupil needs. Individual differences are many and varied, and because teachers and parents are so close to a situation, they often fail to observe the developing problems. An attendance worker is farther away from the situation, not so involved in the daily care of the child, and in a position to give the child individual attention. The superintendent should choose an attendance worker who can give valuable help to school officials and parents in solving individual problems.

Attendance workers find that adults often dismiss as trivial the problems of children, and yet these problems are very real to the child. The child may try to solve his difficulty through types of withdrawal or various expressions of overt behavior. Usually, as this pattern develops and parents become aware of their child's problem, they are in a receptive frame of mind and are willing to accept constructive advice from school personnel. The willingness to accept advice from the school is further enhanced by the basic concern of parents with the welfare and growth of their children and their anxiety to rear them in the best possible way.

Growing up in the modern world is a complex process. A child is subjected to pressures from many sides: his family, his peers, his school, and a society which often appears dichotomous. Attendance workers are in a position to recognize and correct many ill-effects of these social pressures if they fully use available resources, such as health, guidance, and curriculum personnel within the school and public and private agencies outside of the school.

QUALIFICATIONS FOR CHILD WELFARE AND ATTENDANCE WORKERS. The superintendent must weigh carefully the qualifications of applicants before selecting a director of child welfare and attendance. In recent years descriptive titles given to individuals involved in welfare and attendance work indicate the expanded nature of their work. Titles such as "Attendance Counselor," "Attendance Consultant," "School Social Worker," and "Home and School Visitor" are replacing those of "Truant Officer," and "Attendance Officer."

Changing aims in public education require corresponding adjustments in the type of preparation essential to meet new attitudes and new conditions. Few activities in the public school system reflect changed attitudes more clearly than the functions of the school attendance official. This type of service is no longer directed chiefly toward law enforcement; rather, it approaches its responsibility from the standpoint of rendering the greatest assistance for developing children. It is essential, therefore, that a broader and more highly integrated type of professional preparation be provided for those selecting this type of school service.

TRAINING. Professional training requirements currently stress social service. A bachelor's degree is required and usually one or more years of teaching experience. Typical courses required in professional training for child welfare workers include:

1. Counseling Procedures and Techniques.
2. Mental Hygiene.
3. Psychology of Exceptional Children.
4. Home–School Communication.
5. Use of Community Resources.
6. Abnormal Psychology.
7. Case Study and Case Conference Techniques.
8. Supervised Field Experience.
9. Application of the Laws Relating to Children and Child Welfare.

The credential for pupil personnel services should cover positions in counseling, child welfare and attendance, psychology, and psychometry.

PERSONAL TRAITS. The personal traits of a child welfare worker should be the prime consideration in selection since this individual is often the only point of contact between the home and the school. It is necessary that the representative of the school possess a wholesome, well-balanced personality. His most effective tools in bringing about cooperation between home and school are tact, sympathy, and human understanding. He must possess a strength of character that will not allow sympathy for a difficult family situation to interfere with the child's receiving, as a minimum, a basic elementary and secondary school education.

Cooperation between home and school is possible only after mutual confidence is established. With the majority of parents this cooperation and confidence is a natural feeling. But some parents need help and guidance in interpreting what the school and society require of them and their children. When treated with sincerity, a maturity of judgment regarding family problems, and trustworthiness, parents will often respond to help.

Appearance and grooming of the child welfare counselor plays a significant part in home contacts since initial contacts often create lasting impressions. This impression must be favorable in order to put the parent or child in a receptive mood to accept the guidance offered.

HOME CALLS. Home calls are initiated principally as a result of absence from school. The majority of calls are made in a routine effort to verify absence when the school has been unable to contact the home or parents. Most home calls are received by parents with appreciation for the concern shown by the schools. The art of home–school communication is on trial when the parent is one who questions compulsory education and has probably instilled in his children a certain contempt for school. All school personnel as a team want this child to return to school, but to return with a willingness to learn. The principal, teachers, and attendance counselor must impress the parent with a sincere desire to help. They should try to develop some plan of action acceptable to both the parents and the school which should be recorded and left with the parent and child. Parents often have questions that need to be checked with other sources, giving the attendance worker a chance to return to the home on a positive basis. If time permits, in many cases a second call builds up a good relationship, and can be justified in terms of preventative therapy.

Every home contact should be recorded. If a home call is requested on a specific form in the school district, there should be space for recording the disposition or specific recommendations. These data are especially important if the particular case develops into a case conference or juvenile court problem.

RELATIONSHIPS WITHIN THE DISTRICT. Most attendance personnel feel the need for coordination and an effective line of communication with all teachers and administrators. When working with individual schools, they should carry an attitude of service. Coordination between several school agencies is essential. The attendance and health services have many mutual problems and need help from each other; they should be familiar with each other's procedures and records. Guidance and attendance have overlapping features. Since the attendance, health, and guidance services share many problems, some districts are combining these services in the same department. This appears to be a logical organization of "co-related" services. Through amalgamation, the superintendent can secure greater efficiency and reduce overlapping or conflicting services.

ATTENDANCE RECORDS. Attendance records should be kept as simple as possible. They should account for attendance, absences (excused, unexcused, and truancy) and dropouts. All administrators realize that attendance recordkeeping has a definite place in a modern public school. It is the legal record of compulsory attendance as well as the basis in many states for apportionment of funds. It has always been a chore for teachers, seemingly an extra duty to the prime purpose of classroom instruction.

In recent years methods of improving the accuracy of pupil accounting as well as releasing teacher time for teaching have been developed. The most commonly used method of attendance recording is the classroom register. In some states a basic register has so many statistical items of information incorporated that it becomes cumbersome and requires an excessive amount of teacher time to complete and verify at the end of the month. To alleviate this clerical task of the teacher, several systems have been devised.

Centralized attendance is a method whereby a systematic office procedure maintains the individual teacher's attendance records in a central school file. There are several advantages credited to the use of a central attendance program. It relieves the teacher of register keeping. It provides a more accurate record system, in that it is under the supervision of the principal and a clerk whose job concerns attendance. Pupils in elementary grades are given an opportunity to become familiar with reporting to a central attendance office, so that when they matriculate to junior and senior high schools they are not confused. Centralized attendance provides a closer correlation with the school nurse in checking all readmittances; and a better method of recording all verification of illness and absence is provided. There is an opportunity for the child welfare and attendance division to determine more quickly cases in which constructive educational help at home could and should be given. Monthly attendance reports are more easily made and permanent records are more efficiently filed for future reference.[9]

Another method is machine accounting which provides a refinement of centralized attendance by using electronic business machines, not only for attendance, but for pupil records. This development, being used in many parts of the country, is still on a pilot basis; but the resultant saving of clerical and teacher time indicates its potential.

---

[9] Los Angeles County Schools, *Child Welfare and School Attendance Accounting Manual* (Los Angeles, 1958), pp. 31–32.

Many schools also use machines for registration, class cards, transcripts, teachers' class lists, monthly attendance, student programs, and pupil report cards. The main advantage of this system is the ability to use basic information in almost any form desired for lists, reports, summaries, totals, and statistical study. An example of a monthly attendance card is shown in Figure 21–3.

While holding to the basic premise that regular attendance benefits the child, society also recognizes that in practice we must occasionally make exceptions. There are those who cannot benefit from school experience and those who refuse to benefit from school. State laws allow employable preference for certain age groups experiencing problems in school. Certain standards have been established governing their attendance at school.

In states that use the average daily attendance system for apportionment of state funds, the determination of the extent or type of absence can become a major financial problem. Legal and illegal, lawful and unlawful are the usual expressions used by states to determine the type of absence and generally cover similar situations. Illness, medical appointments, and quarantines are the usual legal absences. Illegal absences are those in which the parent and the child do not fully sense the responsibility society has placed on them through compulsory attendance. This includes parental excuses such as entertaining relatives, running errands, attending shows, and refusing to attend school. Some states have a middle ground—

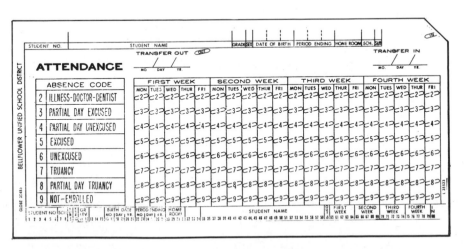

FIGURE 21–3. Example of a Pupil Monthly Attendance Card. Courtesy of the Bellflower Unified School District.

an absence which is illegal for apportionment purposes, but excused (religious holidays, bereavement, a trip with parents, or a court appearance). All absences should be verified whether they are excused or unexcused. Verifications of absence in the form of notes from parents do not necessarily validate the excuse, but are simply a recognition of absence. The attendance laws of the state decide if the absence is considered excused or unexcused. The administrator is concerned a little more deeply with the reasons for non-attendance than with its legality. If he can identify the reasons for non-attendance and isolate its cause, he is much better prepared to suggest a constructive course. Several types of absenteeism are described in the following paragraphs.

TRUANCY. This term is usually applied to willful or continued unexcused absence. Bettleheim states that truancy may be caused by the natural reaction of a child whose needs are not met by the school, or the result of severe anxiety or family disorganization. Measures should be taken to correct these conditions as soon as observed. Placement in a special school may be necessary when corrective measures fail. Truancy, a symptom indicative of underlying disturbances, generally leads to other types of delinquent behavior. It is found in varying degrees, and is not particularly serious if it occurs as an isolated adventure. When repetitive, illegal, and unexcused, it becomes a serious problem, forcing schools to define the offender as an "habitual truant."[10]

Fornwalt maintains that many pupils indulge in mental truancy as a means of escaping an unpleasant atmosphere or of getting away from a boring and meaningless routine. They tolerate the undesirable situation at school, lest they be shamed or humiliated if they become actual truants.[11]

Administrators must accept the challenge of probing for the cause and seeking a solution to the problem of truancy, whether the cause be found in the home, the school, or the child himself. Most administrators are aware that the school itself is probably the greatest single cause. Most truancy cases have multiple causes that complicate the solution. The solution can often be effected through a program change, a school change, or possibly even a curriculum change. Home, school, and community resources

---

[10] Bruno Bettleheim, "Emotionally Disturbed Children," *Forty-Seventh Yearbook,* Part I (Chicago: National Society for the Study of Education, 1947), p. 157.

[11] Russell J. Fornwalt, "Toward an Understanding of Truancy," *School Review* 55 (February 1947), pp. 87–92.

should be utilized to the fullest prior to a legal complaint.   The key to solving truancy is education:

> Education for the teacher, counselor, and school official so they can recognize the truancy problem, react to it swiftly and sympathetically, and provide the counseling to prevent it from happening again.
>
> Education for the community, to spur individuals and organizations into first recognizing the problem and then sponsoring programs to cure it and its related effects.
>
> Education for the parent, so he can determine his responsibilities and deal with the problem effectively in the home.
>
> And most important of all, education for the student, for it is he—now and in later life—who suffers.[12]

Few truancy cases that reach the juvenile courts without a serious attempt for adjustment by the school are justified.

DROPOUTS.   Of general concern to administrators is the increasing number of dropouts from school as students reach the upper limits of the compulsory attendance age.   The most frequently listed reasons for dropping out are: "low academic aptitude, lack of reading ability, insufficient finances, job opportunities, lack of participation in school activities, and needs at home."[13]   Other reasons are: being too old for grade, dislike for school teachers and subjects, and a narrow, required curriculum.[14]   Dropouts occur in affluent areas as well as in low socioeconomic areas.   Lack of family cohesiveness, broken homes, divorce or separation, deceased parents, working mothers, or a lack of parental guidance and encouragement are some of the underlying causes for dropping out.[15]

Dropouts usually have problems that they do not anticipate.   They have difficulty getting and holding jobs; have less earning power than graduates; do not have the opportunity to advance; and are not educationally prepared to hold their jobs for long periods of time.

Schools are partially to blame for dropouts because they have not met the needs of students.   Potential dropouts need a sincere and understanding teacher.   They may need extra help in reading and assistance to

---

[12] Gordon T. Morris, "The Truant," *Today's Education* 61 (January 1972), p. 42.

[13] George R. Cressman and Harold W. Benda, *Public Education in America*, Copyright © 1956, 1961 by Appleton-Century-Crofts, Inc.   Copyright © 1966 by Meredith Publishing Company, published by Appleton-Century-Crofts, New York: 1966, p. 448.

[14] Grieder and Rosenstengel, *Public School Administration*, p. 341.

[15] Cressman and Benda, *Public Education*, p. 448.

improve their study habits.   Above all, they need a functional guidance program that reaches each student on an individual basis.[16]   The curriculum should be flexible and relevant.   Work–study programs can help a student to remain in school.

Any request to drop out should receive a holding effort from the school through counseling, and if this is not successful, a considerate exit interview.   The interview should attempt to guide the student to a job location, possible night or continuation classes to further a job possibility, and should be a pleasant departure.

UNEXCUSED ABSENCE.   Many unexcused absences are due to a lack of understanding or apathy on the part of parents.   In some cases they are not aware of the specific laws that govern attendance.   It is a specific duty of the attendance and welfare worker to relay and explain this information to the home.   In this process tact is paramount; a firm approach should be presented without alienating the parent.   Where the parent continuously treats the problem of unexcused absence lightly, legal recourse should be considered.

EXCUSED ABSENCE.   Excused absence usually involves illness or medical appointments.   The attendance personnel should assist the school health personnel in an attempt to reduce the extent of these absences.   Health education and adequate health habits should receive considerable emphasis, especially with elementary children.   A pupil's home environment is revealed by a home call which often provides a chance to reinforce health education.

The overall reduction of absences, both excused and unexcused, demands coordinated and expanded effort from the fields of attendance, counseling and guidance, health, social services, and school administrative personnel.   Only through cooperation with these services can school personnel uncover the causes and develop a satisfying program to reduce excessive and unwarranted absences.

WORK PERMITS AND EMPLOYMENT OF MINORS.   The control of child labor is the responsibility of the states; the issuance of work permits is usually delegated to the attendance divisions of the public schools.   State laws governing the employment of minors tend to be quite specific.   Federal laws, specifically the Fair Labor Standards Act and the Walsh-

---

[16] Cressman and Benda, *Public Education,* pp. 448–449.

Healy Public Contracts Act, control child labor involved in interstate commerce and government contract work.

Such laws developed from the exploitation of child labor by both employers and parents. This situation existed in rural farming areas as well as in industrialized urban areas, and was a serious social problem until the passage of both state and federal laws. By the year 1909, every state had passed legislation governing child labor in one or more occupations. The scope of this control proved to be so limited in many states as to be almost negligible, especially where the will to enforce it was lacking.

Child labor legislation in the various states established standards for: (1) minimum age, (2) hazardous occupations, (3) maximum daily and weekly hours, and (4) employment or age certificates for minors. The employment certificates are of four types: those furnished to children who desire to work before or after school and on Saturdays; permits to work at specified occupations while school is not in session; permits to work during regular school hours under certain conditions, as age or type of occupation, often with the provision that between certain ages the child attends an extension school; and evidence of age or completion of required minimum education.

Individuals in the school district who are responsible for the issuance and control of work permits must become thoroughly familiar with state and federal laws and regulations of child labor. Before issuing a work permit, they must ascertain that no child will become a source of cheap labor, endanger his physical or mental health, or be denied desired educational opportunities. The superintendent usually delegates this function to the director of child welfare and attendance. Some typical work permit forms are shown in figures 21–4, 21–5, 21–6, and 21–7.

UTILIZATION OF RESOURCES. In a modern approach to attendance enforcement and child welfare, the superintendent realizes a continuing need to draw on other resources, both within and outside of the school. To further the use of specialized facilities, the administrator must be aware of the policies of the specific service offered, who is eligible to receive it, and how the referral is to be made.

SCHOOL SERVICES. The administrator should evaluate the special services which the school is capable of offering. Psychological, social, health, case conference, and counseling services should be reviewed for the possible help they can offer in attendance problems. The principal and the director of child welfare and attendance should plan carefully to use all possible sources.

PRIVATE WELFARE.   Agencies such as Family Service, Salvation Army, Red Cross, YMCA and YWCA, PTA, churches, local boys' clubs and service organizations can offer valuable help in arriving at adjustments. The case of the youngster with a poor attendance and scholastic record because of the inability of the parents to buy needed glasses is typical.   Many service clubs are anxious to provide this type of help by buying glasses, hearing aids, shoes, and other necessities to keep deserving children in school.

PUBLIC AGENCIES.   Public agencies that indirectly aid the work of the schools are bureaus of public assistance, county hospitals, public health and employment services, and many related out-patient clinics.   Referral to these, as well as private agencies, can be of value to the schools when the problems of parents are a basis for the problems of the children.

POLICE AGENCIES.   The administrator should consider the facilities of the juvenile courts, probation departments, and the police department.   Although the courts and probation department are generally used as a last resort, many of them have effective programs for the readjustment of youth.

Police who are assigned to schools as liaison officers have two roles to play: (1) protection of school property, school personnel, and students; (2) development of a positive relationship with youth so that policemen are looked upon as friends, protectors, and confidants.   By being present during school hours, they often prevent trouble.   Their attitude is often more important than their law enforcement.

Since the principal is responsible for his school, police should take their direction from him.   If arrests are necessary, they should be handled with the principal's knowledge and approval.   Many school disturbances are caused by outsiders.   Police should become so well acquainted with the school population that they can recognize and control outsiders before trouble occurs.

Teachers, usually in social studies classes, have invited policemen to explain the functions and responsibilities of the police department and the rights and duties of citizens.   Every school district should have a clear-cut

PERMIT TO EMPLOY
(For Employer's File)

CALIFORNIA STATE
DEPARTMENT OF EDUCATION
FORM NO. 81-3

Name of minor (last name first)

School district_____County_____

Address of minor   ZIP code   Sex   Grade completed

Age of minor   Date of birth   Proof of age accepted   Minor's birthplace

Social Security number   Parent's name (and address if different from minor's)

Employed full time and attending school or classes ☐ or Working outside school hours and attending school in regular session ☐

School to attend   Address   ZIP code

Date to report to class_____ Days and hours enrolled: Mon._____ Tues._____ Wed._____ Thurs._____ Fri._____ Sat._____

Name of person, firm, or corporation employing minor   Address   ZIP code

Phone number of employer   Type of industry   Kind of work minor performs

Hours of employment: Mon. through Fri._____Sat._____Sun._____Weekly total_____

REMARKS:

Issued_____Expires_____   Signature of issuing authority

_____   _____
Signature of minor   Title

FIGURE 21–4. Employer Form. Courtesy of the California State Department of Education.

PERMIT TO WORK AND EMPLOY

_____   _____
Date of issuance   Date of expiration

For High School Graduates Under 18, and Other Minors Under 18 Years of Age Who Are Exempt from Compulsory Education Laws

(This form must be in custody of employer during time of employment and returned to employee when employment terminates.)

Name_____Age_____

Address_____

Sex_____Birthdate_____Proof_____

Social Security Number_____

CALIFORNIA STATE DEPARTMENT OF EDUCATION

FIGURE 21–5. Student Work Permit. Courtesy of the California State Department of Education.

562

REQUEST FOR WORK PERMIT AND STATEMENT OF INTENT TO EMPLOY MINOR

CALIFORNIA STATE
DEPARTMENT OF EDUCATION
FORM NO. B1-4

Name of minor (last name first)		Sex	Social Security number
Address of minor	ZIP code	Phone	County
Age of minor	Date of birth	Proof of age accepted	School district

Employed full time and attending continuation school or classes . . . . ☐
Working outside school hours and attending school in regular session . . . . ☐
Enrolled in work experience education . . . . ☐

School to attend	Address	ZIP code

EMPLOYER'S STATEMENT Name of person, firm or corporation employing minor	Address	ZIP code

Employer's phone number	Employer's signature	Kind of work minor performs

STARTING WAGES $____________

Hours of employment (per day): Monday through Friday______ Saturday______ Sunday______ Weekly total______

PARENT'S SIGNED STATEMENT
This minor is being employed at work described hereon with my full knowledge and consent, and I request a Work Permit be issued.

____________ Date

____________ Signature of parent or guardian

THIS IS NOT A PERMIT TO EMPLOY

Employer's copy of the Permit to Employ will be forwarded to the employer by the issuing authority.

FIGURE 21–6. State Permit Allowing an Employer to Employ a Minor. Courtesy of the California State Department of Education.

CALIFORNIA STATE DEPARTMENT OF EDUCATION

NOTICE OF TERMINATION OF EMPLOYMENT Date____________

This is to certify that________________________
(Name of employee)

whose last known address was____________________

left our employ on____________.
(Date)

Permit issued by____________________

His work was / was NOT satisfactory (circle one).

Remarks:____________________

CHECK ONE: [SIGNED]____________________
(Person, firm, or corporation)

(1) Return to issuing authority ☐

(2) Return to school ☐ By____________________

INSTRUCTIONS FOR USE OF THIS FORM

To be mailed within five (5) days after employment ceases to (1) the issuing authority whose name appears on the work permit; or (2) the school listed on the work permit (checked above). If this notice is returned to the school, the data are to be posted in the registrar's office and the pupil's work record sheet; the card is to be returned to the work permit section if the school district is so organized. This form may be used as a postcard by placing address and stamp on reverse side.

FIGURE 21–7. Form for Termination of Student Employment. Courtesy of the California State Department of Education.

policy that explains the role and duties of policemen when they are on school property or dealing with students and school personnel.

STUDENTS WHO LEAVE SCHOOL. In the normal course of events, the school principal handles cases where the student graduates, moves, is transferred, or is suspended or expelled. For graduates, the cumulative record or necessary information should be sent to the next higher level. Students who move out of a school attendance area should be given a transfer certificate showing their name, address, birth date, and grade assignment. The new school will usually request any other information it needs. Before a student leaves, the school should be sure that all textbooks, library books, school materials, keys, and so forth are turned in. When students want to transfer to another school without changing residence, the principal should follow the district policy as to granting or not granting the request. The district pupil personnel administrator should also be involved or informed.

Suspension and expulsion are more complicated. State and local school board regulations and policies must be followed. It is recommended that the pupil personnel administrator help investigate the case, advise the principal, and inform the school board. Either he or the school board should give final approval and specify the length of the suspension or expulsion.

Complete records in all of the above cases should be reported to the district pupil personnel office where a master file should be kept. When students leave the district, the complete file should be sent to the district office and filed or microfilmed for a permanent record.

Some students are transferred to other schools for specialized teaching upon the advice of the pupil personnel office, since many of them do not have classes for mentally retarded, physically handicapped, or emotionally unstable students. When a student has a lengthy illness and needs to stay at home, he may be transferred to a home teacher.

Guidance Services

Guidance services generally include counseling functions. These services should be coordinated by the district pupil personnel administrator. Tests must be given, case studies made, conferences held, the help of community agencies enlisted, and school counselors assisted. Follow-up work with parents, teachers, and students is necessary.[17]

COUNSELING FUNCTIONS. Counseling is school based but should have coordination and assistance from the district pupil personnel office. It involves much more than merely advising students about their class schedule or rearranging classes. Counselors must be trained in psychology, sociology, test administration, and test interpretation.

Counseling received great impetus as a result of Dr. James Conant's reports on the American high school and junior high school in which he emphasized the need for counselors. The federal government recognized the importance of counseling by appropriating millions of dollars under the National Defense Education Act of 1958 for the purpose of improving guidance, counseling, and testing in American secondary schools.

Counseling helps students adjust to their school environment, their home and family, and their peers. Vocational interests and possibilities can be investigated. Program planning and class scheduling are also counseling functions. Too often, however, this task becomes the major function of counselors.

Most counseling is handled on an individual basis. But most counselors have too many students assigned to counsel effectively on a one-to one basis. Group counseling, less common, has a number of advantages. It permits counselors to spread their services and conserve time. Students may feel more at ease when they meet with their counselor and a peer group, and find that their questions, fears, and problems are shared by others. Group counseling provides a social setting in which students may identify with their peers.[18]

Historically, counseling has been mostly evident in high schools. Later, it was extended to junior high schools. Junior high students in their early adolescence have many personal and social adjustments to make. Junior high counselors have a unique opportunity to counsel and guide students as they attempt to understand themselves and their interpersonal relationships. Students can be helped to participate in their educational planning and in looking toward future vocational choices.

---

[17] Albert L. Ayars, *Administering the People's Schools* (New York: McGraw-Hill Book Co., 1957), p. 307.

[18] Charles F. Combs, Benjamin Cohn, Edward J. Gibian, and A. Mead Sniffin, "Group Counseling: Applying the Technique," *The School Counselor* 11 (October 1963), p. 13.

Most elementary schools have self-contained classrooms with one teacher responsible for the children all day. These teachers know their children and their problems intimately, and become more familiar with parents and home conditions than secondary school teachers. They are then in a position to identify problems in the early stages and counsel students frequently and continuously. However, a few students may need so much counseling that they take an inordinate amount of a teacher's time. In such cases, it is wise to call upon the services of an experienced counselor.

Organized counseling programs, using specialized counselors, have not been carried out in elementary schools with the same intensity as in secondary schools. This is unfortunate because the sooner incipient problems are recognized and isolated, the sooner they can be remedied or solved. When poor habits and attitudes are allowed to continue uncounseled for a period of time or until students reach secondary schools, they are more difficult to change or improve. Many problems that occur in secondary schools might not exist if counseling services were available in the elementary schools. It is important that counselors at the elementary level understand the maturation process of younger children. Trained counselors can work closely with teachers in understanding problems that arise in their classes, freeing the teacher to devote more of his time to actual teaching.

A school's guidance program should be continuous and should complement the instructional program. All students need some guidance whether or not they have problems. Melbo has stated that the school's guidance program should function to help the pupil:

> (1) to understand himself, his abilities and interests, and his personal characteristics; (2) to adjust himself satisfactorily to situations, problems and pressures of his environment; (3) to develop the ability to make his own decisions wisely and solve his problems independently; (4) to make the most effective use of his capacities; and (5) to learn about the educational, occupational, and social opportunities available to him, when he has reached the age or level of maturity at which these knowledges become important in order to make appropriate choices.[19]

THE TESTING PROGRAM. Testing programs have been praised, criticized, and condemned. Some criticisms of educational tests are:

---

[19] Irving Melbo, et al., *Report of the Survey, Ventura City Elementary Schools* (Los Angeles: University of Southern California, 1959), p. 271.

1. They are constructed poorly or vary in quality.
2. Their use is misunderstood.
3. They do not test what they are purported to test.
4. They are often improperly administered.
5. They stamp students as inferior, mediocre, or superior which, in turn, may affect their self-esteem and future social status as an adult.
6. They are used as an infallible record of ability.
7. Their interpretation is subject to error.
8. The scores are kept secret from parents or students.
9. Scores given to parents without complete knowledge of their meaning are incorrectly interpreted.

The proponents of educational testing claim the following purposes:

1. Tests provide the quickest means of determining variability among pupils and identifying the range of achievement.
2. The effectiveness of an educational program can be evaluated, areas of weakness identified, and curriculum revisions determined.
3. A testing program provides a screening device to identify atypical children.
4. Tests provide a starting point for the beginning of class instruction.
5. Teachers have a basis upon which to plan remedial work.
6. Counselors are provided with valuable information.
7. Statistical information is available for many uses.

NORM- VERSUS CRITERION-REFERENCED TESTS. Various types of tests have been used to help determine variabilities among students and to provide information to help teachers and counselors. These include: "measurements of mental ability, scholastic attitude, school achievement, and health and physical development; diagnostic tests of verbal and numerical abilities; interest inventories; and devices to rate and appraise personality, temperament, and emotional and social traits."[20] Their purpose is to help identify weaknesses and to plot remedial instruction to strengthen them.

Norm-referenced or standardized tests are based on national norms. They are descriptive rather than prescriptive, may be biased, and may have little overlap with teacher objectives. However, they are somewhat

---

[20] Ayars, *Administering,* p. 151.

objective, standardized, inexpensive, readily available, and comparable with other samples of the population.[21] They have little application to individualization of instruction and are not concerned with task or behavioral analysis.[22]

In recent years, criterion-referenced tests have been proposed. They provide an ends-oriented approach rather than a means-oriented approach to instruction.[23] Instructional objectives are developed and the degree of their achievement is measured. Objectives should be developed in terms of the following categories: the cognitive domain, the affective domain, and the psychomotor domain.[24] The means are successful if the objectives have been reached.

Criterion-referenced tests evaluate performance in relation to fixed standards, and are not concerned with grade-level descriptions or national student comparisons. They identify those who have mastered instructional objectives; provide information for planning instruction; are specific as to content; apply directly to individualization of instruction; apply directly to task and behavioral analysis; and are not standardized.[25] This type of evaluation is advantageous because it is adaptable, provides feedback, and is congruent with teacher objectives. However, the length of time it takes to reduce instructional objectives to operational terms and the requirement of writing meaningful objectives introduce problems. It is the responsibility of district administrators to see that teachers are trained and have help in developing objectives, criterion-referenced tests, and in using the results to improve individualized instruction.

To achieve the performance objectives that are able to be evaluated, instruction must be adapted to individuals. Many schools have developed learning activity packages in many subject areas. Some schools have developed student learning contracts. If a student's test shows that he has attained the objective, he is permitted to go on to another contract.[26]

---

[21] Thomas E. Neel, "Classroom Performance Standards," *Thrust for Education Leadership,* pp. 17–18.

[22] Jack L. Housden and Lannie LeGear, "An Emerging Model: Criterion-Referenced Evaluation," *Thrust for Education Leadership,* p. 42.

[23] W. James Popham, "The Instructional Objectives Exchange: New Support for Criterion-Referenced Instruction," *Phi Delta Kappan,* p. 174.

[24] John W. Porter, "The Accountability Story in Michigan," *Phi Delta Kappan,* p. 99.

[25] Housden and LeGear, "An Emerging Model," p. 42.

[26] W. James Popham, "Focus on Outcomes: A Guiding Theme of ES '70 Schools," *Phi Delta Kappan,* p. 209.

SCHOOL PSYCHOLOGISTS. Some students have problems or emotional difficulties that require more expert help than most teachers or counselors are prepared to handle. Learning can be impeded unless counseling assistance is provided. The specialized talents of a school psychologist trained in child psychology, child behavior, and learning problems can supply this help. Because of the expense involved, psychologists are more often employed by larger school districts.

Some of the functions that school psychologists can perform are:

1. Helping to remedy emotional problems of students.
2. Helping children with their educational maladjustments.
3. Performing most of the individual testing (but not group testing).
4. Advising teachers in the interpretation of group testing.
5. Analyzing statistical test results.
6. Assisting in curriculum development and the improvement of the learning environment.
7. Having a concern for the mental health of students.

CASE STUDIES. It is often necessary to make a complete case study in order to plan a course of action for a student's problem. To prepare a case study, the following steps should be taken:

1. Group test records should be compiled.
2. Personality traits should be noted.
3. The pupil's social adjustment should be analyzed.
4. Home conditions should be investigated.
5. The physical and health status should be described.
6. School strengths and weaknesses should be noted and analyzed.
7. The teacher should describe what special steps he has taken in attempting to solve the problem.
8. Anecdotal notes should be made at specified times.
9. Individualized tests should be given.
10. Parent conferences should be scheduled.[27]

The skill of a psychologist is needed to help compile a case study, analyze data, and plan a course of action. He should involve a team of

---

[27] Emery Stoops and Russell E. Johnson, *Elementary School Administration* (New York: McGraw-Hill Book Co., 1967), p. 341.

available educational specialists for case-study staff conferences. Input may be needed from the school nurse, doctor, counselor, teacher, and parent. The student must not be overlooked as he alone supplies the key to remedying his problem. The psychologist must plan on continuing a course of action over a period of time. There must be continuous evaluation of progress and revision of remediation as it is deemed necessary.

Control of Behavior

The major purpose of controlling behavior is to provide an environment in which each student is able to receive an education commensurate with his ability to learn. Any kind of behavior that interferes with learning should be considered unacceptable. Control of behavior is a broader term than discipline which connotes only obedience, order, and submission.

Poor behavior previously was dealt with by harsh, immediate, and authoritative means. Students were expected to obey rigid rules and regulations without question. More recently "educators have become convinced that the best discipline exists when the group accepts certain behavior as necessary to the purposes to be achieved."[28] The modern aim is to have groups and individuals develop social control, self-control, and self-direction.

RIGHTS AND RESPONSIBILITIES OF STUDENTS. During the past ten years, students have become more insistent in demanding their rights. They resent it when adults (parents, teachers, or school administrators) tell them what they can or cannot do. They are not willing to accept adult-made rules and regulations. They want the right to help form rules of conduct. Adults must recognize that America's youth are generally more mature and sophisticated than their parents were at the same age.

Administrators and teachers must accept the fact that students have certain rights established by legal precedent in the Bill of Rights. They cannot fight the challenge of youth to influence educational goals and to help formulate school rules. However, administrators must not permit students to take over the control of schools.

Basic standards should be agreed upon by teachers, administrators, parents, and students. The degree of student participation should be

---

[28] Ayars, *Administering,* p. 154.

relevant to their maturity level. Students who help develop their own standards of behavior have a better understanding of the reasons for establishing them and are more likely to assume personal responsibility for supporting them. Accepting rights without assuming responsibility is a one-way street; there must also be self-discipline and respect for the rights of others. However, students need guidance in evaluating the consequences of their actions. Although students should have a voice in setting standards of behavior, no decision is final until the school board approves and adopts it as policy. All students and staff personnel should be informed of adoptions. Behavior or discipline policies should be reviewed periodically and revised as necessary.

CAUSES OF POOR DISCIPLINE. Discipline problems are usually symptomatic of other problems. Some factors that may cause poor discipline are:

Emotional and social factors.
Lack of motivation.
Lack of interest in subject matter or the educational program.
Poor presentation of the subject matter by the teacher.
Emotional repression.
Conflict between the student's behavior and social requirements or the teacher's expectations.
Peer conflicts.
Conflicts between parents and children.
Conflicts between home and school.
Conflicts between teacher and child.
Personal problems.
Malnutrition or physical and health problems.
Thwarted self-expression.
Inferiority complex and feelings of incompetence.
Frustrations in desire to be important.
Lack of sympathy, love, or understanding.
Poor study habits.
Racial, religious, personal, or cultural differences.
Overstimulated life.
Thrill in delinquency that releases tensions.

Causes, such as the above, are related to school, home, or community. The school cannot always solve problems that are not related to it, although it can seek the cooperation of the home and community. It *can* do something about the school environment.

Teachers are usually concerned with dishonesty, disobedience, disorderliness, stealing, cheating, sex, insolence, noisiness, tardiness, and damaging property. Too many are bothered by such trivial behavior as chewing gum, eating candy, or turning around in class. It should be realized that many behaviors are actually normal for an age group, and natural manifestations of growing up. If the solution is punishment, especially for what the student regards as trivial, it causes pressure and rejection, aggravating the problem rather than helping to alleviate it. Nevertheless, the teacher must establish and maintain an orderly classroom climate.

Morphet, Johns, and Reller state that good schools and good teachers have fewer problems than poor schools and poor teachers. Overcrowded classrooms cause more discipline problems than less crowded ones; pupils with emotional difficulties are more likely to have discipline problems; and teacher–principal dominated schools have more problems than those where students share in making school policies. Successful students create fewer discipline problems than those who fail or have unsatisfactory school experiences.[29]

SUGGESTED WAYS OF CONTROLLING BEHAVIOR. Punishment (discussed later in this chapter) is often used to control misbehavior. Except where immediate control is necessary, it is better to diagnose the problem, determine its causes, and then plan a course of action. A positive approach should be used and the cause removed, if possible. A school cannot remove all causes because they do not all originate in the school. The function of the school is to furnish the leadership to gain the cooperation of teachers, parents, pupils, and community service agencies to remedy the causes of misbehavior. The cause should be treated rather than the misbehavior which is the symptom. The ultimate goal is self-discipline for the student. Authoritative force only tends to develop negative attitudes, resistance, and eventually rebellion. If a positive approach is used and cooperation is achieved, misbehavior will have little chance of success. Compromises are necessary since there is little agreement between adults and students on dress codes, hair styles, smoking on school grounds, and so forth. However, workable standards must be worked out and agreed upon.

---

[29] Morphet, Johns, and Reller, *Educational Administration,* p. 386.

ROLE OF THE TEACHER IN CONTROLLING BEHAVIOR. Teachers play a major role in controlling behavior. Good classroom organization, sound planning by the teacher, interesting activities, and well-understood procedures promote good behavior. The day should be filled with stimulating, varied activities. Routines should be established so that students know what to expect and what they should do next. Students and the teacher should understand the limits of behavior.

The teacher should be firm, sincere, and above all, fair. He should not humiliate or embarrass a student. He should be consistent in his expectations of behavior. He should provide the opportunity for every student to experience daily success, if possible. The student should be helped to develop a sense of worth and encouraged to participate creatively in classroom activities. Students should be given responsibilities commensurate with their ability to handle them. Praise should be frequently bestowed to develop pride and a positive attitude.

Teachers should feel free to discuss problems with their principal and to seek his help. In turn, the principal should take the time to help his teachers and to request further help from the district pupil personnel office when it is necessary. Pupil personnel workers and counselors should not administer disciplinary punishment; by doing so, they lose their student trust essential to successful counseling.

PUNISHMENT. Punishment is a stop-gap, first-aid type of control. It is only a momentary help, not a cure, and does not deal with the source of the problem. If used, it should be appropriate to the offense, be understood by the student, and reasonable. It is a temporary restraint that should only be used until the real cause is ascertained and an effective remedy applied. Punishment should be fair, not harsh or cruel, never administered in the heat of anger, and should cause no embarrassment to the student.

Because punishment is at times necessary for control of a disciplinary problem, the school board should adopt clear, concise policies that define the responsibility of teachers, administrators, students, and counselors. The policies should be broad enough to cover as many situations as possible, but not so detailed that they make policemen out of teachers or administrators. Because schools stand *in loco parentis,* they have the right to enforce reasonable rules and regulations and to punish.

Corporal punishment should only be used as a last resort. States vary in their laws regarding corporal punishment; some do not permit it. If permitted, the school board should spell out when corporal punishment is to be used, who is to administer it, what witnesses are required, whether the parents are to be notified, and what report is to be made and to whom. It should be remembered that corporal punishment rules by fear and never solves a problem.

When all else fails, suspension or expulsion may be the only remedy for the protection of the student and others. Suspension is temporary and expulsion is usually for the duration of the semester. The school board should also adopt policies on suspension and expulsion. The district pupil personnel administrator should be involved before a student is suspended or expelled. The student should be counseled so that he understands the reasons for the action. Time limits should be established and parents notified. It is advisable to hold a conference with the parents before readmission to enlist their help. All suspensions and expulsions should be reported to the school board.

Progress Reporting

Schools have an obligation to inform parents of their child's progress in school. Some method of reporting this should be developed. There are two basic methods of grading and reporting to parents as well as informing the student: (1) competitive or norm-referenced and (2) individual progress or criterion-referenced. Parents best understand progress that is related to a norm. They want to know how their child is doing specifically in each subject as well as how he is doing in relation to other children.[30] They confuse reporting with comparative marking.[31]

The student should understand what the grade means before it is reported. Most schools use number or letter rating scales on report cards; here, the grade represents, in the teacher's judgment, the measure of achievement for a student in relation to other students. This type of grading system is norm-referenced.[32] A typical report card lists subjects with assigned grades. Some of the common grading scales are: A, B, C, D, and E or F; 1, 2, 3, 4, and 5; percentages with 100 (perfect) and 70 (usually the lowest passing grade); "pass" and "fail"; N (needs help) or U

---

[30] Henry J. Otto and David C. Sanders, *Elementary School Organization and Administration,* 4th ed., p. 153.

[31] Otto and Sanders, *Elementary School,* p. 155.

[32] Jason Millman, "Reporting Progress: A Case for a Criterion-Referenced Marking System," *Phi Delta Kappan,* p. 226.

(unsatisfactory) and S (satisfactory). Citizenship, work habits, health habits, attitude, effort, and attendance are sometimes added and graded.

Report cards such as these explain very little and leave much to be desired. A "C" grade, for example, can mean that a student is doing "average" work, but can also be a good grade for a slow learner. Without explanation, parents often blame the school or the teacher for a child's poor grade.

A report card based on criterion-referenced testing lists objectives and provides space for indicating those that have been achieved or the proficiency that has been demonstrated. All the objectives that a teacher used cannot be included.[33] This method of reporting does not compare a student with others. The "grade," if a report card is used, shows individual progress toward performance objectives developed by the teacher. The evaluation is based on the individualization of instruction.

No perfect report card has ever been devised. Most school districts, because of complaints or new ideas, revise reporting methods from time to time. There are probably as many types of cards as there are school districts. The trend at the secondary level is toward computerized cards that reduce paper work. Figure 21–8 illustrates an automatically printed type of grade report.

Other methods have been devised to improve the reporting of progress. Letters from the teacher explain progress in narrative form. They may be more personal and explain more fully than report cards, but the method is time-consuming for a teacher, especially at the secondary level where each teacher may be responsible for up to 150 students. Meaningful letters are difficult to compose for large numbers; often the teacher uses a sentence to explain what a single letter or number grade would indicate. Letters to parents tend to become generalized and stereotyped. Some report cards do provide a space for the teacher to write pertinent comments and a space for the parent to make comments or ask questions.

PARENT–TEACHER CONFERENCES. Many school districts achieve success in reporting to parents with parent–teacher conferences that replace report cards or are scheduled at the time report cards are distributed. An extensive study by Henry Otto showed that parents and teachers were in close agreement about the school's objectives and in full agreement that reports to parents should be in terms of objectives. However, both groups were

---

[33] Millman, "Reporting Progress," pp. 226–227.

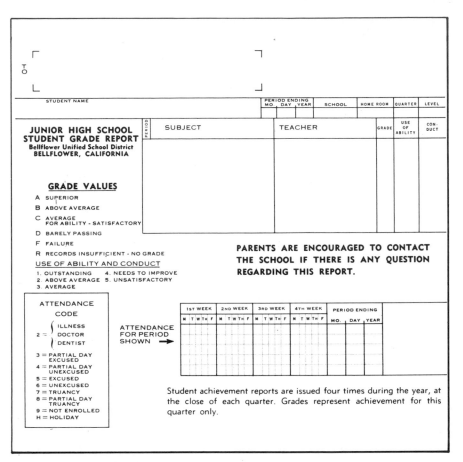

FIGURE 21–8.   Example of a Student Grade Report.   Courtesy
of the Bellflower Unified School District.

vague about what to report.   Parents and teachers alike agreed that any reporting plan should include arrangements for parent–teacher conferences.[34]

If rapport is established and the atmosphere is relaxed, teachers and
parents understand each other better and can cooperate in planning for the
student's educational success.   During a conference, feelings are important.   The teacher must understand how the parent feels and how he may
react.   A conference should be a two-way communication.   Listening is

---

[34] Henry J. Otto et al.   *Four Methods of Reporting to Parents* (Austin, Texas:
The University of Texas Press, 1957).

important on the part of the teacher or counselor. The conferees should discuss:

1. Educational philosophy and expectancies.
2. Objectives that have been developed for the individual student.
3. The degree to which the objectives have been achieved.
4. The meaning of the grades if a report card is used.
5. Problems and suggestions for improvement.
6. Successes.

The conference should end on a friendly and positive note.

It is often difficult to arrange a time that is convenient for both parents and teachers. Many districts permit shortened teaching days during the conference period because of the value of this reporting method. Secondary schools find conferences difficult for two reasons: (1) the average secondary teacher needs to schedule approximately 150 conferences and (2) parents of secondary students do not visit the school as frequently as elementary parents do.

William Glasser believes that there should be few meetings with parents on deficiency reports or disciplinary problems because they do more harm than good. Parents should not be called to the school until all the school's efforts to help the student have failed. At the secondary level, students should always be present when they are discussed by the teacher or counselor and the parent. The conference should not start by trying to fix blame. Constructive suggestions should be the objective of the conference, and the student should have an equal voice in attempts to reach a solution. Recommendations should be brief, to the point, and understandable. When "they have been agreed upon, they should be put in writing and the student should commit himself in writing to following them."[35] Conferences at the secondary level can be successful if they are carefully planned and conducted, and involve the student, as well as the parent and teacher or counselor.

METHODS OF REPORTING STUDENT PROGRESS. According to Henry Otto, most schools use a multiple, rather than a single method of reporting.[36] A teacher opinion poll by the National Education Association supports this statement. The poll asked the question, "What method(s) do you use

---

[35] William Glasser, *Schools Without Failure,* pp. 225–226.
[36] Otto and Sanders, *Elementary School,* pp. 155–156.

TABLE 21–1.   Reporting Pupil Progress to Parents[a]

METHOD OF REPORTING	TOTAL	ELEMEN-TARY	SECOND-ARY
Teacher–parent conferences	69.9%	84.2%	54.4%
Classified scale of letters	67.1	55.9	79.4
Formal letter or written paragraph to parents	23.7	26.0	21.1
Descriptive word grade	20.0	29.2	10.0
Percentage grade	8.9	4.4	13.7
Pass–fail	8.3	7.3	9.3
Classified scale of numbers	7.1	6.4	7.8
Dual marking system	4.4	4.0	4.9
Other	5.0	7.4	2.4

[a] National Education Association, Research Division, "Reporting Pupil Progress to Parents," *Research Bulletin* 49 (October 1971), p. 81.

to report pupil progress to parents?" Table 21–1 shows the responses given by teachers. At the lowest end of the table's scale is a dual marking system in which one mark represents achievement in relation to the teacher's standard and the second represents the amount of effort the student puts forth or the growth toward the listed educational objectives.[37]

Whatever reporting method is used, it should not be totally administratively developed. Parents, teachers, administrators, and students should also be involved. Whether or not all agree, the final compromise on grades and method of reporting should be understood by all.

Pupil Personnel Reports and Records

Some administrators feel that they spend most of their time compiling, analyzing, and reporting data of all types. Since the actual work is largely clerical, clerks should be trained to compile, record, and file or forward reports and records. Some can be trained to analyze and to summarize statistical information to make it more readily available to administrators. The importance of reporting and recording data cannot be underestimated. Records are used to project enrollment in order to determine needs such as: classrooms, teachers, buses, equipment, materials, and services. Actual enrollment or attendance figures determine the amount of finances the school district will receive.

[37] National Education Association, Research Division, "School Marks and Reporting to Parents," *Research Bulletin* 48 (October 1970), pp. 76–86.

The following list shows various types of commonly used pupil personnel records:

Grades earned
Test scores
Case studies
Student cumulative records
Promotion lists
Ethnic summaries
Statistical data: dropouts, suspensions, expulsions, arrests, corporal punishment cases, test summaries, etc.
Attendance area charts
Class loads
Enrollment
Attendance
Psychological studies
School census
Population movement
Student turnover

The student cumulative record contains a great amount of information to help teachers and administrators as they teach, advise, and counsel students. The folder should contain the life history of each student in the school district. Included should be information regarding his family, grades, test scores, health, personality traits, attendance, problems, achievements, co-curricular participation, and leadership. There should be some indication of his potential success in college or employment. The cumulative folder should be used as a reference by teachers, counselors, and the pupil personnel office and referred to for college and employment recommendations.

Much of the information for reports originates in the classroom and therefore is the teacher's responsibility. Teachers should understand the importance of accuracy in reporting and recording data and should have instruction and assistance in performing these tasks. Either the principal or someone from the district pupil personnel office should monitor the information teachers record to ensure accuracy and completeness of information. All records should be checked at the end of the school year. Incorrect recording can affect the future success or employment of a student. Promotion, retention, and graduation lists should be compiled and filed in the office before teachers leave for the summer.

Schools with access to computers have simplified recordkeeping tasks. Data can be recorded on punch cards or tape and run through a computer. Gummed printouts can be used, making it a simple process to stick information on the cumulative folder.

Records and reports have no value unless they are used. An adequate file system is necessary to make information available when needed. There are many types of filing systems; the school district should select the ones that suit their particular needs. Some examples are: Kardex files, visible files, folder files, needle-sort files, and tape files. Space can be saved if older records and reports are microfilmed and stored in a microfilm file. If properly indexed, they can be retrieved easily. The forward-looking school district will look into the possibility of using a newer type of data retrieval system.

Standardization of records greatly facilitates the keeping of records. Numerous attempts have been made to standardize student records so that they may simply be forwarded as the student matriculates, rather than wasting many clerical hours copying information into a new format. Various state, county, city, or federal agencies periodically request student data. If the reporting forms are standardized, many hours are saved in collecting and tabulating similar data.

At the beginning of the school year, each school should have a supply of all forms it will need. The teacher's handbook should be updated to show examples of all forms and explanations of their use. Typical pupil personnel forms used are:

Enrollment blanks
Cumulative record folders
Report cards
Class schedule cards
Attendance slips
Excuse slips
Office pass slips
Athletic eligibility forms
Health forms
Transfer slips
Accident report forms
Nurse referral forms
Office referral forms
Attendance registers or cards

Library cards
Referral for pupil personnel service
Transfer permits and transfer report forms
Readmittance information forms
Lunch passes
Bus passes
Permits for release of child during school hours
Requests for pupil records

CONFIDENTIALITY OF STUDENT RECORDS. It is debatable how much information on students should be made public. What should parents be told? What should prospective employers be told about a student's intelligence, aptitudes, attitudes, or personal qualifications? Perhaps any information that is released should be only for the purpose of helping a student. Parents have a right to know what information about their child is being held on record. Police, governmental agencies, and other schools have a right to expect a school to cooperate in furnishing all necessary, factual information. Employers have a right to information on a student's grades, aptitudes, attendance, and attitudes. Information should be of two types: (1) factual and (2) professional judgments or opinions. Information of a personal nature should not be divulged because the confidentiality of a student must be protected. People or agencies seeking information about a student must prove their (1) need to know and (2) their right to know.

Summary

Pupil personnel services should be centralized under a trained administrator who maintains pupil records and administers testing, psychological, guidance, and other programs. He should first be an administrator and then a specialist in one or several of the services.

Several kinds of school censuses exist, including the grade-progression method, the periodic, and the registration, all annual. The continuous census is recommended, and is almost a necessity for a successful pupil personnel program. It helps in making pre-registration possible and in orienting new students.

Child welfare and attendance are important pupil personnel services. Because school money depends in large part upon average daily attendance, it is important that reasons behind non-attendance be determined.

Reasons for absence include varying cultural patterns, inability of the child to cope with school problems, and family pressures. Welfare and attendance workers should be well trained, with a well-balanced personality and an ability to establish good relationships with parents.

Attendance accounting should be kept simple, as centralized as possible, and use business machines. Regularity of attendance should be stressed with special attention to the two main administrative implications of excessive absences: accounting and guidance. Truancy should be combatted by seeking out the cause and treating it appropriately. The problem of the dropout should be handled similarly.

Work permits are usually handled by the pupil personnel director who also deals with other outside entities such as private welfare groups, public agencies, and police departments. Students who leave school legally must be followed up with transfers of credits and grades. Suspensions and expulsions are also dealt with by the pupil personnel office.

Guidance and counseling functions are coordinated by the director, with trained counselors used wherever possible. Aptitude and personality tests are often administered by the school psychologist, who may assist also in conducting case studies of individual students.

Discipline is a perennial concern of the schools. Today its achievement is complicated by the concept of student rights. Many causes of poor discipline exist, and are usually dealt with by some combination of rewards and punishments administered mainly by the teacher.

Progress reporting, another pupil personnel service, is mostly for the benefit of the parent. Report cards, letters, and parent–teacher conferences are the devices most frequently used. Conferences can be constructive if planned carefully and conducted in a mutually agreeable manner. At the secondary level, the student should be involved along with the parent, teacher, or counselor.

Pupil personnel records should be kept by clerks and made available to those professionally qualified to use them. Cumulative student records are especially valuable if properly kept; they should be kept as confidential as law and professional ethics permit.

Trends

TOWARD MORE ADEQUATE STAFFS. Due to the increasing number of referrals for specialized help, more psychologists, reading specialists, speech and hearing specialists, social case workers, and counselors will be needed.

TOWARD MORE INDIVIDUALIZED INSTRUCTION FOR ATYPICAL STUDENTS. More attention is being paid to helping atypical students receive an education specifically adapted to their needs. The number of classes for the mentally retarded, physically handicapped, emotionally disturbed, and those with reading disabilities will increase. Those who are gifted will receive more appropriate instruction. Bi-lingual students will receive instruction in English, perhaps in a separate class for part of the day. These developments increase the need for more teachers with specialized training to handle the increasing identification and needs of atypical students.

TOWARD BETTER COORDINATION OF PUPIL PERSONNEL SERVICES. Because of the need to expand the pupil personnel services and the increasing number of specially trained personnel, there will be more efficient coordination of their services by the pupil personnel administrator and a clearer definition of functions and duties. Communication avenues, of necessity, will become more clearly defined and opened There will be further development of the natural coordination and communication between all of the allied pupil personnel services.

TOWARD MORE EFFICIENT RECORDING AND REPORTING TECHNIQUES. Pupil personnel administrators will continue to investigate and develop more efficient methods for handling the many time-consuming clerical tasks. Multiple and duplicate records will be eliminated, with standardization the goal. There is a definite trend toward computerized records and reports; smaller districts will use computers as costs decline and computer time is made available by other agencies or school districts.

TOWARD THE CENTRALIZATION OF PUPIL PERSONNEL SERVICES. There is a trend toward the centralization of all pupil personnel services in a single district department, providing better coordination and more efficient management. A teacher who has a student problem will need to make only one request for assistance to receive any and all types of help. Centralizing these services requires the leadership of a top-level administrator; in larger school districts, he should be at the assistant superintendent level.

TOWARD INDIVIDUALIZED PROGRESS REPORTING. Many school districts are moving toward the elimination of norm-referenced or competitive reporting. Student evaluation will be based on criterion-referenced testing which focuses on the concept of mastery and on what knowledge a student is expected to have learned at a particular time.

Administrative Problems

Problem 1

Smithsville is a small urban city. In general, its people are middle- or lower middle-class, and about 15 percent are classified as disadvantaged. It has elected school board members who want academic education stressed. The high school curriculum is oriented to college, despite the fact that only about 20 percent of its graduates go on to college.

Attendance at the high school is poor. Truancy and absences become worse every year as students claim the curriculum is irrelevant and teachers are uninteresting and unsympathetic. Every type of excuse is used and many parents sign notes stating that their children are ill although the school knows it is not true. Many excuses appear to be forged. The district attendance officer spends an inordinate amount of time trying to track down absentees but so far has not been able to improve the attendance.

What can the principal do to improve attendance?
What steps can the attendance officer take?
If you were the superintendent, what would you do?

Problem 2

The superintendent has moved all principals to different schools for the coming school year. Mrs. Goldberg, who is 40 years old, has been assigned as principal to the Clifton Elementary School which has a reputation for lax discipline. The former principal believed in permissiveness to an extreme. There were fights on the playground or on the way to school which were excused as youthful exuberance. Children were often tardy, wandered around the halls, and came into the office without excuse. Classes were noisy; rooms were often left messy. Teachers often complained, but the principal thought the "poor discipline" was part of growing up. He explained that children would learn self-discipline as they matured, if guided properly by the teachers. There were almost no school rules.

Mrs. Goldberg's previous school was noted for its unusually well-mannered children and fine discipline. She was described by others as being strict but fair and understanding. She suspects that the superintendent has assigned her to Clifton to bring order out of chaos.

What procedures can Mrs. Goldberg develop to improve the morale of the school?
What discipline policies should she develop?
How should parents be involved?

Problem 3

The school district described in Problem 1 has 12 elementary schools, 2 junior high schools, and 1 senior high school. Many homes are being sold and demolished as the community changes to an apartment and condominium area. The superintendent is concerned about the effect on enrollment and has asked the director of pupil personnel to make a school census. He is to determine the expected school enrollment for the next school year and the projected figures for the next five and ten years.

How should the director of pupil personnel proceed?

Selected References

AMERICAN ASSOCIATION OF SCHOOL ADMINISTRATORS. *Profiles of the Administrative Team.* Washington, D.C.: The Association, 1971.

BRADLEY, R. C. *Parent-Teacher Interviews, A Modern Concept of Oral Reporting.* Wolf City, Texas: The University Press, 1971.

CAMPBELL, ROALD F.; CORBALLY, JOHN E., JR.; and RAMSEYER, JOHN A. *Introduction to Educational Administration.* 3rd ed. Boston: Allyn and Bacon, 1966.

COMBS, CHARLES R.; COHN, BENJAMIN; GIBIAN, EDWARD J.; and SNIFFIN, A. MEAD. "Group Counseling: Applying the Technique." *The School Counselor* 11 (October 1963).

CONANT, JAMES B. *Slums & Suburbs.* New York: McGraw-Hill Book Co., 1961.

CRESSMAN, GEORGE R., and BENDA, HAROLD W. *Public Education in America.* New York: Appleton-Century-Crofts, 1966.

FENSCH, EDWIN A., and WILSON, ROBERT E. *The Superintendency Team.* Columbus, Ohio: Charles E. Merrill Publishing Co., 1964.

GLASSER, WILLIAM. *Schools Without Failure.* New York: Harper & Row, 1969.

GRIEDER, CALVIN. *Public School Administration.* New York: Ronald Press, 1961.

HOUSDEN, JACK L., and LeGEAR, LANNIE. "An Emerging Model: Criterion-Referenced Evaluation." *Thrust for Education Leadership* 2 (April 1973).

MILLMAN, JASON. "Reporting Progress: A Case for a Criterion-Referenced Marking System." *Phi Delta Kappan* 52 (December 1970).

MORPHET, EDGAR L.; JOHNS, ROE L.; and RELLER, THEODORE L. *Educational Administration: Concepts, Practices and Issues.* Englewood Cliffs, N.J.: Prentice-Hall, 1959.

MORRIS, GORDON T. "The Truant." *Today's Education* 61 (January 1972).

National Education Association, Research Division. "Reporting Pupil Progress to Parents." *Research Bulletin* 49 (October 1971).

NEEL, THOMAS E. "Classroom Performance Standards." *Thrust for Education Leadership* 2 (October 1972).

OTTO, HENRY J., and SANDERS, DAVID C. *Elementary School Organization and Administration.* 4th ed. New York: Appleton-Century-Crofts, 1964.

POPHAM, W. JAMES. "Focus on Outcomes: A Guiding Theme of ES '70 Schools." *Phi Delta Kappan* 51 (December 1969).

———. "The Instructional Objectives Exchange: New Support for Criterion-Referenced Instruction." *Phi Delta Kappan* 52 (November 1970).

PORTER, JOHN W. "The Accountability Story in Michigan." *Phi Delta Kappan* 54 (October 1972).

RISSMAN, F. *The Culturally Deprived School.* New York: Harper & Row, 1962.

SAWREY, JAMES M. *Educational Psychology.* Boston: Allyn and Bacon, 1964.

STOOPS, EMERY, ed. *Guidance Services: Organization and Administration.* New York: McGraw-Hill Book Co., 1959.

———, and RAFFERTY, M. L., JR. *Practices and Trends in School Administration.* Boston: Ginn and Co., 1961.

22

Teacher Education:
Preservice and Inservice

A school is only as good as its teachers and its teachers are only as good as their skills and competencies. Henry Adams believed that "a teacher affects eternity; he can never tell where his influence stops."

It is the purpose of this chapter to establish principles that provide a sound basis for teacher education at both preservice and inservice levels. Procedures are suggested to implement these principles and to make them effective.

This chapter includes a discussion of the following topics:

The Local School's Role in Preservice Teacher Education
The Teacher Education Institution
Standards of Preservice Preparation
Accreditation of Teacher Education Institutions
Teacher Certification
Reciprocal Certification
Continuous Teacher Certification
The State's Role in Teacher Certification
Inservice Improvement in the Local School
Multifaceted Inservice Programs
Constructive Supervision
Democratic Organization of Supervision
Summary
Trends

Material for this chapter was prepared in collaboration with Dr. Joyce Barlow King-Stoops, Professor, University of Southern California, Los Angeles.

The Local School's Role
in Preservice Teacher Education

Schools must take part in shaping their most important tool, the teacher. Fortunately, few schools espouse the statement made by one representative of a school district to the dean of a neighboring college of education: *"You* train the teachers. That's your job. We're too busy to get involved. But let us know when you get a good teacher for first grade—we're going to need one." There is an interdependency between teacher-training institutions and school. Although many other aspects of teacher education have been challenged, the value of a supervised clinical experience in teaching, prior to assuming full responsibility for a class, has been well documented. Conant describes this experience, variously called directed teaching, supervised teaching, or student teaching, as "the one indisputably essential element in professional education."[1]

Regardless of the excellence of the course work, a teacher candidate needs to relate to students in actual situations and master sequential teaching, learning, organization, management, and other skills in order to become competent.

The traditional laboratory training school, located on or near the college or university campus, has largely been supplanted for teacher education purposes by affiliated community schools. Reasons for this development include overcrowding in the laboratory schools, resulting in two or more student teachers simultaneously assigned to one supervising teacher; easier availability of transportation, with many student teachers owning cars; and lack of exposure in the protected campus environment to the broad range of cultural, ethnic, economic, social, emotional, and intellectual problems experienced in the larger community. The broadened base of teacher education involves many more principals and teachers in the process of teacher education.

The University of Minnesota developed cooperative teaching centers in an effort to remedy the limitations of the traditional pattern of assigning individual student teachers. Each teaching center has 12–15 student teachers assigned to it each academic quarter. A center has a resident clinical coordinator available to student teachers and cooperating teachers on a daily basis. The basic objectives of this concept are:

---

[1] James B. Conant, *The Education of American Teachers,* p. 142.

1. To better coordinate preservice and inservice learning experiences to meet the needs and interests of both the undergraduate and the experienced professional and with minimum duplication of effort.
2. To coordinate more fully resources and talents from a college of education, the public schools, and the community, vis-à-vis teacher education and research and development.

THE ROLE OF THE PARTICIPATING SCHOOL.   The school's most significant contribution to the teacher education process is the enriching clinical experience it provides for the student teacher.   Close cooperation between the school and the training institution is particularly essential for the success of the student teaching (or directed teaching) experience.   Because the key person in this process is the supervising teacher, his selection should be given priority, and usually is accomplished best by the school in consultation with the college or university.   Ideally, initial classroom observations are arranged for every student teacher and also arranged for young college people still in the process of career selection.   In addition, child development and educational psychology classes visit the classroom regularly to observe and work with individuals and small groups.   They can relate "what it says in the book" to children and their variety of growth patterns, capabilities, behaviors, feelings, and attitudes; and they can observe teacher methods of working with likenesses and differences in learners.

THE PRINCIPAL'S ROLE.   The principal as the building's educational leader sets the stage for successful directed teaching.   He introduces the new student teacher to the school and to its teachers and other personnel. He sees that rules, regulations, and policies are explained and understood. He uses terminology consistent with that of the training institution.   For example, most colleges avoid the terms "practice teacher" and "practice teaching"; many refer to the student teacher as "associate teacher."   The school principal interprets the directed teaching program to the school and community, and outlines suggested procedures for all involved.   He makes the new student teacher feel welcome in a situation which too frequently is filled with apprehension and anxiety.   He confers with the professor or coordinator from the training institution and maintains open lines of communication for each individual on the teacher education team.

EVALUATION.   The school's participation in evaluation of the student teacher should be clarified.   The principal should be aware of the progress of the student teacher, although his written evaluation usually is not requested by the college or university. However, in cases where such an evaluation is of particular benefit to the school district considering future employment of the individual, or where the college has need of additional input, the principal's written evaluation may have marked value. The principal also may be requested to complete a rating form for placement purposes for the student teacher's file.

EMPLOYMENT OF EDUCATION STUDENTS AS AUXILIARY PERSONNEL. In accordance with recent trends toward employment of paraprofessionals in education, some schools interview, select, and employ education students as paid teacher assistants in the classroom, library, and playground. This provides a ready source of professionally oriented backup personnel and allows for flexibility in differentiated staffing patterns, with benefits accruing to school, training institution, and individuals involved. The prospective teacher gains insights and skills, the working teacher accomplishes more with less time and effort, and the child receives more individual attention and help in the classroom.

An additional advantage to the school, and one which is frequently overlooked, relates to recruitment and selection.[2] The principal and other administrators are able to observe closely and to select early the highly competent prospective teacher. Once selected, the candidate may be groomed specifically for future assignment.

INTERNSHIP. Because the intern role lies somewhere between student teaching and typical first-year teaching, the employment of the intern teacher implies a unique partnership between the school and the college or university. The Association for Student Teaching referred to this joint responsibility for supervision in this statement:

> The intern assumes the major part of the teaching responsibility for a group of children or youth while having the support and guidance of qualified staff members from the college and the school. . . . He is free to extend himself and teach as he will in a regular classroom while still having the assistance of his professional supervisors to aid him in examining his teaching behavior and in reflecting on his decisions relevant to the classroom.[3]

---

[2] Joyce B. King, "Analysis of the Southern California Elementary Teacher Assistant Program" (Unpublished doctoral dissertation, University of Southern California, 1966), pp. 148–50.

[3] Association for Student Teaching, *A Guide to Professional Excellence in Clinical Experiences in Teacher Education,* p. 181.

To be most effective, the program should represent a coordinated team effort in which the school and the college or university share common goals and objectives.

WAYS TO IMPROVE PRESERVICE EDUCATION.   The success of the teacher education program in the schools is measured by its ability to produce competent teachers.   The school and college or university should work together in a continuing effort toward increased accountability, defining competence, pinpointing and working toward performance objectives within larger goals.   Together they should evaluate their program and be ready to revise guidelines, to clarify roles, to try new ways of assigning and scheduling students, and to experiment with ways of conferring and opening all lines of communication, especially feedback.   Better means of concretely measuring competencies of the student teachers are necessary to make written evaluations more meaningful.   The school's acceptance of this professional responsibility is imperative.

THE TEACHER EDUCATION COUNCIL.   A teacher education council (comprised of representatives from college, schools, and students), meeting regularly throughout the year, provides for communication and continuing appraisal of the program.   In some states, the council includes state, county, or professional association representatives.   This enables all members of the team to become acquainted; to mutually develop and continually refine goals, objectives, roles, instruments, guidelines, and procedures; and to communicate with the larger groups.   Activities such as these will lessen the traditional schisms expressed by the old saw, "Well, that may be the way they taught you to do it over there but this is the way it is in the *real* world!"

The Teacher Education Institution

PRESERVICE CURRICULUM.   To qualify for both high school and elementary school credentials today, the would-be teacher must take courses in child and adolescent development, history and sociology of education, guidance, curriculum, and methods.

SCREENING.   Stout found that respondents in 785 teacher education institutions generally believed that teacher candidates could be screened and thereby better selected. The respondents further believed that the better selection would not only improve the *quality* of future teachers, but might improve the *quantity* as well.[4]

Counter to their general image, teacher education institutions are markedly affected by changes in schools. Changing populations, evolving organizational patterns, curriculum and textbook revisions, increased use of instructional technology, and other such developments have caused teacher education curricula and standards to undergo continuous revision. The dwindling market for teachers has major implications for all teacher education institutions. Reduced teacher turnover is bound to result in a greater emphasis placed on upgrading teaching, advanced course work, education of specialists, and research and experimentation.

Standards of Preservice Teacher Preparation

The days of more or less automatic certification are rapidly passing. At one time in America, every high school graduate was a potential teacher; most teachers in the 19th century had never seen a college classroom. Around the turn of the century, the college-trained instructor came upon the scene, and the bachelor's degree became the symbol of the teacher, and remained so until the coming of state certification on a mass scale.

ADVANCED DEGREES IN EDUCATION. Today, a teacher must also hold a credential based upon specified subjects and units prescribed by the state and, in many states, an advanced degree. The master's degree now is required in many states, especially for secondary teaching. The doctorate in education is offered by increasing numbers of universities and is a requirement for teaching education in large colleges and universities. A study of 92 institutions granting the doctorate by the American Association of Colleges for Teacher Education showed that the Ed.D. was identified with teaching, administration, and supervision, and the Ph.D. with educational research. Colleges also felt that all doctoral candidates should possess a common core of knowledge in four areas: the behavioral sciences, the social sciences, philosophy, and measurement and evaluation, and should experience a year of residency. It was also agreed that a

---

[4] Ruth A. Stout, "Selective Admissions and Retention Practices in Teacher Education," *Journal of Teacher Education* 8 (December 1957), p. 429.

doctorate is needed to teach in a teacher education institution. Advanced education has tended to remove the teacher from the teaching arena.[5]

Accreditation of Teacher Education Institutions

The school administrator has the right to expect that a certificated graduate of an accredited teacher education institution possess certain insights and proficiencies. What backgrounds of course work and experience should the new teacher have? What should the college or university provide? Accrediting agencies, often an arm of the state or the profession itself, or both, work to establish standards of excellence and to hold the teacher education institution to these standards. New standards proposed by the American Association of Colleges of Teacher Education for the accreditation of teacher education institutions nationally include the following requirements for basic programs:

1. A thorough general studies component including as much general education as possible in order to produce well-informed, cultivated human beings who will provide acceptable models for children and youth.
2. A professional studies component that includes content and a theoretical practice component.
3. Adequate size and quality of faculty.
4. Sufficient faculty involvement with schools.
5. Adequate resources and facilities (library, instructional media, physical facilities, diverse institutional resources).
6. Evaluation of graduates and use of results to improve programs.[6]

Accreditation procedures still are in a state of flux. Continuous attempts to coordinate efforts between various accrediting agencies should be a priority of the profession.

---

[5] American Association of Colleges for Teacher Education, *The Doctorate in Education*, pp. 10–75.

[6] American Association of Colleges for Teacher Education, *Standards and Evaluative Criteria for the Accreditation of Teacher Education* (Washington, D.C.: National Education Association, 1967), pp. 10–21.

Teacher Certification

Several distinct types of certification have existed for many years. Historically, a school district hired anyone who could read and write and secure a credential of some sort which would enable him to draw a salary for teaching. Various methods existed for qualifying would-be teachers, most of them originating at local levels.

1. Certification through examination. This method involves administering to the applicant a generalized examination of varying degrees of difficulty, depending upon the state which countenances it. Upon successful passage of the test (with a percentage of correct responses agreeing with a predetermined minimum score), the applicant is then credentialed as a teacher by the state or county.
2. Certification through recommendation. Some states authorize teacher credentialing through recommendations by normal schools and other teacher-training institutions, without further qualifications.
3. Certification through previous experience. Some states also permit out-of-state teachers who have completed a given amount of actual teaching experience to qualify for a credential.
4. Certification through local and county offices. Especially in southern and rural states, credentials are bestowed by local educational agencies.
5. Certification through meeting state requirements. State departments of education are demanding more and more that would-be teachers complete approved programs or a minimum number of courses in required subject areas to qualify for the teaching credential. This method has the advantage of virtually standardizing the teacher education program.

THE PURPOSE OF CERTIFICATION. Traditionally, the educational welfare of the pupil has been so closely related to the qualifications of the teacher that even a slight improvement in certification requirements has tended to produce widespread effects upon the educational advancement of a state.[7] In addition, certification protects children from incompetent teachers, acts as a merit system for teachers, and raises the standards of the profession generally.

---

[7] Max M. Appleby, "Organization and Administration of Teacher Certification in California" (Unpublished doctoral dissertation, University of Southern California, 1950).

Most states now require health examinations as prerequisites for the teaching certificate; some require fingerprinting. Psychological testing is required in some states, and most states require no record of felony convictions. Detailed and overly specific loyalty oaths have been declared unconstitutional. Special proficiencies may be asked for, such as audio-visual experience and music ability.

Reciprocal Certification

Teachers are on the move and have been since 1945. Glaring salary differentials in various parts of the country have accentuated the mobility of a profession traditionally mobile.

As teachers move into areas of acute need, states should recognize an equivalency certificate.[8] However, each state tends to insist upon its own certification program for credentialing and issues credentials to out-of-state teachers only when they are able to meet its requirements in toto. Today most states demand that all other state certificates meet the requirements established for its own credential. The free movement of teachers to areas of need is complicated by this lack of state reciprocity.

A device often adopted to enable districts to hire out-of-state teachers and still keep the state's credential standards intact is the "emergency" or "provisional" credential. This is issued upon the application of a local district, usually accompanied by its sworn statement that no "regularly" credentialed state teachers are available. It enables a teacher so certificated to teach in the district in question for a period of time usually not exceeding one or two years. During this time, the teacher is expected to enroll in an approved institution and complete requirements for the regular credential.

The National Council for the Accreditation of Teacher Education, along with professional educators, has worked unceasingly for national accreditation of teachers.[9] Leadership from the U.S. Office of Education in standardizing teacher certification is needed, and its lack is woefully apparent. Certainly a good teacher in Connecticut will also be a good teacher in Washington. The solution would seem to be either the gradual

---

[8] Henry H. Hill, "Major Concerns in Teacher Education," *Twelfth Yearbook*, p. 154.

[9] Richard K. Sparks, "Are We Ready for National Certification of Professional Educators?" *Journal of Teacher Education*, pp. 342–46.

standardization of credentials in the fifty states, or the injection of flexibility into the existing credential requirements. As it is now, veteran teachers from other states are too often compelled to work as "emergency" teachers at the very bottom of most district salary schedules if they move to another part of the country. This penalizes many valuable experts for something over which they can exert absolutely no control.

The task force of the National Commission on Teacher Education and Professional Standards, which accredits teacher education programs in the U.S., recommends that standards for national certification be adopted. It proposes the following standards as a basis for certification:

1. Completion of an approved program at an accredited institution.
2. Recommendation by the institution on the basis of demonstrated competence of the applicant.
3. Recommendation of teacher competence by the appropriate organization of teachers.

The task force recommended that the National Council for Accreditation of Teacher Education enforce professional standards.[10]

Continuous Teacher Certification

The state determines the type of credential granted. If the educational authorities believe in a lengthy and generalized period of teacher education, with candidates exposed to many subject areas and curricular facets, then certification tends to be of the "broad" or "blanket" type. The theory underlying such a credential is that the teacher should be a versatile and broadly capable member of the school staff. He may be better equipped to teach in certain fields, but he is at least theoretically capable of understanding and, if necessary, teaching every subject in the curriculum.

The other type of credentialing has more limited expectations. When adopted by the state as a reflection of its philosophy, it usually takes the form of many certificates, each authorizing the holder to instruct in a particular subject field. A teacher holding a "kindergarten–primary" certificate is fully authorized to teach kindergarten, first, second, and third grades, but is forbidden to instruct fourth, fifth, and sixth grade pupils.

---

10 Margaret Lindsey (ed.), *New Horizons for the Teaching Profession,* p. 238.

The rationale behind this credentialing is the demands of increased specialization. Its result is a proliferation of credentials and certificates, with some states already boasting sixty or seventy.[11]

One of the least salutary features of credentialing is the issuance of the so-called "life credential," which tacitly assumes that once a teacher has secured a certain arbitrary number of units and courses, and has placed behind him enough years of experience, he will be an adequate teacher "for life." The life credential assumes that the same combination of experience and training that renders a teacher qualified to instruct classes in a 1975 social framework will still operate in 1990.

A good system of statewide teacher credentialing should involve a continuous program of inservice training which requires the completion of a given number of courses and units over a specified period of time for credential renewal. As long as a teacher remains in service, he should be expected to keep abreast of developments that exert a profound influence over his subject and techniques. The regular renewal of the teaching certificate, dependent upon the completion of specified university units within the period of time covered by the credential, ensures a teacher aware of current teaching techniques.

Professional organizations are assuming increased responsibility for renewing certification by recommending the form and content of courses, workshops, visitations, and other activities. Minnesota has continuing education committees at the local and state level composed of teachers, administrators, and laymen authorized to certify continuing education units for teachers.

Through more and better training, teachers have risen toward professionalization. Such professionalization is achieved, according to the National Commission on Teacher Education and Professional Standards, by better selection, training, certification, ethics, and general acceptance of higher standards.[12]

The State's Role in Teacher Certification

Teacher certification should be in the hands of the state. At the same time, it must be recognized that universities and teacher education institu-

---

[11] Appleby, "Organization and Administration."

[12] National Commission on Teacher Education and Professional Standards, *The Teacher and Professional Organizations* (Washington, D.C.: National Education Association, 1956), p. 18.

tions actually determine who are to be teachers and who are not. Therefore, the more complete the degree of coordination between the state
department and the teacher education institution, the more effective the
state educational program is apt to be. With a large number of teacher
education institutions in a state, each with a different set of requirements
for the credential over and above the state minimums, teachers tend to
"shop around" for the quickest and easiest way of obtaining a credential.

To prevent this, state requirements for the teaching credential should
coincide with university and teacher education institution requirements for
the same document. A sizable number of states are now mandating
greater control of their teacher education institutions, and they are making
detailed prescriptions for state-approved programs affecting teacher competencies. Thus, the state is able to demand greater accountability for
programs and personnel. State certification of teacher education institutions involves granting graduates of an institution's program a state
teaching credential. Some educators believe that this offers increased
professional autonomy while meeting both state and professional needs.

The fallacy underlying the present certification chaos is the assumption that a given number of units in certain prescribed university courses
will make the difference between a teacher and a non-teacher. There is no
acid test, no accurate prognosis of success or failure. The administrator,
who nine times out of ten will be the would-be teacher's sole and final
judge in years to come, should enter into the training picture. More
participation by school districts and more state department cooperation
should result in increasingly better education for teachers.

Inservice Improvement in the Local School

An inservice program, using the school as a laboratory, might be organized
in the following manner:

1. Through group action and discussion, arrive at a basic agreement upon
    the educational philosophy, goals, and objectives of the school system,
    with the emphasis upon greater accountability.
2. Compare collectively the current practices of the school district with the
    announced objectives.
3. List the conflicts uncovered in order of priority.

4. Set up a schedule for attacking problems, and assign staff members most interested in certain areas to attempt solutions.
5. Invite outside experts and consultants to contribute to the final solutions.
6. Facilitate outside study in related areas so that needed data may be gathered.
7. Experiment under controlled conditions after tentatively adopting a hypothesis indicated by the majority.
8. Evaluate results of the experiment; if a solution to the original problem is found, implement the solution as soon as possible.

Coffey and Golden stress the psychology of change within the individual and within the institution.[13] The institution should recognize the impact of change upon individuals as personnel roles are altered, and it should provide encouragement and official support. Maximum growth within the institution is encouraged by vertical and horizontal communication, participation of all personnel in planning, administration of inservice activities, and evaluation of results.

The essential idea governing the whole program is cooperation. No problem will seem real to a faculty if it is handed down *ex cathedra* from the administration. Teachers must ferret out problems themselves.

Due to constant changes in the learner and society, continuously improved information and understanding about the learning process, increasing diversity and complexity of tools and resources, and other developments in education, even the most astute teacher cannot close the door on continuing education. The well-prepared teacher should be able to evaluate, adapt, and restructure teaching plans and practices for increased effectiveness. Inservice education is an imperative for both teachers and administrators in a rapidly changing, complex environment of systems technology, accountability, needs assessment, and other measures toward explicitness in education.

A modern school, staffed with the most able teachers from training institutions and provided with every material advantage, would deteriorate perceptibly within a few years were it not for inservice education. An educator who does not improve, noticeably and steadily, over the years of his career will slip backward; a school staffed with many such individuals

---

[13] Hubert S. Coffey and William P. Golden, Jr., "Psychology of Change Within an Institution," *Fifty-Sixth Yearbook,* National Society for the Study of Education (Chicago: University of Chicago Press, 1957), chapter IV.

will inevitably decline, regardless of whatever heroic efforts may be brought to bear to stay the decline.[14]

Administrators frequently complain that the crush of "schoolkeeping" responsibilities and crisis-oriented activities tend to consume their energies to the detriment of inservice planning and development. Early involvement of the teaching staff in establishing educational priorities will help to avoid this difficulty.

One of the most important administrative responsibilities is "inservice training" or "inservice education." Barr, Burton, and Brueckner discourage the use of the term, "inservice training," because to some it connotes the doling out of specific procedures to the teacher. It should imply opportunities for growth and development of teacher judgment.[15] In the sense that the best teacher growth occurs under circumstances in which the teacher is afforded opportunities to make selective choices in an atmosphere of professional stimuli, this view is correct.

Marks, Stoops, and King-Stoops define inservice education as including "all activities of school personnel which contribute to their continued professional growth and competence" and give nine basic principles of inservice education:

1. The inservice program emerges from recognized needs of the school and community.
2. All school personnel need inservice education.
3. Proper supervision is an effective means of accelerating the inservice professional growth of personnel.
4. Improving the quality of instruction is the immediate and long-range objective of inservice education.
5. Inservice education leads to a continuous process of reexamination and revision of the educational program. Additionally, it encourages participants to attain self-realization through competence, accomplishment, and security.
6. Inservice education has become an increasing concern of state agencies, colleges and universities, school boards, school administrators, and teachers.

---

[14] Stephen M. Corey and C. Glenn Hass, *Fifty-Sixth Yearbook, In-Service Education,* National Society for the Study of Education (Chicago: University of Chicago Press, 1957), chapters I, II.

[15] A. S. Barr, W. H. Burton, and Leo J. Brueckner, *Supervision,* pp. 565–566.

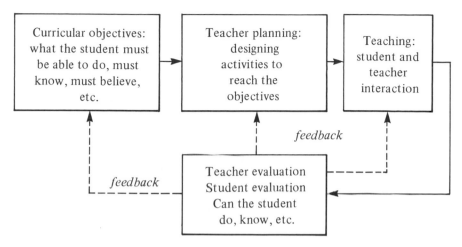

FIGURE 22–1. Relationships Between Curriculum Variables and Teaching. From S. C. T. Clarke, "General Teaching Theory," The Journal of Teacher Education 51 (Fall 1970), p. 407. Reprinted with permission.

7. Supervisors should create an atmosphere that will stimulate a desire on the part of teachers for inservice growth.
8. The inservice program should provide for keeping abreast with research and advances in education.
9. An inservice program is most effective when cooperatively initiated and planned.[16]

It is the responsibility of each individual to seek self-improvement and the responsibility of the school to provide ample opportunities for such improvement. Inservice programs should be based upon competent needs assessment by all individuals involved in the school, including parents, community, and, to a varying degree, students.

An important part of inservice education is the development of objectives. What should the students be able to achieve, create, and produce? Under what conditions? And how will teachers get them there? Figure 22–1 shows relationships between curriculum variables and teaching in the development of objectives.

_____
[16] James R. Marks, Emery Stoops, and Joyce King-Stoops, *Handbook of Educational Supervision,* pp. 219–220.

Inservice programs should be flexible in order to adapt to the changing needs of the community, curriculum, and staff. By identifying student needs, teachers best identify their own needs.

Multifaceted Inservice Programs

Within the framework of local school situations, there are a number of methods whereby problem solving can be implemented and inservice improvement rendered more meaningful. If it is kept in mind that none of these techniques are ends in themselves, but simply means by which the solutions to specific problems can be arrived at, all of them have definite value.

INSTITUTES AND WORKSHOPS. Special presentations and programs arranged either by the school district or by a state or intermediate educational office should be a continuing part of inservice education. Programs should be coordinated with the problem-solving activities of the staff, and should be oriented toward answering questions that have arisen as a result of studies going on within the district.

A favorite device is polling the faculty and staff prior to the institute; subsequently compiling a list of appropriate questions or problem areas for discussion; and securing qualified experts for conducting the workshop sessions. Immediately after the conclusion of the institute, evaluation sheets should be circulated among the participants, soliciting their opinions on the value of the sessions.

UNIVERSITY WORK. Summer sessions, correspondence courses, and year-long extension course work are valuable inservice education devices. Although statistics are not available, it has been reliably estimated that somewhere between one-half and one-third of all teachers pursue a program of study each year at some college or university.[17] When the courses taken are related closely to the individual's teaching assignment, administrators commonly agree on their positive value. An evaluation process or personnel guidance committee should be set up in each school to help teachers choose vital courses and discourage course enrollment solely to advance on the salary ladder.

---

[17] Edwin H. Reeder, *Supervision in the Elementary School,* p. 167.

TRAVEL.   The platitude that travel is broadening is worth remembering when evaluating methods of inservice education.   A teacher whose classes deal with colonial history or westward expansion profits greatly from a tour of New England battlegrounds or a vacation itinerary that includes the Oregon and Santa Fe trails.   A teacher of American government learns from a trip to Washington, D.C.; and a science instructor may conceivably pick up significant teaching data from a tour of the Smithsonian Institute or the Hayden Planetarium.   There is little corroborative evidence, however, that a trip to Coney Island or Catalina may be of value to an instructor of physics.   The indiscriminate use of travel as an inservice educational method is not justified.

TEACHER'S MEETINGS.   Perhaps the most widely neglected inservice training method is the faculty meeting.   Such meetings can be either generalized or particular.   Meetings involving all teachers in a school tend to deal with general policy matters, while those held for teachers of certain grade levels or subject areas may be highly selective in nature.   The former type tends to become a mere "bulletin-board" meeting, at which matters of school routine and administrative activities are dealt with to the point of boredom. The teachers' meeting in inservice training should be used for serious investigation of current problems of real importance.   Such meetings should be well-organized and prepared, with a written agenda, a time schedule, and a definite plan.   A faculty meeting designed to be part of inservice education may receive reports from committees of teachers and staff members, hear presentations from visiting authorities on instructional matters, and arrive at specific recommendations on current educational practice within the district.   In this way, trained observation and evaluation is fostered within the local school personnel, and a valuable inservice adjunct is made possible.

TEACHER VISITATIONS.   The teacher should not be allowed to molder in his classroom.   Several times during the school year, the individual instructor should be encouraged to turn his pupils over to a capable substitute and visit other teachers within or outside the district from whom he may learn new techniques and a variety of methods.   Visits should be carefully planned, and only the best schools and teachers selected for observation.   While the teacher is observing in order to improve his teaching effectiveness, he should continue to receive his daily salary from his school district.   These visits should be arranged by administrator, supervisor, and teacher, with an eye to the existing needs of the teacher. The latter should be encouraged to submit either an oral or a written evaluation of his observations following the visit. If at all possible, the principal should accompany the teacher on at least some visits.

PROFESSIONAL PUBLICATIONS. Every educator should be exposed regularly to professional thinking outside his own immediate surroundings. In many cases, the easiest and most convenient access to such information is professional writings. Books, journals, and bulletins should be provided in a school district's inservice training program. They should be ordered according to some agreed plan and on a regular schedule. After being received by the district, professional publications should be routed into the several schools, provision being made for their eventual destination into the hands of the teachers.

Some districts permit reports on approved professional reading to serve as substitutes for otherwise required college units for advancement on the salary schedule. This procedure, however, tends to put a damper on the free interplay of thought that is such a desirable adjunct to an inservice program. Reading should be done because the teacher has been led to desire it, not as a result of indirect compulsion.

LECTURES AND FORUMS. In rural and relatively isolated school districts, much can be accomplished in inservice development by bringing in ideas, rather than sending teachers to cities to absorb such information. Although the process involves a certain expense, it has repeatedly been found practical to import on a regular monthly schedule certain outstanding figures in education, art, literature, politics, and world affairs to share their special insights with the teachers in local schools.

This inservice device may be broadened with ease to take on a community aspect, with the guest speaker talking to school employees and townspeople. When such a program is decided upon, it is well to organize four or five monthly sessions around one main theme or subject to promote an orderly continuity and development of thought. This also fosters creative group planning and enhances school–community cooperation.

Constructive Supervision

By far the most effective way of improving a teacher's performance is to inform him of his strengths and weaknesses. It is one of the most difficult tasks of school administration. A whole field has grown up around the problem of teacher supervision. Basically, the problem is twofold: first, the supervisory officer and the teacher should reach an agreement on the objectives and how best to attain them; second, the teacher must welcome and be able to profit from suggestions and criticisms that inevitably arise out of supervision. The solution of this problem is the goal of modern supervision.

MODERN SUPERVISION. Instead of a system of routine visitations, notations, and formal conferences, modern supervision stresses cooperative planning and evaluation. Instead of putting a damper on initiative and originality, it attempts to free teachers from routine directives and regulations, and to encourage them to grow in competency according to their own particular abilities. The goal is actually self-supervision. The supervisor operates within the framework of this philosophy as a consulting expert; his services are available freely to all, but are imposed upon none.

Guidance under such a system prevents the undue aggrandizement of any teaching area or department to the detriment of another. Every teacher is encouraged to perceive his proper place in the district's scheme and to fit his activities harmoniously into the whole picture. Such coordination is arrived at through group planning and mutual understanding, rather than through authoritative directives. Instead of regarding supervision as an end in itself, modern theory correctly regards it as an important field of inservice teacher training.

AUTONOMOUS SUPERVISION. Flexibility is an essential quality of supervision. It is vital, therefore, that its administration and programming be left in the hands of individual school principals, with district supervisors acting as visiting resource persons.

There is a great temptation in any sizable school district to set up a centralized, system-wide program, administered from the main office by a specialist in supervision, and applied uniformly throughout the school district. It should be remembered that a building principal is, above all else, a trained supervisor. Each school should develop its own supervisory program tailored to its own needs and, with the cooperation of the district specialists, to administer it satisfactorily.[18]

---

[18] National Education Association, *Twenty-First Yearbook*, reviewed in *Department of Elementary School Principals Bulletin* 21 (June 1942), pp. 310–335.

GROUP SUPERVISION. The older concept of supervision dealt with the individual rather than with the group. Its practitioners believed that their highest function was the development of the maximum potentialities of the individual teacher. Supervisors tended to work with the individual, strengthening his weaknesses and correcting his mistakes. Little attention was given to cooperative supervision by which teachers, meeting together at regular intervals, analyze and discuss common problems and recent developments in teaching techniques. Group supervision ideally should be applied to the needs of both the individual and the faculty as a whole. Cooperative consideration of existing needs and group discussion of research findings in the field of instruction should serve as the basis of any school's supervisory program. The program, once determined by all concerned, should be applied through suitable channels to individual teachers in their daily contacts with pupils. In the final analysis, the only real justification for any supervisory system is the improvement of instruction.

Democratic Organization of Supervision

Nowhere in the entire school program is a spirit of friendliness and understanding more important than in the field of supervision. Such a spirit must be carried into all phases of supervisory organization, including the selection of supervisory personnel, the development of procedures, the organization of the personnel, and the supervision of the supervisory personnel. If, on any one of these levels, the intrusion of autocratic and destructive methods is permitted, the entire supervisory system is correspondingly jeopardized. Barr, Burton, and Brueckner define supervision as leadership within groups that are cooperatively:

1. Evaluating the Educational Product in the Light of Accepted Objectives of Education.
   a. The cooperative determination and critical analysis of aims.
   b. The selection and application of the means of appraisal.
   c. The analysis of the data to discover strength and weakness in the product.

2. Studying the Teacher-Learning Situation to Determine the Antecedents of Satisfactory and Unsatisfactory Pupil Growth and Achievement.
   a. Studying the course of study and the curriculum in operation.

     b. Studying the materials of instruction, the equipment, and the socio-physical environment of learning and growth.

     c. Studying the factors related to instruction (the teacher's personality, academic and professional training, techniques).

     d. Studying the factors present in the learner (capacity, interest, work habits).

3. Improving the Teacher–Learning Situation.

     a. Improving the course of study and the curriculum in operation.

     b. Improving the materials of instruction, the equipment, and the socio-physical environment of learning and growth.

     c. Improving the factors related directly to instruction.

     d. Improving factors present in the learner which affect his growth and achievement.

4. Evaluating the Objectives, Methods, and Outcomes of Supervision.

     a. Discovering and applying the techniques of evaluation.

     b. Evaluating the results of given supervisory programs, including factors which limit the success of these programs.

     c. Evaluating and improving the personnel of supervision.[19]

In organizing the supervisory program in any school system, these are the levels to which particular attention must be paid. On any single level, success or failure depends largely upon such intangibles as the general atmosphere of supervision, the purposes attached to it by the administration, the effects upon all persons involved, and the manner in which supervision is carried out.

Today, Barr, Burton and Breuckner's definition still is useful and appropriate, if their "accepted objectives of education" are expanded. Goals and objectives should be defined at the outset by teachers and administrators and should be agreed upon as a basis for competency, direction, growth, improvement of instruction, and evaluation. This procedure precludes either the teacher's or the administrator's planning alone and fosters cooperation and teamwork. The community should be invited to take part in defining the goals whenever possible, thus broadening involvement. Identification of the more specific objectives usually is the professionals' concern and responsibility.

Measurable, precise, succinct objectives that offer built-in criteria for evaluation of performance are essential for implementation and evaluation of the curriculum and instruction.

---

[19] Barr, Burton, and Brueckner, *Supervision*, pp. 147–148.

SUPERVISORY PERSONNEL. Two traditional classifications exist: general and special. The general supervisor concerns himself with broad aspects of curriculum and teaching competence. The special supervisor is a specialist in single subject fields, as music and art, but increasingly in the more general subjects such as mathematics and science. The general supervisor is enjoying greater popularity and is assuming an increasing role as an internal district employee rather than as an expert from outside. In many cases the principal is the chief supervisory person in a school, and often he may be the only one.

School districts are tending to employ coordinators of instruction as regular staff members and, in larger districts, to use the services of an overall supervisory officer with the title of Assistant Superintendent in Charge of Instruction. Special supervisors are commonly attached today to either state or intermediate educational departments. Their function is to assist several school districts within a given area in problems of specialized subject instruction. The goal of modern supervision is the assistance by all means possible of a program of self-supervision, capable of implementation and direction within the school itself, and operating on at least a semi-autonomous level. Supervision imposed by a centralized agency from outside the school is slowly being abandoned.

ORGANIZATION AND PHILOSOPHY. The organization of the supervisory program is largely dependent upon the philosophy and goals of the school system. A completely centralized and standardized conception of supervision will of necessity stress mechanics, techniques of rating and visitation, regularly spaced visitations, and multitudinous controls, amounting in the end to the negation of good supervision. The line-and-staff pattern will be emphasized, and for the most part, formalized methods will be used. The purpose of such supervision will be to bolster a system-wide curriculum and standardization of the educational product.

Contrasted with traditional supervision, the organization of supervisory procedures on a more modern basis is characterized by four basic goals, discussed in the following paragraphs.

Voluntary rather than compulsory supervision should be sought. Employees should be encouraged to solicit supervisory help, not attempt to avoid it. A faculty committee on supervision meeting regularly throughout the school year to draw up and evaluate the entire supervisory program is the best way to accomplish this end. This committee, including staff members and administrators, schedules class visits and teacher–supervisor conferences; arranges for special supervision in desirable areas; and remains alert to new findings in the field of supervision that might lend themselves to practical use.

Local autonomy is fostered by training school personnel as part of the goals and techniques of good supervision. In a large district, this is best accomplished by encouraging the central office to send its supervisory specialists into the field at regular intervals to work with local supervisors and school principals; the local people in turn can develop the techniques of self-sufficiency with their teachers. Thus, supervision becomes not only one of the areas of inservice training, but also one of its principal goals.

A program of voluntary coordination avoids supervisory laissez faire. In a district with many schools, this aspect of supervision is extremely important; otherwise, a large number of personnel in different school plants, working largely independent of one another, may serve merely to confuse the issue and get in each other's way. The best way to prevent this is to stress the importance of a district-wide standing committee on supervision, composed of representatives selected from several school committees or their chairmen. In this manner, a coordinating group will be available at all times to synchronize the overall goals and objectives of the program from a district point of view.

An important resource may be tapped by including the services of the nearby college or university in establishing practices and procedures for needs assessment, program development, and the like. Inservice programs built around the particular concerns of a school provide the most effective way of upgrading teacher attitudes and skills, but often impartial counsel leads to skilled decision making in establishing of priorities and direction.

AREAS OF SUPERVISION. The scope of supervision oriented toward the total learning process is tremendously broader than it is under a philosophy of supervision as mere improvement of specific techniques. The supervisor, whether general or special, must concern himself at one time or another with the following areas of major importance:

1. Philosophy, goals, and objectives
2. Curriculum
3. Community life
4. Discipline and behavior
5. Equipment and supplies
6. Inservice training

7.   Retention and promotion
8.   Professional relations
9.   Extracurricular activities
10. Personal problems of teachers

APPRAISAL OF SUPERVISION. The superintendent of schools does not supervise instruction; he supervises supervision. Machinery must be set up by him to facilitate regular evaluation of his supervisory program. Pittenger analyzes the functions of the superintendent of schools as follows:

1.   To evaluate the organization and its processes. This may be accomplished through the superintendent's own knowledge of good practice, by the judgments of supervisors and coordinators, by the reactions of teachers, and by the opinions of competent advisers brought in from the outside.
2.   To appraise personnel concerned with supervision. Here one of the best devices is the self-rating plan (ratings by the superintendent and his immediate assistants).
3.   To appraise the outcomes of the educational and supervisory processes. In attempting this, he may employ various types of tests, ratings and measurements, progress and attendance records of pupils, post-school success of graduates, and other similar techniques.[20]

All these methods are of little practical value to the school district if the administration does nothing with the data thus uncovered. The primary duty of the superintendent of schools is the constant improvement of the instructional program. His supervisory personnel are his main contact with that program. Unless he uses the results of various appraisal methods to upgrade the caliber of teaching in his schools, supervision becomes fruitless.

Summary

The value of a supervised clinical experience in teaching prior to assuming full responsibility for a class is obvious. Teacher education represents a partnership venture in which the school should maintain extensive involve-

---

[20] B. F. Pittenger, *Local Public School Administration* (New York: McGraw-Hill Book Co., 1951), pp. 189–190.

ment. To relinquish preservice education to colleges and universities is unrealistic and unwise. Traditional laboratory schools are not equipped to handle large numbers of teacher trainees so that local schools now participate widely to provide laboratory experiences for student teachers. This requires close cooperation in directed teaching between the local school and the training institution, with the principal playing the main role in interpreting the school and the community to the student teacher, and vice-versa. He may also be asked to help evaluate trainees, and increasingly employs them as paid teacher aides. A unique challenge is presented to the nation's schools in this area.

A new development in preservice education is the position of intern teacher, usually a first-year instructor who has just completed student teaching. This is one of several ways to improve preservice education, another being the Teacher Education Council.

Teachers should be given help in instructing novice teachers. They should define their own competencies, pinpoint their objectives, evaluate programs, and learn skills and systems of supervision. They should encourage communication and feedback.

Today's teacher education institution is typically a state college or a private college engaged in large part in educating new teachers. These schools formerly stressed mastery of subject matter; now they also require courses in psychology, guidance, and curriculum. They are important and valuable in the employment screening process.

Teacher certification has become almost wholly a state responsibility. Too often it acts as a block to interstate movement of teachers, making some system of national accreditation highly desirable. Certification requires a working alliance between the training institution and the state department of education. It should become a continuous rather than a terminal process as standards of preservice and inservice teacher preparation continue to improve.

Advanced degrees in education are becoming more common for classroom teachers, a device for raising standards comparable to institutional accreditation and inservice improvement of personnel. The latter should be built upon a formulation of the district's educational philosophy, the development of objectives, and the identification of needs.

Constructive supervision is the most important means of implementing inservice improvement. Modern supervision stresses cooperative planning and evaluation and operates autonomously within individual schools. It must be democratic, and should embrace two classifications of supervisory personnel: general and special. Its organization will depend largely upon the philosophy and goals of the school district. One of the school superintendent's most important jobs is the evaluation of his supervisory program, just as one of the local principal's main jobs is inservice improvement.

A good inservice program is multifaceted, consisting of institutes and workshops, university work, travel, faculty meetings, teacher visitations, professional publications, lectures, and forums.

Trends

Preservice teacher education, certification, accreditation, and inservice education are experiencing pressures from without and from within: from forces of government, community, profession, and sometimes from students. Major current developments are leading to new departures from traditional patterns we have known.[21]

TOWARD EARLIER AND MORE ADEQUATE EXPOSURE TO THE ACTUAL TEACHING SITUATION. General discontent with programs that are too isolated from classroom problems found in the "real" world of teaching will continue to cause education students to use local schools as part of their teaching preparation. Schools will offer more part-time employment opportunities for students to earn and learn and to relate their college course work to applied classroom psychology, methods, and procedures.

TOWARD IMPROVED PREPARATION FOR INNER-CITY TEACHING SITUATIONS. The typical suburban school setting is not meeting the needs of the student who goes into the ghetto to teach. More specialized training preparation for inner-city teaching will focus on understanding and working with parents and community, on communication and language, and on teaching methodology.

TOWARD INCREASING TEAMWORK BETWEEN THE SCHOOL AND THE TEACHER EDUCATION INSTITUTION. The local school is becoming more involved in the process of teacher education, making its needs known,

---

[21] National Commission on Teacher Education and Professional Standards, *A Manual on Certification Requirements for School Personnel in the United States* (Washington, D.C.: National Education Association, 1970), pp. 2–3.

offering ideas and suggestions, and working closely with the college or university to plan unique training experiences for student teachers.

TOWARD A CONTINUING SURPLUS OF TEACHERS. The teacher surplus will result in an increased focus on training specialists. Some feel that there is no teacher surplus, but rather a shortage of funding for salaries and more positions. The surplus also encourages teachers to keep their present positions, resulting in reduced turnover.

TOWARD A STRENGTHENING OF STATE CERTIFICATION AND ACCREDITA-TION PROCEDURES. Greater focus is being placed on state patterns of certification. In 1970, thirty-six states reported extensive use of a system whereby the graduate of a state-approved program is certificated. Teachers will find a simplification of the number of certificates granted, even in the face of increasing specialization.

TOWARD INCREASING RECIPROCITY BETWEEN STATES. A teacher moving to a different state will continue to gain improved chances of being granted a credential in the new state without having to meet additional require-ments. Reciprocity between states will grow.

TOWARD A GREATER NUMBER OF MASTER OF ARTS IN TEACHING PRO-GRAMS. More schools are offering the Master of Arts in Education (many with internships), and more students are working on advanced degrees than ever before; no reversal of this trend is foreseen.

TOWARD NEW COMPETENCIES IN INSERVICE EDUCATION. In the push toward accountability, teachers are experiencing a growing need for skills in formulating an educational philosophy, goals, and objectives. They are writing specific performance objectives prior to evaluating educational out-comes. They will need to analyze and evaluate and speak the language of computers, industry, and technology, as these new insights relate to education.

Teachers will be taught increasingly to work cooperatively with the community to enhance decision making and to improve schools.

TOWARD A GREATER TEACHER VOICE IN INSERVICE EDUCATION. Increas-ing teacher union demands for overtime pay tend to result in fewer school impingements on teacher out-of-class time, with workshops, institutes, and other meeting times cut to a minimum. Implications for the school district relate to careful structuring of content and procedures, with development of alternative approaches to information processing. Teachers will have a comparatively greater voice in planning inservice education, which will continue to develop as a cooperative venture between administrative and teaching staff, with the teacher a major agent of change.

Individualization of instruction will result in greater individualization of teachers' inservice needs.

TOWARD INCREASED PRESSURE ON TEACHERS TO CONTINUE PROFESSIONAL GROWTH.   Teachers will feel countless pressures to keep up-to-date; tenure discussions, merit pay considerations, voucher system challenges, tax election losses, lessened prestige in the eyes of the public and such will contribute to a state of relative insecurity for teachers. School districts with alert leadership will use inservice education to alleviate this insecurity.

With reduced teacher turnover caused by increased numbers of teachers seeking employment, inservice education will shift from emphasis on helping beginning teachers to focusing on the re-education of established teachers.

The challenge is not diminishing in teacher education. With each new departure, each improvement, a host of new, undefined problems emerges. New positions will require instruction, inservice training, and counseling. Preservice and inservice teacher education will be areas of endeavor requiring comparatively greater amounts of energy, time, and money in the coming years.

Administrative Problems

Problem 1

Cambridge School District cooperates with a school of education at a nearby university by placing student teachers in several of its schools. The principal of the Mariposa Elementary School told the assistant superintendent that he had four competent teachers, each of whom had requested the sole student teacher assigned to his school. He is finding it difficult to determine who should supervise the eager, potentially strong candidate for teaching. One of the four teachers plans to rely too heavily on the student teacher; another is rigid but produces high gains in achievement test scores; one is part of a team not wholly committed to having a student teacher; and a fourth expresses a missionary zeal to help because she recalls her student teaching days with horror.

How should the principal select the supervising teacher?
What criteria should be used in selecting the supervising teacher?

Problem 2

Another principal in the Cambridge School District told the assistant superintendent that he could not accommodate any student teacher assigned to his school this year. He claims that his teachers have no time or energy for this activity, and that they regard it as peripheral and deserving of salary supplements. They insist that $20 per student teacher is not an adequate token remuneration. The principal therefore suggests that the student teachers should be reassigned at once before their planned arrival at his school embarrasses them.

What do you see as the real difficulty here?
How would you, as assistant superintendent, handle this situation?

Problem 3

A city school district finds that its teaching staff is maturing and staying in the profession, promising little teacher turnover. Teachers are well entrenched and confident; they feel that their older methods will work well with the new children soon to be bused in. They expect that the newcomers with their different backgrounds and abilities will adjust, and they see no need to make any special effort to prepare for their admission. The principal has great misgivings about this problem and sees it as part of a larger problem of growing inflexibility on the part of his staff.

What should this principal do to prepare his school for the changes to come?
What are the implications for inservice education?

Selected References

ADAMS, HAROLD P. *Basic Principles of Supervision.* New York: American Book Co., 1953.

AMERICAN ASSOCIATION OF COLLEGES FOR TEACHER EDUCATION. *The Doctorate in Education.* Washington, D.C.: National Education Association, 1961.

ANDERSON, K. E., and SMITH, H. A. "Pre-service and In-service Education of Elementary and Secondary School Teachers." *Review of Educational Research* 25 (June 1955), pp. 214–226.

ASSOCIATION FOR STUDENT TEACHING, a national affiliate of NEA. *A Guide to Professional Excellence in Clinical Experiences in Teacher Education.* Washington, D.C., 1970.

BARR, A. S.; BURTON, W. H.; and BRUECKNER, LEO J. *Supervision.* 2d ed. New York: Appleton-Century-Crofts, 1947.

BARTKY, JOHN A. *Supervision as Human Relations.* Boston: D. C. Heath and Co., 1953.

BURTON, WILLIAM H. *Supervision, A Social Process.* New York: Appleton-Century-Crofts, 1955.

CLARKE, S. C. T. "General Teaching Theory." *The Journal of Teacher Education* 21 (Fall 1970), p. 407.

COGAN, MORRIS L. *Clinical Supervision.* Boston: Houghton Mifflin Co., 1973.

CONANT, JAMES B. *The Education of American Teachers.* New York: Mc-Graw-Hill Book Co., 1963.

HARTFORD, ELLIS FORD. "A Look at Teacher Education." *Journal of Teacher Education* 8 (March 1957).

Journal of Teacher Education 24 (Spring 1973).

HILL, HENRY H. "Major Concerns in Teacher Education." *Twelfth Yearbook.* Washington, D.C.: American Association for Teacher Education.

HOUSTON, W. ROBERT, and HOWSAM, ROBERT B., eds. *Competency-Based Teacher Education: Progress, Problems, and Prospects.* Chicago: Science Research Associates, 1972.

KING-STOOPS, JOYCE B. "An Analysis of the Southern California Elementary Teacher Assistant Programs." Unpublished doctoral dissertation, University of Southern California, 1966.

LINDSEY, MARGARET. *Teacher Education: Future Directions.* Washington, D.C.: Association of Teacher Educators, National Education Association, 1970.

————, ed. *New Horizons for the Teaching Profession.* Washington, D.C.: National Commission on Teacher Education and Professional Standards, National Education Association, 1961.

MARKS, JAMES R.; STOOPS, EMERY; and KING-STOOPS, JOYCE. *Handbook of Educational Supervision.* Boston: Allyn and Bacon, 1971.

MELBO, IRVING R., et al. *Report of the Survey of the Pomona Unified School District.* Los Angeles: University of Southern California, 1957.

National Society for the Study of Education. *Fifty-Sixth Yearbook; In-Service Education.* Chicago: University of Chicago Press, 1957.

REEDER, EDWIN H. *Supervision in the Elementary School.* Boston: Houghton Mifflin Co., 1953.

ROSNER, BENJAMIN. *The Power of Competency-Based Teacher Education: A Report of the Committee on National Program Priorities in Teacher Education.* Boston: Allyn and Bacon, 1972.

SPARKS, RICHARD K. "Are We Ready for National Certification of Professional Educators?" *Journal of Teacher Education* 21 (Fall 1970).

SPEARS, HAROLD. *Improving the Supervision of Instruction.* Englewood Cliffs, N.J.: Prentice-Hall, 1953.

STINNETT, R. M. *A Manual on Certification Requirements for School Personnel in the United States.* Washington, D.C.: National Commission on Teacher Education and Professional Standards, National Education Association, 1970.

WILES, KIMBALL. *Supervision for Better Schools.* Englewood Cliffs, N.J.: Prentice-Hall, 1955.

23

Administration of Certificated Personnel

The administration of certificated personnel is an essential function of the school district. The salaries of certificated personnel are the major item in the annual budget. Certificated personnel no longer accept the dictates of administrators without taking part in decisions. An effective school administrator draws from the sincere and intelligent ideas of others to help build a better system of education.

This chapter includes a discussion of the following topics:

Functions of the Personnel Administrator
Personnel Policy Formulation
Procurement of Certificated Personnel
Salaries and Salary Scheduling
Evaluating Personnel Efficiency
Teacher Tenure
Teacher Workload and Working Conditions
Leaves of Absence
Transfer of Certificated Personnel
Separation from Service
Substitute service
Personnel Records and Reports
Summary
Trends

Functions of the Personnel Administrator

Because of the importance of personnel functions, the personnel administrator should be one of the top administrators in a school district and a member of the superintendent's staff. The titles for the position are numerous, the most common being: Personnel Administrator, Administrative Assistant, Director of Personnel, and in larger districts, Assistant Superintendent for Personnel. The position should be equal in rank with business and educational services.

FUNCTIONS OF THE PERSONNEL ADMINISTRATOR. The personnel administrator has numerous functions. In addition, personnel administrators are often asked to perform other duties such as developing policies, preparing news releases, and serving as the negotiator for the school district. The personnel administrator must be a good communicator, have a knowledge of all the personnel functions in his district, and have good understanding and rapport with certificated personnel.

The personnel administrator requires an adequate secretarial and clerical staff to handle applications, correspondence, phone calls; to make reports, keep records, and so forth. In larger school districts, he may have one or more assistants.

PROBLEMS OF THE PERSONNEL ADMINISTRATOR. The major areas of concern for the personnel administrator are: "(1) Recruitment and selection of qualified personnel for certain areas; (2) Communications and relationships between board, central office administration, principals, staff, and parents; (3) Effective and equitable evaluation of staff; and (4) Negotiations and transfer of teachers within the district in order to have a racially integrated, balanced staff."[1] The most common daily administrative problems faced by the personnel administrator are: "(1) Termination of employment for incompetents; (2) Obtaining realistic references and uniform credentials concerning teacher applicants; (3) Contracts binding on the school board but not on the staff member (teachers violating contracts); (4) Data processing and/or other recordkeeping concerning personnel; and (5) Teachers' attitude toward services beyond the normal

---

[1] American Association of School Personnel Administrators, "Problems of Practicing School Personnel Administrators," *AASPA Bulletin,* p. 1.

school day."[2]   The most difficult of these problems is terminating incompetent employees because of the difficulties in meeting legal requirements, building a tenable case, and meeting community pressures over the issue. Another major problem is the handling of negotiations (often in regard to salary and fringe benefits), especially when the district faces severe financial problems.

CONTRACT NEGOTIATION.   Contracts should be offered at the time of employment and reemployment.   They should specify the salary and how it is paid, fringe benefits, days of work, vacations and holidays, inservice, preservice, and institute requirements, hours of work, and any other requirements and duties that the school board has approved.   All of these items are often the subject of negotiation with the teachers' association. The personnel administrator encounters problems especially at the end of the school year and during the summer when he is offering contracts whose specifications and salaries have not yet been resolved.   Unless a deadline has been established for returning teachers to sign contracts, he is unsure of the completeness of his staff and may overemploy or underemploy.   Some districts have had teacher strikes when negotiation is still going on at the start of a school year.   Contract negotiation should start early in the year and all issues should be settled prior to the usual time that contracts are offered.   In fairness to the education of children, negotiation should never carry over into the new school year.

SKILLS NEEDED BY THE PERSONNEL ADMINISTRATOR.   He needs technical training for "prospect appraisal, the building of salary schedules, formulation of job descriptions, personnel research, administration of the numerous records and fringe benefits, and in the specialized type of adult counseling in this post."[3]   He also needs a knowledge of education, general administration, law, data processing, interviewing techniques, evaluation techniques, and practical psychology.[4]   Essential personal attributes that are particularly useful are: "sensitivity and empathy, patience and forbearance, integrity and dependability, imagination and ingenuity, fairness and consistency."[5]

---

[2] American Association of School Personnel Administrators, "Problems," p. 1.

[3] Robert E. Wilson, *Educational Administration,* p. 434.

[4] Wilson, *Educational Administration,* p. 434.

[5] American Association of School Administrators, *Profiles of the Administrative Team,* p. 95.

LINE-AND-STAFF RELATIONSHIPS. There is considerable disagreement as to whether the personnel administrator is a line or a staff officer or a combination of both. In practice, he probably performs both functions. He may be delegated the authority to make some administrative decisions by the school board or the superintendent. Usually, however, he consults with the superintendent first unless the district is very large, in which case he may report to an assistant or deputy superintendent. It is imperative that he be responsible to and report directly to the superintendent. The personnel administrator should serve as a consultant to the building principal. He should also serve as a link between other administrators, teachers, teacher organizations, and the superintendent. The personnel administrator is also involved with classified personnel (*see* chapter 24). There is an increasing trend for personnel administrators to become considerably less involved in administration and to perform more of a staff function providing service to all personnel. It is only when everyone works together, with the personnel administrator serving as a consultant and adviser, that morale is kept at a high level and education improved.

There should be written and oral communication between the personnel office and individual schools on a regular basis to discuss personnel precepts and practices. The personnel administrator who visits schools and offices to observe firsthand and to be available to answer questions personally improves his relationships with personnel. In addition, he should establish relationships with the board of education, the superintendent, professional colleagues, professional organizations, community agencies, the communications media, state agencies, and federal agencies.[6]

Personnel Policy Formulation

Policies are the working agreements that clarify relationships, procedures, and ways of reaching goals and objectives. Without adequate personnel policies, sometimes called rules and regulations, the personnel administrator will be unable to function. Everything that he does or oversees must be done on a policy basis if action is to be consistent. Unfortunately, some school districts operate on an arbitrary basis with few, if any, written personnel policies; others confuse policies with administrative procedures and legal interpretations. Policies are general, broad guidelines for action. Administrative procedures explain the details for making the policy effec-

[6] American Association of School Administrators, *Profiles,* pp. 85–89.

tive.   State laws, however, may require procedures to be made a part of the policy document.

Personnel policies cover every phase of personnel administration, including:

Recruiting procedures	Grievance and appeal procedures
Assignment	Probation and tenure
Promotion	Substitute service
Evaluation	Job descriptions
Dismissal	Personnel records
Salaries	Duties and responsibilities
Fringe benefits	Extracurricular duties
Retirement	Vacations and holidays
Leaves of absence	Guidelines for post-graduate study
Work schedules	Inservice education
Negotiation	

The personnel administrator oversees the formulation of personnel policies, with the help of every individual or group that is affected by a policy.   The board of education and the superintendent should be consulted or informed throughout the procedures.   Broad participation at this stage leads to better understanding and acceptance, even when there is disagreement.   The problems inherent in any new policy can often be eliminated when the knowledge of others is applied to developing it.   The morale of everyone is improved when they are consulted, and problems that may be created when administrative dictums are handed down from above are lessened.

It takes careful planning to formulate personnel policies.   The personnel administrator should develop a schedule and arrange for individuals or representatives of groups to meet.   He should coordinate needed research and employ outside consultants.   His office should prepare tentative agreements as they are reached.   The policy that is finally agreed upon should be sent to the district's legal adviser for interpretation and suggestions.   The final policy must be presented to the board of education for adoption, policy being effective only when officially adopted and recorded in the board's minutes.   After adoption, the personnel administrator is responsible for implementing and enforcing the policies.   Few policies are permanent; they must be studied and revised continuously as conditions and social forces change.

Procurement of Certificated Personnel

The superintendent has responsibility for recommending new employees to the board of education (which has the employing authority). The personnel administrator should have the delegated authority to procure all certificated personnel and to recommend their employment to the superintendent. The success of the educational program is dependent upon the selection of qualified teachers and administrators.

The personnel office should advertise openings, recruit and interview applicants, request references, verify certification, and select qualified prospects to recommend to the superintendent. Now that the teacher shortage seems to be over, it is not as necessary to schedule recruiting trips out of the area. However, if there are not enough qualified minority applicants to achieve an ethnic balance, it may be necessary to travel in order to recruit them.

Job descriptions that accurately define the position, required competencies, experience, and training should be provided.

INTERVIEWING APPLICANTS. The interview, an important aspect of selection, largely determines whether the applicant has the personality and qualifications to be desirable for the district. Interviewing is an art that should be structured so that it is not a waste of time. Direct questions elicit factual information, but non-directive questions determine attitudes and personality. The interviewer should be friendly, avoid debate, and concentrate on listening.

Some districts use tests, district developed or furnished by the Educational Testing Service, prior to the interview. Only those who receive a qualifying score are interviewed. Many doubt the value of tests for selection.

There is an increasing trend toward using a team approach in interviewing applicants, involving the personnel administrator, principals, supervisors, department heads, and teachers. The team should not be so large as to overwhelm an applicant. For interviewing and screening of administrators, most districts use teachers. There are those who think this is inappropriate because they do not believe that teachers should see the personal references of a potential administrator. In the selection of new teachers, the team and the principal should agree on the selection. They usually recommend two candidates for the final decision, usually made by the personnel administrator with the approval of the superintendent. If consideration of an applicant has been discounted, he should be told immediately. Too often an applicant is kept dangling, thinking he is being considered for a position when he is not. Those who cannot be told immediately should be given a date when they will be informed as to whether they have been accepted, are still being considered, or cannot be used. The placement office that sent the candidate's file should also be kept informed as to the status of the applicant and if he is not employed, his file should be returned immediately.

NOTIFICATION AND ASSIGNMENT OF ACCEPTABLE TEACHERS.   Once an applicant has been found acceptable, he should be notified in writing and an offer of employment sent to him. It should contain a deadline for answer so that the district knows whether to hold the position for him or look for other applicants.

When school openings are known, it is wise to let the principal have a strong voice in selecting his teachers. Large school districts, such as New York City, Los Angeles, Detroit, and Chicago, must involve many people in teacher selection since they employ over a thousand teachers each year. They cannot employ for specific positions that are unknown at the time of the interview. Selected applicants must understand that they are employed by the *district* and will be assigned to a new teacher pool until openings occur. Large districts must also use the services of many people to handle the numerous interviews. They should also use data-processing techniques for keeping track of applicants, scheduling, notifying, and assigning. It is a complex task to match vacancies with applicants whose training, qualifications, and certification qualify them for the assignment.

Although the superintendent is responsible for assignment, this is usually delegated to the personnel administrator. As soon as it is known where a new teacher is to be assigned, he should be notified and advised to visit the school and meet the principal. The personnel office should arrange for his orientation. This can be done on a large scale at the beginning of a school year, individually, or in small groups during the year.

Salaries and Salary Scheduling

All educational theory, no matter how excellent, breaks down immediately when compelled to function under poor teaching conditions and pauperizing salaries. Teachers and other employees are, or should be, normal men and women, humanly desirous of the same benefits which have largely become an integral part of the American way of life. School morale is very dependent upon such mundane but vital factors as pensions, leaves of absence, workload, and tenure.

Although teachers have made sizable salary gains in recent years, they have lost ground in the purchasing power of the dollar. However, beginning salaries of teachers have remained slightly above the average increases in the cost-of-living index.[7] Teachers' salaries do not compare favorably with those in other vocations, even where teachers are noted for their high pay. In 1971–72, for example, the average beginning salary for teachers with a bachelor's degree was $7,061. This was 26 percent below the average salary of $9,534 paid for beginning male graduates with a bachelor's degree entering private industry.[8] Table 23–1 compares the average beginning teacher salary (in school systems enrolling 6,000 or more students) with those who entered private business. Although the average salary for all teachers in 1970–71 was estimated by the National Education Association at $9,265, there was a great range. It was estimated that "8.7 percent of the public school teachers are paid less than $6,500; 50.7 percent, from $6,500 to $9,499; 26.2 percent, from $9,500 to $11,499 and 14.5 percent, $11,500 or more."[9]

ESTABLISHED SALARY SCHEDULES. School employees should be paid by cooperatively arrived at salary schedules, providing for minimum and maximum pay and for annual increments in established amounts. Such a device tends to regularize the compensation of employees in accordance with certain categories of employment. Thus, in a given district, there may be different salary schedules, one for teachers, one for administrators, one for clerical employees, one for custodians and maintenance employees, and so on. Such systematic organization allows each employee to project his salary future and eliminates individual bargaining.

PRINCIPLES FOR DEVELOPING TEACHER SALARY SCHEDULES. All schedules and programs should be based on sound principles and policies. A

---

[7] National Education Association, Research Division, "Beginning Salaries for Teachers in Big Districts, 1950–51 to 1970–71," *NEA Research Bulletin,* pp. 83–86.

[8] National Education Association, Research Division, "Starting Salaries: Teachers vs. Private Industry," *NEA Research Bulletin* 50 (March 1972), p. 8.

[9] National Education Association, Research Division, "Facts on American Education," *NEA Research Bulletin* 49 (May 1971), p. 49.

TABLE 23–1. Comparison of the Average Beginning Teacher's Salary with Those Who Entered Private Business in 1971–72[a]

Men and Women Teachers with Bachelor's Degree	
Beginning Teachers	$ 7,061
Men Graduates with Bachelor's Degree	
Engineering	$10,500
Accounting	10,260
Sales–Marketing	8,736
Business Administration	8,424
Liberal Arts	8,292
Production Management	9,792
Chemistry	9,720
Physics	9,636
Mathematics–Statistics	9,192
Economics–Finance	9,216
Other Fields	8,580
Women Graduates with Bachelor's Degree	
Mathematics–Statistics	$ 9,312
Economics–Finance	8,400
General Business	8,016
Chemistry	9,744
Accounting	9,516
Home Economics	7,932
Engineering–Technical Research	10,608

[a] National Education Association, Research Division, "Beginning Salaries for Teachers in Big Districts, 1950–51 to 1970–71," p. 8.

school district's salary program is one of the chief factors in maintaining and improving morale. Individual bargaining is uncertain and leads to lack of trust and confidence. Professional and equitable salary schedules assure teachers that they are receiving a just wage on which they can predict their personal economy. The following principles are recommended for adopting salary schedules:

1. The welfare of the child should be the first consideration in determining teachers' salaries.
2. A salary schedule is one part of a district's total program of personnel administration.
3. A salary schedule should be developed in terms of the basic concept of an annual salary sufficient to attract and hold capable personnel.
4. The salary schedule should be developed by cooperative action of the board, the administration, and the teachers.

5. The salary schedule should be based primarily on training and experience. [However,] techniques for compensating meritorious performance should be cooperatively studied, . . . evaluated [and adopted where possible. Superior teaching is the only ultimate justification for superior salaries.]

6. The salary schedule should provide incentives for satisfactory performance and continued professional growth.

7. Changes in placement from one class to another, or from one step to another within a class, should be accomplished on an annual basis at a fixed point in the fiscal year.

8. Each district should have an "Evaluation of Professional Growth Committee."

9. Extra pay for extra duties should be eliminated as far as possible without creating gross injustice.

10. The salary schedule should be examined annually.

11. Step status should always be maintained.

12. In drawing up a salary schedule, the entire teaching staff should not be penalized because of the inadequacies of a few of its members.

13. The use of the merit concept for the placement of teachers on a salary schedule should not be attempted without adequate study by teachers, administrators, and the governing board.

14. Previous experience outside the district should be recognized.

15. In adopting a new salary schedule, no employee should be penalized by readjustment of placement.

16. Each district should develop its own salary schedule rather than limit its action to that of its neighbors.

17. Sex, race, and creed have no place in the development of a salary schedule.

18. The salary schedule should be supplemented with statements relating to the district's policy on frequency of payment, deductions, and retirement.[10]

For years it has been recommended that salary schedules should have a maximum range of one and one-half the minimum salary. In the last few years, under the urging of the National Education Association, the range has been extended to two times the minimum plus many fringe benefits in numerous school districts.

---

[10] Irving R. Melbo, et al. *Report of the Survey, Laguna Beach Unified School District* (Los Angeles: University of Southern California, 1961), pp. 260–61.

Types of Salary Schedules.   The following list outlines some common salary schedules:

1.   Position schedules pay according to the position the teacher holds: elementary, junior high, high school.   It is practically extinct.
2.   Preparation schedules pay according to the degree held.
3.   Experience schedules pay according to the years of teaching experience.
4.   Cost-of-living schedules base increments upon the Consumer Price Index or some other means of determining the rise in the cost of living.
5.   Merit pay salary schedules are based on the teaching efficiency of the teacher.
6.   Differentiated salary schedules are based on the level of responsibility.
7.   Extra pay for extra duty plans are frequently used to supplement the regular salary schedule.
8.   Fringe benefits supplement the regular salary schedule by providing money for insurance of all types and for retirement benefits.

Longevity increments also have been added to some salary schedules.   An added bonus, for example, may be added every five years after a maximum has been reached.   Some school districts require factors such as "superior" evaluation reports or completion of extra, approved college courses before a teacher can qualify for a salary increase.   Most school districts use various combinations of the above in their schedule development.   The typical salary schedule has several training classifications, such as the bachelor's degree, the bachelor's degree plus required units, the master's degree, and the master's degree plus required units, and in some districts, the doctoral degree.   Step increments are added for each year of experience in each of the classifications.   New teachers are "rated in" according to their academic degree and years of experience.   It is possible to advance on the schedule in two ways: "across," or from one preparation classification to another, and "down," or from one experience step to the next. Placement upon the salary schedule becomes an automatic procedure, facilitating the routine work of the administrator and enabling the teacher to forecast his own salary future.   It has the further advantage of encouraging the teacher to pursue advanced study and degrees.

Table 23–2 shows a sample preparation and experience salary schedule; naturally, the amounts will not remain current.

TABLE 23–2.   Teacher Salary Schedule, 1971–1972

I B.A. OR CREDENTIAL	II B.A. + 15 GRAD. UNITS	III B.A. + 30 GRAD. UNITS	IV B.A. + 45 GRAD. UNITS OR M.A.	V B.A. + 60 INCLUD- ING M.A.	VI B.A. + 75 INCLUD- ING M.A.
7600	7980	8360	8813	9273	9763
7863	8291	8718	9220	9721	10,259
8133	8602	9072	9621	10,170	10,756
8397	8914	9431	10,022	10,618	11,246
8666	9225	9790	10,428	11,067	11,742
8930	9536	10,143	10,829	11,516	12,233
9193	9848	10,502	11,231	11,964	12,729
9463	10,159	10,861	11,637	12,413	13,225
9726	10,471	11,215	12,038	12,856	13,716
9996	10,782	11,574	12,439	13,299	14,212
10,259	11,093	11,932	12,845	13,753	14,703
10,523	11,399	12,286	13,247	14,202	15,200

SALARY SCHEDULE POLICIES.   The following policies are typical of those pertaining to a salary schedule:

1.   All teachers must hold a valid state teaching credential.
2.   All teachers will be placed on a salary schedule commensurate with their units, degrees, and years of credited service.
3.   A maximum of five years credit shall be granted for out-of district teaching service.   Credit for such experience shall be on a year-by-year basis.   Credit will be given for full years of experience only.
4.   Private school experience while holding a valid teaching credential may be given full credit on the salary schedule.
5.   One year (12 months) of verified military service may be counted in lieu of teaching experience.
6.   Teachers employed to teach industrial education subjects may be granted up to four years of credit for work experience, including work as a journeyman, in lieu of teaching experience, whether or not they hold a B.A. degree.
7.   New teachers will be given a tentative placement on the salary schedule by the personnel administrator according to the evidence of experience and training submitted.   Final placement on the salary

schedule will be made when complete college transcripts and verification of experience have been received. All verifications must be received by September 1 of the school year.

8. Units earned in an accredited training institution will qualify the teacher for column or classification status provided such units are in accordance with district policy.

9. Each employee shall advance one experience step per year of experience, provided he has completed a minimum of six semester units of graduate work in an accredited institution each three-year period. In lieu of graduate courses, undertaking workshops, conferences, educational travel, authorship, curriculum development and the like may qualify the employee for step advancement, provided these experiences are designated for credit in advance by an established policy.

10. An evaluation committee may be appointed by the superintendent, the committee to be comprised of two administrators and three teachers. This committee shall approve proposed study or other activities to qualify for advancement on the salary schedule. Any problem relating to salary placement shall be referred to this committee for evaluation. All decisions by the evaluation committee shall be made on a policy basis to eliminate personal bias or special privilege.

11. Each teacher shall advance one step per year on the salary schedule, provided he has received satisfactory ratings or appraisal. Service must be for at least 75 percent of the teaching days of the district's school year.

12. Regulations that are related to the salary schedule, such as leaves of absence, deductions, frequency of payment, institute attendance, and the like, shall be set forth in writing in the *Teachers' Handbook.*

13. Advancement from one training classification to another may be made on September 1 of the fiscal year, provided the teacher furnishes sufficient evidence of specified additional training.

14. A super maximum or anniversary increment of one experience step may be provided for teachers who have taught successfully for each five years on their maximum training classification level. (This is not yet a common practice.)

15. The school year for certificated employees who are paid on the teacher's salary schedule shall be on a calendar month basis from September 1 through June 30. The active days of service shall be approximately 183 working days.

SALARY PROBLEMS.   The preparation–experience schedule so widely used today probably does not do what it purports to do.   It assumes that the accumulation of university units, even on an indiscriminate basis, leads to more effective teaching.   Weber has accumulated evidence which seems to indicate quite the contrary.[11]   To be effective as inservice training, each teacher's proposed course should be approved by the school's evaluation or professional guidance committee.

Putting a dollar sign on a university credit leads too frequently to enrollment in "snap" courses of doubtful value.   Units can be accumulated in widely scattered subject areas bearing little relationship to each other. The acquisition of futile degrees earned by half-hearted research and study in areas of little interest to the teacher is of doubtful value.   Often, there is a sudden or complete cessation of all advanced study after the top rung of the schedule has been reached.   A cynical attitude may develop toward graduate courses in general as a result of enduring classes in which the teacher has no interest and which he is taking merely to satisfy salary schedule requirements.   Such a procedure cannot possibly redound to the advantage of either the teacher or the school system that countenances it. The teaching profession has been susceptible to overrating the value of accumulating advanced degrees, to the neglect of other criteria for judging teacher growth.

When educators are prepared to formulate standards of good teaching and to analyze accurately ways of reaching their goals, then proper stimuli and motivation can be organized to assist in achieving desired objectives. In lieu of academic units, unit credit for salary increases could be granted by the school board for participating in experimental programs judged by teachers, board members, and administrators to be of value to the school district's educational program, for active study of curriculum development, for developing and evaluating new teaching techniques, and for participating in workshops where they cooperatively study problems that have arisen.[12]   Salary rewards should come as the result of demonstrable teaching competency, not solely on the basis of accumulated academic units.

MERIT PAY.   Merit pay as a method of rewarding superior teachers has been discussed in the literature for over fifty years and is still a contro-

---

[11] Clarence A. Weber, *Personnel Problems of School Administrators*, pp. 261–63.
[12] Weber, *Personnel Problems*, pp. 263–64.

versial subject.   Research on the effectiveness of merit pay has been
meager.   Merit pay plans have taken many forms:

1.   Super-maximums
2.   Accelerated increments
3.   Bonus plans
4.   Multiple track
5.   Periodic merit evaluation
6.   Annual outstanding teacher awards
7.   Summer merit teacher projects programs

Many programs combine two or more of these basic plans, most of which
have come into existence since 1946.

PROPONENTS OF MERIT PAY.   Reeder states that "a salary schedule which
gives its awards wholly for preparation and experience, or which operates
automatically toward all teachers, cannot fail to pay many teachers much
more than they deserve and many others much less than they deserve."[13]
Proponents claim that a merit pay plan helps retain superior teachers and
avoids losing them to supervisory or administrative positions or to other
professions.   It recognizes differences in ability, and rewards competence.
Improvement in teaching performance is encouraged and teacher complacency is reduced.

Merit pay appeals to taxpayers because they believe that their tax
dollars will go to teachers who are the most proficient.   Industry has
shown that incentive pay has proven to be successful.

It is unusual that the profession has never devised an accurate
measurement of teaching effectiveness.   Principals and supervisors have
been scrutinizing for generations all sorts and types of teachers, jotting
down virtues and shortcomings, and making various and sundry recommendations to superintendents and school boards.   Thousands of theses,
dissertations, and seminar papers have been written on the general subject
of "the superior teacher," and educational journals for a century have been
full of learned controversy on this topic.   Yet, when the question of merit
pay comes up, many administrators proclaim their inability to select
superior teachers.

---

[13] Reprinted with permission of Macmillan Publishing Co., Inc. from *The Fundamentals of Public School Administration,* 4th ed. by Ward G. Reeder.   Copyright ©
1958 by Macmillan Publishing Co., Inc., p. 164.

MERIT PAY OPPOSITION. The literature for a number of years has included such statements opposing merit pay as the following:

1. Evaluation is too subjective to determine a salary.
2. There is a lack of agreement as to what constitutes good teaching.
3. Many of the aims of education are intangible and difficult or impossible to measure.
4. The validity of scales measuring competence and the reliability of appraisals by raters are of doubtful value.
5. Dissension may be created and resentment between teachers fostered.
6. Professional relationships and morale are destroyed.
7. Strife between teachers and administrators may lead to deterioration of the educational program.
8. Single salary schedules become complicated.
9. Teachers generally resent merit rating salary schedules.
10. Salary schedules based on merit pay are too costly and time-consuming to administer and restrict the number of teachers who deserve the extra salary.
11. Tenure may be weakened.
12. Teacher initiative may be replaced by fear and result in poorer teaching.
13. Many merit pay plans that have been tried have proven unsuccessful.
14. The emphasis on competition encourages professional rivalries and jealousies and damages teaching effectiveness.
15. Constructive supervision is deprived of its purpose.
16. Personal politics may influence the rating.

The National Education Association and the American Federation of Teachers generally oppose merit pay. A survey by the NEA Research Division in 1971 asked the question, "Should each teacher in a school system be paid on the basis of the quality of his work or should all teachers be paid on a standard scale basis?" The results showed the following:

	TEACHER OPINION	PUBLIC OPINION
Quality of work	28%	58%
Standard scale basis	67	36
No opinion	5	6

National Education Association, Research Division, "Merit Pay: Teacher Opinion and Public Opinion," *NEA Research Bulletin,* p. 126.

The poll shows clearly that while the public favors paying teachers according to the quality of their work, teachers overwhelmingly favor the standard pay scale.

DEVISING A MERIT PAY PLAN.   The problem of merit pay is still a difficult one.   At the present time, there seems to be no general solution to developing adequate, fair, and acceptable merit pay plans.   Some of the major problems are the attempts to define what is meant by "excellence," to define the teacher's classroom role, and to institute an acceptable evaluation plan.   There is still much to be learned about merit pay programs.

Merit can be determined, despite a present lack of absolute accuracy in determining its degrees.   The solution to the present dilemma lies, not in outlawing merit as a component of salary schedules, but in determining more precise criteria and mechanisms for identifying it.   A possible method of accomplishing this may be the following:

1.   Develop a preparation–experience type salary schedule generous in its financial provisions and designed to encourage graduate study.
2.   Superimpose on the salary figure in each classification and level of this schedule a substantial and identical bonus for superior performance.
3.   In order to determine the identity of such superior teachers, arrange for the appointment of an evaluating committee composed in each school plant of the principal, a supervisor, and three veteran teachers.
4.   In addition, use standardized achievement tests administered and correlated by the guidance department of the district, so that the improvement of pupils may be measured objectively each year.
5.   Combine classroom visitations, observations, and test results with ratings in extra-curricular leadership, community and staff relations, and professional enthusiasm to identify the top ten percent of teachers with outstanding qualities in their instructional fields.
6.   Superior rating should be valid for one year only, and may be continued or discontinued as a result of annual re-evaluations in accordance with the approved routine.

It is not necessary to overcome *all* objections that can be raised to the merit type of salary schedule.   Any such system will have certain flaws, but the long-range goal will be worthwhile.   For example, the claim that it is impossible to measure the degree to which any teacher has influenced the moral growth or future citizenship of his pupils has some validity.   However, one cannot wait thirty years to give the teacher extra pay. Merit pay should reward on the basis of what we can detect, not on the basis of what we cannot. If an artist does our portrait in oil, and does it well, we pay him immediately upon the completion of his appointed task; we do not wait for a generation to reward his labors until his art hangs in the major museums.

Once the principle of extra financial remuneration for superior teaching is conceded, it is important to implement this principle with total staff participation and with those admittedly inadequate tools presently possessed. We shall certainly not advance the cause of more sensitive and individualized salary scheduling by waiting, apathetically and interminably, for an impossible perfection. At present, the top, middle, and lowest merit can be identified; exceptions do not disprove this working generalization.

During the 1960s, more than 200 California school districts used salary schedules that included merit raises or bonuses. Most of these districts were rural or suburban. Experimentation with merit pay has expanded to other states in the early 1970s.

ADMINISTRATION OF A MERIT PAY PROGRAM. If a school district installs a merit pay program, teachers and administrators must understand and appreciate the purposes of merit pay and the value that can result. All administrators and teachers should participate in developing the plan. There should be sufficient supervisory personnel with competence in subject matter, knowledge of learning processes, skill in evaluation, and the ability to work with others. Creativity and experimentation in the classroom should be permitted. Teachers and observers must recognize that subjectivity in observing methods is an inherent element in the merit pay program and cannot be completely avoided. However, there must be a high degree of trust, sincerity, and fairness by all concerned.

DIFFERENTIATED STAFFING. One of the newest and most controversial salary innovations is that of differentiated staffing. Unlike merit pay, which pays only according to the quality of performance, it pays according to the level of responsibility.[14] Although comparatively few districts use this plan, a great many are showing an interest in it. It is generally considered to be an outgrowth and refinement of team teaching, based on a diversity of teaching tasks and the use of auxiliary personnel to relieve

---

[14] National School Public Relations Association, *Differentiated Staffing in Schools,* Bulletin No. 411–12754 (Washington, D.C.: The Association).

teachers of non-instructional duties. Differentiated teaching goes even further and differentiates a teacher's role and responsibilities according to his interest, ability, and ambition. It assumes that all teachers are not alike in skills; that all cannot participate competently in the decision-making process, nor set their own standards.

Differentiated staffing does not work within the four walls of a self-contained classroom. The prototype school should have multi-shaped lecture halls, small group conference rooms, science and language laboratories, and instructional resource centers. The program is usually found in conjunction with team teaching, nongrading, and flexible scheduling.

Advocates of differentiated staffing claim that it improves the quality of education for children and improves the profession. It permits superior teachers to earn enough to retain them in teaching positions rather than promoting them to non-teaching positions.

No two school systems with differentiated staffing appear to follow the same plan for designating salary differentials, although all permit teachers to earn more than the regular salary schedule. Various titles have been used to differentiate levels of responsibility, such as: associate instructor, instructor, senior instructor, or apprentice teacher, junior resident, and senior resident. Temple City, California, has used the following levels of responsibility for its differentiated staffing plan:

Associate Teacher. A first-year teacher with a B.A. degree who carries a full-time teaching load and is protected by tenure.

Staff Teacher. An experienced teacher with a B.A. degree who is an expert in at least one of several learning modes, such as small group instruction. He has a full-time teaching load and is protected by tenure.

Senior Teacher. A master practitioner in his subject area who must hold a master's degree or equivalent. He teaches other teachers and is responsible for the application of curricular innovations to the classroom. His teaching load varies from 35 to 50 percent and he is protected by tenure as a staff teacher.

Master Teacher. An effective classroom teacher with a scholarly depth of knowledge in his subject matter area who must hold a doctorate degree or equivalent. He maintains a continual program of research and evaluation in his area of curriculum development. His teaching load is 25 percent and he is protected by tenure as a staff teacher.

INITIATION OF A DIFFERENTIATED STAFFING PROGRAM. In the above Temple City organizational plan, it is possible for the Master Teacher, at his highest level, to earn more than the superintendent. Instructional aides assume many of the clerical and housekeeping tasks, freeing the teachers to devote more of their time to the educational program and teaching.

School districts planning to adopt a differentiated staffing program should start slowly and allow twice as much planning time as they have for other innovations. A planning calendar should be developed that leads to the final adoption and implementation of the program. Although it is not absolutely necessary, the differentiated staffing concept emerges more logically from a team teaching program than from any other type of organization. Everyone affected by the program should be involved from the beginning in the planning. The program should not be initiated until all are ready and tentative agreements have been reached. Flexibility should be a built-in feature as many changes will be made as problems arise and new roles are assumed. Reassessment and evaluation should be an integral part of the program. The roles of district and school administrators will change as they become part of an enlarged educational team that contains many skilled specialists teaching from 25 to 50 percent of the time. Because of the controversial nature of the program and its lack of wide acceptance, administrators should investigate existing programs before embarking on one of their own.

SIMPLICITY IN SALARY SCHEDULES. Many salary schedules are effective, not so much for the provisions which they contain as for those which they do not. Factors that should never be considered in determining salary placement are the following: sex, marital status, local residence, or race.

It must be emphasized that the salary schedule has only two proper functions: systematized remuneration and encouragement to improve. If it is made to include other extraneous provisions with no direct bearing on these two primary functions, it becomes a mere device for the implementation of school board or administrative prejudice. Even where such prejudice does not exist, an overly lengthy or complicated schedule tends to defeat its own purposes. Very large school districts, of course, need more employee categories in their schedules; to this extent, they are able to justify moderate complexity. Simplicity, however, is the goal to keep in mind when constructing salary schedules.

Although extra pay for coaching, directing the school play, or putting out the school newspaper or yearbook is usually not recommended, most districts have adopted extra pay schedules. Granting free periods instead of extra pay penalizes other teachers and leads to lowered morale. It also is costly as others must be employed to cover these periods. Those who devote after-class time in the late afternoon, evenings, or on weekends are not willing to accept these duties without extra pay. Industry and business consistently pay overtime and it is only right that teachers be granted the same benefits.

The Research Division of the National Education Association reported in 1970 that over 82 percent of the surveyed districts with an enrollment of 6,000 or more made supplementary payments for athletic or non-athletic activities. Non-athletic activities included musical activities, dramatics, newspapers, magazines, and yearbooks. Annual extra pay ranged from a low of $25 for softball and crosscountry to a high of $5,500 for football. Non-athletic activities ranged from $25 for directing the school newspaper to $2,000 for directing the school band.[15]

ADMINISTRATORS' SALARIES.   Administrators generally receive higher salaries than teachers within the same school system. It is false, however, to assume that they earn considerably more than teachers for a working month. The contracts of most administrators are for twelve months; although they may receive a month's vacation, they usually work through school vacations. There is even less difference on an hourly basis since most administrators attend many meetings after school hours (such as school board and community meetings). Their work day does not end when school is dismissed. Because of the necessity to become involved in community activities, many administrators join community organizations such as service and civic clubs. This involves expense that is not reimbursed but is valuable in the establishment of cooperative, friendly, school–community relationships.

Many principals now earn over $20,000; superintendents' salaries range from $30,000 to over $50,000. The amount depends upon the size of the school district and its ability to finance high salary schedules; larger school districts or those in affluent areas pay the highest salaries. Administrative salaries are arrived at in many ways. Some are based on a ratio to the teachers' salary schedule and rise in proportion to the raises granted teachers. Others include a responsibility factor which may depend

---

[15] National Education Association, Research Division, "Salary Supplements for Extra Duties," *NEA Research Bulletin,* pp. 44–45.

upon the size of the school or the level of administration. Many administrative schedules are negotiated by the administration and the board of education. There appears to be no consensus on the best method for establishing administrative salaries.

Evaluating Personnel Efficiency

No area of school administration is more fraught with perils than personnel appraisal. School administrators retain their positions over a period of years largely because of their ability to attract and retain effective personnel; yet the techniques and devices upon which this ability depends are in a regrettably primitive stage. To compound the problem, teachers seem at times to oppose actively any scientific attempt to evaluate their competence, rendering still more difficult the efforts of the administration to identify employees who deserve most fully to be retained and promoted. If above-average employees are to be obtained and kept by the district, then the district must evaluate its personnel in some way.

All teachers are rated. They are rated by their students and by the parents of the community, regardless of whether there is a formal rating system used by the school district employing them. Their relative status in the community and in the school depends upon this highly informal and sometimes grossly unfair evaluation, based upon second-hand information and subjective impressions. It is apparent that, since teachers are inevitably rated in one way or another, it would be best to accomplish this through some agreed-upon and logically defensible method of evaluation.

Marks, Stoops, and King-Stoops, in their *Handbook of Educational Supervision,* set forth basic principles for teacher evaluation and suggest ways in which evaluation can be used for inservice training. This approach is valuable because it focuses the whole evaluative process on the improvement of instruction for students.[16]

Teacher evaluation has two main functions: managerial and the professional development of the teacher. The managerial function helps the administrator make his decision concerning retention or release. The professional development function facilitates, guides, and directs the teacher as he realistically assesses himself, establishes his educational

---

[16] James R. Marks, Emery Stoops, and Joyce King-Stoops, *Handbook of Educational Supervision: A Guide for the Practitioner,* pp. 517–61.

goals, and develops a practical plan to work toward those goals.[17]   Some
of the purposes of teacher evaluation are:

1.   To secure the best possible education for children through quality in-
     struction.
2.   To provide continued opportunities for each teacher to grow in com-
     petence and through proper recognition of his success, to stimulate him
     to even greater accomplishments.
3.   To assist professional personnel in improving their service to the dis-
     trict.
4.   To provide evidence for the selection and retention of new and per-
     manent teachers.
5.   To provide a record of professional service.
6.   To provide assurance to the public that the utmost care is being taken
     to obtain and retain the best teachers for the children of the community.

PRINCIPLES FOR EVALUATING PERSONNEL.   Professional evaluation involves the formulation of value judgments.   The procedures should be
based on established principles.   The following principles are suggested for
adaptation and use by superintendents:

  1.   Genuinely democratic procedures should be applied.
       a.   The evaluator should demonstrate fairness to the employee.
       b.   The employee should know what is expected of him, and should be
            made fully acquainted with the appraisal techniques.
       c.   The employee should know the exact nature and degree of any dis-
            satisfaction with his services, and be given time and aid for correc-
            tion of these deficiencies.
       d.   Employees desiring a review of their evaluations should feel free to
            contact the principal or superintendent.
       e.   Age, sex, marital status, religion and other personal matters which
            do not affect the employee's performance of his duties should not be
            considered in the evaluation.
       f.   Ratings, though necessarily subjective, should be based on as much
            positive, objective evidence as possible.
  2.   The first step in setting up an evaluation program should be development
       of a set of performance standards.
  3.   The community and the school system should be informed about the
       evaluation program and given a chance to improve it.

---

[17] M. Dale Lambert, "Refocussing Teacher Evaluation: A Process of Guided Self-
Analysis," *Thrust for Education Leadership,* p. 41.

4. An evaluation program should be studied critically, and always be subject to revision.

5. Evaluation should be a professional improvement and guidance device.

6. Evaluation is of little value without an attempt to correct weaknesses discovered.

7. Appraisal should be a continuous process.

8. Each employee should be given a copy of evaluation policies when first hired; evaluation policies should be set forth in detail in the district handbook, school handbook, or similar publication.

9. The evaluator should demonstrate impartiality to all employees.

10. Self-appraisal by teachers and others should be encouraged.

11. The primary factor in the success of an evaluation program is the quality of human relations governing use of the evaluation instruments, not the quality of the instruments themselves.

12. The evaluator should rate only those aspects with which he is most familiar, omitting comment on other items.

13. Evaluation programs should discourage comparison of one employee with another.

14. The latest rating of an employee should be the major one considered, rather than an average of all ratings.

15. The evaluator should be alert for symptoms of incipient mental, social, and physical maladjustments, and prescribe preventive activities.

16. Follow-up conferences should accompany the written evaluation.

17. Purposes of the evaluation program should be both administrative and supervisory in nature, the emphasis being on improvement of instruction.

FUNCTIONS OF THE DISTRICT PERSONNEL OFFICE IN THE EVALUATION PROGRAM. The personnel office, although it is not usually responsible for evaluating personnel, has functions such as: coordinating the evaluation program, preparing evaluation forms, orientation of new personnel, inservice training in evaluation procedures, recordkeeping, counseling evaluators and evaluees, and working with the committee responsible for the evaluation process.[18] The personnel office has an intrinsic interest in teacher evaluation because it has the major responsibility for recruiting, employing, and assigning teachers. The personnel administrator, whether

---

[18] American Association of School Administrators, *Profiles,* pp. 81–82.

or not he helps evaluate, should assume a responsibility for visiting new teachers in their classrooms. What he observes will help him in future selections, and the teacher will also appreciate his continued interest.

The personnel office should see that teachers are evaluated according to the policies of the district; that time schedules for reports are met; that eligibility for tenure is established; and that earned tenure is granted. In cases involving dismissal, the personnel office notifies the school board and the teacher; notifies the teacher of his rights; sees that legal requirements are followed; and prepares the case for possible hearings or court action.

VARIOUS EVALUATION METHODS. Completely objective evaluation is an ideal but unattainable goal. However, it is necessary for the administrator to adopt one or more of the methods of rating available to him.

Traditionally, principals have rated teachers on a checklist type of sheet or card which included such items as: skill as an instructor, attitude toward young people, supervision, judgment and tact, emotional stability, ability to control a class, initiative, daily preparation, knowledge of subject field, classroom environment, accuracy in keeping records, promptness, physical and emotional health, personal appearance, and relationships with staff and parents. Research does not clearly indicate that any of these factors affect pupil progress. Formerly the rating sheet or card was composed by the administration and used exclusively by the supervising officer. Often, the teacher was never informed of his rating score, and was downgraded or discharged with no actual reasons given. The rating was usually based on one or two short classroom visitations that might or might not have been followed by a conference. Tenured teachers were usually evaluated only once every year or two, often without classroom observations. "Such perfunctory procedures have obvious weaknesses—they are one-sided and subjective; they have little value as documentation in dismissal hearings; they do not provide for any participation by the teacher; they provide no real help for the teacher needing improvement; and they assess the teacher rather than the teaching act."[19]

Today, the trend is toward the use of rating devices as an aid to improvement of instruction rather than solely as a basis for rehiring or dismissal. Regardless of how they are used, the written instrument itself should be developed cooperatively by teachers working on a committee with administrators and supervisors. In this way, the product of the think-

---

[19] National Education Association, Research Division, "New Approaches in the Evaluation of School Personnel," *Research Bulletin* 50 (May 1972), p. 41.

ing of the group will tend to be acceptable to all, and thus will achieve its maximum utility.

NEW APPROACHES TO TEACHER EVALUATION. Teacher competence is multi-dimensional and difficult to determine. The usual rating sheet does not provide a satisfactory method of evaluating competence. Some of the new experimental methods that presently are used by only a few school systems are discussed in the following paragraphs.[20]

USE OF MULTIPLE EVALUATORS. To overcome the one-sided (by only the principal) evaluation, assessments are made by a committee of superiors, peers, subordinates, students, and parents. The final evaluation can be made by individuals or by a consensus.

USE OF PERFORMANCE OBJECTIVES. The management-by-objectives program is the most revolutionary evaluation procedure. Long- and short-range goals are determined by the superintendent, district administrators, and the board of education for the district. Sometimes parents, and even students, help to develop the goals. The principal, assistant principal, and teachers determine the goals for a school, for a department, and for a classroom. The teacher may determine goals for each student. The objectives should be attainable, measurable, and as precisely written as possible. Once the objectives for a classroom and the students have been agreed upon, standards of performance should be developed to determine whether the accomplishment can be considered successful. The results should be predetermined as accurately as possible. Acceptable evaluation means that the agreed-upon goals have been met. Since goals may change, evaluation must also change. (It should be pointed out that the one who worries the most is the insecure teacher. He will need the most help and understanding.)

The evaluation of the goal achievement of the individual teacher should be based on objective judgment and may be made by a single evaluator, the evaluator and the evaluee, or may include opinions from peers, parents, or students.

Teachers and teacher associations have been reluctant to accept evaluation based on performance objectives because they have not been able to control the variables necessary for satisfactory achievement of their

---

[20] National Education Association, Research Division, "New Approaches," pp. 41–44.

performance. These include such factors as: the learning environment, classroom load, materials, supplies, equipment, and support services. This reluctance will continue until:

1. Teachers have a strong voice in helping to develop policies.
2. Job descriptions for teachers spell out what is expected of a teacher and what services will be available to help him.
3. Teachers are involved in developing performance objectives, expected standards of performance, and the evaluation program.
4. Teachers help determine their classroom load, supplies, materials, and equipment.
5. Administrators are evaluated as to their performance standards in reaching their performance objectives.

It is obvious that the objectives for teachers in one school or other schools in the same district will be different. The achievement of a class in a culturally disadvantaged neighborhood will usually be less than that in an upper-class community. The percentage of gain in achievement in relation to other similar groups can be measured if the data can be made available. For example, a 10 percent gain in reading in a bilingual area in relation to other similar areas may be just as great as the same gain in an upper-class community in relation to its similar areas. Yet the actual reading level of the two classes may be totally different. These things must be considered when performance objectives are developed and the teacher is evaluated on his achievement in reaching the objectives.

Evaluation by performance objectives implies that the principal cannot make the evaluation by himself. Too many principals, especially in secondary schools, may evaluate 60 to over 100 teachers. This is an impossible task, even without using performance objectives. The principal must use the help of department heads and grade level chairmen, and employ relevant statistical data. One of the advantages of evaluation by performance objectives is that it promotes better communication between the teacher and the administrator.

CLIENT-CENTERED EVALUATION. There is a growing trend for the "evaluee" to evaluate the "evaluator," although the concept of client-oriented evaluation is still in its infancy. Client-centered evaluation applies to the evaluation of administrators at all levels. The Educational Research Service reported in 1970 that of 67 school systems asked to submit information on client-oriented evaluation, only 19 stated that teachers were permitted to evaluate principals.[21] Client-oriented evaluation programs were usually voluntary and annual.

Client-centered evaluation allows clients to be more involved in controlling matters that affect their lives. Teachers, parents, and students can furnish a general evaluation of a principal's overall performance in areas where they have direct contact with him. There is an obligation to be objective and constructive. The performance objectives on which the evaluation is based should be cooperatively developed with input from those being guided as well as from their leader. Client-centered evaluation seeks to assess the degree to which the objectives are achieved. If principals are sincere in accepting the evaluation of others of their success, they can reassess objectives and seek improved output.[22]

USE OF MULTIPLE EVALUATION BASES. This combines an evaluation of effective teaching techniques and performance objectives. These two types of evaluation may be made at different times and by different evaluators.

USE OF IN-BASKET DATA. In this evaluation procedure, all good and bad data regarding incidents and facts are placed in the teacher's file. They could include classroom observation reports, transcripts of courses taken, letters of complaint or commendation, reports of participation in school or community activities, achievements earned, leadership positions, inservice participation, and statements regarding suggestions for improvement. Specific documentary data, such as this, is valuable when evidence is needed to justify retention, advancement, or dismissal.

USE OF STUDENT PERFORMANCE. This controversial evaluation procedure is based solely on the achievement of a teacher's students. Achievement goals are established for the class and the evaluation is based on the percentage of students who reach the goals. In 1971, only one school system was using this program on an experimental and optional basis.

---

[21] American Association of School Administrators and NEA Research Division, "The Evaluee Evaluates the Evaluator," pp. 1–4.

[22] George B. Redfern, "Client-Centered Evaluation," *The School Administrator,* pp. 7–10. The Educational Research Service, sponsored jointly by the NEA Research Division and the American Association of School Administrators, has published the following booklets: *Evaluating Administrative/Supervisory Performance,* ERS Circular No. 6, 1971, Stock No. 219–21504, and *Evaluating Teaching Performance,* ERS Circular No. 2, 1972, Stock No. 219–21510.

SELF-EVALUATION. One of the best methods for a teacher to determine how he is teaching and progressing is to evaluate himself. The Purdue Teachers Examination is one of a number of instruments that lend themselves to self-criticism and appraisal.[23] Another valuable device is the National Teacher Examination, which enables a teacher to test himself on his proficiency in areas such as child development, methods of teaching, and major subject fields.[24] Self-evaluation is usually not the complete answer to the rating problem in any school system. Some teachers will refuse to cooperate with the program. Human nature being what it is, many of the personnel who need to take stock of themselves most thoroughly will be the very ones who will decline to do so.

CO-EVALUATION. This method is sometimes called multiple evaluation. No teacher should be evaluated in the course of a year by only one person. As many supervisory officers as possible should participate in the evaluation. Further, the ratings conducted by these several supervisory persons should be made as many different times as possible. The reason for this injunction is a simple one: even the best of the rating score cards or scales is fundamentally subjective, in the sense that no two supervisors are apt to agree in every respect as to a certain teacher's worth.

In a district of moderate size, it is advisable to schedule rating sessions throughout the year by the superintendent, the assistant superintendent, and the principal. A composite rating can be secured for each teacher from the combined evaluations with reasonable confidence that an injustice was not being worked upon a teacher.

Co-evaluation also includes participation in the rating process by the teacher himself. A common practice is for the supervisor to invite the teacher to fill out his own rating card during the same period of time that the administrator is filling one out for the teacher. On a specified date, the two then meet to go over the items covered by the rating instrument, and a genuine attempt is made to achieve a meeting of minds. It is usually possible to resolve all differences. In cases where it proves impossible, both the teacher's and the administrator's cards should be turned in to the superintendent, with a brief note attached to explain the discrepancy.

---

[23] I. B. Kelly and J. K. Perkins, *Purdue Teachers Examinations: How I Teach* (Minneapolis: Educational Test Bureau, Educational Publishers, Inc.).

[24] *National Teacher Examinations,* Bulletin of Information (Princeton, N.J.: Educational Testing Service).

The value of this method lies partly in its use of the democratic process to achieve results; partly in its retention of the expert opinion of the supervisory officer as an important feature of rating; and partly in its ability to compel self-analysis on the part of the teacher. It is probably the most efficient instrument of rating yet to be developed. It should be emphasized that it is far from objective. Any type of employee evaluation is of necessity subjective in most of its phases.

EVALUATION OF PRINCIPALS AND ADMINISTRATORS. If the chief purpose in appraisal is the diagnosis of strengths and weaknesses in an effort to bring about professional improvement, the principal as leader of the school requires appraisal even more than teachers. Principals and district administrators must be rated by the superintendent for purposes of retention; usually they are assessed in terms of doing a satisfactory or unsatisfactory job. Too often, administrators are not evaluated formally by the superintendent for constructive purposes, aside from retention. They often wonder how they are doing and what their strengths and weaknesses are. An evaluation conference recognizes their importance, builds their confidence, and helps them to grow professionally. The only evaluation the superintendent usually receives is when the board of education either reemploys him or dismisses him, sometimes without warning.

Rating of administrators as a means of helping them grow professionally is extremely complicated because of the complexity of their responsibilities and functions. A diagnostic rating blank defining and measuring their functions runs into considerable length. In California, a law (1972) requires all certificated personnel to be evaluated, including administrators.

Whether or not the administrator is evaluated formally, he should develop his own objectives and the procedures he expects to use to attain them. He can list all his functions and responsibilities and develop a checklist to analyze his strengths and weaknesses. Self-evaluation is as important for the administrator as for a teacher.

SUPERVISORY EVALUATION. Districts that for one reason or another have not progressed as far as some in implementing the newer methods of evaluating teachers should rely on their supervising principals for ratings.

Some administrators, noting that teachers are usually dissatisfied with their ratings, have decided that the best way to upgrade faculty morale is to abolish rating altogether. To their surprise, they often find that the very teachers who had protested the rating procedure now complained because no one ever visited their classrooms or evaluated their work. What teachers really want is sound evaluation. Frivolous ratings based on the lighting in the room, the arrangement of desks, and the appearance of murals or mobiles in the corners of the room are justly regarded with suspicion by the average teacher. On the other hand, ratings that contain good, sound comments on assignments, recitations, and pupil participation are welcomed by all sincere instructors. The evaluation conference must be conducted in an informal and friendly fashion.

In a school district that relies on unilateral rating, such an evaluation should be simple, brief, and easily understood. It should provide for several classroom visits by the supervisory officer at different times of the day over a period of several months. It should assess the totality of the teacher's influence on his pupils, colleagues, administrators, and community, and should be known by the teacher in ample time for him to secure maximum benefit from it.

PUPIL ACHIEVEMENT FOR TEACHER EVALUATION. This pragmatic approach denies the importance of teachers' characteristics and stresses the predominant significance of teachers' results. The only results that can be satisfactorily measured within a reasonable length of time are in the areas of pupil subject achievement and behavior. Such intangibles as social, moral, and emotional progress are at present impossible to measure objectively, yet unquestionably are of great importance. Rating that depends wholly or in large part on ascertainable pupil progress places emphasis on types of conduct and achievement that lend themselves most readily to objective appraisal. Such rating should always be administered in the light of partial rather than total evaluation.

Procedures discussed here will not solve all the difficult and complicated evaluation problems. However, they offer possibilities for improving the traditional checklist type of evaluation so commonly used. They provide a better and broader means of assessing schools and teachers and rendering them more accountable.

Evaluations should never serve as the sole basis for dismissal or teachers will regard the entire evaluative process with fear and mistrust. When evaluation is regarded by the administration as a teaching aid and, more importantly, is actually operated as such, then teachers will welcome rating as an opportunity to improve their teaching potential.

CHARACTERISTICS OF A GOOD TEACHER. If teachers are to be evaluated, the evaluator should be able to distinguish good teachers and poor teachers. Hamachek reports on research regarding the dimensions of teacher personality and behavior; his findings are discussed in the following paragraphs.

Personal characteristics. Effective teachers are more humane, have a sense of humor, are fair, empathetic, democratic, teach with more spontaneity, and are adaptable to change.[25]

Instructional procedures. Good or effective teachers reflect more of the following behaviors in their classroom behavior, interaction patterns, and teaching styles:

1. Willingness to be flexible, to be direct or indirect as the situation demands.
2. Ability to perceive the world from the student's point of view.
3. Ability to "personalize" their teaching.
4. Willingness to experiment.
5. Skill in asking questions (as opposed to seeing self as a kind of answering service).
6. Knowledge of subject matter and related areas.
7. Provision of well established examination procedures.
8. Provision of definite study helps.
9. Reflection of an appreciative attitude (evidenced by nods, comments, smiles, etc.).
10. Use of conversational manner in teaching—informal, easy style.[26]

Self-perceptions. Good teachers see themselves as good people, have positive self-perceptions, are optimistic, and evidence healthy self-acceptance.[27]

Perceptions of others. Good teachers, according to Hamachek, exhibit the following attitudes toward others:

1. They seem to have generally more positive views of others—students, colleagues, and administrators.
2. They do not seem to be as prone to view others as critical, attacking

---

[25] Don Hamachek, "Characteristics of Good Teachers and Implications for Teacher Education," *Phi Delta Kappan,* p. 342.

[26] Hamachek, "Characteristics of Good Teachers," p. 342.

[27] Hamachek, "Characteristics of Good Teachers," p. 343.

people with ulterior motives; rather they are seen as potentially friendly and worthy in their own right.

3. They have a more favorable view of democratic classroom procedures.
4. They seem to have the ability and capacity to see things as they seem to others—i.e., the ability to see things from the other person's point of view.
5. They do not seem to see students as persons "you do things to," but rather as individuals capable of doing for themselves once they feel trusted, respected, and valued.[28]

Hamachek summarizes by stating that good teachers enjoy life, possess a sense of humor, enjoy other people, do not have a neurotic need for power and authority, do not have a host of anxieties, are flexible, have a positive view of themselves, are well informed, and can communicate what they know so that it makes sense to their students. One further characteristic: their students learn more than do students of poor teachers.

DISMISSAL OR NON-REEMPLOYMENT. Dismissal refers to removal during the term of a contract. Non-reemployment is failure to recommend employment at the end of the contract period. The term dismissal is commonly used for both situations.

One of the most troublesome duties of a school administrator is to terminate a certificated employee. It is never a painless process and deserves to be bulwarked by the best possible evaluation procedures. Justice toward all concerned is the main objective, and the welfare of the pupils a prime consideration. The wishes and feelings of the individual employee are important but of secondary concern. Teachers should be retained or dismissed in general accordance with their effectiveness or incompetence, not as a result of personal prejudices or purely subjective impressions.

Typical causes for dismissal are those in effect in California:

1. Immoral or unprofessional conduct.
2. Commission of, or aiding or advocating the commission of, acts of criminal syndicalism.
3. Dishonesty.
4. Incompetency.
5. Evident unfitness for service.

---

[28] Hamachek, "Characteristics of Good Teachers," p. 343.

6. Physical or mental condition unfitting a teacher to instruct or associate with children.
7. Persistent violations of or refusal to obey school laws or reasonable regulations of the board or the state board.
8. Conviction of a felony or of any crime involving moral turpitude.
9. Advocating or teaching Communism with intent to indoctrinate pupils.
10. Present membership in the Communist Party.
11. Refusal to answer questions by the school board or legislative investigating committees concerning Communist Party membership or present personal advocacy of the violent overthrow of the government of the United States or of any state.

More and more teachers are appealing to the courts over dismissal decisions. If the court is to uphold the dismissal action, evidence to support the cause must prove the persistent nature of the difficulties, show that repeated warnings have been given, and frequent assistance has been provided. Dismissal evidence must be specific in nature, extensive in scope, recorded, dated, and timed. Written evidence must consist of the original drafts made at the time or immediately after the observation or conference. State laws must be followed regarding reasons for dismissal, notification dates, legal deadlines that must be met, and notifications given to the teacher. Most districts lose cases in the courts because of failure to meet legal requirements and lack of sufficient, documented evidence to show that a fault existed. States, as well as counties within a state, differ in their interpretations of the dismissal laws.

Information must be specific. The "use of foul language," for example, is not specific enough. Evidence must show what words were actually used. The "reasonableness" of a school board's rules also influences a court's decision. [In recent years, court decisions have not favored administrators so it is imperative that they prepare themselves thoroughly when they plan to dismiss an unsatisfactory teacher.]

Dismissal should usually be regarded as a confession of failure on the part of the administration. Logic leads inexorably to one of two conclusions in the case of the discharged teacher: (1) Improper or inadequate screening led to the original employment of an unfit person. (2) Lack of proper supervisory assistance resulted in either deterioration or failure to improve while in service.

There are unquestionably cases where the welfare of the pupils and of the school system demands the dismissal of the teacher, but in all too many of these instances the fault lies with the administration. Since this is true, it is to the advantage of the administrator to use every tool at his command to avoid the necessity of discharging a teacher. If he has sufficient supervisory help, he can use semi-annual ratings as an invaluable aid in assigning his specialists on a priority basis to teachers most in need of immediate assistance. Ratings serve as an alarm, calling attention insistently to those whose professional future may depend upon expert help. Evaluation fulfills a constructive rather than destructive purpose.

SATISFACTORY EVALUATION THROUGH THE USE OF MANY TECHNIQUES. All evaluative methods described in this chapter have their proper place in the operation of teacher evaluation. The danger lies in relying too exclusively on any one technique. The ideal rating procedure would be a continuous process, going on throughout the school year and embracing teacher graduate study and travel during the summer. It would combine the evaluations by full-time supervisory officers with self-ratings of teachers; provide for the examination of pupil progress and for the opinions of the pupils themselves; and bring all the resources of modern psychology and psychometry to bear upon the problem of evaluation. The end product of all this activity would be the accurate evaluation of each teacher in life-size and multi-dimensional form, and in his capacity as an educator. The evaluators should constantly bear in mind that the picture thus evoked would be only an incomplete representation of the actual person. Rating will never be an infallible process. At best, it will always be just a little more true than false.

CONSTRUCTIVE USE OF EVALUATION. Although it is inevitable that rating will always be used to justify the retention or termination of employees, *the principal constructive use of evaluation should be the improvement of the individual in his chosen field*. Rating can and should be the most effective instrument to diagnose strengths and weaknesses. In this connection, the evaluation program should be put to practical use in the following specific ways:

1. Teachers should use rating sheets to compare their opinions of their own teaching ability with those of the evaluators. All discrepancies should be noted, and an honest effort made to ascertain whether or not

indicated weaknesses have any basis in actuality. When the teacher becomes aware of areas of his teaching where improvement is shown to be needed, he then will be in a position to undertake the necessary steps toward self-improvement.

2. Teachers can engage in cooperative analysis of teaching weaknesses and strengths. Often certain patterns of general strengths and failings can be discerned within a school system and profitably studied.

3. Administrators also should use the evaluation program to map out a long-range plan for continuing betterment in the implementation of the program itself. Any district-wide rating plan is capable of improvement. The danger lies in complacency.

4. The board of education in any district should use the rating system as an important facet in its appraisal of the success or failure of the entire program of supervision. While it is probably unsuitable and impractical for a school board to engage in examinations of individual ratings, it is certainly appropriate for board members to be constantly informed of the results of the evaluation program.

Teacher Tenure

Teacher tenure guarantees maximum security to today's teachers. The principle behind tenure is that of freedom from arbitrary dismissal. Its strength lies in its assurance to the teacher of years of security in which he is free to grow professionally and teach constructively, as long as he does not violate established rules and regulations of the state and school district in which he is employed. Its weakness lies in the perpetuation of the occasional poor teacher who survives preliminary screening and probationary scrutiny to achieve permanence.

Tenure usually is acquired either by statutory provision or by act of the governing body of the school district. Many states provide that a teacher shall be classified as *probationary* until he has completed a prescribed number of years of service in a given district, at which time he achieves permanency. This probationary period should be longer than one year but less than five; three years is probably the optimum period. Most tenure laws provide for dismissal for cause only after the teacher has achieved permanent status.

Since there has been considerable misunderstanding about the function of employee tenure in school systems, the following basic concepts or principles will serve as guidelines for administering the tenure program:

1. The principal reason for tenure should be child benefit; sound and properly administered tenure programs must promote child welfare.
2. Tenure should be considered a privilege, not an inherent right.
3. Tenure policies should be established on a statewide basis.
4. Tenure should be restricted to certificated personnel.
5. Careful initial selection and a successful probationary period (which may actually be considered part of the selection process) should precede the granting of tenure.
6. Tenure provisions should not prevent prompt dismissal of ineffective employees.
7. Tenure legislation should define dismissal procedures in detail.
8. Tenure should recognize the principle of seniority in the event of unavoidable reduction of staff.

STATE REGULATIONS OF TENURE.   More than half the states have laws sanctioning some form of tenure for teachers.   Most of these laws provide for a teacher to automatically qualify for permanency after completion of a prescribed number of years of service.   Some states restrict compulsory or automatic tenure to districts with an enrollment of more than a certain minimum number of pupils.   Most state and national teacher organizations spend much time and energy promoting state tenure legislation.

FLEXIBILITY IN TENURE.   Tenure owes its remarkable growth and general acceptance to the abuses that grew up in teacher hiring during the Depression of the 1930s.   At that time, it was common for teachers to be discharged capriciously, largely due to the fact that other equally good instructors could be found to fill the vacancies created.   The resulting low state of teacher morale caused organized groups of educators to devote their efforts over a period of many years to the elimination of these evils. Eventually, states and school districts adopted tenure laws of varying degrees of rigidity.

Teachers now possess a degree of independence and a favorable bargaining position.   The average teacher today is in a position to remedy unjust or discriminatory treatment.   Summary dismissals of teachers without substantial cause are rare today, minimizing rigid tenure practices.

More elastic tenure regulations would avoid mandatory court hearings to discharge a teacher whom board and administration find incompetent. Causes for termination of employment should be set forth by law, and the tenured teacher should have the right to appeal a board decision of dismissal. Such an appeal should be made to an impartial group of former or inservice teachers appointed by the state department of education and trained to evaluate teacher competence. It should be forced to observe formal legal procedures or precedents, but should be able to freely discuss the entire situation, including background and reputed shortcomings. Procedures of this nature would safeguard the tenure rights of the employee, without dragging administrators and board members into prolonged court sessions. The expenses of such appeal machinery should be borne entirely by the state.

It also has been suggested that renewable contracts of from two to five years duration be used. If, after proper evaluation, the teacher is deemed unsatisfactory, he should be entitled to a hearing.

Teacher Workload and Working Conditions

There is less confidence today in the reliability of the several formulas used to measure teacher workload. It is becoming increasingly apparent that the workload is heavily affected by other and more imponderable factors than the classic list compiled by Harl Douglass. His formula for a secondary school arrives at an arbitrary unit based on a class of twenty-five taught for a period of forty-five minutes in a subject requiring an average amount of preparation. His list of items that constitute a heavy load are: number of classes taught daily; number of students per class (there is little or no research which shows that class size affects the achievement of pupils); number of preparations involved; length of class periods; subject or grade taught; and age and characteristics of the pupils.[29] On the other hand, teachers have enumerated overload factors such as administrative interruptions; correcting papers; adapting procedures to individual pupil differences; extra-curricular work; planning requirements; and clerical duties.

The crux of the excessive work load problem seems to be the individual teacher himself. If he is one who regards teaching as a chore rather than as a rewarding experience, as a job rather than as a form of creative

---

[29] Harl R. Douglass, "The 1950 Revision of the Douglass High School Teaching Load Formula," *Bulletin of the NASSP* (May 1951), pp. 13–24.

expression, then almost any minute transgression will constitute an excessive load. If, on the other hand, the teacher is encouraged to develop his talent in a creative direction and to regard his profession as a thrilling and rewarding personal experience, then he will assume willingly and successfully a load which, as expressed by most formulas, is excessive.

The problem of overloading can be prevented or lessened if elementary classes have thirty or fewer pupils and secondary classes twenty-five or fewer pupils. The provision of qualified substitute teachers, adequate clerical services, adequate classrooms, facilities, supplies, and equipment help teachers with large classes. Teachers also do a better job if they are assigned to duties closely related to their interests, preparation, and experience. Program and assignment changes should be kept within reasonable bounds. A teacher load that proves excessive in one type of school environment may be quite tolerable under other circumstances. The inservice program should be directed toward developing time-saving, energy saving, and efficiency building methods and procedures.[30] Excessive teacher load can be significantly ameliorated by inspirational and meaningful leadership and the application of basic principles of good personnel management.

WORKING CONDITIONS. In addition to a well-ventilated, well-lighted, and well-heated classroom, teacher satisfaction is affected by factors such as: convenient parking facilities, storage cupboards for personal belongings, quiet eating area, adequate restroom facilities, and restful lounge rooms. It is never a waste of money to provide facilities that help maintain morale.

Leaves of Absence

A teacher who has provided faithful and competent service, and whom the district wishes to retain, should apply for and receive some type of leave of absence. There are several varieties of leaves of absence: sabbatical, maternity, political, military, bereavement, sick, and personal.

SABBATICAL LEAVE. School districts customarily pay a teacher for time spent on professional duties outside his classroom. Such duties may in-

---

[30] B. F. Pittenger, *Local Public School Administration* (New York: McGraw-Hill Book Co., 1951), pp. 167–168.

clude conventions, conferences, visitations, programs, and professional organization duties. In addition to these short-term absences, teachers properly should be granted long-term leaves at stated intervals in order to pursue advanced degrees, formal or independent study, travel, or a combination of these. In 1972, twenty-four states and the District of Columbia had laws regarding sabbatical leaves for teachers. Most of the other states permit local boards of education to develop their own sabbatical leave rules and regulations, causing great variance in sabbatical leave policies from state to state.[31]

Sabbatical leaves are granted by the board of education on recommendation of the superintendent. Districts vary on the requirements for length of the sabbatical and on payment of full or partial salary. Leaves are usually granted after six to seven years of service in the district, seven years being the most common term. The number of those on leave is limited usually to a percentage, commonly 2 percent of the certificated personnel.

Those requesting sabbatical leaves should make a formal request, stating their purpose. At the expiration of the leave, the teacher usually is required to return to the district for a year or two or rescind his salary. Upon return, he should be reinstated in his previous position or, if that is not possible, assigned to work in an area appropriate to his training. He should also file a written report of his activities, stating their professional value to him, and the educational benefit of the experience or knowledge he gained. The time spent on sabbatical leave should be applied toward salary advancement and retirement credit on the same basis as active teaching.

MATERNITY LEAVE. Educators now generally feel that granting maternity leaves is a humane and prudent policy. Although some state laws prohibit granting such leaves with pay, it is to the advantage of the district to pay wherever it may legally do so. Some districts attempt to terminate teachers rather than grant them maternity leave; this should never be permitted. Maternity leave policies generally require the discontinuance of teaching at a specific time, usually about the fourth or fifth month of pregnancy. The National Education Association claims that policies requiring pregnant teachers to take a leave at a designated time are discriminatory and that individual cases should be decided upon individual charac-

---

[31] National Education Association, Research Division, "Sabbatical Leave for Teachers in State Statutes," *NEA Research Bulletin*, p. 22.

teristics.[32]   While court decisions increasingly rule in favor of maternity leaves, the district is not prevented from setting up reasonable regulations for maternity leaves of absence, based on agreed-upon factors of health and safety.

Districts vary as to the time of return to service, but often the leave is for one year, renewable for a second year.   Whatever policy is adopted for maternity leaves, it should be realistic and reasonable.

POLITICAL OR CIVIC LEAVE.   More and more teachers are exerting their constitutional right to run for political office.   As employees, not as officers of the school district, they have a legal right to hold public office.   If elected, they should be granted a leave of absence without pay for the duration of their term.   A teacher with an interest in helping in government should not be penalized by dismissal.   In fact, he should return to the classroom with more political maturity and experience to enhance his teaching.   The district policy should spell out clearly the procedure to be followed, such as: (1) campaigning shall not take place during working hours; (2) public school supplies, materials, or equipment shall not be used during the campaign or after election; (3) undue influence, based upon teacher status, shall not be exerted before or after election.

MILITARY LEAVE.   Military leaves must be granted when the employee is called into the armed services for training or extended duty.   Whether full or partial salary is paid and for what length of time should be spelled out in the policy statement, sometimes required by state law.   Upon the termination of the teacher's tour of duty, he is to be reassigned to the same or similar position held before his military service.

BEREAVEMENT LEAVE.   Bereavement leave should be granted with pay when an employee loses a member of his immediate family.   The term "immediate family" must be defined.   Most school districts specify the allowable number of bereavement days, the most common being five days (three days is the next most frequent provision).   Some districts combine bereavement leave with sick leave provisions.   District policy should spell out the definitions, provisions, and the method of requesting, verifying, and reporting bereavement leave.

---

[32] National   Education   Association,   "Discriminating   Against   the   Pregnant Teacher," *Today's Education*, pp. 33–35.

SICK LEAVE.   The practice of compelling sick teachers to take non-pay leaves, once common, has now happily diminished almost to the vanishing point.   State laws, district policies, or teacher contracts generally specify provisions for sick leave.   It is common procedure, especially in larger school districts, to grant five to ten days of sick leave each year with full pay.   Some states grant one day of sick leave yearly for each month worked, with the stipulation that the employee works at least 75 percent of the working days in the month.   Cumulative sick leave allows those who maintain good health to accrue thirty, fifty, or an unlimited number of sick leave days to use when emergencies arise.   The limit of accumulation depends upon state and district regulations.   In contrast to this cumulative principle is the bonus method, whereby a teacher is rewarded financially at the end of the year by a pay overage based on his approach to perfect attendance, or penalized by subtraction of a portion of his regular salary for each day's absence.   Teacher organizations advocate payment of accumulated sick leave days upon retirement.

Various laws pertain to payment for sick leave after the earned days are used up.   Provisions include full pay for up to three months if no substitute teacher is employed, or the difference in pay between the employee's salary and the substitute's for up to five months.   Under extenuating circumstances, the school board may decide on the amount of pay and the length of the leave.

To avoid abuse of sick leave pay, some districts require a statement from the doctor that the employee was ill and now may return to work.   It is not fair, however, to make it difficult for most teachers because of the abuses of the few.   District policy should state how sick leave is earned, how it is compensated for, how it is to be verified, and what physical examinations, if any, are required.

The adept administrator always handles leaves of absence on a policy basis.   The American Association of School Administrators has published a list of criteria to aid school personnel in handling sick leaves.   A summary of the criteria follows:[33]

1. Sick leave should be treated as a way of improving instruction, not as a generous gesture by a school board.

---

[33] American Association of School Administrators, *Administering a Sick-Leave Program for School Personnel* (Washington, D.C.: The Association, 1954).

2. Features should be added only when they have been agreed upon and found acceptable.
3. Measures designed to keep to a minimum absences due to illness should be a part of sick-leave policies. A check of physical fitness at time of original employment and periodic health inventories thereafter are recommended procedures.
4. All provisions should be clearly and completely stated, and should be given official sanction through board adoption and incorporation into the minutes.
5. Sick leave should be clearly distinguished from other types of leave.
6. Though some safeguards against abusers may be necessary, they should not receive primary attention.
7. Necessary financing must be provided.
8. Provision for competent substitutes strengthens acceptance of plans granting sick leave for regular teachers.
9. Proper procedures for reporting absences, maintaining records, and obtaining substitutes should be worked out in detail and should be clearly understood by all.

PERSONAL LEAVE. Personal leave has generally been granted without compensation. Some states and many forward-looking districts provide leaves with pay for emergencies such as bereavement or serious illness in the immediate family. California permits certificated employees to use up to six days of accumulated sick leave for reasons such as death of a member of the immediate family, attendance of the funeral of close relatives, the birth of a child, or in cases of personal necessity that are serious in nature, involve circumstances the employee cannot reasonably disregard, and require his attention during assigned hours of service. Regulations of personal leave and methods of verification should be clearly stated in the district policy.

Although they may not be granted such leaves with pay, teachers should be permitted to absent themselves for overriding personal reasons. The difficulty lies in defining carefully what causes are to be considered acceptable for non-illness absences. Lack of such a definition may generate much ill feeling, and the benefits of non-illness leaves of absence may be largely dissipated. Teacher organizations are proposing a plan of granting several days of personal leave each year with pay and without stating the reason.

OTHER TYPES OF LEAVES OF ABSENCE. There is a trend toward broadening the types of leave that may be granted, either with or without pay. Some school districts, for example, grant leaves for:

1. Jury duty as provided by law.
2. Court appearances as a witness, a litigant, or on behalf of the district.
3. Religious leave for faiths other than Christian.
4. Paternity leave.

An effective method for raising the level of teacher involvement is to provide leaves for attendance at conferences and for visitations to other classrooms within or without the district. District policy should be specific in stating the provisions for such leaves.

Transfer of Certificated Personnel

Certificated personnel are transferred from one assignment to another for various reasons. Although most transfers involve teachers, principals may also be transferred. Some superintendents believe that a principal may become too entrenched or that a move every few years is good for the community and is a challenge to the principal. Moves may also be made to give a principal an opportunity to use his abilities more successfully in a new situation. Some principals object to transfers because they become involved with their community and tend to develop a staff that conforms to their personality and thinking. A transfer discourages them and they feel that they must start over.

Teachers may request changes because of unhappy teacher–principal relationships, heavy classroom loads, excessive pupil turnover, desire to work under another principal, desire to work in a new school, desire to work closer to home, or desire to work in a lower or higher socioeconomic area. Principals may request transfers for teachers whom they find incompatible or in order to give a weak teacher an opportunity to achieve in another situation. Teachers who do not do well at one school, or who are misassigned, may do very well in another school or at another level, improving both the satisfaction of the teacher and the educational program. Care in original assignment will help to lessen the need to make changes such as these.

Experienced teachers tend to request assignments to upper socioeconomic areas. Transfers made on the basis of seniority can result in the staffing of lower socioeconomic areas, where the need is greatest, with inexperienced or less satisfactory personnel. Some teachers consider any transfer a form of punishment. Principals also may not want to accept weak teachers.

Transfer complications can be lessened if pre-established policies and guidelines are followed. Too often the teacher is not aware of an impending transfer and principals are not consulted by the personnel administrator prior to the final transfer decision.

A teacher who wishes to transfer should fill out a transfer request form stating his reasons, hold a conference with his principal (who should indicate whether or not he approves the request), and forward the form to the personnel office. The principal who wishes to have a teacher transferred should follow a similar procedure. The personnel office should collect all requests and reassign teachers, as far as possible, on a fair and equitable basis. If fair, clearly understood procedures are followed and all people are informed of the reasons for making or not making transfers, many of the transfer problems will be eliminated.

Separation from Service

There are only four ways that a certificated employee can be separated from service: decease, resignation, dismissal, or retirement. When an employee dies, the state department of education must be notified. The personnel administrator can assist in a significant way by helping the members of the family with the paper work involved in collecting state death benefits. School district friends of the deceased teacher will appreciate hearing about the funeral arrangements.

When a teacher resigns, he should discuss it with his principal and notify the personnel office or superintendent in writing, setting the effective date of the resignation and the reason. Notice should be given at an early date so that a satisfactory replacement can be employed. At the end of the school year, the opening can be filled from the new teacher pool that was selected during the summer. It is a good procedure for the personnel administrator to hold a conference with the teacher to determine his reasons for leaving and to advise him regarding his rights particularly reemployment at a later date. The administrator should also explain the circumstances of withdrawing his retirement contributions if he is leaving the teaching profession. The dismissal of teachers is discussed in the section on evaluation in this chapter.

Retirement preparations should be started at least one year prior to the retirement date. Planned retirement should be discussed with the principal, the superintendent, or the personnel administrator. The personnel office should assist the teacher in preparing the necessary forms for submission to the state, and advise him about retirement benefits and available options. Membership in the American Association of Retired Persons (AARP) or the National Retired Teachers Association (NRTA) provides many advantages and benefits.

Most states use a joint contributory retirement system in which the teacher contributes a percentage of his salary and the district or state matches this amount.[34] The minimum age for retirement is usually 60 years and the maximum age is 65 to 70 years. In a good system, retirement can be accomplished at an earlier age if hastened by total physical disability.[35] Most school retirement systems are better than Social Security coverage. It is possible for teachers of a state or a subdivision to decide whether or not they wish to qualify for Social Security. In most states, teachers are covered by Social Security supplemented by existing teacher retirement systems or integrated with them.[36] Retirement benefits vary from state to state and are determined by a set formula that involves age and length of service. An example of the different retirement provisions has been listed by the National Education Association: "Alaska, at age 55 with 30 years' service; Florida, at any age with 35 years' continuous service or with 10 years' service at age 62; Kentucky, at any age with 30 years' service; and New York, at age 55 with as little as 2 years of service if rendered after age 53 and June 1967."[37]

Many problems complicate provisions for adequate retirement. Most states do not apply out-of-state service toward retirement, although a few permit teachers to purchase a limited amount of credit. A system of interstate retirement reciprocity should be established so that qualified teachers are not unnecessarily penalized. The rising cost of living dilutes

---

[34] George R. Cressman and Harold W. Benda, *Public Education in America,* Copyright © 1956, 1961 by Appleton-Century-Crofts, Inc. Copyright © 1966 by Meredith Publishing Company, p. 184.

[35] Cressman and Benda, *Public Education,* p. 185.

[36] Cressman and Benda, *Public Education,* p. 184.

[37] National Education Association, Research Division, "What's New in Teacher Retirement Systems," *NEA Research Bulletin,* p. 111.

the value of retirement benefits. Only a few states provide fixed increases or automatic retirement adjustments and the percentages vary considerably. The most desirable method would be to provide an automatic percentage increase based on changes in the Consumer Price Index.

Substitute Service

Supplying substitutes is one of the important functions of the personnel office. The quality of substitute teachers helps to determine the quality of the school district's educational program. The ideal substitute is one who can instruct the class to which he is assigned with the lesson plans left by the regular teacher. Regular teachers should prepare a folder for their substitutes containing information on lesson plans, seating arrangements, duty schedules, time schedules, where to get help if needed, and notes on any classroom problems.

The personnel office has the responsibility for recruiting qualified substitutes and orienting them to district procedures. A district *Substitute's Handbook* should explain some of the district's policies and procedures on time to report and leave, renewal of assignment, pay, reports, discipline, attendance reporting, release of students prior to dismissal, fire drills, lunch periods, illness and accidents, and so forth. A workshop for the substitute staff at the beginning of each school year is helpful. A substitute's job is always difficult and often thankless. Administrators and other teachers should make substitutes feel welcome, offer assistance, and give recognition as contributing members of the school system.

There are two types of substitutes: long-term and day by day. Long-term substitutes carry on as the regular teacher would. Short-term substitutes do not have this total responsibility but should be prepared with lessons in case the regular teacher has not left any plans.

Procedures should be developed that explain what to do when substitutes are not available. In secondary schools, the principal may require teachers to give up a free or preparation period to cover a class, sometimes for extra pay. In elementary schools, classes might be divided between several teachers or the principal may teach the class until a substitute can be found.

SUBSTITUTE CALLING SYSTEM. The district should have clearly defined procedures for a teacher to follow in requesting a substitute such as who, when, and how to notify the district office. The following is a typical list of procedures for handling substitutes that can be adapted to fit the special needs of any school district.

PROCEDURES FOR HANDLING SUBSTITUTES

Regular Teacher's Responsibility

1. The following materials should be prepared and updated:
   a. Seating chart
   b. Roll of class
   c. Weekly program
   d. Daily lesson plan
   e. Next day's schedule and assignments
   f. Room committees
   g. Location of general supplies and equipment and names of two responsible students who can help

2. Items *a* to *g* should be in the large drawer of the desk and the desk should be unlocked

3. Request for substitute services should be made before 2:00 P.M. on the day preceding absence or immediately after 6:30 A.M. if the need for absence is not known until the day of absence. Call to report your absence and give the following information:
   a. Your name
   b. Your school
   c. Your grade or subject
   d. Your parking assignment (if necessary)
   e. Reason for your absence
   f. Date of your expected return

4. All absentees must call their principal by 2:00 P.M. *each day* of continued absence in order to report a return or continued absence.

5. Make clear to students that they are as responsible to the substitute teacher as to the regular teacher.

Substitute's Responsibility

1. Report to the school's office one-half hour prior to the beginning of the first class.

2. Read all notices on the bulletin board and take all messages, etc., from the teacher's box.

3. Pick up keys and yard or cafeteria duty schedule.

4.   Check class attendance carefully and accurately at the beginning of the day. Send this report to the office.

5.   Take roll after each recess and lunch.

6.   Carry out the teacher's plans and assignments as outlined.

7.   Hold students accountable for work, citizenship, attendance, etc.

8.   Leave a written report for the teacher giving:
     a.   Work covered
     b.   Plans and assignments for the next day
     c.   Any other pertinent information covering students, bulletins, etc.

9.   Adhere to the same school hours as the regular teacher.

10. Check with the school office before leaving to see whether you are released or are to return the next day.

School Office Responsibility

1.   Call Personnel Office for a substitute as soon as an impending absence is known.

2.   Schedule relief teachers from the faculty when no substitute is available.

3.   Keep an accurate record of each teacher's absence for payroll purposes.

4.   Notify the Personnel Office each day as to the status of substitute teachers assigned.

There are different methods of handling calls from teachers who are unexpectedly absent. The call can be made to the school or the district office. This method has the advantage of clarifying information on a personal basis, but involves extra clerical help. Large districts may use an automatic recording machine with 60 seconds allowed for the message. This sometimes results in garbled or incomplete information because the caller could not give the required information in the time allowed by the automatic machine. Some districts use an answering service to handle calls from absent teachers because they find it cheaper and more efficient. Each school district must determine what method is best for its own situation.

EVALUATION OF SUBSTITUTES.   As far as it is practical, substitutes should be evaluated by the principal. Personal observation is the best way to gain information on teaching effectiveness. Follow-up conferences can be held if time permits. The regular teacher can report on the substitute's performance. Brief substitute evaluations channeled to the personnel office from the principal's office can serve as a reference for future regular employment.

Personnel Records and Reports

Numerous records that are important for the employee as well as for the district must be kept in the personnel office. A partial listing includes:

Employment applications.
Contracts.
Assignment sheets.
Lists of employees by school, department, or office.
Payroll listings.
Individual Kardex-type card for each employee.
Cumulative folders for each employee containing references, health information, credentials, application, training and experience information, evaluation reports, letters of commendation, recommendations for improvement, contracts, information on leadership roles and community activities, and service credits.
Credentials: active and due to be renewed.
Staff ethnic surveys.
Probationary and tenure lists.
Leaves of absence of all types.
Folders of employees who have left the district or a microfilm file with the same information.
Special teaching categories.
Lists of openings and expected openings.
Substitute teachers.
Statistical records of many types.

It is an endless task to keep all personnel information accurate and up to date. Furthermore, many personnel offices are understaffed. It is helpful if the office has access to a computer to record information and furnish printout data. Large districts are compelled to use computer equipment.

The personnel office also must make many reports to the superintendent, the school board, the teacher association, various governmental agencies, and the county and state boards of education. They concern almost every activity carried on by the personnel office. Most personnel offices receive many requests for data on personnel from all the agencies mentioned above, as well as from graduate students seeking data for their theses. It takes many hours of administrative and clerical time to compile the required or requested data. Most school districts should seriously consider computerizing information to keep up with the increasing quantity of required reports and records. A simplified data retrieval system should be used.

Summary

There should be a specially trained personnel administrator to handle all problems of recruitment, termination, and negotiations; he should operate under cooperatively developed, written policies. Procurement of personnel should follow a set pattern, with the building principal actively involved in selection.

Districts should have salary schedules, with placement and rate of progress made clear, and with a range of two times the minimum salary, plus fringe benefits. The two basic types of salary schedules are position and preparation schedules. Before any schedule is adopted, the district should adopt salary schedule policies, including a position on merit pay, currently the most controversial issue in such scheduling. An innovation related to salary scheduling is that of differentiated staffing. Whatever schedule is used, it should be kept as simple as possible.

One of the most difficult areas of school administration is personnel evaluation, which should be based upon established principles that stress democratic procedures and professional improvement. Evaluation should be coordinated by the personnel office and should include the use of multiple evaluators, performance objectives, in-basket data, and student performance. Other types of evaluation include self-evaluation and co-evaluation, in which attention is also given to evaluation of administrators and principals. The good teacher usually possesses desirable personal characteristics, effective instructional procedures, and a positive perception of himself. Dismissal should be based on the most extensive evaluation procedures possible. The evaluations should be written and detailed and should employ many techniques; above all, constructive evaluation should occur *before* dismissal.

Teacher tenure is dependent upon state law, which is currently too rigid. Periodic evaluation and renewal of certification would bestow more flexibility to tenure.

Teacher work load is a highly subjective topic. Little or no evidence, for example, suggests that class size affects pupil achievement, although there is considerable evidence that it affects teacher morale. Meaningful leadership and good personnel management will alleviate unfair work loads.

Leaves of absence are essential under certain conditions. Typical leaves are sabbatical, maternity, political or civic, military, bereavement, sick, and personal.

Teachers are often transferred from one assignment to another. Pre-established policies and guidelines lessen complications. The same principle applies to separation from service. Here, the personnel office can be of vital help (whether the separation is caused by decease, resignation, dismissal, or retirement), by assisting with advice, preparation of forms, and explanation of options and alternatives.

Another important function of the personnel office is supplying substitute teachers, either long-term or day by day. A *Substitute's Handbook* should be prepared and made available by the office.

Finally, the chapter identifies the necessary components of record-keeping and report making.

Trends

Many trends are apparent in personnel administration. However, the many complexities in this area make it difficult to predict the future. Some of the most apparent trends are mentioned in the following paragraphs.

TOWARD MORE AND MORE LEGISLATION. Because of the many personnel problems, state legislatures, governmental agencies, and school boards are frantically trying to solve them through legislation. Actually, this creates confusion, more problems, more legal interpretations, and more legislation. There are now so many laws regarding personnel that no district can be sure of its legality in every respect. There appears to be no cessation of such legislation.

TOWARD A CHANGE IN THE ROLE OF THE PERSONNEL ADMINISTRATOR. The clerical functions of the personnel administrator will be handled more often by additional clerical assistance and computerized equipment. This should free the administrator to devote more time to more personal counseling of teachers and guidance of staff development. In addition to orienting new teachers, the personnel administrator will spend more time improving relationships and adjusting individual problems of teachers. Because of the many personnel laws, teachers will need more personnel counseling.

There are others, however, who believe there will be less time for personal relationships and teacher counseling because of increased external demands, a more aggressive public, the creation of larger districts that require more services, teacher militancy, and increasing demands for negotiation of every personnel policy. Depersonalization of the role of the personnel administrator, at a time when teachers need more counseling, would be unfortunate. . The trend should be directed toward more personal services for teachers.

TOWARD INCREASING SALARIES. Teachers' salaries, including fringe benefits, have more than doubled since World War II. The rising cost of living has offset much of this gain, generating more demands for salary increases. No immediate interruption of this trend can be foreseen.

TOWARD MORE CONSTRUCTIVE EVALUATION. Less rigid and more constructive rating of personnel should occur. Instead of a multiple form, stressing percentage points and sub-categories, the rating device of the future promises to be a comparatively brief instrument that condenses key attributes of good teaching into a few major headings. It will be administered informally, and in an atmosphere of mutual understanding and desire to improve the instruction of children.

TOWARD THE USE OF COOPERATIVELY DEVELOPED RATING INSTRUMENTS. The function of the rating supervisor will continue to become more circumscribed. Evaluation will become increasingly a democratic process; even in school districts that persist with unilateral rating, the use of a cooperatively devised rating card will become more common. A commonly developed instrument of this type promotes greater confidence in its fairness and validity among all persons concerned. Evaluation will accordingly be more apt to result in willingness on the part of the teacher to accept findings and to follow the recommendations for improvement made by the rating officer.

TOWARD CO-EVALUATION. As more school systems develop adequate supervisory staffs, the trend toward co-evaluation will become more pronounced. The teacher's rating of his own ability in several categories will be an important part of the final picture, as will ratings by supervisors and building principals. Such a rating system will streamline visitation and conference time, but will be the result of evaluations by more supervisory officers than can now be assigned.

TOWARD THE USE OF EVALUATION AS A VALUABLE INSERVICE IMPROVEMENT DEVICE. The old policy of justifying dismissals almost exclusively on the basis of rating scores is passing out of use. The trend is now toward the use of rating as a method of retaining rather than of eliminating personnel. Diagnostic rating cards are coming into general use; they permit either supervisory evaluation, self-evaluation, or both. A teacher will be made aware early in his career of both his strong and weak points as they appear to his supervisors. He will be invited to analyze these aspects of his professional competence, and will be given expert assistance in overcoming the weak points in his teaching. Proper evaluation will thus be equated with a salvaging function, and potentially serviceable teachers will not be so cavalierly dismissed.

TOWARD THE PRINCIPLE OF MULTIPLE EVALUATION. Evaluation by one person is little better than no evaluation at all. The trend toward multiple evaluation will be largely governed by size of the district and the money available for hiring supervisory personnel. Assuming that school districts in the future will tend toward larger size and increased wealth, it should prove possible to employ enough supervisory help to enable each teacher to be evaluated by several different persons each year.

TOWARD EXTENSION OF STATE-GRANTED TENURE TO TEACHERS. Eventually, every American teacher with more than three years' experience in any given school district will be protected by tenure governed by the state laws. This extension of tenure will probably be accompanied, however, by the increasing recognition that tenure laws should not be so drawn as to protect incompetent or indolent instructors.

TOWARD BROADENING OF LEAVE OF ABSENCE REGULATIONS. It is becoming increasingly evident that liberal leave of absence provisions are a relatively inexpensive but exceedingly potent means of strengthening employee morale. Leaves will be used more and more in the future as a method of reducing the teacher work load, which is coming to be recognized as a psychological problem. There is a trend toward the granting of more sick leave, an increase in the days for accumulated sick leave, and the right to transfer sick leave to other regional areas.

TOWARD INCREASING FRINGE BENEFITS. Fringe benefits for school employees have increased considerably during the last two decades and will increase more. School boards have been slower to use fringe benefits as a way of procuring and retaining high caliber workers than have leaders in business and industry. More provisions for leaves, vacations, hospitalization, and on-the-job training will be offered as a means of competing in the professional labor market.

TOWARD MORE SPECIALIZED AND SPECIFIC ASSIGNMENTS. Greater specialization on the part of school employees, combined with written assignments and job descriptions, are coming to characterize good personnel management. Clarification of duties and responsibilities in written form is a continuing trend.

Administrative Problems

In Basket

Problem 1

The transfer of teachers between schools has been a problem in the Gettysburg Consolidated School District for a long time. The district policy is vague and no procedure has been established for effecting transfers.

Teachers have complained that they are sometimes reassigned to other schools without reason. Principals believe that weak teachers are sometimes forced on them because other principals are afraid to evaluate them for dismissal. During the summer, the personnel director sometimes reassigns teachers to fill openings created by resignation if he cannot find a new teacher to fill the spot. Teachers and principals often do not know about the changes until September when they return from vacation. Although the district office thinks that a transfer is made to strengthen a school or a subject area, the teacher often fears that something is wrong with him.

The teacher's association resents the way transfers are handled and is demanding that a comprehensive policy be developed. Principals have joined the teachers in desiring a strong voice in personnel assignment and reassignment.

The superintendent has asked the personnel director to develop a transfer policy to meet the district's needs.

What procedure should the personnel administrator use in developing the policy?
What items should the policy cover?

Problem 2

The evaluation program in the Coldwood Unified School District requires the principal to evaluate probationary teachers twice a year and permanent teachers once a year. The evaluation form is a checklist covering such items as: teaching ability, classroom control, personal characteristics, and professional growth. Under each topic, there are several sub-items and a small space for comments. Principals are required fill out the checklist and schedule a teacher conference. At the end of the conference, the teacher is asked to sign the checklist, indicating that it has been discussed with him. One copy of the evaluation is given to the teacher and one is sent to the personnel office. A record of classroom visitations is also required.

The teachers have raised many objections to the evaluation system. They say that some principals do not visit their classes and others stay only a few minutes. (Secondary principals retort that with over 80 teachers, it is impossible to visit all of them.) Teachers feel that the checklist is an outdated evaluation procedure; that evaluations by a single person—the principal—are not satisfactory and often show personal bias; that evaluation conferences are not always a two-way exchange of ideas and are more often dominated by the principal.

Permanent teachers feel that they should be exempted from yearly evaluation.

The teacher's association, as a result of the complaints, has asked the superintendent to appoint a committee to revise the evaluation procedure. The superintendent has delegated this responsibility to the personnel director.

Whom should the personnel director select for the committee?
What schedule should be established for committee meetings?
What procedure should the committee follow as it works at developing a new evaluation policy?
If you were a member of the committee and were asked for your ideas about an evaluation policy, what would you recommend?

Problem 3

Teachers in the Jefferson Elementary School are rather traditional, most of them having taught five or more years. Elaine Robertson is a new third grade teacher who has recently graduated from college. She has enthusiastically introduced innovative concepts into her teaching. For example, instead of the usual three-group reading program, Ms. Robertson has developed an individualized reading program. Some of her advanced pupils are reading fourth and fifth grade books. Her pupils are excited and are eager to go to school each day.

Several teachers have been vocal in their resentment of Ms. Robertson, who has sensed their attitude. One day she enters the teacher's lounge as Ms. Green, a veteran fourth grade teacher, is complaining about how her reading program will be ruined when Ms. Robertson's pupils, who have read most of the books she is planning to use, enter her class. Ms. Robertson is very upset over what she hears and goes to her principal and tells him what has been happening.

How should the principal counsel Ms. Robertson?
How should he proceed with the other teachers?
What should Ms. Robertson do?

Selected References

American Association of School Administrators. *Profiles of the Administrative Team.* Washington, D.C.: The Association, 1971.

American Association of School Administrators and NEA Research Division, "The Evaluee Evaluates the Evaluator." ERS Circular, No. 5 (August 1970).

American Association of School Personnel Administrators. "Problems of Practicing School Personnel Administrators." *AASPA Bulletin* 9 (June 13, 1969).

BARRO, STEPHEN M. "An Approach to Developing Accountability Measures for the Public Schools." *Phi Delta Kappan* 52 (December 1970).

CAMPBELL, ROALD F.; CORBALLY, JOHN E., JR.; and RAMSEYER, JOHN A. *Introduction to Educational Administration.* 3rd ed. Boston: Allyn and Bacon, 1966.

CRESSMAN, GEORGE R., and BENDA, HAROLD W. *Public Education in America.* 3rd ed. New York: Appleton-Century-Crofts, Division of Meredith Publishing Co., 1966.

EBEL, ROBERT L. "Behavioral Objectives: A Close Look." *Phi Delta Kappan* 52 (November 1970).

GRIFFITH, DANIEL E.; CLARK, DAVID L.; WYNN, D. RICHARD; and IANNACCONE, LAURENCE. *Organizing Schools for Effective Education.* Danville, Illinois: Interstate Printers and Publishers, 1962.

HAMACHEK, DON. "Characteristics of Good Teachers and Implications for Teacher Education." *Phi Delta Kappan* 50 (February 1969).

LAMBERT, M. DALE. "Refocussing Teacher Evaluation: A Process of Guided Self-Analysis." *Thrust for Education Leadership* 1 (February 1972).

MARKS, JAMES R.; STOOPS, EMERY; and KING-STOOPS, JOYCE. *Handbook of Educational Supervision: A Guide for the Practitioner.* Boston: Allyn and Bacon, 1971, pp. 517–561.

MORPHET, EDGAR L.; JOHNS, ROE L.; and RELLER, THEODORE L. *Educational Organization and Administration.* 3rd ed. Englewood Cliffs, N.J.: Prentice-Hall, 1967.

National Education Association. "Discriminating Against the Pregnant Teacher." *Today's Education* 60 (December 1971).

————, Research Division. "Beginning Salaries for Teachers in Big Districts, 1950–51 to 1970–71." *NEA Research Bulletin* 48 (October 1970).

————, Research Division. "Merit Pay: Teacher Opinion and Public Opinion." *NEA Research Bulletin* 49 (December 1971).

————, Research Division. "New Approaches in the Evaluation of School Personnel." *NEA Research Bulletin* 50 (May 1972).

————, Research Division. "Sabbatical Leave for Teachers in State Statutes." *NEA Research Bulletin* 50 (March 1972).

————, Research Division. "Salary Supplements for Extra Duties." *NEA Research Bulletin* 48 (May 1970).

————, Research Division. "What's New in Teacher Retirement Systems." *NEA Research Bulletin* 48 (December 1970).

REDFERN, GEORGE B. "Client-Centered Evaluation." *The School Administrator* (March 1972).

STINNET, R. M. "Merit Rating for Teachers." *The Instructor* 70 (January 1961).

WEBER, CLARENCE A. *Personnel Problems of School Administrators.* New York: McGraw-Hill Book Co., 1954.

WILSON, ROBERT E. *Educational Administration.* Columbus, Ohio: Charles E. Merrill Publishing Co., 1966.

24

Administration of
Classified Personnel

The administration of classified personnel within school districts is assuming a steadily increasing degree of importance. Factors contributing to this trend are the continual increase in the number of non-certificated employees serving within a school district, particularly paraprofessionals or aides to the certificated staff, and the general increase in the caliber of persons seeking types of civil service positions. A trend toward codification of rules and regulations governing the operation of the classified system has resulted from pressures by civil service employee unions and other organizations that are rapidly developing to serve and advance the cause of the classified employee.

This chapter includes a discussion of the following topics:

Administrative Areas of the Classified Service
Classification and Description
The System of Job Classification
Wage and Salary Administration
Procurement, Selection, Training, Evaluation, and Advancement
Management Principles
Administration of Equitable Rules and Regulations
Summary
Trends

Material for this chapter was prepared in collaboration with Dr. Danforth White, Director of Personnel, Lynwood Unified School District, Lynwood, California.

Administrative Areas of Classified Service

The scope of responsibility for the operation of the classified service may be categorized into three broad but interlocking areas: (1) the classification and description of the various jobs within an organization into a definable interrelationship that is hierarchical in nature for the purpose of salary assignment, promotion, examination, and evaluation; (2) procurement, selection, training, and advancement procedures; and (3) the employment of positive management practices to attain high employee morale.

Modern management principles are being applied to the previously neglected area of support, or classified, personnel. These principles include (1) the emergence of a much more systematized and equitable manner in which employees are initially recruited and subsequently compensated, including provisions for merit recognition and security benefits, in addition to an equitable basic wage; (2) provision for additional training and impartial advancement to higher positions of responsibility; and (3) most importantly, the use of supervisory techniques that not only provide the employee with knowledge of how well he is performing on the job, but enable him to feel that he is a vital and contributing member of the educational system. Trends developing within civil service in general, and within education specifically, are making it imperative that school administrators at all levels recognize the importance of developing a sound system for the administration of the classified personnel.

A sound organizational definition appearing on paper can only fulfill its stated purpose if it is adhered to. Failure on the part of administration to follow an adopted definition can easily contribute to poor morale among employees. Employee confidence is further diminished by unfair administration of policies, such as those dealing with establishment of wage compensation, promotional opportunities, or the processing of a grievance. A figurative triangle can be formed in which a strong system of classification and compensation form one leg; merit selection and advancement another; and positive employee management the third (*see* Figure 24–1). Only upon these three elements can a sound system of classified personnel administration be built.

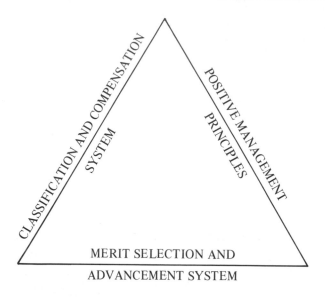

FIGURE 24–1.   Administrative Functions Involving Classified
Personnel.

The System of Job Classification

Establishing a relationship between each job in the school district is the
first step toward developing a sound classified service.   In order to establish this relationship, the scope, duties, and skills required for each position within an organization must be accurately defined.   To accomplish
this, job descriptions for each function are written.   For purposes of
exactness as well as building employee morale, many personnel administrators request the employee (or a representative of a group) to initiate written descriptions about the exact nature of his duties.   Job descriptions
from one group, custodians, for example, are then edited and combined
into one statement covering the tasks performed by the group.   The edited
description is then returned to the employees for their comments and ultimate approval.   It is essential that the content of the job description include the degree of education required for the position, the minimum
amount of experience necessary, the number of people to be supervised (if
any), and the extent of responsibility.   Although information may be presented in a variety of ways, the typical job description should contain the
following headings:

  I. Definition of Position

 II. Example of Duties

III. Qualifications
    A. Knowledge
    B. Ability
    C. Experience

As an example, a typical job description for a clerk–typist might be written in this manner:

CLERK–TYPIST

Definition

Under supervision, performs a variety of clerical jobs of average difficulty; operates office machines, a mainly repetitive activity; and performs other work as required.

Job Characteristics

Positions in this class perform general clerical work, such as typing, maintaining files, acting as a receptionist and operating various office machines and appliances. Positions in this class require typing skill, though this requirement varies in degree from position to position. The clerical duties assigned to positions in this class require a working knowledge of subject matter and clerical functions, and good clerical ability. Incumbents exercise initiative and independent judgment within a limited number of standardized procedures. Supervision of other clerical employees normally is not assigned to positions in this class, although assistance in training new or seasonal employees is sometimes required.

Examples of Duties

Types, proofreads, files, checks, and enters information on records; answers telephones and waits on a public counter, giving information on routine, procedural, or directional questions; types a wide variety of materials, including records, tests, reports, memoranda, tables, lists, and requisitions, from oral, rough-draft copy, or notes; cuts stencils; post information, including attendance and scholarship records; operates office appliances and machines; sorts and files documents and records according to predetermined classifications, maintaining alphabetical, index, and cross-reference files; makes arithmetical calculations; checks records and papers for clerical and arithmetical accuracy and completeness, and for compliance with established standards or procedures; mails out letters, forms, and applications; receives, sorts, and distributes incoming and outgoing mail; acts as receptionist; assists in making out forms; inspects incoming shipments or materials for conformance with orders.

Qualifications

KNOWLEDGE OF: Modern office methods, appliances, and practices; proper English usage, grammar, spelling, and punctuation.

ABILITY TO: Compose routine correspondence independently; make simple arithmetical calculations with speed and accuracy; meet the public tactfully and courteously and answer questions in person or over the telephone; understand and follow oral and written directions.

EXPERIENCE: One year of responsible clerical experience.

EDUCATION: Equivalent to graduation from high school.

SKILLS: Typing speed of at least 40 net words per minute.

RANKING JOBS.   Following the development, or revision, of descriptions for each job within the organization, each individual position is then ranked in relation to similar jobs within its group.   To accomplish this task, two major systems for job ranking have been developed: the quantitative method, in which either the job ranking plan or grade description plan may be used; and the non-quantitative method, in which point rating or factor comparison are the principal means by which tasks are ranked.

Next an organizational chart is developed to show graphically the hierarchical relationship each job bears to another.   A number of jobs of similar nature becomes a "group," while two or more groups performing similar, but not identical, duties become a "class."   In turn, classes are clustered together into a hierarchy and ultimately into a total "service." An example of a service might be the segment of classified personnel charged with the maintenance and operation of a district's vehicles.   They would be known as "the transportation service," encompassing all employees required to repair, maintain, operate, and supervise the trucks, buses, and mobile mechanical equipment of the district.

The advantage of defining position requirements and representing each graphically becomes readily apparent when using the information for recruitment, selection, training, and evaluation of employees. These guidelines, established by the personnel administrator, serve as a basis for composing advertisements for job openings circulated among employment agencies, posted on public bulletin boards, and advertised in other media. They also provide a basis for measuring employees for purposes of inservice training, pay recognition, and promotion, demotion, or dismissal.

Wage and Salary Administration

Wage and salary administration relies on accurate job classification and description which provides for the development of wages, salaries, and other benefits for the employee. The absence of a sound policy of salary administration quickly contributes to a decline in morale among employees. The basic job description or classification forms the basis on which equitable salary policy is formulated.

Initially, rules and policies for salary administration should be developed prior to entry into actual salary negotiations. Factors to be taken into account in developing a classified salary system are the relationships between each position class, comparison data, and the internal structure of the schedule itself. Most salary systems in common use today employ a grid system in which a range of salaries is represented on a percentage increase from a base figure. Table 24–1 represents a typical arrangement in which each range represents a 2½ percent increase over the previous one. Each position is assigned a range. For example, a clerk–typist is range 19 so the starting salary is $459. The five steps in the horizontal direction represent five percent increases and are used, one step at a time, to automatically advance the employee for each year of service. The clerk-typist would receive $559 at the beginning of the fifth year. Hourly equivalents are used for temporary or part-time employees in each position range.

Relationships between various jobs within a group can be determined

TABLE 24–1. *A Typical Classified Salary Schedule*

RANGE NUMBER	ANNUAL SALARY INCREMENTS					HOURLY EQUIV- ALENT
	1	2	3	4	5	
1	$294	$309	$325	$341	$358	$1.70
2	301	317	333	349	367	1.74
3	309	325	341	358	376	1.79
4	317	333	349	367	386	1.83
5	325	341	358	376	395	1.87
6	333	349	367	386	405	1.92
7	341	358	376	395	415	1.97
8	349	367	386	405	426	2.02
9	358	376	395	415	436	2.07
10	367	386	405	426	447	2.12
11	376	395	415	436	459	2.17
12	386	405	426	447	470	2.23
13	395	415	436	459	482	2.28
14	405	426	447	470	494	2.34
15	415	436	459	482	506	2.40
16	426	447	470	494	519	2.46
17	436	459	482	506	532	2.52
18	447	470	494	519	545	2.58
19	459	482	506	532	559	2.65
20	470	494	519	545	573	2.71
21	482	506	532	559	587	2.78
22	494	519	545	573	602	2.85
23	506	532	559	587	617	2.92
24	519	545	573	602	632	2.99
25	532	559	587	617	648	3.07
26	545	573	602	632	664	3.14
27	559	587	617	648	681	3.22
28	573	602	632	664	698	3.30
29	587	617	648	681	715	3.39
30	602	632	664	698	733	3.47
31	617	648	681	715	751	3.56
32	632	664	698	733	770	3.65
33	648	681	715	751	789	3.74
34	664	698	733	770	809	3.83
35	681	715	751	789	829	3.93

by surveying business, industry, and/or nearby school districts. Each position is then assigned a range position on the grid. A typical salary hierarchy for a secretarial group showing position titles, salary ranges, and the relationship of each position to other positions within the group is illustrated in Table 24–2.

TABLE 24–2. An Example of a Salary Hierarchy for a Secretarial Group

POSITION	SALARY RANGE NUMBER	POSITION (BENCH MARK) RELATIONSHIP
Clerk–Typist	19	Bench Mark
PBX Operator	19	Direct alignment with Clerk–Typist
Senior Clerk–Typist	23	Four (4) schedules above Clerk–Typist
Library Clerk	23	Four (4) schedules above Clerk–Typist
Elementary School Clerk	24	Five (5) schedules above Clerk–Typist
Secretary	24	Five (5) schedules above Clerk–Typist
Adult School Clerk	24	Five (5) schedules above Clerk–Typist
Continuation School Clerk	24	Five (5) schedules above Clerk–Typist
Senior Secretary	29	Five (5) schedules above Elementary School Clerk
Secondary School Secretary	29	Direct alignment with Senior Secretary
Administrative Secretary	31	Two (2) schedules above Senior Secretary

THE BENCH MARK SYSTEM.   A hierarchical system simplifies the annual task of reviewing salaries with bench marks.   To implement this system, one position within the group is chosen as a comparison position, or bench mark.   Salary rates paid to the particular position in other school districts, industries, and businesses are compared.   If the results of the survey indicate that the salary organization is "low," the bench mark position is up-graded, and all other positions related to it are adjusted.   This system not only simplifies the determination of salary for each particular classification, but satisfies one of the major elements of good salary administration: keeping salaries internally consistent.   In choosing the bench mark position, the lowest position in the hierarchy is generally selected for the following reasons: (1) Incumbents in the position are generally more numerous.   (2) Mobility for the position is generally greater, thus enabling wages to more accurately reflect prevailing rates. (3) Duties assigned to lower level positions are generally similar to those in business and industry.   In other words, the duties of a custodian or clerk typist are the same in any industry.

JOB COMPARISON SYSTEM.   In contrast to the bench mark system, the method of salary determination through job-by-job salary comparison is much more time-consuming and does not provide for the continuation of internal salary consistency.   On the other hand, the use of job-by-job comparisons does enable wages paid to each individual classification to more accurately reflect prevailing wages paid for that particular position. The principle of "like pay for like work" is more readily fulfilled.

FRINGE BENEFITS.   In addition to considering actual wages, increasing attention has been focused on the use of ancillary or fringe benefits for employees.   This trend in public education has been prompted by the example of business and industry; by the employee's demand for ever increasing job security and protection both for himself and his family; and by the fact that in some states, monies derived for the payment of fringe benefits come from separate tax sources and do not constitute a drain on the general funds of the school district.   Thus, in a time of increasingly tight s/ 1ool budgets, fringe benefits provide a means for the employee who otherwise might not be awarded cash salary increases to be compensated. Common fringe benefits are:

1.   Major medical health insurance for the employee and his family.
2.   Dental coverage.
3.   Income protection in case of severe illness.
4.   Life insurance.
5.   Tax sheltered annuities.

Many districts are offering insurance through the so-called "cafeteria plan."   Under this plan, each employee is granted a sum of money to be used for insurance coverage; he selects coverages best suited to his particular desires and needs.   Due to the wide diversity of economic and marital status of the employees in a school district, the "cafeteria plan" ensures that each employee is receiving coverage appropriate to his particular situation.   Fringe benefits for classified employees should be comparable to those for certificated employees.

GUIDING PRINCIPLES.   Three principles of wage and salary benefits should govern their administration: (1) The administration of wages and benefits should be executed according to a predetermined plan, adopted long before employee–employer salary negotiations are undertaken.   (2) The system used should ensure that the internal relationships developed between classifications are maintained when salaries are revised.   At the same time, salaries adopted for a particular group should be equal to those paid for similar work in other businesses or industries.   (3) Fringe benefits should reflect the needs and desires of each individual employee, rather than of a particular group of employees. The "cafeteria" plan most nearly fulfills this requirement.

Procurement, Selection, Training, Evaluation, and Advancement

The second area of responsibility in the administration of classified personnel pertains to the establishment of procurement procedures; the selection of qualified employees; orientation and training; evaluation; and providing opportunities for advancement. This area is referred to as the merit system in the triangle described earlier in the chapter.

JOB ANNOUNCEMENTS. A job announcement seeking applicants is an important off-shoot of the basic job description. They are designed to accomplish three main purposes: to attract qualified persons to investigate the merits of the position through its salary and advancement potential; to outline the duties and requirements of the position; and to explain various mechanics of application, testing, and selection procedures. The artistic layout of the job announcement and its content should attract the individual to the school. It should promise advancement opportunities and outline how the individual is identified with the growth and success of the organization as a whole.

Recent civil rights interpretations by the Equal Employment Opportunities Commission and the U.S. Supreme Court have held that job qualifications should not contain "artificial barriers to employment." Specifically, this includes stipulations that bar an individual from applying for a position because he does not possess qualifications or requirements not directly related to the skills necessary for the position.

EXAMINATION PROCESS. The system of job classification also enables the employing organization to construct an examination process that directly relates to the requirements of the position and to determine the individual's potential success in the position. The Federal government has decreed that examination procedures must be directly related to the requirements of the position and must fairly measure the individual's potential for success in the position. From the basic job description, the school organization can construct or purchase test materials that directly relate to the requirements of the position. No test, however, should be used unless it has been validated with job success.

A personal interview should also be a part of the examination process for classified employees. It helps to determine the personality of the applicant and how he will fit into the school system and also offers an opportunity to delve in depth into his qualifications to perform the job. The interviewer should have training in interview techniques.

ORIENTATION, SUPERVISION, AND EVALUATION. The job description enables the individual who is hired to know what is expected of him. Prudent supervisory practice should provide for a review of job requirements for the new employee by his immediate superior, the employee should confirm his understanding of the position. If the employee is later terminated for poor performance, his signature will not allow him to claim that he did not know the requirements of the position.

The system of classification also serves to measure the performance of the individual against his job specification. It is upon the job description criteria that ratings are made and the inservice training needs of the employee are met. Ratings developed from established job criteria also provide valuable data to determine potential for future promotion into higher classifications. Success within one classification often predicts an individual's ability to handle positions demanding a higher degree of skill and responsibility.

TRAINING PROGRAM. Once the individual has been selected as an employee of the school district, the responsibility of the organization shifts to a program of continuous training that will enable the individual to carry out the responsibilities of his classification and to learn new skills.

In considering various aspects of the training program, it must be kept in mind that all activities in which the employee engages are part of a training program, and that each of these activities should be preplanned with the welfare of both the employee and the organization in mind. Although most training is of the "how to" type, some school districts provide leadership training for those looking for advancement. Training programs should have the endorsement, acceptance, and participation of top school administrators. Although training can be costly, it is essential. Rosenberger states:

> There is a limit to the amount of training that can be done economically. Although training involves cost, it is far more costly not to provide

training that is needed. It is impractical to train all employees extensively, and yet poor management to neglect urgent employee training needs.[1]

Most large school districts have specialists to conduct inservice training. They can also serve as consultants to smaller school districts. Specialists outside the field of education can also be employed to conduct training programs, although the cost may be prohibitive in smaller districts. In general, there are four varieties of employee training that are discussed in the following paragraphs.

PRE-ENTRY. This is a program conducted on an apprenticeship basis. The individual is given some training for the position he is to occupy prior to actual performance on the job. This program may involve classroom work dealing with practices of the trade or work with the actual tools of the trade.

INDUCTION. This type of inservice program is aimed at specifically orienting the employee to the tasks of his classification. Since it is assumed he has the general knowledge required for the position, this program is not as extensive as that of the apprentice program. Training is usually conducted in the actual working situation.

ON-THE-JOB TRAINING. One of the most frequently used programs, on-the-job training takes the employee where he is and extends his knowledge and skills. For example, in training a new custodian, the supervisor is cognizant of the individual's potential to prepare him to assume a more responsible role. Training aimed at enabling a custodian to assume a more advanced role might include knowledge of the latest custodial practices, techniques of supervision, and methods of assisting others in doing a better job. Supervisory roles require not only superior knowledge of the technical aspects of the work, but knowledge of the skills needed to impart this information to others.

SUPPLEMENTARY. This type of inservice activity parallels on-the-job training, but is carried out away from the specific job location. The most common type of supplementary training is received through educational courses at local trade schools or colleges. The school organization itself

---

[1] Homer T. Rosenberger, *Employee Training Incentives,* p. 1.

can set up courses, conducted either by district employees or outside consultants. Supplementary work should deal with either the technical aspects of the job or the techniques of supervision.

In sum, the inservice program should be evaluated to see what it is accomplishing in the areas of:

1. Improving morale and decreasing turnover.
2. Preparing workers for jobs for which pretrained employees are not available.
3. Decreasing the amount of initiation time.
4. Reducing the necessary time to determine whether or not the new employee is suitable for the job.
5. Increasing the worker's effectiveness on the present job.
6. Improving the product.
7. Increasing the number of workers available to step into jobs of greater responsibility.
8. Decreasing absenteeism.
9. Decreasing accidents.[2]

The purpose of any inservice program is to meet the needs of the individual and to train him to carry out his job adequately, as well as to gain new skills for advancement.

EVALUATION.   As important an aspect of the employee's growth as his inservice training is the evaluation of his performance by the employee himself and his supervisor. As indicated previously, evaluation is closely related to the basic job description because the employee is initially made aware of what is expected of him through this medium. It is important that initially the duties be clarified and that the employee be made aware of how he is performing.

The evaluation form in and of itself is an important part of the process as it serves as a guideline upon which judgment of the employee's performance is based. In order to let the employee know where he stands, the document should be simple in its construction and content. It should be specific in indicating performance levels associated with evaluative terms such as good, poor, superior, and so forth. At the same time, it

---

[2] Homer T. Rosenberger, *Organizing and Administering an Employee Training Program*, p. 32.

should be flexible enough to measure the individuality of the person being rated.

In order to avoid rating inconsistencies, school districts provide training in rating procedures that specifically focus on what is being rated, what to look for, and what behaviors are being observed. The evaluation form should indicate what behaviors are associated with various levels of performance. The necessity of specifically determining behavioral characteristics cannot be emphasized too greatly. Current employment practices emphasize employment testing that is validly related to the requirements of the job. If entry tests are to be proven valid in a statistical sense, so must the evaluation of the employee be defined to directly relate to the initial content of the test.

The primary purpose of evaluation is to enable the employee to improve his work performance. Management practices now stress a method of evaluation whereby the employee himself sets his performance goals and then at some future date determines his degree of accomplishment. Through the identification of his own desired areas of improvement, the employee feels more committed to professional growth.

ADVANCEMENT. Employees in a school district should be given every opportunity to advance. If the district has an effective inservice training program, employees interested in advancement will be prepared to apply for higher positions. A school district spends unnecessary funds if it goes outside the district to select personnel for higher positions when it may have qualified people within the district. This also causes resentment from qualified employees. If the training program is a sound one and evaluation procedures are based on well-understood, cooperatively developed policies, employees should not feel disgruntled if they do not receive a promotion.

The Administration of Equitable Rules and Regulations

The employment, classification, and compensation of employees imply a need for developing and adhering to specific administrative rules and regulations to govern the operation of the classified personnel service. The development and administration of sound personnel practices constitutes the third portion of the triangle in Figure 24–1 (p. 678).

While the mechanics of recruiting, selecting, and rewarding the employee are important in developing and maintaining positive morale within the organization, increasingly sophisticated management trends emphasize the importance of developing positive, overall working relationships as well. The development of specific procedures contributes to positive morale. On the other hand, areas of human relations and personnel management do not consist of isolated procedures. In order to develop a sound program of organizational health, the "whole" must be encompassed. To attempt to emphasize one or two elements of a program is to assure failure; one aspect cannot exist without the other.

The conscientious administrator in industry, business, or education must construct a sound, all-encompassing personnel program. Administrators must be aware of the importance of motivation, participation, and interpersonal relations. Without commitment to these concepts, the employee morale will suffer. Personnel programs require conscientious efforts of administrators to be aware of the needs of each employee and to make an attempt to equate these needs to the particular organization. The employee can no longer be expected to merely do his job, draw his check, and go home contented. Instead, he must be made to feel that he is a part of the organization and that his contribution to the overall good of the organization is appreciated. His suggestions and contributions for the improvement of his job or of the organization should be sought and welcomed by supervisors.

Cooperative Development of Rules and Regulations. The increase in employee participation has caused a growing trend toward cooperative development of rules and regulations by which employees will be governed.

In any area of administration where there may be potential misinterpretation or disagreement between an employee and his supervisor, solutions should be considered and a means of resolution outlined before problems occur. Cooperatively developed rules and regulations should be based on school board-adopted policies concerning:

Employment.
Classification and assignment: job descriptions, vacancies, changes in assignment, and transfer.
Compensation: salary schedules for full-time, part-time, temporary, and substitute employment, and overtime pay.
Work periods: school calendar, hours of work.

Insurance: accident, health, workmen's compensation.

Tax-sheltered annuities.

Probation and permanency: probationary period, promotion, and reinstatement.

Suspensions, demotions, and termination: grounds for demotion, suspension or dismissal, disciplinary action, hearings, resignations, layoffs, and retirement.

Leaves of absence: sick, industrial, accident, personal, bereavement, maternity, military, emergency, and jury duty.

Vacations.

Performance and evaluation: periodic evaluations, inservice training, and complaints.

Rules and regulations should be compiled in a policy or regulations handbook which explains, in simple language, the policies under which various programs are administered. Handbooks should be printed in a compact, handy form and distributed to all employees. As policies and regulations are changed or superseded, revisions should be distributed to all employees. Periodically, the handbook should be reviewed by the administration and a representative employee group, and, if need be, completely revised and reprinted.

GROUNDS FOR DEMOTION, SUSPENSION, OR DISMISSAL. The continued employment of personnel should be contingent upon proper performance of assigned duties and personal fitness. Typical causes for demotion, suspension, or dismissal are the following:

1. Incompetency or inefficiency in the performance of duties.
2. Insubordination (including, but not limited to, refusal to do assigned work).
3. Carelessness or negligence in the performance of duty or in the care or use of district property.
4. Offensive or abusive conduct or language toward other employees, pupils, or the public.
5. Dishonesty.
6. Drinking alcoholic beverages on the job or reporting to work while intoxicated.
7. Narcotic addiction.
8. Personal conduct unbecoming to an employee of the district.

9. Engaging in political activity during assigned hours of employment.
10. Conviction of any crime involving moral turpitude.
11. Arrest for a sex offense.
12. Repeated and/or unexcused absence or tardiness.
13. Abuse of illness leave privileges.
14. Falsifying any information supplied to the school district, including, but not limited to, information supplied on application forms, employment records, or any other school district records.
15. Persistent violation or refusal to obey safety rules or regulations made applicable to public schools by the board of education or by any appropriate state or local governmental agency.
16. Offering of anything of value or any service in exchange for special treatment in connection with the employee's job or employment, or accepting anything of value or any service in exchange for granting any special treatment to an employee or to any member of the public.
17. Willful or persistent violation of the state's *Education Code* or the rules of the board of education.
18. Any willful failure of good conduct tending to injure the public service.
19. Abandonment of position.
20. Advocacy of overthrow of federal, state, or local government by force, violence, or other unlawful means.
21. Membership in the Communist Party.[3]

GRIEVANCE PROCEDURES.   All regulations being subject to misapplication or misinterpretation, a grievance procedure whereby the employee has a recourse if he feels he has been unfairly treated is vital.   While grievance procedures vary from organization to organization, all grievance procedures contain certain common elements.   Initially, the basis for most grievances is an alleged violation of an existing rule or regulations; the absence of any rules or regulations may also lead to filing a grievance and to the necessity of developing a policy to cover the grievance situation.

The initial step in any grievance procedure generally includes an informal conference between the grievant and his superior (assumed to be the individual against whom the grievance has been lodged) which at-

---

[3] Vista Unified School District, *Classified Personnel Rules and Regulations* (Vista, Calif.: 1966), pp. 507–507.1.

tempts to resolve the problem on a low-level, informal basis. If the grievance cannot be resolved at this point, mechanics should be developed to formally register the grievant's complaint in written form and to forward it to higher authority. The grievant's employee organization should step in at this point in an effort to solve the problem or to assist in the processing of the grievance. Additional mechanics provided for the processing of the grievance should include: the steps through which it is to be channeled; time intervals or limitations for administrative reply to the grievance, as well as a time limitation in which the grievant must act in order to continue his case; and the individual or group by whom the final resolution of the grievance will be made.

In many states, the resolution of a grievance within an educational organization lies with the board of education and/or a type of civil service commission. There is also an increasing trend toward resolution of grievances through the use of a third party or outside mediator. In the latter case, however, many state laws still rest ultimate decision-making power in the board of education, rendering the third party an advisory body. In other states, arbitration is binding on both parties regardless of the mechanics of the grievance procedure or the means by which the problem is settled.

Proper management of employees necessitates a procedure by which problems can be brought forth and attempts at resolutions made. The employee should be encouraged to register a grievance if he feels it is of genuine concern to him. In addition, he should be assured that the registration of such a grievance will in no way be held against him or jeopardize his position in the future.

Summary

The administration of classified personnel should emphasize the importance of systematic development of rules and procedures to guide classified employee and administrator in providing the vital auxiliary services of the school district. As more and more non-certificated employees enter the educational ranks as paraprofessionals charged with assisting teaching personnel, it is vital that the rules and regulations under which they work be clearly developed and understood by all. The federal government's emphasis on improving employee selection, promotion, and working conditions tends to reinforce the importance of such a system.

While the administration of classified personnel can be divided into several broad areas, this chapter attempts to show that the key aspect of any system of administration lies in the proper definition and description of each of the jobs within the classified service. Job description should be clearly expressed in written form and made thoroughly familiar to the employee.

The development of a basic job description leads to the identification of a complete hierarchy of classified positions. Such a system, once identified and reproduced in graphic or organizational form, enables administrators to grasp the overall functioning of the organization. In addition, an organizational scheme lends itself to the identification of salary determination, promotional opportunities, and inservice training needs. The identification of specific job requirements enables the individual to know what skills are required to obtain a given position, the type of examination procedures he will encounter to prove he possesses these skills, and the responsibility and duties connected with the position. His performance as measured against this job definition enables the employee and his supervisor to assess his success in the position, and to identify further training and the structure of inservice programs. This assessment of the employee and his job also enables the worker to identify skills required for promotion.

The process by which job descriptions and procedures are developed is as important an administrative task as the procedures themselves. Increasing emphasis of this aspect of personnel administration comes from the field of industrial psychology. The individual is no longer to be looked upon as merely a "tool" of the organization, but rather as an individual who must be able to fulfill his basic needs through identification with the goals of the organization for which he works. He should also feel that he shares in the determination of the success or failure of the organization, thus becoming in some degree "master of his own fate."

Educational policies for administering classified personnel parallel movements in the modernization of other organizational systems. Emphasis is now placed on employee participation in determining job conditions and in assisting in the development of organizational rules, regulations, or procedures. Commitment to these modern principles fosters the employee's feelings of worth and usefulness which in turn lead him toward increased participation and commitment to the overall aims of the organization.

Trends

TOWARD INCREASED EMPHASIS ON NEGOTIATION. Classified employees no longer accept dictates from the administration. Under the impetus of employee associations, they are organizing themselves into local groups that are becoming more powerful in their demands for higher salaries, more fringe benefits, and better working conditions. They are demanding an increasing voice in developing policies, rules, and regulations that concern them. Collective bargaining between the school board and the classified employee association or union will increase. As districts grow in size and complexity, this trend will probably intensify.

TOWARD THE USE OF JOB DESCRIPTIONS. Carefully developed job descriptions help to clarify job expectations. Written descriptions make it easier for the employee to know what he is to do and, further, help in evaluating his services. Most districts will use job descriptions instead of easily misunderstood oral declarations.

TOWARD MORE SOPHISTICATED SELECTION PROCEDURES. There is an increasing trend in the use of more sophisticated selection procedures which test the individual's potential skills for a given job. Tests that are irrelevant to a particular position will be discontinued.

TOWARD THE ELIMINATION OF ARTIFICIAL BARRIERS. Barriers to employment that do not pertain directly to the requirements of the job are being eliminated. Criteria such as age, sex, race, color, or creed are having less and less effect on employment because federal laws prevent discrimination.

TOWARD EQUITABLE PAY SCALES. There is a trend toward pay scales that are equal to comparable positions in business and industry. More and more school districts are surveying business and industry as they develop classified salary schedules.

TOWARD MORE FRINGE BENEFITS. Fringe benefits are becoming more common as a means of increasing employee remuneration. Some of these include insurance protection of all types, increased vacation allowances, and longevity rewards. More districts will follow the lead of business and industry in providing these benefits.

TOWARD INCREASED USE OF TRAINING PROGRAMS.   Employee failure was previously considered the fault of the employee. Forward-looking school districts, as they assume responsibility for employee success, are providing on-the-job training and inservice programs for their classified personnel.

TOWARD BETTER EVALUATION PROCEDURES.   Elaborate rating scales are being abandoned as a means of evaluating classified personnel. Performance evaluation will become more directly related to job specifications.

Administrative Problems

Problem 1

The new director of classified personnel finds that there are few job descriptions for classified personnel. This situation has caused problems with relationships between various groups of personnel, particularly in regard to duties and salaries.

How should the director proceed in the development of job descriptions?
When developed, how can he remedy discrepancies?

Problem 2

Bill Gray, the head custodian at Mayfair Elementary School, has been performing poorly, although in the past he has done outstanding work. Specifically, he has not followed district custodial regulations in certain instances, such as poor cleaning, leaving early, taking long coffee breaks, not training his helpers, and occasionally failing to secure the buildings. There have been numerous teacher complaints.

The principal, Mr. Redfern, has held numerous conferences with Mr. Gray. Although he has given him written suggestions about what he must do to improve, there has been little improvement. His last two evaluations have been below district standards. Mr. Redfern has decided that Mr. Gray should be dismissed.

How should Mr. Redfern proceed to effect Mr. Gray's dismissal?
What evidence will he need?

Problem 3

Assume the same situation as in Problem 2. Bill Gray has been given due notice that he is being terminated. He believes that the principal is unfair in his evaluation, that the complaints are not valid, and that he should be given another chance to improve. He appeals to his Grievance Committee which accepts his case. The district personnel director has become involved.

What should the principal do?
How should the personnel director proceed?

Selected References

ARGYRIS, CHRIS. *Integrating the Individual with the Organization.* New York: John Wiley and Sons, 1964.

CASTETTER, W. A. *Administering the School Personnel Program.* New York: Macmillan Co., 1969.

COLE, DAVID. *The Quest for Industrial Peace.* New York: McGraw-Hill Book Co., 1967.

DAVIS, KEITH. *Human Relations at Work.* New York: McGraw-Hill Book Co., 1967.

FINLEY, ROBERT E., ed. *The Personnel Man at His Job.* New York: American Management Association, 1962.

FRENCH, WENDELL. *The Personnel Management Process.* Boston: Houghton Mifflin Co., 1964.

GELLERMAN, SAUL W. *Management by Motivation.* New York: American Management Association, 1968.

GORTON, RICHARD A. *Conflict, Controversy and Crisis in School Administration Supervision: Issues, Cases and Concepts for the 70's.* Dubuque, Iowa: Wm. C. Brown, 1972.

MCGREGOR, DOUGLAS. *The Human Side of Enterprise.* New York: McGraw-Hill Book Co., 1960.

————. *The Professional Manager.* New York: McGraw-Hill Book Co., 1967.

PIGORS, PAUL, et al. *Management of Human Resources.* New York: McGraw-Hill Book Co., 1969.

————, and MYERS, CHARLES A. *Personnel Administration.* New York: McGraw-Hill Book Co., 1965.

ROSENBERGER, HOMER T. *Employee Training Incentives.* Pamphlet No. 16. Washington, D.C.: Society for Personnel Administration, May 1958.

————. *Organizing and Administering an Employee Training Program.* Pamphlet No. 11. Washington, D.C.: Society for Personnel Administration, April 1956.

STRAUSS, GEORGE, and SAYLES, LEONARD R. *Personnel: The Human Problems of Management.* Englewood Cliffs, N.J.: Prentice-Hall, Inc., 1960.

WARNER, KENNETY D. *Developments in Public Employee Relations.* Chicago: Public Personnel Association, 1965.

25

Employee Organizations

Change has occurred in all aspects of employee representation in the education field, but the extent of this change has been most substantial in the last two decades. A national, unified, and multifaceted teachers' organization in this century would surely not have been predicted a generation ago. The present status of teacher organizations and organizations of other school personnel is a matter worthy of serious study as an administrator looks toward the future.

This chapter deals with teacher, administrator, and non-certificated employee organizations. The real and periphery objectives of such groups may or may not be similar; but they have all undergone drastic and traumatic revisions. They are equally deserving of consideration in the context of their respective or cumulative effects on the educational structure. Teachers and non-certificated coworkers are not merely extending the industrial union concept. Nor do administrators and their organizations represent the antithesis of this concept. All of these groups, individually and collectively, represent industry counterparts to some degree; but a deeper analysis is required before too many inferences are drawn.

This chapter includes a discussion of the following topics:

Development and Progress of Employee Organizations
General Areas of Involvement
Specific Areas of Involvement

Material for this chapter was prepared in collaboration with Dr. Paul E. Dundon, Superintendent, Garden Grove Unified School District, Garden Grove, California.

Summary
Trends

Development and Progress of Employee Organizations

Teacher, administrator, and non-certificated (or classified) organizations have developed at different rates and for somewhat different reasons. One of the first and primary interests was to increase salaries, followed by attempts to improve working conditions. Business, industry, and unions have provided some impetus. Some factors that have led to the upsurge of teacher organization movements are:

1. Teachers are better prepared and more competent.
2. Teaching has become a life career for many.
3. Schools have grown larger.
4. Urbanization.
5. Greater control by teachers of their professional standards.[1]

Teacher organizations have been the strongest and most aggressive, although non-certificated groups, depending upon their leadership, have been quite forceful. In most cases, administrator organizations have been slower to develop strength and have tended to be more professional and less militant in demanding recognition.

TEACHER ORGANIZATIONS. Without attempting a specific chronological study of teacher professional groups, it is clear the present direction is toward involvement and negotiation. Until the 1950s, this involvement consisted generally of local chapters of educators, a state organization, and the only national teacher representative structure, the National Education Association (NEA).

However, there was often strong division in the local units over the necessity, desirability, or propriety of direct affiliation with the respective state or the national organization. As pressure grew to make enrollment in a local unit conditional upon state and national membership, the philosophical disparity among professional educators became apparent.

---

[1] American Association of School Administrators, *School Administrators View Professional Negotiation*, p. 16.

Many teachers, in the sixties and continuing into the seventies, believed that the only real and lasting control of teachers over their destinies lay in political power. This idea has led to voting drives and service as party volunteers and office holders, particularly at the local level where teachers have been elected to city councils and boards of education.[2] (Other professional groups, such as the American Medical Association, operate in a similar manner.) Prior to the fifties, militancy as defined today was not yet apparent, but there were those in education who felt that teachers should actively demand more adequate salaries and raise their prestige.

The dominant opinion at this time, however, held that teaching, freely entered into as a profession, should be so considered and honored. Moreover, salaries should not be the prime or only concern of educators. Continued and intensified power struggles were not deemed worthy of the profession or in the best interests of the students toward whom the whole process was directed. Until rather recently, this philosophical position seemed to prevail, and in certain portions of the country it still does.

Gradually (but more rapidly in urban areas such as New York City, Pittsburgh, Detroit, and Buffalo), teacher groups were recognized as a political force. In a relatively few years, politicians, particularly in state legislatures, began to respond to and cultivate this force. Quite naturally, counterforces were developed and the entire manner of dealing with educational matters was transformed. Salaries and benefits are now (in the seventies) only a portion of the items under consideration by all parties. The number and variety of demands have been substantially altered.

Political philosophies and even party platforms reflect the magnitude of this new force. As teachers become more militant and achieve collective negotiation arrangements, they determine the conditions under which they will work and the services they will render. This has put them in conflict with the public, reacting through its elected representatives. The power struggle between teachers and the public over control of education is on a collision course.[3] Lay citizens have begun to polarize, strongly supporting or opposing teacher organizations and their politics. Candidates for local, state, and national offices have taken stands.

Perhaps even more important to those in education, administrators

---

[2] T. M. Stinnett, "Teachers in Politics: The Larger Roles," *Today's Education* 57 (October 1968), p. 37.

[3] Arthur E. Salz, "Formula for Inevitable Conflict: Local Control vs. Professionalism," *Phi Delta Kappan,* p. 333.

have begun to fully recognize that a massive organizational response from their group is necessary. Collective bargaining by teacher associations received a boost in 1973 when the National School Board Association president told the School Board Convention that collective bargaining in Connecticut had improved education and had produced many special services for students.

Clearly, a direction has been established, although some believe that public education suffers from collective bargaining rights for teachers. Caution against prejudging or predicting the pattern of the future power structure in education is well advised. It would appear safe to conclude, however, that teacher organizations have achieved a power base from which no real return to the past is possible, even if desired. Power offers opportunity, as well as responsibility. The future of public education in the United States depends in no small measure on how teacher organizations implement this force and recognize leadership responsibilities. The transformation of teacher organizations from "docile, semiactive, and socially oriented [groups] into dynamic, strongly active, welfare-focused associations" is one of the most important developments in recent years.[4]

Teacher organizations are moving more and more toward joining with labor as they attempt to work toward common goals and to increase their power base. Nine states (Michigan, Iowa, Wisconsin, Maryland, Hawaii, Connecticut, New Mexico, Illinois, and Delaware) have formed a state-wide coalition of public employees that includes teachers, firefighters, police, and state and local government employees. The president of the National Education Association says that the potential of the 14 million people represented by this labor coalition will become "the outstanding labor phenomenon of the 1970s." Teachers will seek all the rights of employees in the private sector, creating another situation with which administrators must cope.[5]

As movement is made toward mandatory enrollment in both state and national groups by local teacher units, an apparent unification of purpose probably will occur. Whether or not this is translated into a lasting unification will depend essentially upon the nature of the role, collectively and individually, that society demands of the teacher. Accountability, in one form or another, has always been the final determinant. In the past,

---

[4] American Association of School Administrators, *Profiles of the Administrative Team,* p. 91.

[5] National Education Association, "Connecticut Public Employees Coalition Set," *NEA Reporter* 13 (April 1974), p. 2.

failures or shortcomings in education have not been ascribed to employee organizations. This situation will be altered as involvement in the decision-making process becomes more common for teacher associations. Moreover, the National Education Association (NEA) and the American Federation of Teachers (AFT) will accelerate competitive drives for membership. Those opposing mandatory membership in any state or national group create an internal matter of some concern for present teacher organizations.

Should a merger of both the NEA and AFT occur in the near future and become enforceably binding on teacher units throughout the nation, the internal dissension will be no different than is presently noted in the AFL–CIO or Teamsters groups.

ADMINISTRATOR ORGANIZATIONS. Traditionally, administrators have organized themselves in a more effective manner than teachers. The local educational power structure generally was assumed to lie with the school principal or district superintendent. State and national organizational structure was efficient enough to reinforce these individuals from a professional standpoint. Membership dues were ample to provide staff services on a rather sophisticated level. Common areas of concern and methods of successful problem solving were shared with the membership.

A factor in the development of administrator groups was the cooperative and supportive attitude of school board members. State and national school board associations generally set up organizations to parallel administrators. These arrangements should not really be surprising since the operation and direction of schools were generally assumed to rest with such individuals. Legal and financial matters of concern to both school boards and administrators require consultant firms to advise both groups and bind them together in an alliance that perhaps has become too close. Positions on matters are commonly defined and set forth as the establishment positions on a particular issue.

Colleges and universities also tend to work directly with administrator organizations. Innovations in educational theory and practice often appeared through this union. Textbooks and educational articles were published and put into practice by this partnership. It would probably not be unfair or inaccurate to state that not only were administrators recognized as more effectively organized, but leadership in educational matters was continually deferred to them. Decisions were made and implemented without a great deal of equivocation. This is not to say there was no disagreement expressed from teachers or others, but the operational decisions were generally more a matter of direction by fiat than anything else. These operational techniques are not completely lost today.

Moreover, this arrangement was not without the consent of the entire educational community. In a sense, other educators abdicated the role of responsibility and accountability that passed naturally to administrators and school boards. It was against such a background, to a greater or lesser degree, that the more recent moves toward total staff involvement were directed.

There are many responsible and knowledgeable professionals who believe that today's collective bargaining procedures for teachers have received rapid acceptance essentially because of so many years of nearly complete capitulation in decision making by the vast majority of teachers. Individuals who do not want to see teachers take to the streets in direct or supportive strike situations maintain that the educational etsablishment is reaping the harvest it sowed by not providing for a natural "give and take" in human affairs. Certainly, the field of education centers primarily on human relationships. Some writers believe that unless significant moves are made education will be organized and operated in a manner very similar to business and industry.

Another equally responsible and knowledgeable group of educational leaders are convinced that there is no method of compromise available at this point. Their contention is that the only way to restore any sort of input into the management of education is through political action. These people advocate entering the political arena to elect individuals at all levels (including school boards) who will be receptive to the teacher's point of view. Strong teacher group ties with state and national organizations and higher education are reminiscent of the previous power structure of administrator organizations.

Today's educational administrator must cope with a power struggle that will determine the leadership of the profession. In the present climate, the role of the administrator is being questioned, opening the role to some redefinition. The public's attitude and expectations, and the changing nature and dynamics of education have all contributed to this situation.

NON-CERTIFICATED ORGANIZATIONS. Sole emphasis on teacher and administrator organizations, to the neglect of non-certificated groups, repeats the error made by boards of education and administration toward teacher groups. There is no effective way in which school districts can function without the cooperative efforts of non-certificated personnel.

The development of organizational patterns of growth for classified personnel is not especially clear. As school districts grew in size and number, the work force in secretarial, clerical, maintenance and the like groups expanded proportionately. In some instances, local organizations were started and affiliated with state associations. Very often, though, no formal group was set up to speak for these individuals. Gradually, each state experienced an effort to organize this segment of the school community into an official association. Groups attempting to organize the non-certificated personnel range from local employee organizations to the AFL–CIO. Although generally about one-half the size of the teacher group, the importance of this group of school personnel cannot be over-emphasized.

Many states have an agency specifically for non-certificated personnel. Titles for this agency vary; some are called personnel commissions or merit commissions. The function of such a commission generally is to ensure the fairness of testing and hiring procedures, job classifications, evaluations, and grievance procedures. This agency could be compared to the federal government's civil service operation. Such administrative structures are set up by election of the employees themselves or by legislative mandate, depending upon the state. In some cases, the employees or the public may also vote the agency out of existence.

Especially in areas where unions are powerful, there has been an increasing move to do away with these agencies, as well as with non-union employee organizations. State personnel commissions have been criticized because they operate as bargaining agents jealously guarding their position. An agency established to safeguard employee rights should not function as a bargaining agent or solicit membership. The agency originally set up to ensure equity and fairness is now the target of employee organizations that believe they should be the guardians of employee rights. The motivation of those who seek to become employee representatives is rather clear. After all, what more desirable attraction to membership could there be than sole responsibility for defense of employees' rights and working conditions?

As the employee gains more representation on a formal and binding basis, he may also have to forfeit some of the individual or personal relationships inherent in an informal process. It will be an interesting and challenging time for all those involved in the formation of the new procedures.

General Areas of Involvement

Over the past decade, expressions of concern for teacher groups have grown in number and intensity. Teacher interest in decision making has complicated the administrator's task. Teacher associations have criticized school boards, superintendents, and more recently, building-level administrators.[6] Matters on which administration previously could make unilateral decisions without challenge have diminished greatly. Moderate and militant teacher organizations have made almost all areas of administrative discretion eligible for negotiation.

The extent to which teachers are persistent in their desire to become involved in decision making is dependent upon the strength of their local organization and the extent of state legislation on the subject. In California, a representative Certificated Employee Council is named by the state as the negotiating agency for teachers. Appropriate issues for negotiation are set forth generally and include curriculum, staff transfers, class size and the like, along with salary, fringe benefit, and welfare items, improvement of working conditions, provision of remedial reading teachers, more guidance counselors,[7] and fewer noninstructional duties.

Teacher groups apparently will make concerted efforts toward implementation of collective bargaining and a companion closed-shop arrangement. A parallel effort will be made to unify the present National Education Association with the American Federation of Teachers so that conflict within the profession will not jeopardize possible gains.

In areas or districts where more than one teacher organization has been or is in existence, loyalties are divided. Recent moves have been made to make local membership valuable and viable, especially by local chapters of the NEA and the AFT. Teachers traditionally have shied away from group membership, presenting a major obstacle to be overcome in organizing teachers.

In recent years, states have granted more recognition to matters directly involving teachers. Legislation in some states ensures that the

---

[6] Luvern L. Cunningham, "The Magnificent Pandora of Decentralization," *The School Administrator* (June 1970), p. 6.

[7] Salz, "Formula for Inevitable Conflict," p. 333.

process of negotiation is not only mandated but specifically patterned for teacher organizations. A few years ago a team of educators (comprised of teachers, counselors, and administrators) could meet rather informally with the school board's representative to discuss matters of mutual concern. However, common negotiations are now prohibited and membership rather clearly defined in an ever-increasing number of states. Most teacher groups now specifically negotiate for teachers, with the balance of educators often in a gray and undefined area of representation.

Specific Areas of Involvement

An attempt will be made in this section to provide the essential points of employee organization involvement, with some appropriate remarks for the reader's consideration and study on each.

SALARIES AND BENEFITS. Educators are not unlike other wage-earning groups, although their approach to salary discussions has become more stringent than in the past.

Teachers' organizations have accelerated efforts to establish the idea that their membership is underpaid and without the fringe benefit protection of other employee groups. To the extent that salaries and other benefits have improved for educators, these organizations have a right to claim some measure of success and credit. The degree to which credit can be ascribed to local, state, or national teacher organizations is disputable.

The teacher organization outlines of fringe benefits and salary proposals for negotiation are formulated with the knowledge that the association will usually have to compromise or back off; an alternate set of proposals are also ready before negotiation begins. Administration or management also has alternate proposals. Neither side knows what the other is willing to give up as they bargain between fringe benefits and salary. It is a give-and-take game until the final agreement is negotiated.

Teacher negotiations over salaries and benefits occupy longer and longer periods of time. A few years ago the teacher salary committee would sit down with the school board's representative (either the superintendent or his delegated representative) to draw up a salary schedule and insurance program for the following school term in a few days' or weeks' time. Negotiations are presently formally scheduled for months. In larger districts, teacher–board negotiations are a year-round proposition.

More and more sessions are being called by one side or the other throughout the year.

Administrator groups have also modified their techniques of negotiating for their own salary and benefit arrangements in recent years. In some states, recent statutes require administrators and others to discuss salary and supplemental benefits through their own structures. Because they have been excluded from negotiations with teacher groups, administrators must develop negotiating techniques to a much greater extent. They find themselves part of a trend to sustain professional identity that is in part compelled by law and by practicality.

In terms of strategy and knowledge of the art of negotiation, the administrator group should be quite formidable across the bargaining table. Whether or not this group will find it necessary to exert its political muscle is problematical. Will administrators claim the right to strike?

Non-certificated employee organizations are generally more involved with salaries and fringe benefits than with working conditions and employee rights, important as these are. Employees are more likely to join their organizations if they are effective in raising salaries and benefits. Salaries or wages are relatively lower for this group and except for job placement, classification, and grievance procedures, there is not the same incentive for diverse involvement in educational decision making as with certificated groups.

EMPLOYEE RIGHTS. Perhaps today's political and social climate dictates that this topic be a top priority, especially in teacher organization policy. Within this general category falls a wide variety of peripheral subjects; but when a delineation of specific areas is attempted it very quickly becomes apparent that several concepts are closely interrelated. For example, one cannot discuss evaluation of performance without touching tenure status, peer or student evaluation, staffing policies and procedures, administrative prerogative and legitimate jurisdiction, curriculum structure and freedom of expression.

Salaries and fringe benefits are basic demands but employee rights form the touchstone of the entire movement. Although timing and economic conditions affect tactical judgments, the overall strategy is to move ahead on both issues. In the long run, the issue of employee rights may become the major thrust.

Administrators generally do not display the intensity of teachers toward employee rights. They commonly feel that employee rights are an

internal concern to be resolved through unstructured and infomal arrangements. Administrators diplomatically hesitate to resort to a critical
and antagonistic position that teacher representatives feel compelled to
take against them. Administrators' rights that are allegedly violated or
compromised may be more expeditiously handled by assuming a management posture.

Employees represented by non-certificated organizations (classified
employees) have their rights protected by their local groups. Both union
and independent state organizations have similar operational procedures.

CURRICULUM AND STAFFING ITEMS. Teachers have and will continue to
have more effect on curricular and staffing aspects of district operations
and policy. In states where legislation has set up negotiating councils of
some form or another, there is no question that these items are legitimate
ones for inclusion in a negotiating agenda. However, there are few states
where a governing board is legally bound to do more than "meet and
confer in good faith."

There are other professionals, such as counselors, who have not as yet
decided on a philosophical stance. Should they be considered as teachers
on special assignment, or as more closely aligned with the administrative
group? (Previously, they have not been thought of as part of administration.) Both positions have practical and philosophical advantages and
liabilities. Teacher organizations have not catered to counselor membership. If administrators ask counselors or other ancillary personnel to join
them, it would remove them from the close relationship they should have
with teachers.

The non-certificated groups generally do not directly confront strictly
educational matters. However, most personnel administrators believe that
the implementation of any agreement will in no small measure be dependent upon this group.

OPERATION AND MANAGEMENT. The militancy of teacher organizations
has made the past five to ten years a difficult period for educators. As
teacher organizations mature and demand a more important role in decision making, they are becoming "a source of anxiety to school boards and
administrators." The traditional method of decision making by administrators and school boards is being altered by teacher organization demands

and negotiation.[8]   Large teacher organizations are becoming more powerful and aggressive and are using strikes and the threat of strikes as
powerful weapons.[9]   These developments have affected attitudes of both
school administration and the lay public.

The rapid rise of effective teacher organizations has created a great
momentum directed toward changing patterns of public education.   Administrators, according to some teachers, have not functioned receptively
or responsively.   Perhaps nothing could have prevented the confrontation
atmosphere that now pervades the educational establishment.   However,
little real and innovative effort was devoted to constructive change which
might have taken some of the driving power and emotional impetus out of
anti-administration feelings, all of which reinforces the axiom that good
leadership is not static or monolithic.

Administrator, teacher, and non-certificated organizations can be
helpful in improving, not only education, but the administration of a school
district.   If they act in a positive, constructive, open, and sincere manner,
they have much to contribute to decision making.   Administrators who
realize this and can develop a good working relationship with the district's
organizations can benefit.

Summary

The changing patterns of employee organizations over the past twenty
years are related to social patterns that have changed at an even more rapid
rate.   Because education is charged with passing on to new generations the
knowledge and values of past and present society, it is forced to focus on
social realities.

For better or worse, challenges to educators have been made both
internally and externally.   The public charges that educators have not done
an effective job and accountability is almost nonexistent.   The pressures
internal to the profession are also intriguing and critical to our national
system of education.   Democracy is a rare, precious, and unpredictable
way of life; the issue to which this chapter addresses itself is truly reflective
of the entire process.

---

[8] Archie R. Dykes, "Democracy, Teachers, and Educational Decision-Making,"
School & Society 92 (April 4, 1964), p. 156.

[9] Cunningham, "The Magnificent Pandora," p. 7.

Trends

It is a presumptuous undertaking to attempt to project trends in the volatile area of employee relations. Employee relations practices in public education are in a great state of flux. However, some trends for the future are submitted for study and discussion. Readers from different sections of the country will perhaps respond differently because what is now reality in one section may be only conversation in another.

TOWARD MANDATORY CONFERRING PROCEDURES. This prediction does not necessarily mean binding arbitration will prevail in all certificated or non-certificated relations. It does mean that the relaxed and rather informal atmosphere of many school negotiations will give way to a more structured pattern set forth by law. Most likely the organization representing the greatest segment of the staff will be designated a negotiating agent. A compulsory "dues" arrangement will probably be authorized to cover expenses of the representation responsibility.

TOWARD LESS USE OF THE TERM "PROFESSIONAL" FOR TEACHERS. In order to gain political leverage, teacher organizations will not permit the popular conception of "professional" to act as a liability. Tenure status will be an item to be traded for representation by the bargaining agent. There is some doubt that this trade-off will be viewed as a bargain by all teachers.

TOWARD NEGOTIATIONS FOR ADMINISTRATORS. This prognostication may appear to be too encompassing or without sufficient indication at this time, but there is a trend to place administrators in representative situations of their own. Negotiations will be defined further as counselors and other ancillary personnel are given representation.

TOWARD GREATER USE OF ACCEPTED MANAGEMENT PROCEDURES. The use of these techniques will be intensified by all groups, not only by administrators. As the size and complexity of inter- and intra-organizational problems become apparent, reliance on proven effective and efficient procedures will increase. All representative groups will sharpen their abilities to perform, benefitting education generally.

Toward Non-Certificated Organizational Sophistication. These groups will rapidly become more structured and sophisticated in their approach to challenges to represent their membership. Personnel commissions and similar quasi-governmental agencies will not be looked upon with a great deal of favor. Unions and independent employee organizations will emphasize that the individual can be more appropriately represented by membership in an employee group, and that watchdog agencies only serve as a confusing bureaucracy. Job protection will be a strong selling point for membership campaigns in unions or state employee groups.

Toward Some Competition Between Certificated and Non-Certificated Groups. The inevitable confrontation that results from two or more groups trying to get a larger share of the same dollar source will bring these groups into a competitive position. The confrontation will probably be based on mutual respect, and the non-certificated group will gain more since they will be starting from a lower base.

Toward a Greater Direct Accessibility to Boards of Education. There will be a movement to place matters of organizational interest directly before local boards of education, excluding the administrative staff from decision making. However, the local boards will not encourage this arrangement. It will become apparent that open communication and access are sensible and reasonable public relations goals, although only to the extent that they serve to provide accurate and reliable input for decisions. Local governing bodies will move to ensure that staff members supplying input are aware of the critical nature of the process of good management, as well as the philosophy of the local board.

Toward Greater Involvement in Decision Making by Employee Groups. As a corollary to the preceding prediction, employee groups will definitely become involved in greater decision-making roles.

Administrative Problems

In Basket

Problem 1

A high school administrative staff has found evidence that circumstantially confirms what parents have suspected for about two years concerning a male history teacher. The teacher has been making inappropriate remarks to female students in his class. The evidence against the teacher is only available from students. The teacher has been continually rated average or above and no indication has been given that his performance has changed recently. Community pressure has begun to insist upon some definitive action against this teacher, but there is also some noticeable support by parents of students with whom the teacher is especially friendly.

How should the administrative staff proceed with the interrogation of students with firsthand knowledge of the teacher's behavior?

Should the principal ask the central office to transfer the teacher at the first available opportunity to another school since there is no indication that the students are suffering academically?

How should the school principal approach the teacher about his future performance which will become a matter for close scrutiny and evaluation?

If you were the principal, would you request dismissal of the teacher, using student testimony and students as witnesses? Why or why not?

What would you do if the local teacher association becomes involved?

Problem 2

The local executive director of the teacher organization has asked to meet with the district administrator in charge of personnel services to discuss a matter that has come to his attention involving one of the teacher members and the teacher's principal. The executive director has suggested a luncheon meeting.

If you were the district personnel administrator, how would you handle this request?

Problem 3

A local non-certificated group representing the majority of employees has asked for a meeting with the Board of Education's representative to establish jurisdiction in a maintenance department. A job classification study requested by this group indicates that two of five painters should be downgraded in salary by 5 percent; this compromising situation has been complicated by the demands of another non-certificated organization to represent the painters because of the outcome of the survey.

What are the criteria for determining jurisdiction, assuming there is no statewide or national contractual arrangement?

What obligation is there for the district to follow the job classification survey? Can it accept some portions and ignore others?

Would it be proper and/or more logical from an administrative standpoint to encourage the non-certificated employees to select a single bargaining unit (assuming no formal contractual arrangements now exist with any organization)? Explain the reason for your answer.

Selected References

ALLEN, RAY B., and SCHMIDT, JOHN. *Collective Negotiations in Educational Administration.* Fayetteville, Ark.: University of Arkansas College of Education, 1966.

AMERICAN ASSOCIATION OF SCHOOL ADMINISTRATORS. *Profiles of the Administrative Team.* Washington, D.C.: The Association, 1971.

————. *School Administrators View Professional Negotiation.* Washington, D.C.: The Association, 1966.

BEAUBIER, EDWARD W., and THAYER, ARTHUR N., eds. *Participative Management: Decentralized Decision Making.* Burlingame, Calif.: Association of California School Administrators, 1973.

BENNIS, WARREN G. *Changing Organizations.* New York: McGraw-Hill Book Company, 1969.

DROR, YEHEZKEL. *Public Policymaking Reexamined.* San Francisco: Chandler Publishing Co., 1968.

DRUCKER, PETER F. *The Age of Discontinuity.* New York: Harper & Row, 1969.

EVANS, JOHN. *The Evolving Role of Systems Analysis in Educational Management.* Burlingame, Calif.: Operation PEP, 1970.

HARMAN, WILLIS W. *The Nature of Our Changing Society: Implications for Schools.* Palo Alto, Calif.: Stanford Research Institute, 1969.

HASKINS, K W. "Case for Local Control." *Saturday Review* (Jan. 11, 1969).

NATIONAL EDUCATION ASSOCIATION TASK FORCE ON URBAN EDUCATION. "Trying to Find the Pony: Decentralization, Community Control, Governance of the Education Profession." *Today's Education* 58 (February 1969).

NELSON, D. LLOYD, and PURDY, WILLIAM M. *School Business Administration.* Lexington, Mass.: D. C. Heath Co., 1971.

SALZ, ARTHUR E. "Local Control vs. Professionalism." *Phi Delta Kappan* 50 (February 1969).

SVENNING, LYNNE L. *Collective Decision-Making in Organizations.* San Mateo County, Calif.: Board of Education, 1970.

STINNETT, T. M. "Teachers in Politics: The Larger Roles." *Today's Education* 57 (October 1968).

WILDMAN, WESLEY A., and PERRY, CHARLES R. "Group Conflict and School Organization." *Phi Delta Kappan* 47 (January 1966).

ZIEGLER, WARREN L. *An Approach to the Future: Perspectives in American Education.* Syracuse, N.Y.: University Research Corporation, 1970.

ZIMMERMAN, H. M. "Community and the Schools: Who Are the Decision-Makers?" *Bulletin of the National Association of Secondary School Principals* 53 (May 1969).

26

The Administration of Professional Negotiation

Collective action by teachers emerged as a new factor in personnel administration in the 1960s and has become an increasing concern to teachers, administrators, and school board members in the 1970s. Teacher associations now focus primarily upon issues for negotiation and school personnel administrators devote considerable time to dealing with issues and procedures involved in the negotiation process. Non-certificated groups, as well as certificated associations, are demanding the right to negotiate.

This chapter includes a discussion of the following topics:

The Era of Professional Negotiation
Goals for Negotiation
Principles of Negotiation
What Should Be Negotiated?
Who Negotiates?
The Negotiation Process
Grievance Procedures
Work Stoppages and Strikes
Negotiating Salaries
Non-Certificated Negotiation
The Superintendent's Role in Negotiation
Summary
Trends

Material for this chapter was prepared in collaboration with Dr. James E. Black, Assistant Superintendent—Personnel, Culver City Unified School District, Culver City, California.

The Era of Professional Negotiation

The era of professional negotiation or collective bargaining is here and cannot be overlooked by school administrators. Collective bargaining by teachers began in 1961 when a local chapter of the American Federation of Teachers won the right to bargain for the teachers of New York City. In 1972, twenty-nine states had some public education collective bargaining laws and over 70 percent of the nation's teachers were covered by collective agreements. Lieberman states that:

> In less than a decade personnel administration has been forced away from its historic orientation toward individual contracts and from an approach which emphasized relations between administrators and individual teachers, totally ignoring teacher organizations. Teacher organizations now play a crucial role in formulating and implementing personnel policies affecting teachers.[1]

The advent of negotiation has brought about a rivalry between the National Education Association and the American Federation of Teachers. Many elections have been held to determine which organization shall represent the majority of teachers. Although the NEA has won more elections, the AFT has made membership gains. It is predicted that the two associations will merge within the next few years. A schism appears to be developing between administrators and teachers over administrator membership in both the NEA or AFT and their own administrator groups. This dual membership causes a conflict when the administrator, who must support the board of education position in negotiations, finds that position incompatible with the teacher organization's demands. Teacher strikes have further aggravated teacher–administrator relations. Teacher groups believe that administrators should recognize a strike and close their schools accordingly. Administrators generally believe that the schools should remain open at all costs. In California seven separate state administrator organizations merged to form a single, strong association in 1971. Administrators are now organizing to compete with the increasing power of teacher organizations.

TEACHER MILITANCY. Teacher militancy, which has led to the demands to negotiate, is motivated by many grievances: large classes, slow salary

---

[1] Myron Lieberman, "The Future of Collective Bargaining," *Phi Delta Kappan,* p. 214.

advancement, lack of financial support at every level, lack of teacher representation in policy development, poor teaching conditions, and an unsympathetic administration.

Teachers are now better trained, more competent, and less naive than in the past. They are not willing to accept a curriculum which they had no voice in developing or policies which they did not help to formulate. They want to propose policies, not merely be invited to participate in their formulation.

Goals for Negotiation

If it is professionally accomplished, negotiation can lead to a strengthened partnership between teachers, administration, and the school board. Negotiation is based on the democratic concept that those who are governed should have a voice in their government. Intelligent, professionally trained teachers have skills and knowledge to contribute.

Four goals that should be considered in the negotiation process are:

1. To develop better two-way channels of communication.
2. To develop a problem-solving basis for action.
3. To seek common values.
4. To develop effective continuing relationships.

To be most effective and professional, teachers should be more concerned with the improvement of education than with their own economic welfare or free lunch periods, important as these items are. Responsibilities should receive as much attention as rights; i.e., the economic welfare of teachers should not take precedence over the improvement of education. Administrators can gain strength if they are willing to listen and develop empathy for teachers. Members of negotiating teams should be given sufficient authority to reach mutually satisfactory solutions. The ultimate goal is to serve the educational welfare of children which can only be accomplished by the full cooperation of all employees.

Principles of Negotiation

There are a number of principles that will help to make the negotiation process easier.

1.   Proceed carefully. Agree on general principles before discussing specific proposals.
2.   Show that all parties have a mutual interest, although there is seldom identity of interest.
3.   Demonstrate a sincere attitude and purpose.
4.   Know and admit the impact of budget demands on educational programs.
5.   Use persuasion to help people make up their own minds.
6.   Try to win agreements rather than arguments; hostility and argumentation waste time and divert energies.
7.   Try to reach an agreement, even on one item, as it tends to spawn other agreements.
8.   Never confuse opposition with hostility.
9.   Negotiate in good faith and assume that others are doing likewise.
10. Separate facts from opinion and be able to interpret facts correctly.[2]
11. Respect the intelligence, skill, and resource of the adversary.
12. Keep a sense of humor.
13. Listen attentively and without interruption.
14. Concede to win a concession.
15. Submit a proposal but be prepared to accept amendments.
16. Use the caucus.
17. Present proposals early, preferably at the first meeting.
18. Dispel myth of non-economic demands.
19. Raise questions on precise application of each proposal.
20. Anticipate questions from adversary.
21. Find out why proposal is rejected; a simple change in phrasing might make it acceptable.
22. Agreement on parts of a proposal should be tentative until agreement is reached on the entire proposal.
23. Be prepared to make counter-proposals.
24. Keep careful, accurate, and complete notes.
25. Begin session on positive note; review areas of tentative agreement reached at last meeting.

Negotiation can be effective if sound principles of human relations are utilized. The conferring parties should have mutual trust, confidence, respect, and appreciation of opposing points of view:

---

[2] *Ten Principles of Negotiations,* Professional Services Office Bulletin.

The most productive negotiating sessions will result when both teams enter a relationship in which (1) the purpose of the meeting is to seek agreement on agenda items; (2) each participant has respect for the other team; (3) the basis for positions taken rests in use of fact and reason (*what* is right, not *who* is right); and (4) the major objective of the process is the improvement of the educational program and the welfare of students.[3]

What Should Be Negotiated?

Almost every issue related to education and teacher employment has been put forth for negotiation. The following list illustrates some of the items that are commonly negotiated by teachers:

Grievance procedures
Salaries
Teaching hours and work loads
Class size
Use of specialists
Non-teaching duties
Teacher employment and assignment
Transfers
Vacancies and promotions
Summer school and night school
Teacher evaluation
Discipline of teachers
Individual teacher contracts
Teacher facilities
Use of school facilities
Leaves of absence: sick, temporary, extended, sabbatical
Student control and discipline
Protection of teachers
Insurance: health, life, family, or dependent coverage
Retirement
Professional development and educational improvement
Textbooks
Dues deduction

---

[3] John Donaldson, "The Process of Negotiation," *CTA Journal*, p. 14.

The school administration should prepare its own list of items for negotiation. Generally it is concerned with new policies or policy changes. A few examples are:

1. Teachers are to remain in their respective building thirty minutes beyond the regular school closing time for parent and/or pupil conferences, lesson preparation, faculty meetings, and inservice meetings.
2. New teachers will be given 39-week contracts, one of these weeks to be used for inservice preeducation, the week immediately prior to the opening of school.
3. Unassigned periods are to be used for pupil and/or parent conferences, lesson preparation, or other related instructional effort in the building.
4. Teachers are to accept special substitute assignments, for a special substitute rate of pay, when a volunteer plan is insufficient to cover classes because of lack of substitutes.
5. All employees will be required to submit a doctor's certificate verifying illness when sick leave extends to five or more consecutive school days, including paid or declared holidays.

Who Negotiates?

If there is only one teacher organization and all teachers are members, teachers should be represented by a duly elected negotiation committee. But in many districts, there may be two or more teacher organizations; and some teachers may not belong to any of them or may belong to more than one. There is no universally accepted way to handle this situation, and state laws and local procedures vary. However, each district should develop a policy that explains how representation is to be attained.

Another complex problem relates to administrator representation. If administrators have dual membership in the teacher organization and the administrator organization, what is their status in the negotiation process? These problems should be clarified if negotiation is to be fair and equal.

Opinions differ over who should represent the school board and the administration. Traditionally, the superintendent represented teachers to the school board and the school board to the teachers. In representing the board and administration, the superintendent may serve as a negotiator with full authority; negotiator with limited authority; adviser to negotiators for the board; adviser to negotiators for both board and teachers; neutral

resource person; or nonparticipant.[4]   Opinions also differ as to whether
the superintendent or the school board should be actively involved in
negotiation.   If the people responsible for making final recommendations
and decisions participate in the negotiation process, it complicates the
issues and the autonomy of the superintendent may be eroded.   The superintendent, as a leader of people, must retain his ultimate authority to
communicate recommendations to the board of education.

Some superintendents delegate responsibility to the personnel administrator to negotiate for the district and the school board.   This creates
a problem for the personnel administrator because he must uphold and
enforce the policies he has helped negotiate.   However, since employee
relations are an important personnel function, "the personnel administrator
must not be left out of negotiation dialogue between top-level administrators and leaders of teacher organizations when matters of great significance to good personnel administration are being considered."[5]

Teacher associations are employing professional negotiators to advise
and represent them, intensifying the negotiation process.   Few administrators have the expertise at this time to negotiate effectively so they should
also employ professional negotiators.   In any case, whoever represents the
board must have full authority to negotiate.[6]   If he does not have this
authority, negotiation cannot take place.

The Negotiation Process

The negotiation process should be conducted in a business-like manner
following agreed-upon rules.   Arrangements should be made to release
negotiators from their duties and substitutes employed to fill their vacancies.   There is disagreement as to whether negotiation meetings should
take place during or after school hours.   Both sides should submit agenda
items.   Although some states do not permit closed-door sessions for public
employees, the news media should not be permitted to observe negotiation
meetings.   Some items may take weeks of discussion before any agreement
is reached so a tight schedule should be avoided.   In some cases, a great
deal of research is necessary.   Each side should record its own minutes

---

[4] National Education Association, Research Division, "State Patterns in Negotiation," *NEA Research Bulletin,* pp. 15–17.

[5] American Association of School Administrators, *Profiles of the Administrative
Team,* p. 81.

[6] Lieberman, "The Future," p. 215.

and news releases should be made jointly by both sides. Final agreements should be specific and written. It is advisable to have an attorney look them over to determine whether they are legally sound.

Figure 26–1 is a negotiations process model for assessing needs, setting goals, presenting proposals, defining the negotiation process, solving impasses, and reaching agreement. Administrators who follow the diagrammed procedures should be able to arrive at agreed-upon decisions without going off on tangents and creating problems.

After decisions have been agreed upon, they should be presented to the board of education for approval. Further study and revision may be suggested since the board has the final authority over adoption of the negotiated decision. After board adoption, it is necessary that new policies be communicated to all personnel and implemented as soon as possible. Since most negotiation involves personnel problems or policies, the personnel administrator must carry out most of the decisions.

If logical, planned procedures are followed, negotiation can be a worthwhile process. The following checklist has been developed to help administrators check off important points during the negotiation process.

NEGOTIATION PROCESS CHECKLIST

I.   Select negotiating team
     ____ **A.**   Determine membership
     ____ **B.**   Clarify roles
     ____ **C.**   Set goals

II. Prior to submission of association demands:
     A.   Review
          ____ **1.**   Last negotiation meeting and board rules
          ____ **2.**   Management's proposals
               ____ **a.**   List suggestions for change
               ____ **b.**   Review board policies in other districts for beneficial language
               ____ **c.**   Identify what provisions adversely affect efficiency
               ____ **d.**   Describe what provisions result in excessive grievances
               ____ **e.**   Avoid vague and ambiguous provisions
               ____ **f.**   Identify provisions restricting management's right to act
               ____ **g.**   Anticipate unforeseen costs
               ____ **h.**   Draft new proposals

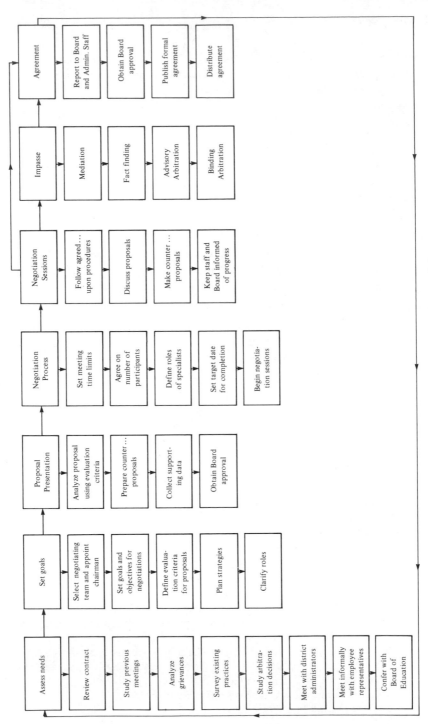

FIGURE 26–1.   *Negotiations Process Model.*

_____ **3.** Anticipate association demands
    _____ **a.** Study demands by associations in other districts
    _____ **b.** Research resolutions passed at association convention
    _____ **c.** Analyze speeches by association officials
    _____ **d.** List of grievances filed

_____ **4.** Inservice training of administrative personnel
    _____ **a.** Identify roles of administrators in the negotiation process
    _____ **b.** Explain the negotiation process

_____ **5.** Apprisal of the rights of management
    _____ **a.** Clarify right to maintain efficiency of operations
    _____ **b.** Describe right to hire, dismiss for cause, etc.
    _____ **c.** Identify right to take all necessary action in emergency situations
    _____ **d.** State right to administer, innovate, and change the educational program

_____ **6.** Advise of any rules or regulations that affect employees
    _____ **a.** Ensure uniform application
    _____ **b.** Read sections and keep them current

_____ **7.** Set forth permissive conduct with respect to association activities
    _____ **a.** Use of bulletin boards
    _____ **b.** Role of building representatives
    _____ **c.** Furnishing of non-confidential information

III. Analyze association demands
  A. Each demand should initially be analyzed as to:
    _____ **1.** Affect on legal responsibility
    _____ **2.** Cost
    _____ **3.** Tax rate
    _____ **4.** Impact on instructional program

  B. Questions to be asked on every proposal:
    _____ **1.** Is there a real problem?
    _____ **2.** Is it a continuing problem?
    _____ **3.** Is it general in nature or specific and limited?
    _____ **4.** Will the proposal change the problem?
    _____ **5.** Does the proposal address the problem?
    _____ **6.** Is the proposal free from adverse operating effects or unanticipated costs, now or in the future, and does it infringe on management's rights?
    _____ **7.** Is the cost reasonable in relation to the problem?
    _____ **8.** Is the cost reasonable in relation to the total cost impact of the settlement?

  C. Administrative personnel should always be involved with the implication of the demands and their affect on the operations of a department. This involvement also allows for uniform application of adopted proposals.

   D. Analyzing cost factors

      1. Internal data

        ____ **a.** Current wage and fringe-benefit levels and their cost

        ____ **b.** Number of employees in each job classification

        ____ **c.** Breakdown of the number of employees by sex, marital status, number of dependents, and age

        ____ **d.** Total fringe benefits including days off

        ____ **e.** Actual dollar amount per employee

        ____ **f.** What a one-cent increase and multiples thereof will mean in total cost

        ____ **g.** Affect on tax rate

        ____ **h.** Budget and review projections for year to be covered

        ____ **i.** Analysis of effect of changes on employees not covered in the unit

      2. External data

        ____ **a.** Information on recent settlements in other cities

        ____ **b.** Comparative data surveys

        ____ **c.** Cost of living and base period

        ____ **d.** Surveys of fringe benefits in surrounding areas

        ____ **e.** Salary surveys in both public and private sector

        ____ **f.** Other pertinent surveys

IV. Analyze the association negotiator and:

   ____ **A.** Learn as much as possible about the negotiator and his committee

   ____ **B.** Does the negotiator live up to his commitments?

   ____ **C.** What approach does he take in the negotiating process?

   ____ **D.** Will he control his committee or will they control him?

   ____ **E.** Will he wait until there is no other alternative to a quick settlement?

   ____ **F.** Will he make a deal outside the negotiating room?

   ____ **G.** Is any member of the committee emotional, unreasonable, or involved in a particular crusade?

   ____ **H.** Identify each member of committee as to job, militancy, capabilities, or other pertinent information

V. Administration's goals and objectives

   ____ **A.** Set guidelines for management's negotiator

      ____ **1.** Long-term goals

      ____ **2.** Short-term goals

      ____ **3.** Salary objectives

      ____ **4.** Supplemental benefit objectives

      ____ **5.** Alternative objectives

      ____ **6.** Negotiating plan

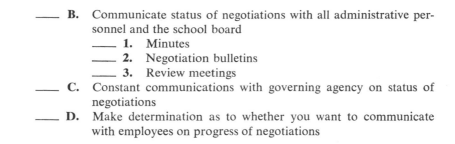

_____ **B.** Communicate status of negotiations with all administrative personnel and the school board
  _____ **1.** Minutes
  _____ **2.** Negotiation bulletins
  _____ **3.** Review meetings
_____ **C.** Constant communications with governing agency on status of negotiations
_____ **D.** Make determination as to whether you want to communicate with employees on progress of negotiations

---

NEGOTIATION PROBLEMS.   Despite the procedures that have been outlined to make negotiation effective, the art of negotiation is so new in education that a number of problems exist.   One of the main problems is the lack of experience and skill in negotiating techniques on the part of teachers and administrators.   Teacher associations have been able to receive professional assistance through their state and national chapters.   School boards and school administrators have had less assistance and advice.   Insufficient time during the school day and the unavailability of negotiating council members during summer months also hamper the negotiation procedure.

When the American Federation of Teachers has been involved as the bargaining agent strikes often occur.   The National Education Association has taken action by calling for sanctions against a school district where unsatisfactory conditions exist.   Toward the end of 1969, the traditionally conservative NEA became more liberal in viewpoint.   It took steps toward merging with the AFT and began to void its "no strike" position.   "Sick outs" occurred where masses of teachers reported that they were "sick."   Teachers began demanding that their requests be met.   Protest marches and picketing took place when boards of education were reluctant to engage in meaningful negotiations.

It will take time to work out the solutions to these and other problems, but it is imperative that they be reached as soon as possible.   It is the children who suffer when conflicts that are not resolved upset the equilibrium of the teaching staff or result in strikes.

IMPASSES.   An impasse may result if negotiation fails to solve an issue or if negotiation is refused.   Policies should be developed for the resolution of an impasse.   However, skillful negotiations avoid most impasses.

There are four ways to resolve an impasse: mediation, fact finding, conciliation, and arbitration.   If there is persistent disagreement and an impasse is reached, the problem should be mediated.   Mediation uses a neutral person, approved by both sides, who attempts to open channels of communication and coax the parties into agreement. The mediator does not judge or rule but merely helps. This is the most satisfactory procedure for settling persistent disagreements.

If mediation is not successful, the next step is fact finding without recommendation. This is essentially an attempt to establish the real facts underlying a dispute and to re-establish the meet-and-confer process. If no solution is reached, it may be necessary to initiate fact finding with recommendation, using the services of a third person who tells the school board and the employee organization what the terms of the agreement should be. The board and the organization may either accept or reject the recommendation.

Conciliation is a third way to solve an impasse. It can be successful if neither party makes initial unreasonable demands. Facts should be found and presented honestly. An approach that builds on the positive is necessary. Both sides should keep an open mind. If there is friendliness and mutual understanding, conciliation is an effective way to resolve an impasse.

If an impasse persists, the final step is binding arbitration. The third party tells the board and the employee organization what the settlement will be and the decision must be accepted whatever it is.

Grievance Procedures

Problems often arise over the interpretation of or adherence to a policy. Nothing should prevent an employee from resolving a complaint informally outside the grievance procedure, as long as the adjustment of the complaint is consistent with the statutes, board policies and regulations, or administrative rules and procedures. For these reasons, the school district must have clearly defined grievance procedures. The purpose of a grievance procedure is to assure a certificated employee that he has direct communication with the person responsible for the alleged grievance and that he has channels open for redress of a grievance if not settled at a lower level. It will also eliminate fear of reprisal and raise morale.

DEFINITIONS. A "grievant" is usually an employee or group of employees or the Certificated Employee Council filing a grievance. A "grievance" is a written statement by a grievant stating that a controversy, dispute, or disagreement exists. The grievance must involve interpretation or application of statutes, board policies and regulations, or administrative rules and procedures; or, that a condition exists that jeopardizes employee health and safety. "These conditions or circumstances, whether real or imaginary, may be either directly or indirectly related to written documents, verbal instructions, or environment."[7] "Employer" refers to the board of education or school administration. "Days" imply working days.

A "grievance procedure" has been defined as "a method by which an individual employee can express a complaint, problem, or dispute without fear of reprisal and obtain a fair hearing at progressively higher administrative levels."[8]

TYPES OF GRIEVANCES. The most common types of grievance problems are:

1. Legal problems: professionally connected, personal, or both.
2. Professionally related personal problems: disagreement with evaluation, assignment practices, personality conflicts, physical or mental health problems, and failure to follow procedures.
3. Teacher organization problems: administrator-teacher relationships, teacher–board relationships, teacher–teacher organization relationships, and ethics.

PROCEDURE AND STEPS. Grievance procedures provide equitable interpretation and application of personnel policies and practices and should be negotiated and made a part of the negotiation agreement.

The grievance procedure should:

1. Define a grievance.
2. Explain the procedure for filing a grievance.
3. Specify the time schedule for filing a grievance, holding discussions, reporting decisions, appealing decisions, and holding hearings.
4. Designate eligible participants.
5. Provide for investigation of the problem.
6. Explain appeal procedures.
7. Explain how impasses shall be handled.

---

[7] National Education Association, Research Division, "Hearing Teachers' Grievances," *NEA Research Bulletin,* p. 81.

[8] National Education Association, "Hearing Teachers'," p. 81.

8. Establish rules for mediation.
9. Explain how communications are to be handled.

The following steps show the procedures that can be followed in solving a grievance:

Step 1:   Informal Complaint

Within sixty days from the event upon which the grievance is based, or within sixty days of knowledge of the act or condition that is the basis of the complaint, the grievant may file a grievance with the school principal or his immediate supervisor.

Within five days following the filing of the grievance, the aggrieved shall discuss the problem at a pre-arranged meeting with the principal or his immediate supervisor.   At the informal conference a conscientious attempt should be made to resolve the complaint.   Step 2 of the grievance policy should be initiated only when this informal effort fails to accomplish a satisfactory and equitable resolution of the problem.

The school principal or his designated representative, or the immediate supervisor or his designated representative, shall have five days following the informal conference to render a written decision to the grievant.

Step 2:   The Superintendent's Level

If the grievance is not settled in Step 1, the grievant may move to Step 2 through written notice to the superintendent of schools within ten days. The superintendent of schools or his designated representative has ten days to give a written decision after receipt of the grievance.

Step 3:   The Board of Education Level

If the grievance is not settled in Step 2, the grievant may move it to Step 3 by written notice to the board of education within ten days after receiving the superintendent's reply.   The board shall meet with the aggrieved employee within ten days after receipt of the appeal; seventy-two hours notice of the meeting shall be given the aggrieved employee.   The board shall notify the aggrieved employee in writing of its decision within five school days after the hearing.

Step 4:   Arbitration

If the grievance is not settled in Step 3, the grievant may within ten days move the matter to arbitration under the voluntary labor arbitration rules of the American Arbitration Association. Neither party to the grievance shall refuse to proceed to arbitration upon the grounds that the matter in question is not arbitrable. If a question of the right to arbitrate an issue is raised by either party, such questions shall be determined in the first instance by the arbitrator. The parties further agree to accept the arbitrator's award as final and binding upon them.

Many districts do not accept the idea of binding arbitration but prefer fact finding with recommendation or "non-binding arbitration." There is little question, however, that binding arbitration will be required in all school districts before too long.

COUNCIL REPRESENTATION. All employees should have the right of Certificated Employee Council representation at each step of the grievance procedure and should not be required to be present themselves at any step.

Any individual employee or group of employees should have the right at any time to present grievances to their employer and to have such grievances adjusted with the intervention of the Certificated Employee Council. Copies of employer decisions given at any step of the grievance procedure should be speedily delivered to the Certificated Employee Council. The Certificated Employee Council submits any grievance filed and later dropped to arbitration, provided that the grievance involves the application or interpretation of statutes, board policies and regulations, or administrative rules and procedures. A grievant should not be represented by any person who might be required to take action, or against whom action might be taken, in order to adjust the grievance.

RELEASED TIME. Grievances ordinarily should be processed during the regular work day, and released time provided for all participants in the investigation and processing of representatives and witnesses.

GENERAL STATEMENTS ON THE GRIEVANCE PROCEDURE. The time limits specified in any level of the procedure may be modified by mutual agreement. Failure by an employee to process the grievance from one level to the next within the time limits provided for should result in a disposition of the grievance unfavorable to the grievant; conversely, a failure of an administrator, superintendent, or school board to reply or act within the specified time limits should result in a disposition of the grievance favorable to the grievant.

Once a grievance is submitted, the subject matter should be treated as confidential personnel information. Nothing in the bringing of a grievance, favorably or unfavorably resolved, should operate to impair the professional rights and privileges of an employee (specifically, personnel file entries or information communicated to others by board members or employees).

At any level of the grievance procedure the aggrieved should have the right to be represented by a person or persons of his choosing.

Work Stoppages and Strikes

Unfortunately, teacher organizations are becoming increasingly unwilling to accept final decisions and are resorting to work stoppages or strikes that impair the instructional needs of children. State courts have ruled that it is illegal for public employees to strike; the United States Supreme Court declined to review such cases in 1970. There have been over 500 teacher strikes in the last ten years. Some state laws have been passed that allow strikes if the board does not accept arbitration.

Administrator associations believe that the district has a responsibility to keep the schools open as long as possible to protect students who report to school and to maintain communication between the schools, the teachers, the students, the parents, and the general public. The board of education should adopt clear-cut policy and procedures to be followed during a work stoppage.

Negotiating Salaries

Salaries are extremely important to all school personnel. Constant salary increases concern administrators and school boards because they are the largest expenditures in the school district's budget. Teachers, under the urging of their national- and state-affiliated local associations, have become more militant in demanding salaries and salary negotiations, and strikes over salaries have become numerous. Teachers no longer are willing to accept administratively developed schedules.

Throughout the United States, salary contracts are being arrived at through negotiation. These master contracts are written documents containing the policies and decisions mutually agreed upon by teachers and the board of education. Both sign in good faith. The master contract contains the terms and conditions under which a teacher will work and the provisions for an equitable salary, fringe benefits, nondiscrimination, grievance procedure, and involvement in curriculum development. Administrators are also increasingly requesting the same rights as teachers.

Personnel handbooks are being replaced by negotiated agreements. Because the boundary limits for carrying out the terms of the contract are specifically defined in the agreement, a personnel administrator has limited freedom to apply rules and regulations to fit individual cases or circumstances.[9]

Non-Certificated Negotiation

Non-certificated or classified personnel, as well as certificated personnel, are demanding the right to negotiate. They believe that they have important jobs in the school district, are not second-class employees, and should have the same privileges as certificated personnel. Their associations have encouraged them to negotiate and have helped them to do so. One of the most forceful associations is the California School Employees Association (CSEA).

Most non-certificated personnel consider salaries the most important item to be negotiated. However, they also want to negotiate some of the following items:

Fringe benefits
Vacations
Working hours
Working conditions
Evaluation
Overtime pay
Policies that concern them
Job descriptions

Since disputes usually arise over salaries or working conditions, job descriptions become important to non-certificated personnel. They believe that evaluations, continued employment, or dismissal should be based on

---

[9] American Association of School Administrators, *Profiles,* p. 84.

job descriptions that they have helped to develop or that have been negotiated.

The negotiation process for non-certificated personnel should follow the same procedures as those outlined for certificated personnel.

The Superintendent's Role in Negotiation

Within the framework of permissive legislation, superintendents must see that cooperatively written and mutually agreed-upon policies and procedures are adopted for negotiation. This should be done *before* problems arise. The superintendent who is alert to the demands that exist will involve teachers in decision making as soon as possible. If decisions are made on a partnership basis, there should be fewer problems to be negotiated.

The superintendent's responsibilities in the negotiation process are in a state of flux and have not yet been clearly defined. A few years ago, the National Education Association surveyed 6,115 districts throughout the United States and found that only 25 percent had written negotiation procedures.[10] Lack of written procedures complicates the superintendent's ability to function properly in this area.

Table 26–1 shows the role of the superintendent in negotiation. Although legislation establishes the superintendent's role, it appears to be

TABLE 26–1.   Role of the Superintendent in Negotiation[a]

ROLE OF SUPERINTENDENT	RESPONSES	PERCENT
Negotiator with full authority	324	21.4
Negotiator with limited authority	239	15.8
Advisor to negotiators for school board only	201	13.3
Advisor to negotiators for school board and teachers	614	40.5
Neutral resource person	101	6.7
Nonparticipant	16	1.0
Other	20	1.3
Totals	1,515	100.0

[a] National Education Association, "The Superintendent's Role in Negotiation," *NEA Research Bulletin* 45 (October 1967), p. 84.

---

[10] National Education Association, Research Division, "The Superintendent's Role in Negotiation," *NEA Research Bulletin,* pp. 84–86.

influenced by the size of the school district. In larger school districts, the superintendent is generally a negotiator with full authority. But as enrollment decreases, his role shifts to that of adviser to the negotiators. The superintendent's role should be defined more clearly during the next few years as more states adopt negotiation legislation.

Summary

Professional negotiation or collective bargaining has been established in education. Teacher associations have furnished the impetus and leadership. Negotiations have also created a rift between teachers and administrators. There are many reasons why teachers have demanded negotiation at this time. Today teachers are better trained and more competent and believe they have something to contribute to policy development.

If negotiation is professionally accomplished, it can lead to a stronger partnership between teachers, administrators, and school boards. The goals of negotiation include the development of better two-way channels of communication and the seeking of common values. The ultimate goal should be the improvement of education for the benefit of children.

The principles of negotiation stress human relationships, sincerity, use of persuasion, and compromise. Good faith and respect by both parties is essential. Recommendations for conducting productive negotiations are presented.

Teachers believe that almost everything that pertains to their professional life is negotiable. Since negotiation should not be one-sided, administrators should also present policies for negotiation.

Teachers usually negotiate through their representative committee or council. Their association may employ a professional negotiator; school boards and/or administrators should do likewise. The superintendent's role is not clear; he may negotiate, delegate his function, advise, or remain neutral.

The negotiation process should be planned, negotiated, and adopted. It should be business-like and follow agreed-upon rules. When an item has been finalized, it should be written, published, and put into effect. A negotiation process checklist is presented for administrators to follow a logical plan in reaching negotiated solutions.

Impasses are sometimes reached when negotiation fails. They can be solved by mediation, fact finding, conciliation, or arbitration.

Grievances occur when there are problems over the interpretation of or adherence to a policy. They may be related to legal, personal, or teacher organization problems. Grievances must be defined, filed, investigated, and solved. The procedural steps for solving grievances are: (1) informal complaint; (2) the superintendent's level; (3) the board of education level; and (4) arbitration.

More work stoppages and strikes are occurring because teacher organizations are increasingly unwilling to accept final decisions.

Master contracts containing the conditions under which a teacher will work, salary, and fringe benefits are negotiated in many districts. Master contracts limit the freedom of personnel administrators in applying policies, rules, and regulations to individual cases.

Non-certificated personnel, supported by their associations, are also demanding the right to negotiate, especially in regard to salaries, fringe benefits, working conditions, and job descriptions.

Every school district should have clearly defined, agreed-upon policies for negotiating, handling impasses, solving grievances, and dealing with strikes and work stoppages.

Trends

TOWARD AN INCREASE IN PROFESSIONAL NEGOTIATION. Teacher involvement in administration is here and will not diminish. In the future, personnel policies will be negotiated. There will be better clarification of the role of the personnel administrator because of the impact of collective bargaining on personnel policies and personnel procedures. Negotiation will move from the school district toward state and national levels as teacher organizations become more powerful.

TOWARD MORE TEACHER INVOLVEMENT IN DECISION MAKING. Teachers can no longer be ignored as school boards and administrators develop policies, curriculum, and courses of study. During the next few years there will be an increase in the number of school districts negotiating with teachers. Negotiation policies, formalizing the negotiation procedure, will become common. As a result, the paternalistic attitude of administrators will lessen.

TOWARD MORE STRIKES AND TEACHER MILITANCY. Until districts involve teachers actively in decision making, they will become more forceful in making their demands known. Strikes and picketing will become more commonplace. The National Education Association will relax its no-strike stand. Teachers will become more vocal and demanding at board of education meetings. Full-time negotiators will be employed by teacher organizations and by school boards.

TOWARD MORE INVOLVEMENT OF THE PERSONNEL ADMINISTRATOR IN THE NEGOTIATION PROCESS. As collective bargaining increases in public education, the role of the personnel administrator will become that of the district advocate or the coordinator of district negotiations. He will be in charge of the negotiation process for district administration, either engaging in the actual negotiation or coordinating the efforts of a professional negotiator.

TOWARD MORE INVOLVEMENT OF CLASSIFIED EMPLOYEES IN THE DECISION-MAKING PROCESS. As more and more states adopt collective bargaining laws for public employees, the classified staff will demand a more active role in decisions that affect them. They will no longer take a backseat to the professional staff and will demand an equal status in the bargaining process.

Administrative Problems

In Basket

Problem 1

Although the small Mountain Empire School District has had few personnel problems and no negotiation process, the superintendent realizes that teachers are becoming increasingly militant. He thinks it would be wise to develop a negotiation process before problems arise.

How should he proceed?
Whom should he involve?

Problem 2

The Amherst Unified School District has had an established negotiation policy for several years that has worked well. This year the local teacher's association has elected several dynamic and forceful officers whose program includes smaller class loads, a 12 percent salary raise, more fringe benefits, and a broader leave-of-absence policy. In particular they threaten to strike if their salary and fringe benefit demands are not met.

In the past, the personnel administrator has been delegated to be the negotiator for the board of education. Now, the teacher's association has hired a professional negotiator to work with their committee and to speak for them. Administration has no professional negotiator. Furthermore, the teacher's negotiation committee is refusing to meet with the personnel administrator and says that it will meet only with the superintendent.

What action should the superintendent take?
What can the board of education do?

Selected References

ANGELL, GEORGE W. "Grievance Procedures under Collective Bargaining: Boon or Burden?" *Phi Delta Kappan* 52 (April 1972).

AMERICAN ASSOCIATION OF SCHOOL ADMINISTRATORS. *Profiles of the Administrative Team.* Washington, D.C.: The Association, 1971.

————. *School Administrators View Professional Negotiation.* Washington, D.C.: The Association, 1966.

ASSOCIATION OF CALIFORNIA SCHOOL ADMINISTRATORS. "Persistent Disagreement." *Management Action Paper* 1, n.d.

DONALDSON, JOHN. "The Process of Negotiation." *CTA Journal* 64 (October 1968).

KOYAYASHI, SHIGERU. *Creative Management.* New York: American Management Association, 1971.

LIEBERMAN, MYRON. "The Future of Collective Bargaining." *Phi Delta Kappan* 53 (December 1971).

NATIONAL EDUCATION ASSOCIATION, Research Division. "Hearing Teachers' Grievances." *NEA Research Bulletin* 45 (October 1967).

————, Research Division. "State Patterns in Negotiation." *NEA Research Bulletin* 46 (March 1968).

————, Research Division. "The Superintendent's Role in Negotiation." *NEA Research Bulletin* 45 (October 1967).

Relationship of Grievance Processing to Negotiations. Professional Services Office Bulletin. Los Angeles: California Teachers Association, 1967.

STINNETT, TIMOTHY M., et al. *Professional Negotiations in Public Education.* New York: Macmillan Co., 1966.

PART SEVEN

Instruction,
the Public,
and the Future

27

The Administrator's Role
as Instructional Leader

In developing a role for administrators as leaders of the instructional program within a school district, there are three levels to be considered: (1) the superintendency, (2) district-level administrators to whom the superintendent delegates this responsibility (e.g., the assistant superintendent or director), and (3) the building principal. In the ensuing material, an approach or rationale is presented that is generic in nature and applicable to each of these levels. The approach presented can be used by any individual involved in curriculum planning and implementation, regardless of his position in the district. Because so many school districts have varying organizational patterns that depend on size, tradition, community composition, and the like, a generic approach to instructional leadership is not only feasible but practical. The term "administrator" hereafter will apply to any member of the administrative team with which the reader may wish to identify.

This chapter includes a discussion of the following topics:

Instructional Responsibilities of the Superintendent
The Administrator and Meeting the Challenge of Change
The Administrator and Postwar Educational Change
The Administrator Surveys the Changing Scene
Administrative Tools and Strategies
Educational Needs Assessment and Goal Development

This chapter was prepared in collaboration with Dr. Sarkis A. Takesian, Assistant Superintendent of Educational Services, Redondo Beach City Schools, Redondo, California.

Instructional Responsibilities of the Superintendent

The superintendent has many responsibilities in connection with the instructional program, all of which are continuously changing. The following list is an example of some of the instructional responsibilities for which he must furnish leadership:

1. Selection of high caliber teachers, counselors, and administrators.
2. Provision for inservice training.
3. Budgeting for the instructional program, materials, supplies, and ·equipment.
4. Provision for supervision.
5. Encouraging continuous curriculum planning and development.
6. Promoting articulation between various school levels.
7. Encouraging vertical and horizontal communication.
8. Improving public relations for the instructional program.
9. Strengthening guidance services.
10. Providing for special instruction for atypical children.
11. Ensuring proper placement and promotion for students.
12. Providing health services, adult education, attendance, child-welfare, and library services to aid the instructional program.
13. Providing for educational research.
14. Providing evaluation of all educational programs and services to assure that developing programs are moving in proper directions.

The superintendent cannot be an expert in all administrative duties, nor does he have enough time to do all things personally. He should organize a management team representative of all areas of administration. The team should not be so large that it becomes unwieldy. In small districts, all administrators should be members. The team should meet regularly with the superintendent and participate actively in planning, sharing information, and in helping to make decisions. Issues and concerns that confront any member of the team are pondered cooperatively. In a team situation, each member has the means to clarify relationships and to relate his responsibilities to other members. When the superintendent delegates responsibility to any team member, he must also grant the commensurate authority.

The Administrator and Meeting the Challenge of Change

Since World War II, the school administrator has been concerned with change on a vast and varying scale. Meeting the instructional needs of a growing and diversified school population has been a demanding preoccupation. A variety of programs has been developed to meet the needs of students throughout the country. The successes have been admirable, but an inordinate number of attempts have not been successful.

Instructional programs should be designed according to an assessment of needs. Questions to pose before implementation are:

1. How were the needs of the students determined?
2. Who determined student needs?
3. Was an overall systematic procedure used to relate all of the component parts of curriculum design?
4. Was there school–community cooperation in determining student needs?
5. Were teachers involved in the process of needs assessment and planning?

It has been common practice in the past for the district office personnel to specify student needs and design programs with relatively little teacher or community involvement. As a result, many well-intentioned programs have not worked out as envisioned. Today's administrator must cope with change by using management techniques that enable him to assess needs more accurately, establish instructional goals and objectives, determine available resources and alternative procedures, and use more precise evaluation methods.

This chapter provides the school administrator with some systems approach tools with which to meet the challenge of change in an orderly manner (*see* figures 27–1, 27–2, and 27–3 on pp. 749, 750, 752–753). Some of the systems ideas to be considered are:

1. Perceiving functional relationships in education, a school management model.
2. Employing a systems approach model.
3. A generic model for effecting change.
4. A curriculum development model.

The administrator can use these concepts as instruments for meeting change in a systematic manner.   The first idea is the theoretical framework upon which the others are based.   These tools enable the administrator to establish a frame of reference upon which school and community needs can be based.   With this knowledge, the administrator plans the specifics of the program and determines its success.   He is able to plan more precisely because of the greater control exercised by being able to envision the entire procedure from beginning to end because the various components are related.   These tools can be used by any administrative level for planning.

The Administrator and Post-War Educational Change

Immediately after World War II, the primary educational concern was to provide classroom space for the phenomenal increase in school population. The need was so great that almost all of the administrator's time and energy centered about growth and the factors associated with it.   Relatively little time was spent on curriculum change or innovation because of the concern with growth.   There also was little felt need for change in instructional programs because existing curricula were considered basically adequate.

In 1957, when the Russian sputnik was launched, the apathy toward instruction changed to one of near frenzy for change.   The entire country thought that its school instructional programs were inadequate because another nation had demonstrated a scientific feat unmatched by the United States.   There was a general wounding of the American pride which manifested itself in the demand for greater achievement and emphasis in schools on science, mathematics, and foreign languages. With the enactment of the National Defense Education Act, federal funds became available to school districts for development and implementation of new programs in these areas.

Several factors have combined to force another look at the democratic process in the United States, particularly at the plight of minority and ethnic groups. With the large-scale mass movement of civilian and military personnel during World War II, the development of mass media, especially television, and the increased opportunities for rapid transportation, ethnic and other minority groups have had another look at what has been taking place in our nation. They have asked why the guarantees of the Constitution and the Bill of Rights are not extended to *all* citizens of this nation. Educators have also been forced to take another look at educational structures. They have taken up the challenge to improve instruction. In substance, the second great change in educational practices is being caused by social factors that embody concern for the individual. Along with a continuing thrust for academic opportunity, there is an accompanying force for greater consideration for the individual's self-concept. There is also a greater demand for a variety of educational opportunities beyond that of a college preparatory course. The present thrust is embodied in an age-old educational axiom which is only partially realized: Fit the curriculum to the student and not the student to the curriculum.

In looking at curriculum change, the administrator is now faced with a less tangible factor, that of designing instructional programs that include the building of a student's self-concept. This dimension previously was largely ignored in curriculum design for two general reasons. First, cognition and cognitive factors have been the traditional foundation of curriculum design. Second, affective areas are much more difficult to incorporate into instructional programs. In spite of education's known thoughts on the individual and his uniqueness, very little was done to promote this idea in curricula.

Another educational direction, apparently in conflict with the emphasis on enhancing student self-concept, is the advocacy of management theory to conduct school district affairs. The primary force in this area came from the U.S. Office of Education as a condition of the National Defense Education Act (NDEA) and the Elementary and Secondary Education Act (ESEA) funding. The use of systems analysis as a management technique within the federal government and its military establishments during and after World War II made its way into school planning by way of the U.S. Office of Education and various private sectors. Along with rising taxes and increased costs of school operations, the public has become somewhat resistive to continued generous support of public schools. Educators, as a result, are beginning to apply management theory to the operation of schools and to use systems analysis principles to achieve curriculum improvement. Terms such as accountability, Planning–Programming–Budgeting Systems (PPBS), behavioral objectives, and management by objectives are being accepted by more and more administrators and have had effects on curriculum planning.

Systems analysis application to education has disturbed some educators who feel that education is an art and not an endeavor in which expectations can be preordained. Further, these educators see systems approaches as a cold and dehumanizing influence which by its nature precludes individual human considerations. Advocates of the systems analysis idea claim that it is simply another planning tool. A tool only does what the user intends.

The Administrator Surveys the Changing Scene

Today's administrator of public schools must be extensively involved in planning, implementation, and evaluation of the instructional program. Whatever his position—superintendent, district-level curriculum specialist, or building principal—he must always remember that educators serve students through instructional programs and counseling. All other school-related matters serve as support factors to the instructional programs. As such, the administrator must be cognizant of the changing scene dominating the social and cultural environment to accurately translate his perceptions into meaningful instructional programs. It is extremely important to be able to effect change in a systematic manner that provides for accurate and meaningful adaptation of instructional experiences tuned to the needs of the community and school.

A new era of educational thinking, behavior, experimentation, and criticism has developed. A classification of educational objectives has been advanced by Bloom, Krathwahl, Dave and others into the following areas:

Cognitive Domain[1]	Affective Domain[2]	Psychomotor Domain[3]
Knowledge	Receiving	Imitation
Comprehension	Responding	Manipulation
Application	Valuing	Precision
Analysis	Organization	Articulation
Synthesis	Characterization	Naturalization
Evaluation		

Educators must develop abilities to recognize and specify individual components of the complex behavior of learning. The Taxonomy of Educational Objectives is a system for standardizing the classification of educational goals. It gives precision to defining the curriculum and educational objectives and it helps in evaluating the achievement of objectives. It can be useful as a strategy for the specification of the affective, cognitive, and psychomotor domains. Perhaps the Taxonomy serves its greatest purpose in distinguishing between levels of intellectual activity (cognition) and levels of "affect" (one's feelings as they relate to learning). Education has long had as its cornerstone these related levels of intellectual endeavor. However, it is relatively new for educators to emphasize the feelings and attitudes of students in curriculum design. Perhaps the Taxonomy will further serve to remind educators that learning involves many factors and that curriculum design should include more consideration of *how* students learn, in addition to *what* they learn.

Purkey presents considerable evidence to show that school achievement is related to self-concept.[4] In other words, a student is able to achieve in relation to how much he thinks he is able. If self-concept is enhanced in teacher–pupil relationships, there is a corresponding increase in student achievement. It becomes very important for the teacher to practice positive encouragement in every relationship with his students. Implicit in this concept is the realization of how students can be "put down" unknowingly by teachers.

Glasser places heavy emphasis on the positive relationships between

---

[1] Benjamin S. Bloom (ed.), *Taxonomy of Educational Objectives, The Classification of Educational Goals, Handbook I: Cognitive Domain*, p. 18.

[2] David R. Krathwahl, Benjamin S. Bloom, and Bertram B. Masia, *Taxonomy of Educational Objectives, The Classification of Educational Goals, Handbook II: Affective Domain*, p. 35.

[3] As proposed by Dr. R. H. Dave, National Institute of Education, New Delhi, India.

[4] William W. Purkey, *Self-Concept and School Achievement* (Englewood Cliffs, N.J.: Prentice-Hall, 1970), pp. 14–26.

teacher and student.[5]   He states that many students feel that teachers cater to more productive students and tend to disregard the less academically inclined.   Quite often teacher neglect of the poorer student or the misbehaving one instills a feeling of rejection.   As a result, the student often continues his misbehaving patterns or his poor academic achievement.

Holt states that the organizational and methodological patterns of the typical public school promote failure for students.[6]   Under current instructional patterns, mass mediocrity can be expected because the individual is given little consideration.

In an exhaustive survey of instructional practices in public schools, Silberman found many practices that should be discarded in favor of approaches capitalizing on the uniqueness of the individual student.[7]   He writes extensively about the British Infant Schools that place heavy emphasis on the interests of students and a classroom environment to promote their interests.

The administrator must be alert to the growing demands of accountability.   Management theory in the operation of schools allows administrators to justify and account for costs and student achievement.   Mager's book on the writing of instructional objectives was a major force in the preparation of instructional programs oriented to measurable student output.[8]   Popham[9] has long been an advocate of measurable instructional objectives.

Throughout the educational scene, numerous attempts have been made to adapt management theory to school district operation.   In addition to the notion of general accountability to the taxpayer, federal grants to school districts have forced the development of systems analysis in public schools.   School districts are becoming acquainted with terms such as educational goals, measurable objectives, alternative approaches, monitoring systems, and evaluation of results based on prestated objectives.   In California, legislative action in 1971 provided for evaluation of certificated personnel based on student achievement.[10]   The result has been a state wide effort by local school districts to use systems approach measures to

---

[5] William Glasser, *Schools Without Failure* (New York: Harper & Row 1969), p. 63.

[6] John Holt, *How Children Fail* (New York: Dell Publishing Co., 1964), p. 13.

[7] Charles E. Silberman, *Crisis in the Classroom,* p. 54.

[8] Robert F. Mager, *Preparing Instructional Objectives,* p. 3.

[9] *See* W. James Popham et al., *Instructional Objectives,* pp. 32–52.

[10] Assembly Bill 293, California state legislature, signed into law on July 20, 1971.

develop instructional programs and evaluation procedures reflecting educational goals and measurable student objectives.

Administrators must recognize that all teachers have not accepted wholeheartedly the concept of accountability. Some feel that accountability in education is an indictment and a threat since the initial idea came from individuals and groups with little or no experience in teaching: the conservative community, disadvantaged groups, and liberal spokesmen concerned with the value received from their tax money for education.[11] Teachers also feel threatened because accountability is assessed in terms of output, not input. Bernard McKenna states that "performance itself is important, no matter what its relation to learning outcomes," although better teaching "leads to better results with students." He explains further that teaching performance is an end in itself "whether or not it can be demonstrated to result in specific outcomes.[12] Teachers generally believe they should only be held accountable if:

1. They share in the development of goals and objectives.
2. There is adequate funding of the educational program.
3. Salaries are commensurate with other professions.
4. Teachers and the school board share jointly in the negotiation of comprehensive contracts and in the development of policies.
5. Clearly defined goals are developed cooperatively by teachers, school board, administrators, students, parents, and the community.
6. There is appropriate evaluation of all instructional goals.
7. The educational process is as highly valued as learning outcomes.
8. Students participate in decision making.
9. Teachers are assigned only to classes they are qualified to teach.
10. The teacher has time to carry out all teaching tasks and is free from nonteaching duties.
11. There are adequate facilities, resources, and support personnel.
12. The teacher has a voice in the selection, evaluation, and purchase of educational equipment and supplies.
13. There is strong administrative backing for the maintenance of discipline.
14. The teacher shares in evaluation and testing programs.[13]

---

[11] Joseph Stocker, "Accountability and the Classroom Teacher." *Today's Education,* p. 42.
[12] Bernard H. McKenna, "Teacher Evaluation: Some Implications." *Today's Education,* p. 56.
[13] Stocker, "Accountability," pp. 47–49.

The National Education Association believes that teachers can be held accountable only if school boards and administrators also are accountable.

Through greater individual attention for each student promoted by the use of paid school aides, volunteer aides, student tutorial assistance, and diagnosis and prescription approaches, the classroom teacher has the personnel, materials, and techniques to launch an individualized instructional program for children. A great amount of literature has been written about individualizing instruction, although little substantial progress has been made in reorganizing the traditional patterns of classroom instruction.

Administrative Tools and Strategies

The administrator's role as instructional leader involves many facets of total operation of the school. He has the primary responsibility, with staff and community involvement, for planning his school's curriculum and support services. Planning also involves articulation between elementary, junior high, and senior high schools. Implementation is achieved by staff inservice as well as by administering and coordinating support services such as pupil personnel, guidance and counseling, health, cocurricular activities, the instructional media center, special education classes, and federal and state programs. He must continuously evaluate curriculum, support services, effectiveness of his teaching staff, and his communication with the school community.

With such an array of diversified responsibilities in instructional leadership, the administrator must be able to function effectively in all areas. Figure 27–1 represents a generic management model applicable to the resolution of educational problems. The model illustrates three separate but related functions that encompass a systems analysis mode. Identifying the purpose of any proposed activity or project becomes the first task. This is done in terms of educational goals and objectives based on the considered rationale. With the purpose or direction delineated, the process is continued by employing the secondary functions listed under "process." To complete the program or project, a system of evaluation directly related to the specified objectives stated under "purpose" must be developed. Monitoring, a part of the evaluation structure and an on-going process, ensures that the procedure is within the boundaries set by the objectives.

The dashed lines in Figure 27–1 indicate feedback information for

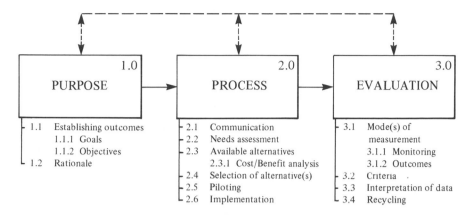

FIGURE 27–1. Perceiving Functional Relationships in Education.

the modification of any factor or component in the model. No part of the model is static. Recycling of information is vital to the success of the project (stressed by the monitoring of progress). One of the great advantages of this approach over traditional methods is the greater chance for success because of more thorough planning and constant monitoring of progress to keep the program on course. Usually, traditional approaches do not consider evaluation until the program or project is completed. By then, it is too late to make mid-course corrections. In traditional procedures, evaluation has not been related to specifics and usually is simply a matter of procedure. Under these conditions, the evaluation of instructional programs does not have very much significance and has a detached relationship to the program.

A DELINEATION OF OBJECTIVES IN A SYSTEMS MODEL. Objectives for instructional programs should answer the following questions:

1. What is a learner able to measurably demonstrate following a lesson, unit, period, etc., of instruction? (The learner writes, says, describes, demonstrates, etc.)
2. What conditions should exist to guide the learner toward some desired outcome or objective? (Time limitations, number of pages of a report, etc.)
3. What criteria are designed to show how well a learner or a class progresses toward the desired end? (The learner is to complete 30 out of

35 items; 90 percent of the class are expected to complete the assignment, etc.)

An objective must be compressed in more precise terms in order to eliminate or reduce the possibility of misinterpretation. A goal has no precision to it. Words such as "knowing, understanding, or appreciation" belong to expressions of goals and not to objective statements. Objectives described in the previous list focus on observable and measurable behavior of the learner. One cannot observe what a learner "knows" except by what he says, does, demonstrates, explains, etc.

The use of Figure 27–1 and an understanding of goals and objectives provide the administrator with a powerful tool with which to plan, develop, implement, and measure the success of any instructional need.

A BASIC SYSTEMS ANALYSIS MODEL. Figure 27–2 is a basic systems analysis model incorporating its characteristic components. It is related to Figure 27–1 in regard to the designations of purpose, process, and evaluation. A systems model is usually characterized by two modes, the analysis phase and the synthesis phase. Analysis refers to the detailed inspection of every available resource and alternative that could possibly work toward meeting stated objectives. Synthesis results when only alternatives and resources from the total array are selected as best meeting the needs of the objectives.

In Figure 27–2, analysis components include 0.0 to 6.0; synthesis components encompass 7.0 to 10.0. In this figure, as in other systems

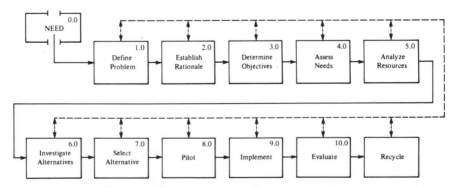

FIGURE 27–2. Basic Components in a Systems Approach Model.

flow designs, the dark continuous lines indicate the direction of task resolution. The dashed lines indicate feedback from each component of the system. Feedback or component information is important because it serves to show how various aspects of the project are progressing. Figure 27-2 represents a "closed-loop system"; the continuous lines represent direction of activity and the dashed lines indicate feedback or monitoring information which can be fed back to the beginning, or any part, of the system for a continuous, closed-loop system of information flow. In Figure 27-3, a model for effecting change, the dashed lines are omitted so that only the continuous flow or lines of direction appear. In any systems flow diagram, whether or not the dashed lines appear, one always assumes that the feedback mechanism is a part of the system.

A valuable aspect of a systems approach for the administrator exercising leadership in instruction is a planning model. Heavy emphasis is placed on consideration of factors that indicate direction or purpose. It is upon this action that the success or failure of the program or project rests. Since every component of a systems model is related to another component, no activity is executed in isolation. In this manner, all are tied together in a common thrust or effort directed toward reaching stated objectives.

DEALING WITH CHANGE Figure 27-3 depicts a generic change model using the concepts previously covered. The administrator now has tools that specify a step-by-step approach to the resolution of instructional problems. It does not matter which of his responsibilities require change. All the responsibilities listed in the beginning of this section and others can be approached by this systems format.

Figure 27-3 indicates a "need" (0.0) which at this point is neither defined nor fully recognized. The Change Model requires defining the problem with substantive characteristics (1.0). In 2.0 and 3.0, there are statements relating to goal formation, objectives considerations, and so forth. They are designed so that a needs assessment can be conducted; 2.0 indicates an assessment of what presently is and 3.0 indicates what ought to be. The difference between the two is needed to formulate a needs assessment. Not all of the components of 3.0 require change as a part of the needs assessment. In the Change Model, 4.0 through 17.0 are procedural in nature. Once components from 0.0 to 3.0 are clarified, the other components point the way to getting the job done.

With this additional tool, the instructional leader has the background

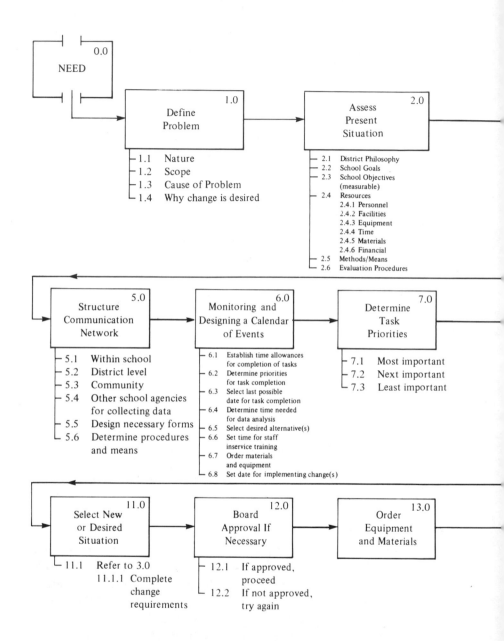

FIGURE 27–3. A Generic Model for Effecting Change.

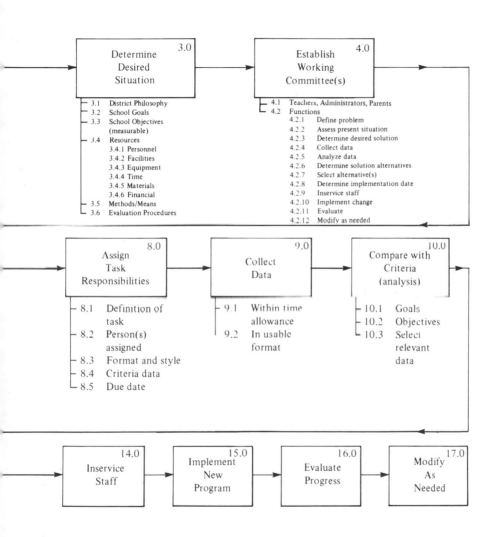

FIGURE 27–3. Continued.

753

to determine the degree of need and to further specify it in terms of objectives. He knows what human and material resources are available to him and can determine what alternative methods best fit the program within budgetary allowances. He is aware of the communication channels he must employ and when the program can be implemented. He further knows that measurement of the program is based upon prestated objectives so that evaluation results have some frame of reference.

Educational Needs Assessment and Goal Development

In assessing needs and developing goals, a district should establish a schedule for the following steps:

1. The board of education commits itself to the program by official action.
2. Through community–school cooperation, the district's educational philosophy is developed.
3. The needs are assessed with staff and community working together as a team.
4. Decisions are made on the goals and goal indicators, based on the needs.
5. The board of education approves and publishes the goals.
6. The goals are translated into workable plans or program objectives.
7. Priorities for action are developed.
8. Goals and objectives are implemented.
9. The degree of attainment of objectives is assessed.
10. Areas requiring change are identified.
11. Changes and alternatives are developed to shorten the distance between "what is" and "what ought to be."
12. Re-evaluation and re-assessment continue.

A program such as the above can be adapted by any school district to meet its particular situation. Needs, goals, and objectives should be identified for the school district, particular school, classroom, and individual student. Figures 27–1, 27–2, and 27–3 illustrate step-by-step processes for effecting change.

Instructional programs in the United States are characterized more by process than by purpose. Educational offerings are typically concerned with techniques, methodology, materials, and equipment to a much greater degree than they are with clarifying the direction education should take. Most textbooks, curriculum guides, instructional materials, whether commercially or district prepared, and other instructional support materials reveal almost complete concern with how-to-do-it instructions. Relatively few materials deal with educational purpose or rationale to support their use. Lack of emphasis on purpose and direction often results in failure of innovative programs.

FORMULATION OF AN EDUCATIONAL PHILOSOPHY LEADING TO GOAL STRUCTURE. Most school districts have a statement of educational philosophy. However, most school district statements on their philosophy are so general that many differing interpretations can be drawn from the same document. As a result, not much attention is given to the existing philosophy. A systems approach model is extremely valuable for the administrator as he can create a systematic delineation of philosophical expression. The translation of district philosophy through educational goals to specific instructional objectives reveals a common expression to school personnel and the community, and the expressed philosophy bears meaning at the instructional level.

NEEDS ASSESSMENT. Typically, educators formulate educational policy through elected board members with little community involvement, assuming knowledge of the needs and desires of the community. For this reason, many innovative programs have failed. It should occur to educators at some point in time that the instructional program must be in concert with the needs of the community.

Throughout the nation, legislatures are passing a rash of laws forcing school districts to assess the value structure of their communities in order to plan the best educational program to meet the needs of their particular districts. The relatively new term, "needs assessment," is a management tool that assists "in making more systematic and rational decisions."[14] An educational need is defined as "the situation which occurs when

---

[14] Arthur N. Thayer, "Needs Assessment: Component I." *Thrust for Education Leadership,* p. 34.

student performance is below that which is specified in a behavioral objective." It can only be identified by assessing "stated performance objectives to determine whether or not objectives are being accomplished."[15]   ESEA Title III programs, for example, demand educational needs assessment which identifies local educational deficiencies.   The assessment can be carried out by using measurable objectives developed by the district or the community.   Community and students rank the objectives to be included in the school's curriculum.   When the rankings are averaged, enlightened determinations of the curriculum preferences of the school's constituents can be made.   Needs assessments can also be made in any area of the school district's responsibilities: finance, administration, personnel evaluation, transportation services, and so forth.

Needs can be assessed by questionnaires, surveys, discussions, and publications.   Parents, businessmen, teachers, administrators, and students should be involved in helping the district identify needs.   All economic, ethnic, and geographic segments of the community must be involved directly.   James Popham[16] states that "many astute school people will see the use of objectives-based needs assessments as a reasonable vehicle for allowing appropriate groups to express their educational preferences."[17]

In the selection of assessment techniques, the following questions should be asked:

1.   Are the objectives to be measured the truly important ones?
2.   Is the technique of assessment the most efficient means of determining the achievement of the desired objectives?
3.   What is the effect of the assessment technique on its user?
4.   What is the effect of accountability practices on the student?[18]

GOAL SETTING.   After the district's educational philosophy has been shaped and its special needs assessed, educational goals and sub-goals must be established in a cooperative venture with the community.   This reduces the credibility gap that so often exists between community and school. The goal structure is born out of the district philosophy.   Goals are broad

---

15 *Needs Assessment*, Booklet for Developing Evaluative Skills, 8 (Tucson, Ariz.: Educational Innovators Press, 1970), p. 8.
16 W. James Popham, "Objectives '72." *Phi Delta Kappan*, p. 434.
17 Popham, "Objectives," p. 434.
18 Arthur W. Combs, *Educational Accountability: Beyond Behavioral Objectives*, pp. 2–3.

statements but more definitive than the original philosophical framework. Goals are not usually measurable but are the most specific descriptions of the values expressed in the school's philosophy. Throughout the process of educational goal development, the administrator as instructional leader plays a vital role. His active participation in all facets of the project is important to subsequent instructional direction. It is this determination of purpose that provides meaning to the process of educating students.

PERFORMANCE OBJECTIVES.   Following the agreement on goals, performance or behavioral objectives should be developed which indicate:

1. Who is going to perform the specified behavior.
2. The behavior that is expected to occur.
3. The situation in which the behavior will be observed.
4. The expected proficiency level.
5. The time needed to bring about the behavior.
6. The method by which the behavior is going to be measured.[19]

Performance objectives are difficult to write because of the many variables that must be considered. They must be defined for the level or for the person to which they apply and they should be specific. Performance objectives as they are applied to classrooms are described more fully in chapter 29.

EVALUATION.   After classroom or performance objectives have been written and implemented, they must be evaluated to determine whether they are being met. In the past, school districts, schools, and educational programs have been evaluated quantitatively. Needs assessment focuses attention on quality. In the evaluation process, information must be collected and analyzed to make valid decisions on attainment levels. This process leads to accountability in education.

Needs assessment is a step-by-step development of an educational accountability model through the implementation of educational goals and objectives involving community, profession, and students. It is one of the major tasks of all school administrators as schools are forced to assess the

---

[19] *Needs Assessment*, p. 8.

value structure of their communities in order to plan the best program for the needs of their particular districts.

The Administrator
and a Curriculum Development Model

Whether it is a matter of developing an entirely new curriculum for a school district or simply designing a new course or program, the same theoretical background of systems analysis prevails. The whole idea for developing instructional programs on a systematized or integrated basis is to relate all facets of the program to the district philosophy and educational goals. In this manner, all instructional effort stems from the same source, the philosophy of the district as an expression of the community value standards. It is therefore appropriate to consider a related or structured approach to developing curriculum. The approach to curriculum design suggested in this chapter has as its basis the framework described below:

A CURRICULUM DEVELOPMENT MODEL

1.0 Expression of Purpose
    1.1 District philosophy statement
    1.2 District educational goals
    1.3 Measurable objectives at district, building, and classroom levels

2.0 Process Sequence
    2.1 Re-examine learning process
    2.2 Redefine teaching/learning relationships
    2.3 Balance emphasis between cognitive and affective factors
    2.4 Establish curriculum based on how children learn
    2.5 Determine subject concepts with staff
    2.6 Integrate related methods, materials, facilities, and equipment
    2.7 Staff inservicing
    2.8 Curriculum piloting
    2.9 Curriculum implementation

3.0 Evaluation Components
    3.1 Establish clear knowledge of objectives (1.3)
    3.2 Establish evaluation procedures related to objectives
    3.3 Evaluate
    3.4 Interpret results
    3.5 Communicate information
    3.6 Modify curriculum as needed or as desired

Since this model is generic in nature, its application to curriculum development can be effected rather easily.

The "process" sequence described here denotes all factors to be considered to reach the "purpose" statements. The process sequences place considerable emphasis on taking another look at how children learn and what the teaching process is and how it relates to the learning process. (All too often classroom procedures are heavily oriented to what the teacher does, neglecting how children learn.) There is also emphasis on the cognitive/affective factors in classroom instruction. Schools have been heavily oriented toward the teaching of skills and the accumulation of knowledge, disregarding the feelings and attitudes of students toward instructional programs. Consideration must be given to student attitude; if student attitude is indifferent, learning will be indifferent. If instruction is appealing and of interest, learning will increase proportionately.

EVALUATION COMPONENTS. Evaluation components are also related to purpose and process by way of the objective statements. If objectives determine the extent and degree of effort, then evaluation must be objective oriented. In this manner, purpose, process, and evaluation are integrated in such a way that each function and its subfunctions are related to other functions and their subfunctions.

The Administrator's Role as Instructional Leader

This has to do with the human characteristics so necessary in person-to-person relationships that will yield the most in educational productivity. Because of existing laws and district policies that empower the administrator with authority, he is in a position to be a vital force in instructional leadership.

Far too often the administrator's authority is used as a unilateral force which excludes the thinking of subordinates. This is not to say that the administrator has no responsibility for decision making. Rather, the organization of any sector of the school district can be such that decision making by the administrator materializes through the cooperative effort of the entire staff. The basic involvements of the total staff, including administrators, should contain the elements of confidence, trust, and respect.

The basic operation of the school enterprise lies in the classroom environment. All other activities and personnel are in support of this function. The administrators are the change agents that provide the necessary environment for change. Teachers also must be included in all facets of instructional planning that involve them. Thus, administrative leadership involves perceiving the changing environment, possessing the know-how by which changes can be made, and using the strengths of all staff members in a humane manner for maximum effort. This combination of skills allows the administrator to function effectively as the instructional leader.

Summary

Nowhere in administration has change been so far-reaching as in the area of instructional leadership. This chapter provides systems approach tools with which to meet the challenge of this change, including (1) perceiving functional relationships in education; (2) employing a systems approach model; (3) a generic model for effecting change; and (4) a curriculum development model.

Two recent reasons for instructional change were Sputnik, resulting in new stress on science and mathematics, and the civil rights movement, resulting in a move to fit the curriculum to the student. As a result, the administrator must now be conversant in both the cognitive and affective domains of educational objectives.

He must also develop tools and strategies to cope with changing instructional needs, specifically a systems approach as a planning tool. This enables the administrator to plan, develop, implement, and measure their success or failure.

Instructional programs have long been more concerned with process than with purpose. Lack of direction is one reason so many innovative programs fail. Here the systems approach model can be extremely valuable in translating district philosophy into educational goals and then into specific instructional objectives. Goals and objectives should be on a planned needs assessment program.

One curriculum development model starts with district philosophy and adds the notion of measurable objectives. Its "process" sequence stresses cognitive/affective factors related to instruction, and integrates manner, purpose, process, and evaluation.

Trends

In the past, the superintendent's attention has been taken up with problems of building construction, business management, personnel, and public relations to the extent that little time was left for the consideration of instruction, the main business of education. The trend today is toward allotting more administrative time to the instructional program. All other matters are considered as supplementary. So many changes and innovations are taking place, and at an increasingly faster rate, that the alert administrator must be acutely aware of these trends.

TOWARD INCREASED SCHOOL–COMMUNITY INVOLVEMENT. No longer will the school remain an entity apart from the community. The school exists as a part of the community, and more interaction should result to develop meaningful programs consistent with the needs of the community and its value structure.

TOWARD GREATER SYSTEMIZED ORGANIZATION OF THE CURRICULUM. There is a need to have a more meaningful relationship between components of the instructional program. There will be greater emphasis on a theory or model for curriculum development so that order prevails in translating the district philosophy into relevant classroom instruction.

TOWARD MORE PRECISE MEASUREMENT PRACTICES. There is a greater demand for the justification of the tremendous expenditure of money for public education. This type of accountability necessitates more careful evaluation of instructional results.

TOWARD PROGRAM AUDITING. To reduce the credibility gap between expenditures and results in education, independent auditors will audit instructional programs to determine whether instructional objectives are being met. Program auditing is in operation primarily in federally related programs but will be common to regular district programs.

TOWARD MORE CONCERN FOR THE INDIVIDUAL. With more assistance provided to the classroom teacher by paid and volunteer aides and student tutorial programs, the teacher will be able to manage classroom procedures so that individual programs ·can be prescribed for students following a period of diagnosis and evaluation.

TOWARD INCREASED EMPHASIS ON THE SOCIAL SCIENCES. The social sciences embody the relationships of people to people. With today's increased concern for the individual and his welfare, there will be increased pursuit of the social sciences. This area of the curriculum will form a powerful basis for change in the face of man's continued inhumanity to man.

TOWARD GREATER CONCERN FOR ENVIRONMENTAL FACTORS. In the future, curricula will reflect man's concern for his fate on this planet. With the knowledge available today about pollution of all types, instructional programs will be developed to teach future generations how to live in a cleaner environment.

TOWARD INCREASED PARTICIPATION IN MANAGEMENT BY ALL STAFF MEMBERS. There is a wealth of energy and skill available at every staff level in every school district. Participative management of school affairs will make available many resources that have been virtually untapped before. Cooperative effort by teachers and administrators will yield instructional programs meaningful to students and staff alike.

TOWARD GREATER FEDERAL INVOLVEMENT. As school district sources of income continue to shrink, greater involvement in federal programs is to be expected.

TOWARD GREATER EMPHASIS ON CRITERION-REFERENCED EVALUATION. Testing and evaluation traditionally have been norm-referenced. Comparisons are made to others or to standardized averages. There is a definite trend toward criterion-referenced testing and evaluation which uses individualized tests and objectives for evaluation. This procedure will be applied to administrators, teachers, and other personnel, as well as to students.

Administrative Problems

Problem 1

The Mar Vista Consolidated School District has an average daily attendance of 15,000. It has been a relatively stable, conservative, middle-class area for years with little turnover in school personnel. About five years ago, the community began to change. Minority families have been moving in at an increasing rate each year. They have not adopted the mores of the community. The formerly strong Parent Teacher Associations at various schools are having problems and bickering is common.

Discipline, tardiness, truancy, and vandalism are becoming problems for the district. The highly academic curriculum is no longer relevant and does not meet the needs of a changing student population. Bi-lingualism has also created teaching and learning problems. Personnel turnover of teachers, administrators, and classified personnel is upsetting the stability of the school district. The superintendent and Board of Education seem to spend most of their time "putting out fires." They have been unable to cope with the rapidity of the changes that are taking place.

If you were the superintendent, what management techniques would you use to cope with the changes?

Problem 2

Assume the same situation as in Problem 1. The superintendent has asked you, the senior high school principal, to design a new curriculum for your school with a goal of meeting the needs of the changing student population.

How would you proceed?
What type of curriculum changes do you envision?
What immediate objectives should you achieve?

Problem 3

Assume the same situation as in Problem 1. The superintendent has asked you, an elementary principal, to head up an investigation of the elementary school curriculum in the district and to make recommendations for possible changes.

How would you proceed?
What curriculum changes do you envision?

Selected References

AMERICAN ASSOCIATION OF SCHOOL ADMINISTRATORS. *Administrative Technology and the School Executive: Applying the Systems Approach to Educational Administration.* Washington, D.C.: The Association, 1969.

BLOOM, BENJAMIN S., ed. *Taxonomy of Educational Objectives: The Classification of Educational Goals, Handbook I: Cognitive Domain.* New York: David McKay Co., 1956.

Booklet for Developing Evaluative Skills. *Needs Assessment,* Booklet 8. Tucson, Ariz.: Educational Innovators Press, 1970.

COMBS, ARTHUR W. *Educational Accountability: Beyond Behavioral Objectives.* Washington, D.C.: Association for Supervision and Curriculum Development, 1972.

CONNER, FORREST E., and ELLENA, W. J., eds. *Curriculum Handbook for School Administrators.* Washington, D.C.: American Association of School Administrators, 1967.

ELLENA, WILLIAM. *Curriculum Handbook for School Executives.* Washington, D.C.: American Association of School Administrators, 1973.

FLANDERS, NED A. *Helping Teachers Change Their Behavior.* Rev. ed. Ann Arbor: School of Education, University of Michigan, 1965.

GLASSER, WILLIAM. *Reality Therapy.* New York: Harper & Row, 1965.

———. *The Identity Society.* New York: Harper & Row, 1972.

GERHARD, MURIEL. *Effective Teaching Strategies with the Behavioral Outcomes Approach.* West Nyack, N.Y.: Parker Publishing Co., 1971.

KRATHWAHL, DAVID R.; BLOOM, BENJAMIN S.; and MASIA, BERTRAM B. *Taxonomy of Educational Objectives: The Classification of Educational Goals, Handbook II: Affective Domain.* New York: David McKay Co., 1964.

LESSINGER, LEON M. *Every Kid a Winner: Accountability in Education.* New York: Simon and Schuster, 1970.

MAGER, ROBERT F. *Preparing Instructional Objectives.* Palo Alto, Calif.: Fearon Publishers, 1962.

MEALS, DONALD W. "Heuristic Models for Systems Planning." *Phi Delta Kappan* 48 (January 1967).

MCKENNA, BERNARD H. "Teacher Evaluation: Some Implications." *Today's Education* 62 (February 1973).

MILLER, DONALD R. *An Analytical Framework for Public Education and Educational Management.* Operation PEP, Burlingame, California (September 1969).

———. *A System Approach to Educational Management.* Operation PEP, Burlingame, California (October 1968).

———. *A System for Comprehensive Planning.* Operation PEP, Burlingame, California (May 1969).

POPHAM, W. JAMES. *Instructional Objectives.* American Educational Research Monograph. Chicago: Rand McNally, 1969.

———. "Objectives '72." *Phi Delta Kappan* 53 (March 1972).

PURKEY, WILLIAM W. *Self-Concept and School Achievement.* Englewood Cliffs, N.J.: Prentice-Hall, 1970.

SILBERMAN, CHARLES E. *Crisis in the Classroom.* New York: Random House, 1970.

STOCKER, JOSEPH. "Accountability and the Classroom Teacher." *Today's Education* 60 (March 1971).

THAYER, ARTHUR N. "Needs Assessment: Component I." *Thrust for Education Leadership* 1 (December–January 1972).

U.S. Department of Health, Education, and Welfare, Office of Education, Bureau of Educational Personnel Development. *How Teachers Make a Difference.* Washington, D.C.: U.S. Government Printing Office, 1971.

28

Public Relations

No other area of school administration betrays the dilemma of the average educator more vividly than the difficult but essential art of public relations. The entire concept of this recent adjunct to administration is alien and basically repugnant to those who have begun professional lives as classroom teachers. The scholarly mind is the antithesis of the public relations mind; it tends to be introverted, while public relations requires a gregariousness and extroversion more typical of the salesman or advertising man than of the educator. It is significant that efforts have been made for many years to supplant the term "public relations" with something less obnoxious. In recent years, the term "school–community relations" has come into common use by many writers and agencies, including the American Association of School Administrators.[1] Educators seem to feel that there are certain negative and unfortunate connotations attached to public relations that should have no place in the world of education.

We live in an era of publicity and publicity is a one-way process. The public schools, which mirror and stem from the body politic, cannot retreat and plead professional immunity from the same compulsion to inform the public that afflicts other occupations and businesses. Unless school administrators accurately inform the people of what the schools are doing, someone else will tell them, and probably inaccurately. Public relations, then, has become a necessity; whether or not the necessity becomes an unpleasant one depends almost entirely on how well the administrator organizes and administers his program of public information. Public relations is communication and communication is human relations.

---

[1] American Association of School Administrators, *Profiles of the Administrative Team*, p. 123.

Its effectiveness is largely dependent upon the personal relationships that exist between the communicating parties. It should be a two-way process.

This chapter includes a discussion of the following topics:

Interpretive Public Relations Programs

Many schools equate public relations with press agentry. They assume the desirability of defending the status quo or justifying any or all of the ramifying activities of the schools.

The so-called "preventive" school of public relations designs its public information program to meet possible future criticism in certain specific or general fields. It piles up ammunition for contingencies, and maintains a constant attack on the critics of the schools, hoping that a continuous offensive will help prevent attacks on the schools by diverting attention. This is not good public relations either, and often amounts to manipulation of public relations for personal reasons.

The administrator who interprets public relations for school districts as equivalent to public relations for private business is also wrong. Industrial public relations are set up to sell products. Any superintendent who organizes his public relations program primarily to "sell" his school system ignores its weak points, whitewashes acknowledged flaws, and over-emphasizes desirable features. Business, highly competitive and operating within a framework of public tolerance for "pardonable" exaggerations, manages to escape potent criticism. Public education clearly cannot.

The sole purpose of school public relations should be to explain the school district's educational program, activities, and general operation. Everything that the district does is a matter of public interest and concern. Public relations should not attempt to justify, to palliate, or to cover up. It should not be used to aggrandize the status or reputation of the superintendent. The goal should and must be to tell the truth. If the pursuit of this goal requires the admission of errors or shortcomings in certain departments, such confession should be made, along with details of what is being done to correct the situation. The people of a community will be far more apt to respect and support a school system that candidly admits its own failings than one that pretends to uphold an impossible standard of perfection.

Basic Criteria for a School District Public Relations Program

A public relations program should not operate as a reflex response to a specific stimulus. A district that spontaneously invents some method of informing the public about a forthcoming bond election often establishes a system permanently oriented toward a financial interpretation of school affairs. Similarly, a superintendent may hurriedly create machinery designed to sway community opinion as a reaction to an actual or threatened attack upon his own tenure, with the resulting system becoming a lasting personal bulwark to an individual employee of the district. Any such origin for a public relations program is at once inadequate and one-sided. To avoid this, it is necessary to erect a school information program on certain well-grounded principles.

CRITERIA FOR AN EFFECTIVE PUBLIC RELATIONS PROGRAM. The school district should develop certain criteria for an effective public relations program. The following criteria developed by Bloom might be used as a guide:

Philosophy

The board of education should adopt a general statement of philosophy of education as a foundation for policies which would give direction to the public information program of the school district.

Policy

The public information program should be based upon written policies adopted by the board of education.

Dynamics

The public information aspects of successful school public relations must be founded upon an outstanding educational program.

Form

The public information program should be vigorous but dignified.

Scope

All operations of the school district should be included in a comprehensive public information program.

Completeness

The community should be afforded access to all the facets of school operations through the public information program.

Sensitivity

School public relations should be a two-way process. The public information program should establish channels of communication through which the school can be kept sensitive to the attitudes and desires of the community.

Agents

The public information program should be organized to make effective use of all officials and employed personnel of the school district.

Agencies

All possible agencies, written, oral and social, should be utilized in the public information program by selecting the best media for the specific purpose to be achieved.

Integrity

The information given to the community should accurately reflect the practices within the schools of the district.

Continuity

The public information program should provide a continuous flow of interpretive information to the community.

Review

There should be an annual review of the public information program by the superintendent and board of education and revisions made according to the findings of the review.[2]

POLICY BASIS FOR A SCHOOL DISTRICT PUBLIC RELATIONS PROGRAM. Few school districts have policies relating to a sound public relations program. Public information is a function of administration and particularly of the superintendent, even if he delegates it to another administrator. Administration is responsible to the board of education which establishes policy. A public relations policy should:

1. Be based on the district's educational philosophy.
2. Define objectives.
3. Develop an organizational chart with clear and understandable lines of communication.
4. Specify the methods to be used for internal communication (pupils, teachers, staff, central office) and for external communication (parents, public, organizations, local government, news media).
5. Designate who is to be responsible for public relations and provide a position description.
6. Establish the means for periodically evaluating the effectiveness of the public relations program.

Many superintendents have little experience in the field of public relations and may waste valuable time handling the program. If the school system has 4,000 or more students, it would be wise to employ a full-time public relations professional, and one on a part-time basis in smaller districts. He can do a better job and allow other administrators to pursue their educational responsibilities.

PUBLIC RELATIONS AS A FACET OF THE EDUCATIONAL PROGRAM. Once it is realized that public relations fits comfortably into the overall function of education, the dissemination of information in an organized manner becomes a recognized function of public education. This realization is essential to the construction of a good information program because it leads inevitably to publicizing, on an equal basis, all phases of the school

---

[2] Clarence H. Bloom, "Appraisal of Schools by Certain Community Groups: A Study of Public Information Programs" (Unpublished doctoral dissertation, University of Southern California, 1965), pp. 212–215.

program. Curriculum and guidance as well as sports and social activities should be stressed in releases to the various media of public information. In addition, the activities and accomplishments of the board of education, teachers, administrators, and nonteaching personnel should be publicized. The varied activities of a school district should present a well-rounded picture, not a distorted caricature. All public relations should be student centered and educationally oriented.[3]

An advantage of integrating public relations into the school program is its ability to assume an inconspicuous role in the existing scheme of things. It does not present a glaring target for unthinking criticism by either district employees or taxpayers. When public information is handled by working educators, as distinguished from professional press agents faintly disguised as administrative assistants, it becomes more sensitive and legitimate. It is only as an extension of education that school public relations can achieve its optimum possibilities.

PUBLIC RELATIONS AND THE COMMUNITY. It is a mistake to glorify the schools. They exist as servants of society and creatures of the state. Any public relations design must take this fundamental truth into direct cognizance. Public relations programs attempt to reconcile the apparently conflicting stereotypes of the school as the servant versus the school as the leader.

Schools cannot diverge too greatly from the community way of life. If they do, they find themselves increasingly out of touch with the society they seek to serve. On the other hand, it is the duty of the schools to stress aspects of culture and learning, and to constantly press for the acceptance of higher standards of citizenship and morality. In so doing, a school acts as a leader instead of a servant. It is not only possible but essential that leadership be equated with service. Good public relations places these two functions in proper focus.

PUBLIC RELATIONS IS A TWO-WAY STREET. Good public relations involves receiving information as well as giving it. Educators must understand what is going on around them. District employees directly concerned with public relations should develop appropriate devices to collect, tabulate, and measure community opinion and reactions. on a continuing basis. Polls, surveys, and questionnaires are useful, as well as

---

[3] American Association of School Administrators, *Profiles*, p. 133.

contacts with chambers of commerce, church groups, and fraternal organizations.

A citizens' committee interested in working with the schools to communicate lay opinions and criticisms to school personnel is very effective. Each school person affiliated with Rotary or Kiwanis also serves to detect and transmit community opinion about the schools. Most important and difficult to measure is the role of friendly individuals scattered among the homes and businesses of the school district. When on personal terms with representatives of the schools, these people can be invaluable carriers of community comment and thought. Face-to-face communication is one of the most effective means of communicating because public relations is really the practice of human relations. A good public relations program evaluates the importance of all these information sources and provides for fostering them. Too often, the system becomes a one-way transmitter—sending, not receiving, information.

USE OF ALL AVAILABLE CHANNELS FOR PUBLIC RELATIONS. A school system may establish excellent contacts with the press, but fail to exploit the possibilities of radio and television. Another may work effectively with civic and fraternal groups, but lose sight of the importance of pupil and teacher contacts with the public. Specialized abilities of the public relations director often are the cause of this imbalance. Occasionally, one-sidedness stems from some combination of local circumstances, such as the presence of the newspaper editor or radio station owner on the board of education.

No school system can afford to rely exclusively upon a limited use of public relations media. The best way to achieve a balanced use of media is to adopt a carefully organized plan, using the several instruments of news dissemination, with ample materials and time allotted to each one.

PUBLIC RELATIONS AND PUBLIC UNDERSTANDING. There is more to public relations than a constant pitch for community support. An uninformed support for school activities is the antithesis of good public relations. Public relations should furnish a constant stream of suggestions and constructive criticisms to the school. If a philosophy is adopted that strives solely or largely for indiscriminate applause, this stream of ideas is dammed up. If the school authorities hear only what they wish to hear, they lose all awareness of the reality of public opinion that may oppose the policies and practices which they had fondly believed to be universally accepted.

If mutual understanding rather than support is established as the goal, the problem tends to solve itself. The administration is then constantly engaged in an evaluative process, questioning practices that outside sources of information have criticized. One of two results occur: either a practice is abandoned or modified, or a release of accurate information convinces the citizenry of its desirability. In either case, the outcome redounds to the ultimate advantage of the schools.

CONTINUOUS PUBLIC RELATIONS. Public relations as a continuing process involves a positive approach to the community. Continuing public relations programs are preventive programs. In contrast to public relations programs that react only to specific crises, continuous programs avoid creating the impression of immediate urgency or an avoidance of criticism. By building a clear and easily understood picture of community education in the public's mind over a period of years, the long-range program will ensure an accurate representation of the schools' activities.

Intermittent public relations, on the other hand, only operate to confront temporary crises, such as the need for a tax or bond referendum, or to meet criticism of the schools. Otherwise, they are not active on a continuing basis.

PUBLIC RELATIONS: INFORMAL, INTERESTING, AND VARIED. To be effective, public relations programs should be honest, inclusive, understandable, dignified, comprehensive, and sensitive to the public. Statistical data from school offices used as public relations are insufficient. The vast majority of people in any community are only mildly interested in the problems of the schools. They are not apt to wade through budget material. The reservoir of public goodwill runs dry rather quickly if it is frequently subjected to long and dreary proclamations from the superintendent's office.

Public relations programs must face reality. Because people are understandably unwilling to be bored by figures, they should be eliminated as much as possible. Verbosity in bulletins and messages home should be replaced with short, humorous notes designed to catch the eye and hold attention. In both written and spoken communications, short sentences, concrete terminology, and specific examples should be used. Written communications should keep in mind:

The central idea you wish to convey.
Relating all other ideas to the central theme.
For whom the material is written.
How and where the people will get the material.
What reaction is sought.
Organizing the material logically.
Making sentences simple and clear.
Using familiar terms where possible.
Making writing sound like informal talking.
Giving concrete examples and illustrations.
Summarizing briefly and clearly.[4]

Statistics should be presented to the public with charts and diagrams. The information should be carefully packaged with an eye to the particular audience for whom it is intended. A technician or professional man reacts quite differently than a day laborer. A rural population's response differs from that of an urban citizenry. It follows that the school representative charged with a public relations responsibility must develop a profound knowledge of the makeup of his community which he should be prepared to use in preparing his releases.

Agents of Good School Public Relations

School public relations is not exclusively the job of the professional expert. The most valuable and lasting contacts that the school has with the general public are oral, not written. Although the public relations professional can help a school district communicate with the public, pupils and school personnel are usually more effective.

PUPILS AND THE PUBLIC RELATIONS PROGRAM. A dissatisfied student body can negate all administrative efforts in public relations. On the other hand, pupils who are satisfied with their school and who admire and respect their teachers are worth dozens of highly paid press agents.

---

[4] Albert L. Ayars, *Administering the People's Schools* (New York: McGraw-Hill Book Co., 1957), pp. 63–64.

Natural public relations by students occurs if:

1. The pupils are taught with a well-balanced curriculum stressing content which the parents understand and appreciate.
2. The pupils are reminded shortly before the closing bell of the various accomplishments of the school day. The most satisfactory way to bring this about is to schedule a five-minute period at the end of each high school class period, or at the end of each elementary school day, for a brief but intensive review of the day's work.
3. The pupils are taught a unit on Education. *About Our Schools,* a 1955 unit-text designed to teach high school pupils about public education, should be adapted and used by local administrators for students.[5]

SCHOOL PERSONNEL. The administrator has a considerable public relations impact upon the people of his district. The better trained he is to present the facts to his public, the greater his impact; this principle also applies to principals, supervisors, and board members. Nevertheless, it is the rank and file of school employees who contact the public most regularly and frequently, and who consequently achieve the greatest effect upon public opinion. Whether or not a public relations administrator is employed, public relations is the responsibility of every employee.

Teachers who complain openly about their jobs and their superiors harm the morale of the entire school district. Custodians who joke publicly about the relative ease of their work and the slipshod manner in which they perform their duties raise doubts in the minds of the taxpayers which public relations programs have difficulty allaying. Most school people also have families who, in turn, have friends; these many contacts with the community are of tremendous importance to any plan of public information.

The school bus driver who brags about his fine new equipment and the good behavior of the children who ride his bus is a walking, talking advertisement for the school district. So is the school secretary who tells her friends about the well-organized accounting procedures used in her office, and the polite behavior of the pupils who bring absence notes to her desk.

---

[5] *See* Emery Stoops and M. L. Rafferty. *About Our Schools, A Unit on Public Education.*

School personnel are often uninformed about their school district. Bacon, in a survey of California teachers, found that:

1. Fewer than 25 percent of the teachers had correct information about the school district.
2. At least 50 percent of the teachers were incorrectly informed about the government, service organizations, and fraternal groups of the area in which they taught.
3. Teachers were not well informed about employment in the community.
4. Teachers who were residents of the district were better informed.
5. Many statements about school–community relationships given high priority by writers were rejected by teachers.[6]

Bacon recommends that:

1. Representatives of community organizations should have more opportunities to work with teacher groups on school projects.
2. Teachers should examine the many community avenues open to them to enrich both their instructional programs and their social interaction in the school community.
3. There should be better communication between teachers and administrators in defining mutual roles and in sharing information.
4. A teacher's most effective role in public relations is that of creating a favorable image of the institution he represents.
5. Educators should seek to build channels of school–community interaction.
6. Teachers' associations should re-emphasize to the profession and public that their chief aim is to further functions that contribute to the optimum educational opportunities for youth.[7]

One of the first duties of the person charged with the proper functioning of school public relations should be the thorough introduction of district philosophy to school personnel. They should be the target of an active campaign of information designed to acquaint them with what is going on in departments other than their own; what is being taught in the

---

[6] Leonard Bacon, "Teacher-Community Interaction Viewpoints Regarding Teacher Public Relations" (Unpublished doctoral dissertation, University of Southern California, 1965), pp. 279–280, 297.

[7] Bacon, "Teacher-Community Interaction," pp. 297–301.

classrooms; and how the administration is working to overcome existing problems and difficulties.

In addition, school employees should be appealed to directly and frequently to remember that they are representatives of the school system, whether on duty or off. Staff complaints should initially be discussed with administrators. This tends to minimize publicized complaints by channeling problems properly. If such cooperation is secured, it reduces greatly the amount of grumbling and gossiping which otherwise would be brought to the ears of citizens and improperly magnified. A school system with happy, informed employees seldom worries about poor public relations.

LAY COMMITTEES. A citizens' committee or lay advisory group composed of prominent and representative members of the local citizenry, most of whom presumably are in close touch with crosscurrents of community thought, is a helpful adjunct to public relations. Committees may be specialized, such as recreation commissions, school band supporters, athletic team booster clubs, and similar groups. Organizations of this type are admirable points of contact with representative segments of special community interests, and as such should be cultivated by the school administration. Decisions pending in their particular areas of interest should be discussed fully with them before being translated into action. Soliciting the advice of their members and weighing it carefully before taking action will usually enhance public relations for the district, and also promote an efficiency of operation.

Another increasingly common type of lay committee is one set up to advise the board of education on policy. A committee of this nature may be short-term (e.g., to consult on a bond issue or building program) or long-term (e.g., intended to meet at regular intervals over an extended period of time for consultation on a wide range of school problems). Such organizations should be permanent and their membership widely representative of the whole community.[8] The permanent committee customarily concerns itself with problems of long-range building needs, curriculum questions, and school–community relations. Many superintendents, however, believe that lay committees should not be permanent but should have an assigned task which, once completed, ends the life of the committee. Lay committees with no specifically assigned task possibly may interfere

---

[8] J. H. Hull, "Lay Advisory Committees to Boards of Education in the United States" (Unpublished doctoral dissertation, University of Southern California, 1949), pp. 259–261.

with normal district operation. Some citizens' groups become self-appointed and unwanted "boards of education," taking it upon themselves to issue decisions and statements about matters that are properly beyond their domain. Good leadership that stresses subordination to the legal authority of the school board and unwaveringly emphasizes the strictly advisory function of the lay committee avoids this pitfall and exploits the proper public relations value of such a group.

SCHOOL–COMMUNITY COUNCILS. Sometimes called citizen advisory committees or advisory boards, they are a type of lay committee organized at the school, rather than the district, level. They are the answer to many criticisms of school administration. Minority groups have felt that their desires about curriculum and school administration have not been represented at the district level. There has been criticism of overcentralization of authority in a few people too far removed from the local school community. Boards of education, especially in large cities, have been accused of not understanding the educational desires of the community. There has been an increasing emphasis on decentralizing authority and increasing the autonomy of the local schools. In order for the school to satisfy the educational desires of its attendance area, it must involve the parents in the decision-making process. The principal should consult his school–community council on all substantive matters.

Controversies have arisen about the method of selecting these councils. In some cases, they have been appointed by the principal, often creating a bias in their composition. Minority groups resent this method because they do not believe such a council is truly representative of the whole school community. Some states and school districts require the election of council members. However, the method of nominating or electing members is not always spelled out. Decisions are not always made about what to do with an on-going, appointed council once elections have been mandated. Some of these problems will be clarified and solved in the future. It is generally agreed that these councils should be democratically elected so that all people and segments of the community have a voice in selecting members. Council members, whether elected or appointed, should be willing to serve, represent varying points of view, reflect the ethnic composition of the school, be reasonable, have imagination, and be concerned about the welfare of the school. Teachers should also be members of the council.

Once it has been decided to create a school–community council, certain decisions must be made:

1. The purposes of the council must be defined.

2. The method of selecting the council members must be determined.
   a. If elected: How are prospective members nominated? How is the election conducted?
   b. If appointed: Who appoints? Who should be appointed?

3. The size of the council must be established.

4. Determination must be made regarding meetings.
   a. Time of meetings.
   b. Place of meetings.
   c. Frequency and dates of meetings.

5. Officers must be selected.
   a. There must be a presiding chairman who should be appointed by the council rather than by the principal.
   b. A secretary should be appointed to keep the minutes.

6. The order of business should be agreed upon. A decision should be made as to what should be discussed in the council meeting.

7. There should be agreement as to what action should be taken after the council has made a decision or recommendation.

Whether a lay council is established at the school or the district level, it should be *advisory* only. If it does make decisions, they should not be binding on the school administrator; he is the ultimate authority on what is best for the administration of the school. A community council should never expect or be permitted to dictate a school or district program. Statesmanship is necessary if the administrator is to keep the council's role and his administrative leadership in proper perspective.

PARENT–TEACHER ASSOCIATIONS. A school–home association should be intended primarily as a device to bring about better understanding between the parent and the instructor for the benefit of the child. As such, it is only indirectly an instrument for improving school public relations. However, such an organization may be of tremendous value in building a better understanding between groups and individuals. In the final analysis, this is the principal goal of public relations. Particularly important is the stress placed by parent–teacher associations on cooperative leadership by lay people and professional personnel. It is always highly advisable to associate as many lay persons as possible in any process that involves interpreting school policy to the citizenry. The cooperative aspect of parent–teacher organizations should be especially useful in this respect.

Parent–teacher groups have been accused in recent years of alleged domination by school administrators. In view of such criticism, it behooves educators to encourage lay leadership in these associations and to accept constructive suggestions from the nonprofessional membership. Administrators must develop a genuine partnership with responsible lay members of parent–school organizations if they wish such groups to be of maximum service in relaying information about school policy to the community and in reporting community attitudes and criticisms to the schools.

ADULT EDUCATION.   The best way to gain support for a good school program is to expose a maximum number of people to its effects. Because most public relations programs are aimed at adults, an extensive system of adult education is one of the best investments a school district can make. This program may include night classes, lectures, forums, organized recreation, discussion groups, or a combination of all of these. Courses are now offered in hundreds of schools in subjects ranging from agriculture to typing; the variety of offerings seems certain to multiply during the next few years.

The administrator who is conscious of public relations will strengthen his adult curriculum and make every reasonable effort to increase the number of participants. Each person who can be persuaded to visit the school and familiarize himself with what is being done there is an almost certain future supporter. These people tend to identify themselves with the school, to take a personal interest in its problems, and to react strongly against capricious and unfounded criticism of the local school.

An adult program that has been designed to meet specific community needs and that has been worked out cooperatively by educators and civic leaders is of greater value from a public relations standpoint than one that is purely the product of school planning.

Types of Media
in a Good Public Relations Program

In addition to the various individuals and groups that may be drawn into a good school public relations program as effective agents for news dissemination, certain institutions and organizations should also be relied upon for rapid spreading of news and general information. Most of them are commercial in nature, so they tend to be susceptible to a business-like approach, and to handle information with brevity and color.

NEWSPAPERS. Despite the billions spent on other forms of advertising, the daily newspaper is still the most effective means of communicating an idea to the public. The school public relations director should give a great deal of thought to the preparation of copy especially designed to meet the standards set by the press of his community. What the editor may see as important school news may not necessarily coincide with what the administrator feels is significant. In fact, there is almost certain to be a strong divergence of opinion here.

Newspapers usually indicate that they are interested in receiving announcements of activities at individual schools; materials about district administration; curriculum changes and offerings, including class schedules; special achievements of individuals or groups; special feature or human interest material; adult education services; and provision for scholarships and awards for students. Most school news reported in newspapers covers co-curricular activities, especially athletic events and personalities. Other topics that are focused upon by the news media are: school vandalism, test scores and student achievement, school taxes and finance, board of education meetings, administrative problems, and new educational programs, particularly if they are controversial. Administrators, on the other hand, usually consider desirable topics to be: the value of education, student progress and achievement, student health, school building programs, courses of instruction, and methods of instruction. A file of feature articles about school district activities can be developed and released during quiet news periods.

The school administrator and the newspaper editor have a long way to go before they can achieve basic agreement as to what constitutes important school news. The worst mistake the school representative can make, however, is to assume that the editor is deliberately downgrading the important items to glorify the less important. Actually, the editor probably does not care one way or another. He is headlining the categories of school news which he believes to be of primary interest to the casual reader. It is up to the school to demonstrate that the editor is wrong in his emphasis or, if he is proved right, to tackle the much harder task of reeducating the reading public.

Curricular and related news that is cleverly written, informal, and condensed increases newspaper coverage. Especially in smaller communities, busy editors are usually eager to print such material verbatim. Basic principles of good journalistic style should be followed.

Community people are interested in the daily affairs of a school, particularly human interest items—if they are related in an interesting style. Some examples are:

A teacher who has had his class develop an unusual science experiment.
The custodian who works hard to keep the classrooms and building clean and sparkling.
A day in the life of a school secretary, especially her method of dealing with an angry parent.
The many tasks of a principal, many of which are not known by the general public.
How the cafeteria manager prepares tasty food to help maintain the health of children.
How supplies are ordered and delivered so that they are always available when needed.
How the bus driver maintains his sanity as he transports 70 children safely to and from school.

SCHOOL PUBLICATIONS AND BULLETINS. The school newspaper is a potentially potent medium of news dissemination. However, most high school papers are put out simply as a function of the journalism classes, reporting campus news sporadically, but with little organized attempt to interpret the school to the public.

Other school publications such as handbooks for students, teachers, and other district employees are often widely distributed throughout the community, and may be read by persons other than school employees. Folders and brochures designed to attract prospective teachers to the district can become important media for public relations. Even the report card can fill a useful niche if it is constructed to express the purposes of the school. It is often the main written contact between school and parent, and as such should carefully explain the school's intent and the objectives of the reporting system. Leaflets, prepared by the superintendent's office, can be designed to interpret proposed or existing departures from previous practice, to explain school finances and the budget, personnel changes, testing programs, and reports of various kinds.

RADIO AND TELEVISION. Most schools using the highly specialized media of radio and television to disseminate information place themselves at the mercy of studio programmers and script writers. The production of radio and television programs is complex and technical, and few school districts employ people with the necessary skill and experience to perform creditably in this medium. Although there are many apparent similarities between radio and the newspaper, the former has not attained the importance of the latter in the school public relations picture. Radio and television are more commercialized than newspapers, and desirable evening time is seldom available for school programs. These media are more interested in sensational reporting events such as teacher or student strikes, school board arguments, unsatisfactory test reports, minority dissatisfactions, and transportation problems. Many school activities do not lend themselves readily to audio-visual presentation. Radio and television audiences are accustomed to evaluating all programs in terms of their entertainment value; most school programs are informative rather than entertaining.

The increasing use of filmed programs in television and transcriptions in radio should result eventually in better use by the schools of these media. Tape recordings allow for program editing, making possible a more polished product. Unless a community boasts an extraordinarily public-spirited station owner, however, commercialism and scheduling will continue to minimize use of television and radio for school public relations. Where a cooperative station management exists, the schools should make every effort to present programs free from excessive lecturing, unimaginativeness, and sloppy workmanship.

PUBLIC SCHOOL WEEK. The public has been conditioned for many years to think seriously about its schools only once or twice a year, during such special events as Public School Week and American Education Week. While this may be undesirable to an educator who wants to make his public relations program a continuing operation, it should not preclude making use of the limited opportunities presented by these special occurrences.

A large percentage of the general public rarely enters the door of the school except to attend programs of this sort. The administrator should seize the opportunity to get as much of his message across as possible during the brief time involved in such events. "Open house" should be made a part of the evening's program. "Back to school" nights, with parents visiting classes and teachers, can also be used to good advantage. The printed announcements and schedules of events should contain meaningful material about the educational picture. Both the needs and accomplishments of the schools should be tastefully stressed, and an effort made to encourage those who attend to visit their schools more regularly and purposefully.

ADULT FORUMS. Adult forums are particularly valuable if the school district funds can accommodate visiting speakers monthly. Especially in rural or semi-isolated communities, the cultural opportunities offered by a series of such forums tends to inhibit their provincialism. Larger groups of lay people are attracted into the schools by this method than by any other. Furthermore, members of forum audiences are apt to be among the more thoughtful and serious-minded citizenry of the community, i.e., the people that the typical public relations program attempts to inform. A public relations program has a far greater chance of success if the persons at whom it is aimed are already convinced that the schools are places dedicated to vital and cultural activities and to the exchange of topical information.

TEACHER APPRAISAL AND USE OF PUBLIC RELATIONS TECHNIQUES. Teachers are the key agents of a school's public relations program. To most parents, the school centers around the child's teacher. Research reveals that most teachers' understanding of good public relations procedures exceeds their actual practice. The Research Division of the National Education Association studied the reactions of 3,046 teachers with respect to what they considered to be effective public relations devices and to what extent they used those devices. Figure 28–1 shows the results of the NEA survey.

Organized Public Relations Programs

Even a one-room school should consider its public relations. In a school district employing only a few teachers, a definite proportion of their time

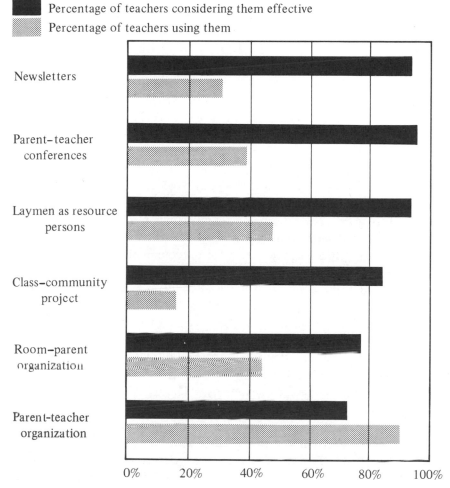

■ Percentage of teachers considering them effective

▨ Percentage of teachers using them

Newsletters

Parent–teacher conferences

Laymen as resource persons

Class–community project

Room–parent organization

Parent-teacher organization

0% 20% 40% 60% 80% 100%

FIGURE 28–1. Public Relations Techniques and Their Use. Source: *National Education Association, "Teachers View Public Relations,"* NEA Research Bulletin *37 (April 1959), p. 35.*

and effort should be allocated and directed to informing the community about the school and its work. When several schools and a substantial number of personnel are involved, it often becomes both prudent and effective to assign the organization and conduct of the public relations program to certain district employees. Whether the emphasis should be placed on public relations at the local school level or at the district level depends upon the underlying philosophy of the district which should be clarified by the school board's policy statements. District administration should implement the adopted policy by clear-cut administrative procedures.

LOCAL SCHOOL PROGRAM. In a district that places stress on the autonomous operation of public relations at a local school level, the principal is the key individual. He should work out with his personnel a program that seems best suited to his school and its needs. An appropriate percentage of his time and of his faculty's time should be devoted to the production of regular and significant news releases to press, television, and radio outlets located in the area served by his school. He should arrange for his teachers and staff members to make themselves available for talks before civic and fraternal organizations on topics within their spheres of competence. He should work with PTA groups and citizens' committees, telling the school's story and listening acutely for the community's reactions.

In a situation placing emphasis on local orientation, the best organizational plan is a three- or five-member committee of certificated and noncertificated school employees interested in public relations. All school publicity should be planned by this body, and the principal should act as chairman of it. He should require all written handouts to be channeled through his office so that school publicity is coordinated and duplications are avoided. One or two key lay citizens attached to this committee in an advisory capacity enhance its legitimacy. The local newspaper editor or radio station owner also can serve in his capacity as an expert.

The program that results from the deliberations of this group should be a continuing one, tailored to the idiosyncrasies of the community supporting the school. Factors such as economic levels, cultural backgrounds, and political bias should be taken into consideration in planning the program. Every effort should be made to achieve simplicity and to avoid pomposity, educational terminology, and excessive verbiage. Ideally, the result should be a well-rounded process of news dissemination, well received by the citizenry and characterized by reciprocity.

CENTRALIZED DISTRICT PROGRAM. The heart of a systemwide program is the superintendent's office. In districts of moderate size, the superintendent himself may handle most of the details involved in editing and releasing school news. Superintendents consider school–community relations to be one of their three most important functions. A 1964–65

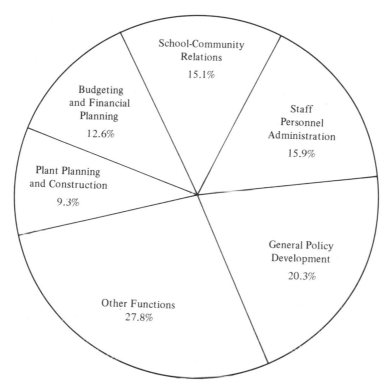

FIGURE 28–2. Percentage of Time Spent by Superintendents on Various Functions. Source: *Robert Filbin, "Do Superintendents Spend Enough Time on PR?" Phi Delta Kappan 53 (November 1971), p. 193.*

study showed that 76 superintendents representing school districts in 26 states with school populations ranging from 1,055 to 95,263 spent an average of 15.1 percent of their time in some function of community relations (*see* Figure 28–2).[9]

Many school districts distribute monthly or weekly publications designed to acquaint the average lay citizen with what the schools are doing. These bulletins should be issued from a central administrative point and individual school bulletins with conflicting viewpoints should be avoided. District bulletins can be made more attractive and readable when they are illustrated with charts, diagrams, or pictures. To be effective, their distribution should be on a regularly scheduled basis. It is better to mail

[9] *See* Robert Filbin, "Do Superintendents Spend Enough Time on PR?" *Phi Delta Kappan,* p. 193.

them than to depend upon student delivery. Mailing also makes it possible to include citizens and community organizations as well as parents.

Where districts are more sizable, the superintendent may select one of his assistants or employ a part-time administrator to perform public relations functions. The centralized method, however, necessitates the employment of a full-time public relations director. He should be a specialist in public relations with training in educational methods and administration, and his office should be solely concerned with public relations. All public communications should be cleared through his office, although this does not mean that he should monopolize functions of public relations. Public relations is peculiarly and inescapably a function of the board and the superintendent. The expert is employed to advise them, not to govern their affairs. Perhaps the best way to avoid the appearance of press agentry is to work through a coordinating council composed of representatives of youth groups, the PTA, civic and fraternal organizations, and various school facilities. In establishing such a council, a policy of limited goals is advisable at first.

The director of public relations may have many different titles. Fugate found that of the 45 public relations specialists employed in 65 California districts, 37 were identified by different position titles.[10] For large school systems, the American Association of School Administrators recommends the title of Assistant Superintendent for School–Community Relations. The assistant superintendent, as a member of the superintendent's staff, should be a

. . . specialist in public relations, counselor to superintendent and board of education, promoter of effective school–community relations, adviser in preparation of brochures, newsletters, and house organs, facilitator of in-system communication, confidant of top leadership of school system, friend of principals and teachers, communicator of educational objectives and purposes, closer of communications gaps between school system and its public, conductor of advertised and unadvertised campaigns, specialist in communication techniques.[11]

The major duties and responsibilities of the public relations administrator should be:

---

[10] Kathryn Fugate, "Policy and Practice in the Administration of School Public Relations," *California School Administrator,* p. 1.

[11] American Association of School Administrators, *Profiles,* p. 123.

1. Press, radio, and TV contacts.
2. Writing press releases.
3. Staff newsletter and publications.
4. Community newsletter and publications.
5. Election and bond referendum campaigns.
6. Superintendent's annual report.
7. Working with community, civic, and service groups.
8. Special projects (American Education Week, B.I.E. Day, etc.).
9. Publicity on federal projects.
10. Editorial services for central office staff.
11. Writing speeches, reports, or papers for central office staff and board of education.
12. Speakers bureau.
13. Inservice PR training for school staffs.
14. Assessment of public attitudes.
15. Development of teacher recruitment materials.
16. Photographic services.[12]

Because all problems in which the public is involved eventually reach the superintendent, the community relations administrator must work closely with him. The superintendent, in turn, must have complete confidence in his administrator. The superintendent, as in all other educational activities, is the ultimate authority for the direction of any public relations program.

Coordination is the most difficult achievement for the centralized system; the larger the district, the greater the difficulty. Public relations-minded principals should not be allowed to furnish the majority of the publicity or to dominate the entire program. The best way to avoid this is to assign percentage quotas to the several schools and to apply these quotas to the sum total of all releases. Each school should have a contributor selected cooperatively by the public relations director and the building principal. His duty should be to serve largely as a liaison between his school personnel and the central office, regularly submitting news in previously selected priority areas. Where a flow of news has been properly encouraged and organized, the job of the public relations director then

---

[12] National Education Association, Research Division, "The School Public Relations Administrator," *NEA Research Bulletin,* p. 30.

becomes one of editing, writing, and supervising, rather than ferreting out news on his own initiative.

The centralized program is outlined as follows:

1. A director of public relations is hired by the district and given whatever assistance may be needed.
2. The director should work closely with a coordinating council composed of school and lay people.
3. The council should map out areas of needed publicity, and re-evaluate the program at regular intervals.
4. The director should assign to each school in the district an appropriate role in gathering and promulgating school information.
5. The director should constantly strive to keep the balance of publicity even, insofar as the individual schools are concerned.
6. The director should be the final judge of the form, style, and choice of material to be released to the various news media.

Internal communication is as important as external communication. Procedures must be established for easy two-way communication between schools, departments, central office, individuals, administration, and the school board. Teacher–administrator communication is as important, if not more so, than administrator–teacher communication. The public relations administrator should be responsible for internal communication.

Evaluating the Public Relations Program

There are many ways to evaluate a school district's public relations program: listing public relations activities; checking upon results; polling the various publics; studying the qualifications of public relations personnel; calling upon outside consultants; and using checklists. A valuable checklist for superintendents has been developed by the American Association of School Administrators.[13] Superintendents should look upon evaluation as a continuous process and use varied techniques. They can ask themselves questions such as:

---

13 American Association of School Administrators, "ABC's of School Public Relations: A Check List."

1. Am I aware of the needs of the community?
2. Are all the available news media such as newspapers, the radio, and television used?
3. Are we using all community resources?
4. Do we have a representative public relations committee that meets regularly to consider ways in which the school and the community can communicate with each other?
5. Are newsletters or bulletins sent regularly to parents and others in the community?
6. Are people reading or paying attention to our public relations efforts? Do they understand them?
7. If failures are found in our public relations program, what efforts are being made to remedy the problem?
8. How many of our employees participate actively in community organizations?
9. Do we have staff members who are able and available to speak before local civic and club groups?
10. Do we have clearly defined policies and procedures for our public relations program? Are they revised periodically?
11. Is our educational program good enough? Are we doing all that we can to let people know about the "good" things?[14]

Summary

School public relations programs, increasingly becoming an absolute necessity for successful administration, should be interpretive rather than offensive or defensive. School public relations differs from industrial public relations, which is designed only to sell products. School public relations exists only to explain the school district's program, activities, and operation.

A public relations program should be erected on these basic concepts: (1) development of district criteria; (2) its establishment on a policy basis; (3) recognition that the public relations program is one facet of the entire educational picture; (4) portrayal of the schools in their proper relation to the community; (5) acknowledgment that public relations is a

---

[14] Emery Stoops and Russell E. Johnson, *Elementary School Administration*, p. 275.

two-way street; (6) use of all available media; (7) attempts to achieve public understanding rather than support; (8) recognition that the program should be continuous, not spasmodic; and (9) constant attempts to render public relations releases informal, interesting, and varied.

Good school public relations should use many agents: pupils, school personnel, lay committees, parent–teacher associations, and adult education. Similarly, one test of a good public relations program is the number and variety of media it uses, including newspapers, school publications and bulletins, radio and television, Public Schools Week, adult classes and forums, and teacher appraisal.

All districts require organized public relations programs. In a district with considerable autonomy, the principal is the key individual, preferably acting as chairman of a committee of district employees that generates the program. In a centralized district, the superintendent handles most of the public relations, in conjunction with a director of public relations. Coordination of duties and responsibilities is essential and can best be accomplished by using a coordinating council of school and lay people.

Trends

As we have seen in so many other aspects of modern school administration, the trend in public relations is away from the simple and toward the complex. The older method of school public relations either reacted spasmodically to criticisms or was activated at irregular intervals to put over a revenue project. It was seldom a coherent, continuous project, developed over a long period of time. The apparent trends in this specialized field are all in the direction of more enlightened professionalism.

TOWARD THE USE OF PUBLIC RELATIONS TO INTERPRET THE SCHOOL PROGRAM. The old concept of school public relations as a form of advertising is passing. A new type of public information program strives to portray the schools accurately and moderately, to explain their functioning thoroughly, and to let the public draw their own conclusions. As education becomes more confident of its own importance and status in the public eye, and as it grows more representative of what the people want, this trend will accelerate.

TOWARD THE INTEGRATION OF PUBLIC RELATIONS INTO THE EDUCATIONAL PROGRAM AND THE ADMINISTRATIVE ORGANIZATION. More and more trained and credentialed administrators are specializing in public relations, indicating that school public relations in the future will become increasingly professionalized. If the program of school information is to reflect accurately the many activities of the schools, those charged with the administration of the program must be members of the school staff, not apart from them. Public relations in the schools of tomorrow will be administered in the same way as curriculum development or the guidance program—by educators with a profound knowledge of what their schools are trying to do.

TOWARD THE USE OF PUBLIC RELATIONS TO COLLECT AND EVALUATE PUBLIC OPINION. It will be just as important in the future for a public relations director to be able to tell the schools what the public is thinking as to be able to tell the public what the schools are doing. The use of polls and other opinion-measuring devices will become a part of the educational public relations man's professional equipment.

TOWARD CONTINUOUS RATHER THAN INTERMITTENT PUBLIC RELATIONS. Hiring well-known publicity firms to organize special drives or elections for embattled school districts will decline. In place of this sporadic approach to enlisting public support, continuous public relations programs will emerge, operating daily to inform the people of the school's needs and accomplishments. Continuing public relations should enable the schools to go to the people with confidence when special needs arise. The citizens of the school district will have been kept apprised of these needs and their origins for a long time before the final necessity for action arose.

TOWARD BROADENING THE BASE OF PUBLIC RELATIONS. The function of the public relations expert will grow to be the organization of a broadly based committee of interested citizens who will chart the future of the program and help to implement it. By involving representative members of the community as well as the school personnel, the public relations director will place his program on a solid foundation of general co-operation.

TOWARD CENTRALIZED PROFESSIONAL DIRECTION OF SCHOOL PUBLIC RELATIONS. In small districts, the superintendent or principal will continue to direct the public relations program. In large districts, the director will be a school administrator who has specialized in this field of education.

In either case, the school district's program of public information increasingly will be in the hands of well-qualified and specially trained experts. Within a short time, school districts will insist upon achieving maximum results from their professional efforts, along with public realization and recognition of the work of the schools. This can only mean centralized and professionally expert public relations programs.

TOWARD MORE EMPHASIS ON THE STUDENT. News releases from the school district will feature more of the learning, accomplishments, and activities of students rather than fiscal policies and board of education activities. There will be more extensive use of visual presentations such as photographs, short film sequences, and videotape displays featuring students. Students will be revealed in their new role as participants on district and school committees, in the superintendent's administrative council, and in board meetings.

Administrative Problems

In Basket

Problem 1

The people in the city of Sanger claim that they know little about their school system. Although school board meetings are open, few people attend. The local newspaper publishes short summaries of Board of Education decisions and sporadic news items, although many people do not subscribe to the paper. Some schools send bulletins home from time to time. Businessmen, in particular, resent that the only time the district really communicates is during a tax or bond election.

    Young, dynamic Dr. Conger has been employed as the school district's new superintendent. The Board selected him because of his outgoing personality and interest in good school–community relations as well as his successful administrative experience.

How can Dr. Conger proceed in improving communication between the school district and the community?
What channels can be used?

Problem 2

Assume the same situation as in Problem 1. The superintendent has decided that one of the first things he will do to help communication is to send a monthly district bulletin to every home.

Whom should Dr. Conger involve to write articles for the bulletin?
What topics should be covered?
What format should be developed for the bulletin?

Problem 3

Assume the same situation as in Problem 1. Dr. Conger, believing that each school can be a major factor in improving school–community relations in its attendance area, has asked each principal to develop a plan for improving communication with the public in his school community. He has also explained that communication should not entirely be from school to community but should be also from community to school.

If you were one of the principals, what would you propose?
On what basis would you make your decision?
Whom would you involve? In what way?

Selected References

AMERICAN ASSOCIATION OF SCHOOL ADMINISTRATORS. "ABC's of School Public Relations: A Check List." Washington, D.C.: The Association, 1959.

————. *Profiles of the Administrative Team.* Washington, D.C.: The Association, 1971.

DE MARE, GEORGE. *Communicating for Leadership.* New York: Ronald Press, 1968.

DUBIA, DOROTHY E. "Developing Goals, Planning, and Implementing a Positive PR Program." *Thrust for Education Leadership* 3 (October 1973).

FILBIN, ROBERT. "Do Superintendents Spend Enough Time on PR?" *Phi Delta Kappan* 53 (November 1971).

FREY, GEORGE T. "Improving School-Community Relations." *Today's Education* 60 (January 1971).

FUGATE, KATHRYN. "Policy and Practice in the Administration of School Public Relations." *California School Administrator* 23 (August 1968).

GELMS, KENNETH J. "To Be or Not to Be Read." *Thrust for Education Leadership* 3 (October 1973).

JAY, ANTHONY. *Corporation Man.* New York: Random House, 1971.

JONES, MAXWELL, and STANFORD, GENE. "Transforming Schools into Learning Communities." *Phi Delta Kappan* 60 (November 1973).

MARROW, ALFRED J. *Management by Participation.* New York: Harper & Row, 1967.

MOEHLMAN, ARTHUR B., and VAN ZWOLL, JAMES A. *School Public Relations.* New York: Appleton-Century-Crofts, 1957.

NATIONAL EDUCATION ASSOCIATION, Research Division. "The School Public Relations Administrator." *Research Bulletin* 46 (March 1968).

NORTON, MICHAEL M. "PR Program Runs Farther, Faster with Volunteer 'People Power'." *Thrust for Education Leadership* 3 (October 1973).

STOOPS, EMERY, and JOHNSON, RUSSELL E. *Elementary School Administration.* New York: McGraw-Hill Book Co., 1967.

STOOPS, EMERY, and RAFFERTY, M. L. *About Our Schools, A Unit on Public Education.* Los Angeles: California Education Press, 1955.

29

Educational Reform
and Innovation

All innovations do not necessarily result in the improvement of the educational system. But improvement will only come about with change. For change in school systems to be successful, administrators must give thoughtful analysis and time to planning desirable innovation. They cannot afford to spend all their energies on routine matters or to be preoccupied with procedural and budgetary demands. Reforms and innovations require careful planning, forward-looking leadership, and involvement of many people. They must be tested by pilot programs in the field.

This chapter includes a discussion of the following topics:

Rationale for Educational Reform
Review of Processes of Change in Education
The Role of One Professional Organization in Effecting Change
One School System's Approach to Educational Reform
Summary
Trends

Rationale for Educational Reform

Educational reform is and has been for a number of years a topic of widespread interest. Daily accounts in the news media underscore how the subject is of growing concern to parents, taxpayers, and educators alike.

This chapter was prepared in collaboration with Dr. Edward W. Beaubier, Assistant Executive Director of the Association of California School Administrators.

American society has changed dramatically in the past decade. Our pattern of education, based primarily on an agrarian way of life, no longer serves the purposes and problems of our society. Because over 70 percent of our population live in cities, the problems of the megalopolis and its large schools and school districts are of crucial significance.

Technology has made possible unimaginable frontiers for change in society and has revolutionized American working life. Education must reflect the influence of technology in this area. Today many people are employed in jobs that did not exist ten years ago, and obsolescence of job skills increases at a frightening pace. It is estimated that three-quarters of the jobs that will exist in the year 2000 do not exist today. Educators must teach today's generation of students to be able to adapt to these changes. Adult education must continue to be part of this effort. Basic, traditional curricula no longer fully prepare a student to meet the challenge of his environment.

Education today should reach out and encompass all persons, including those formerly thought uneducable, while simultaneously defining in more rigorous terms the powers to be developed through education. Educational advancement and adaptation to new needs require speedy incorporation of applicable knowledge and techniques to the content and organization of curriculum, to methods and materials of instruction, and to ways in which the educational enterprise is organized and administered.

Review of Processes of Change in Education

Many persons are concerned with speeding up the processes of change in education; yet it is apparent that not all kinds of change in education constitute fitting or effective responses to the transformations in culture and society. Existing literature on educational innovation and social change provides little in the way of either empirical data or verifiable hypotheses on how to accelerate the process of making education a more effective instrument, either for the realization of social goals or for the development of individual capacities and talents. Without an adequate understanding of the forces influencing change in education or the processes through which educational institutions interact with culture and society, it is difficult to predict the direction and amount of future change or to specify the probable determinants of change in the future. Without this understanding, attempts to intervene in educational change processes are likely to be inept and ineffective.

Innovations are often resisted. Resistance may be caused (1) by the organizational structure of the educational system or (2) by negative attitudes of professional personnel.[1] Some sources of resistance to change are:

1. The threat that change repudiates past practice, giving the appearance of approval to those better prepared to follow the new practice.
2. Change may appear to benefit one part of the organization at the expense of the other parts.
3. Resentment may occur when change is imposed from above in a hierarchical organization.
4. Teachers may believe that they lack the skill to implement a particular innovation.
5. Teachers and principals fear that liberalizing changes may directly affect student control.[2]

Unless the public understands the need for making changes and is convinced that changes will result in improvements in education, changes are not likely to be made.

The Role of One Professional Organization in Effecting Change

The Association of California School Administrators places great emphasis on the preparation of school administrators to implement appropriate strategies for the improvement of education through appropriate reform plans. One example of a comprehensive reform strategy is ACSA's Project Leadership, described in the following section. Although unique to California, the strategies and procedures described in this chapter can be adapted for use in any state or school district.

INVOLVEMENT. ACSA's Project Leadership brings to educational leadership a program designed to demonstrate in a practical way the new skills

---

[1] Howard Baumgarten, *Guidelines for Staffing: A Study of the Ways to Facilitate Constructive Change in California School Districts* (San Francisco: Arthur D. Little, Inc., 1966), p. 31.

[2] Baumgarten, *Guidelines*, p. 32.

needed by today's successful school administrator to bring about educational reform. It has been proven successful by practicing administrators throughout the state. The Project is an involvement process; only by "getting into the action" of Project Leadership will the individual administrator really learn how to apply these new skills.

WHAT IS PROJECT LEADERSHIP? Project Leadership is one component of the ACSA Professional Development Program. Latest concepts and successful programs in school management are part of this comprehensive training program. The Project's primary focus is to assist school administrators to become more effective education leaders. It seeks to help school administrators identify and attain high priority goals. Project Leadership objectives (in sequence) are the following:

1. First phase: Identify a top priority goal to serve as a focus of Project activity. Specify a set of planned procedures for attaining the goal and for determining whether the goal has been achieved.
2. Second phase: Complete field testing and evaluation of procedures selected for attaining the goal.
3. Third phase: Implement in one or more schools a field-tested set of procedures for attaining at least one high priority educational goal.

BENEFITS OF ACSA PROJECT LEADERSHIP. Participants in ACSA Project Leadership will learn how to:

1. Train district personnel to become resource consultants for their own district.
2. Obtain access to nationally known educators.
3. Use training materials.
4. Use computerized information retrieval.
5. Develop communication networks.

PROJECT LEADERSHIP COMPONENTS. Following is a brief description of the phases of the ACSA Project Leadership program:[3]

---

[3] Edward W. Beaubier, "Project Leadership: Association of California School Administrators," *Thrust for Education Leadership* 1 (December–January 1972), pp. 14–16.

Introductory. Presents an overview of the Project rationale and mission statement, and includes a self-assessment instrument to assist the individual in identifying his participation level.

Needs Assessment. The Project Leadership plan is a generic model that suggests how community, staff and students may be involved in the goal-setting process, which is based upon needs.

Problem Solving. The problem-solving component (used with the needs assessment and administrative support components) sets up a workable system for resolving complex problems. It includes resources and products developed by Project Leadership and educational agencies.

Administrative Support. This component is a planned model to assist the building principal.

Assessment Alternatives. Consists of instruments an administrator may use to assess items such as school climate, operation, citizen opinion, inservice needs, decision and action behaviors, and patterns of influence, as well as self-assessment instruments of leadership techniques.

Time Management. A component designed to assist the practicing administrator to become more efficient in the use of his work day, and thus more efficient in his leadership skills.

PROJECT LEADERSHIP ENTRY TRAINING COMMITMENT. Numerous management-training packages have been field tested and made available to participating school districts. Major areas of school management and related management-training packages are contained in an ACSA professional development program kit.[4] Included in the entry level component are training needs surveys, strategies, and instruments to identify needs and determine where training for an individual or group of administrators should begin in relation to Project Leadership.

Participants have the opportunity to meet with an educational management counselor to determine the most appropriate instrument. Based upon data from one of the training needs surveys and the individual's particular professional interests, the counselor helps to determine the appropriate entry point to Project Leadership. The alternative entry level possibilities are illustrated in Figure 29–1.

---

[4] Arthur N. Thayer, "Needs Assessment: Component 1," *Thrust for Education Leadership* 1 (December–January 1972), p. 36.

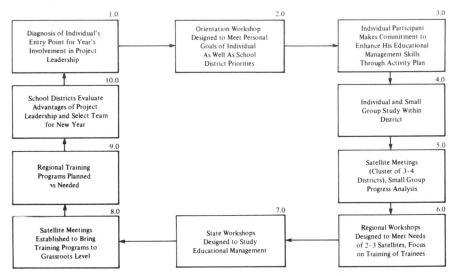

FIGURE 29–1. Training Cycle to Implement Management Change.

Each participant in Project Leadership has the opportunity to determine, through self-assessment of his personal professional leadership skills, an entry point into the Educational Management Training Program. This model is open and flexible, capitalizing on innovative and proven educational management-training products.

ADDITIONAL TRAINING MANAGEMENT SKILLS. In addition to major components, Project Leadership features training management skills in the following areas:

Alternative Educational Management Models
American Management Association Training Program
Building Trust
Communication Skills
Cross-Age Teaching
Decentralized Administration
Developing Student Self-Image
Differentiated Staffing
Effective Use of Professional Negotiators
Employer–Employee Relations

Ernstspiel-Problem Solving
How to Use SMERC
Individualized Instruction
Master Planning
Measuring Effective Goals
Non-Graded School
Objectives Writing
Organizing Resources
Performance Evaluation
Personnel Standards
Practicum: Resources within the School
Priority-Setting Textbook Media
Program Evaluation
Resource Unit Allocation Budgeting
Simulation of Decentralized Budgeting

TRAINING STRATEGIES. Project Leadership has found the greatest success in the implementation of the management change model through the training cycle illustrated in Figure 29–2.

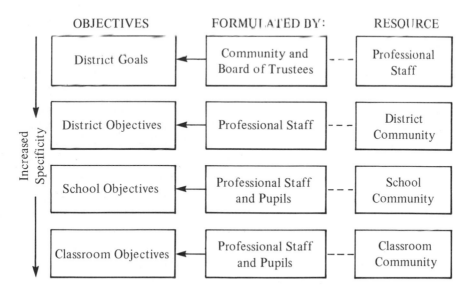

FIGURE 29–2. Model Illustrating Increasing Specificity and Involvement in the Development of Objectives.

PROJECT LEADERSHIP SUBSCRIPTION. Project Leadership is financed through subscription by individual school districts, county offices, and/or other educational agencies (private and public). Contracts are designed for school districts and other agencies as follows:

1. Under 500 Average Daily Attendance: One representative, either district office or site administrator.
2. Under 1,000 ADA: One district office and one site administrator.
3. Under 10,000 ADA: One district office and one site administrator.
4. Over 10,000 ADA: One district office and two site administrators.
5. For a very large district: Two three-man teams comprised of one district and two site administrators on each team.
6. County Schools Office Representatives.
7. Private Institution: One representative, either district office or site administrator.

One School System's Approach to Educational Reform

The Fountain Valley School District Board of Trustees recognized the need for planned educational reform that was reflected in recent legislation obligating school districts to implement a system for rational curriculum planning and program accountability.

Because needs differ from one community to another, if educational reform is to be effective, it must be initiated in a systematic fashion at the local school district level. A plan for reform that does not include concise objectives and a system for measurement is meaningless and represents a waste of tax dollars, as well as human effort. If initial educational reform is to incorporate precision, it will cost money. Private industry has shown that long-range, systematic planning becomes a sound investment.

Currently, curriculum development and implementation appear to be an affair of intuition or a business of trial and error. The march of change makes it absolutely essential that we reassess our position. An acceptable position should become totally immersed in (1) objectives, (2) relevancy, (3) values, (4) measurement, and (5) productivity. Educators must ask themselves: "What changes in student behavior can be accomplished by new programs that were not possible under the old curriculum?" And educators must structure new programs in a manner that will enable them to present objective evidence showing that the expected changes actually took place. They need carefully selected structures to guide themselves toward the systematic production of programs leading to stated objectives. If they fail to structure a process, they might find themselves with a hodgepodge curriculum that would be less effective than the original state-mandated program.

Traditionally, educational objectives were stated in vague, poorly defined terms. Until now, this presented no real problem to some because they were not their objectives but those mandated from the outside. Whether a child reached the stated objectives was nearly impossible to determine because of the lack of clarity with which the objectives were written.

This position is untenable today with the demand for precise evidence on learner performance. Any curriculum must provide for the measurement of "post-instructional learner behavior." Specific learning results must be compared with stated objectives to enable us to determine program effectiveness.

Once a district makes a commitment to precise evidence of learning results, a rational plan for program development must be developed. This plan should include:

1. Clearly defined educational objectives.
2. The selection of appropriate learning opportunities to meet the objectives.
3. A systematic plan of organization designed to facilitate the selected learning opportunities.
4. A method of evaluation to measure the degree to which stated pupil objectives have been met.

This concept for curriculum development intends to point a direction for reform, not to present a recipe. Specifically, the description to be presented here contains some vital considerations for developing a curriculum in the future. However, this description should not be interpreted as a universal model. Each school district must develop a model for curriculum development tailored to its own requirements.

A DISTRICT POINT OF VIEW. Before a plan for implementing stated objectives can be developed, consideration must be given to the perspectives of children, how they learn, and their physical and emotional development. When combined with hereditary factors, these factors produce a wide range of differences between individuals.

The Fountain Valley School District professional staff believes the emphasis in education has changed from "teaching" to "learning." Since it is impossible to provide true experts in each subject area, the staff's effort focuses upon the learning act rather than the teaching act. This focus, combined with the psychological and physiological uniqueness of the learner, gives the school district its direction in the establishment of a program of learning.

As a prelude to developing a model for program improvement, the school district Board of Trustees adopted ten broad goals reflecting the purposes for the schools in this community. These broad goals represent the feelings of the community assessed by the answers to extensive questionnaires and oral interviews from parents in the district. The student goals are:

1. Efficiency in the use of the fundamental skills of communication (reading, writing, calculating).
2. The ability to think and evaluate constructively and creatively; the habit of objective self-examination.
3. Respect for human values and for the rights, beliefs, and property of others; acceptance of responsibility for good citizenship.
4. The recognition of personal worth, and pride in the quality of personal achievement; respect for all forms of honest work.
5. An understanding and appreciation of the American heritage; ethical behavior based on a sense of moral and spiritual values.
6. An appreciation of art, music, and literature.
7. An understanding of the physical world and the need for wise use of natural resources.
8. Sound mental, physical, and emotional health.
9. The constructive use of personal time.
10. A respect for learning and a readiness for further education.

These goals are specifically designed only to give staff direction for concrete program development and implementation.

Following the establishment of the goals, the essentials of program development include: (1) setting objectives; (2) selecting appropriate learning opportunities; (3) providing for effective organization; and (4) outlining a systematic procedure for evaluation.

OBJECTIVES. At the district level, an example of a more specific educational objective might be:

> The *student* (institution) will demonstrate his *knowledge* (behavior) of *mathematical skills* (instruction) at a performance level commensurate with his ability (evaluation).

At the school level, the objective would be more specific:

> The *student* (institution) will demonstrate his *knowledge* (behavior) of the *skills of mathematics* (instruction) by *completing the developmental skills sequence identified in the District Mathematics Guide* (evaluation) at a sequential rate commensurate with his ability.

At the classroom level, the objective would be even more specific:

> The *student* (institution) will demonstrate his *knowledge* (behavior) of *two-place multiplication* (instruction) by *deriving the correct answers to 9 of 10 teacher-prepared problems* (evaluation).

Each objective becomes more concise as the learning situation moves closer to the classroom and to the student, allowing for the individual differences between local districts, schools, teachers, and students. Figure 29–2 illustrates the increasing specificity and involvement in the development of objectives.

LEARNING OPPORTUNITIES. The selection of learning opportunities for students should be made to modify behavior to meet the stated objectives. Modification of human behavior takes place in three domains: (1) the cognitive domain, (2) the affective domain, and (3) the psychomotor domain. Each domain contains a sequential hierarchy of increasingly abstract processes intended to modify, by degrees of sophistication, intellectual, attitudinal, and physical behavior. If proper communication is to take place between those involved in the development of workable educa-

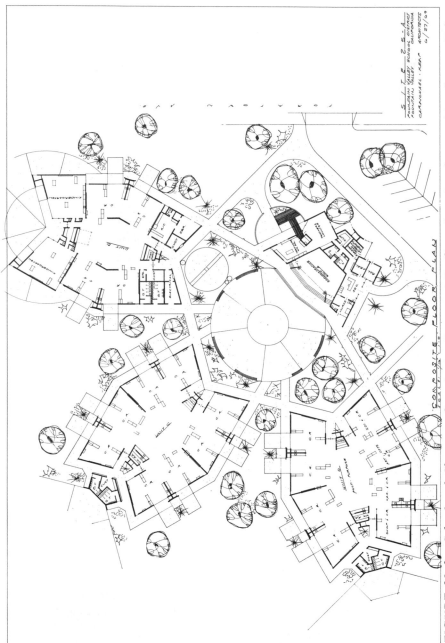

FIGURE 29–3. *School and Classroom Organization Pattern to Facilitate Learning Opportunities. Source: Fulton School, Fountain Valley School District. Carmichael-Kemp, Los Angeles, California, architects. Dr. Edward Beaubier, Superintendent. Reproduced by permission.*

tional objectives, it is essential that they agree on the meaning of the language used to describe their objectives. The selection of appropriate learning opportunities is made after this clarification of terms.

ORGANIZATION. The district, school, and classroom organizational patterns must be selected to facilitate learning opportunities. Figure 29–3 illustrates such a classroom organizational pattern. Too often, organizational patterns emerge because of tradition, current fad, building design, or other factors unrelated to district purpose.

To reach identified objectives, the district professional staff developed an organizational plan based on the concept of the self-contained classroom. It expanded upon this to incorporate the strengths of differentiated staffing, multimedia learning materials, and the flexible use of space.

In order to ensure proper diagnosis of learning needs, the teacher must be as familiar as possible with each student's individual strengths and weaknesses. Because the teacher works with a relatively small number of students in this plan, the chances for in-depth diagnosis are enhanced.

The need for consistency in program organization and implementation is essential in the individualization of instruction. If one teacher has the basic responsibility for the management of the educational program of a small number of students, the consistency within and between various areas of the curriculum is enhanced.

Flexible scheduling of time is critical to the implementation of an individualized program. Flexibility permits the allocation of instructional time to meet each pupil's needs and interests as diagnosed by the teacher.

Providing for an adequate variety of learning opportunities and selecting instructional materials to intensify these learning opportunities is a difficult task indeed. But if adequate individualization of instruction is to take place, learning alternatives must be provided for each student.

The Fountain Valley School District believes that the expanded, self-contained classroom provides the basis for the implementation of an individualized instructional program. To expand upon the advantages inherent in the self-contained classroom and to better meet student needs, the school district developed the Learning Center. The Learning Center extends the self-contained classroom through the addition of extra teaching space, certificated and auxiliary personnel, and instructional materials.

School design should support and enhance the educational program. The goal of the Fountain Valley School District professional staff is to provide a stage for learning that develops the individual talents and abilities of each child.

A variety of teaching and learning station areas should be provided to allow for an extension and enrichment of the basic curriculum. Equal consideration is given to spaces that allow for learning skills, and encouraging use of skills (i.e., inquiry training, research, and an extended application of learned concepts).

Development of specific areas within the Learning Center may be permanent or changing. This is determined largely by the cooperating teachers as they identify short-term, intermediate, and long-range objectives for individual students.

EVALUATION. A district that establishes clearly defined educational goals, supported by pupil objectives stated in measurable terms, takes a major step towards true accountability for the quality of the instructional program. If objectives are stated in concise, measurable terms, the specific choice of learning opportunities and organizational plans for learning implementation will become more purposeful and justified.

Once these steps have been taken, it becomes necessary to establish a structure for evaluation. This should allow for accurate assessment of pupil behavior during and after the specified period. Evaluation should measure the degree to which students have met intended objectives established by the school and the district.

An evaluation model should first establish a program calendar designed to define the necessary tasks and period of time required to accomplish the evaluation process. The program calendar should indicate *who* will be evaluated and *how* the evaluation process will be accomplished. Following development of a program calendar of evaluation, the implementation of the actual program begins.

During implementation of the actual program, an in-process monitoring system should be established for an on-going program evaluation. The in-process program of evaluation is tied closely to the time sequence established in the program calendar. As the actual program comes to a close, analysis of behavior change is made by an evaluation of the degree of success a student has made toward achieving the program product or behavioral objective. One of the following should be determined: (1) Has the objective been met? (2) If the objective has not been met, what was the probable cause?

Following this assessment, a recycling process begins. A decision is made whether or not to redefine or modify currently stated objectives and program implementation or to select an entirely new set of objectives for program continuation. The data gathered during the in-process and terminal stages of the evaluation model furnish the data necessary for program planners to make these determinations.

VEHICLES FOR EDUCATIONAL REFORM. If effective, total educational reform is to take place, a series of systematically developed pilot programs must be placed in operation to assess the reliability of the selected educational reform before it is adopted on a districtwide basis.

The Fountain Valley School District chose to use every resource at its disposal for these pilot programs, including budgeted local funds, private funding sources, and federally funded projects.

Specific projects are based upon one or more of ten identified district goals. Each specific project model was developed in accordance with the previously identified plan for rational program reform. Some sample innovative programs follow:

Reform: Learning Resource Center Project

District Goal No. 1
Efficiency in the use of the fundamental skills of communication (reading, writing, and calculating).

District Objective

> Students (institution) will demonstrate comprehension (behavior) in the skill area of reading (instruction) as measured by their performance on selected, standardized tests (measurement).

School Objective

> Students (institution) will demonstrate comprehension (behavior) of learned library science skills (instruction) by their use of teacher-presented procedures to locate and select reference material relevant to a teacher-assigned topic (measurement).

Classroom Objective

> Students (institution) will demonstrate comprehen-
> sion (behavior) of the Dewey Decimal System
> (instruction) by using this procedure in the resource
> center to locate a teacher-assigned reference
> (measurement).

PROJECT DESCRIPTION.   Under ESEA Title II, Phase 2, the Harry C.
Fulton School project was granted $64,000 to develop a Multimedia
Learning Resource Center.   The Multimedia Learning Resource Center
provides a vehicle for the extension of a self-contained classroom by providing additional teaching space, multimedia materials, certificated and
auxiliary personnel (*see* Figure 29–4).   Specifically, the Learning Resource Center is:

1.   A reading, listening, and viewing center where academic skills and cul-
     tural tastes are developed.
2.   A learning laboratory for research and study where pupils learn to
     work independently and in groups.
3.   A collection of learning materials that enables pupils to explore and
     satisfy their varied curiosities and interests.
4.   A center contributing to the personal, social, educational, and voca-
     tional guidance of students.
5.   An instructional center for improving the use of multimedia throughout
     the school.
6.   An extension of the regular classroom program.
7.   A laboratory of specialists to meet the needs of individual students.

The Learning Resources Center contains:

10,000 library books	Independent study carrels
50 magazine subscriptions	Cooperative teaching stations
1,000 filmstrips	Film projectors
150 super-8 film cartridges	Tape recorders with headsets
750 study prints	Reading laboratories
1,000 disc records	Reference books

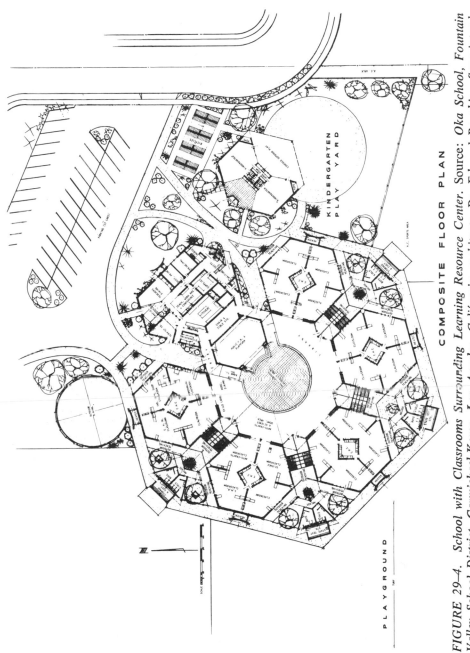

COMPOSITE FLOOR PLAN

FIGURE 29–4. School with Classrooms Surrounding Learning Resource Center. Source: Oka School, Fountain Valley School District. Carmichael-Kemp, Los Angeles, California, architects. Dr. Edward Beaubier, Superintendent. Reproduced by permission.

The Learning Resources Center is staffed by:

1. The librarian, a specialist in multimedia, who works cooperatively with children and teachers to bring instructional materials into the learning and teaching process.
2. Two coordinating teachers assigned the task of providing additional learning activities for the children. Enrichment, remedial, and supplementary learning experiences are provided under their guidance.
3. The psychologist, teacher of educationally handicapped, and the speech and hearing therapist are resources of diagnostic information and prescription for learning alternatives which contribute to the environment of the Learning Resource Center.
4. The library clerk and teacher aides act as circulating assistants for the Center. They assist with audio-visual equipment, recordkeeping, and clerical tasks.
5. The volunteer aides help with processing, circulation, filing, and shelving of materials.
6. The responsibility of the principal is to provide the team leadership that moves the program toward ultimate objectives of developing self-actuating children.

Reform: Primary Level Economics Project

District Goal No. 3
Respect for human values and for the rights, beliefs, and property of others; acceptance of responsibility for good citizenship.

District Objective

> Students (institution) will demonstrate respect for the property of others (instruction) by their response (behavior) while attending school.

School Objective

> Following classroom instructions, students (institution) will demonstrate their response (behavior) to the concept of respect for the rights of others (instruction) by conforming to established school rules related to rights of fellow students (evaluation).

Classroom Objective

> Following classroom instruction identifying eight
> rules of behavior relating to the respect for the prop-
> erty of others (instruction), students (institution)
> will respond (behavior) by conforming to the estab-
> lished rules related to the respect of the property
> rights of others (evaluation).

PROJECT DESCRIPTION. Applying cooperatively with two other school districts, the Fountain Valley School District was granted $64,000 by ESEA Title III to implement a primary economics curriculum. Primary teachers at three schools are teaching children basic principles of economics through a program that emphasizes:

1. Teacher inservice education in economics.
2. Provision for books, records, filmstrips, and other media related to economics.
3. Study trips into the community.

"Discovering the Working World" is a primary program that spotlights economic education within the framework of social sciences. The study of economics develops an understanding of economic roles and responsibility as citizens, producers, and consumers.

The local community is the laboratory for learning as the students observe the economic growth and planning of their own cities. Parents of students involved in the study are invited to learn along with their children. Parent involvement includes study trips to the school and to the classrooms, and field trips throughout the community and surrounding areas with their children on Saturdays.

Reform: League of Cooperating Schools Project

District Goal No. 4

The recognition of personal worth and pride in the quality of personal achievement; respect for all forms of honest work.

District Objective

> Students (institution) will demonstrate value (be-
> havior) toward learning (instruction) by becoming
> self-actuating learners.

School Objective

> Students (institution) will demonstrate value (be-
> havior) towards learning (instruction) by becoming
> self-actuating in an "open structure" model of school
> organization (evaluation).

Classroom Objective

> In an open structure plan of classroom organization,
> students (institution), when given the choice to
> attend or not to attend class, will demonstrate value
> (behavior) towards learning (instruction) by choos-
> ing to attend (evaluation).

PROJECT DESCRIPTION. The League of Cooperating Schools is a tri-
partite arrangement between the Institute for the Development of Educational Activities (IDEA), the University of California at Los Angeles,
Teaching and Research Development Division, and eighteen schools
located in Southern California. The main purpose of the League is to
initiate and disseminate information on educational innovations. The
participants in this League receive consultant aid through the IDEA office
which, in the case of one, amounts to over $2,000 per year.

The Fountain Valley School District also has the use of the Research
and Development facilities through this relationship. The support received
through the League facilitates innovative practices in educational techniques and organization which are implemented at Arevalos School.

Of the several reforms currently being implemented at the Arevalos
School is the concept of an "open structure" of classroom organization.
This pattern allows a student to choose how his school day will be spent.
The theory behind open structure is that when youngsters are allowed to
make decisions, the chosen activity will become more meaningful to them.

Other features of the project include:

1. Techniques and strategies for implementing individualized instruction.
2. Assessing styles of leadership.
3. Assessing staff climate.

Reform: Community Resource Project

District Goal No. 6
An appreciation of art, music, and literature.

District Objective

> Student (institution) knowledge (behavior) of litera-
> ture, music, and art (instruction) will be increased as
> a result of classroom implementation of the com-
> munity resource project.

School Objective

> Following input by community-based, free-lance
> writers, students (institution) will demonstrate in-
> creased knowledge (behavior) of current Fountain
> Valley community efforts in the field of literature
> (instruction) by their response on a teacher-prepared
> pre- and post-test (evaluation).

Classroom Objective

> As a result of a directed lesson by a community-
> based, free-lance writer, students (institution) will
> demonstrate knowledge (behavior) of the five steps
> necessary to have a fiction story published (instruc-
> tion) in a national magazine by listing, in writing,
> these five steps (evaluation).

PROJECT DESCRIPTION. The Community Resource Program is a system
designed to use human and material resources of the community to provide

an enriched program for children.   Specifically, the purposes of the Community Resource Project are:

1.   To expand and enrich the scope of the basic instructional program.
2.   To provide an additional source of materials.
3.   To better involve the community in the total effort of educating children.
4.   To provide a vehicle for vocational guidance for students at the 7th and 8th grade levels.
5.   To expand the relevancy of the curriculum for children.

To achieve these purposes, the following strategy was implemented:

1.   Questionnaires were distributed to each adult in Fountain Valley.
2.   Through the guidance of the School Community Resource chairman and staff, children of the district developed posters and other ways to publicize the project.
3.   The Community Resource chairman contacted community agencies and civic organizations such as the Woman's Club, Chamber of Commerce, parent–teacher groups, etc., for the purpose of describing the project and requesting assistance in its implementation.

To assist in the establishment of the program and the assessment of its worth, a retrieval system is currently being developed to rapidly gather data on available community resources.   The system includes a process by which teachers and students will be able to identify, request, and receive community resource assistance in a systematic fashion.

Reform: Special Education Project

District Goal No. 8
Sound mental, physical, and emotional health.

District Objective

> As a result of the Title VI Inservice Education Project (instruction) for Special Education Staff (institution), cognitive and affective pupil–teacher relationships will be modified (behavior).

School Objective

> The Special Services Staff (institution) will demonstrate knowledge (behavior) of cognitive and affective teacher–pupil interaction (instruction) as a result of their scores on the Roberson Interaction Analyses coding instrument (evaluation).

Classroom Objective

> The teacher (institution) will demonstrate comprehension (behavior) of the five levels of affective behavior (instruction) by coding teacher behavior at the 80th percentile of reliability on the Roberson Interaction Analysis Scale (evaluation).

PROJECT DESCRIPTION. The Title VI Project is an Inservice Training Program for Special Education personnel. The inservice process will guide the participants through a hierarchical sequence of cognitive and affective objectives. The inservice training is aimed at developing relevant educational or academic tasks, as well as sensitizing the participants to the reactions and attitudes of children.

The program is appropriate for all personnel with contact with the exceptional child; the major focus will be on change of teacher behavior. The process is sequential insofar as each problem or behavior is (1) diagnosed; (2) a prescription or solution for it is researched and recommended; and (3) an evaluation of the diagnosis and prescription takes place by the teacher and the interdisciplinary team. They cooperatively attempt to provide for the youngster with learning problems.

Reform: Learning Centers

District Goal No. 9
The constructive use of personal time.

District Objective

> When given unscheduled time blocks, students (institution) will demonstrate their respect for the use of personal time (instruction) by their response (behavior) in the Learning Center.

School Objective

> Following classroom instruction about the use of personal time (instruction), students (institution) will demonstrate their response (behavior) by applying learned skills in the Learning Centers when given unscheduled blocks of time (evaluation).

Classroom Objective

> When assigned unscheduled blocks of time in the Learning Centers, students (institution) will demonstrate response (behavior) to the use of personal time (instruction) by selecting with greater frequency activities that require independent study, rather than activities directed by the Coordinating Teacher (evaluation).

PROJECT DESCRIPTION.   Each school in the district contains three modular instructional areas surrounded by self-contained classrooms.   These modules are identified as Learning Centers.

The Learning Center is an extension of the basic self-contained classroom.   This extension provides additional teaching space, supporting staff, and additional instructional materials.

A variety of teaching and learning areas are provided to allow for an extension and enrichment of the basic curriculum.   Development of specific areas within the Learning Center may be permanent or changing. This is determined largely by the classroom teachers and Coordinating

Teachers as they identify short-term, intermediate, and long-range objectives for individual students.

Reform: Culturally and Educationally Disadvantaged Student Project: Title I

District Goal No. 10
The respect for learning to promote a readiness for further education.

District Objective

> Students (institution) will demonstrate comprehension (behavior) of reading skills (instruction) as demonstrated by their response on the SPACHE Reading Diagnostic Test (evaluation).

School Objective

> Students (institution) will demonstrate comprehension (behavior) of language skills (instruction) as demonstrated by their response on the Illinois Test of Psycholinguistic Abilities (evaluation).

Classroom Objective

> Students (institution) will demonstrate comprehension (behavior) of ten new directional verbal commands (instruction) by following them when given by the teacher verbally (evaluation).

PROJECT DESCRIPTION. The current Title I Project was designed to implement two major components:

1. Teacher inservice training directed toward the culturally and educationally disadvantaged child.
2. Development of a school organizational model that would expand pupil learning opportunities to meet identified affective and cognitive needs.

Specifically, project objectives include:

1. Staff inservice: The development of staff understanding of the needs for individualizing instruction and the development of alternative classroom processes for personalized learning.
2. The instigation of a rationale for the development of a school organization that will best facilitate the individualization of instruction for the culturally and educationally disadvantaged child.
3. The establishment of a criteria for the selection and use of auxiliary personnel needed to adequately support a program of individualized instruction for culturally and educationally disadvantaged.
4. Effective "target area" parent involvement in the Title I Project.
5. A greater emphasis on pupil language development.
6. A greater emphasis on bridging the cultural gap inherent in the "target" area population.

The proposed project is designed to meet these six identified needs through a Language Development Center. In addition, the proposed project expands the current plan of differentiated staffing to provide greater opportunities for cultural and language development. An additional facet of the project has been designed to create a better school–community liaison and responsibility in the educational program of the "target area" school.

Summary

This chapter emphasizes that if true educational reform is to take place, a concise plan for change must be developed that is relevant to the educational goals of the community and the specific needs of the pupils of that community. The plan for reform must contain: concise pupil objectives stated in behavioral terms; a process for organizing and implementing appropriate learning activities; and staff preparation and renewal programs.

The plan for reform must be field tested by carefully controlled pilot projects to ensure that any potential reform on a districtwide scale will indeed be a more expedient means of reaching desired objectives.

Unfortunately, most districts are not able to finance the field testing or the implementation of the reforms. The support of private, state, and federal funding as it currently exists is not adequate if meaningful reform is to be initiated. Financial reform at all levels to support local district effort is needed, if the educational program is to be improved.

Trends

The trend toward making school districts accountable for educational programs is causing more of them to explore innovative teaching and administrative techniques. It is difficult to predict with any degree of accuracy which innovative programs will become definite trends because they are being continuously evaluated, refined, or eliminated. However, the following general trends appear to be definite, although individual programs will vary.

TOWARD MORE INDIVIDUALIZED LEARNING. We have experienced emphasis on this trend for many decades. The Elementary and Secondary Education Act of 1965 provided impetus for renewed efforts to seek alternative instructional strategies to meet individual student learning.

TOWARD PRESCRIPTIVE TEACHING. This practice was discussed for several decades, but more recently put into practice as more accurate diagnosis of the individual learner's educational needs has been developed. Prescriptive teaching approaches the individual's priorities in learning. In the ensuing years, more teachers will use techniques of diagnosis involved in prescriptive teaching.

TOWARD QUALITY INSTRUCTIONAL MEDIA TO ASSIST STUDENT LEARNING. Based upon diagnostic instruments to identify the learner's needs, instructional materials have been designed to enable the learner to attain his priorities in education. More extensive use will be made of instructional media as teachers become more familiar with and less fearful of the newer, more sophisticated hardware and software.

TOWARD THE CONCEPT OF OPEN SPACE. The open space concept emerged as a result of diagnostic approaches to individualized learning needs of children. Alternatives related to instructional materials and to learning centers which can no longer be offered by the traditional self-contained classroom are influential. An increasing number of schools will take education outside of the classroom's four walls. Students will be freer to use instructional media centers and go out into the community.

TOWARD FLEXIBLE TIME SCHEDULING. Flexible time scheduling relates directly to the open classroom where walls do not inhibit the time which each individual needs to perform. Students will be free to follow their interests for the length of time necessary to reach objectives developed for them. There will be fewer schedules with arithmetic from 9 to 10 AM, English from 10 to 11 AM, and so forth.

TOWARD MORE LONG-RANGE PLANNING. In order to fully use flexible time scheduling, results of diagnostic testing, prescriptive teaching, and quality instructional materials, a long-range time plan for learning needs to be put together. Considering all variables, quality learning takes time. Teachers and administrators will establish written goals and objectives for semester and year-long periods of time, rather than on a daily or weekly basis. School board and superintendent plans will be projected for at least three to five years.

Administrative Problems   In Basket

Problem 1

Tom Brown is the new, young, and dynamic principal of the Hilgard Elementary School. There are 22 teachers covering the kindergarten through the sixth grade, eighteen of whom are tenured. There are two new teachers in the first grade, one in the fourth grade, and one in the fifth grade. In the first few weeks, Tom is disappointed to find that pupils are instructed in rather traditional fashion. The teachers plan well, and there are no discipline problems, but there is little freedom for students. The four new teachers request a conference with Tom Brown. They have decided that they would like to try something different from teaching in a rigid, structured, and graded system. In college, they studied the nongraded school and saw it in action. They would like to see this system installed in their school. Tom is delighted!

At the next faculty meeting, he announces that the new teachers want to make the school nongraded and that he will start making plans to commence this program next September. He was too inexperienced to notice the raised eyebrows and whisperings. During the next few weeks, rumors began to fly and the new teachers report to Tom that they are looked upon as outcasts by the other teachers. He also hears one of the sixth grade teachers say, "Who does Mr. Brown think he is, telling us how we are going to teach next year?"

What mistakes did Mr. Brown make?
How should he have proceeded?
Now that a problem has arisen, what can Tom do to solve it?

Problem 2

The superintendent of the Newark Unified School District has just returned from a state conference where accountability, goals, objectives, and needs assessment were the major topics of discussion. The district has 4 elementary schools and a small junior–senior high school. The community is stable and has always been supportive of its schools. The budget is adequate and finances are no problem. At the weekly administrative council meeting, the superintendent asks each member of his administrative team to draw up a plan for developing broad student goals for the district. Following this, he requests that the administrators develop a set of specific educational objectives for their schools.

What procedures should the superintendent suggest for developing the goals?
If you were a principal, how would you go about developing your school's objectives?
What must be done to assess students' needs?

Selected References

BALDRIDGE, J. V., and JOHNSON, R. *The Impact of Educational R & D Centers and Laboratories: An Analysis of Effective Organizational Strategies.* Palo Alto, Calif.: Stanford University, 1972. Mimeographed.

BEAUBIER, E. W., and THAYER, A. N., eds. *Participative Management/Decentralized Decision Making: Working Models.* Burlingame, Calif.: Association of California School Administrators, 1973.

BEAUBIER, E. W., ed. "Evaluating Personnel Performance." *Thrust for Education Leadership* 2 (October 1972).

BEAUBIER, E. W., ed. "ACSA Project Leadership Management Support Systems." *Thrust for Education Leadership* 1 (December–January 1973).

BEAUBIER, E. W. "Goals, Processes and Products." *California Elementary Administrator* 31 (October 1968).

BEAUBIER, E. W. "Fountain Valley Invests in Human Talent." *California School Boards* 24 (February 1968).

BENNIS, W. G.; BENNE, K. D.; and CHIN, R. *The Planning of Change.* New York: Holt, Rinehart and Winston, 1962.

CARLSON, R. D. *Adoption of Educational Innovations.* Eugene, Oregon: The Center for the Advanced Study of Educational Administration, 1965.

CULVER, C. M., and HOBAN, G. J., eds. *The Power to Change: Issues for the Innovative Educator.* New York: McGraw-Hill Book Co., 1974.

GOODLAD, J. I. *Thought, Invention and Research in the Advancement of Education*. In Committee for Economic Development, *The Schools and the Challenge of Innovations*. New York: McGraw-Hill Book Co., 1969.

GROSS, N.; GIAQUINTA, J.; BERNSTEIN, M. *Implementing Organizational Innovations: A Sociological Analysis of Planned Educational Change*. New York: Basic Books, Inc., 1971.

GUBA, E. *Methodological Strategies for Educational Change*. Washington, D.C.: ERIC Document Reproduction Service (November 1965).

MAGUIRE, L. M.; TEMKIN, S.; and CUMMINGS, C. P. *An Annotated Bibliography on Administering for Change*. Philadelphia: Research for Better Schools, Inc., 1971.

MILES, M. B. *Innovation in Education*. New York: Bureau of Publications, Teachers College, Columbia University, 1964.

MILLER, D. R. *Planned Change in Education*. Report of Operation PEP: A Statewide Project to Prepare Educational Plans for California, 1968.

RITTENHOUSE, C. D. *Innovation Problems and Information Needs of Education Practitioners*. ERIC Report, vol. 1. Washington, D.C.: Department of Health, Education, and Welfare, Education Resources Information Center, 1970.

STUFFLEBEAM, D. L. *Proposal to Design New Patterns for Training Research, Development, Demonstration/Dissemination and Evaluation Personnel in Education*. Washington, D.C.: United States Department of Health, Education, and Welfare, 1970.

30

The Future of
Educational Administration

This chapter is designed to pique the school administrator's imagination and to invite him to speculate upon his changing role in the '70s, '80s, and '90s. Society today is characterized by a baffling and accelerated rate of change. Fast moving changes in schools, homes, churches, industry, government, values and mores will tax the school administrator's training, experience, and initiative. Americans give wholehearted support to their educational institutions. The job of the school administrator in the future will be to help his staff and community to find the most efficient ways of improving school organization, instruction, personnel management, business procedures, and public relations.

This chapter includes a discussion of the following topics:

Patterns of School Organization
Administering the Improvement of Instruction
Administering School Personnel
Support and Business Management
Improvement of School and Community Relations
Summary
Trends

Patterns of School Organization

Organizational patterns of school jurisdiction have evolved from the one-room school house to consolidated, unified, and merged districts with larger populations and huge campus buildings. In the early one-room school days, there was no need for a school administrator; the teacher worked directly with the governing board. The county superintendent was little more than a bookkeeper, and the state department of education was too remote to arouse much attention. With the growth of physical plants and the expansion of district boundaries, more nonteaching managers at the district and building levels, the county office, state department, and the United States Office of Education were needed to administrate the widening functions and jurisdictions of public schools.

The bureaucratic buildup of principals, assistant principals, counselors, supervisors, psychologists, coordinators, administrative assistants, assistant superintendents, associate superintendents, directors, superintendents, and many others is unequaled anywhere in the world. This growth of administrative support positions may be slowed in the future, but will continue. The greatest change will be a modification of the role of administrators rather than an increase in their numbers. The growth and cost of administration has been criticized, but state legislatures continue to pass educational statutes invariably requiring more supervision, reporting, apportionment of funds, and employment of new personnel.

THE LOCAL SCHOOL DISTRICT. The size of the local school district in America has increased greatly and caused serious problems. Although district consolidation will occur less frequently, the process will continue in some elementary school districts that will combine with high school districts. More articulation and less isolation is needed here. The unification process in general will be slowed in future years as problems of centralization force its reconsideration.

The thrust of teachers and teacher organizations into some areas of school administration may lessen the need for executive expansion, particularly in the areas of instruction, supervision, and curriculum planning. A slowdown in the birthrate will decrease the numbers of students and lessen the need for administrative support personnel.

The 1954 Brown decision, urbanization, and improved transportation have done much to stimulate the organization of adequate school districts. Modern equipment allows for greater efficiency in large districts. However, some sociologists feel that overcrowding and large campuses are environments that foster narcotic habits, belligerence, and apathy. Student mores have changed most in the big inner-city schools. Parents find it difficult to locate the responsible individual in the bureaucratic layers of big school districts. They do not know or influence "downtown" members of the board of education. The lack of close contact with members of the administration and board has led to a credibility gap. This gap between school supporters and school decision makers has led to defeats of tax override and school bond elections. The drift from rural to urban areas such as New York, Chicago, and Los Angeles has brought a reverse trend of decentralization. People are demanding closer relationships with their own schools.

The administrator of the future will determine the appropriate size for a school district to benefit students, teachers, and taxpayers. Problems of ethnic balance, school discipline, learning efficiency, community support, and good economy will be solved by administrators of the future. Administrators can solve these problems by the application of sound research, community leadership, hard work, and a large portion of common sense.

STATE SCHOOL ORGANIZATION. Because education is a state function, the state has complete responsibility for all aspects of organization and maintenance of schools at the local level. The people through their legislators have devised a *School Code* that provides for a state department of education, a county office or intermediate unit, and local school districts. This pattern (with variations such as in Hawaii where the local, intermediate, and state units are combined) is a consistent organizational design.

Most state school systems are comprised of the state superintendent of public instruction with his support staff and a state board of education. Sometimes the superintendent is elected by the people and the state board is appointed by the governor. This brings about a dual responsibility that often leads to conflict and blockage of good educational leadership and services to schools. It is probable in the future that more boards will be elected by the people who own the schools. These boards then will select a superintendent to administer their policies.

State departments have grown significantly in the last decade and will grow even more as the state assumes greater financial support for local school districts, and particularly as the federal government funnels billions of dollars through the state department to local districts. The federal government has appropriated large sums of money to strengthen the machinery of the state departments of education.

The increased importance of the state department of education makes it essential that the state superintendent and state board work in harmony

to improve education for children and youth locally. The expanding role
of the state department of education should not be limited to the allocation
of funds, but should concentrate chiefly upon leadership to improve instruction for a changing, proliferating, complex society. The state department of education should help lead youth into new and more fulfilling
lives.

REORGANIZING THE INTERMEDIATE UNIT. Although some intermediate
units have reorganized into more efficient units, more will need to do so in
the future. Many county superintendencies throughout the United States
are vestiges of the 19th century. Now transportation technology has facilitated the creation of larger jurisdictions, allowing some physical reorganization of these units to take place. For example, in the state of Washington where county offices were abandoned, about one-third of the
intermediate units were established with boundaries drawn to expedite the
needs of the intermediate unit program.

The term "regionalism" describes situations in which a number of
counties form a consortium to provide area services such as audio-visual
aids, computer printouts, vocational or special educational centers, and
larger area coordination. The areas are fluid and may vary depending
upon the service rendered. These attempts at reorganization are good and
will be accelerated in the future.

The intermediate unit is the right arm of the state department of
education and serves as the first source of help for the local district. The
state capitol is often remote from outlying districts and the number of
personnel in the state department is woefully inadequate to serve the needs
of school districts with urgent problems. As a go-between agency, the
intermediate unit has the responsibility of statute and regulation enforcement, but its greatest use is in conveying the service and leadership aspects
of the state department.

The intermediate unit must be reorganized for greater efficiency in
meeting the demands of changing programs in local districts. It should
provide services that districts cannot provide, or which they provide less
effectively. In providing services, specialists from the intermediate unit
will work increasingly with higher district administrative echelons, spreading assistance to greater numbers of educators. Larger intermediate units
with expanded capabilities will serve high-level district administrators and
focus more and more on instructional service and leadership.

THE FEDERAL GOVERNMENT AND EDUCATION.   Although education is a state function, it is a vital national interest.   The federal government was slow to recognize its role in educational support, but now that such support has occurred, it will continue and grow larger.

The United States Office of Education and other governmental agencies involved in education are destined to play greater roles.   They should coordinate their efforts and funnel support and assistance to local agencies in ways most beneficial to the people.   Since the federal government lays first claim to the nation's taxable resources, greater support should be dispersed from Washington.

State or local control may be sacrificed by accepting federal funds. To remedy this, many teachers, administrators, board members, and organizations are making a strong plea for less categorical and more general aid.   Those closest to education can better discern its needs and design ways for its improvement.   Local educators must exert great pressure upon their congressional representatives to lessen bureaucratic decision making in Washington and preserve a people's choice over their own schools.

Education is too important to be ruled by federal bureaucrats or to have tax money from the people appropriated to sustain bureaucracy in Washington that drains funds from more direct educational needs.   Local educators and citizens must be sure that the schools of the people and by the people will receive federal funds for the people.

The greatest good comes from the federal government when it enhances equalization of educational opportunity, provides unique educational leadership, and supports programs that would otherwise unfortunately be limited if left to the dwindling funds from local property taxation.   School administration in the future must secure the maximum from federal participation and avoid the hazards of remote control and waste.

Administering the Improvement of Instruction

Education has experienced a revolution in curriculum content and orientation that parallels the growth of administrative personnel and district size.   This revolution was in response to contemporary student needs and developments in transportation, manners and morals, politics, psychological outlooks, business and industry, and religion.

With space age perspective, we look back upon a comparatively short period and we see more real change in education than took place from Socrates or Diogenes to John Dewey and E. L. Thorndike. A new terminology has emerged: the Lancastrian system, the Dalton plan, democracy in education, correlation, integration, fusion, work experience, team teaching, relevance, programmed learning, pontooning, modular scheduling, behavioral objectives, microteaching, contracting, competency based instruction, multiple tracking, nongrading, multigrading, open classrooms, alternative schools, and countless more.

What is the administrator of today looking into the future to do with the curriculum? Change it, of course! But in what direction and to what extent? Do greater men and women come out of bigger schools than out of the limited one-room, one-textbook schools? Can a full-time principal, superintendent, and staff of specialized experts do as well? Or better?

The beginning administrator should realize that all instructional planning does not rest upon his shoulders or those of his staff. The schools still belong to the people who can share in making them better. Because the schools do not belong to the students, the teachers, or the board of education, but to the whole people, the administrator should set some priorities. He should begin by understanding that the instructional program as it serves the welfare of children is primary. School finance, personnel management, organization and public relations are only support systems that add to the effectiveness of teaching and learning.

ADMINISTERING CURRICULUM DEVELOPMENT. A curriculum design should be a sincere attempt to facilitate the learning process for all involved in it. Therefore, curriculum development should be a cooperative process, involving teachers, supervisors, administrators, community representatives, students, and representatives from the intermediate unit or state department of education. The curriculum team represents the emphasis of the future.

Traditional curricula offered fewer subjects, most of which were required courses. In contrast, today a large comprehensive high school has enough departments, multiple tracks, work experience, extension and adult courses to allow a student to enroll in new courses each fall for most of his adult life.

Many fear that bigness in education results in a mass educational product with no powers of discretion or individuality. However, the large high school with diversified course offerings clearly provides for individual interests. In elementary schools, children are not mass educated. The ungraded school allows children to travel at different rates and in different directions. First grade pupils have rather common interests and needs in that they all learn reading and number skills, but the further up the elementary ladder they go, the more diverse they become. The ultimate goal is complete individualization of teaching and learning. Upper grade elementary classes with their interest groups, team teaching, programmed learning, teaching machines, and wide reading and study choices are emphasizing individualization and will surely continue the trend.

Special education is a good example of provision for widely diverse curriculum experiences for very different children. The hard-of-hearing, blind, paraplegic, brain-damaged, emotionally disturbed, educationally handicapped, and genetically deformed children are now being helped with specific programs. Before World War I, almost nothing was done for these children. The almost complete individualization in special education classes is a forerunner to trends in so-called normal classes in the future.

Administrators who work with experts in curriculum development soon learn the advantages of a psychological approach. Curriculum specialists sometimes overuse esoteric psychological terms, but the practical administrator should consider the benefits of their expertise for students. The administrator of the future should strive to offer such a variety of worthwhile experiences that the needs of all students will be met adequately.

As he tries to fashion and administer an instructional program that will provide for a vast and expanding range of interests and needs, the administrator must remember the vast range of learners to be served. This range spans early childhood education to adult education. The extension of schools to serve prekindergarten and post-high school students requires special schools with various methods of instruction. For example, the multiple-handicapped child will learn better in a special development center than in a special education class. Early childhood classes operate better close to home (in a housing tract, for example) than in an elementary school. Adult education classes may be held in the day or evening, in a school, or in churches and synagogues, stores, business establishments, and clubrooms.

Ideally, the administrator of the future should plan to meet the broad spectrum of learner needs. He should enlist the help of all available persons and agencies, and remember that the people should have the final decision as to what should be taught in their schools.

PRIVATE SCHOOLS. Unless public school administrators respond to the people, the people will establish private schools to satisfy their goals for their children. When public schools become standardized, apathetic, and unresponsive to public demands, then private schools will grow. There are signs that private schools may increase all over the country to meet the growing disparity of student needs.

The dilemma of the private school is that it has great freedom and opportunity to innovate, but lacks financial support. Large numbers of private and parochial schools have closed their doors or discarded innovative programs due to lack of finances.

The private school is not an adequate answer to the growing demand for variety and specialization. To the extent that such schools meet the people's desires even on restricted funds, they will grow. But the public school administrator with vision should anticipate the changing needs of learners and provide the special programs and special schools that a dynamic world demands.

CHANGING CLASSROOM METHODOLOGY. The greatest educational change in the latter part of this century will not be in curriculum content, the size and shape of buildings, or innovations in school finance, but in instructional methodology. Students will learn many different subjects, skills, and appreciations faster and with more satisfaction.

School administrators of the future will be aware of many elements that change and improve classroom methodology, particularly psychology and technology. Teachers are now trained in psychology and the science of learning as never before. In the future, they will motivate students, expedite learning, and reward success. More varied, illustrated, and interesting study materials are available; tests have been improved; learning environments have been adapted; and technology has provided a host of learning aids to better-trained teachers who wish to improve their methods.

Technology in education has provided and will continue to provide sophisticated audio-visual devices for learning—from overhead projectors to instant information retrieval. In contrast to the school equipment of the beginning of this century (consisting of pencil and pad, copy book and slate), the modern elementary classroom has TV projectors, electronic calculators, intercommunication systems, free reading book racks, easels, and a library of films and slides. This collection of learning equipment is growing daily and will continue to grow in the future.

Heavy responsibility rests upon highly skilled teachers for the use of this technology in their teaching methods. The teacher must be proficient in choosing the best methods to apply the most appropriate technology. Student achievement will be verified by increasingly sophisticated testing devices. Because learning at its best stresses individualization, the teacher will employ as many methods, settings, and aspects of technology as he has students.

Administering School Personnel

Human relations is both an art and a science, and it is in this area that most administrators succeed or fail. It is easy for an administrator to set down the right numbers in the right column of a budget. It is much more difficult to say the right words to an irate teacher, a discouraged custodian, or to a failing student.

The administration of employed personnel involves the selection, management, and separation of certificated and classified staff members. The administration of pupil personnel involves five essential steps:

1. Keeping adequate information about the individual.
2. Gathering extensive information about opportunities.
3. Counseling, or matching the individual with his opportunities.
4. Individual choice and planning.
5. Follow-up and redirection.

ADMINISTERING CERTIFICATED PERSONNEL. The administration of certificated personnel begins with recruitment, selection, orientation, and assignment to duties. The wise administrator gives much time to this process. He knows that his program can never rise above the competency of his staff. He also knows that during this process the new employee acquires an idea of what will be expected of him, how much he can shirk, or how eagerly he can work to improve the program. It is better for the administrator to spend many hours screening for just the right candidate than to go through agonies of dismissal later. The team selection device will be used in the future. Use of consultants from a nearby university or intermediate unit is a sound investment for productive team selection services.

The management of certificated employees involves such processes as assignment of duties, supervision, evaluation, negotiations, and provision of benefits, both direct and fringe.

If teachers and administrators are to be held responsible for assigned duties, the assignment should be in writing with oral clarification. Supervision should be a team process of achieving the assigned duties with evaluation based upon the performance of these same duties. Some administrators have surprised teachers by including duties not previously clarified in evaluation forms. Naturally, resentment, inefficiency, and lowered employee morale result. Teachers should participate in the formulation of their own evaluation criteria and instruments. They should see, confer over, and sign their own evaluation reports in the presence of the evaluator.

Negotiation is a relatively new term in personnel nomenclature. Teachers and teacher organizations have made strong demands, particularly in the area of benefits, and have relied upon the process of negotiation to achieve their demands. This beginning in negotiations has led to much more teacher involvement in decision making, to conflict between professional associations and unions, and to many hours of administrator–teacher committee time. Teacher organizations have battled over professional negotiations and collective bargaining.

EMPLOYEE ORGANIZATIONS. Professional associations support negotiation, whereas teacher unions prefer collective bargaining with teacher strikes as the ultimate weapon. Much discussion has taken place about the merger of professional associations and unions. The professional associations are bending sharply toward the unions, and this direction will continue as the associations adopt union methods to achieve more benefits for their members. As we move further into the seventies, more and more professional associations will use strikes or the threat of strikes to force compliance with their demands. As professional associations and unions increasingly use similar tactics to gain member support, they will essentially become duplicate groups.

TEACHER SUPPLY. After World War II there were severe teacher shortages and demands for better teacher salaries. Significant salary increases, automatic increments for years of service, added compensation for graduate degree credits, extra pay for extra work, and generous fringe benefits occurred in the postwar era. Tenure of position, though not measured in dollars, does have security value. Holidays, vacations, and sick leaves also account for generous benefits. Teachers work about 180 of the 365 days of the year, but according to associations and unions, they must be paid an annual salary. Teacher benefits have increased markedly in recent years and will continue to constitute about 80 percent of school budgets.

The last phase of personnel administration is separation from service. Certificated personnel separate from service by resignation, death, retirement, or dismissal. The administrator of the future should pay more attention to separation interviews, counseling toward retirement, help for relatives, such as beneficiary allotments in case of death, and serious supervisory help before dismissal.

The administrator of the future can improve instruction by relying more and more upon better and extended preservice and inservice training. Teaching becomes more complicated and demanding each year. The sweep of student interest is paralleled by the multiplicity of instructional materials, machines, strategies, and parental expectations. Both certificated and classified employees need continuous inservice training to meet changing conditions and to perform the multiplicity of duties.

ADMINISTERING CLASSIFIED PERSONNEL. Most suggestions that have been made for the successful administration of certificated personnel can also be made for handling classified personnel. In fact, the two groups should be treated as equally as possible. Both are important to the education of students; if either group fails, learning will be impaired.

Classified employees often feel that teachers and administrators look down upon them or upon their positions. Every position in the school system is vital and should be so recognized, or eliminated. Administrators should not allow policies and procedures to exist that exaggerate the importance of any group of workers. A glaring example of this was found in a school system that allowed certificated employees five days of bereavement leave, but allowed classified employees only three days.

Administrators of the future will give more attention to the selection, management, and separation of classified as well as certificated personnel. They will be sure that their benefits compensate them for their service and that their service is oriented toward better instruction for all students in the school.

ADMINISTERING PUPIL PERSONNEL SERVICES. The wise administrator will assign all certificated personnel the responsibility of guiding students and not rest all responsibility in guidance counselors. School secretaries, bus drivers, custodians, and cafeteria workers can have a wholesome impact upon children too. Specialized guidance personnel will handle the technical processes of information gathering, formal counseling, and career planning.

The administration of pupil personnel services has been greatly enhanced by supporting psychologists, reading specialists, speech and hearing therapists, caseworkers, psychometrists, and other counselors. Test refinements, data gathering, counseling rooms, and scheduled guidance periods all add to effectiveness.

Special personnel services are needed for students with handicaps such as mental retardation, physical disability, emotional disturbances, bilingual problems, and poor home conditions. Administrators can do much to provide the conditions that will help these students and to coordinate the efforts of the school with the home, church, clubs, and other community associations.

Much controversy surrounds the rights of access to pupil personnel records. More and more the pupil personnel file will be used as an information bank, open only to responsibly and legitimately concerned people.

Administering School Support
and Business Management

Reduced to their simplest terms, school support and business management involve (1) obtaining funds and (2) spending them to complete planned programs. The chief sources of support are local property taxes, state allocations, and federal subsidies. School monies usually are spent for salaries, supplies, equipment, capital outlay, maintenance and operation, transportation, food services, and insurance.

ADMINISTERING SOURCES OF SUPPORT. Traditionally, schools were primarily supported by the local property tax. This form of taxation has become increasingly unfair and inadequate as great islands of wealth and troughs of poverty have developed as a result of urbanization and other socioeconomic problems. The local property tax no longer provides sufficient funds. It negates equalization of educational opportunity and overburdens the owners of real property.

Increasing support from the state and the federal government will minimize the property tax. State legislatures have been quick to accept the concept of education as a state function but were slow to provide sufficient support. However, the state share of financial support has grown and will grow more. State monies will come from multiple sources, broadening the tax base by obtaining revenue from income, sales, transfers, luxuries, and estates taxes. By using this broader tax base, the state can set a floor, or minimum program, for all schools in the state. Local districts may enrich the program by adding to state allotments with local funds. The state may provide a minimum amount for every district or massive amounts for impoverished districts and smaller amounts for the islands of wealth. The latter option is more ideal but stands less chance politically. Education support bills tend to be passed when they offer something for every legislator's constituency.

When the state legislature mandates a program such as teaching space science or second languages, the state should furnish the money so that the local district can carry out the state's mandate. Greater state participation in financing local school districts should lead toward a uniform state salary schedule for teachers.

The federal government has also increased its portion of support, but must make a greater financial effort in the future. There are poor and wealthy states within the nation just as there are poor and wealthy districts within the state. Greater federal support will lead to the equalization of educational opportunity.

Many educators who lead the fight for greater federal funding are now somewhat disillusioned because much of the federal money is drained off by bureaucracy or highly paid consultants. Too much federal money is siphoned off in this manner and never reaches the students in the classroom. A second disillusionment has come with the provision of categorical rather than general aid. For local districts to receive federal funds they have to write extensive projects, adding burdens upon their already overworked staffs. These projects are granted or refused by officials in Washington who are very remote from the local scene and lack understanding of local needs. Local teachers and administrators should have more voice and control. However, categorical aid has thrust monies into some areas of education poorly served by local districts.

The concept of local control of school systems is as old as our nation and is based upon the fact that people own the schools. If this concept is to continue, then local citizens as well as local teachers and administrators must put enough pressure upon their representatives in Congress to receive more general than categorical aid. This will surely come to pass as the federal government with its great taxing powers will furnish more dollars for education in America.

ADMINISTERING TAX ELECTIONS.   School bond issues increasingly have failed to gain voter support as citizens have witnessed rises in property taxes and increases in school salaries without apparent increase in student achievement.   Student riots, drug traffic on campuses, an increase in vandalism and destruction of school property, and teacher strikes have shaken public confidence in schools.   The public still wants their schools to teach their children indispensable fundamental processes, to guard their health and safety, to maintain campus conditions that will promote morality and citizenship, and to teach students some loyalty to their country— concepts that taxpayers see as good old-fashioned patriotism.   Radical outbursts by students or teachers have led to an alarming credibility gap between the schools and their supporters.

The modern administrator has the impossible task of providing adequate school facilities and keeping his operating budget in balance when the public is defeating more tax proposals at the ballot box.   Looking to the future, more money for capital outlay must be provided from state and federal sources.   Locally, schools must give the public what they are paying for.   The financial burden must be spread.   Furthermore, radical elements in the faculty, encouraged by militant teacher organizations, must tone down and give the people what they want in their schools, or be satisfied to do without the people's support.

Administering School Expenditures

More money is expended for personnel salaries than for all other costs combined.   For this reason, the administrator of the future must be much more careful and astute in selecting both certificated and classified employees.   After selection, clear, definite, written assignments must be provided for each employee.   The process of supervision must be adequate and directed toward helping each employee fulfill the purposes of the school system.   Provision for an appropriate and sufficient amount of inservice training is essential.   Following this kind of personnel improvement, the administrator may then justifiably continue or dismiss the employee from service.   The ultimate criterion must be the welfare of the students.   Tenure laws must be responsive to this principle also.   Teacher organizations should also stress student welfare to maintain public support.

ADMINISTERING SCHOOL BUILDING PROGRAMS.   The administrator of the future should understand that school buildings are constructed to accommodate changing educational programs.   The buildings should be flexible to adapt to changes such as open-space instruction or portable, individualized teaching stations.

During the planning of new facilities or the revision of old, architects, instructional specialists, the community, and others can offer practical suggestions.   Teachers are especially helpful.   Extensions of the school program such as early childhood education and adult education programs must be taken into consideration.   Advanced vocational training with expensive machines and materials and education of multiple-handicapped persons should be in regional development centers planned and built to suit the specific needs of the students.

As we learn to control the environment, provision should be made for the regulation of temperature through heating and air conditioning, the elimination of dust and noxious fumes (especially in big cities), and the control of noise pollution.   Air conditioning, warm air flow, carpeting, filters, and humidifiers will be a reality and a necessity for maximum learning in the future.

MAINTENANCE AND OPERATION.   Economical and efficient maintenance and operation of school facilities requires the future administrator to have a high degree of expertise in helping classified employees to preserve the investment of the people and to exploit the expensive facilities for the better education of students.   Costly facilities can be used not only for regular day students, but in the future to a greater extent for adult education and other community interests.

As districts grow larger, there will be an increasing trend toward centralization of the maintenance staff, with traveling crews servicing the needs of each school unit.   There will also be an increasing trend toward the specific assignment, scheduling, supervising, and inservice training of custodians.   This will help them to supplement learning programs and to preserve valuable property.

ADMINISTERING STUDENT TRANSPORTATION. Greater numbers of students will be delivered to classrooms in buses. This increased transportation activity makes increased demands upon already strained school budgets. In the future, an increased percentage of transportation costs must come from state or federal sources.

There will be greater state control and regulation of school buses and bus drivers. The U.S. Department of Transportation's Standard No. 17 (see chapter 16) requires safety and efficiency standards for school buses and rigid licensing standards for bus drivers. These standards will be enforced and perhaps expanded in the future. Inservice training and close supervision of bus drivers are essential.

School district ownership and maintenance of school buses and other transportation equipment are preferred to contracting with private companies. District ownership has been found to be more economical, more efficient, and safer. Superintendents and principals have more control over bus drivers and their relationships to children when the total operation is owned by the district.

In some communities school busing has been singled out as the panacea for ethnic integration. Others feel that school busing cannot solve a great social issue that has been with us for decades. They argue that monies spent for busing programs to integrate would be better spent for educational purposes and that other means of solving social issues outside the school should be sought. The purpose of school transportation should be to deliver students safely to school and in the best emotional state to begin the day's learning activities.

ADMINISTERING SUPPLIES, EQUIPMENT, AND FOOD SERVICE. As students become more diverse in their interests and needs, as educational offerings proliferate, and as teachers become more versatile, the variety of supplies and equipment will multiply. The days of the writing pad and the slate have given way to the overhead projector, xeroxing, closed-circuit TV, erasable ink, and the self-teaching textbook. There seems to be no end to the variety and amount of instructional materials designed to hasten the speed and accuracy of student learning.

The trend in supply and equipment administration has gone from the student purchase of slate and pencils to total supply of all materials needed by the school district. In this way, the student from a home on welfare has access to the expensive equipment needed for his education equal to the child from the richest home in the district. This equalization of opportunity is good.

More and more, the teaching staff has been called upon to choose the type and amount of materials needed. This trend will continue because administrators are less qualified to determine the proper color of art paper that will be used in grade six of the Abraham Lincoln School than is the teacher who uses it. For the sake of efficiency, all requests for materials will be made far in advance of need and will be purchased from standardized supply and equipment lists. Volume purchasing is economical and may be accomplished by cooperation with neighboring districts and with the intermediate unit.

The actual use and disbursal of supplies should be handled by teachers rather than by clerks and administrators. The "open stockroom system" should replace the practice of weekly teacher requisitions. When teachers participate in supply and equipment administration from selection to use, the learning increment will be greater.

Food service in the schools is increasingly important. As schools become larger and as more students are transported from greater distances, it is necessary to serve a well-balanced lunch that is sometimes the student's most nutritious meal of the day. Most school cafeterias are supposedly self-supporting, but are subsidized by the free use of school facilities and equipment, a paid director's salary, and by various grants of federal food and allotments.

Administrators of the future will handle school food services efficiently, but more importantly will make certain that the highest standards of cleanliness, hygiene, and nutrition are maintained. The school cafeteria can be a learning laboratory for teachers and students where only the most healthful foods are served. The cafeteria is a means for the display and use of the most nutritious foods. The school should be the place where students learn to make the best choices. Teachers should not only help students make wiser selections but to understand some basic principles including the importance of good nutrition.

One school decided to eliminate carbonated cold drinks at the snack bar and replace them with fruit juices. Administrators and teachers expected patronage to decline and cause loss in the snack bar account. With some advance classroom instruction, it was found that when carbonated drinks were replaced by nutritional fruit juices, student participation increased 19 percent. Dentists, doctors, and other interested citizens may work well with teachers and administrators in planning better nutrition in the food services program.

ADMINISTERING THE SCHOOL INSURANCE PROGRAM.　Insurance programs are becoming as complex and diversified as the schools themselves.　As facilities, supplies, equipment, and employee risks become more diversified, the insurance program must become more varied to protect the people's investment.

School replacement costs have risen sharply as the diversity in school equipment has mushroomed.　Not only is it necessary for the administrator to determine the types of facilities, supplies, and equipment that have to be replaced in case of fire or other disaster, but he must take into account the necessity of sustaining the educational program with replacements made on the most expeditious timetable possible.　The security of school property and the continuity of the school program will be a much greater concern in the future.

The administrator must consider coverage of life, health, disability, and liability of the district's employees.　Group insurance, health and accident insurance, income protection, and bodily injury are becoming standard coverages and will be completely accepted as the responsibility of the school district.

Since school districts are increasingly vulnerable to damage suits, the administrator of the future must provide liability insurance for those who may be hurt in classrooms, on buses, or become ill from eating food in the cafeteria.　The school must secure liability coverage for visitors, students, and employees against falls on wet or icy entrances and against accidents that often occur in halls or on stairways.

Many administrators have run into trouble in obtaining claims when they have purchased piecemeal insurance.　If one company carries liability insurance for the buses and another carries liability insurance for the buildings and grounds, who pays when a child breaks his ankle stepping off the bus?　Was he on the bus or on the school grounds?

There is a trend developing, which will gain momentum, for the purchase of more package-type policies.　All provisions of the insurance package, including physical facilities and personal protection, should be carried by a single company and written into a single policy.　The free enterprise competition could come between packages rather than between the fragmented segments of the total insurance needs of the district.

Since more and more insurance of different types is becoming necessary, the cost factor is a serious item in the budget. Larger districts with more schools and greater financial capability can reduce insurance costs by "underinsuring." This is called co-insurance in which the company and the district each carry a portion of the risk. Since it is unlikely, if not impossible, that any sizable number of schools in Cleveland or Pittsburgh would be destroyed at one time, it is good economic policy for the district to carry a portion of its own risk. This portion will differ with each large school district. The future administrator will have to seek consultant help from insurance specialists in companies, universities, intermediate units, and state departments if he is to provide the safest and most economical protection for persons and property. Proper explanation of the co-insurance plan to students, staff, and public creates an awareness of their responsibility for helping to protect school persons and property.

It is likely that in the future state and federal government may participate to a greater extent in helping the local school district meet its insurance needs. This would be a means of equalizing school burdens, and guaranteeing that educational programs would continue with the least possible interruption.

BUDGETING AND BOOKKEEPING. Budget making should not be an annual procedure, but should be continuous. Those who are most concerned with the budget should supply budget requests throughout the year. These requests should be placed in a priority list with the greatest emphasis upon requests that improve the district's instructional program. This type of budget procedure is optional with the district, but recent emphasis has given heavy weighting to the "planning–programming–budgeting–system" (PPBS). In any event, budgets should reflect multiyear programs and take into account the goals and objectives of the school system. This implies that there should be an evaluation of budgetary results.

Bookkeeping and accounting are systems designed to allow for constant monitoring of the budget's income and expenditures. The best systems are those that keep all concerned persons aware of the monies that have been spent and the monies available for accomplishing the goals of the school system. A good method is to account for all funds expended as well as for all funds encumbered. At a glance this method reveals amounts still available for unplanned needs and emergencies.

With the help of the intermediate unit, the standardization of bookkeeping and accounting procedures will become more common in the future. There should be careful auditing by nonschool auditing services.

The public should be kept informed at all times of the use of its money and the benefits derived from expenditures.

TECHNOLOGICAL ADVANCES IN SCHOOL MANAGEMENT.   An increased use of machines and systems is as necessary and economical in school business management as it is in the manufacturing of automobiles or processing of food products.   The diversity of curricular and co-curricular programs increases the job of engineering the budgeting and accounting procedures.

The cutting edge of the future calls for administrators who can institute and supervise automated systems with standardized forms and reports. Permanent records will be on microfilm with instantaneous retrieval possibilities.   Data processing centers and data banks will be commonplace and at the immediate disposal of the business administrator.   School business administrators and their assistants will require greater training in all aspects of technology and a continuous process of inservice training to cope with the sophisticated equipment and systems now becoming available for use in the future.   All sophisticated equipment and systems should be employed for economic efficiency and for stimulating better student learning.

Administering School Public Relations

School public relations practices are no longer oriented to advertising; today, school–community communication and participation are emphasized.   *School public relations is an integral part of the total school program, cooperatively planned and administered.*

Public relations is not a fund raising or approval seeking activity carried on outside the school program.   A good public relations program begins with a good educational program and is continuous.   If a public relations program is to be worthwhile, the administrator must establish the best possible instructional program for students and then communicate it in many ways.

Public relations is everybody's job.   Administrators, teachers, counselors, classified employees, and particularly students are all public relations agents.   So, too, is the public, the people who own the schools. When school public relations programs are initially organized, community representatives should participate with all responsible school personnel. School programs should solicit community queries or suggestions to teachers and administrators. This intercommunication system keeps all interested persons informed and working toward the same goals.

ADMINISTERING A PROGRAM WORTHY OF PUBLICATION. The effective administrator develops quality learning programs, economically and efficiently run, and seeks continuously the highest caliber staff available. The administrator of the future will not be able to let words replace accomplishments when he speaks to PTA meetings, service clubs, or is interviewed by reporters. He must have quality results to announce as chief executive and manager of the public relations process.

The administrator should focus public relations interest on the programs available and the accomplishments of students rather than emphasizing how much money he is saving by cutting down on needed transportation or spelling books. In improving programs, he needs participation by parents, students, teachers, and others. Identification of public relations as an important element of the school program results in favorable attitudes. Parents appreciate a program that they have helped to plan and accomplish.

PERSONNEL IN THE PUBLIC RELATIONS PROGRAM. The standard question at the evening dinner table is often, "What did you learn in school today?" The importance of students in the public relations program is often overlooked. PTA meetings that draw the largest attendance are those that feature students rather than speakers. Teachers and administrators should seize every opportunity to impress students and parents with successes rather than harping upon failures or less than satisfactory work. One administrator who witnessed a bond issue go down to defeat provided for complimentary notes rather than "cinch" notices to go to the homes weekly. As suspected, the next bond issue passed by more than a two-thirds majority.

Parent participation is a strong element in good school public relations. Taxpayers without children are also important. A school administrator in the deep South received considerable harassment from a local businessman who objected to the cost of schools and their "woeful lack" of history instruction. This businessman had spent many hours studying the campaigns of General Lee's armies. After the superintendent invited him to speak to the senior United States history class, this critic of the schools became one of its strongest supporters. He knew they were teaching history because he himself had helped in the instruction!

Both certificated and classified personnel have essential roles to play in public relations. A good administrator should work with his classified staff to let them know how indispensable their support service is to the welfare of students. Teachers should not just teach, but should be ready to communicate with others. At every bridge game, at the store, in conferences, teachers can help their own cause by increasing understanding of the importance of learning programs. They should never criticize their colleagues or programs in other departments to bolster their own positions. Internal conflicts should be kept internal. Internal problems should be solved so that constructive programs are shared with the public. All certificated and all classified employees should perform well so that they can be truthful traveling ambassadors for a highly successful school system.

The job of the future administrator is to use continuously the help of all classes of personnel to improve and then to publicize the people's schools. If he does this, his position is secure because he has given top priority to the highest type of educational program for learners.

Summary

The superior administrator of the future will experience the thrill of having developed the best possible learning situation at the least cost, with the highest caliber of personnel, and the broad participation of all those concerned with improving education. Parents, students, secretaries, custodians, bus drivers, and teachers will comprise a winning team, a team that will help to develop the maximum capacities of learners in the direction most beneficial to the community, the state, and the nation.

Trends

Great changes are taking place in the areas of instruction, organization, finance, personnel management, and public relations. The competent administrator must be prepared for these emerging conditions.

TOWARD GREATER DIVERSIFICATION IN ADMINISTERING THE INSTRUCTIONAL PROGRAM. There will be curricula within the curriculum, schools within the school, groups within the classroom, and individual study within the groups. Different types of specialized schools will spring up as developmental centers or as private schools. Early childhood education and adult education will increase. Student interests, abilities, and needs are expanding outward in all directions. The job of the future administrator will be to provide for these divergencies.

TOWARD THE GOLDEN MEAN IN DISTRICT REORGANIZATION. Small school districts will merge and larger ones will decentralize. An ideal district size will be approached as most efficient for all aspects of the learning program. The administrator of the future must find the ideal size for school districts and intermediate units. He must also provide leadership in attaining the best external and internal organization for the school system.

TOWARD GREATER PARTICIPATION BY THE STATE AND FEDERAL GOVERNMENT IN SCHOOL SUPPORT. School support will change from chief reliance on the property tax to a much broader tax base created by state and federal governments. Greater state and federal support will enhance equalization of educational opportunity. More generalized aid with local control is a fight that must be won by future administrators.

TOWARD TEAM PARTICIPATION IN THE MANAGEMENT OF SCHOOL SYSTEMS. Administrators, teachers, students, parents, and taxpayers should all function as a school management team. The time is coming when the superintendent or principal will no longer be able to administer the district or building level alone. He will need the help of the teachers and others. Cautious administrators will not allow aggressive teacher organizations to seize control. The people own the schools and have final control through their elected representatives on the school board. Paid and community personnel will be advisory rather than decision-making agents.

TOWARD TOTAL COMMUNITY INVOLVEMENT IN SCHOOL PUBLIC RELATIONS. School public relations will become a continuous, integral part of the total school program, involving both school and community personnel. The program has evolved from a one-man, one-shot publicity campaign to a year round campaign with participation of all concerned. Instead of being informed about the program, patrons will become a part of the program. When the school's business is everybody's business, there will be fewer bond election failures and more general support for a sound educational program.

Administrative Problems

Problem 1

You have been named the new superintendent of a unified school district with 10,000 students in average daily attendance. The community includes a small city but has rural students too, ranging from lower- to upper-middle class. The instructional program at both the elementary and secondary levels has been quite traditional and limited, with much more offered in academic than vocational or commercial subjects. The faculty for the most part supports this program. The community is proud of its very low tax rate. Two administrative positions are open: Assistant Superintendent for Business and Assistant Superintendent for Instruction.

What qualifications would you look for in an Assistant Superintendent for Business? Why?

What qualifications would you look for in an Assistant Superintendent for Instruction? Why?

What would you say at your first principals' meeting?

Would you announce any planned changes at the first teachers' meeting in September?

How would you implement any changes you plan?

Problem 2

As the high school principal in the district described in Problem 1, with only three more years until retirement:

Would you enthusiastically help the superintendent make changes in the high school course offerings?

If the community were satisfied with your program, would you keep the status quo *and resist the progressive ideas of your superintendent?*

How would you justify your stand?

Problem 3

You are a young elementary school principal and the only elementary school principal that agrees with the superintendent who wants to make considerable change in the instructional program. Your teachers are divided, but most favor the current instructional program.

How can you help to change the attitudes of your fellow principals?

What would you do to change their minds and get the support of your teachers for needed changes?

What kind of reports would you give to the community?

Selected References

BROWN, REX V. *Research and the Credibility of Estimates.* Homewood, Ill.: Richard D. Irwin, Inc., 1971.

CAMPBELL, ROALD R., et al. *The Organization and Control of American Schools.* 2nd ed. Columbus, Ohio: Charles E. Merrill Publishing Co., 1970.

ELLENS, WILLIAM. *Curriculum Handbook for School Executives.* Washington, D.C.: American Association of School Administrators, 1973.

GRANGER, ROBERT L. *Educational Leadership: An Interdisciplinary Perspective.* Scranton, Penn.: Intext Educational Publishers, 1971.

HUMMEL, RAYMOND C., and NAGLE, JOHN M. *Urban Education in America: Problems & Prospects.* New York: Oxford University Press, 1973.

IANNACCONE, LAURENCE, and LUTZ, FRANK W. *Politics, Power and Policy: The Governing of Local School Districts.* Columbus, Ohio: Charles E. Merrill Publishing Co., 1970.

KIRST, MICHAEL W. *State, School, and Politics.* Lexington, Mass.: D. C. Heath and Co., 1972.

KOYAYASHI, SHIGERU. *Creative Management.* New York: American Management Association, 1971.

LUTZ, FRANK W., and IANNACCONE, LAURENCE. *Understanding Educational Organizations: A Field Study Approach.* Columbus, Ohio: Charles E. Merrill Publishing Co., 1969.

MCCARTY, DONALD J., and RAMSEY, CHARLES E. *The School Managers.* Westport, Conn.: Greenwood Publishing Corp., 1971.

MCGARTH, J. H. *Planning Systems for School Executives: The Unity of Theory and Practice.* Scranton, Penn.: Intext Educational Publishers, 1972.

MARKS, JAMES R.; STOOPS, EMERY; and KING-STOOPS, JOYCE. *Handbook of Educational Supervision.* Boston: Allyn and Bacon, 1971.

MALTZ, MAXWELL. *Psycho-Cybernetics.* New York: Pocket Books, 1971.

MERANTO, PHILLIP. *School Politics in the Metropolis.* Columbus, Ohio: Charles E. Merrill Publishing Co., 1970.

MATTHEWS, DON Q. *The Design of the Management Information System.* Philadelphia: Auerbach Publishers, 1971.

MYERS, M. SCOTT. *Every Employee a Manager.* New York: McGraw-Hill Publishing Co., 1970.

NELSON, D. LLOYD, and PURDY, WILLIAM M. *School Business Administration.* Lexington, Mass.: D. C. Heath and Co., 1971.

NUNNERY, MICHAEL Y., and KIMBROUGH, RALPH B. *Politics, Power, Polls, and School Elections.* Berkeley, Calif.: McCutchan Publishing Co., 1971.

PERRY, WILDMAN. *The Impact of Negotiations in Public Education.* Worthington, Ohio: Jones Publishing Co., 1970.

Phi Delta Kappa. *Educational Evaluation and Decision Making.* Itasca, Ill.: F. E. Peacock Publishers, 1971.

RUBIN, LILLIAN B. *Busing and Blacklash.* Berkeley, Calif.: University of California Press, 1972.

SCHMUCK, RICHARD A., and MILES, MATTHEW B. *Organization Development in Schools.* Palo Alto, Calif.: National Book Press, 1971.

STOOPS, EMERY, and JOHNSON, RUSSELL E. *Elementary School Administration.* New York: McGraw-Hill Book Co., 1967.

STOOPS, EMERY, and KING-STOOPS, JOYCE. *Discipline or Disaster.* Bloomington, Ind.: Phi Delta Kappa Foundation, 1972.

THOMPSON, ROBERT B. *A Systems Approach to Instruction.* Hamden, Connecticut: Shoe String Press, 1971.

TOFFLER, ALVIN. *Future Shock.* New York: Random House, 1970.

TOWNSEND, ROBERT. *Up the Organization.* New York: Alfred A. Knopf, 1970.

UNRUH, ADOLPH, and TURNER, HAROLD E. *Supervision for Change and Innovation.* Boston: Houghton Mifflin, 1970.

WIRT, FREDERICK M., and KIRST, MICHAEL M. *The Political Web of American Schools.* Boston: Little, Brown, 1972.

Rating Checklist for Principals

There is a trend toward management by use of objectives established by teachers, principals, supervisors, and district administrators. The objectives should be related not only to what now exists in a school district, but to what ought to be most useful in the future. Evaluation should be in terms of how closely the objectives are reached.

The checklist presented here can be adapted to apply to any administrative position, although it was designed primarily to help the principal in cooperation with the superintendent and staff. This instrument allows a principal to view himself in action, and to evaluate his administration in terms of how effectively he is working with the people of the school and the community in planning and carrying out the educational program. By using this checklist as an example, teachers and principals can develop similar objectives for teacher self-evaluation or for the principal's evaluation of a teacher.

The following rating scale should be kept in mind as each number is circled indicating the extent to which each administrative practice or action exists in the principal's school:

N . . . . . . Cannot evaluate principal regarding this practice because of insufficient evidence.
0 . . . . . . This practice is not found to any extent.
1 . . . . . . This practice is found to a very limited degree.
2 . . . . . . This practice is found to a fair degree.
3 . . . . . . This practice is found to an average degree.
4 . . . . . . This practice is found to a large degree.
5 . . . . . . This practice is found to an extent that leaves little to be desired.

Constructive remarks by those cooperating in the evaluation can be of value in analysis of the evaluation materials. Space can be provided for this purpose at the end of areas "A," "B," and "C."

A. Competencies Required to Carry out the Role of Democratic Leadership.

A competent and successful school principal is a person who:

1. *Understands and practices democratic administration.*
   The principal:
   a. Shows an understanding of the nature of democracy
   N 0 1 2 3 4 5
   b. Demonstrates faith in the capacities of others and relies heavily on their capacities .... N 0 1 2 3 4 5
   c. Encourages teacher participation in policy formation and evaluation .... N 0 1 2 3 4 5
   d. Encourages student participation in policy formation and evaluation .... N 0 1 2 3 4 5
   e. Encourages lay people in policy formation and evaluation
   N 0 1 2 3 4 5
   f. Is effective in leading individuals and groups to discover problems .... N 0 1 2 3 4 5
   g. Works toward common understanding of the school's objectives and their relation to problems that the principal, staff, and all concerned have jointly set out to solve .... N 0 1 2 3 4 5
   h. Leads individuals and groups in arriving at decisions on the basis of factual analysis and interpretation of data
   N 0 1 2 3 4 5
   i. Uses committee techniques with keen understanding to solve problems .... N 0 1 2 3 4 5
   j. Understands and uses accepted parliamentary procedure as a means of giving form to cooperative activity ... N 0 1 2 3 4 5
   k. Accepts rightful share of responsibility in initiating policies of the school .... N 0 1 2 3 4 5

2. *Demonstrates a keen understanding of group dynamics.*
   The principal:
   a. Demonstrates the belief that a group of people, by applying reflective thought to their problems, can arrive at more reliable conclusions than can individuals working alone ... N 0 1 2 3 4 5
   b. Defends the rights of people to express their views
   N 0 1 2 3 4 5
   c. Attracts individuals to the idea of group planning and action
   N 0 1 2 3 4 5

d. Provides for cooperative agenda for goal formulation in group meetings .... N 0 1 2 3 4 5

e. Examines his role and behavior as a member of each group with which he works .... N 0 1 2 3 4 5

f. Is willing to allow others to evaluate him as a member of a group
N 0 1 2 3 4 5

g. Inspires respect and loyalty for the leader of the group, whoever the leader might be at any specific time ... N 0 1 2 3 4 5

h. Encourages every member of a group to serve as a resource person .... N 0 1 2 3 4 5

i. Exercises patience with groups when their deliberations require considerable time .... N 0 1 2 3 4 5

j. Helps to clarify thought by well-timed, pertinent questions
N 0 1 2 3 4 5

k. Presents thought-provoking information and situations to those concerned with improvement of the school program
N 0 1 2 3 4 5

l. Provides information pertinent to the solution of the problem at hand .... N 0 1 2 3 4 5

m. Allows time for groups to mature in their relationships and to learn to work together effectively .... N 0 1 2 3 4 5

n. Keeps before the group clear statements of what they are trying to do and what has been attained in approaching the solution of school problems .... N 0 1 2 3 4 5

o. Encourages groups at work to suspend judgment until all pertinent facts have been examined .... N 0 1 2 3 4 5

p. Brings out action implications of all group discussions
N 0 1 2 3 4 5

q. Stays in the background a reasonable amount of the time
N 0 1 2 3 4 5

3. *Takes the lead in planning a program of inservice growth for himself and his staff.*
The principal:

a. Reflects the belief that people learn from one another
N 0 1 2 3 4 5

b. Sets an example for the staff by carrying out a planned program of professional improvement for himself ...... N 0 1 2 3 4 5

c. Encourages and makes possible professional improvement on the part of staff members .... N 0 1 2 3 4 5

d. Recommends policies to superintendent and board that will encourage professional growth among teachers ... N 0 1 2 3 4 5

e. Promotes active participation in professional organizations

N 0 1 2 3 4 5

f. Realizes that professional growth is a lifelong process

N 0 1 2 3 4 5

g. Credits his school as he works professionally with other principals .... N 0 1 2 3 4 5

h. Gives others credit for their achievements ... N 0 1 2 3 4 5

4. *Shows a sense of timeliness in taking action.*
The principal:

a. Keeps himself informed on how the staff, pupils, and community feel about vital issues .... N 0 1 2 3 4 5

b. Analyzes carefully the school situation before planning any improvement program .... N 0 1 2 3 4 5

c. Times changes and improvements to correspond with the growth and educational thinking of the community .... N 0 1 2 3 4 5

d. Establishes sufficient facts to support any proposed change

N 0 1 2 3 4 5

e. Plans a reasonable and practical program of improvement that can be carried through to successful completion in a definite period of time .... N 0 1 2 3 4 5

f. Initiates action promptly in emergency situations

N 0 1 2 3 4 5

5. *Maintains physical, mental, and emotional vitality and adjustment.*
The principal:

a. Possesses professional honesty and courage .. N 0 1 2 3 4 5

b. Has energy sufficient to meet demands of job . N 0 1 2 3 4 5

c. Is well adjusted in home and community life . N 0 1 2 3 4 5

d. Participates in hobbies to afford physical and mental relaxation

N 0 1 2 3 4 5

e. Maintains·emotional stability in all situations . N 0 1 2 3 4 5

f. Is consistent in his behavior .... N 0 1 2 3 4 5

g. Maintains neat, well-groomed appearance .. N 0 1 2 3 4 5

h. Accepts criticism objectively .... N 0 1 2 3 4 5

i. Enjoys being with people . . . . N 0 1 2 3 4 5
j. Is a good listener . . . . N 0 1 2 3 4 5

6. *Develops and maintains high morale among all school personnel.*
The principal:
a. Creates a feeling on the part of each staff member that he or she is a member of a whole team, and that what he or she does is a contributing factor to the success of the school program
N 0 1 2 3 4 5
b. Makes every effort to provide desirable working conditions
N 0 1 2 3 4 5
c. Encourages constructive criticism of administrative decisions and activities . . . . N 0 1 2 3 4 5
d. Encourages maximum representation of teachers in decisions involving the welfare of the staff . . . . N 0 1 2 3 4 5
e. Defends the school and its personnel against unwarranted criticism . . . . N 0 1 2 3 4 5
f. Accepts all actions of individual staff members as the responsibility of the school . . . . N 0 1 2 3 4 5
g. Encourages the total staff to assist individual members toward improvement . . . . N 0 1 2 3 4 5
h. Displays a genuine interest in personal, social, and family interests of staff members . . . . N 0 1 2 3 4 5
i. Works with staff in determining relationships between salary schedules, workloads, and responsibilities . . . . N 0 1 2 3 4 5
j. Alters his viewpoint when presented with evidence that does not support his position . . . . N 0 1 2 3 4 5
k. Keeps administrative rules and regulations at a minimum
N 0 1 2 3 4 5
l. Demonstrates the belief that school administration is not an end unto itself, but exists only for the improvement of instruction and for the welfare of the children . . . . N 0 1 2 3 4 5

7. *Expresses himself well, especially orally and in public.*
The principal:
a. Makes proper preparation before all public talks
N 0 1 2 3 4 5
b. Understands and applies good techniques of public speaking
N 0 1 2 3 4 5

c. Gives careful thought to form of letters and all written communication .... N 0 1 2 3 4 5

d. Is a good conversationalist .... N 0 1 2 3 4 5

e. Is able to express ideas so clearly that there is little chance of being misunderstood or misinterpreted .... N 0 1 2 3 4 5

8. *Budgets time to best advantage.*
   The principal:
   a. Organizes the school program and delegates responsibility to free himself from a multiplicity of routine administrative tasks

   N 0 1 2 3 4 5

   b. Has a planned schedule of his activities publicized within the school to facilitate discharging his administrative responsibilities

   N 0 1 2 3 4 5

   c. Displays punctuality in fulfilling his duties .. N 0 1 2 3 4 5

   d. Shows proficiency in the expenditure of time on necessary unscheduled activities (such as visits by salesmen) . N 0 1 2 3 4 5

   e. Devotes part of day to activities specifically designed for the improvement of instruction .... N 0 1 2 3 4 5

   f. Provides time-saving equipment for school offices

   N 0 1 2 3 4 5

9. *Recognizes and assumes the social and civic responsibilities of the school administrator in a community.*
   The principal:
   a. Is an active member of community organizations (such as Red Cross, Community Chest, Chamber of Commerce)

   N 0 1 2 3 4 5

   b. Is an active member of some community church group

   N 0 1 2 3 4 5

   c. Interprets educational needs and the school program to community organizations .... N 0 1 2 3 4 5

   d. Works with community organizations in promoting school programs and satisfying the needs of the students and community

   N 0 1 2 3 4 5

   e. Lends the aid and influence of the school to the promotion of deserving community projects .... N 0 1 2 3 4 5

B. Competencies Required to Work Effectively with School Personnel.
   A competent and successful school principal is a person who:

10. *Works with the superintendent, board of education, staff, and students to develop a philosophy of education appropriate to the school and community setting and does not overlook objectives pertinent to state, national, and world needs.*

The principal:

a. Invites teachers to participate in formulating and evaluating the philosophy, objectives, and policies of the school. N 0 1 2 3 4 5
b. Invites pupils to participate in formulating and evaluating the philosophy, objectives, and policies of the school. N 0 1 2 3 4 5
c. Meets with the board of education (by invitation of the superintendent) to formulate and evaluate the philosophy, objectives, and policies of the school . . . . N 0 1 2 3 4 5
d. Promotes recognition and discussion of community problems (such as health and adult education) . . . . N 0 1 2 3 4 5
e. Promotes recognition and discussion of state problems that relate to education . . . . N 0 1 2 3 4 5
f. Promotes recognition and discussion of national and international problems that relate to education . . . . N 0 1 2 3 4 5
g. Discusses local, state, and national problems frequently with pupils to encourage active citizenship . . . . N 0 1 2 3 4 5

11. *Selects personnel capable of attaining the accepted objectives of the school and assigns them to positions in which they will be most effective.*

The principal:

a. Makes it possible for teachers to participate in the selection of new teachers . . . . N 0 1 2 3 4 5
b. Makes recommendations for the employment of personnel to the superintendent of schools on the basis of their ability to fulfill needs made evident by careful job analysis . . . . N 0 1 2 3 4 5
c. Makes it possible for staff members to select extra-class duties to use their special aptitudes more extensively . . . . N 0 1 2 3 4 5
d. Sets up a program of orientation and assistance for teachers new to the system . . . . N 0 1 2 3 4 5
e. Shows appreciation for good teaching by recommending promotions, commendations, and salary increases . . . . N 0 1 2 3 4 5
f. Furnishes job applicants with information pertinent to the position . . . . N 0 1 2 3 4 5

12. *Organizes school personnel for a cooperative approach to all educational problems.*

The principal:

a. Makes provision for staff cooperation in working on pertinent problems presented by individual teachers ..... N 0 1 2 3 4 5

b. Invites the superintendent to visit the school to discuss educational problems with the staff .... N 0 1 2 3 4 5

c. Encourages and provides opportunity for teachers to visit the homes of pupils .... N 0 1 2 3 4 5

d. Provides released time for teachers to study and plan solutions to educational problems .... N 0 1 2 3 4 5

e. Organizes and makes use of workshops and other problem-solving techniques .... N 0 1 2 3 4 5

f. Provides for continuous study of educational problems

N 0 1 2 3 4 5

g. Clarifies relationships and responsibilities of school personnel

N 0 1 2 3 4 5

h. Provides opportunity for progress reports from individuals, committees, and organizations .... N 0 1 2 3 4 5

i. Provides opportunities for teaching and nonteaching personnel to discuss their responsibilities in relation to school objectives

N 0 1 2 3 4 5

j. Plans with nonteaching personnel so that their work does not interfere unduly with the work of teachers and pupils

N 0 1 2 3 4 5

k. Is systematic and consistent in dealing with noncertificated staff

N 0 1 2 3 4 5

l. Provides workshops, short courses, and demonstrations for noncertificated staff .... N 0 1 2 3 4 5

13. *Plans and works with school personnel for the continuous development and improvement of the school's curriculum.*

The principal:

a. Schedules staff meetings for the purpose of formulating and evaluating curriculum objectives .... N 0 1 2 3 4 5

b. Uses knowledge of available resources in curriculum planning

N 0 1 2 3 4 5

c. Is open minded and receptive to ideas about new curricula that show promise .... N 0 1 2 3 4 5

d. Gears the curriculum objectives to present and future student needs .... N 0 1 2 3 4 5
e. Holds joint meetings in which staff members in the elementary school discuss their work and objectives with those in the high school and vice versa .... N 0 1 2 3 4 5
f. Considers college-bound students in designing the school program .... N 0 1 2 3 4 5
g. Considers students who will not attend college in designing the school program .... N 0 1 2 3 4 5
h. Holds staff meetings to discuss individual and collective pupil progress .... N 0 1 2 3 4 5
i. Makes it possible for pupils to participate in planning the curriculum .... N 0 1 2 3 4 5

14. *Provides learning experiences designed to induce desirable patterns of student behavior as outlined by curriculum objectives.*
The principal:
a. Leads in the formulation of broad goals for the school
                                        N 0 1 2 3 4 5
b. Encourages each teacher to formulate specific objectives designed to achieve the broad goals of the school .. N 0 1 2 3 4 5
c. Provides environment favorable to pupil learning
                                        N 0 1 2 3 4 5
d. Works with each teacher to help her provide for desirable classroom experiences .... N 0 1 2 3 4 5
e. Stimulates student participation in school activities to include all students .... N 0 1 2 3 4 5
f. Stresses democratic principles as fundamental in all phases of school organization and life .... N 0 1 2 3 4 5
g. Practices the philosophy that the school is a laboratory where growing children are assisted in dealing intelligently and effectively with social, spiritual, and moral values .... N 0 1 2 3 4 5
h. Provides pupils with experiences designed to help them develop abilities and habits of discrimination, constructive citizenship, cooperation, and self-reliance .... N 0 1 2 3 4 5
i. Includes experiences in the school curriculum that lead toward understanding and appreciation of the cultures and needs of the people of foreign countries .... N 0 1 2 3 4 5

j. Gives attention to the training of pupils in preparing for local, state, and national careers of public leadership . N 0 1 2 3 4 5
k. Recognizes in the curriculum the importance of science in the contemporary world . . . . N 0 1 2 3 4 5

15. *Establishes appropriate procedures for evaluating pupil progress toward objectives and for making changes in the curriculum organization and content when needed.*
The principal:
a. Makes provision for continued evaluation of the school's instructional program . . . . N 0 1 2 3 4 5
b. Demonstrates willingness to make changes when needed
N 0 1 2 3 4 5
c. Obtains staff participation in designing the school's forms and methods for reporting to parents . . . . N 0 1 2 3 4 5
d. Obtains student participation in designing the school's forms and methods for reporting to parents . . . . N 0 1 2 3 4 5
e. Obtains parents' participation in designing the school's forms and methods for reporting to them . . . . N 0 1 2 3 4 5
f. Encourages discussion with parents concerning student progress
N 0 1 2 3 4 5
g. Encourages discussion with students concerning their individual progress . . . . N 0 1 2 3 4 5
h. Provides training in the administration of commercial evaluative devices and the interpretation of results . . . . N 0 1 2 3 4 5
i. Makes available commercial evaluative devices for use by the staff . . . . N 0 1 2 3 4 5
j. Provides training for teachers in evaluative techniques such as anecdotal records, case studies, and sociometric procedures
N 0 1 2 3 4 5
k. Uses results of the testing program to help determine whether or not the objectives of the school are being achieved
N 0 1 2 3 4 5
l. Uses the results of the testing program as an aid in revising the curriculum . . . . N 0 1 2 3 4 5
m. Works with the individual staff members to use test results in diagnosis and remedial services . . . . N 0 1 2 3 4 5
n. Integrates the testing program with the guidance program
N 0 1 2 3 4 5

16. *Plans and works with school personnel for the continuous improvement of instruction.*

The principal:

a. Assumes direct responsibility for the improvement of instruction
N 0 1 2 3 4 5

b. Encourages teachers to assume responsible freedom in exercising their judgment and initiative in the choice and arrangement of activities, subject matter, and method . . . . N 0 1 2 3 4 5

c. Provides cooperatively selected instructional materials and assists teachers in their use . . . . N 0 1 2 3 4 5

d. Leads teachers and their committees in the preparation of instructional materials . . . . N 0 1 2 3 4 5

e. Conducts classroom observations skillfully . . N 0 1 2 3 4 5

f. Gives suggestions concerning classroom methods whenever and wherever he feels competent . . . . N 0 1 2 3 4 5

g. Uses conferences with teachers as means for cooperative study of instruction (both individual and group) . . . . N 0 1 2 3 4 5

h. Makes full use of standard tests . . . . N 0 1 2 3 4 5

i. Encourages improvement of teacher-constructed tests
N 0 1 2 3 4 5

j. Encourages improvement of grading and promoting
N 0 1 2 3 4 5

k. Encourages teacher exchange of ideas on classroom techniques
N 0 1 2 3 4 5

l. Provides opportunities for teachers to visit each other's classes within the school . . . . N 0 1 2 3 4 5

m. Provides opportunities for teachers to observe other teachers in other schools . . . . N 0 1 2 3 4 5

n. Provides consultants when needed . . . . N 0 1 2 3 4 5

o. Develops professional library for the school staff
N 0 1 2 3 4 5

p. Plans for favorable teacher–pupil ratio to achieve maximum learning . . . . N 0 1 2 3 4 5

17. *Leads in the development and improvement of the school's guidance services.*

The principal:

a. Uses surveys of the school community as an aid in guidance
N 0 1 2 3 4 5

b. Provides leadership for staff studies designed to improve the counseling of students in the school .... N 0 1 2 3 4 5
c. Provides time in the daily work schedule for one or more staff members to devote some time to guidance work . N 0 1 2 3 4 5
d. Helps to correlate guidance work with classroom work

N 0 1 2 3 4 5
e. Designs testing program to determine pupil interests and abilities

N 0 1 2 3 4 5
f. Provides an organized follow-up of students after they leave school .... N 0 1 2 3 4 5
g. Makes student records accessible and encourages their use

N 0 1 2 3 4 5
h. Provides educational and occupational information services

N 0 1 2 3 4 5

18. *Uses the resources of the community to enrich the school program.*
The principal:
a. Surveys and analyzes resources of the community to determine their implications for enriching the educational program

N 0 1 2 3 4 5
b. Encourages teachers to provide experiences that will familiarize students with the occupations and industry in the community

N 0 1 2 3 4 5
c. Maintains directory of community resource persons

N 0 1 2 3 4 5
d. Plans for the use of local resource people to enrich the educational program .... N 0 1 2 3 4 5
e. Cooperates by providing time and means for off-campus pupil experiences .... N 0 1 2 3 4 5

19. *Makes use of teacher and student potential to plan and carry out school activities.*
The principal:
a. Develops an educational environment conducive to staff and pupil growth .... N 0 1 2 3 4 5
b. Acquaints everyone in school organization with his duties

N 0 1 2 3 4 5
c. Organizes the school program so that it functions smoothly in his absence .... N 0 1 2 3 4 5

d. Encourages students to assume responsibility and take initiative in school activities .... N 0 1 2 3 4 5
e. Develops cooperatively with teachers and students a handbook containing information about school organization, objectives, philosophy, and responsibilities .... N 0 1 2 3 4 5
f. Organizes teacher committees to plan for the assignment of special duties .... N 0 1 2 3 4 5
g. Provides adequate and continuous supervision of student activities during noon hours, recess, and play periods . N 0 1 2 3 4 5
h. Encourages students to assume responsibility in regulating the use of vehicles on school grounds .... N 0 1 2 3 4 5

20. *Understands and uses the implications of research and experimentation for developing the best possible school program.*
The principal:
a. Understands and applies the scientific method . N 0 1 2 3 4 5
b. Keeps informed on current educational research

N 0 1 2 3 4 5
c. Encourages carefully planned experimentation in teaching methods .... N 0 1 2 3 4 5
d. Aids in providing for teacher demonstrations, films, and discussion to clarify elements of a good learning situation

N 0 1 2 3 4 5
e. Places emphasis on the teacher's understanding of child growth and development .... N 0 1 2 3 4 5
f. Encourages teachers to focus attention on the individual learner

N 0 1 2 3 4 5

21. *Establishes open communication among school personnel.*
The principal:
a. Is accessible to teachers and students and willing to discuss any problems .... N 0 1 2 3 4 5
b. Encourages teachers to visit the principal's office for discussing school and personal problems .... N 0 1 2 3 4 5
c. Encourages students to visit the principal's office for discussing school and personal problems .... N 0 1 2 3 4 5
d. Keeps the superintendent and board of education informed of the school's activities through reports supplementary to those required by the state department of education .... N 0 1 2 3 4 5

e. Recognizes the influence of students as present and future public relations agents .... N 0 1 2 3 4 5

f. Uses to advantage available standard media (such as personal and group conferences, bulletins, school newspaper)

N 0 1 2 3 4 5

g. Plans for communication between teaching and nonteaching staff members .... N 0 1 2 3 4 5

22. *Maintains adequate records.*

The principal:

a. Formulates policies pertaining to recordkeeping with help of the school staff .... N 0 1 2 3 4 5

b. Maintains records on present and potential employees

N 0 1 2 3 4 5

c. Makes use of information on school staff in determining duties necessary for the proper functioning of the school

N 0 1 2 3 4 5

d. Maintains adequate cumulative records on each student

N 0 1 2 3 4 5

e. Makes periodic reports to the staff and students about the finances of the school .... N 0 1 2 3 4 5

23. *Applies sound principles of school economy in obtaining and dis-*
tributing school supplies and equipment and in maintaining school
property.

The principal:

a. Buys wholesale whenever it means an appreciable saving to the school .... N 0 1 2 3 4 5

b. Asks for competitive bids where justified by size of expenditure

N 0 1 2 3 4 5

c. Plans in advance to prevent emergency buying

N 0 1 2 3 4 5

d. Provides for systematic storage and distribution of supplies

N 0 1 2 3 4 5

e. Stresses economy in the use of supplies and respect for property as an important phase of the educational program

N 0 1 2 3 4 5

f. Plans for a continuous maintenance program of buildings and grounds .... N 0 1 2 3 4 5

24. *Understands and applies sound school building principles to house the educational program.*
    The principal:
    a. Keeps well informed on present-day trends in school building use and construction .... N 0 1 2 3 4 5
    b. Uses competent architectural advisers in school-building planning .... N 0 1 2 3 4 5
    c. Insists on adequate supervision of actual construction
    N 0 1 2 3 4 5
    d. Considers the needs of the total school program in the use of buildings and grounds .... N 0 1 2 3 4 5
    e. Advocates long-term building plans which conform to the findings of continuous surveys of the community and its educational needs .... N 0 1 2 3 4 5
    f. Includes teachers, parents, and pupils in designing the educational program and projecting building requirements necessary for that program .... N 0 1 2 3 4 5

25. *Provides for safe and convenient transportation of pupils.*
    The principal:
    a. Demonstrates belief that the school bus is an educational tool to be used for educational purposes .... N 0 1 2 3 4 5
    b. Provides adequate supervision for students while loading, unloading, and riding school buses .... N 0 1 2 3 4 5
    c. Provides effective and well-trained school patrols for school buses .... N 0 1 2 3 4 5
    d. Prescribes seating arrangement for pupils ... N 0 1 2 3 4 5
    e. Requests periodic inspection of school buses . N 0 1 2 3 4 5
    f. Encourages employment of well-qualified bus drivers
    N 0 1 2 3 4 5
    g. Holds conferences with bus drivers on safety . N 0 1 2 3 4 5
    h. Works with bus drivers in establishing and adhering to time schedules .... N 0 1 2 3 4 5
    i. Cooperates with agencies concerned with highway safety
    N 0 1 2 3 4 5
    j. Keeps everyone concerned informed of laws regarding transportation .... N 0 1 2 3 4 5

26. *Understands and applies with skill state and board of education regulations.*

The principal:

a. Applies appropriate legal principles and uses fully the rights provided therein for the advancement of education

N 0 1 2 3 4 5

b. Keeps informed about state school laws .... N 0 1 2 3 4 5

c. Keeps informed about the rules and regulations of the state board of education and the state department of education

N 0 1 2 3 4 5

d. Interprets the content and purpose of board regulations to faculty, students, and public .... N 0 1 2 3 4 5

e. Accepts and applies all board regulations as if they were his own

N 0 1 2 3 4 5

f. Provides channels through which teachers, students, and parents can make constructive suggestions about rules and regulations

N 0 1 2 3 4 5

g. Defends rules and regulations of the board of education from unfair and unwarranted criticism .... N 0 1 2 3 4 5

27. *Demonstrates a functional conception of the place of office work in the total pattern of administrative responsibilities.*

The principal:

a. Administers office work without allowing it to consume a disproportionate amount of his time .... N 0 1 2 3 4 5

b. Has regular but flexible schedule for accomplishing routine office work .... N 0 1 2 3 4 5

c. Organizes office work to win respect of teachers, pupils, and parents .... N 0 1 2 3 4 5

d. Emphasizes the importance of prompt and accurate recording of office work .... N 0 1 2 3 4 5

e. Establishes policies concerning services to be provided by the school office .... N 0 1 2 3 4 5

C. Competencies Required to Work Effectively with the Community and Its Organizations.

A competent and successful school principal is a person who:

28. *Enlists the help of parents and other representatives of the community to develop a philosophy of education appropriate to the*

*school and the community setting and does not overlook objectives
pertinent to state, national, and world needs.*
The principal:
a. Provides opportunities for parents to participate in formulating
and reviewing the philosophy of the school .... N 0 1 2 3 4 5
b. Carries out studies of public opinion about schools

N 0 1 2 3 4 5

c. Interviews patrons and community leaders to determine what
they wish the school to do for their children .... N 0 1 2 3 4 5
d. Aids the community to recognize and evaluate social, economic,
ethical, and political trends at work in the community

N 0 1 2 3 4 5

29. *Knows the community through planned study.*
The principal:
a. Studies the community continuously .... N 0 1 2 3 4 5
b. Shows a working knowledge of the power structure of the community .... N 0 1 2 3 4 5
c. Understands the value system of the community

N 0 1 2 3 4 5

d. Understands the interdependence of people and the need to help
reduce the force of factors that produce antagonisms among individuals and groups in the community .... N 0 1 2 3 4 5
e. Recognizes the crucial social problems that have been created by
the progress of science and technology .... N 0 1 2 3 4 5
f. Uses the school program to contribute toward the understanding
and solution of problems of living and working together

N 0 1 2 3 4 5

g. Contributes to the design of community programs that stress the
basic freedoms inherent in our democratic way of life

N 0 1 2 3 4 5

30. *Stimulates the community to recognize and support its school needs.*
The principal:
a. Recognizes community needs as of paramount importance in
studying and designing the school program .... N 0 1 2 3 4 5
b. Promotes faculty–community meetings to discuss community
needs and the part the school can play in providing for these needs

N 0 1 2 3 4 5

c. Plans assemblies and other school programs around community problems .... N 0 1 2 3 4 5
d. Invites parents and other lay people to attend assemblies and other school programs .... N 0 1 2 3 4 5
e. Provides time for staff to participate in community organizations
N 0 1 2 3 4 5
f. Uses educational committees of community organizations to promote an understanding of school–community relationships
N 0 1 2 3 4 5
g. Makes use of the combined efforts of students, teachers, and other school personnel in acquainting the community with school activities, goals, and accomplishments .... N 0 1 2 3 4 5
h. Publicizes studies that show a need for major change in the educational program .... N 0 1 2 3 4 5
i. Develops a well-organized plan to enlist support of the public for the school .... N 0 1 2 3 4 5
j. Is active in promoting needed school legislation
N 0 1 2 3 4 5
k. Interests citizens in the support of educational programs in social institutions other than the school .... N 0 1 2 3 4 5

31. *Organizes laymen of the community for cooperative approaches to all educational problems.*
The principal:
a. Understands and applies a sound methodology of problem solving .... N 0 1 2 3 4 5
b. Invites parents, interested laymen, and representatives of the PTA to the school to discuss educational problems
N 0 1 2 3 4 5
c. Does not hesitate to visit the homes of pupils to discuss educational problems with parents .... N 0 1 2 3 4 5
d. Organizes interested laymen and consultants and the administrative and teaching staff to study the needs of the youth in the community .... N 0 1 2 3 4 5
e. Clearly explains the purpose of a meeting ... N 0 1 2 3 4 5
f. Is skilled in leading the community to release its energies toward the improvement of educational opportunities .. N 0 1 2 3 4 5
g. Promotes meetings of lay people to discuss educational needs of the community .... N 0 1 2 3 4 5

h. Provides training situations for those who assume a place of community leadership .... N 0 1 2 3 4 5

32. *Encourages the community to make wide use of the facilities of the school.*
The principal:
a. Cooperates with the superintendent, school board, and lay leaders in determining policies for the use of school plant
N 0 1 2 3 4 5
b. Publicizes the policies pertaining to use of the school plant
N 0 1 2 3 4 5
c. Encourages the community to make wide use of the school facilities within the limits of predetermined policies .. N 0 1 2 3 4 5
d. Schedules school–community use of the school plant
N 0 1 2 3 4 5
e. Provides facilities for adult education ...... N 0 1 2 3 4 5

33. *Helps improve the quality of living in the community through the school program.*
The principal:
a. Understands all community educational influences that relate to pupils .... N 0 1 2 3 4 5
b. Provides physical examinations as part of the school program
N 0 1 2 3 4 5
c. Plans adult classes as part of the total school program
N 0 1 2 3 4 5
d. Cooperates with vocational and other teachers in planning projects designed to improve family living conditions N 0 1 2 3 4 5
e. Participates actively in community improvement projects
N 0 1 2 3 4 5
f. Plans experiences in the school program designed to improve physical and mental health .... N 0 1 2 3 4 5
g. Plans experiences designed to improve family relations as a part of the educational program .... N 0 1 2 3 4 5

34. *Uses available local, state, and regional resources to solve educational problems.*
The principal:
a. Makes use of staff members of the state department of education in approaching educational problems .... N 0 1 2 3 4 5

b. Makes use of staff members of colleges and universities

N 0 1 2 3 4 5

c. Solicits the aid of instructional supervisors .. N 0 1 2 3 4 5

d. Uses the special qualifications and abilities of the visiting teacher or other attendance personnel .... N 0 1 2 3 4 5

e. Makes use of community resources such as recreational centers, libraries, business establishments, and industries N 0 1 2 3 4 5

f. Provides work experiences for students through the cooperation of the school with community business concerns N 0 1 2 3 4 5

g. Provides conferences for students with representatives of business, industry, civic, and service agencies as part of the educational program .... N 0 1 2 3 4 5

h. Makes use of local concerns with educational significance

N 0 1 2 3 4 5

i. Makes extensive use of services, personnel, and materials provided by private, county, state, and federal agencies

N 0 1 2 3 4 5

j. Obtains a list of free and inexpensive materials available for schools .... N 0 1 2 3 4 5

k. Maintains an inventory of natural and physical resources in the community .... N 0 1 2 3 4 5

l. Maintains an inventory of community social organizations

N 0 1 2 3 4 5

35. *Establishes open communication between school and community.* The principal:

a. Makes use of newspapers, radio stations, TV stations, films, and other mass media to promote understanding and improvement of the educational program .... N 0 1 2 3 4 5

b. Shows good judgment in conversing with individuals about the school and its program .... N 0 1 2 3 4 5

c. Supports parent–teacher organizations and encourages teachers to take an active part .... N 0 1 2 3 4 5

d. Assumes responsibility of informing news agencies about the needs of the school .... N 0 1 2 3 4 5

e. Keeps patrons informed through school publications

N 0 1 2 3 4 5

f. Demonstrates the belief that one of the most effective ties between the school and the community is the child N 0 1 2 3 4 5

g. Analyzes and uses constructive criticism for the betterment of the school and its program .... N 0 1 2 3 4 5

36. *Engages community lay people in the evaluation of the school and its program.*
The principal:
a. Sets up and uses whatever organization is needed to meet with lay people for the purpose of evaluating the school's curriculum
N 0 1 2 3 4 5
b. Sets up and uses whatever organization is needed to bring lay people into the process of evaluating the school's guidance services
N 0 1 2 3 4 5
c. Sets up and uses whatever organization is needed to bring lay people into the process of evaluating the school's instruction
N 0 1 2 3 4 5
d. Is attentive to the comments of community groups about the values of the educational program and of changes made in it
N 0 1 2 3 4 5
e. Progresses only as fast as the community can follow
N 0 1 2 3 4 5
f. Encourages frequent evaluation of the school plant by community groups considering the school's objectives N 0 1 2 3 4 5

37. *Demonstrates knowledge and skill of budget making and financial accounting that meet the conditions of public trust.*
The principal:
a. Makes a budget for the school only after consultation with his teachers and lay leaders .... N 0 1 2 3 4 5
b. Provides for keeping accurate records of all school monies received and spent .... N 0 1 2 3 4 5
c. Provides for auditing all school financial records
N 0 1 2 3 4 5
d. Makes periodic reports to the superintendent and board of education about the finances of the school .... N 0 1 2 3 4 5
e. Makes periodic reports to the public about the finances of the school .... N 0 1 2 3 4 5

Author Index

Subject Index